Race, Identity, and Representation in Education

second edition

Edited by

Cameron McCarthy, Warren Crichlow,
Greg Dimitriadis, and Nadine Dolby

Routledge
Taylor & Francis Group

NEW YORK AND LONDON

Published in 2005 by
Routledge
Taylor & Francis Group
270 Madison Avenue
New York, NY 10016

Published in Great Britain by
Routledge
Taylor & Francis Group
2 Park Square
Milton Park, Abingdon
Oxon OX14 4RN

© 2005 by Taylor & Francis Group, LLC
Routledge is an imprint of Taylor & Francis Group

Printed in the United States of America on acid-free paper
10 9 8 7 6 5 4 3 2 1

International Standard Book Number-10: 0-415-94992-0 (Hardcover) 0-415-94993-9 (Softcover)
International Standard Book Number-13: 978-0-4159-4992-7 (Hardcover) 978-0-4159-4993-4 (Softcover)
Library of Congress Card Number 2004022357

Trademark Notice: Product or corporate names may be trademarks or registered trademarks, and are used only for identification and explanation without intent to infringe.

Library of Congress Cataloging-in-Publication Data

Race, identity, and representation in education / edited by Cameron McCarthy ... [et al.].-- 2nd ed.
    p. cm. -- (Critical social thought)
   Includes bibliographical references and index.
   ISBN 0-415-94992-0 (hardback : alk. paper) -- ISBN 0-415-94993-9 (pbk. : alk. paper)
   1. Education--Social aspects--United States. 2. Multicultural education--United States. 3. Minorities--Education--United States. 4. Race awareness--United States. 5. Discrimination in education--United States. 6. Educational equalization--United States. 7. Curriculum change--United States. I. McCarthy, Cameron. II. Series.

LC191.4.R33 2005
371.829'00973--dc22   2004022357

Taylor & Francis Group
is the Academic Division of T&F Informa plc.

Visit the Taylor & Francis Web site at
http://www.taylorandfrancis.com

and the Routledge Web site at
http://www.routledge-ny.com

Contents

v

**Part Three: Racial Affiliation, Racial Resentment, Racialized Citizenship:
State and Educational Policy Dilemmas in the Twenty-First Century**

Acknowledgments

Race, Identity, and Representation in Education, Second Edition was nurtured into being by the collective efforts of the editors and contributors alike and the steady support of a wonderful band of graduate students and research assistants in the Institute of Communications Research who served as the volume's principal interlocutors and editorial collective. We are particularly grateful to members of the collective—Susan Harewood, Jin-Kyung Park, Alice Filmer, Michael Giardina, Miguel Malagreca, David Monje, Soochul Kim—for their editorial advice and theoretical and methodological insights and suggestions. They helped to shepherd the second edition from conception to production. We would also like to thank Paula Treichler and Bruce Williams, outgoing and incoming directors of the Institute of Communications Research, for their support and suggestions on this volume. The Editors are grateful for the funding and research support of the Institute of Communications Research at the University of Illinois at Urbana. Further support was provided in the form of a Communications Scholar Award to Cameron McCarthy and advance support funds from Routledge. Next, we would like to express our sincerest thanks for the remarkable conceptual advice and unwavering encouragement offered to us by Routledge's brilliant acquisitions editor, Catherine Bernard. Finally, we would like to offer our special thanks to Michael Apple, distinguished editor of the *Critical Social Thought* series.

Versions of the chapters by Michael Omi and Howard Winant, Edward Said, Christine Sleeter, and Cornel West appeared in the first edition of *Race, Identity, and Representation in Education.* Versions of the following chapters were published elsewhere:

Appadurai, A. "Diversity and Disciplinarity as Cultural Artifacts." In *Disciplinarity and Dissent in Cultural Studies*, edited by C. Nelson and D. Goankar, 23–36. New York: Routledge, 1997.

Bhabha, H. "'Race', Time and the Revision of Modernity." In *The Location of Culture*, 236–276. New York: Routledge, 1994.

Coffey, M. "What Puts the 'Culture' in 'Multiculturalism'? An Analysis of Culture, Government, and the Politics of Mexican Identity." In *Multicultural Curriculum*, edited by R. Mahalingham and C. McCarthy, 37–55. New York: Routledge, 2000.

Fine, M., and L. Weis. "Crime Stories: A Critical Look through Race, Ethnicity and Gender." *Qualitative Studies in Education*, 11, no. 3 (1998): 435–459.

Lebeau, V. "The Unwelcome Child: Elizabeth Eckford and Hannah Arendt." *Journal of Visual Culture*, 3, no. 1 (2004): 51–62. Copyright 2004. Reprinted by permission of Sage Publications Ltd.

Lipsitz, G. "Whiteness and War." In *The Possessive Investment in Whiteness,* 69–98. Philadelphia: Temple University Press, 1999. Copyright 1988 by Temple University Press. All rights reserved.

Lugo, A. "Reflections on Border Theory, Culture, and the Nation." In *Border Theory: The Limits of Cultural Politics*, edited by S. Michaelson and David D. Johnson, 43–67. Minneapolis: University of Minnesota Press, 1997. Copyright 1997 by the Regents of the University of Minnesota.

McCarthy, C. and G. Dimitriadis. "Governmentality and the Sociology of Education: Media, Educational Policy, and the Politics of Resentment." *British Journal of Sociology of Education* 21, no. 2 (2000):169–85.

Roman, L. "States of Insecurity: Cold War Memory, "Global Citizenship" and Its Discontents, *Discourse: Studies in the Cultural Politics of Education*, 25, no. 2 (2004): 1–24.

Shohat, E. "Taboo Memories, Diasporic Visions: Columbus, Palestine, and Arab-Jews." In *Performing Hybridity*, edited by M. Joseph and J. Fink, 131–56. Minneapolis: University of Minnesota Press, 1999.

Spivak, G. "The Women's Texts and a Critique of Imperialism." *Critical Inquiry*, 12 (1985): 243–61.

West, C. "The New Cultural Politics of Difference." *October* 53 (Summer 1990): 93–109. Copyright 1990 by October Magazine Ltd. and the Massachusetts Institute of Technology.

Willis, P. "Foot Soldiers of Modernity: The Dialectics of Cultural Consumption and the 21st-Century School." *Harvard Educational Review,* 73, no. 3 (Fall 2003): 390–415. Copyright 2003 by the President and Fellows of Harvard College. All rights reserved.

Series Editor's Introduction

I begin a book of mine, *Official Knowledge* (2000), with a story of an African American child who is trying to stop a fight between two of his classmates. He isn't participating in the altercation, but *he* is the one who is literally pulled into the principal's office and suspended for fighting. The child in question in this instance was my son—and the reality of constantly being constructed as the "other" and the extremely powerful effects of this on him are too distressing to retell. Instances such as these are "ordinary" and that is exactly the point. They speak to the ways in which differential power relations are ongoingly built and experienced in our daily lives. They also speak to a powerful politics of whiteness in which even supposedly "liberal" institutions, filled with supposedly "liberal" people, construct identities and relations of dominance and subordination—and the resistances that ensue from these relations—that enable such institutions and people to act on their common sense in ways that are more than a little damaging (Lipman 2004).

I wanted to begin my Series Editor's Introduction to this important book with this example because it points to some of the ways race works, in this case on a school playground. It's a mundane example; but it also can serve as a reminder about the power of race in the ordinary interactions of daily life in all of our institutions.

In their exceptional analysis of the way the discourses of race have operated in the United States, Omi and Winant argue that race is not an "add-on," but is truly constitutive of many of our most taken for granted daily experiences.

> In the U.S., race is present in every institution, every relationship, every individual. This is the case not only for the way society is organized—spatially, culturally, in terms of stratification, etc. —but also for our perceptions and understandings of personal experience. Thus as we watch the videotape of Rodney King being beaten, compare real estate prices in different neighborhoods, size up a potential client, neighbor, or teacher, stand in line at the unemployment office, or carry out a thousand other normal tasks, we are compelled to think racially, to use racial categories and meaning systems in which we have been socialized. Despite exhortations both sincere and hypocritical, it is not possible or even desirable to be "color-blind." (Omi and Winant 1994, pp. 158–159)

Not only is it not possible to be color-blind, as they go on to say, "Opposing race requires that we notice race, not ignore it." Only by noticing race can we challenge it, "with its ever-more-absurd reduction of human experience to an essence attributed to all without regard for historical or social context." By placing race squarely in front of us, "we can challenge the state, the institutions of civil

xi

society, and ourselves as individuals to combat the legacy of inequality and injustice inherited from the past" and continually reproduced in the present (Omi and Winant 1994, p. 159).

In the above statements, Omi and Winant set an agenda that is ambitious conceptually, historically, and politically. But there have been volumes that have taken up that ambitious agenda and have pushed it further along each of these dimensions. The volume you are reading is a powerful extension of one of the most important of these books. The first edition of *Race, Identity, and Representation in Education* appeared a decade ago. It quickly was hailed as a major contribution to the ways in which educators, social and cultural theorists, and activists might better think about the realities of "race" as both a social construction and a set of oppressive realities and relations. This second edition not only furthers this important agenda, but it goes even deeper into the material, conceptual, and empirical—and intensely political—issues that are involved in any serious understanding of race, its history, how it is mobilized, and its effects.

McCarthy, Crichlow, Dimitriadis, and Dolby bring together some of the very best authors inside and outside of education to interrogate what Edward Said argued was the ultimate task of education—to rethink the linkages of knowledge, culture, and association among all people. In the words of the editors, this means that we need to think "contextually, relationally, and contrapuntally." Doing this requires that we be diachronic and synchronic at the same time.

The implications of the chapters in this book are profound. The authors ask us to not be satisfied with the accepted answers involving such things as "multiculturalism" and "diversity." Instead, they challenge us to think across boundaries—disciplinary, conceptual, and geographic. In doing so, they clearly recognize that race is not an "it," a biological entity; nor can it be analyzed apart from its relations to the multiple relations of power that construct "it" and which it helps construct (see Ladson-Billings and Gillborn 2004).

Taking race and its complexities seriously of course requires us not only to think synchronically across these borders, but diachronically as well. That is, the concepts by which we have understood race not only need to be seen as having a history, but these very concepts must be put to the test of the constant insurgent resistance to and struggles against their use. They must be reconstructed to take account of the major transformations, both destructive and creative, that our societies are undergoing. Without a sense of this diachronicity, we cannot grasp the inherent tensions and collective histories behind the actors who make these histories and the actors who try to grab onto these histories to make some sense out of them. Nor can we get a picture of the rich processes that create those new possibilities of association to which Edward Said was directing our attention.

The late French sociologist Pierre Bourdieu points to some of these issues when he says:

> What appears to us today as self-evident, as beneath consciousness and choice, has often been the stake of struggles and instituted only as the result of dogged confrontations between dominant and dominated groups. The major effect of historical evolution is to abolish history by relegating to the past, that is to the unconscious, the lateral possibilities it eliminated. (Bourdieu 1998, pp. 56–57)

Bourdieu implies that this is not simply an academic agenda. For, just as there are multiple ways in which race has been and is understood and acted upon, and multiple sets of relations in which it is involved, there are multiple sites for potential democratization and struggle (Sheller and Urry 2003, p. 108). However, our ability to engage in critical forms of association and of critical citizenship and democracy, to create what Crossley (2003) so nicely calls a "radical habitus," depends on an engaged understanding of the complex ways in which public and private spheres, state and civil society, region and nation, person rights vs. property rights, cultures and ethnicities—all of which have participated in racial and racializing, as well as classed and gendered, logics and histories (see, e.g., Mills 1997; Fraser 1989; Foner 1998)—are all being reconstituted. Our previous dichotomous ways of understanding these relations are no longer sufficient.

The editors and authors of the second edition of *Race, Identity, and Representation in Education* have produced a book that takes up all of these challenges in truly serious ways.

In combination with the concrete attempts to radically reconfigure state social and educational policy and to reconstruct the relations among the state, education, and the most marginalized members of our societies (see, e.g., Apple et al. 2003), this is a volume that points the way towards a much more robust and nuanced sensitivity to the problems and possibilities of uniting theory, policy, and practice. It constitutes a lasting contribution.

Michael W. Apple
*John Bascom Professor of Curriculum and
Instruction and Educational Policy Studies
University of Wisconsin, Madison*

References

Apple, M.W. (2000). *Official Knowledge*, 2nd edition. New York: Routledge.

Apple, M. W. et al. (2003). *The State and the Politics of Knowledge*. New York: RoutledgeFalmer.

Bourdieu, P. (1998). *Practical Reason*. Cambridge: Polity Press.

Crossley, N. (2003). From reproduction to transformation: Social movement fields and the radical habitus. *Theory, Culture & Society* 20: 43–68.

Foner, E. (1998). *The Story of American Freedom*. New York: Norton.

Fraser, N. (1989). *Unruly Practices*. Minneapolis: University of Minnesota Press.

Ladson-Billings, G. and Gillborn, D. (Eds.) (2004). *The RoutledgeFalmer Multicultural Reader*. New York: RoutledgeFalmer.

Lipman, P. (2004). *High Stakes Education*. New York: RoutledgeFalmer.

Mills, C. (1997). *The Racial Contract*. Ithaca: Cornell University Press.

Omi, M. and Winant, H. (1994). *Racial Formation in the United States*. New York: Routledge.

Sheller, M. and Urry, J. (2003). Mobile transformations of "public" and "private" life. *Theory, Culture & Society* 20: 107–125.

Introduction

Transforming Contexts, Transforming Identities
Race and Education in the New Millennium

CAMERON McCARTHY, WARREN CRICHLOW, GREG DIMITRIADIS,
AND NADINE DOLBY

This second edition of essays on race, identity, and representation in education offers an occasion not for celebration, but for a careful and rigorous consideration of key developments associated with racial formation in the past decade and a half—now more insistent since 9/11—and their ramifications for education broadly defined. The second edition of *Race, Identity, and Representation in Education* is edited against the backdrop of dramatic shifts in governmentality taking place on a global scale—dynamics that have profound implications for racial affiliation and "its" cultural and sociopolitical uses. In the first edition (1993), the authors called attention to an intensifying pattern of instability and uncertainty in the processes of racial affiliation and communal identification that had become increasingly apparent since the late 1980s. Particularly in advanced capitalist nations such as the United States, much of this uncertainty was informed by the material reality of downturns in the industrial economy, retrenchment of social welfare systems, and the influx of immigrants and refugees (legal and illegal) into the heart of public sphere institutions of citizenship, and secondary labor markets burgeoning in metropolitan centers. These transnational movements of people and aspirations set in motion new logics of identity—cultural, linguistic, gendered, religious, and sexual—making it difficult for cultural purists in given racial groups to hold onto "their" putative constituencies or to offer racial manifestos that could guarantee narrow historical demands or insular self-interests. These associated cultural politics of difference (West in this edition) all had a particularly poignant inflection in education as various custodians of culture stood ready to carve up the school curriculum like a carbuncle, presumably to assign different resources, culturally determined expectations, and determinate knowledge outcomes to mutually exclusive groups.

In addition to critiques of reconstituted pedagogical boundaries, the authors wrote against the grain of the disciplinary insulation that had marked the production of knowledge within schooling and particularly undermined the power and reach of scholarship on racial antagonism. This confinement and parochialism within the disciplines was not solely endemic to the reigning paradigmatic formulae but also inherent to reform discourses such as multiculturalism. While multiculturalist intervention into the hierarchical space of race thinking and cultural absolutism was important, it also served to celebrate otherness and diversity within narrowly construed notions of shared values and assimilable ways of life. We argued that such an ameliorative antidote to cultural exclusion and nonrecognition avoided engagement with critical knowledges, privileging instead a managerial discourse of cultural sampling in which all contending ethnic groups would be given their preserve in both the curriculum and private confines of consumer culture (see Appadurai in this edition). Similar reform-driven discourses were also associated with a vigorous retreat from popular culture, which both liberal and conservative critics deemed corrosive to the morals and values traditionally transmitted in schools to the young (McCarthy et al. 1999). These themes fueled the culture wars, which were waged over the representation of the present and future of democratic recognition and redistribution of public resources (Yudice 2003). Simultaneously, the modern configuration of the nation was elsewhere being reordered by global capitalism, mass migration, and the amplification and rapidity of movement of images around the world. Educators, at least in the United States, seemed oblivious to the turbulence of global change and the subtle resurgence of old racial codes in a brooding patriotic nationalism. With tacit belligerence some insisted on negotiating demands for inclusion in the "canon" and in school knowledge by clinging onto a transcendent, idealized sense of the past as both the organic and moral fruition of Western Civilization, Western Culture (Ravitch 1990).

What then had appeared to us in the early 1990s as emergent cracks in the racial order, and the scholarly paradigms that had been advanced to understand these developments, had by the end of the last century grown into a full-blown metamorphosis in the terms and conditions in which race could and would be articulated and struggled over. No longer could the old defenders of the status quo school curriculum comfortably hold Western Culture before the onslaught of racial and ethnic multiplicity like a vast antiballistic shield of protection. No longer could liberal and progressive scholars comfortably "place" culture with race into predictable multicultural slots. For as Ernest Hemingway's narrator had noted in a moment of premature exultation in *For Whom the Bell Tolls* (1940/1996), "the ground had moved from beneath [our] feet." Culture and identity had been "dirempted" from place. And, the cultural porosity precipitated by the movement of people, economic and symbolic capital, and the proliferation, amplification, and circulation of images across the globe has deeply unsettled ethnic enclaves, even the dominant Eurocentric preserves. This is the moment in which we live—a historical moment of radical reconfiguration and re-narration of the relations between centers of power and their peripheries.

Nothing has, for us, more powerfully illustrated and underscored these unmistakable dynamics of world reordering than the current state of global conflict intensified after the dreadful events of September 11, 2001. The idea that we live in a deeply interconnected world in which centers and margins are unstable and are constantly being redefined and rearticulated was underscored that morning, under the brilliant September sky in downtown Manhattan. Within this new landscape, it is striking how it is now possible to send shock waves from the margins to the epicenters of the modern world. In the prescient language of Michael Hardt and Antonio Negri (2004), we are vividly aware of how the postcolonial, postcold war center—periphery settlement has been swiftly reordered and subsumed in a new, perilous network of imperial rule. World system stability is brazenly sustained through war, placing the most vulnerable civilian populations at risk. At the same time, it is important to recall that representational technologies, mass migration, enormous movements of capital across national borders, and everyday imaginative labor among diverse human actors (the volatile forms of cultural reproduction that Arjun Appadurai talks about in *Modernity at Large* [1996]) also mobilize vital linkages between the margins and the epicenters of the modernist life. These productive social relations and cultural vernacular contents can potentially embody collectivist counternarratives that sustain capacities to aspire, and thus the possibility to imagine, to

oppose exclusion, and to act together across differences to transform global life toward a new organization of social justice, ethicality, and humane uses of social power (Appadurai 2004).

The cataclysmic ripple effects of 9/11 cascade around the world: the U.S.-led declaration and
prosecution of the war on terrorism and its tactical policies of regime change and preemptive
strikes, the occupation of Iraq and the attendant pacification of democracy domestically and con-
travention of law internationally, and the transnational extension of the policing and detaining
power of the state. All of these developments complicate matters of race, identity, and representation considerably. We see, in the United States, for example, very tenuous feelings of alliance built
among former antagonists under the symbolic umbrella of nation and patriotism. Otherwise
excluded racial minorities such as African Americans, Latinos, and Asian Americans are interpol-
lated, along with traditionally reactionary classes, into a newly expanded cultural dominant built
around jingoistic symbolism and service to country. This combination of ideological coercion and
individuated processes of self-interested commonsense making, particularly in a context of uncertainty about national and personal security, effectively abets the wholesale naming of "others," particularly Arab (or Arab-looking) Americans, as the conspicuous enemy within and abroad (see Ono
and Rizvi in this edition). Greater regulation and domestic surveillance of the citizenry are also
manifested in increased xenophobic security on borders shared with Mexico to the south and Canada to the north. These politics, "all in the name of security" (Said 2004), produce degrading
effects on profiled groups and inhibit wider flows of regional trade that ironically hurt local economies. In addition, these anxious biopolitical regimes of insularity also served to normalize authoritarian state responses—particularly at the intersection of gender and cultural difference—toward
"low-skilled" migrants, guest workers, and so-called third world refugees seeking economic and
political asylum in the land of opportunity (see Roman in this edition). At present, there seem to be
no constitutive limits to pervasive biometric technologies of information gathering associated with
face scanning, finger printing, and DNA sampling that implicate all of us—tourists and vagabonds
(Bauman 1998)— in a global network of security and surveillance that is flourishing (Gates 2003).

New Millennium: Second Edition

The central purpose of this second edition, then, is to contribute considered theoretical, methodological, and policy reflection on this present historical conjuncture characterized by new dynamics
of racial formation and extraordinary developments in global structures. In detailed and complex
readings of sociopolitical, psychic, and cultural contexts, contributors invite readers to consider the
seriousness of the malaise of mainstream culture and schooling, underwritten as they are by state
and corporate-driven imperatives of neoliberalism, marked by an intensification of privatization
and multiplication of racialization, injustice, exploitation, and resentment enhanced by deepening
poverty. There is a great need for us to move beyond disabling conventionalisms of "political correctness" and institutional practices of epistemological confinement of difficult and political
knowledges. Against the massive discursive and material systems of hierarchy and exclusion that
encourage dehumanization and hopelessness, there remains active space to embrace more scholarly, critical, and imaginative command of power and knowledge—to recognize the ways that this
couplet can contain productive resources for critical, reflexive, and participatory interventions in
the contemporary field of education and broader contours of social life. This idea of interdisciplinary movement and collectivist change is, in this collection, directed toward articulation of different answers that look through and beyond the stasis and the confounding circumstances that
underwrite the lives of modern racialized subjects.

Our suggestion here of movement and change is drawn from Herman Melville's novel *Moby
Dick*. Its still relevant narrative of rigid nineteenth-century regimes of social classification (also see

Willinsky 1998) portrays human movement in the context of stasis, an experience parallel to what George Lipsitz (2004) describes as a "locked on this earth" feeling evident among many American inner-city minority youth. For us, movement and stasis are powerful contemporary tropes, particularly where bureaucratic deployment in school and social service institutions recode race in order to routinize cultural plurality and to homogenize heterogeneous forms of identity formation (see Anyon, Fine and Weis, Grossberg in this edition). Contributors seek to confront and interpret the present cultural and political complex—this network of new relations that defines race relations and schooling in an era of globalization. Our inquiry both probes and offers new considerations and approaches to questions of race, identity, and representation that have endured, albeit under much changed circumstances, into the twenty-first century. How might educational scholars and activists not only work to critically understand the globalization of educational regimes, broadly conceived, but also recognize principled alternative practices to them in local situations? How might we theorize social change and its conjunctural relationship to schools? What general organizing principles or terms might we deploy to both sum up these developments and identify their dominant vectors, both for individuals and collectivities? In varied ways, the essays collected here suggest that it is not enough to offer self-complacent formulations at the level of abstraction of the mode of social production. Neither is it enough to seek to isolate the variable of race from other complicating factors of modern life, social or psychic, in the pursuit of some vain form of methodological individualism reduced to identity politics and the authenticity of origins. Our attempt is to pay proper attention to patterns of historical incorporation and the spontaneous work of culture and identification practices in specific institutional contexts and programmatic applications. These are the challenges at stake as we set out from what Dennis Carlson (2003) calls the "safe harbors" of mainstream education.

Organizing Categories: Matters of Culture, Matters of Identity, Matters of State/Public Policy

Across the varied contributions, *Race, Identity, and Representation in Education, Second Edition* foregrounds philosophical, theoretical, empirical, and policy-inflected studies of some of the pivotal modern dynamics that are related to the topic of race in education. We look, collectively, away from the traditional opposition of theory versus practice, abstraction versus concrete studies, and so forth that now dominate both mainstream and radical approaches to race. Our aim here is not to separate out these different strategies of race analysis as is customarily done, but to model research that cuts across and integrates the theoretical and the empirical, the poetic and practical. Moreover, to adequately address the complexities of race in this contemporary historical moment, students of race cannot study race alone (Hall 1980, 339) but must pay greater attention to contextualization, relationality, and conjunctural analysis. Accordingly, contributors to this collection highlight patterns of historical incorporation and the work of culture and identification practices in specific institutional contexts, as well as the spread of effects across and beyond local settings, linking the urban/local to the cosmopolitan/global.

The edition is thematically structured around three key categories: popular culture, identity, and state/public policy. These critical organizing categories materially and discursively embody principal contradictions and tensions through which twenty-first-century race relations in education are expressed. They also force us to think about the operation of racial logics beyond the school, and to move our analysis into society and the globalizing world context where individual relations intersect with popular culture and state/public policy. Within the cultural complex of these critical fault lines the authors attempt to envision new opportunities and responsibilities required for the transformation and reconfiguration of race relations in the twenty-first century as improvised and variously expressed in popular politics and solidarity today (e.g., Rao and Walton 2004).

Part One of the book is comprised of chapters in which contributors broadly examine the theme "Race, Globalization, and the Management of Popular Culture." "Contested Identities, Contested Desires: Racial Experience and Curriculum Dilemmas in the Twenty-First Century" is the overarching topic explored in the eight chapters of Part Two. In Part Three, contributors examine the topic "Racial Affiliation, Racial Resentment, Racialized Citizenship: State and Educational Policy Dilemmas in the New Century." Paul Willis brings the collection to a close with a powerful riposte to glib analytic uses of the category "globalization" in his Afterword essay entitled "Foot Soldiers of Modernity."

Part One: Race, Globalization, and the Management of Popular Culture

In this section, contributors consistently work toward the reformulation of the concept of "culture," offering retheorizations and reformulations in ways that are not often pursued in educational analysis. One such area of debate, explored in detail in the *First Edition*, is the status of discourses of "culture." Often undertheorized, "culture" is still commonly treated in education as a preexistent, unchanging deposit, consisting of a rigidly bounded set of elite or folkloric knowledges, values, experiences, and linguistic practices specific to particular groups. In this new edition, we argue that even the critical perspective of the cultural studies paradigm, which we invoked in the first edition, is now inadequate to a discussion of the new work of culture in a globalizing and information age, especially as it bears upon race.

Instead, we maintain that it might now be more useful to think about "culture" along the lines suggested by Tony Bennett in "Putting Policy into Cultural Studies" (1996), *The Birth of the Museum* (1995), and "Culture and Governmentality" (2003) as well as the work of Toby Miller (1998). These approaches combine the neo-Gramscian understandings that underpin the cultural studies paradigm with Foucauldian insight on the role of the discursive and the cultural in the differential production of citizenship and power discriminations in modern society. Here, too, theorization of culture moves beyond the "whole way of life" formulation in the Raymond Williams sense (although his linking of culture to moral sensibility and feeling and his discussion of hegemony as a form of cultural saturation in *The Long Revolution* [1961] clearly apply). Rather, we conceptualize culture as a set of dynamic, productive, and generative material and immaterial practices in the regulation of social conduct and social behavior that emphasize personal self-management (i.e., the modification of habits, tastes, style, and physical appearance) and the expanded role of civil society in the state and vice versa in the rule of populations—"rule at a distance." By way of this emphasis, contributors to the *Second Edition* link work in education to the politics of popular culture and public policy and the imbedded discriminations in the instrumental and expressive orders of the racialized state.

Drawing on a variety of disciplines and subdisciplines—cultural studies, postcolonial theory, anthropology, sociology, psychoanalysis, media studies, and literary criticism—Michael Omi and Howard Winant ("The Theoretical Status of the Concept of Race"), Homi Bhabha ("'Race', Time, and the Revision of Modernity"), and Cornel West ("The New Cultural Politics of Difference") open up this section by casting a backward historical glance on the conceptual, cultural, and ideological work of the category of race in the evolution of dominant–subordinate relations in modern society. Together, these contributors suggest that racial logics do not follow one simple trajectory but indeed show considerable historical variability. It is the difficult methodological process of trying to understand this variability that might help us to better grasp contemporary developments with respect to race after 9/11—developments associated with globalization, postcolonialism, and specific forms of racism such as "Islamophobia" (Omi and Winant in this edition).

In their essay "The Theoretical Status of the Concept of Race," Omi and Winant critique both idealist and positivist and essentialist and antiessentialist theorization of race, insisting instead on the materialist basis of race and the need to make complex readings of changing global and national contexts. Engaging an array of literary, philosophical, and sociological references and allusions, Homi Bhabha ("'Race', Time and the Revision of Modernity") indicts contemporary scholarship on modernity for its tendency to separate the topic of race from the narrative of the Enlightenment and the marginalization of postcolonial third world subjects from the discourse of the modern. Like Edward Said ("The Politics of Knowledge" in this edition), Bhabha argues that this separation is illegitimate and that the perspective of race on the Enlightenment shatters all claims to linearity in the account of the modern. A raced perspective on modernity shows in fact Western savagery at the heart of the Enlightenment project as revealed in the genocidal acts of the modern West on to the third world, the institution of slavery, and the like. Cornel West ("The New Cultural Politics of Difference") offers a genealogy of race and the evolution of the modern by tracing the work of decolonizing actors and practices and their activist commitments to social transformation, intellectual, existential, and political. Unlike Habermas's insistence on the still becoming of the Western modern, West argues that Enlightenment thinking and the great projects it produced and consolidated on the backs of the colonies and minorities have been overtaken by a history of counterhegemonic struggles since the post–World War II period. On a global scale, we live in a new age, the age of difference and multiplicity where the relations between the center and the periphery are rewritten and rescripted from the bottom up.

Issues of globalization, migration, and terrorism have increased this sense of instability in center–periphery relations, argue Alejandro Lugo ("Reflections on Border Theory, Culture, and the Nation") and Kelly Gates ("Technologies of Identity and the Identity of Technology: Race and the Social Construction of Biometrics"). These analysts' fast forward concerns over race to consider contemporary patterns of racialization associated with the policing of the U.S. border and consequent management of the new populations now entering the porous nation from Latin America, Asia, the Caribbean, and Africa. Gates and Lugo find that in the language of official policy, problems of immigration and terrorism are fundamentally connected through the category of race. Lugo argues that the dominant preoccupation with the physical boundaries and border checkpoints of "the" nation must be "re-imagined," particularly with regard to the way the modern state manages populations through the creation of cultural border lines of distinction and categorization that demarcate desirable from undesirable populations. While Lugo focuses on the matter of movement and migration across borders, Gates's analysis directs our attention to the racializing processes associated with the management of terror, specifically the deployment of biometric technologies for the production of digitally generated information profiles on the global flow of travelers, migrant or otherwise.

For Leslie Roman ("States of Insecurity: Cold War Memory, 'Global Citizenship' and Its Discontents") and George Lipsitz ("Whiteness and War"), the issue of the border is related to and deeply rooted in the warmaking and imperialist project of the United States. Roman argues that this is a project that is fundamentally informed by "whiteness" and the privileging of Anglo-American interests in state policy.

Three more chapters move the discussion of race toward a consideration of the nexus between nation, identity, and citizenship in the light of globalization and 9/11. Nikos Papastergiadis's essay ("The Homeless Citizen"), a personally inflected social analysis of the predicament of modern forms of affiliation, calls attention to the uneasy truce that exists between modern citizens and state rule in Anglo-Liberal democracies such as Australia and the United States. He maintains that the threat of terrorism and the calculated use of 9/11 by politicians have served to undermine the moral bond between country and citizen. Drawing on his father's immigrant experience in

Australia, Papastergiadis complexly argues that increasingly culture is being separated from place in the modern world as mass migration and electronic mediation alter the terms of existence and the relationships of social actors to modern institutions and states. Rereading assumptions of modern world divisions, Ella Shohat ("Taboo Memories and Diasporic Visions: Columbus, Palestine, and Arab-Jews") returns to the 1492 expulsion of Jews and Moors from Spain. From an incipient moment in the violence of European imperialist history, the time of the launching of Columbus's exploration, Shohat highlights an unexpected and undertheorized connection between the Arab–Jewish relationship and mainstream history of the West. As taught in schools, the voyages of Columbus and the "Age of European Exploration" are discussed without reference to this story of ethnic cleansing in fifteenth-century Spain that had as its object both Jews and Muslims. More importantly, her historical analysis reasserts an empirically, philosophically, and ethically grounded proposition; that is, there are weak boundaries and unsuspected lines of association and exchange between even the most embattled of groups. These unsuspected lines of affiliation and relationality place ethnic absolutism, jingoism, and unreflexive patriotism in grave doubt as forms of culture-based identity politics that first and foremost seek to silence voice and the capacity to dissent among subordinated groups. Cameron McCarthy, Michael Giardina, Susan Harewood, and Jin-Kyung Park ("Contesting Culture: Identity and Curriculum Dilemmas in the Age of Globalization, Postcolonialism and Multiplicity") look at the dynamic philosophical and practical challenges that the ethnic multiplicity associated with globalization, migration, and electronic mediation of images pose to the organization of knowledge in the university and schooling. They insist that a rethinking of the school curriculum to address issues of multiplicity, heterogeneity, and variability in patterns of historical incorporation of different populations into schooling is long overdue: this must begin with recognition of the heterogeneous basis of all knowledge.

Finally, Fazal Rizvi ("Representations of Islam and Education for Justice") and Deborah Britzman ("A Note to 'Identification with the Aggressor'") bring Part One to a close with trenchant discussions of the dangers, and indeed, limitations of the insider/outsider perspective in mainstream teaching of North American children about "other" groups and peoples. Though their methodological approaches are very different—Rizvi's sociological and philosophical and Britzman's psychoanalytical and interpretive—they make compelling appeals to educators, reminding them of their responsibility to examine violent representations of the other and to interrogate the meaning of aggression itself. Rizvi looks at religious discourse and its use in the politics of representation of Islam in the West, particularly after 9/11. He ultimately argues for an ethical, moral encounter between education, religion, and citizenship in which the educator has potentially a pivotal social and interventionary role in addressing racial and ethnic differences. Britzman concludes Part One with a deeply thoughtful reply to the other contributors to this first section of the *Second Edition,* offering a compassionate plea for contemporary students of race relations to attend to the nuance and complexity of the topic of aggressor/victim relations. Making the case for a psychoanalytic reading of the modern subject's relation to violence, Britzman suggests that the capacity for aggression resides in all of us. She maintains that the tendency to see aggression as simply and only a destructive force operating outside of "us," residing in "bad" people or anomic or deviant social actors (deviant adolescents being the often-used example), dominates mainstream thinking on schooling. This is especially true in the way we deal with aggression in research on curriculum and classroom management practice associated with children and adolescents. Britzman's chapter suggests that aggression in fact may have creative as well as destructive dimensions. In a powerful reply to the other contributors, Britzman submits that considerations of social difference that take the difficult knowledge of aggression for granted, or ignore its pedagogical complexity, risk the reproduction of normative thinking about the psychical dimensions of racial antagonism and foreclose useful insights into seemingly unresolvable conflicts of subjectivity that continue the slippery play of fantasy and reality in social learning. Tension, contradiction, heterogeneity, and contingency do not simply reside in the world outside or, for that matter, after education (Britzman 2003). All modern subjects—black white, Asian, Latino, or Native American—are transformed, divided, first and foremost internally, in the remainder of the fantasy/reality dynamic to which Britzman points.

Part Two: Contested Identities, Contested Desires: Racial Experience and Curriculum Dilemmas in the Twenty-First Century

The second organizing category foregrounded in this book is "identity." As migration, electronic mediation, and biometric and information technologies have separated culture from place, "identity" is similarly transformed. Here, the discussion of race focuses on the complexity of racial identities produced in postcolonial experience and in modern institutions of social and cultural reproduction. As Stuart Hall writes, racial identity is conceptualized as a contextualized performance "produced within specific historical and institutional sites, within specific discursive formations and practices, and by specific enunciative strategies" (Hall 1996, 4). Contributors therefore call attention to, for example, the ways in which minority urban cultural forms, linked especially to music and sports, such as basketball and football (cultural forms that are deeply alluring to school youth) are the vital carriers of the new messages of neoliberal imperatives now operating in U.S. education and society and elaborated on an expanded global scale (see King in this edition). In looking at the field of sport for guidance on the matter of racial identity, we are also pointing to expanded terms of reference for understanding educational dynamics, pointing beyond the walls of the institution of schooling itself to the wider culture and society where we believe the practices of the entertainment media, cultural practices of fashion and style, and the general circulation of popular images serve to instruct and educate the young in patterns of identity formation and forms of affiliation, forms of inclusion and exclusion (Dolby 2001).

In the first two chapters in this section, Gayatri Spivak ("Three Women's Texts and a Critique of Imperialism") and Rishma Dunlop ("One Living Female Child: The Education of a Sirdar's Daughter in Canada") examine the bitter fruit of colonialism and the specific ideological and cultural workings of the relationship between colonial whiteness, Western forms of social civility and trusteeship, and their subordinating impact on the colonized or native woman. In her chapter, "Three Women's Texts and a Critique of Imperialism," Spivak generates a spell-binding postcolonial deconstruction of three classic Western novels—*Jane Eyre*, *Wide Sargasso Sea*, and *Frankenstein*—pointing to their contradictory treatment of the native woman and the role of the Western woman as a carrier of imperialism. Dunlop's "One Living Female Child: The Education of a Sirdar's Daughter in Canada" employs a tapestry of history and autobiographical memory, poetry, and prose to interrupt social normative understandings of race—black versus white, the lighter versus the darker races, men versus women.

Vicky Lebeau ("The Unwelcome Child: Elizabeth Eckford and Hannah Arendt") and Christine Sleeter ("How White Teachers Construct Race") return us to the issue of racial antagonism and the complexity of racial identity formation, specifically in the United States. Both of these contributors focus our attention on ethical dilemmas that are imbricated in race relations and the performance of racial identities. Lebeau calls our attention to an example of an ethical dilemma taken from the beginnings of the civil rights movement in the 1950s in which the great German refugee philosopher, Hannah Arendt, sharply rejected the idea of broad liberal support for the movement's campaign to end segregation in Southern schools. Arendt's unorthodox objection was that the terms of the demand for desegregation were too narrow and that there was a need for parents to protect their children from the harshness of political life. She also insisted that issues such as the right to sexuality and sexual desire and the fear of miscegenation were being avoided by both the protesters as well as the racist opponents of the struggle for racial equality. Lebeau analyzes Arendt's arguments and the responses of those of her critics, such as Ralph Ellison and Sidney Hook, in light of contemporary thinking, particularly over the issue of the status of representation and power in identity politics and the struggle for change. Christine Sleeter ("How White Teachers Construct Race") also takes up the issue of moral dilemmas associated with the politics of policy intervention in the area of race relations in schooling. In a perceptive assessment of a two-year racial sensitivity training program for teachers in a small Midwestern town, Sleeter calls attention to patterns of aberrant decoding of the program by white teachers and to the unintended effects of its implementation. In her qualitative research study of the perspectives of teachers involved in this multicultural, racial sensitivity training program aimed at positively affecting white teachers' attitudes toward minorities in their classrooms, Sleeter illustrates the flaws in idealist policy making on race relations in education. In the study, teachers' negative attitudes to minorities seemed to harden rather than transform over the period of exposure to the staff development program in the sensitivity training in question.

Mary Coffey ("What Puts the 'Culture' in 'Multiculturalism'? An Analysis of Culture, Government, and the Politics of Mexican Identity") also offers an unsentimental view of multiculturalism and its susceptibility to appropriation by the state and dominant groups. She is philosophically and empirically interested in the work of culture and popular education in the mobilization of modern populations around ethnic and nationalistic core values—in brief, the deployment of multiculture for neoliberal political ends. Coffey offers a discursive analysis and a multisite case study of the appropriation of indigenous culture and the muralism of the Mexican revolutionary artists such as Diego Rivera by the PRI government in the 1920s and 1930s. Her conclusion is sobering: that "authentic" indigenous culture can be appropriated and reconstructed into a useable multiculture of the Mestizo; that authentically radical painting can also help to build this national popular view of mixed-race people in the service of the state's interest in domesticating and neutralizing resistance and elaborating governmental control over the entire Mexican population. Samantha King ("How to Be Good: The NFL, Corporate Philanthropy, and the Racialization of Generosity") revisits similar themes raised by Coffey, showing how urban sport-based philanthropy and associated multiculture can be put to work in the project of cause-related marketing of multinational corporations. This neoliberal project links urban cultural forms, corporate sponsors such as Nike, huge corporate sport businesses such as the NFL, and philanthropic projects such as fundraising for breast cancer research, into one expanded system of privatization of social welfare, health, education, and culture—areas once controlled by state policy. King documents the rise of this form of ironic Keynesianism on the part of multinational corporations, and the deepening appropriation of urban sport in this system of neoliberal appropriation and redirection of social welfarism and volunteerism.

Luis Mirón, Antonia Darder, Jonathan Xavier Inda, and Angharad Valdivia, in the section's final two essays, force us to consider the meaning of hybridity, transnationalism, and the new terms they present to the educational and social contexts of race relations in the United States. While Mirón et al. view the hybridity reflected in the transnationalism of Mexican and Latin American migrants crossing the border as offering positive challenges to U.S. education and culture, Valdivia cautions, as does Coffey earlier, that hybridity as the discursive and policy interpretation of the variability in the Latino and migrant populations may in fact serve to neutralize the politics of these subordinate racial groups so constrained. In a nuanced reading of the responses of students from Santa Ana, California, to the ideologies of language competence as embodied in Proposition 227 (California's "English for the Children" Proposition voted into law in the late 1990s), Mirón et al. maintain that these students see themselves as part of a globalizing world context where dexterity in English and Spanish is, and will continue to be, a vital asset. On the other hand, Valdivia, in her survey of the emergent discipline of Latino studies, argues that Latino studies lays bare the untenability of binary racial coding because of the radical hybridity within Latinidad but that this same hybridity opens up a space for erasure and displacement at the level of culture and bodies.

Part Three: Racial Affiliation, Racial Resentment, Racialized Citizenship: State and Educational Policy Dilemmas in the Twenty-First Century

This concluding section is structured by the question "What is the specific character of the modern racialized state and its relationship to educational policy?" While there is no simple answer, it is a vital question since contemporary research seems to be pointing us in contradictory directions about the nature of the state in light of radical global transformations. On the one hand, scholars such as Henry Giroux (1996), Naomi Klein (2002), and Anthony Giddens (1991, 2000) suggest that with respect to the racially and socially disadvantaged, the state is decomposing: disinvesting in programs of social welfare and support. As the state retreats from its public commitments, it simultaneously centers the (contradictory and ironic) programs of altruism, volunteerism, and philanthropy underwritten by multinational corporations and nongovernmental organizations. On the other hand, Michael Apple (in this edition), Kelly Gates (2003), Andy Green (1997), and Saskia Sassen (2002, 2003), among others, argue that the state is consolidating: digging itself back into modernist borders that are paradoxically reinforced by the new postindustrial biometric information technologies of surveillance and regulation, accompanied by an emphasis on self-regulation and a Foucauldian headless body politic. These scholars, too, point to the expanded and critical role of the state in brokering the interests of global capital as it seeks out new areas of value in the process of opening up new markets and colonizing new labor forces in the third world and on the periphery of the first.

But it may be the case that both sides of this story of the recomposing state are valid, tendencies that are seen in the No Child Left Behind Act of 2001 (NCLB), which simultaneously tightens state control over educators while it redirects public funds to private educational organizations in a move to sever "public" from "schooling." In the process, NCLB siphons money from the racially disadvantaged, aggravating racial and educational inequality. In this section, we call attention to these features of the racialized state, recognizing that developments in the United States are deeply connected to a wider world reality, linking up the particularity of the local/urban realities with the global and the planetary.

Cameron McCarthy and Greg Dimitriadis, Michael Apple, and Lawrence Grossberg open Part Three by calling attention to larger patterns in culture and society that connect race to globalization and neoliberalism. In these essays, the authors maintain that popular culture, in a variety of expressions across race and class formations, has become a theater for competing views of the present and the future of "lived" democracy in the United States. While Cameron McCarthy and Greg Dimtriadis ("Governmentality and the Sociology of Education: Media, Educational Policy, and the Politics of Resentment") and Michael Apple ("Patriotism, Democracy, and the Hidden Effects of Race") point to the rise of popular resentment and patriotism as responses to the disembeddedness associated with globalization and 9/11, Grossberg ("Cultural Studies, the War against Kids, and the Rebecoming of U.S. Modernity") foregrounds the folding in of state responsibility to the young into corporatist neoliberal agendas. However, none of these analysts is willing to accept outright the notion of the irrelevance of the state or of its demise. McCarthy and Dimitriadis make the case that state and public policy, corporate interest and popular culture must be read in tandem to understand the deepening racial inequality in schooling. Apple points to the Bush administration's No Child Left Behind Act as indicating the state's announcement of a trend toward the marketization and privatization of schooling. And, Grossberg identifies the cuts in federal spending and tax cuts for the rich, beginning in the 1980s, as the clearest possible sign of material disinvestment in both minority and majority youth. This, for Grossberg, is not simply a policy issue but an ethical issue. It is symptomatic of the fact that as both the left and the right attack the modernization of institutional and cultural life in the United States, both minority and majority kids are the principal victims of their misguided policies.

This theoretical and methodological emphasis on materialist analysis linking state and corporate policy to urban education and culture is continued with even greater specificity of focus on the inner city in the chapters of Jean Anyon, Michelle Fine and Lois Weis, and Michael Giardina and CL Cole that follow. Jean Anyon's "A Political Economy of Race, Urban Education, and Educational Policy" adds a necessary depth of political economic analysis of the status of the urban poor to this collection. The thrust of her argument is that the lack of jobs and decent incomes for African American and Latino families in U.S. cities is a pervasive phenomenon that serves to undermine the educational achievement and job futures of black and brown working class youth. Anyon maintains that with the rise of globalization and neoliberal agendas across both state and corporate sectors we have entered into a new post-civil-rights period in which access to economic opportunity is undermined in part by deindustrialization and new labor market demands for "soft" as opposed to "hard" skills. Despite the impersonal veneer of structural adjustments to the domestic economy, Anyon points out that older forms of racial bias in job recruiting and hiring and educational preparation remain a persistent impediment in the lives of young workers. Analysis of neoliberalism is given a somewhat different twist by Michael Giardina and CL Cole. They point to the conflation of the post-civil-rights political culture and the neoliberal entrepreneurial instincts of a new class of urban businessmen, like Magic Johnson, who have sought to exploit their connections to the inner city itself. Giardina and Cole report on the case of Harlem in New York City, illustrating the interconnection between business and gentrification across race and class. In this study, black businessmen like Johnson join with global multinational interests like McDonald's and Starbucks in deepening the exploitation and displacement of the urban population. Meanwhile, third world as well as both black and white suburban middle-class renters and condo buyers displace long-time, working-class African American and Latino residents, transforming this historic neighborhood enclave into a elite bedroom community for the downtown Manhattan business district.

In their chapter entitled "Crime Stories: A Critical Look through Race, Ethnicity, and Gender," Fine and Weis also lead us away from the simplistic media labeling of the inner city. Analyzing data from 154 life histories of urban poor-zone residents, they point to the variability of the perspectives of urban residents on crime and violence. For Fine and Weis, the nonsynchronous intersection of race, ethnicity, and gender articulated across multiple stories of everyday life foreground three different types of crime/violence discourses. While African American and Latino men emphasized the menace of state-based (police) violence and white men expressed concern about street violence, women of all races and ethnicities in the study expressed as a principal concern the issue of domestic violence. In "The Queer Character of Racial Politics and Violence in America," William Pinar's account of inmate-on-inmate rape complicates the discussion of racial violence considerably and reverses the historical story of the use of rape by white males to subjugate black women and men. The queerness of contemporary rape in the post-civil-rights prison context that Pinar discusses is heterosexual-on-heterosexual, black on white. It is ironic that it is within the context of a coercive institution of the state itself—the state-run maximum-security prison—that black men seek revenge for abuses conducted both in the present but also, historically, in the era of lynching, and even further back, to slavery. Of course, the homoerotic issue of both black men's and white men's desires for each other remains a historical subtext in this essay.

Arjun Appadurai, Kent Ono, and Edward Said bring Part Three to a close with chapters that interrogate the very meaning of race and ethnicity—a discussion that Michael Omi and Howard Winant launched at the beginning of this book. Each of these chapters seeks to bring the debate over racial antagonism and ethnicity back onto the field of knowledge itself—back onto the specific terrain of the institutionalization of subjugated knowledges and curriculum reform in the areas of race/ethnic relations, area studies, and postcolonial studies. In his essay, "Diversity and Disciplinarity as Cultural Artifacts," Appadurai makes the case for moving beyond the kind of representational identity politics that dominate current thinking about race and curriculum reform in education. The matter of diversity understood as cultural diversity (multiculturalism), argues Appadurai, is a particular interpretation of difference that privileges the practice of cultural and political representativeness as a bounded identity in curriculum organization while bracketing knowledge and epistemology. By contrast, critical methodological diversity foregrounds heterogeneity in knowledge making and production but often brackets experience, practice, and place, thus generating hypothetical subjects. Appadurai argues for the conjoining of discourses such as multiculturalism, ethnic studies, and area studies with cultural studies in the founding of a new multidisciplinary approach to curriculum reform in the area of race and ethnic relations. Kent Ono's essay ("Asian American Studies after 9/11") complements Appadurai's argument, suggesting that there is a need to connect the ethnic studies disciplines (using Asian American studies as an example) to broader political issues beyond the sanitized world of the academy. Ono insists on the need to think about the link between epistemology and politics, as well as the need to think beyond the limited interests of one's putative group of cultural or political affiliation. These ideas have demonstrable practical dimensions, as Ono observes, in activism to resist conservative social policies such as Proposition 187 (the California statewide referendum on the proposal to eliminate health, education, and welfare benefits for undocumented migrants). On the basis of these observations, Ono outlines, in tentative and transitional terms, possible conditions for a post–civil rights interdisciplinary activism in the university built on the knowledge base of ethnic studies.

In the final section of Part Three, the late Edward Said ("The Politics of Knowledge") issues a counterblast against ethnocentric identity politics in education as well as the smug, self-satisfied dominance of the Eurocentric curriculum in schooling. Consistent in this thematic over a lifetime's work, Said warned that: "A single overmastering identity at the core of the academic enterprise, whether that identity be Western, African, or Asian is a confinement, a deprivation. The world is made up of numerous identities interacting, sometimes harmoniously, sometimes antithetically" (Said in this edition). Published in the first edition of *Race, Identity, and Representation in Education*, this observation has proven prophetic. Said was one of the earliest public intellectuals to advise us that the powerful cultural, political, and economic forces released by globalization could not be adequately addressed by educational institutions operating on outmoded theories of disciplinary knowledge. He maintained that the difference and multiplicity precipitated by developments such as mass migration, the amplification of images in electronic mediation, and the movement of people and cultural capital could not be contained in schooling by doctoring the curriculum through models of content addition. His argument, then, still stands now: that the great challenge of education in the modern world is to rethink the linkages of knowledge and culture, exchange and association among all people. The implication, in the language of Said's secular humanism, is the intellectual requirement to think contextually, relationally, and contrapuntally about the organization of school knowledge and classroom pedagogy—and to think against the grain of normative assumptions about the nature and role of race and difference in contemporary life, in and outside of schooling.

In a provocative Afterword, Paul Willis reminds us that the issue at stake in these debates over the nature and future of race and schooling concerns real, warm-bodied youth, who are in his view vulnerable class actors, first and foremost. They are—he argues, echoing Grossberg earlier—the "unconscious foot soldiers in the long front of modernity." Instead of using the term *globalization* (a word that is often used too glibly), Willis points instead to the reorganization of capital, material production, and consumption. With others in this collection, Willis characterizes the present era as the "third wave" of modernization, a period in which working class children (particularly male youth) and poor-zone inner-city youth have been effectively displaced by deindustrialization, outsourcing, and the changing information and service-based nature of the economy. Culture and diversity are important in this story about the contradiction and tensions in the global modern. Willis argues for an engaged (rather than neutral) reading of culture in relation to the economic and social transformations actually taking place in the lives of modern youth. On this basis, theory and practice may discover relevancy to the myriad challenges facing teachers and students learning to live in a complex world. This same spirited commitment to praxis also extends to the ongoing tasks of diverse publics participating in battles over the future of a global modern, indeed learning in a multiplicity of local contexts to sustain the capacity to imagine, to aspire, and to make the world differently.

Conclusion: New Conversations about Race and Education

This collection's thirty chapters take us across a wide range of substantive and methodological concerns, as read through a variety of disciplinary and interdisciplinary lenses. The chapters are linked, however, in an endeavor to highlight how tensions around culture, racial identity, and public policy are now playing out in the realm of education and social life since 9/11, and more broadly in the face of ongoing global transformations. Throughout this introduction we have articulated a now widely expressed awareness, shared by our collaborators and others (e.g., Hargreaves 2003), that our age is one of fundamental insecurity and vulnerability—one with profound implications for education and cultural practice writ large. As with any interdisciplinary project, the collection of chapters expresses distinct points of view and occupies sundry theoretical standpoints that do not usually coincide in the analysis of race. Despite differences of approach and analytic method—from the sociological to the psychoanalytical, the material to the immaterial—the contributors' concerns overlap on three interrelated categories that organize the collection: popular culture, dynamics of identity, and state/public policy.

First, with respect to the category of popular "culture," contributors consistently endeavor to work to reformulate the concept of culture by offering empirical analyses, case examples, and theorizations of mass mediated consumption that are often not pursued concurrently in race-related debates in educational studies. Through this emphasis, contributors to the *Second Edition* link education to the politics of popular culture and public policy, with imbedded discriminations in the instrumental and expressive orders of the racialized state, both local and global. Second, the categories of "identity" and identification are critical to understanding the performative impact of racial affiliation and antagonism in education and society. And like culture, identity is understood to animate material and imaginary terrains of struggle, where aggression but also abiding possibilities for future productive forms of affliation and collaboration both reside—neither reducible to the other. Finally, authors give emphasis to key issues of state and public policy and the regulatory landscape in which racial antagonism and forms of affiliation are administered and modulated. We agree with the now common observation that a suprastate system has emerged, characterized by an adventurous project of policing a racialized Empire at great distances overseas (in places such as Iraq and Afghanistan) for purposes of extending privatized conditions of market advantage and uninhibited capitalist accumulation. Yet, at the same time, while the state's role in extending the rapacious reach of capital requires covert pacification abroad it also engenders a rigorous regime of controls and overt intrusions at "home" in the name of domestic security, revealing a state that is vulnerable, porous, and deeply insecure.

Of course, the role and function of schools have been profoundly complicated in this context. The traditional roles of schooling—for example, preparing young people for work and citizenship—no longer provide clear mooring. If nothing else, our moment is marked by difference, and multiplicity, in ways indexed throughout this edition. However, public policy initiatives around schools and schooling have tended to elide this complexity, opting instead to claim a kind of fullness of knowledge and control over the curricula. Working against the tide of difference, many educators have tended to draw a bright line of distinction between the established school curriculum and the teeming world of multiplicity that flourishes in the everyday lives of youth beyond the school. These educators still insist on a project of homogeneity, normalization, and the production of the socially functional citizen. Such technocratic approaches to difference insist on bringing the problems of multiplicity and difference into a framework of institutional intelligibility and manageability. We see "resentment" logics informing a range of school activities today, from high stakes testing such as No Child Left Behind to narrow technichist approaches to multiculturalism (Dimitriadis and McCarthy 2001; McCarthy 1998; McCarthy and Dimitriadis this edition).

It should not be surprising, then, that many youth are turning away from school when engaging the issues and concerns most relevant in their lives. Indeed, as we have (individually and collectively) shown elsewhere, young people are turning to popular culture and alternative schooling institutions in the face of these realities. Young people are using a wide span of cultural forms to navigate their everyday lives today, including popular music, fashion, dance, and art (Dimitriadis 2001; Dolby 2001). More and more, as this work makes clear, we must ask ourselves what kinds of curricula—broadly defined—young people draw on to understand, explain, and live through the world around them. This is messy terrain, one that exceeds a priori notions about identity often privileged by educators. Young people in the United States and around the world are elaborating complex kinds of social and cultural identifications through music like hip hop and techno in ways that challenge predictive notions about texts, practices, and identities. As contributors to this collection and others make clear, the multiple uses to which popular culture is put challenge and belie easy notions of "cultural identification."

In closing, the enormous social, cultural, and material dislocations since the mid-1990s have destabilized any certainty around the traditional roles of learning in schools. And yet pedagogical work remains central to possibilities for a different global future—early childhood literacy and communication, the preparation of young learners for meaningful work, the fostering of capacity for political participation in civil society and citizenship. This contested landscape of global inequality and marginalization, we argue, demands a different set of understandings as to what constitutes an engaged "research imaginary" in education today. That is, how to contextualize and envision pedagogy and cultural work that might make a difference beyond privileged market-driven solutions as individuated identity consumption. This capacity for intervention seems at the heart of any discussion of race, identity, and representation in education today—where the idea that theory is not enough, that critique is not an end in itself is taken seriously. Here contributors have followed an imperative not just to rewrite geographies of gender, to theorize diasporic memory, and to critique racial logics in the context of state-networked globalization after 9/11. Seeking to expand these critical terms, authors reimagine possibilities of alternative policy and collaborative practice that respond to aspirations for participation and self-determination still pulsing in the everyday lives of the historically excluded and their allies in the centers and peripheries that divide our world. Above all else, we hope these chapters will provoke debate that helps to nurture a more expansive notion of "education" itself, thus inviting further contributions from a broad range of cultural critics and intellectual workers.

References

Appadurai, A. *Modernity at Large*. Minneapolis: Minnesota Press, 1996.

Appadurai, A. "The Capacity to Aspire: Culture and the Terms of Recognition." In *Culture and Public Action*, edited by V. Rao and M. Walton, 59–84. Stanford: Stanford Social Sciences/Stanford University Press, 2004.

Bauman, Z. "Tourists and Vagabonds." In *Globalization: The Human Consequences*, edited by Z. Bauman, 77–102. Cambridge, UK: Polity, 1998.

Bennett, T. *The Birth of the Museum*. New York: Routledge, 1995.

Bennett, T. "Putting Policy Back into Cultural Studies." In *What Is Cultural Studies*, edited by J. Storey, 307–21. London: Arnold, 1996.

Bennett, T. "Culture and Governmentality." In *Foucault, Cultural Studies and Governmentality*, edited by J. Bratich, J. Packer, and C. McCarthy, 47–66. Albany: SUNY Press, 2003.

Britzman, D. *After Education: Anna Freud, Melanie Klein, and Pyschoanalytic Histories of Learning*. New York: State University of New York Press, 2003.

Carlson, D. *Leaving Safe Harbors*. New York: RoutledgeFalmer, 2003.

Dimitriadis, G. *Performing Identity/Performing Culture: Hip Hop as Text, Pedagogy, and Lived Practice*. New York: Peter Lang, 2001.

Dimitriadis, G. and C. McCarthy. *Reading and Teaching the Postcolonial: From Baldwin to Basquiat and Beyond*. New York: Teachers College Press, 2001.

Dolby, N. *Constructing Race: Youth, Identity, and Popular Culture in South Africa*. Albany: SUNY Press, 2001.

Gates, K. "Biometrics at the Border: Automated Identification and Race." Paper presented at the University of Illinois at Urbana, Institute of Communications Research, 2003.

Giddens, A. *The Consequences of Modernity*. Stanford: Stanford University Press, 1991.

Giddens, A. *Runaway World: How Globalization Is Refashioning Our Lives*. London: Routledge, 2000.

Giroux, H. *Fugitive Cultures: Race, Violence, and Youth*. New York: Routledge, 1996.

Green, A. *Education, Globalization and Nation State*. London: Macmillan, 1997.

Hall, S. "Race, Articulation and Societies Structured in Dominance." In *Sociological Theories: Race and Colonialism*, 305–45 Paris: UNESCO, 1980.

Hall, S. "Introduction: Who Needs Identity?" In *Questions of Cultural Identity*, edited by S. Hall and P. DuGay. London: Sage, 1996, 1–17.

Hardt, M. and A. Negri. *Multitude: War and Democracy in the Age of Empire*. New York: Penguin Press, 2004.

Hargreaves, A. *Teaching in the Knowledge Society*. New York: Teachers College Press, 2003.

Hemingway, E. *For Whom the Bell Tolls*. New York: Simon and Schuster, 1996. (Orig. pub. 1940.)

Klein, N. *No Logo*. 2nd ed. New York: Picador, 2002.

Lipsitz, G. "Locked on This Earth: Movement and Stasis in Black Culture." Lecture delivered at Levis Center, University of Illinois at Urbana, March 6, 2004.

McCarthy, C. *The Uses of Culture*. New York: Routledge, 1998.

McCarthy, C. and W. Crichlow, eds. *Race, Identity and Representation in Education*. 1st ed. New York: Routledge, 1993.

McCarthy, C., G. Hudak, S. Miklaucic, and P. Saukko, eds. *Sound Identities*. New York: Peter Lang, 1999.

Miller, T. *Technologies of Truth: Cultural Citizenship and the Popular Media*. Minneapolis: Minnesota Press, 1998.

Rao, V. and M. Walton, eds. *Culture and Public Action*. Stanford, CA: Stanford Social Sciences/Stanford University Press, 2004.

Ravitch, D. "Diversity and Democracy: Multicultural Education in America." *American Educator* 14 (1990): 16–48.

Said, W. E. "Afterword." In *From Oslo to Iraq and the Road Map: Essays*. New York: Pantheon Books, 2004.

Sassen, S. *Global Networks/Linked Cities*. New York: RoutledgeFalmer, 2002.

Sassen, S. *Denationalization: Economy and Polity in a Global Digital Age*. Princeton, NJ: Princeton University Press, 2003.

Willensky, J. *Learning to Divide the World: Education at Empire's End*. Minneapolis: University of Minnesota Press, 1998.

Williams, R. *The Long Revolution*. London: Chatto and Windus, 1961.

Yeats, W.B. "The Second Coming." In *The Variorum Edition of the Poems of W. B. Yeats*, edited by P. Allen and R. Alspach, 401–2. New York: Macmillan, 1957. (Orig. pub. 1921.)

Yudice, G. *The Expedience of Culture: Uses of Culture in the Global Era*. Durham, NC: Duke University Press, 2003.

Part One
Race, Globalization, and the Management of Popular Culture

1

The Theoretical Status of the Concept of Race

MICHAEL OMI AND HOWARD WINANT

Introduction

Race was once a relatively intelligible concept; only recently have we seriously challenged its theoretical coherence. Today there are deep questions about what we actually mean by the term. But before (roughly) World War II, before the rise of Nazism, before the end of the great European empires and particularly before the decolonization of Africa, before the urbanization of the U.S. black population and the rise of the modern civil rights movement, race was still largely seen in Europe and North America (and elsewhere as well) as an essence, a natural phenomenon, whose meaning was fixed, as constant as a southern star.

In the earlier years of the twentieth century, only a handful of pioneers, people like W. E. B. Du Bois and Franz Boas, and Robert E. Park of the Chicago School, conceived of race in a more social and historical way. Other doubters included avant-garde racial theorists emerging from the intellectual and cultural ferment of the Negritude movement and the Harlem Renaissance, pan-Africanists and nationalists, and Marxists electrified by the Russian revolution. Many of these had returned from the battlefields of France to a Jim Crow United States, swept in 1919 by antiblack race riots. Others went back to a colony—Senegal, India, Trinidad, the Philippines—where they found the old racist imperialism proceeding undisturbed. So now they sought to apply to the mother continent of Africa or other colonial outposts, or to the United States or Europe itself, the rhetorics of national self-determination expressed at Versailles, in the Comintern, in the various pan-Africanist conferences that had been occurring, or in the music, art, and literature that was now being produced by colored hearts and minds all around the world.

These were but the early upsurges of twentieth-century challenges to the naturalistic and essentialized concept of race that had dominated Western thought for centuries; that had indeed been invented in Europe and had evolved in tandem with the Enlightenment and European imperial rule. To be sure, doubts about the eternality of racial categories, however important, were still very much on the margins of accepted knowledge. Early racial critics were not only peripheral to the global system of racial hierarchy; they too were marked, still marked, by its power and ubiquity. Even the pioneers just mentioned still paid homage to race theories we would now view as archaic at best.[1] All made incomplete breaks with essentialist notions of race, whether biologistic or otherwise deterministic, as do we still today.

3

Although racial essentialism remains very much with us, at the dawn of the twenty-first century, the theory of race has been significantly transformed. The social construction of race, which we have labeled the *racial formation process* (Omi and Winant 1994), is widely recognized today, so much so that it is now often conservatives who argue that race is an illusion. The main task facing racial theory today, in fact, is no longer to critique the seemingly "natural" or "common sense" concept of race, although that effort has not been entirely completed by any means. Rather, the central task is to focus attention on the continuing significance and changing meaning of race; it is to argue against the recent discovery of the illusory nature of race; against the supposed contemporary transcendence of race; against the widely reported death of the concept of race; and against the replacement of the category of race by other, supposedly more objective categories like ethnicity, nationality, or class. All these initiatives are mistaken at best, and intellectually dishonest at worst.

In order to substantiate these assertions, we must first ask, what is race? Is it merely an illusion: an ideological construct utilized to manipulate, divide, and deceive? This position has been taken by many theorists, and activists as well, including many who have served the cause of racial and social justice in the United States. Or is race something real, material, objective? This view too has its adherents, including both racial reactionaries and racial radicals.

In our view both of these approaches miss the boat. The concept of race is neither an ideological construct, nor does it reflect an objective condition. Here we first reflect critically on these two opposed viewpoints on the contemporary theory of race. Then we offer an alternative perspective based on racial formation theory.

Race as an Ideological Construct

The assertion that race is an ideological construct, understood in the sense of an "illusion" that explains other "material" relationships in distorted fashion, seems highly problematic. Though today it is usually seen as a core tenet of conservative racial theory—think of "colorblindness" (Connerly 2000) and the main neoconservative positions (Murray 1984; Thernstrom and Thernstrom 1997; Glazer 1997; see also Winant 1997)—as noted, this view is held across the political spectrum from right to left. For example, the prominent radical historian Barbara Fields takes this view in her 1990 article "Slavery, Race and Ideology in the United States of America." Although Fields inveighs against various uses of the race concept, she directs her critical barbs most forcefully against historians who "invoke race as a historical explanation" (Fields 1990, 101).

According to Fields, the concept of race arose to meet an ideological need: its original effectiveness lay in its ability to reconcile freedom and slavery. The idea of race provided "the means of explaining slavery to people whose terrain was a republic founded on radical doctrines of liberty and natural rights..." (Fields 1990, 114).

But, Fields says, to argue that race, once framed as a category in thought, an ideological explanation for certain distinct types of social inequality, "takes on a life of its own" in social relationships is to transform (or "reify") an illusion into a reality. Such a position could be sustained "[o]nly if *race* is defined as innate and natural prejudice of color... ":

> [S]ince race is not genetically programmed, racial prejudice cannot be genetically programmed either, but must arise historically.... The preferred solution is to suppose that, having arisen historically, race then ceases to be a historical phenomenon and becomes instead an external motor of history; according to the fatuous but widely repeated formula, it "takes on a life of its own." In other words, once historically acquired, race becomes hereditary. The shopworn metaphor hus offers camouflage for a latter-day version of Lamarckism. (Fields 101, emphasis original)

Thus race is either an illusion that does ideological work or an objective biological fact. Since it is certainly not the latter, it must be the former. No intermediate possibility—consider, for example, the Durkheimian notion of a "social fact"—is considered.[2]

Some of this account, for example, the extended discussion of the origins of North American race thinking, can be accepted without major objection.[3] Furthermore, Fields effectively demonstrates the absurdity of many commonly held ideas about race. But her position at best can only account for the *origins* of race thinking, and then only in one social context. To examine how race thinking evolved from these origins, how it responded to changing sociocultural circumstances, is ruled out. Why and how did race thinking survive after emancipation? Fields cannot answer, because the very perpetuation of the concept of race is ruled out by her theoretical approach. As a relatively orthodox Marxist, Fields could argue that changing "material conditions" continued to give rise to changes in racial "ideology," except that even the limited autonomy this would attach to the concept of race would exceed her standards. Race cannot take on "a life of its own"; it is a pure ideology, an illusion.

Fields simply skips from emancipation to the present, where she disparages opponents of "racism" for unwittingly perpetuating it. In denunciatory terms Fields concludes by arguing for the concept's abolition:

> Nothing handed down from the past could keep race alive if we did not constantly reinvent and re-ritualize it to fit our own terrain. If race lives on today, it can do so only because we continue to create and re-create it in our social life, continue to verify it, and thus continue to need a social vocabulary that will allow us to make sense, not of what our ancestors did then, but of what we choose to do now. (Fields 1999, 118)

Fields is unclear about how "we" should jettison the ideological construct of race, and one can well understand why. By her own logic, racial ideologies cannot be abolished by acts of will. One can only marvel at the ease with which she distinguishes the bad old slavery days of the past from the present, when "we" anachronistically cling, as if for no reason, to the illusion that race retains any meaning. We foolishly "throw up our hands" and acquiesce in race thinking, rather than—doing what? Denying the racially demarcated divisions in society? Training ourselves to be "color-blind"?[4]

In any case the view that race is an illusion or piece of false consciousness is held not only by intellectuals, based on both well-intentioned and ulterior motivations; it also has a commonsense character. One hears in casual discussion, for example, or in introductory social science classes, variations on the following statement: "I don't care if a person is black, white, or purple, I treat them exactly the same; a person's just a person to me...." Furthermore, some of the integrationist aspirations of racial minority movements, especially the civil rights movement, invoke this sort of idea. Consider the famous line from the "I Have a Dream" speech, the line that made black conservative cultural critic Shelby Steele's career: "that someday my four little children will be judged, not by the color of their skin, but by the content of their character...."

Our core criticisms of this "race as ideology" approach are two. First, it fails to recognize the salience a social construct can develop over half a millennium or more of diffusion, or should we say enforcement, as a fundamental principle of social organization and identity formation. The longevity of the race concept, and the enormous number of effects race thinking (and race acting) have produced, guarantee that race will remain a feature of social reality across the globe, and a fortiori in the United States, despite its lack of intrinsic or scientific merit (in the biological sense).[5] Second, and related, this approach fails to recognize that at the level of experience, of everyday life, race is a relatively impermeable part of our identities. For example, U.S. society is so thoroughly racialized that to be without racial identity is to be in danger of having no identity. To be raceless is akin to being genderless. It is to be invisible or ghostly.[6] Indeed, when one cannot identify another's race, a microsociological "crisis of interpretation" results, something perhaps best interpreted in ethnomethodological or Goffmanian terms. To complain about such a situation may be understandable, but it does not advance understanding.

Race as an Objective Condition

On the other side of the coin, it is clearly problematic to assign objectivity to the race concept. Such theoretical practice puts us in quite heterogeneous, and sometimes unsavory, company. Of course the biologistic racial theories of the past do this: here we are thinking of the prototypes of fascism, such as Gobineau and Chamberlain (Mosse 1978), of the eugenicists, such as Lothrop Stoddard and Madison Grant, and of the "founding fathers" of scientific racism such as Agassiz, Broca, Terman, and Yerkes (Kevles 1985; Chase 1977; Gould 1981). Indeed an extensive legacy of this sort of thinking extends right up to the present.

But much liberal and even radical social science, though firmly committed to a social as opposed to biological interpretation of race, nevertheless also slips into a kind of objectivism about racial identity and racial meaning. This is true because race is all too frequently treated as a discrete variable. It is considered, investigated, or "controlled for" as if it were an objective phenomenon, rather than a sociohistorical construct that is deeply unstable and internally contradictory (Zuberi 2001). Thus, to select only prominent examples, Daniel Moynihan, William Julius Wilson, Milton Gordon, and many other mainstream thinkers theorize race in terms that downplay its variability and historically contingent character. So even these major writers, whose explicit rejection of biologistic forms of racial theory would be unquestioned, fall prey to a kind of creeping objectivism of race. For in their analyses a modal explanatory approach emerges as follows: sociopolitical circumstances change over historical time, racially defined groups adapt or fail to adapt to these changes, achieving mobility or remaining mired in poverty. In this logic there is no reconceptualization of group identities, of the constantly shifting parameters through which race is thought about, group interests are assigned, statuses are ascribed, agency is attained, and roles performed.

Contemporary racial theory, then, is often "objectivistic" about its fundamental category. Although abstractly acknowledged to be a sociohistorical construct, race in practice is often treated as an objective fact. One simply *is* one's race; in the contemporary United States, for example, if we discard euphemisms, we have five color-based racial categories: black, white, brown, yellow, or red.

This is problematic, indeed ridiculous, in numerous ways. Nobody really belongs in these boxes; they are patently absurd reductions of human variation. But even accepting the nebulous "rules" of racial classification (e.g., what Harris [1964] calls "hypodescent"), many people don't fit anywhere: Into what categories should we place Arab Americans? Brazilians? Argentinians? South Asians? Such a list could be extended indefinitely; every racial identity is unstable. Objectivist treatments, lacking a critique of the constructed character of racial meanings, also clash with experiential dimensions of the issue. If one doesn't *act* black, white, and so on, that's just deviance from the norm. There is in these approaches an insufficient appreciation of the performative aspect of race, as postmodernists or pragmatists might call it.[7]

To summarize the critique of this "race as objective condition" approach, then, it fails on three counts: First, it cannot grasp the processual and relational character of racial identity and racial meaning. Second, it denies the historicity and social comprehensiveness of the race concept. And third, it cannot account for the way actors, both individual and collective, have to manage incoherent and conflictual racial meanings and identities in everyday life. It has no concept, in short, of what we have labeled *racial formation*.

Toward a Critical Theory of the Concept of Race

The foregoing clearly sets forth the agenda that any adequate theorization of the race concept must fulfill. Such an approach must be theoretically constructed so as to steer between the Scylla of "race as illusion" and the Charybdis of "racial objectivism." Such a critical theory can be consistently developed, we suggest, drawing upon racial formation theory. Such a theoretical formulation must be explicitly historicist: it must recognize the importance of historical context and contingency in the framing of racial categories and the social construction of racially defined experiences.

What would be the minimum conditions for the development of such a critical, processual theory of race? Beyond addressing the standard issues to which we have already referred,[8] such as equality, domination/resistance, and micro–macro linkages, we suggest three such conditions for such a theory:

- It must apply to contemporary *politics*.
- It must apply in an increasingly *global context*.
- It must apply across *historical time*.

Contemporary Political Relationships

The meaning and salience of race is forever being reconstituted in the present. In the last half century new racial politics emerged in a process, usually decades long, that constituted a hegemonic shift or postcolonial transition. Along the lines of what we have called the "trajectory of racial politics" (Omi and Winant 1994, 84–88) the meanings of race, and the political articulations of race, have proliferated.

Examples include the appearance of competing racial projects, by which we mean efforts to institutionalize racial meanings and identities in particular social structures: notably those of individual, family, community, and state. As equality- and difference-oriented movements contend with racial "backlash" over sustained periods of time, as binary logics of racial antagonism (white/ black, Latino/Indio, settler/native, etc.) become more complex and decentered, political deployment of the concept of race comes to signal qualitatively new types of political domination, as well as new types of opposition.

Consider the United States example. In the United States today it is now possible to perpetuate racial domination without making any explicit reference to race at all. Subtextual or "coded" racial signifiers, or the mere denial of the continuing significance of race, usually suffice. Similarly, in terms of opposition, it is now possible to resist racial domination in entirely new ways, particularly by limiting the reach and penetration of the political system into everyday life, by generating new identities, new collectivities, new (imagined) communities that are relatively less permeable to the hegemonic system.[9] Much of the rationale for Islamic currents among blacks in the United States, and to some extent for the Afrocentric phenomenon, can be found here. Thus the old political choices, integration vs. separatism, assimilation vs. nationalism, are no longer the only options.[10]

In the "underdeveloped" world, proliferation of so-called postcolonial phenomena also have significant racial dimensions, as the entire Fanonian tradition (merely to select one important theoretical current) makes clear. Crucial debates have now been occurring for decades on the question of postcolonial subjectivity and identity, the insufficiency of the simple dualism of "Europe and its others," the subversive and parodic dimensions of political culture at and beyond the edges of the old imperial boundaries (Said 1978; Bhabha 1990).

The Global Context of Race

Once seen in terms of imperial reach, in terms of colonization, conquest, and migration, racial space has always been globalized. In the postcolonial period, however, a new kind of racial globalization has become visible.[11] Today the distinction "developed/underdeveloped" has been definitively overcome. Obviously by this we don't mean that now there are no disparities between North and South, rich and poor. Rather we mean that the movement of capital and labor has internationalized all nations, all regions. Today we have reached the point where "the empire strikes back,"[12] as former (neo)colonial subjects, now redefined as "migrants" and "undocumented" persons (sometimes called "denizens"), challenge the majoritarian status or cultural domination of the formerly metropolitan group (the whites, the Europeans, the "Americans," the "French," etc.). Meanwhile, such phenomena as the rise of "diasporic" models of blackness, the creation of "panethnic"[13] communities of Latinos and Asians (in such countries as the United Kingdom or the United States), and the breakdown of borders in both Europe and North America, all seem to be internationalizing and racializing previously national polities, cultures, and identities. To take just one example, popular culture now divulgates racial awareness almost instantaneously, as reggae, rap, samba, or various African pop styles leap from continent to continent.

Comparing hegemonic racial formations in the contemporary global context suggests that diasporic solidarity and race consciousness is taking new forms as it emerges (or reemerges) in the twenty-first century. There are also new theoretical and practical efforts to understand national and regional racial dynamics in light of the globalization framework. For example, the attention given to "the black Atlantic" as an evolving sociohistorical complex of domination and resistance (Gilroy 1993; Linebaugh and Rediker 2001) is being supplemented by work on regional diasporas like the Luso-Brazilian Atlantic (Miller 1988; Stam 1997), and the Caribbean (James 1998). Recent scholarship on Africa situates the motherland much more centrally in global political economic development than was previously the case (Cooper 1993).[14] In similar fashion, African ideas and "the idea of Africa" (Mudimbe 1994; see also Appiah 1985/1992) now challenge formerly hegemonic Northern and Western worldviews much more comprehensively than could ever have been imagined in the past. A burgeoning new literature on processes of continuity and change in the African diaspora points to the unrecognized (and ongoing) political dynamism of that global complex (Patterson and Kelley 2000). The world is learning once again, as it has over and over throughout the modern age, about the centrality of race on the global stage: racial identity continues to shape "life-chances" worldwide; transnational organizing along racial lines is evident among indigenous, black, and many dispersed/diasporic peoples; and racial stigma is continually being reallocated (and resisted) everywhere. Although space is not available to develop these points fully here, we can offer two brief examples of the latter: resurgent Islamophobia and the increasing racialization of white identities.

By Islamophobia (Halliday 1999) we mean anti-Islamic (and by extension, anti-Muslim) prejudice. Although religious bigotry and hostility are certainly at work here, the racial components of Islamophobia should now be obvious, particularly in the United States, but elsewhere in the world as well. Very old patterns are resurfacing here; for example, the United States affords itself a civilizing mission in the Arab world, the Muslim world, much as the British and French (not to mention the Crusaders) did in the past. Arabs in the United States and Europe are subject to widespread racial profiling; this is particularly true after the September 11, 2001, attacks. The United States has been deluged with a flood of periodical ink and broadcast soundbites devoted, for example, to the problematic and mysterious essence of Islam: political Islam, fundamentalist Islam, sex and gender under Islam, the putative "backwardness" of Islam in comparison to the enlightened and democratic West, the tutelary role of Christianity and obligation of proselytization in the Islamic world.

All of this signals a regression in the West, and particularly in the United States, to orientalism at its worst (Said 1978). It hardly needs repeating that, like the nineteenth-century phenomenon Said analyzed so influentially, twenty-first-century orientalism is also a discursive set of variations on the theme of racial rule; it is redolent of the old colonial and imperial arrogance. The uplifting mission of the West is proclaimed (e.g., in the values of "freedom," "democracy," "pluralism," "secularism," etc.), while beneath the surface the old agendas advance: most notably political–military power and the capture of natural resources.

The dissolution of the transparent racial identity of the formerly dominant group, that is to say, the *increasing racialization* of whites in Europe, the United States, and elsewhere, must also be recognized as proceeding from the increasingly globalized dimensions of race. As previous assumptions erode, white identity loses its transparency, the easy elision with "racelessness" that accompanies racial domination. "Whiteness" enters into crisis; it becomes a matter of anxiety and concern.[15] Harking back to the eugenic panics that swept the United States and the colonial "mother countries" a century ago (Grant 1916/1970), mainstream political thinkers now lament the demise of colonial order, hanker for a new imperial system (Ignatieff 2003) that would bring order to the chaotic postcolonial "ends of the Earth" (Kaplan 1997), and worry about racial "swamping," the loss of cultural integrity, and declining white fertility in the world's West and North (Brimelow 1995).

The Emergence of Racial Time

Some final notes are in order regarding the question of the epochal nature of racial time. Classical social theory had an Enlightenment-based view of time, a perspective that understood the emergence of modernity in terms of the rise of capitalism and the bourgeoisie. This view was by no means limited to Marxism. Weberian disenchantment and the rise of the Durkheimian division of labor also partake of this temporal substrate. Only rarely does the racial dimension of historical temporality appear in this body of thought, as, for example, in Marx's excoriation of the brutalities of "primitive accumulation":

> The discovery of gold and silver in America, the extirpation, enslavement, and entombment in mines of the aboriginal population, the beginning of the conquest and looting of the East Indies, the turning of Africa into a warren for the commercial hunting of blackskins, signalized the rosy dawn of the era of capitalist production. These idyllic proceedings are the chief momenta of primitive accumulation. On their heels treads the commercial war of the European nations with the globe for a theater. It begins with the revolt of the Netherlands from Spain, assumes giant dimensions in England's AntiJacobin War, and is still going on in the opium wars with China, etc. (Marx 1967, 351)

Yet even Marx frequently legitimated such processes as the inevitable and ultimately beneficial birth pangs of classlessness—by way of the ceaselessly revolutionary bourgeoisie. Today such teleological accounts seem hopelessly outmoded. Historical time could well be interpreted in terms of something like a racial *longue durée*: for has there not been an immense historical rupture represented by the rise of Europe, the onset of African enslavement, the *conquista*, and the subjugation of much of Asia? We take the point of much poststructural scholarship on these matters to be quite precisely an effort to explain "Western" or colonial time as a huge project demarcating human "difference," or more globally as Todorov, say, would argue, of framing partial collective identities in terms of externalized "others" (Todorov 1985). Just as, for example, the writers of the *Annales* school sought to locate the deep logic of historical time in the means by which material life was produced (diet, shoes, etc.),[16] so we might usefully think of a racial *longue durée* in which the slow inscription of phenotypical signification took place upon the human body, in and through conquest and enslavement to be sure, but also as an enormous act of expression, of narration.

In short, just as the noise of the "big bang" still resonates through the universe, so the overdetermined construction of world "civilization" as a product of the rise of Europe and the subjugation of the rest of us, still defines the race concept. Such speculative notes as these, to be sure, can be no more than provocations. Nor can we conclude this effort to reframe the agenda of racial theory with a neat summation. There was a long period (centuries) in which race was seen as a natural condition, a human essence. This was gradually supplanted, although not entirely superseded, during the twentieth century by new ways of thinking about race: it was now seen as subordinate to the supposedly more concrete, "material" relationships of culture, economic interest, and national identity. Centuries of essentialist and "naturalizing" views of race were replaced (though not entirely) with more critical perspectives that envisioned dispensing with the "illusion" of race. Perhaps now we are approaching the end of that racial epoch too.

To our dismay, we may have to give up our familiar ways of thinking about race once more. If so, there may also be some occasion for delight. For it may be possible to glimpse yet another view of race, in which the concept operates neither as a signifier of comprehensive identity, nor of fundamental difference, both of which are patently absurd, but rather as a marker of the infinity of variations we humans hold as a common heritage and hope for the future.

Notes

1. Du Bois's invocations in *The Souls of Black Folk* of Germanic concepts of race derived from Herder and Fichte are but one example of this. Boas's critique of the physical anthropology of his time also preserved some of its racial stereotypes. Marxism's Eurocentric elements contained significant racist residues, and pan-Africanism and Negritude often appealed to quasi-religious or nonrational black or African essences (e.g., *nomo*), in their accounts of racial difference.
2. For a similar "left" argument against the usefulness of the concept, see Appiah (1985/1992).
3. Minor objections would have to do with Fields's functionalist view of ideology, and her claim that the race concept only "came into existence" (Fields 1990, 101) when needed by whites in North American colonies beginning in the late seventeenth century. The concept of race, of course, has a longer history than that.
4. David Roediger, who is generally in agreement with Fields, also criticizes her on this point. "At times she nicely balances the ideological creation of racial attitudes with their manifest and ongoing importance and their (albeit ideological) *reality.*... But elsewhere, race disappears into the 'reality' of class" (Roediger 1991, 7–8; emphasis original).
5. A famous sociological dictum holds that "If men (sic) define situations as real, they are real in their consequences" (Thomas and Thomas 1928, 572), a claim that would clearly apply to racial "situations" of all sorts.
6. Avery Gordon has suggested that race "haunts" U.S. society and culture as a consequence of the fierce contradictions it embodies: its simultaneous omnipresence and disavowal throughout American life (Gordon 1997).
7. "The question of identification is never the affirmation of a pregiven identity, never a self-fulfilling prophecy—it is always the production of an image of identity and the transformation of the subject in assuming that image" (Bhabha 1990, 188).
8. Although only in passing. There can be no extended racial theorizing here. In other work we have developed a more systematic theoretical approach to race (see Omi and Winant 1994).
9. The work of Paul Gilroy (1991) on the significance of black music in Afro-Diasporic communities is particularly revealing on this point.
10. Our point here is that previously marginalized identities and positions are now politically more salient, have more "voice," and influence current political conflicts more than they did in the past. Of course there is nothing new about the particular examples we have cited. Islam has always been present among African Americans (as well as in every other racially identified group). For all its controversies and problems (Moses 1994), Afrocentrism justifiably claims its heritage in pan-Africanism, Ethiopianism, and so on.
11. For a more extensive treatment of these large issues, see Winant (2001).
12. We borrow this phrase, not from George Lucas but from the book of that title edited at the Centre for Contemporary Cultural Studies, 1982.
13. David Lopez and Yen Espiritu define panethnicity as "the development of bridging organizations and solidarities among subgroups of ethnic collectivities that are often seen as homogeneous by outsiders." Such a development, they claim, is a crucial feature of ethnic change: "supplanting both assimilation and ethnic particularism as the direction of change for racial/ethnic minorities." They conclude that while panethnic formation is facilitated by an ensemble of cultural factors (e.g., common language and religion) and structural factors (e.g., class, generation, and geographical concentration), a specific concept of race is fundamental to the construction of panethnicity (Lopez and Espiritu 1990, 198).

14. Thus confirming Du Bois's claims to this effect ("Semper novi quid ex Africa") nearly a century after he made them (Du Bois 1915/1995).
15. Once again this is an old story. Among a vast literature, see Roediger (1991), Harris (1993), Jacobson (1999).
16. For example, the magisterial work of Fernand Braudel (1975).

References

Appiah, Kwame Anthony. "The Uncompleted Argument: Du Bois and the Illusion of Race." In *My Father's House: Africa in the Philosophy of Culture.* New York: Oxford University Press, 1992. (Orig. pub. 1985.)

Bhabha, Homi K. "Interrogating Identity." In *Anatomy of Racism,* edited by David Theo Goldberg. Minneapolis: University of Minnesota Press, 1990.

Braudel, Fernand. *Capitalism and Material Life, 1400–1800,* translated by Miriam Kochan. New York: Harper Colophon, 1975.

Brimelow, Peter. *Alien Nation: Common Sense about America's Immigration Disaster.* New York: Random House, 1995.

Centre for Contemporary Cultural Studies. *The Empire Strikes Back: Race in 70s Britain.* London: Hutchinson, 1982.

Chase, Allan. *The Legacy of Malthus: The Social Costs of the New Scientific Racism.* New York: Knopf, 1977.

Connerly, Ward. *Creating Equal: My Fight against Race Preferences.* San Francisco: Encounter Books, 2000.

Cooper, Frederick. "Africa and the World Economy." In *Confronting Historical Paradigms: Peasants, Labor, and the Capitalist World System in Africa and Latin America,* edited by Frederick Cooper et al. Madison: University of Wisconsin Press, 1993.

Du Bois, W. E. B. "The African Roots of the War." In *W. E. B. Du Bois: A Reader,* edited by David Levering Lewis. New York: Henry Holt, 1995. (Orig. pub. 1915.)

Fields, Barbara. "Slavery, Race and Ideology in the United States of America." *New Left Review* (May/June 1990).

Gilroy, Paul. *There Ain't No Black in the Union Jack: The Cultural Politics of Race and Nation.* Chicago: University of Chicago Press, 1991.

Gilroy, Paul. *The Black Atlantic: Modernity and Double Consciousness.* Cambridge, MA: Harvard University Press, 1993.

Glazer, Nathan. *We Are All Multiculturalists Now.* Cambridge, MA: Harvard University Press, 1997.

Gordon, Avery F. *Ghostly Matters: Haunting and the Sociological Imagination.* Minneapolis: University of Minnesota Press, 1997.

Gould, Stephen Jay. *The Mismeasure of Man.* New York: Norton, 1981.

Grant, Madison. *The Passing of the Great Race.* New York: Arno, 1970. (Orig. pub. 1916.)

Halliday, Fred. "'Islamophobia' Reconsidered." *Ethnic and Racial Studies* 22 (September 1999).

Harris, Cheryl. "Whiteness as Property." *Harvard Law Review* 106 (1993).

Harris, Marvin. *Patterns of Race in the Americas.* New York: Walker, 1964.

Ignatieff, Michael. "American Empire (Get Used to It)." *The New York Times Magazine,* January 5, 2003.

Jacobson, Matthew Frye. *Whiteness of a Different Color: European Immigrants and the Alchemy of Race.* Cambridge, MA: Harvard University Press, 1999.

James, Winston. *Holding Aloft the Banner of Ethiopia: Caribbean Radicalism in Early Twentieth-Century America.* New York: Verso, 1998.

Kaplan, Robert B. *The Ends of the Earth: From Togo to Turkmenistan, from Iran to Cambodia, a Journey to the Frontiers of Anarchy.* New York: Vintage, 1997.

Kevles, Daniel J. *In the Name of Eugenics: Genetics and the Uses of Human Heredity.* New York: Knopf, 1985.

Linebaugh, Peter, and Marcus Rediker. *The Many-Headed Hydra: The Hidden History of the Revolutionary Atlantic.* Boston: Beacon, 2001.

Lopez, David, and Yen Le Espiritu. "Panethnicity in the United States: A Theoretical Framework." *Ethnic and Racial Studies* 13 (1990).

Marx, Karl, *Capital* Vol. 1. New York: International, 1967. (Orig. pub. 1867.)

Miller, Joseph C. *Way of Death: Merchant Capitalism and the Angolan Slave Trade, 1730–1830.* Madison: University of Wisconsin Press, 1988.

Moses, Wilson Jeremiah. *Afrotopia: The Roots of African American Popular History.* New York: Cambridge University Press, 1998.

Mosse, George L. *Toward the Final Solution: A History of European Racism.* New York: Howard Fertig, 1978.

Mudimbe, V.Y. *The Idea of Africa.* Bloomington: Indiana University Press, 1994.

Murray, Charles A. *Losing Ground: American Social Policy, 1950–1980.* New York: Basic Books, 1984.

Omi, Michael and Howard Winant. *Racial Formation in the United States: From the 1960s to the 1990s.* Rev. ed. New York: Routledge, 1994.

Patterson, Tiffany Ruby, and Robin D. G. Kelley. "Unfinished Migrations: Reflections on the African Diaspora and the Making of the Modern World." *African Studies Review* 43, no. 1 (April 2000).

Roediger, David R. *The Wages of Whiteness: Race and the Making of the American Working Class.* New York: Verso, 1991.

Said, Edward. *Orientalism.* New York: Viking, 1978.

Stam, Robert. *Tropical Multiculturalism: A Comparative History of Race in Brazilian Cinema and Culture.* Durham, NC: Duke University Press, 1997.

Thernstrom, Stephan and Abigail Thernstrom. *America in Black and White: One Nation, Indivisible.* New York: Simon and Schuster, 1997.

Thomas, W. I. and Dorothy Swaine Thomas. *The Child in America.* New York: Knopf, 1928.

Todorov, Tsvetan. *The Conquest of America: The Question of the Other*, translated by Richard Howard. New York: Harper and Row, 1984.

Winant, Howard. *The World Is a Ghetto: Race and Democracy Since World War II*. New York: Basic, 2001.

Winant, Howard. "Behind Blue Eyes: Contemporary White Racial Politics," *New Left Review* 222 (September–October 1997).

Zuberi, Tukufu. *Thicker Than Blood: How Racial Statistics Lie*. Minneapolis: University of Minnesota Press, 2001.

2

'Race', Time and the Revision of Modernity

HOMI K. BHABHA

'Dirty nigger!' Or simply, 'Look, a Negro!'

— Frantz Fanon
The Fact of Blackness

I

Whenever these words are said in anger or in hate, whether of the Jew in that *estaminet* in Antwerp, or of the Palestinian on the West Bank, or the Zairian student eking out a wretched existence selling fake fetishes on the Left Bank; whether they are said of the body of woman or the man of colour; whether they are quasi-officially spoken in South Africa or officially prohibited in London or New York, but inscribed nevertheless in the severe staging of the statistics of educational performance and crime, visa violations, immigration irregularities; whenever 'Dirty nigger!' or, 'Look, a Negro!' is not said at all, but you can see it in a gaze, or hear it in the solecism of a still silence; whenever and wherever I am when I hear a racist, or catch his look, I am reminded of Fanon's evocatory essay 'The fact of blackness' and its unforgettable opening lines.[1]

I want to start by returning to that essay, to explore only one scene in its remarkable staging, Fanon's phenomenological performance of what it means to be *not only a nigger* but a member of the marginalized, the displaced, the diasporic. To be amongst those whose very presence is both 'over-looked'—in the double sense of social surveillance and psychic disavowal—and, at the same time, overdetermined—psychically projected, made stereotypical and symptomatic. Despite its very specific location—a Martinican subjected to the racist gaze on a street corner in Lyons—I claim a generality for Fanon's argument because he talks not simply of the historicity of the black man, as much as he writes in 'The fact of blackness' about the temporality of modernity within which the figure of the 'human' comes to be *authorized*. It is Fanon's temporality of emergence—his sense of the *belatedness of the black man*—that does not simply make the question of ontology inappropriate for black identity, but somehow *impossible* for the very understanding of humanity in the world of modernity:

You come too late, much too late, there will always be a world—a white world between you and us. (My emphasis)

13

It is the opposition to the ontology of that white world—to its assumed hierarchical forms of rationality and universality—that Fanon turns in a performance that is iterative and interrogative—a repetition that is initiatory, instating a differential history that will not return to the power of the Same. Between *you and us* Fanon opens up an enunciative space that does not simply contradict the metaphysical ideas of progress or racism or rationality; he distantiates them by 'repeating' these ideas, makes them uncanny by displacing them in a number of culturally contradictory and discursively estranged locations.

What Fanon shows up is the liminality of those ideas—their ethnocentric margin—by revealing the *historicity* of its most universal symbol—Man. From the perspective of a postcolonial 'belatedness', Fanon disturbs the *punctum* of man as the signifying, subjectifying category of Western culture, as a unifying reference of ethical value. Fanon performs the desire of the colonized to identify with the humanistic, enlightenment ideal of Man: 'all I wanted was to be a man among other men. I wanted to come lithe and young into a world that was ours and build it together'. Then, in a catachrestic reversal he shows how, despite the pedagogies of human history, the performative discourse of the liberal West, its quotidian conversation and comments, reveal the cultural supremacy and racial typology upon which the universalism of Man is founded: 'But of course, come in, sir, there is no colour prejudice among us…. Quite, the Negro is a man like ourselves…. It is not because he is black that he is less intelligent than we are'.

Fanon uses the fact of blackness, of belatedness, to destroy the binary structure of power and identity: the imperative that 'the Black man must be Black; he must be Black in relation to the white man'. Elsewhere he has written: 'The Black man is not. [caesura] Any more than the white man' (my interpolation). Fanon's discourse of the 'human' emerges from that temporal break or caesura effected in the continuist, progressivist myth of Man. He too speaks from the signifying time-lag of cultural difference that I have been attempting to develop as a structure for the representation of subaltern and postcolonial agency. Fanon writes from that temporal caesura, the time-lag of cultural difference, in a space between the symbolization of the social and the 'sign' of its representation of subjects and agencies. Fanon destroys two time schemes in which the historicity of the human is thought. He rejects the 'belatedness' of the black man because it is only the opposite of the framing of the white man as universal, normative—*the white sky all around me*; the black man refuses to occupy the past of which the white man is the future. But Fanon also refuses the Hegelian-Marxist dialectical schema whereby the black man is part of a transcendental sublation: a minor term in a dialectic that will emerge into a more equitable universality. Fanon, I believe, suggests another time, another space.

It is a space of being that is wrought from the interruptive, interrogative, tragic experience of blackness, of discrimination, of despair. It is the apprehension of the social and psychic question of 'origin'—and its erasure—in a negative side that 'draws its worth from an almost substantive absoluteness … [which has to be] ignorant of the essences and determinations of its being … an absolute density … an abolition of the ego by desire'. What may seem primordial or timeless is, I believe, a moment of a kind of 'projective past' whose history and signification I shall attempt to explore here. It is a mode of 'negativity' that makes the enunciatory present of modernity disjunctive. It opens up a time-lag at the point at which we speak of humanity through its differentiations—gender, race, class—that mark an excessive marginality of modernity. It is the enigma of this form of temporality which emerges from what Du Bois also called the 'swift and low of human doing',[2] to face Progress with some unanswerable questions, and suggest some answers of its own.

In destroying the 'ontology of man', Fanon suggests that 'there is not merely one Negro, there are *Negroes*'. This is emphatically not a post-modern celebration of pluralistic identities. As my argument will make clear, for me the project of modernity is itself rendered so contradictory and unresolved through the insertion of the 'time-lag' in which colonial and postcolonial moments emerge as sign and history, that I am sceptical of those transitions to postmodernity in Western academic writings which theorize the experience of this 'new historicity' through the appropriation of a 'Third World' metaphor; 'the First World ... in a peculiar dialectical reversal, begins to touch some features of third-world experience.... The United States is ... the biggest third-world country because of unemployment, nonproduction, etc.'[3]

Fanon's sense of social contingency and indeterminacy, made from the perspective of a postcolonial time-lag, is not a celebration of fragmentation, *bricolage*, pastiche or the 'simulacrum'. It is a vision of social contradiction and cultural difference—as the disjunctive space of modernity—that is best seen in a fragment of a poem he cites towards the end of 'The fact of blackness':

> As the contradiction among the features
> creates the harmony of the face
> we proclaim the oneness of the suffering
> and the revolt.

II

The discourse of race that I am trying to develop displays the *problem of the ambivalent temporality of modernity* that is often overlooked in the more 'spatial' traditions of some aspects of postmodern theory.[4] Under the rubric 'the discourse of modernity', I do not intend to reduce a complex and diverse historical moment, with varied national genealogies and different institutional practices, into a singular shibboleth—be it the 'idea' of Reason, Historicism, Progress—for the critical convenience of postmodern literary theory. My interest in the question of modernity resides in the influential discussion generated by the work of Habermas, Foucault, Lyotard and Lefort, amongst many others, that has generated a critical discourse around historical modernity as an epistemological structure.[5] To put it succinctly, the question of ethical and cultural judgement, central to the processes of subject formation and the objectification of social knowledge, is challenged at its 'cognitivist' core. Habermas characterizes it as a form of Occidental self-understanding that enacts a cognitive reductionism in the relation of the human being to the social world:

> Ontologically the world is reduced to a world of entities *as a whole* (as the totality of objects ...); epistemologically, our relationship to that world is reduced to the capacity of know[ing]... states of affairs... in a purposive-rational fashion; semantically it is reduced to fact-stating discourse in which assertoric sentences are used.[6] (My emphasis)

Although this may be a stark presentation of the problem, it highlights the fact that the challenge to such a 'cognitivist' consciousness displaces the problem of truth or meaning from the disciplinary confines of epistemology—the problem of the referential as 'objectivity' reflected in that celebrated Rortyesque trope, the mirror of nature. What results could be figuratively described as a preoccupation not simply with the reflection in the glass—the idea or concept in itself—but with the frameworks of meaning as they are revealed in what Derrida has called the 'supplementary necessity of a parergon'. That is the performative, living description of the *writing* of a concept or theory, 'a relation to the history of its writing and the writing of its history also'.[7]

If we take even the most cursory view of influential postmodern perspectives, we find that there is an increasing *narrativization* of the question of social ethics and subject formation. Whether it is in the conversational procedures and 'final vocabularies' of liberal ironists like Richard Rorty, or the 'moral fictions' of Alisdair Macintyre that are the sustaining myths 'after virtue'; whether it is the *petits récits* and *phrases* that remain from the fall-out of the grand narratives of modernity in Lyotard; or the protective but ideal speech community that is rescued *within* modernity by Habermas in his concept of communicative reason that is expressed in its pragmatic logic or argument and a 'decentred' understanding of the world: what we encounter in all these accounts are proposals for what is considered to be the essential gesture of Western modernity, an 'ethics of self-construction'—or, as Mladan Dolar cogently describes it:

> What makes this attitude typical of modernity is the constant reconstruction and the reinvention of the self.… The subject and the present it belongs to have no objective status, they have to be perpetually (re)constructed.[8]

I want to ask whether this synchronous constancy of reconstruction and reinvention of the subject does not assume a cultural temporality that may not be universalist in its epistemological moment of judgement, but may, indeed, be ethnocentric in its construction of cultural 'difference'. It is certainly true, as Robert Young argues, that the 'inscription of alterity within the self can allow for a new relation to ethics';[9] but does that *necessarily* entail the more general case argued by Dolar, that 'the persisting split [of the subject] is the condition of freedom'?

If so, how do we specify the historical conditions and theoretical configurations of 'splitting' in political situations of 'unfreedom'—in the colonial and postcolonial margins of modernity? I am persuaded that it is the catachrestic postcolonial agency of 'seizing the value-coding'—as Gayatri Spivak has argued—that opens up an interruptive time-lag in the 'progressive' myth of modernity, and enables the diasporic and the postcolonial to be represented. But this makes it all the more crucial to specify the discursive and historical temporality that interrupts the enunciative 'present' in which the self-inventions of modernity take place. And it is this 'taking place' of modernity, this insistent and incipient *spatial* metaphor in which the social relations of modernity are conceived, that introduces a temporality of the 'synchronous' in the structure of the 'splitting' of modernity. It is this 'synchronous and spatial' representation of cultural difference that must be reworked as a *framework* for cultural otherness *within* the general dialectic of doubling that postmodernism proposes. Otherwise we are likely to find ourselves beached amidst Jameson's 'cognitive mappings' of the Third World, which might work for the Bonaventura Hotel in Los Angeles, but will leave you somewhat eyeless in Gaza.[10] Or if, like Terry Eagleton, your taste is more 'other worldly' than Third World, you will find yourself somewhat dismissive of the 'real' history of the 'other'—women, foreigners, homosexuals, the natives of Ireland—on the basis 'of certain styles, values, life-experiences which can be appealed to now as a form of political critique' because 'the fundamental political question is that of demanding an equal right with others of what one might become, not of assuming some fully-fashioned identity which is merely repressed'.[11]

It is to establish a *sign of the present*, of modernity, that is not that 'now' of transparent immediacy, and to found a form of social individuation where communality is *not predicated on a transcendent becoming*, that I want to pose my questions of a contra-modernity: what is modernity in those colonial conditions where its imposition is itself the denial of historical freedom, civic autonomy and the 'ethical' choice of refashioning?

III

I am posing these questions from within the problematic of modernity because of a shift within contemporary critical traditions of postcolonial writing. There is no longer an influential separatist emphasis on simply elaborating an anti-imperialist or black nationalist tradition 'in itself'. There is an attempt to interrupt the Western discourses of modernity through these displacing, interrogative subaltern or postslavery narratives and the critical-theoretical perspectives they engender. For example, Houston Baker's reading of the modernity of the Harlem Renaissance strategically elaborates a 'deformation of mastery', a vernacularism, based on the enunciation of the subject as 'never a simple coming into being, but a release from being possessed'.[12] The revision of Western modernism, he suggests, requires both the linguistic investiture of the subject and a practice of diasporic performance that is metaphorical. The 'public culture' project that Carol Breckenridge and Arjun Appadurai have initiated focuses on the transnational dissemination of cultural modernity. What becomes properly urgent for them is that the 'simultaneous' global locations of such a modernity should not lose sense of the conflictual, contradictory locutions of those cultural practices and products that follow the 'unequal development' of the tracks of international or multinational capital. Any transnational cultural study must 'translate', each time locally and specifically, what decentres and subverts this transnational globality, so that it does not become enthralled by the new global technologies of ideological transmission and cultural consumption.[13] Paul Gilroy proposes a form of populist modernism to comprehend both the aesthetic and political transformation of European philosophy and letters by black writers, but also to 'make sense of the secular and spiritual *popular* forms—music and dance—that have handled the anxieties and dilemmas involved in a response to the *flux of modern life*'.[14]

The power of the postcolonial translation of modernity rests in its *performative, deformative* structure that does not simply revalue the contents of a cultural tradition, or transpose values 'cross-culturally'. The cultural inheritance of slavery or colonialism is brought *before* modernity *not* to resolve its historic differences into a new totality, nor to forego its traditions. It is to introduce another locus of inscription and intervention, another hybrid, 'inappropriate' enunciative site, through that temporal split—or time-lag—that I have opened up (specifically in Chapter 9) for the signification of postcolonial agency. Differences in culture and power are constituted through the social conditions of enunciation: the temporal caesura, *which is also the historically tranformative moment*, when a lagged space opens up *in*-between the *inter*subjective 'reality of signs ... deprived of subjectivity' and the historical development of the subject in the order of social symbols.[15] This transvaluation of the symbolic structure of the cultural sign is absolutely necessary so that in the renaming of modernity there may ensue that process of the active agency of translation—the moment of 'making a name for oneself' that emerges through 'the undecidability ... [at work] in a struggle for the proper name within a scene of genealogical indebtedness'.[16] Without such a reinscription of the sign itself—without a transformation of the site of *enunciation*—there is the danger that the mimetic contents of a discourse will conceal the fact that the hegemonic structures of power are maintained in a position of authority through a *shift in vocabulary* in the position of authority. There is for instance a kinship between the normative paradigms of colonial anthropology and the contemporary discourse of aid and development agencies. The 'transfer of technology' has not resulted in the transfer of power or the displacement of a neo-colonial tradition of political control through philanthropy—a celebrated missionary position.

What is the struggle of translation in the name of modernity? How do we catachrestically seize the genealogy of modernity and open it to the postcolonial translation? The 'value' of modernity is not located, a priori, in the passive fact of an epochal event or idea—of progress, civility, the law—but has to be negotiated *within* the 'enunciative' present of the discourse. The brilliance of Claude Lefort's account of the genesis of ideology in modern societies is to suggest that the representation of the rule, or the discourse of generality that symbolizes authority, is ambivalent because it is split off from its effective operation.[17] The *new or the contemporary* appear through the splitting of modernity as event and enunciation, the epochal and the everyday. Modernity as a *sign* of the present emerges in that process of splitting, that *lag*, that gives the practice of everyday life its consistency as *being contemporary*. It is because the present has the value of a 'sign' that modernity is iterative; a continual questioning of the conditions of existence; making problematic its own discourse not simply 'as ideas' but as the position and status of the locus of social utterance.

IV

'It is not enough … to follow the teleological thread that makes progress possible; one must isolate, within the history [of modernity], an event that will have the value of a sign'.[18] In his reading of Kant's *Was ist Aufklärung?* Foucault suggests that the sign of modernity is a form of decipherment whose value must be sought in *petite récits*, imperceptible events, in signs apparently *without* meaning and value—empty and ex-centric—in events that are outside the 'great events' of history.

The sign of history does not consist in an essence of the event itself, nor exclusively in the *immediate consciousness* of its agents and actors, but in its form as a *spectacle*; spectacle that signifies *because of* the distanciation and displacement between the event and those who are its spectators. The indeterminacy of modernity, where the struggle of translation takes place, is not simply around the ideas of progress or truth. Modernity, I suggest, is about the historical construction of a specific position of historical enunciation and address. It privileges those who 'bear witness', those who are 'subjected', or in the Fanonian sense with which I began, historically displaced. It gives them a representative position through the spatial distance, or the *time-lag* between the Great Event and its circulation as a historical sign of the 'people' or an 'epoch', that constitutes the memory and the moral of the event *as a narrative*, a disposition to cultural communality, a form of social and psychic identification. The discursive address of modernity—its structure of authority—decentres the Great Event, and speaks from that moment of 'imperceptibility', the supplementary space 'outside' or uncannily beside (*abseits*).

Through Kant, Foucault traces 'the ontology of the present' to the exemplary event of the French Revolution and it is there that he stages his sign of modernity. But it is the spatial dimension of 'distance'—*the perspective distance from which the spectacle is seen*—that installs a cultural homogeneity into the sign of modernity. Foucault introduces a Eurocentric perspective at the point at which modernity installs a 'moral disposition in mankind'. The Eurocentricity of Foucault's theory of cultural difference is revealed in his insistent spatializing of the time of modernity. Avoiding the problems of the sovereign subject and linear causality, he nonetheless falls prey to the notion of the 'cultural' as a social formation whose discursive doubleness—the transcendental and empirical dialectic—is contained in a temporal frame that makes differences repetitively 'contemporaneous', regimes of sense-as-synchronous. It is a kind of cultural 'contradictoriness' that always presupposes a correlative spacing. Foucault's *spatial distancing* seals the sign of modernity in 1789 into a 'correlative', overlapping temporality. Progress brings together the three moments of the sign as:

> a *signum rememorativum*, for it reveals that disposition [of progress] which has been present from the beginning; it is a *signum demonstrativum* because it demonstrates the present efficacity of this disposition; and it is also *signum prognosticum* for, although the Revolution may have certain questionable results, one cannot forget the disposition [of modernity] that is revealed through it.[19]

What if the effects of 'certain questionable results' of the Revolution create a disjunction, between the *signum demonstrativum* and the *signum prognosticum*? What if in the geopolitical space of the colony genealogically (in Foucault's sense) related to the Western metropolis, the symbol of the Revolution is partially visible as an unforgettable, tantalizing promise—a *pedagogy* of the values of modernity—while the 'present efficacy' of the sign of everyday life—its *political performativity*—repeats the archaic aristocratic racism of the *ancient régime*?

The ethnocentric limitations of Foucault's spatial sign of modernity become immediately apparent if we take our stand, in the immediate postrevolutionary period, in San Domingo with the Black Jacobins, rather than Paris. What if the 'distance' that constitutes the meaning of the Revolution as sign, the *signifying lag* between event and enunciation, stretches not across the Place de la Bastille or the rue des Blancs-Monteaux, but spans the temporal difference of the colonial space? What if we heard the 'moral disposition of mankind' uttered by Toussaint L'Ouverture for whom, as C. L. R. James so vividly recalls, the signs of modernity, 'liberty, equality, fraternity ... what the French Revolution signified, was perpetually on his lips, in his correspondence, in his private conversations.'[20] What do we make of the figure of Toussaint—James invokes Phédre, Ahab, Hamlet—at the moment when he grasps the tragic lesson that the moral, *modern* disposition of mankind, enshrined in the sign of the Revolution, only fuels the archaic racial factor in the society of slavery? What do we learn from that split consciousness, that 'colonial' disjunction of modern times and colonial and slave histories, where the reinvention of the self and the remaking of the social are strictly out of joint?

These are the issues of the catachrestic, postcolonial translation of modernity. They force us to introduce the question of subaltern agency, into the question of modernity: what is this 'now' of modernity? Who defines this present from which we speak? This leads to a more challenging question: *what is the desire of this repeated demand to modernize? Why does it insist, so compulsively, on its contemporaneous reality, its spatial dimension, its spectatorial distance?* What happens to the sign of modernity in those repressive places like San Domingo where progress is only heard (of) and not 'seen', is that it reveals the problem of the disjunctive moment of its utterance: the space which enables a postcolonial contra-modernity to emerge. For the discourse of modernity is *signified* from the time-lag, or temporal caesura, that emerges in the tension between the epochal 'event' of modernity as the symbol of the continuity of progress, and the interruptive temporality of the sign of the present, the contingency of modern times that Habermas has aptly described as its 'forward gropings and shocking encounters'.[21]

In this 'time' of repetition there circulates a contingent tension within modernity: a tension between the *pedagogy* of the symbols of progress, historicism, modernization, homogeneous empty time, the narcissism of organic culture, the onanistic search for the origins of race, and what I shall call the 'sign of the present': the performativity of discursive practice, the *récits* of the everyday, the repetition of the empirical, the ethics of self-enactment, the iterative signs that mark the non-synchronic *passages* of time in the archives of the 'new'. This is the space in which the question of modernity *emerges as a form of interrogation*: what do I belong to in this present? In what terms do I identify with the 'we', the intersubjective realm of society? This process cannot be represented in the binary relation of archaism/modernity, inside/outside, past/present, because these questions block off the forward drive or teleology of modernity. They suggest that what is read as the 'futurity' of the modern, its ineluctable progress, its cultural hierarchies, may be an 'excess', a disturbing alterity, a process of the marginalization of the symbols of modernity.

Time-lag is not a circulation of nullity, the endless slippage of the signifier or the theoretical anarchy of aporia. It is a concept that does not collude with current fashions for claiming the heterogeneity of ever-increasing 'causes', multiplicities of subject positions, endless supplies of subversive 'specificities', 'localities', 'territories'. The problem of the articulation of cultural difference is not the problem of free-wheeling pragmatist pluralism or the 'diversity' of the many; it is the problem of the not-one, the minus in the origin and repetition of cultural signs in a doubling that will not be sublated into a similitude. What is *in* modernity *more* than modernity is this signifying 'cut' or temporal break it cuts into the platitudinous notion of Culture splendidly reflected in the mirror of human nature; equally it halts the endless signification of difference. The process I have described as the sign of the present—*within modernity*—erases and interrogates those ethnocentric forms of cultural modernity that 'contemporize' cultural difference: it opposes both cultural pluralism with its spurious egalitarianism—different cultures in the same time ('The Magicians of the Earth', Pompidou Centre, Paris, 1989)—or cultural relativism—different cultural temporalities in the same 'universal' space ('The Primitivism show', MOMA, New York, 1984).

V

This caesura in the narrative of modernity reveals something of what de Certeau has famously described as the non-place from which all historiographical operation starts, the lag which all histories must encounter in order to make a beginning.[22] For the emergence of modernity—as an ideology of *beginning, modernity as the new*—the template of this 'non-place' becomes the colonial space. It signifies this in a double way. The colonial space is the *terra incognita* or the *terra nulla*, the empty or wasted land whose history has to be begun, whose archives must be filled out; whose future progress must be secured in modernity. But the colonial space also stands for the *despotic* time of the Orient that becomes a great problem for the definition of modernity and its inscription of the history of the colonized from the perspective of the West. Despotic time, as Althusser has brilliantly described it, is 'space without places, time without duration'.[23] In that double-figure which haunted the moment of the enlightenment in its relation to the *otherness* of the Other, you can see the historical formation of the time-lag of modernity. And lest it be said that this disjunctive present of modernity is merely my theoretical abstraction, let me also remind you that a similar, signifying caesura occurs within the invention of progress in the 'long imperialist nineteenth century'. At the mid-point of the century questions concerning the 'origin of races' provided modernity with an ontology of its present and a justification of cultural hierarchy within the West and in the East. In the structure of the discourse, however, there was a recurrent ambivalence between the developmental, organic notion of cultural and racial 'indigenism' as the justification of supremacy, and the notion of evolution as abrupt cultural transition, discontinuous progress, the periodic eruption of invading tribes from somewhere mysterious in Asia, as the guarantee of progress.[24]

The 'subalterns and ex-slaves' who now seize the spectacular event of modernity do so in a catachrestic gesture of reinscribing modernity's 'caesura' and using it to transform the locus of thought and writing in their postcolonial critique. Listen to the ironic naming, the interrogative repetitions, of the critical terms themselves: black 'vernacularism' repeats the minor term used to designate the language of the native and the housebound slave to make demotic the grander narratives of progress. Black 'expressivism' reverses the stereotypical affectivity and sensuality of the stereotype to suggest that 'rationalities are produced *endlessly*' in populist modernism.[25] 'New ethnicity' is used by Stuart Hall in the black British context to create a discourse of cultural difference that marks ethnicity as the struggle against ethnicist 'fixing' and in favour of a wider minority discourse that represents sexuality and class. Cornel West's genealogical materialist view of race and Afro-American oppression is, he writes, 'both continuous and discontinuous with the Marxist tradition' and shares an equally contingent relation to Nietzsche and Foucault.[26] More recently, he has constructed a prophetic pragmatic tradition from William James, Niebuhr and Du Bois suggesting that 'it is possible to be a prophetic pragmatist and belong to different political movements, e.g., feminist, Black, chicano, socialist, left-liberal ones'.[27] The Indian historian Gyan Prakash, in an essay on postorientalist histories of the Third World, claims that:

> it is difficult to overlook the fact that ... third world voices ... speak within and to discourses familiar to the 'West'.... The Third World, far from being confined to its assigned space, has penetrated the inner sanctum of the 'First World' in the process of being 'Third Worlded'—arousing, inciting, and affiliating with the subordinated others in the First World ... to connect with minority voices.[28]

The intervention of postcolonial or black critique is aimed at transforming the conditions of enunciation at the level of the sign—where the intersubjective realm is constituted—not simply setting up new symbols of identity, new 'positive images' that fuel an unreflective 'identity politics'. The challenge to modernity comes in redefining the signifying relation to a disjunctive 'present': staging the past as *symbol*, myth, memory, history, the ancestral—but a past whose iterative *value as sign* reinscribes the 'lessons of the past' into the very textuality of the present that determines both the identification with, and the interrogation of, modernity: what is the 'we' that defines the prerogative of my present? The possibility of inciting cultural translations across minority discourses arises because of the disjunctive present of modernity. It ensures that what *seems* the 'same' within cultures is negotiated in the time-lag of the 'sign' which constitutes the intersubjective, social realm. Because that lag is indeed the very structure of difference and splitting within the discourse of modernity, turning it into a performative process, then each repetition of the sign of modernity is different, specific to its historical and cultural conditions of enunciation.

This process is most clearly apparent in the work of those 'postmodern' writers who, in pushing the paradoxes of modernity to its limits, reveal the margins of the West.[29] From the postcolonial perspective we can only assume a disjunctive and displaced relation to these works; we cannot accept them until we subject them to a *lagging*: both in the temporal sense of postcolonial agency with which you are now (over) familiar, and in the obscurer sense in which, in the early days of settler colonization, to be lagged was to be transported to the colonies for penal servitude!

In Foucault's Introduction to the *History of Sexuality*, racism emerges in the nineteenth century in the form of an historical retroversion that Foucault finally disavows. In the 'modern' shift of power from the juridical politics of death to the biopolitics of life, race produces a historical temporality of interference, overlapping, and the displacement of sexuality. It is, for Foucault, the great historical irony of modernity that the Hitlerite annihilation of the Jews was carried out in the name of the archaic, premodern signs of race and sanguinity—the oneiric exaltation of blood, death, skin—rather than through the politics of sexuality. What is profoundly revealing is Foucault's complicity with the logic of the 'contemporaneous' within Western modernity. Characterizing the 'symbolics of blood' as being retroverse, Foucault disavows the time-lag of race as the sign of cultural difference and its mode of repetition.

The *temporal* disjunction that the 'modern' question of race would introduce into the discourse of disciplinary and pastoral power is disallowed because of Foucault's spatial critique: 'we must conceptualize the deployment of sexuality on the basis of the techniques of power that are *contemporary* with it' (my emphasis).[30] However subversive 'blood' and race may be they are in the last analysis merely an 'historical retroversion'. Elsewhere Foucault directly links the 'flamboyant rationality' of Social Darwinism to Nazi ideology, entirely ignoring colonial societies which were the proving grounds for Social Darwinist administrative discourses all through the nineteenth and early twentieth centuries.[31]

If Foucault normalizes the time-lagged, 'retroverse' sign of race, Benedict Anderson places the 'modern' dreams of racism 'outside history' altogether. For Foucault race and blood interfere with modern sexuality. For Anderson racism has its origins in antique ideologies of class that belong to the aristocratic 'pre-history' of the modern nation. Race represents an archaic ahistorical moment outside the 'modernity' of the imagined community: 'nationalism thinks in historical destinies, while racism dreams of eternal contaminations … outside history'.[32] Foucault's spatial notion of the conceptual contemporaneity of power-as-sexuality limits him from seeing the double and overdetermined structure of race and sexuality that has a long history in the *peuplement* (politics of settlement) of colonial societies; for Anderson the 'modern' anomaly of racism finds its historical modularity, and its fantasmatic scenario, in the colonial space which is a belated and hybrid attempt to 'weld together dynastic legitimacy and national community ... to shore up domestic aristocratic bastions'.[33]

The racism of colonial empires is then part of an archaic acting out, a dream-text of a form of historical retroversion that 'appeared to confirm on a global, modern stage antique conceptions of power and privilege'.[34] What could have been a way of understanding the limits of Western imperialist ideas of progress within the genealogy of a 'colonial metropolis'—a hybridizing of the Western nation—is quickly disavowed in the language of the *opéra bouffe* as a grimly amusing *tableau vivant* of 'the [colonial] bourgeois gentilhomme speaking poetry against a back-cloth of spacious mansions and gardens filled with mimosa and bougainvillea'.[35] It is in that 'weld' of the colonial site as, contradictorily, both 'dynastic and national', that the modernity of Western national society is confronted by its colonial double. Such a moment of temporal disjunction, which would be crucial for understanding the colonial history of contemporary metropolitan racism in the West, is placed 'outside history'. It is obscured by Anderson's espousal of 'a simultaneity across homogeneous empty time' as the modal narrative of the imagined community. It is this kind of evasion, I think, that makes Partha Chatterjee, the Indian 'subaltern' scholar, suggest, from a different perspective, that Anderson 'seals up his theme with a sociological determinism ... without noticing the twists and turns, the suppressed possibilities, the contradictions still unresolved'.[36]

These accounts of the modernity of power and national community become strangely symptomatic at the point at which they create a rhetoric of 'retroversion' for the emergence of racism. In placing the representations of race 'outside' modernity, in the space of historical retroversion, Foucault reinforces his 'correlative spacing'; by relegating the social fantasy of racism to an archaic daydream, Anderson further universalizes his homogeneous empty time of the 'modern' social imaginary. Hidden in the disavowing narrative of historical retroversion and its archaism, is a notion of the time-lag that displaces Foucault's spatial analytic of modernity and Anderson's homogeneous temporality of the modern nation. In order to extract the one from the other we have to see how they form a double boundary: rather like the more general intervention and seizure of the history of modernity that has been attempted by postcolonial critics.

Retroversion and archaic doubling, attributed to the ideological 'contents' of racism, do not remain at the ideational or pedagogical level of the discourse. Their inscription of a structure of retroaction returns to disrupt the enunciative function of this discourse and produce a different 'value' of the sign and time of race and modernity. At the level of content the archaism and fantasy of racism is represented as 'ahistorical', outside the progressive myth of modernity. This is an attempt, I would argue, to universalize the spatial fantasy of modern cultural communities as living their history 'contemporaneously', in a 'homogeneous empty time' of the People-as-One that finally deprives minorities of those marginal, liminal spaces from which they can intervene in the unifying and totalizing *myths* of the national culture.

However, each time such a homogeneity of cultural identification is established there is a marked disturbance of temporality in the *writing of modernity*. For Foucault it is the awareness that retroversion of race or sanguinity haunts and doubles the contemporary analytic of power and sexuality and may be subversive of it: we may need to think the disciplinary powers of race as sexuality in a hybrid cultural formation that will not be contained within Foucault's logic of the contemporary. Anderson goes further in acknowledging that colonial racism introduces an awkward weld, a strange historical 'suture', in the narrative of the nation's *modernity*. The archaism of colonial racism, as a form of cultural signification (rather than simply an ideological content), reactivates nothing less man the 'primal scene' of the modern Western nation: that is, the problematic historical transition between dynastic, lineage societies and horizontal, homogeneous secular communities. What Anderson designates as racism's 'timelessness', its location 'outside history', is in fact that form of time-lag, a mode of repetition and reinscription, that *performs* the ambivalent historical temporality of modern national cultures—the *aporetic coexistence*, within the cultural history of the *modern* imagined community, of both the dynastic, hierarchical, prefigurative 'medieval' traditions (the past), and the secular, homogeneous, synchronous cross-time of modernity (the present). Anderson resists a reading of the modern nation that suggests—in an iterative time-lag—that the hybridity of the colonial space may provide a pertinent problematic within which to write the history of the 'postmodern' national formations of the West.

To take this perspective would mean that we see 'racism' not simply as a hangover from archaic conceptions of the aristocracy, but as part of the historical traditions of civic and liberal humanism that create ideological matrices of national aspiration, together with their concepts of 'a people' and its imagined community. Such a privileging of ambivalence in the social imaginaries of nation*ness*, and its forms of collective affiliation, would enable us to understand the coeval, often *incommensurable* tension between the influence of traditional 'ethnicist' identifications that coexist with contemporary secular, modernizing aspirations. The enunciative 'present' of modernity, that I am proposing, would provide a political space to articulate and negotiate such culturally hybrid social identities. Questions of cultural difference would not be dismissed—with a barely concealed racism—as atavistic 'tribal' instincts that afflict Irish Catholics in Belfast or 'Muslim fundamentalists' in Bradford. It is precisely such unresolved, transitional moments within the disjunctive present of modernity that are then projected into a time of historical retroversion or an inassimilable place outside history.

The *history* of modernity's antique dreams is to be found in the *writing out* of the colonial and postcolonial moment. In resisting these attempts to normalize the time-lagged colonial moment, we may provide a *genealogy* for postmodernity that is at least as important as the 'aporetic' history of the Sublime or the nightmare of rationality in Auschwitz. For colonial and postcolonial texts do not merely tell the modern history of 'unequal development' or evoke memories of underdevelopment. I have tried to suggest that they provide modernity with a modular moment of *enunciation*: the locus and locution of cultures caught in the transitional and disjunctive temporalities of modernity. What is in modernity *more* than modernity is the disjunctive 'postcolonial' time and space that makes its presence felt *at the level of enunciation*. It figures, in an influential contemporary fictional instance, as the contingent margin between Toni Morrison's indeterminate moment of the 'not-there'—a 'black' space that she distinguishes from the Western sense of synchronous tradition—which then turns into the 'first stroke' of slave rememory, the *time* of communality and the narrative of a history of slavery (see pp. 191–2 for an elaboration of this issue). This translation of the meaning of time into the discourse of space; this catachrestic seizure of the signifying 'caesura' of modernity's presence and *present*; this insistence that power must be thought in the hybridity of race and sexuality; that nation must be reconceived liminally as the dynastic-in-the-democratic, race-difference doubling and splitting the teleology of class-consciousness: it is through these iterative interrogations and *historical initiations* that the cultural location of modernity shifts to the postcolonial site.

VI

I have attempted, then, to designate a postcolonial 'enunciative' present that moves beyond Foucault's reading of the task of modernity as providing an ontology of the present. I have tried to open up, once again, the cultural space in the temporal doubling of sign and symbol that I described in Chapter 9 (pp. 192–3): from the stroke of the sign that establishes the intersubjective world of truth 'deprived of subjectivity', back to the rediscovery of that moment of agency and individuation in the social imaginary of the order of historic symbols. I have attempted to provide a form of the writing of cultural difference in the midst of modernity that is inimical to binary boundaries: whether these be between past and present, inside and outside, subject and object, signifier and signified. This spatial-time of cultural difference—with its postcolonial genealogy—erases the Occidental 'culture of common sense' that Derrida aptly describes as 'ontologizing the limit between outside and inside, between the biophysical and the psychic'.[37] In his essay 'The uncolonized mind: Postcolonial India and the East', Ashis Nandy provides a more descriptive illustration of a postcolonial India that is neither modern nor anti-modern but non-modern. What this entails for the 'modern antonyms' of cultural difference between the First and Third Worlds, requires a form of time-lagged significa-tion, for as he writes:

> this century has shown that in every situation of organized oppression the true antonyms are always the exclusive part versus the inclusive whole … [N]ot the past versus the present but either of them versus the rationality which turns them into co-victims.[38]

In splitting open those 'welds' of modernity, a postcolonial contra-modernity becomes visible. What Foucault and Anderson disavow as 'retroversion' emerges as a retroactivity, a form of cul-tural reinscription that moves *back to the future*. I shall call it a 'protective' past, a form of the future anterior. Without the postcolonial time-lag the discourse of modernity cannot, I believe, be written; with the *projective past* it can be inscribed as a historical narrative of alterity that explores forms of social antagonism and contradiction that are not yet properly represented, political identities in the process of being formed, cultural enunciations in the act of hybridity, in the process of translating and transvaluing cultural differences. The political space for such a social imaginary is that marked out by Raymond Williams in his distinction between emergent and residual practices of oppositionality that require a 'non-metaphysical and non-subjectivist' sociohistorical positionality.[39] This largely unexplored and undeveloped aspect of Williams's work has a contemporary relevance for those burgeoning forces of the 'cultural' left who are attempting to formulate (the unfortunately entitled) 'politics of difference', grounded in the experience and theory of the 'new social movements'. Williams suggests that in certain historical moments, the 'profound deformation' of the dominant culture will prevent it from recognizing 'practices and meanings that are not reached for' and these potentially empowering perspectives, and their political constituencies, will remain profoundly unsignified and silent within the polit-ical culture. Stuart Hall takes this argument forward in his attempt to construct an alternative 'modernity' where, he suggests, 'organic' ideologies are neither consistent nor homogeneous and the subjects of ideology are not unitarily assigned to a singular social position. Their 'strangely composite' construction requires a redefinition of the public sphere to take account of the histor-ical transformation by which it follows that an alternative conception of socialism must embrace this struggle to democratize power across all the centres of social activity—in private as well as in public life, in personal associations as well as in public obligations.… If the struggle for socialism in modern societies is a war of position, then our conception of society must be of a *society of positions*—different places from which we can all begin the reconstruction of society of which the state is only the anachronistic caretaker.[40]

Such a form of the social (or socialist) imaginary 'blocks' the totalization of the site of social utterance. This encounter with the time-lag of representation insists that any form of political emergence must encounter the *contingent place* from where its narrative *begins* in relation to the temporalities of other marginal 'minority' histories that are seeking their 'individuation', their vivid realization. There is a focus on what Houston Baker has emphasized, for Black Renaissancism, as 'the processual quality [of meaning] … not material instantiation at any given moment but the effi-cacy of passage'. And such a passage of historical experience lived through the time-lag opens up quite suddenly in a poem by the Afro-American poet, Sonia Sanchez:

> life is obscene with crowds
> of black on white
> death is my pulse.
> what might have been
> is not for him/or me
> but what could have been
> floods the womb until I drown[41]

You can hear it in the ambiguity between 'what *might* have been' and 'what *could* have been'—the contingency, the closeness of those rhetorics of indeterminacy. You read it in that considerable shift in historical time between the conditions of an obscene past—*might have been*—and the conditionality of a new birth—*could have been*; you barely see it in the almost imperceptible shift in tense and syntax—*might:could*—that makes all the difference between the pulse of death and the flooded womb of birth. It is the repetition of the 'could-in-the-might' that expresses the marginalized disjunctive experience of the subject of racism—*obscene with crowds/of black on white*: the passage of a 'projective past' in the very time of its performance.

The postcolonial passage through modernity produces that form of repetition—the past as projective. The time-lag of postcolonial modernity moves *forward*, erasing that compliant past tethered to the myth of progress, ordered in the binarisms of its cultural logic: past/present, inside/outside. This *forward* is neither teleological nor is it an endless slippage. It is the function of the *lag* to slow down the linear, progressive time of modernity to reveal its 'gesture', its *tempi*, 'the pauses and stresses of the whole performance'. This can only be achieved—as Walter Benjamin remarked of Brecht's epic theatre—by damming the stream of real life, by bringing the flow to a standstill in a reflux of astonishment. When the dialectic of modernity is brought to a standstill, then the temporal action of modernity—its progressive, future drive—is *staged*, revealing 'everything that is involved in the act of staging *per se*'.[42] This slowing down, or lagging, *impels* the 'past', *projects* it, gives its 'dead' symbols the circulatory life of the 'sign' of the present, of *passage*, the quickening of the quotidian. Where these temporalities touch contingently, their spatial boundaries metonymically overlapping, at that moment their margins are lagged, sutured, by the indeterminate articulation of the 'disjunctive' present. *Time-lag keeps alive the making of the past.* As it negotiates the levels and liminalities of that spatial time that I have tried to unearth in the postcolonial archaeology of modernity, you might think that it 'lacks' time or history. Don't be fooled!

It may appear 'timeless' only in that sense in which, for Toni Morrison, Afro-American art is 'astonished' by the figure of the ancestor: 'the timelessness is there, this person who represented this ancestor'.[43] And when the ancestor rises from the dead in the guise of the murdered daughter, Beloved, then we see the furious emergence of the projective past. Beloved is not the ancestor as the 'elder' whom Morrison describes as benevolent, instructive and protective. Her presence, which is profoundly time-lagged, moves forward while continually encircling that moment of the 'not-there' which Morrison sees as the stressed, dislocatory absence that is crucial for the rememoration of the narrative of slavery. Ella, a member of the chorus, standing at that very distance from the 'event' from which modernity produces its 'sign', now describes the projective past.

> The future was sunset; the past something to leave behind. And if it didn't stay behind you might have to stomp it out…. As long as the ghost showed out from its ghostly place … Ella respected it. But if it took flesh and came in her world, well, the shoe was on the other foot. She didn't mind a little communication between the two worlds, but this was an invasion.[44]

Ella bears witness to this invasion of the projective past. Toussaint bears witness to the tragic dissolution, in San Domingo, of the sign of the Revolution. In these forms of witness there is no passivity; there is a violent turning from interrogation to *initiation*. We have not simply opposed the idea of progress with other 'ideas': the battle has been waged on hybrid territory, in the discontinuity and *distanciation* between event and enunciation, in the time-lag *in-between* sign and symbol. I have attempted to constitute a postcolonial, critical discourse that contests modernity through the establishment of other historical sites, other forms of enunciation.

In the figure of the witness of a postcolonial modernity we have another wisdom: it comes from those who have seen the nightmare of racism and oppression in the banal daylight of the everyday. They represent an idea of action and agency more complex than either the nihilism of despair or the Utopia of progress. They speak of the reality of survival and negotiation that constitutes the moment of resistance, its sorrow and its salvation, but is rarely spoken in the heroisms or the horrors of history. Ella says it, plainly: '*What is to be done in a world where even when you were a solution you were a problem.*' This is not defeatism. It is an enactment of the limits of the 'idea' of progess, the marginal displacement of the ethics of modernity. The sense of Ella's words, and my chapter, echo in that great prophet of the double consciousness of modern America who spoke across the veil, against what he called 'the colour-line'. Nowhere has the historical problem of cultural temporality as constituting the 'belatedness' of subjects of oppression and dispossession been spoken more pertinently than in the words of W. E. B. Du Bois—I like to think that they are the prophetic precursor of my discourse of the time-lag:

> So woefully unorganized is sociological knowledge that the meaning of progress, the meaning of swift and slow in human doing, and the limits of human perfectibility, are veiled, unanswered sphinxes on the shores of science. Why should Aeschylus have sung two thousand years before Shakespeare was born? Why has civilization flourished in Europe and flickered, flamed and died in Africa? So long as the world stands meekly dumb before such questions, shall this nation proclaim its ignorance and unhallowed prejudices by denying freedom of opportunity to those who brought the Sorrow Songs to the Seats of the Mighty?[45]

Du Bois makes a fine answer in the threnody of the Sorrow Songs, their eloquent omissions and silences that 'conceal much of real poetry beneath conventional theology and unmeaning rhapsody'.[46] In the inversion of our catachrestic, critical process, we find that the 'unmeaning', the non-sense of the sign discloses a symbolic vision of a form of progress beyond modernity and its sociology—but not without the enigmatic riddle of the sphinx. To turn Ella's words: what do we do in a world where even when there is a resolution of meaning there is a problem of its performativity? An indeterminacy which is also the condition of its being historical? A contingency which is also the possibility of cultural translation? You heard it in the repetition of Sonia Sanchez as she turned the historical obscenity of 'what might have been' into the projective past, the empowering vision of 'what could have been'. Now you see it in the gaze of the unanswered sphinxes: Du Bois' answer comes through the rhythm of the swift and slow of human doing itself as he commands the certain shores of 'modern' science to recede. The problem of progress is not simply an unveiling of human perfectibility, not simply the hermeneutic of progress. In the performance of human doing, through the veil, emerges a figure of cultural time where perfectibility is not ineluctably tied to the myth of progressivism. The rhythm of the Sorrow Songs may at times be swift—like the protective past—at other times it may be slow—like the time-lag. What is crucial to such a vision of the future is the belief that we must not merely change the *narratives* of our histories, but transform our sense of what it means to live, to be, in other times and different spaces, both human and historical.

Notes

1. All citations from Fanon in the following pages come from 'The fact of blackness', in *Black Skin, White Masks*, Foreword by H. Bhabha (London: Pluto, 1986), pp. 109–40.
2. W. E. B. Du Bois, *The Souls of Black Folk* (New York: Signet Classics, 1982), p. 275.
3. 'A conversation with Fredric Jameson', in A. Ross (ed.) *Universal Abandon: The Politics of Postmodernism* (Edinburgh: Edinburgh University Press, 1988), p. 17.
4. See my reading of Renan in Chapter 8, 'DissemiNation'.
5. Each of these writers has addressed the problem of modernity in a number of works so that selection becomes invidious. However, some of the most directly relevant are the following: J. Habermas, *The Philosophical Discourse of Modernity* (Cambridge: Polity Press, 1990), esp. chs 11 and 12; M. Foucault, *The History of Sexuality. Volume One: An Introduction* (London: Allen Lane, 1979); see also his 'The art of telling the truth', in L. D. Kritzman (ed.) *Politics, Philosophy and Culture* (New York: Routledge, 1990); J.-F. Lyotard, *The Differend* (Minneapolis: University of Minnesota Press, 1988); C. Lefort, *The Political Forms of Modern Society*, J. B. Thomason (ed.) (Cambridge: Polity Press, 1978), especially Part II, 'History, ideology, and the social imaginary'.
6. Habermas, *The Philosophical Discourse of Modernity*, p. 311.
7. J. Derrida, *The Post Card: From Socrates to Freud and Beyond*, A. Bass (trans.) (Chicago: Chicago University Press, 1987), pp. 303–4.
8. M. Dolar, *The Legacy of the Enlightenment: Foucault and Lacan*, unpublished manuscript.
9. R. Young, *White Mythologies: Writing, History and the West* (London: Routledge, 1990), pp. 16–17. Young argues a convincing case agains the Eurocentrism of historicism through his exposition of a number of 'totalizing' historical doctrines, particular in the Marxist tradition, while demonstrating at the same time that the spatializing anti-historicism of Foucault remains equally Eurocentric.
10. Cf. Young, *White Mythologies*, pp. 116–17.
11. T. Eagleton, *The Ideology of the Aesthetic* (Oxford: Blackwell, 1990), p. 414.
12. H. A. Baker, Jr., *Modernism and the Harlem Renaissance* (Chicago: Chicago University Press, 1987), p. 56.
13. C. Breckenridge and A. Appadurai, The Situation of Public Culture, unpublished manuscript. For the general elaboration of this thesis see various issues of *Public Culture: Bulletin of the Project for Transnational Cultural Studies* (University of Pennsylvania).
14. P. Gilroy, 'One nation under a groove', in D. T. Goldberg (ed.) *Anatomy of Racism* (Minneapolis: University of Minnesota Press, 1990), p. 280.
15. Although I introduce the term 'time-lag' more specifically in Chapters 8 and 9, it is a structure of the 'splitting' of colonial discourse that I have been elaborating and illustrating—without giving it a name—from my very earliest essays.
16. J. Derrida, 'Des Tours de Babel', in *Difference in Translation*, J. F. Graham (ed.) (Ithaca: Cornell University Press, 1985), p. 174.
17. Lefort, *The Political Forms of Modern Society*, p. 212.
18. Foucault, 'The art of telling the truth', p. 90.
19. ibid., p. 93.
20. C. L. R. James, *The Black Jacobins* (London: Allison and Busby, 1980), pp. 290–1.
21. J. Habermas, 'Modernity: an incomplete project', in H. Foster (ed.) *Postmodern Culture* (London: Pluto, 1985).
22. M. de Certeau, 'The historiographical operation', in his *The Writing of History*, T. Conley (trans.) (New York: Columbia University Press, 1988), p. 91.
23. L. Althusser, *Montesquieu, Rousseau, Marx* (London: Verso, 1972), p. 78.
24. P. J. Bowler, *The Invention of Progress* (Oxford: Blackwell, 1990), ch. 4.
25. Gilroy, 'One nation under a groove', p. 278.
26. C. West, 'Race and social theory: towards a genealogical materialist analysis', in M. Davis, M. Marable, F. Pfeil and M. Sprinker (eds.) *Towards a Rainbow Socialism* (London: Verso, 1987), pp. 86 ff.
27. C. West, *The American Evasion of Philosophy* (London: Macmillan, 1990), pp. 232–3.
28. G. Prakash, 'Post-Orientalist Third-World histories', *Comparative Studies in Society and History*, vol. 32, no. 2 (April 1990), p. 403.
29. Robert Young, in *White Mythologies*, also suggests, in keeping with my argument that the colonial and postcolonial moment is the liminal point, or the limit-text, of the holistic demands of historicism.
30. Foucault, *The History of Sexuality*, p. 150.
31. M. Foucault, *Foucault Live*, J. Johnstone and S. Lotringer (trans.) (New York: Semiotext(e), 1989), p. 269.
32. B. Anderson, *Imagined Communities* (London: Verso, 1983), p. 136.
33. ibid., p. 137.
34. ibid.
35. ibid.
36. P. Chatterjee, *Nationalist Thought and the Colonial World* (London: Zed, 1986), pp. 21–2.
37. J. H. Smith and W. Kerrigan (eds.) *Taking Chances: Derrida, Psychoanalysis, Literature* (Baltimore: Johns Hopkins University Press, 1984), p. 27.
38. A. Nandy, *The Intimate Enemy* (Delhi: Oxford University Press, 1983), p. 99.
39. R. Williams, *Problems in Materialism and Culture* (London: Verso, 1980), p. 43. See also Chapter 8, p. 149
40. S. Hall, *The Hard Road to Renewal* (London: Verso, 1988), pp. 10–11, 231–2.

41. H. A. Baker, Jr., 'Our Lady: Sonia Sanchez and the writing of a Black Renaissance', in H. L. Gates (ed.) *Reading Black, Reading Feminist* (New York: Meridian, 1990).
42. W. Benjamin, *Understanding Brecht*, S. Mitchell (trans.) (London: New Left Books, 1973), pp. 11–13. I have freely adapted some of Benjamin's phrases and interpolated the problem of modernity in the midst of his argument on epic theatre. I do not think that I have misrepresented his argument.
43. T. Morrison, 'The ancester as foundation', in M. Evans (ed.) *Black Women Writers* (London: Pluto, 1985), p. 343.
44. T. Morrison, *Beloved* (London: Pluto, 1985), pp. 256–7.
45. W. E. B. Du Bois, *The Souls of Black Folk* (New York: Signet Classics, 1969), p. 275.
46. ibid., p. 271.

3

The New Cultural Politics of Difference

CORNEL WEST

In the last few years of the twentieth century, there is emerging a significant shift in the sensibilities and outlooks of critics and artists. In fact, I would go so far as to claim that a new kind of cultural worker is in the making, associated with a new politics of difference. These new forms of intellectual consciousness advance new conceptions of the vocation of critic and artist, attempting to undermine the prevailing disciplinary divisions of labor in the academy, museum, mass media, and gallery networks while preserving modes of critique within the ubiquitous commodification of culture in the global village. Distinctive features of the new cultural politics of difference are to trash the monolithic and homogeneous in the name of diversity, multiplicity, and heterogeneity; to reject the abstract, general, and universal in light of the concrete, specific, and particular; and to historicize, contextualize, and pluralize by highlighting the contingent, provisional, variable, tentative, shifting, and changing. Needless to say, these gestures are not new in the history of criticism or art, yet what makes them novel—along with the cultural politics they produce—is what constitutes difference and how it is constituted, the weight and gravity it is given in representation, and the way in which highlighting issues like exterminism, empire, class, race, gender, sexual orientation, age, nation, nature, and region at this historical moment acknowledges some discontinuity and disruption from previous forms of cultural critique. To put it bluntly, the new cultural politics of difference consists of creative responses to the precise circumstances of our present moment—especially those of marginalized first world agents who shun degraded self-representations, articulating instead their sense of the flow of history in light of the contemporary terrors, anxieties, and fears of highly commercialized North Atlantic capitalist cultures (with their escalating xenophobias against people of color, Jews, women, gays, lesbians, and the elderly). The nationalist revolts against the legacy of hegemonic party henchmen in second world excommunist cultures, and the diverse cultures of the majority of inhabitants on the globe smothered by international communication cartels and repressive postcolonial elites (sometimes in the name of communism, as in Ethiopia) or starved by austere World Bank and IMF policies that subordinate them to the North (as in free-market capitalism in Chile), also locate vital areas of analysis in this new cultural terrain.

The new cultural politics of difference are neither simply oppositional in contesting the mainstream (or *male*stream) for inclusion nor transgressive in the avant-gardist sense of shocking conventional bourgeois audiences. Rather they are distinct articulations of talented (and usually

29

privileged) contributors to culture who desire to align themselves with demoralized, demobilized, depoliticized, and disorganized people in order to empower and enable social action and, if possible, to enlist collective insurgency for the expansion of freedom, democracy, and individuality. This perspective impels these cultural critics and artists to reveal, as an integral component of their production, the very operations of power within their immediate work contexts (i.e., academy, museum, gallery, mass media). This strategy, however, also puts them in an inescapable double bind—while linking their activities to the fundamental, structural overhaul of these institutions, they often remain financially dependent on them. (So much for "independent" creation.) For these critics of culture, theirs is a gesture that is simultaneously progressive and co-opted. Yet without social movement or political pressure from outside these institutions (extraparliamentary and extracurricular actions like the social movements of the recent past), transformation degenerates into mere accommodation or sheer stagnation, and the role of the "co-opted progressive"—no matter how fervent one's subversive rhetoric—is rendered more difficult. In this sense there can be no artistic breakthrough or social progress without some form of crisis in civilization—a crisis usually generated by organizations or collectivities that convince ordinary people to put their bodies and lives on the line. There is, of course, no guarantee that such pressure will yield the result one wants, but there is a guarantee that the status quo will remain or regress if no pressure is applied at all.

The new cultural politics of difference faces three basic challenges—intellectual, existential, and political. The intellectual challenge—usually cast as a methodological debate in these days in which academicist forms of expression have a monopoly on intellectual life—is how to think about representational practices in terms of history, culture, and society. How does one understand, analyze, and enact such practices today? An adequate answer to this question can be attempted only after one comes to terms with the insights and blindnesses of earlier attempts to grapple with the question in light of the evolving crisis in different histories, cultures, and societies. I shall sketch a brief genealogy—a history that highlights the contingent origins and often ignoble outcomes—of exemplary critical responses to the question.

The Intellectual Challenge

An appropriate starting point is the ambiguous legacy of the Age of Europe. Between 1492 and 1945, European breakthroughs in oceanic transportation, agricultural production, state consolidation, bureaucratization, industrialization, urbanization, and imperial dominion shaped the makings of the modern world. Precious ideals like the dignity of persons (individuality) or the popular accountability of institutions (democracy) were unleashed around the world. Powerful critiques of illegitimate authorities—the Protestant Reformation against the Roman Catholic Church, the Enlightenment against state churches, liberal movements against absolutist states and feudal guild constraints, workers against managerial subordination, people of color and Jews against white and gentile supremacist decrees, gays and lesbians against homophobic sanctions—were fanned and fueled by these precious ideals refined within the crucible of the Age of Europe. Yet the discrepancy between sterling rhetoric and lived reality, glowing principles and actual practices, loomed large.

By the last European century—the last epoch in which European domination of most of the globe was not substantively contested or challenged—a new world seemed to be stirring. At the height of England's reign as the major imperial European power, its exemplary cultural critic, Matthew Arnold ([1855] 1969), painfully observed in his "Stanzas from the Grand Chartreuse" that he felt some sense of "wandering between two worlds, one dead/the other powerless to be born" (p. 302). Following his Burkean sensibilities of cautious reform and fear of anarchy, Arnold acknowledged that the old glue—religion—that had tenuously and often unsuccessfully held together the ailing European regimes could not do so in the mid-nineteenth century. Like Alexis de Tocqueville in France, Arnold saw that the democratic temper was the wave of the future. So he proposed a new conception of culture—a secular, humanistic one—that could play an integrative role in cementing and stabilizing an emerging bourgeois civil society and imperial state. His famous castigation of the immobilizing materialism of the declining aristocracy, the vulgar philistinism of the emerging middle classes, and the latent explosiveness of the working-class majority was motivated by a desire to create new forms of cultural legitimacy, authority, and order in a rapidly changing moment in nineteenth-century Europe.

For Arnold ([1869] 1925), this new conception of culture

> seeks to do away with classes; to make the best that has been thought and known in the world current everywhere; to make all men live in an atmosphere of sweetness and light....
>
> This is the *social idea* and the men of culture are the true apostles of equality. The great men of culture are those who have had a passion for diffusing, for making prevail, for carrying from one end of society to the other, the best knowledge, the best ideas of their time, who have laboured to divest knowledge of all that was harsh, uncouth, difficult, abstract, professional, yet still remaining the best knowledge and thought of the time, and a true source, therefore, of sweetness and light. (p. 67)

As an organic intellectual of an emergent middle class—as the inspector of schools in an expanding educational bureaucracy, professor of poetry at Oxford (the first noncleric and the first to lecture in English rather than Latin), and an active participant in a thriving magazine network—Arnold defined and defended a new secular culture of critical discourse. For him, this discursive strategy would be lodged in the educational and periodical apparatuses of modern societies as they contained and incorporated the frightening threats of an arrogant aristocracy and especially of an "anarchic" working-class majority. His ideals of disinterested, dispassionate, and objective inquiry would regulate this secular cultural production, and his justifications for the use of state power to quell any threats to the survival and security of this culture were widely accepted. He aptly noted, "Through culture seems to lie our way, not only to perfection, but even to safety" (Arnold, [1869] 1925, p. 200).

For Arnold, the best of the Age of Europe—modeled on a mythological mélange of Periclean Athens, late republican/early imperial Rome, and Elizabethan England—could be promoted only if there were an interlocking affiliation among the emerging middle classes, a homogenizing of cultural discourse in the educational and university networks, and a state advanced enough in its policing techniques to safeguard it. The candidates for participation and legitimation in this grand endeavor of cultural renewal and revision would be detached intellectuals willing to shed their parochialism, provincialism and class-bound identities for Arnold's middle-class-skewed project: "Aliens, if we may so call them—persons who are mainly led, not by their class spirit, but by a general humane spirit, by the love of human perfection" ([1869] 1925, p. 107). Needless to say, this Arnoldian perspective still informs much of academic practice and secular cultural attitudes today: dominant views about the canon, admission procedures, and collective self-definitions of intellectuals. Yet Arnold's project was disrupted by the collapse of nineteenth-century Europe—World War I. This unprecedented war—in George Steiner's words, the first of the bloody civil wars within Europe—brought to the surface the crucial role and violent potential not of the masses Arnold feared but of the state he heralded. Upon the ashes of this wasteland of human carnage—including some of the civilian European population—T.S. Eliot emerged as the grand cultural spokesman.

Eliot's project of reconstituting and reconceiving European highbrow culture—and thereby regulating critical and artistic practices—after the internal collapse of imperial Europe can be viewed as a response to the probing question posed by Paul Valéry in "The Crisis of the Mind" ([1919] 1962) after World War I:

> Will Europe become *what it is in reality*—that is, a little promontory on the continent of Asia? Or will it remain *what it seems*—that is, the elect portion of the terrestrial globe, the pearl of the sphere, the brain of a vast body? (p. 31)

Eliot's image of Europe as a wasteland, a culture of fragments with no cementing center, predominated in postwar Europe. And though his early poetic practices were more radical, open, and international than his Eurocentric criticism, Eliot posed a return to and revision of tradition as the only way to regain European cultural order and political stability. For Eliot, contemporary history had become, as James Joyce's Stephen declared in *Ulysses* ([1922] 1934), "a nightmare from which he was trying to awake" (p. 35); "an immense panorama of futility and anarchy," as Eliot put it in his renowned review of Joyce's modernist masterpiece (Eliot, [1923] 1948, p. 201). In his influential essay, "Tradition and the Individual Talent" ([1919] 1950), Eliot stated that:

> Yet if the only form of tradition, of handing down, consisted in following the ways of the immediate generation before us in a blind or timid adherence to its successes, "tradition" should positively be discouraged. We have seen many such simple currents soon lost in the sand; and novelty is better than repetition. Tradition is a matter of much wider significance. It cannot be inherited, and if you want it you must attain it by great labour. (p. 4)

Eliot found this tradition in the Church of England, to which he converted in 1927. Here was a tradition that left room for his Catholic cast of mind, Calvinist heritage, puritanical temperament, and ebullient patriotism for the old American South (the place of his upbringing). Like Arnold, Eliot was obsessed with the idea of civilization and the horror of barbarism (echoes of Joseph Conrad's Kurtz in *Heart of Darkness*), or, more pointedly, the notion of the decline and decay of European civilization. With the advent of World War II, Eliot's obsession became a reality. Again, unprecedented human carnage (fifty million died)—including an indescribable genocidal attack on Jewish people—throughout Europe as well as around the globe put the last nail in the coffin of the Age of Europe. After 1945, Europe consisted of a devastated and divided continent, crippled by a humiliating dependency on and deference to the United States and Russia.

The second historical coordinate of my genealogy is the emergence of the United States as *the* world power (in the words of André Malraux, the first nation to do so without trying to do so). The United States was unprepared for world power status. However, with the recovery of Stalin's Russia (after losing twenty million lives), the United States felt compelled to make its presence felt around the globe. Then, with the Marshall Plan to strengthen Europe, it seemed clear that there was no escape from world power obligations.

The post-World-War-II era in the United States, or the first decades of what Henry Luce envisioned as "The American Century," was a period not only of incredible economic expansion but of active cultural ferment. The creation of a mass middle class—a prosperous working class with bourgeois identity—was countered by the first major emergence of subcultures among American non-WASP intellectuals; the so-called New York intellectuals in criticism, the abstract expressionists in painting, and the bebop artists in jazz music. This emergence signaled a vital challenge to an American male WASP elite loyal to an older and eroding European culture.

The first significant blow was dealt when assimilated Jewish Americans entered the higher echelons of the cultural apparatuses (academy, museums, galleries, mass media). Lionel Trilling is an emblematic figure. This Jewish entree into the anti-Semitic and patriarchal critical discourse of the exclusivistic institutions of American culture initiated the slow but sure undoing of male WASP cultural hegemony and homogeneity. Trilling's aim was to appropriate Arnold's project for his own political and cultural purposes—thereby unraveling the old male WASP consensus while erecting a new post-World-War-II liberal academic consensus around cold war, anticommunist renditions of the values of complexity, difficulty, variousness, and modulation. In addition, the postwar boom laid the basis for intense professionalization and specialization in expanding institutions of higher education—especially in the natural sciences, which were compelled to respond somehow to Russia's successful ventures in space. Humanistic scholars found themselves searching for new methodologies that could buttress self-images of rigor and scientific seriousness. The close reading techniques of New Criticism (severed from their conservative, organicist, anti-industrialist ideological roots), the logical precision of reasoning in analytic philosophy, and the jargon of Parsonian structural-functionalism in sociology, for example, helped create such self-images. Yet towering cultural critics like C. Wright Mills, W.E.B. Du Bois, Richard Hofstadter, Margaret Mead, and Dwight MacDonald bucked the tide. This suspicion of the academicization of knowledge is expressed in Trilling's well-known essay "On the Teaching of Modern Literature" ([1961] 1965):

> Can we not say that, when modern literature is brought into the classroom, the subject being taught is betrayed by the pedagogy of the subject? We have to ask ourselves whether in our day too much does not come within the purview of the academy. More and more, as the universities liberalize themselves, turn their beneficent imperialistic gaze upon what is called Life Itself, the feeling grows among our educated classes that little can be experienced unless it is validated by some established intellectual discipline. (p. 10)

Trilling laments the fact that university instruction often quiets and domesticates radical and subversive works of art, turning them into objects "of merely habitual regard." This process of "the socialization of the anti-social, or the acculturation of the anti-cultural, or the legitimization of the subversive" leads Trilling to "question whether in our culture the study of literature is any longer a suitable means for developing and refining the intelligence" ([1961] 1965, p. 26). He asks this question in a spirit not of denigrating and devaluing the academy but rather of highlighting the possible failure of an Arnoldian conception of culture to contain what he perceives as the philistine and anarchic alternatives becoming more and more available to students of the '60s—namely, mass culture and radical politics.

This threat is partly associated with the third historical coordinate of my genealogy—the decolonization of the third world. It is crucial to recognize the importance of this world-historical process if one wants to grasp the significance of the end of the Age of Europe and the emergence of the United States as a world power. With the first defeat of a Western nation by a non-Western nation—in Japan's victory over Russia (1905); revolutions in Persia (1905), Turkey (1908), Mexico (1911–12), and China (1912); and much later the independence of India (1947) and China (1948) and the triumph of Ghana (1957)—the actuality of a decolonized globe loomed large. Born of violent struggle, consciousness raising, and the reconstruction of identities, decolonization simultaneously brings with it new perspectives on that long-festering underside of the Age of Europe (of which colonial domination represents the *costs* of "progress," "order," and "culture"), and requires new readings of the economic boom in the United States (wherein the black, brown, yellow, red, white, female, gay, lesbian, and elderly working class live the same *costs* by supplying cheap labor at home as well as in U.S.-dominated Latin American and Pacific Rim markets).

The impetuous ferocity and moral outrage that motor the decolonization process are best captured by Frantz Fanon in *The Wretched of the Earth* (1963):

Decolonization, which sets out to change the order of the world, is, obviously, a program of complete disorder.... Decolonization is the meeting of two forces, opposed to each other by their very nature, which in fact owe their originality to that sort of substantification which results from and is nourished by the situation in the colonies. Their first encounter was marked by violence and their existence together—that is to say the exploitation of the native by the settler—was carried on by dint of a great array of bayonets and cannons....

In decolonization, there is therefore the need of a complete calling in question of the colonial situation. If we wish to describe it precisely, we might find it in the well-known words: "The last shall be first and the first last." Decolonization is the putting into practice of this sentence....

The naked truth of decolonization evokes for us the searing bullets and bloodstained knives which emanate from it. For if the last shall be first, this will only come to pass after a murderous and decisive struggle between the two protagonists. (pp. 36–37)

Fanon's strong words describe the feelings and thoughts between the occupying British Army and the colonized Irish in Northern Ireland, the occupying Israeli Army and the subjugated Palestinians on the West Bank and Gaza Strip, the South African Army and the oppressed black South Africans in the townships, the Japanese police and the Koreans living in Japan, established armies and subordinated ethnic groups in the former Soviet Union. His words also partly invoke the sense many black Americans have toward police departments in urban centers. In other words, Fanon is articulating century-long, heartfelt, human responses to being degraded and despised, hated and hunted, oppressed and exploited, and marginalized and dehumanized at the hands of powerful, xenophobic European, American, Russian, and Japanese imperial nations.

During the late 1950s, the '60s, and the early '70s in the United States, these decolonized sensibilities fanned and fueled the civil rights and black power movements, as well as the student, antiwar, feminist, gray, brown, gay, and lesbian movements. In this period we witnessed the shattering of male WASP cultural homogeneity and the collapse of the short-lived liberal consensus. The inclusion of African Americans, Latino/a Americans, Asian Americans, Native Americans, and American women in the culture of critical discourse yielded intense intellectual polemics and inescapable ideological polarization that focused principally on the exclusions, silences, and blindnesses of male WASP cultural homogeneity and its concomitant Arnoldian notions of the canon.

In addition these critiques promoted three crucial processes that affected intellectual life in the country. First is the appropriation of the theories of postwar Europe—especially the work of the Frankfurt School (Marcuse, Adorno, Horkheimer), French/Italian Marxisms (Sartre, Althusser, Lefebvre, Gramsci), structuralisms (Levi-Strauss, Todorov), and poststructuralisms (Deleuze, Derrida, Foucault). These diverse and disparate theories—all preoccupied with keeping alive radical projects after the end of the Age of Europe—tend to fuse versions of transgressive European modernisms with Marxist or post-Marxist left politics and unanimously to shun the term "postmodernism." Second, there is the recovery and revisioning of American history in light of the struggles of white male workers, African Americans, Native Americans, Latino/a Americans, gays and lesbians. Third is the impact of forms of popular culture such as television, film, music videos, and even sports on highbrow, literate culture. The black-based hip-hop culture of youth around the world is one grand example.

After 1973, with the crisis in the international economy, America's slump in productivity, the challenge of OPEC nations to the North Atlantic monopoly of oil production, the increasing competition in high-tech sectors of the economy from Japan and West Germany, and the growing fragility of the international debt structure, the United States entered a period of waning self-confidence (compounded by Watergate) and a nearly contracted economy. As the standards of living for the middle classes declined—owing to runaway inflation and escalating unemployment, underemployment, and crime—the quality of living fell for most everyone, and religious and secular neoconservatism emerged with power and potency. This fusion of fervent neoconservatism, traditional cultural values, and "free market" policies served as the groundwork for the Reagan-Bush era.

The ambiguous legacies of the European Age, U.S. preeminence, and decolonization continue to haunt our postmodern moment as we come to terms with both the European, American, Japanese, Soviet, and third world *crimes against* and *contributions to* humanity. The plight of Africans in the New World can be instructive in this regard.

By 1914 European maritime empires had dominion over more than half of the land and a third of the peoples in the world—almost seventy-two million square kilometers of territory and more than 560 million people around colonial rule. Needless to say, this European control included brutal enslavement, institutional terrorism, and cultural degradation of black diaspora people. The death of roughly seventy-five million Africans during the centuries-long, transatlantic slave trade is but one reminder, among others, of the assault on black humanity. The black diaspora condition of New World servitude—in which people of African descent were viewed as mere commodities with production value, who had no proper legal status, social standing, or public worth—can be characterized, following Orlando Patterson, as natal alienation. This state of perpetual and inheritable domination that diaspora Africans had at birth produced the *modern black diaspora problematic of invisibility and namelessness*. White supremacist practices—enacted under the auspices of the prestigious cultural authorities of the churches, print media, and scientific academics—promoted black inferiority and constituted the European background against which African diaspora struggles for identity, dignity (self-confidence, self-respect, self-esteem), and material resources took place.

An inescapable aspect of this struggle was that the black diaspora peoples' quest for validation and recognition occurred on the ideological, social, and cultural terrains of non-black peoples. White supremacist assaults on black intelligence, ability, beauty, and character required persistent black efforts to hold self-doubt, self-contempt, and even self-hatred at bay. Selective appropriation, incorporation, and rearticulation of European ideologies, cultures, and institutions alongside an African heritage—a heritage more or less confined to linguistic innovation in rhetorical practices, stylizations of the body as forms of occupying an alien social space (e.g., hairstyles, ways of walking, standing, and talking, and hand expressions), means of constituting and sustaining camaraderie and community (e.g., antiphonal, call-and-response styles, rhythmic repetition, risk-ridden syncopation in spectacular modes in musical and rhetorical expressions)—were some of the strategies employed.

The modern black diaspora problematic of invisibility and namelessness can be understood as the condition of relative lack of power for blacks to present themselves to themselves and others as complex human beings, and thereby to contest the bombardment of negative, degrading stereotypes put forward by white supremacist ideologies. The initial black response to being caught in this whirlwind of Europeanization was to resist the misrepresentation and caricature of the terms set by uncontested non-black norms and models and to fight for self-recognition. Every modern black person, especially the cultural disseminator, encounters this problematic of invisibility and namelessness. The initial African diaspora response was a mode of resistance that was moralistic in content and communal in character. That is, the fight for representation and recognition highlighted moral judgements regarding black "positive" images over and against white supremacist stereotypes. These images "re-presented" monolithic and homogeneous black communities in a way that could displace past misrepresentations of these communities. Stuart Hall has discussed these responses as attempts to change the "relations of representation."

These courageous yet limited black efforts to combat racist cultural practices uncritically accepted non-black conventions and standards in two ways. First, they proceeded in an *assimilationist manner* that set out to show that black people were really like white people—thereby eliding differences (in history and culture) between whites and blacks. Black specificity and particularity were thus banished in order to gain white acceptance and approval. Second, these black responses rested upon a *homogenizing impulse* that assumed that all black people were really alike—hence obliterating differences (class, gender, region, sexual orientation) between black peoples. I submit that there are elements of truth in both claims, yet the conclusions are unwarranted owing to the basic fact that non-black paradigms set the terms of the replies.

The insight in the first claim is that blacks and whites are in some important sense alike—i.e., positively, in their capacities for human sympathy, moral sacrifice, service to others, intelligence, and beauty; or negatively, in their capacity for cruelty. Yet the common humanity they share is jettisoned when the claim is cast in an assimilationist manner that subordinates black particularity to a false universalism, i.e., non-black rubrics and prototypes. Similarly, the insight in the second claim is that all blacks are in some significant sense "in the same boat"—that is, subject to white supremacist abuse. Yet this common condition is stretched too far when viewed in a *homogenizing* way that overlooks how racist treatment vastly differs owing to class, gender, sexual orientation, nation, region, hue, and age.

The moralistic and communal aspects of the initial black diaspora responses to social and psychic erasure were not simply cast into binary oppositions of positive/negative, good/bad images that privileged the first term in light of a white norm, so that black efforts remained inscribed within the very logic that dehumanized them. They were further complicated by the fact that these responses were advanced principally by anxiety-ridden, middle-class black intellectuals (predominantly male and heterosexual) grappling with their sense of double-consciousness—namely their own crisis of identity, agency, audience—caught between a quest for white approval and acceptance and an endeavor to overcome the internalized association of blackness with inferiority. And I suggest that these complex anxieties of modern black diaspora intellectuals partly motivate the two major arguments that ground the assimilationist moralism and homogeneous communalism just outlined.

Kobena Mercer has talked about these two arguments as the reflectionist and the social engineering arguments. The reflectionist argument holds that the fight for black representation and recognition—against white racist stereotypes—must reflect or mirror the real black community, not simply the negative and depressing representations of it. The social engineering argument claims that since any form of representation is constructed—i.e., selective in light of broader aims—black representation (especially given the difficulty for blacks to gain access to positions of power to produce any black imagery) should offer positive images, thereby countering racist stereotypes. The hidden assumption of both arguments is that we have unmediated access to what the "real black community" is and what "positive images" are. In short, these arguments presuppose the very phenomenon to be interrogated and thereby foreclose the very issues that should serve as the subject matter to be investigated.

Any notions of "the real black community" and "positive images" are value laden, socially loaded, and ideologically charged. To pursue this discussion is to call into question the possibility of such an uncontested consensus regarding them. Hall has rightly called this encounter "the end of innocence or the end of the innocent notions of the essential Black subject … the recognition that 'black' is essentially a politically and culturally constructed category" (Hall, 1988, p. 28). This recognition—more and more pervasive among the postmodern African diaspora intelligentsia—is facilitated in part by the slow but sure dissolution of the European Age's maritime empires and the unleashing of new political possibilities and cultural articulations among ex-colonized peoples across the globe.

One crucial lesson of this decolonization process remains the manner in which most third world authoritarian bureaucratic elites deploy essentialist rhetorics about "homogeneous national communities" and "positive images" in order to repress and regiment their diverse and heterogeneous populations. Yet in the diaspora, especially among first world countries, this critique has emerged not so much from the black male component of the left as from the black women's movement. The decisive push of postmodern black intellectuals toward a new cultural politics of difference has been made by the powerful critiques and constructive explorations of black diaspora women (e.g., Toni Morrison). The coffin used to bury the innocent notion of the essential black subject was nailed shut with the termination of the black male monopoly on the construction of the black subject. In this regard, the black diaspora womanist critique has had a greater impact than have the critiques that highlight exclusively class, empire, age, sexual orientation, or nature.

This decisive push toward the end of black innocence—though prefigured in various degrees in the best moments of W.E.B. Du Bois, James Baldwin, Amiri Baraka, Anna Cooper, Frantz Fanon, C.L.R. James, Claudia Jones, the later Malcolm X, and others—forces black diaspora cultural workers to encounter what Hall has called "the politics of representation." The main aim now is not simply access to representation in order to produce positive images of homogeneous communities—though broader access remains a practical and political problem. Nor is the primary goal here that of contesting stereotypes—though contestation remains a significant albeit limited venture. Following the model of the African diaspora traditions of music, athletics, and rhetoric, black cultural workers must constitute and sustain discursive and institutional networks that deconstruct earlier modern black strategies for identity formation, demystify power relations that incorporate class, patriarchal, and homophobic biases, and construct more multivalent and multidimensional responses that articulate the complexity and diversity of black practices in the modern and postmodern world.

Furthermore, black cultural workers must investigate and interrogate the other of blackness/whiteness. One cannot deconstruct the binary oppositional logic of images of blackness without extending it to the contrary condition of blackness/whiteness itself. However, a mere dismantling will not do—for the very notion of a deconstructive social theory is oxymoronic. Yet social theory is what is needed to examine and *explain* the historically specific ways in which "whiteness" is a politically constructed category parasitic on "blackness," and thereby to conceive of the profoundly hybrid character of what we mean by "race," "ethnicity," and "nationality." Needless to say, these inquiries must traverse those of "male/female," "colonizer/colonized," "heterosexual/homosexual," et al., as well.

Demystification is the most illuminating mode of theoretical inquiry for those who promote the new cultural politics of difference. Social structural analyses of empire, exterminism, class, race, gender, nature, age, sexual orientation, nation, and region are the springboards—though not the landing grounds—for the most desirable forms of critical practice that take history (and herstory) seriously. Demystification tries to keep track of the complex dynamics of institutional and other related power structures in order to disclose options and alternatives for transformational praxis; it also attempts to grasp the way in which representational strategies are creative responses to novel circumstances and conditions. In this way the central role of human agency (always enacted under circumstances not of one's choosing)—be it in the critic, artist, or constituency, and audience—is accented.

I call demystificatory criticism "prophetic criticism"—the approach appropriate for the new cultural politics of difference—because while it begins with social structural analyses it also makes explicit its moral and political aims. It is partisan, partial, engaged, and crisis centered, yet it always keeps open a skeptical eye to avoid dogmatic traps, premature closures, formulaic formulations, or rigid conclusions. In addition to social-structural analyses, moral and political judgements, and sheer critical consciousness, there indeed is evaluation. Yet the aim of this evaluation is neither to pit art objects against one another like racehorses nor to create eternal canons that dull, discourage, or even dwarf contemporary achievements. We listen to Laurie Anderson, Kathleen Battle, Ludwig van Beethoven, Charlie Parker, Luciano Pavarotti, Sarah Vaughan, or Stevie Wonder; read Anton Chekhov, Ralph Ellison, Gabriel García Márquez, Doris Lessing, Toni Morrison, Thomas Pynchon, William Shakespeare; or see the works of Ingmar Bergman, Le Corbusier, Frank Gehry, Barbara Kruger, Spike Lee, Martin Puryear, Pablo Picasso, or Howardena Pindell—not in order to undergird bureaucratic assents or enliven cocktail party conversations, but rather to be summoned by the styles they deploy for their profound insights, pleasures, and challenges. Yet all evaluation—including a delight in Eliot's poetry despite his reactionary politics, or a love of Zora Neale Hurston's novels despite her Republican Party affiliations—is inseparable from, though not identical or reducible to, social structural analyses, moral and political judgements, and the workings of a curious critical consciousness.

The deadly traps of demystification—and any form of prophetic criticism—are those of reductionism, be it of the sociological, psychological, or historical sort. By reductionism I mean either one-factor analyses (crude Marxisms, feminisms, racialisms, etc.) that yield a one-dimensional functionalism or hypersubtle analytical perspectives that lose touch with the specificity of an artwork's form and the context of its reception. Few cultural workers of whatever stripe can walk the tightrope between the Scylla of reductionism and the Charybdis of aestheticism—yet demystificatory (or prophetic) critics must. Of course, since so many art practices these days also purport to be criticism, this also holds true for artists.

The Existential Challenge

The existential challenge to the new cultural politics of difference can be stated simply: How does one acquire the resources to survive and the cultural capital to thrive as a critic or artist? By cultural capital (Pierre Bourdieu's term), I mean not only the high-quality skills required to engage in cultural practices but more importantly, the self-confidence, discipline, and perseverance necessary for success without an undue reliance on the mainstream for approval and acceptance. This challenge holds for all prophetic critics, yet it is especially difficult for those of color. The widespread modern European denial of the intelligence, ability, beauty, and character of people of color puts a tremendous burden on critics and artists of color to "prove" themselves in light of norms and models set by white elites whose own heritage devalued and dehumanized them. In short, in the court of criticism and art—or any matters regarding the life of the mind—people of color are guilty (i.e., not expected to meet standards of intellectual achievement) until "proven" innocent (i.e., acceptable to "us").

This is more a structural dilemma than a matter of personal attitudes. The profoundly racist and sexist heritage of the European Age has bequeathed to us a set of deeply ingrained perceptions about people of color, including, of course, the self-perceptions that people of color bring. It is not surprising that most intellectuals of color in the past exerted much of their energies and efforts to gain acceptance and approval by "white normative gazes." The new cultural politics of difference advises critics and artists of color to put aside this mode of mental bondage, thereby freeing themselves both to interrogate the ways in which they are bound by certain conventions and to learn from and build on these very norms and models. One hallmark of wisdom in the context of any struggle is to avoid knee-jerk rejection and uncritical acceptance.

Self-confidence, discipline, and perseverance are not ends in themselves. Rather they are the necessary stuff of which enabling criticism and self-criticism are made. Notwithstanding inescapable jealousies, insecurities, and anxieties, one telling characteristic of critics and artists of color linked to the new prophetic criticism should be their capacity for and promotion of relentless criticism and self-criticism—be it the normative paradigms of their white colleagues that tend to leave out considerations of empire, race, gender, and sexual orientation, or the damaging dogmas about the homogeneous character of communities of color.

There are four basic options for people of color interested in representation—if they are to survive and thrive as serious practitioners of their craft. First, there is the Booker T. Temptation, namely the individual preoccupation with the mainstream and its legitimizing power. Most critics and artists of color try to bite this bait. It is nearly unavoidable, yet few succeed in a substantive manner. It is no accident that the most creative and profound among them—especially those who have staying power beyond being mere flashes in the pan to satisfy faddish tokenism—are usually marginal to the mainstream. Even the pervasive professionalization of cultural practitioners of color in the past few decades has not produced towering figures who reside within the established white patronage system, which bestows the rewards and prestige for chosen contributions to American society.

It certainly helps to have some trustworthy allies within this system, yet most of those who enter and remain tend to lose much of their creativity, diffuse their prophetic energy, and dilute their critiques. Still, it is unrealistic for creative people of color to think they can sidestep the white patronage system. And though there are indeed some white allies conscious of the tremendous need to rethink identity politics, it is naive to think that being comfortably nested within this very same system—even if one can be a patron to others—does not affect one's work, one's outlook, and most important, one's soul.

The second option is the Talented Tenth Seduction, namely, a move toward arrogant group insularity. This alternative has a limited function—to preserve one's sanity and sense of self as one copes with the mainstream. Yet it is, at best, a transitional and transient activity. If it becomes a permanent option it is self-defeating in that it usually reinforces the very inferiority complexes promoted by the subtly racist mainstream. Hence it tends to revel in parochialism and encourage a narrow racialist and chauvinistic outlook.

The third strategy is the Go-It-Alone Option. This is an extreme rejectionist perspective that shuns the mainstream and group insularity. Almost every critic and artist of color contemplates or enacts this option at some time in his or her pilgrimage. It is healthy in that it reflects the presence of independent, critical, and skeptical sensibilities toward perceived constraints on one's creativity. Yet it is, in the end, difficult if not impossible to sustain if one is to grow, develop, and mature intellectually, as some semblance of dialogue with a community is necessary for almost any creative practice.

The most desirable option for people of color who promote the new cultural politics of difference is to be a Critical Organic Catalyst. By this I mean a person who stays attuned to the best of what the mainstream has to offer—its paradigms, viewpoints, and methods—yet maintains a grounding in affirming and enabling subcultures of criticism. Prophetic critics and artists of color should be exemplars of what it means to be intellectual freedom fighters, that is, cultural workers who simultaneously position themselves within (or alongside) the mainstream while clearly being aligned with groups who vow to keep alive potent traditions of critique and resistance. In this regard one can take clues from the great musicians or preachers of color who are open to the best of what other traditions offer, yet are rooted in nourishing subcultures that build on the grand achievements of a vital heritage. Openness to others—including the mainstream—does not entail wholesale co-optation, and group autonomy is not group insularity. Louis Armstrong, Ella Baker, W.E.B. Du Bois, Martin Luther King, Jr., Jose Carlos Mariategui, Wynton Marsalis, M.M. Thomas, and Ronald Takaki have understood this well.

The new cultural politics of difference can thrive only if there are communities, groups, organizations, institutions, subcultures, and networks of people of color who cultivate critical sensibilities and personal accountability—without inhibiting individual expressions, curiosities, and idiosyncrasies. This is especially needed given the escalating racial hostility, violence, and polarization in the United States. Yet this critical coming together must not be a narrow closing of ranks. Rather it is a strengthening and nurturing endeavor that can forge more solid alliances and coalitions. In this way prophetic criticism—with its stress on historical specificity and artistic complexity—directly addresses the intellectual challenge. The cultural capital of people of color—with its emphasis on self-confidence, discipline, perseverance, and subcultures of criticism—also tries to meet the existential requirement. Both are mutually reinforcing. Both are motivated by a deep commitment to individuality and democracy—the moral and political ideals that guide the creative responses to the political challenge.

The Political Challenge

Adequate rejoinders to intellectual and existential challenges equip the practitioners of the new cultural politics of difference to meet the political ones. This challenge principally consists of forging solid and reliable alliances to people of color and white progressives guided by a moral and political vision of greater democracy and individual freedom in communities, states, and transnational enterprises—i.e., corporations and information and communications conglomerates. Jesse Jackson's Rainbow Coalition is a gallant yet flawed effort in this regard: gallant due to the tremendous energy, vision, and courage of its leader and followers; flawed because of its failure to take seriously critical and democratic sensibilities within its own operations.

The time has come for critics and artists of the new cultural politics of difference to cast their nets widely, flex their muscles broadly, and thereby refuse to limit their visions, analyses, and praxis to their particular terrains. The aim is to dare to recast, redefine, and revise the very notions of "modernity," "mainstream," "margins," "difference," "otherness." We have now reached a new stage in the perennial struggle for freedom and dignity. And while much of the first world intelligentsia adopts retrospective and conservative outlooks that defend the crisis-ridden present, we promote a prospective and prophetic vision with a sense of possibility and potential, especially for those who bear the social costs of the present. We look to the past for strength, not solace; we look at the present and see people perishing, not profits mounting; we look toward the future and vow to make it different and better.

To put it boldly, the new kind of critic and artist associated with the new cultural politics of difference consists of an energetic breed of new world *bricoleurs* with improvisational and flexible sensibilities that sidestep mere opportunism and mindless eclecticism; persons of all countries, cultures, genders, sexual orientations, ages, and regions, with protean identities, who avoid ethnic chauvinism and faceless universalism; intellectual and political freedom fighters with partisan passion, international perspectives, and, thank God, a sense of humor to combat the ever-present absurdity that forever threatens our democratic and libertarian projects and dampens the fire that fuels our will to struggle. We will struggle and stay, as those brothers and sisters on the block say, "out there"—with intellectual rigor, existential dignity, moral vision, political courage, and soulful style.

Published with the permission of the author. This essay first appeared in October 53 (Summer 1990), pp. 93–109.

References

Arnold, M. ([1869] 1925). *Culture and Anarchy: An essay in political criticism*. New York: MacMillan.
———. ([1855] 1969). Stanzas from the Grand Chartreuse. In C. B. Tinker & H. F. Lowry (eds.), *Poetical Works* (299–306). London: Oxford.
Eliot, T. S. ([1919] 1950). Tradition and the individual talent. In *Selected Essays* (pp. 3–11). New York: Harcourt.
———. ([1923] 1948). Ulysses, order, and myth. In S. Givens (ed.), *James Joyce: Two decades of criticism* (198–202). New York: Vanguard.

Fanon, F. (1963). *The Wretched of the Earth*. New York: Grove.

Hall, S. (1988). New Ethnicities. In K. Mercer (ed.), *Black Film, British Cinema*. ICA documents, 7 (27–31). London: ICA.

Joyce, J. ([1922] 1934). Ulysses. New York: Random.

Trilling, L. ([1961] 1965). On the teaching of modern literature. In *Beyond Culture: Essays on literature and learning* (3–30). New York: Viking.

Valéry, P. ([1919] 1962). The crisis of the mind. In D. Folliot & J. Mathews (eds.), *The Collected Works of Paul Valéry* (Vol. 10, 23–36). New York: Bollingen.

4

Reflections on Border Theory, Culture, and the Nation

ALEJANDRO LUGO

border *n* 1: an outer part or edge 2: BOUNDARY, FRONTIER ... 4: an ornamental design at the edge of a fabric or rug

syn BORDER, MARGIN, VERGE, EDGE, RIM, BRIM, BRINK

borderland *n* 1a: territory at or near a border: FRONTIER b: an outlying region

borderline *n*: a line of demarcation

bordure *n*: a border surrounding a heraldic shield

Webster's New Collegiate Dictionary

frontera (de frontero.) f. *Confín de un Estado* [Limit of a state]

2. *Fachada* [ornamental design]... 5. *Límite*

frontería (de frontero) f.ant. *Frontera; hacer frente* [To confront]

frontero, ra *Puesto y colocado enfrente* [Situated in front]

Diccionario de la Lengua Española

Heterotopia: disorder in which fragments of a large number of possible orders glitter separately in the dimension, without law or geometry, of the heteroclite....in such a state, things are laid, placed, arranged in sites so very different from one another that it is impossible to find a place of residence for them.

Michel Foucault, *The Order of Things*

We live in a time and space in which borders, both literal and figurative, exist everywhere.... A border maps limits; it keeps people in and out of an area; it marks the ending of a safe zone and the beginning of an unsafe zone. To confront a border and, more so, to cross a border presumes great risk. In general people fear and are afraid to cross borders.... People cling to the dream of utopia and fail to recognize that they create and live in heterotopia.

Alejandro Morales, *Dynamic Identities in Heterotopia*

The Borders of Border Theory

If we wanted to carry out an archaeology of border theory, how would we identify its sources and its targets? Where would we locate its multiple sites of production and consumption, formation and transformation? What are the multiple discourses producing images of borders almost everywhere, at least in the minds of academics? In trying to answer these questions, more with an exploratory spirit than with a definitive one, let us say that the sites, the sources, the targets, and the discourses can be variably characterized by the following: previously marginalized intellectuals within the academy (i.e., women and other minorities), the outer limits of the nation-state (i.e., the U.S.-Mexico border region), the frontiers of culture theory (i.e., cultural borderlands vis-à-vis cultural patterns), the multiple fronts of struggle in cultural studies (i.e, the war of position), the cutting edge (at the forefront) of theories of difference (i.e., race, class, gender, and sexual orientation), and finally (at) the crossroads of history, literature, anthropology, and sociology (i.e., cultural studies).

In this essay I argue that in order to understand its political and practical importance, we must reimagine border theory in the realm of the inescapable, mountainous terrains of Power (Foucault, 1978) as it has operated in the past two hundred years in the West (Foucault, 1978; Derrida, 1966), and as it has been imbricated in the academy, in culture theory, in the global contexts of late capitalism, and in the last analysis, and perhaps most important, in the realms of the changing "nation" (Anderson, 1991) and "state" (Hall, 1986).[1]

This privileging of the "nation/state," on my part, relates to a current theoretical and political concern that has practical implications for the opening of more inclusive spaces under globalization, especially for the coming twenty-first century: *the deterritorialization* of the nation, politics, culture and border theory, and, finally, human agency (Ong, 1995; Morales, 1996; Martín-Rodríguez, 1996). For Alejandro Morales, "Michel Foucault's concept of heterotopia explains border culture," and "life in the chaos of heterotopia is a perpetual act of self-definition gradually deterritorializing the individual" (1996, 23, 24). Regarding feminist practice in the global setting, Aihwa Ong argues that "diasporic feminists (and we should all be somewhat mobile to be vigilant) should develop a denationalized and deterritorialized set of cultural practices. These would have to deal with the tough questions of gender oppression not only in that 'other place'… but also in one's own family, community, culture, religion, race, and nation" (1995, 367). Finally, just as Manuel Martín-Rodríguez, following Deleuze and Guattari, argues that a "minor language" can erode a "major language from within," I argue that the border region and border theory can erode the hegemony of the privileged center by denationalizing and deterritorializing the nation/state and culture theory: "In other words, minor languages erode, as it were, a major language from within, deterritorializing it, breaking up its system's supposed homogeneity" (Martín-Rodríguez, 1996, 86).[2]

Much more specifically, my analytic framework is the following: I will try to draw the contours of two theoretical parallelisms, both of which are constituted by seemingly disconnected conceptual preoccupations. On the one hand is the critical articulation between Gramsci's notion of *the state and its dispersal* and Foucault's notion of *power and its deployment*;[3] on the other is Anderson's critique of the nation and Rosaldo's critique of culture in anthropology. I am particularly interested in Gramsci's uses of the terms "state," "force relations," and "war of position" and how they might relate to Foucault's "relations of force" and his faith in "the strategical model rather than the model based on law" as well as his strategic belief that "politics is *war* pursued by other means" (Foucault, 1978, 93; emphasis added). I argue here that these connections of resistance against folk notions of the "head of the king [and] the spell of monarchy" (Foucault, 1978, 88–89)—that is, "the state/the law"[4]—are quite telling in themselves about the ways in which we have come to think about social life and culture inside and outside anthropology, which is my interest here. These critiques call for multiple discourses, wars of position, situated knowledges, positioned subjects, and different arenas of contestation in everyday life. Thus, the analysis presented here should help explain the recent production of theories of borders in our Westernized imagination. I will examine this articulation between border theory and the West, within anthropology, by juxtaposing Anderson's critique of the nation as an imagined community with Rosaldo's critique of culture as shared patterns of behavior.[5]

By reflecting on these parallelisms—that between Gramsci's notion of the state and Foucault's notion of power (both being *dispersed* entities) and that between Anderson's notion of the imagined community and Rosaldo's cultural patterns (both being *homogeneous* entities)—I hope to show how border theory in the late twentieth century in anthropology (i.e., Rosaldo's "cultural borderlands") cannot be properly understood unless it is situated, willy-nilly, vis-à-vis changing discourses about the state, the nation, and culture in the nineteenth and twentieth centuries, at least as these imagined categories and periodizations are examined in the works of Rosaldo himself (*Culture and Truth*, 1993), Anderson (*Imagined Communities*, 1991), Foucault (*History of Sexuality*, 1978), and Stuart Hall ("Gramsci's Relevance for the Study of Race and Ethnicity," 1986).

By locating border theory at the crossroads of culture theory in anthropology, and at the crossroads of ideologies of the state and the nation, which in turn produced "anthropologies" that represented national hegemonic traditions (American, British, and French), I hope to show the political and epistemological limits under which we teach, write, do research, and theorize. My main argument here is that border theory itself can contribute effectively to the exploration of these limits, as long as it is recognized to be (as theories of social life tend to be) a product of the codification of a "multiplicity of force relations … which by virtue of their inequalities, constantly engender states of power" (Foucault, 1978, 93).

The Current State of Culture: Cultural Borderlands vis-à-vis Cultural Patterns

Cultural borderlands should be understood, first of all, in relation to the previous dominant discourse about culture: cultural patterns. Renato Rosaldo has been very precise about the limitations of what he calls the "classic vision of unique cultural patterns":

> It emphasizes shared patterns at the expense of processes of change and internal inconsistencies, conflicts, and contradictions. By defining culture as a set of shared meanings, classic norms of analysis make it difficult to study zones of difference within and between cultures. From the classic perspective, cultural borderlands appear to be annoying exceptions rather than central areas of inquiry. (1993, 27–28)

Although I agree with Rosaldo's critical assessment of the social and political implications of the ideology of "cultural patterns," my vision of the way those cultural patterns have been constituted in the theoretical imagination of classic anthropologists is a bit different. In fact, the historical process through which we have come to theorize and think about culture, society, cultural patterns, and borderlands should not be taken for granted, or as a given, if we want, as Foucault puts it, "to cut off the head of the king" (1978, 88).

I propose here that the attempt to decipher the complex relation between "structure and practice" was and has been a dominant thinking channel or tool through which the concept of culture has been imagined, though more implicitly than explicitly. Let us see how the latter contention is manifested in the writings of some of anthropology's major and recent practiioners. By considering the sociopolitical and historical context in which anthropologists wrote, I hope to shed some light on why, after all, a discourse on culture and society emerged. The following discussion will eventually bring us back to an analysis of the roles of the state, the law, and the nation in shaping our formulations of the concept of culture and of social life in general.

Marshall Sahlins has explicitly associated the concept of culture with a double existence: "In the dialectic of culture-as-constituted and culture-as-lived we ... discover some possibility of reconciling the most profound antinomy of social science theory, that between structure and practice: reconciling them, that is, in the only way presently justifiable—as a symbolic process" (1982, 48). Regarding "society," however, Sherry Ortner has also identified a dialectical polarity in what she calls "practice theory," which constitutes the attempt to understand "how society and culture themselves are produced and reproduced through *human intention and action*" (1984, 158; emphasis added). Ortner argues that "the modern versions of practice theory ... appear unique in ... that society is a system, that the system is powerfully constraining, and yet that the system can be made and unmade through human action and interaction" (159). Ortner's similar treatment of both "society" and "culture" is less conspicuous, for our purpose here, than the way she imagines these theoretical constructs through pervasive critical dualisms: system and action, human intention and action. Sahlins's imaginings about culture, as lived and as constituted, also reproduce the pattern I am exposing here: the double existence of culture.[6]

Sahlins subjects this dialectic in culture to his "structure and history" approach (1981, 1982, 1985; see also Rosaldo, 1980), whereas Ortner associates the dialectic in society with a general theory of "practice" (1984). Ortner in fact argues that this focus on "practice" emerged in the early 1970s as a result of such historical conjunctures as the New Left movement; she also suggests that "practice theory" became articulated in American anthropology when Bourdieu's *Outline of a Theory of Practice* was translated into English in 1978.[7]

In what follows, I suggest that the anthropological notion of culture constituted by the articulation of beliefs and action, structure and practice, culture as constituted and culture as lived, system and action, was the historical product of a specific "academic" response to the political relation between the state/the nation and its citizens—a relationship that can be traced to the nineteenth century. In fact, these larger sociohistorical forces became crystallized in Western academia through Durkheim's (1933[1893], 1965[1912]) invention of society and through Matthew Arnold's (1963[1867–68]) production of culture.

Culture and the State

Previous to the late 1960s, certain socioeconomic and political events of the Victorian era contributed to the continued suppression of the explicit treatment of the structure/practice relation embedded in the concepts of "culture" and "society": to talk about human practice or praxis was to talk about history, conflict, change, and social transformation—theoretical concepts that could easily expose the colonial and capitalist encounters/enterprises of the nineteenth century and the first half of the twentieth century. Thus, until the early 1970s, the discourse on culture and society in the social sciences, and especially in anthropology, was dominated by the systematic analysis of the coordination of such dualisms as the individual and society, the individual and culture—ignoring the political implications of "practice" (for examples of this pattern, see Durkheim, 1933[1893], 1965[1912]; Malinowski, 1944; Benedict, 1934; Radcliffe-Brown, 1952; Barth, 1966).

Consequently, due to the political suppression of conceptual binaries, which included "practice," the notions of "society" and "culture" were to be discussed in terms of "order," "harmony," "rules" (Durkheim, 1933[1893], 1965[1912]), "shared patterns of beliefs" (Boas, 1963[1911]; Benedict, 1934), and an antichaotic condition (Weber, 1977[1905]). Political scientist Perry Anderson has appropriately noted that the work of Durkheim, like that of Weber and Pareto, was haunted by "a profound fear of the masses and premonition of social disintegration" (1968). He claims quite explicitly that sociology at the turn of the twentieth century "emerged as a bourgeois counter-reaction to Marxism," which, of course, was arguing at the time that class conflict was inevitable. It must be noted, however, that Durkheim was as much against the greedy capitalist on the loose at the time as against the "immorality" of the masses. Both of these threats confirmed for him, as an employee of the French state, the need of rules to monitor and control both the working classes and the utilitarian entrepreneur.

The intensification of class conflict had emerged as a product of industrial capitalism within the "West"; additionally, broader sociopolitical tensions were generated as a result of the retraction of some European colonialisms due to the nineteenth-century nationalist movements in Spanish America and Central Europe. The expansion of U.S. colonialism at the turn of the twentieth century also contributed to a generalized problem of the body politic within and outside the West (see Anderson, 1991; Foucault, 1978; Hall, 1986). Foucault and Stuart Hall treat 1870 as a key historical moment regarding, respectively, the production of new sexualities and the expansion of the new imperialist colonialisms.[8] According to Gramsci and Hall, this period in the later part of the nineteenth century constitutes a historical transition in the nature of the "State" from a monarchical, dynastic body politic and its *subjects* to a "State" (read: nation/nation-state) in which the *subjects* become *citizens*, and thus become loosely tied to the direct control of a centralized, lawlike apparatus; in this new political regime, individuals are indirectly monitored through the state's *dispersal of power* (Hall, 1986; Foucault, 1978). This process must be properly explained in the historical and geographic contexts of each newly emerging nation around the world.[9]

Stuart Hall describes Gramsci's vision of this critical transformation in Western history:

> Gramsci bases this "transition from one form of politics to another" historically. It takes place in "the West" after 1870, and is identified with "the colonial expansion of Europe," the emergence of modern mass democracy, a complexification in the role and organization of the state and an unprecedented elaboration in the structures and processes of "civil hegemony." What Gramsci is pointing to, here, is partly the diversification of social antagonisms, the "dispersal" of power, which occurs in societies where hegemony is sustained, not exclusively through the enforced instrumentality of the state, but rather, it is grounded in the relations and institutions of civil society [schooling, the family, the factory, churches and religious life, and so on]. (1986, 18)[10]

Weber documented the bureaucratization of modern institutions around the same time, after 1870 and into World War I (1958[1920]). The "war of position" necessary for effective political resistance against the dispersal of power, and characterizing the new state of the "State" is powerfully stated in military terms:

> The "war of position"… has to be conducted in a protracted way, across many different and varying fronts of struggle.… What really counts in a war of position is not the enemy's "forward trenches" (to continue the military metaphor) but "the whole organizational and industrial system of the territory which lies to the rear of the army in the field"—that is, the whole structure of society, including the structures and institutions of civil society. (Hall, 1986, 17, paraphrasing Gramsci)

Today's realization of the transformation of the nature of *the cultural* (from homogeneity to heterogeneity) as manifested by both "cultural studies" and the postmodern preoccupation with "dispersal," has clearly influenced Renato Rosaldo's redefinition of "culture" in terms of "borderlands," fragmentation, and contestation (as opposed to the exclusivity of shareability, coherence, and uniformity). It is necessary to quote Rosaldo at length from his book *Culture and Truth* (1993):

The fiction of the uniformly shared culture increasingly seems more tenuous than useful. Although most metropolitan typifications continue to suppress border zones, human cultures are neither necessarily coherent nor always homogeneous. More often than we usually care to think, our everyday lives are crisscrossed by border zones, pockets and eruptions of all kinds. Social borders frequently become salient around such lines as sexual orientation, gender, class, race, ethnicity, nationality, age, politics, dress, food, or taste. Along with "our" supposedly transparent cultural selves, such borderlands should be regarded not as analytically empty transitional zones but as sites of creative cultural production that require investigation. (207–8)

In the past, however, from the moment Marxism became a threat to late-nineteenth-century European order, Marx and his followers were not only negatively sanctioned (suppressed) in major sociological and anthropological circles, but "metropolitan typifications" of culture and society (i.e., Durkheimian and Weberian traditions) quite willingly continued "to suppress" any alternative means of studying and analyzing social life in its entirety, that is, in a manner that such phenomena as disorder, chaos, fragmentation, contestation, resistance, and "the border zones" could be rigorously scrutinized. The notion of "cultural borderlands" seems to be closely associated with social identities or subjectivities—that is, age, gender, class, ethnicity—however, for purposes of explaining what Sherry Ortner calls "human intention and action" or what Sahlins denotes as "structure and practice," Renato Rosaldo still depends on the dual aspect of social life that, I have argued, has characterized our imaginings about both culture and society.

For example, while analyzing the work of literary theorist Kenneth Burke, Rosaldo wrote:

Recent social thinkers [Giddens, 1979; Ortner, 1984] have updated Burke's style of analysis by identifying the interplay of "structure" and "agency" as a central issue in social theory. Most central for them, in other words, is the question of *how received structures shape human conduct, and how, in turn, human conduct alters received structures.* (1993, 104; emphasis added)

Thus, if the initial understanding of the "state" was complicitly associated with rules, laws, and order, which must be followed or obeyed by its citizens or subjects, Victorian anthropologists (British, American, and French) quite willingly, with the same juridical attitude and "morality," traveled to other "non-Western" societies uncritically searching for the rules, traditions, orders, and coherent social systems to which human subjects (or informants, in the anthropologists' case) must accommodate and adhere. By "uncritical," I mean that these early-twentieth-century scholars did not necessarily articulate in their writings the impact of the state on the production of social science itself. It is also true, however, that the dominant discourse on "law and society" had a key humanitarian angle that was used against an earlier vision of "natives" as lacking law and therefore having no rights to life and property.

Nonetheless, the Victorian focus on morality, order, and the law, with its many angles, dominated the anthropology practiced until the early 1970s, when the civil rights, New Left, and feminist movements and the decolonization of previously colonized "nations" disinterred both critical thought and critical theory from the academic cemetery deliberately constructed by "metropolitan scholars" (see Rosaldo, 1993, chap. 1). Now that we recognize that "modern societies" constitute "arenas" of different social contestations, are we looking for similar contestations, fragmentations, dispersals, disorders, and chaos within and in "other" societies," just as our ancestors looked for order, shared patterns, and coherent systems here and elsewhere?

Perhaps what is of major importance here is that our metaphors of social life have also been transformed along with our notions of culture, society, and the state. There has been a very persuasive replacement, not only displacement, of a metaphoric trope: the biological organism, which was supposed to maintain itself in equilibrium through systemic (political) order and (social) harmony, has been decidedly supplanted by the "war" metaphor, which sheds light on how "society" and "culture" constitute hegemonic battlefields where contestation itself (instead of reciprocity) is inescapably pervasive. As Foucault suggestively questions, "Should ... we say politics is *war* pursued by other means?" (1978, 93; emphasis added).[12]

Thus, although Gramsci's work on the state and culture seems to have been "discovered" as late as the 1950s and 1960s as a result of the sociopolitical movements of Birmingham, England (see Raymond Williams's *Politics and Letters*, 1979), through Gramscian "cultural studies," the state has come to be imagined vis-à-vis its dispersal of power within "civil society" by being deployed on a battlefield of multiple social relations. Since the mid-1980s, through the critiques of such scholars as Renato Rosaldo, Donna Haraway (1986), and James Clifford (1986), American anthropologists have begun rigorous (re)search on the deployment, dispersal, and, ergo, fragmentation of society and culture, where identities and experiences are constantly being contested in specific sites or localized centers of power, such as the factory, the cafeteria, the bus, and even the restroom.[13]

Nonetheless, despite the influence of cultural Marxism, the notion of culture used in cultural studies has its strong connection to the culture concept constituted by "structure and practice" and that has characterized most academic conceptions or imaginations about the social and the cultural. Paul Willis, author of the classic *Learning to Labor*, says the following with regard to his use of the "cultural": "I view *the cultural*, not simply as a set of transferred internal *structures* (as in the notion of socialisation) nor as the passive result of the action of dominant ideology downwards (as in certain kinds of marxism) but at least in part as the product of collective human *praxis*" (1977, 3; emphasis added; note the inevitable duality—structure/praxis). Based on Gramsci, Hall presents the following definition of culture:

> One might note the centrality which Gramsci's analysis always gives to the cultural factor in social development. By culture, here, I mean the actual, grounded terrain of practices, representations, languages and customs of any specific historical society.... I would also include that whole distinctive range of questions which Gramsci lumped together under the title, the "national popular."... They are a key stake as objects of political and ideological struggle and practice. (1986, 26)

The dual aspect (ideology/practices, structure/praxis) associated with a general definition of culture, although not central, is self-evident. Along with this implicit double existence, in the past decade or so, as I have noted, we have simultaneously treated, much more explicitly, culture as an arena of different social contestations. James Clifford notes, "Culture, and our views of it, are produced historically, and are actively contested" (1986, 18). He adds, "Culture is contested, temporal and emergent" (19). Its temporality, its instability, its contingency, and thus its fragmentation all give form and content to the theory of borderlands that Rosaldo (1993) and Anzaldúa (1987) call for in and outside social analysis.

Yet to limit the concept of culture to "contestations" while not recognizing its double life (as we tend to do regarding new theories of borders, culture, and social life) is to confuse culture with Gramsci's notion of the "State" in "modern societies." As Stuart Hall correctly argues about Gramsci:

> Gramsci elaborates his new conception of the state.... it becomes, not a thing to be seized, overthrown or "*smashed*" with a single blow, but a complex formation in modern societies *which must become the focus of a number of different strategies and struggles because it is an arena of different social contestations.* (1986, 19; emphasis added)

In fact, I must emphasize that Gramsci associated culture not only with practices and representations, but also with the "national popular." Why is culture and the idea of nation or nationalism so closely interrelated by Gramsci?

Culture and the Nation: Imagined Communities

In the late twentieth century, both culture and the state are perceived to be dispersed as well as consolidated or centralized. Yet we have privileged, in the past ten years, the dispersed and the fragmented. How were nationalism, the state, the nation, and culture perceived in the nineteenth century? In a pre-Rosaldo phase, culture was imagined, almost exclusively, to be shared, patterned, and homogeneous. So, in a similar way, throughout the nineteenth century and the first half of the twentieth century, the nation, according to Benedict Anderson, came to be imagined in homogeneous time, and as an imagined community: "The nation is always conceived as a deep, horizontal comradeship. Ultimately it is this fraternity that makes it possible, over the past two centuries, for so many millions of people, not so much to kill, as willingly to die for such limited imaginings" (1991, 7).

These imaginings—whether from the first decade of the 1800s (Creole nationalism, i.e., Mexico) or from the 1820s or the 1850s of Central Europe (so-called vernacular/linguistic nationalisms, which were opposed to the hegemony of Latin) or from the "official nationalism" prior to the end of World War I (a nation/dynasty combination)—all culminated in the now threatened "nation-state" that became the international norm after 1922 and at least until the 1970s. By the 1970s the nation-state was politically and economically transcended, or at least challenged, by the strategic fragmentation of the manufacturing production process around the globe in late capitalism. In the specific case that has concerned my larger writing project (Lugo, 1995), the Mexican state has been challenged by the deployment of *maquiladoras* not only throughout Mexico, but throughout the border metropolis of Ciudad Juarez; they are located in more than ten industrial parks strategically established in different sections of the city.

Thus, the imagined community Anderson identifies in the idea of the nation is the imagined (shared) community Rosaldo identifies in the classic anthropological concept of culture, which was conceptualized in the period of "official nationalism" (around and after 1850; Arnold published *Culture and Anarchy* in 1868) and discursively deployed throughout the consolidation of the "nation-state" (between 1922 and 1970).[14]

Two major historical forces (or, in Gramsci's terms, *force relations*) that led to the nation as an imagined community were the emergence of print capitalism (the novel and the newspaper) and the gradual collapse of the hegemony of Latin (a collapse that gave rise to vernacular nationalisms within Europe). Before these major historical and complicated political processes led to the initial versions of the nation (before the nineteenth century—more specifically, before 1776), the political imagination regarding such taken-for-granted conceptualizations as "society" or "social groups" was characterized by fragmentation, intermarriage, and cultural and social heterogeneity—all predating a homogeneous imagined community.

For instance, Benedict Anderson has written in relation to this prenation, premodern stage, "The fundamental conceptions about 'social groups' were centripetal and hierarchical, rather than boundary-oriented and horizontal" (1991, 15). With regard to the dynastic, monarchic realm, Anderson notes that,

> in the older imagining, where [kingship] states were defined by centres, borders were porous and indistinct, and sovereignties faded imperceptibly into one another. [Are not these border crossings?] Hence, paradoxically enough, the ease with which pre-modern empires and kingdoms were able to sustain their rule over immensely heterogeneous, and often not even contiguous, populations for long periods of time. (19)

Regarding sexual politics, Anderson makes it very clear that, "in fact, royal lineages often derived their prestige, aside from any aura of divinity, from, shall we say, miscegenation? For such mixtures were signs of Superordinate status [thus]… What 'nationality' are we to assign to the Bourbons?" (20–21). Consequently, assigning an essentialized "national" or "cultural" identity to any subject (as opposed to *citizen*) or to any, let us say, intersubjective collectivity, before the nation, was not only difficult, but probably impossible.[15]

It is evident that heterogeneity preceded the "imagined community"—the nation, the nation-state, nationalism, all of which, I argue, influenced our notions of culture and society during the nineteenth and most of the twentieth century. Thus, the heterogeneity discovered in the late twentieth century in theories of borderlands and fragmentation should not be limited exclusively to the collapse of classic norms—from the mid-1960s to the mid-1980s—rather, our theories of culture, society, and identity should be analyzed in the contexts of much longer historical processes, such as (1) the first attempts "to cut off the head of the king" in the early nineteenth century and (2) the political transformation and/or reproduction of the nation-state, throughout and in the late twentieth century. Even more productively, we must conduct additional comparative research on the heterogeneity of the late twentieth century and the heterogeneity associated with prenation contexts and politics—not that heterogeneity cannot coexist with homogeneity, but this strategy might serve as a point of departure from a possible prison house of border thought.[16] At the same time, however, we must recognize that such identities as class, gender, sexuality, and ethnicity, as they are articulated in the late twentieth century, are products of the 1900s; in particular, they are products of a long history of resistance—the working-class, feminist, gay and lesbian, and civil rights movements of the 1960s, as well as of the decolonization of Africa and Asia since the late 1950s (Rosaldo, 1993).

We can now claim, then, that in the 1990s the "State" has been strategically dispersed, both by current Gramscian thinking and by late capitalist multinational corporations in this historic moment characterized by the dispersal of manufacturing production processes throughout the world. Unfortunately, Benedict Anderson not only ignores the role of late capitalism in the redefinition of the nation-state after 1965, but also does not perceive that the fascism of Mussolini had been produced through and by the ideology of the nation, which Anderson himself limits to an amorous feeling of patriotism. Anderson also ignores the major threat to the formation of the nation-state in the first decades of the twentieth century: the attempt to internationalize (read: denationalize; deterritorialize) the working classes.

It is perhaps at this analytic juncture that we must systematically articulate Rosaldo's theory of multiple subjectivities (so much needed for our understanding of the politics of difference under state citizenry) with pervasive late capitalism—which can be characterized not only by the fragmentation of the production process, but also by the fragmentation of the labor force. Is it possible to reconcile the following seemingly irreconcilable statements about the politics (and economics) of difference? First, Rosaldo argues:

> Social borders frequently become salient around such lines as sexual orientation, gender, class, race, ethnicity, nationality, age, politics, dress, food, or taste…. such borderlands should be regarded not as analytically empty transitional zones but as sites of creative cultural production that require investigation. (1993, 207–8)

And second, June Nash notes, regarding the current global accumulation of capital: "Sectors of the labor force based on gender, ethnicity, age, and education within both industrial core and peripheral nations are differentially rewarded and these differences, along with wage differences, between nations, determine the long-run movement of capital" (1983, 3).

Adding the wage differential to the "borderlands" equation or theory does not allow us to separate "border zones" as "sites of creative cultural production" from "border zones" as "sites of lucrative manufacturing production" in the globalization of capital. Thus, is the theory of borderlands a critique or handmaid of capitalist discipline in this historical moment? Historically and theoretically, it can be both. Just as we must extend cultural borderlands into a critique of late capitalist production, so we must transform the political economy of June Nash into a critical, global theory of multiple cultural subjectivities, which in fact Rosaldo offers. After all, one alternative lies in situating our theoretical concepts about social life not only in the larger contexts of history, nationalism, and power, but also in micro contexts of cultural specificity as well as in the Foucauldian recognition that academic research is a question of orienting ourselves to a conception of power which replaces ... the privilege of sovereignty with the analysis of a *multiple and mobile field of force relations*, wherein far-reaching, but never completely stable, effects of domination are produced.... And this, not out of a speculative choice or theoretical preference, but because in fact *it is one of the essential traits for Western societies that the force relationships which for a long time had found expression in war, in every form of warfare, gradually became invested in the order of political power.* (1978, 102; emphasis added)

From the Nature of the State to the State of Nature

The foregoing emphasis on war, contestation, and power relations in society and culture, more than a faithful commitment to communist utopias, constitutes a heterotopic strategy of resistance and opposition to the extreme conservatism permeating Durkheimian thinking. The latter influential paradigm, however, is tied more to Hobbes, who wrote for an earlier British monarchy, than to Durkheim himself, who was reacting against late-nineteenth-century labor unrest (Anderson, 1968). In assigning the generalized transformations of societies to specific historical periods—for example, to 1870s historical events (both Durkheim and Gramsci) or, for that matter, to 1970s political occurrences and outcomes—one runs the danger of reducing the complexity of human relations to socially situated experiences (practice), which are in turn transformed into generalized visions of the world (structure). The problematic trick presents itself when the latter (structure) are confused with the former (practice), not in the recognition that one can lead to or challenge the other. The unfixity of either "structure" or "practice" allows for the analysis of the *unintended* consequences of culture and its politics, past or present.

"Situated knowledges" (Haraway, 1986) in themselves are not necessarily, and have not always been, part of the "war of position" that Gramsci promoted. Durkheim's position about the state, morality, and society was consciously situated as well, but vis-à-vis the state's need, of the times, to restore so-called social order—both from capitalist rapacity (the greedy capitalist) and from worker unrest. Under late capitalism, Durkheim's vision of the state is in fact being dismantled by multinational corporations, particularly in Mexico, more specifically at the U.S.-Mexico border, and by a much-needed border theory that is produced by border subjects who claim citizenships that transcend boundaries (see Anzaldúa, 1987; Rosaldo, 1993; Morales, 1996; Lugo, 1996).

Throughout most of the history of social science thinking, and, in fact, as early as 1642, Hobbes argued in *Leviathan* (1978[1642]), and in Latin (that is, before "the nation"), that the state of nature is inherently about chaos, disorder, and war, and that the only remedy is to impose a sovereign—the king—so that order and harmony will exist. Thus, we must realize that actual social life does not tend to obey "official mandates" or the most recent "theoretical paradigms." Human relations did not necessarily transform themselves from "chaos" to "order" under Hobbes, nor from "order" to "chaos" under Marx, nor from "chaos" to "order" (back again) under Durkheim, nor will they change from pure "order" to pure "disorder" under Gramscian, postmodernist, and/or borderland thinking.[17] Thus, just as culture changes, so does the state; needless to say, our concepts about them are also transformed, according to distinct historical specificities.

Social life changes and reproduces itself both through cultural-historical contingencies and through the arbitrary, though still symbolically constituted, imposition of a politically legitimated force. It is our business to study the former and a matter of human integrity not only to scrutinize the latter, but, more important, to prevent it. It is necessary that we continue our analytic flow from "Culture" to "culture," from the "State" to the "state," from "Order" to "order," from "Patterns" to "patterns," and, lastly, from "Chaos" to "chaos." As Geertz persuasively noted in 1973, the anthropologist still "confronts the same grand realities that others ... confront in more fateful settings: Power, Change, Faith, Oppression ... but he confronts them in obscure enough [I'd say dear enough]—places ... to take the capital letters off them" (21). It seems, after all, that one of postmodernism's major contributions to sociocultural analysis is, as Benítez-Rojo argues in *The Repeating Island: The Caribbean and the Postmodern Perspective*, its "lens," which "has the virtue of being the only one to direct itself toward the play of paradoxes and eccentricities, of fluxes and displacements" (1992, 271)—that is, toward the simultaneous play of order and disorder, coherence and incoherence, chaos and antichaos, contestation and shareability, practice and structure, culture and history, culture and capitalism, and, finally, patterns and borderlands (Rosaldo, 1993). We should not privilege a priori one or the other; instead, we must continuously suspend each category in order to analyze their eccentricities. It seems to me that only by following these suggestions was I able to juxtapose the analysis of assembled goods in *maquiladoras* with the analysis of the fragmented lives of the *maquila* workers who assembled them, both in the larger contexts of history and the present, the global economy and the local strategies of survival, and, finally, in the more intricate, micro contexts of culture and power.

Conclusion

By examining Gramsci's notion of the state and its dispersal, Foucault's notion of power and its deployment, Anderson's critique of the nation, and Rosaldo's critique of culture, I have tried to spell out my critique of cultural analysis, cultural studies, and culture and border theory, as these are imbricated, willy-nilly, in nationalist, capitalist, late-capitalist, and related projects of politically legitimated force. My specific argument throughout the essay, however, has been fourfold. First, I have argued that dominant (and dominating) anthropological conceptions of culture and society have been historically constituted by such dialectic dualities as beliefs and practices (Boas, 1940[1920]), "symbolic structures and collective behavior" (Geertz, 1973b, 251), structure and agency (Rosaldo, 1980,1993; Bourdieu 1978), human action and intention (Ortner, 1984), and culture as constituted and culture as lived (Sahlins, 1981, 1982, 1985).[18] Second, I have asserted that received academic conceptions of culture and the border, and of social life for that matter, have been heavily (but, for the most part, unconsciously) influenced by our capacity and incapacity to acknowledge the distinct transformations that the nature of the Westernized "state" has gone through in the past two hundred years (the recent academic recognition of everyday experiences along the U.S.-Mexico border region is a recent manifestation of this transformation, especially with the creation of Free Trade [Border] Zones around the world). Third, I have contended that these academic conceptions of culture and border have been the historical products of either political suppressions or political persuasions and of other types of resistance (i.e., the emergence of minority scholars who have experienced life at the borderlands) to the center's domination. Finally, I have argued in this essay that culture, constituted by both beliefs and practices, is not necessarily shared or contested, and that the crossroads and the limits or frontiers of these beliefs and practices (border theory) constitute, in turn, the erosion of the monopoly of culture theory as "cultural patterns," *from within* (to follow Martín-Rodríguez, 1996, 86).

What is the role of anthropologists in the production of a cultural theory of borderlands in the interdisciplinary arena? Anthropologists today can certainly redefine themselves vis-à-vis the emergent and newly formed academic communities that now confront them. In the late twenti-eth century, as Renato Rosaldo (1994) consistently argues, anthropologists must strategically (re)locate/(re)position and "remake" themselves in the current scholarly battlefield of power relations.

In order to be effective in this conceptual/political relocation, however, both anthropologists and nonanthropologists who think seriously about the cultural must ask themselves the following question (which Roland Barthes would pose to anybody regarding the nature of interdisciplinarity): Is the concept of culture an object of study that belongs to no particular discipline? Only an *anti*disciplinary mood would provide an answer in the affirmative. A cultural theory of borderlands challenges and invites academics to recognize the crossroads of *inter*disciplinarity, where "ambassadors" are no longer needed. Once the challenge and the invitation are accepted, border theory itself can simultaneously transcend and effectively situate culture, capitalism, and the academy at the crossroads, but only if it is imagined historically and in the larger and dispersed contexts of the nation and of Power (Foucault, 1978).

Otherwise, the *deterritorialization* of the state, theory, and power—and, thus, effective resistance against them—is impossible. Yet those of us who theorize about the border (especially previously marginalized theorists) must recognize that our border has been simultaneously a *bordure*: a border surrounding *a shield*. Unfortunately, shields against capitalism and other agents of oppression are not common among less privileged border subjects, such as factory workers and other working-class men and women inhabiting the U.S.-Mexico border region (Lugo, 1995; Limón, 1994). Until we democratically distribute these shields, those who perhaps need them the most will remain marginalized. After all, as Alejandro Morales argues in "Dynamic Identities in Heterotopia," "In general people fear and are afraid to cross borders.... People cling to the dream of utopia and fail to recognize that they create and live in heterotopia" (1996, 23).

Although much remains to be done, there is no doubt that border theory has proven to be an effective alternative for some of us who used to fear not only to cross borders but to challenge them.

Notes

This essay is part of a larger project titled "Fragmented Lives, Assembled Parts: A Study in Maquilas, Culture, and History at the Mexican Borderlands." I am very grateful to Nancy Abelmann, Jane Collier, George Collier, Bill Kelleher, Bill Maurer, Renato Rosaldo, and Marta Zambrano for commenting on earlier versions of this essay. I am, of course, solely responsible for any errors. With much respect, admiration, *cariño*, and gratitude, I dedicate this essay to Professor Renato Rosaldo.

1. In this essay, *the nation* and *the state*, though usually imbricated with each other, are used to refer, respectively, to a changing imagined community (Anderson, 1991) and to a changing governance apparatus (Hall, 1986). These specific uses, and their implications for culture and border theories, are examined throughout the essay. The examination of these categories and their implications, however, is intended to be illustrative of the social and political problems that must be, and have not yet been, addressed in the literature that concerns us here; thus, though this essay reflects on the state of culture and the nation during the past two hundred years, it does not constitute in itself an exhaustive historical project. I wish mainly to point out some limitations and some new readings of these topics.
2. "Deterritorializing" from "within" is a multilinear process and a complicated political project. It is multilinear because there are several fronts of struggle: the nation-state, contested communities, theory itself, and the individual subject, among many others. It is a complicated political project because agents inhabit multiple locations. For instance, I write this essay from diverse, but interconnected, positions: as a cultural anthropologist who did fieldwork among *maquila* (factory) workers and who was trained in American institutions; as a Mexican who was born in Ciudad Juárez, Mexico, but who became Chicano while continuing my elementary, secondary, and university schooling in Las Cruces, New Mexico. While living in Las Cruces, I visited Ciudad Juárez every weekend until I was twenty-two years of age; thus, I am also a borderer (*fronterizo*) whose everyday experiences could be unpredictably located at the Mexico (Ciudad Juárez)/Texas (El Paso)/New Mexico (Las Cruces) borders. Whatever my multiple locations and possibilities, however, in this essay I would particularly like to reflect on why, as academics, we have come to think seriously about "culture" and "borders" to begin with.
3. In *The History of Sexuality*, Foucault writes, "The purpose of the present study is in fact to show how deployments of power are directly connected to the body" (1978, 151). These "deployments of power" are imbricated with the deploy-

ments of sexuality in the modern West. In part 4 of the same work, titled "Deployment of Sexuality," Foucault examines in detail the objectives, methods, domains, and periodizations through which power operated and dispersed itself from the late eighteenth century to the late nineteenth century in Europe (see 75–131). He also argues that power is omnipresent: "The omnipresence of power: not because it has the privilege of consolidating everything under its invisible unity, but because it is produced from one moment to the next, at every point, or rather in every relation from one point to another" (93).

4. Foucault writes: "Law was not simply a weapon skillfully wielded by monarchs; it was the monarchic system's mode of manifestation and the form of its acceptability. In Western societies since the Middle Ages, the exercise of power has always been formulated in terms of law" (1978, 87). He adds: "One is attached to a certain image of power-law, of power-sovereignty, which was traced out by the theoreticians of right and the monarchic institution. It is this image that we must break free of, that is, of the theoretical privilege of the law and sovereignty, if we wish to analyze power within the concrete and historical framework of its operation. We must construct an analytics of power that no longer takes law as a model and code" (90).

5. Interestingly, in his analysis of the nation, Anderson uses the same periodization that Foucault uses to examine the deployment of sexuality—the late eighteenth and nineteenth centuries. For the most part, Rosaldo limits himself to the twentieth century.

6. In fact, Sherry Ortner organizes her highly influential essay on "practice theory" (1984) along such dialectics as system/action and structure/practice.

7. In "Cultural Reproduction and the Politics of Laziness," I try to show how this double life of culture (in the work of Sahlins, Ortner, and Bourdieu) is manifested inside an electronic *maquila* through an analysis of how specific notions of laziness at the workplace reproduce ideologies of masculinity and machismo (Lugo, 1995; also see Lugo, 1990).

8. Foucault associates this periodization—"1870"—with the production of the homosexual as "a personage, a past, a case history, and a childhood, in addition to being a type of life" (1978, 43). He adds: "We must not forget that the psychological, psychiatric, medical category of homosexuality was constituted from the moment it was characterized—Westphal's famous article of 1870 [*Archiv für Neurologie*] on 'contrary sexual relations' can stand as its date of birth.... The sodomite had been a temporary aberration; the homosexual was now a species" (43).

9. In the case of Mexico, the question of *mestizaje* and *lo mexicano*, as national projects, emerged at the same time the nation-state was trying to consolidate itself immediately after the Mexican Revolution of 1910–20.

10. In addition to these institutions of civil society, Foucault adds "a multiplicity of discourses produced by a whole series of mechanisms operating in different institutions ... demography, biology, medicine, psychiatry, psychology, ethics, pedagogy, and political criticism" (1978, 33). Regarding their *dispersal*, Foucault explicitly and forcefully notes, "So it is not simply in terms of a continual extension that we must speak of this discursive growth; it should be seen rather as a dispersion of centers from which discourses emanated, a diversification of their forms, and the complex deployment of the network connecting them (34).

11. Of course, the "self/other" distinction has been both contested and problematized in recent writings of culture.

12. In his experimental ethnography *Dancing with the Devil*, José Limón applies the metaphor of war in ways I am suggesting here, but following Gramsci's "war of maneuver" and "war of position." In the following quotation, Limón uses the metaphor of war quite appropriately to depict the racial struggle between Mexicans and Anglos in South Texas: "For it is a basic premise and organizing metaphor for this essay that since the 1830s, the Mexicans of south Texas have been in a state of social war with the 'Anglo' dominant Other and their class allies. This has been at times a war of overt, massive proportions; at others, covert and sporadic; at still other moments, repressed and internalized as a war within the psyche, but always conditioned by an ongoing social struggle fought out of different *battlefields*" (1994, 15–16).

13. See chapter 6 of my manuscript "Fragmented Lives, Assembled Parts" (1995). Also, feminist anthropologists have been at the forefront of this "new" and exciting anthropology (see especially the provocative and theoretically sophisticated volumes *Uncertain Terms*, 1990, edited by Faye Ginsburg and Anna Tsing, and *Women Writing Culture*, 1995, edited by Ruth Behar and Deborah Gordon).

14. Of course, this notion of culture, as shared patterns of behavior, still reigns in some quarters.

15. See my analysis of prenation, dynastic, monarchic, and heterogeneous New Spain and New Mexico in my chapter titled "Hegemony and History in the Invention of Borderlands Geography" (Lugo, 1995).

16. See Lugo (1995, chap. 2) for the encounters of conquest both Hernán Cortés and Juan de Oñate had with uncertain, unidentified, and perhaps yet unnamed groups of people in the coast of "México" and in what came to be New Mexico.

17. One of the most important contributions of Renato Rosaldo's thinking is precisely Rosaldo's sensitivity to analysis of power as it is found in *both* patterns and borderlands, chaos and order, subjectivity and objectivity, and culture and politics. None of these entities holds a monopoly on truth. This is Rosaldo's most important message regarding culture, identity, and power/knowledge.

18. I have also argued that within anthropology, if "practice and structure," "beliefs and action," do not explicitly appear in early anthropological debates about culture and the individual, the individual and society, the individual and social structure, or culture and the environment, it is because "practice," as category of analysis, was suppressed due to its implication for political mobilization on the part of colonized subjects, the working poor, and other subaltern subjects—the usual targets of anthropologists throughout most of the twentieth century. Also, anthropologists have historically privileged such analytic domains as cognition, symbols, the environment, decision making, the superorganic and personality, among many others, in trying to get to the cultural or the social in human beings. Yet all these categories acquire meaning for academics only to the extent that they can explain or interpret people's "beliefs and actions." Thus, we return to the structure/practice duality that, I argue, has constituted our dominant discourse on culture—so far.

References

Anderson, Benedict. 1991. *Imagined Communities: Reflections on the Origin and Spread of Nationalism*. London: Verso.

Anderson, Perry. 1968. "Components of the National Culture." *New Left Review* 50.

Anzaldúa, Gloria. 1987. *Borderlands/La Frontera: The New Mestiza*. San Francisco: Aunt Lute.

Arnold, Matthew. 1963[1867–68]. *Culture and Anarchy*, ed. J. Dover Wilson. Cambridge: Cambridge University Press.

Barth, Frederik. 1966. *Models of Social Organization* (Occasional Paper No. 23). London: Royal Anthropological Institute.

Behar, Ruth, and Deborah A. Gordon, eds. 1995. *Women Writing Culture*. Berkeley: University of California Press.

Benedict, Ruth. 1934. *Patterns of Culture*. Boston: Houghton Mifflin.

Benítez-Rojo, Antonio. 1992. *The Repeating Island: The Carribean and the Postmodern Perspective*, trans. James E. Maranis. Durham, N.C.: Duke University Press.

Boas, Franz. 1940[1920]. *Race, Language, and Culture*. New York: Free Press.

———. 1963[1911]. *The Mind of Primitive Man*. New York: Collier.

Bourdieu, Pierre. 1978. *Outline of a Theory of Practice*. New York: Cambridge University Press.

Clifford, James. 1986. "Introduction: Partial Truths." In *Writing Culture: The Poetics and Politics of Ethnography*, eds. James Clifford and George E. Marcus, 1–26. Berkeley: University of California Press.

Derrida, Jacques. 1978[1966]. *Writing and Difference*, trans. Alan Bass. Chicago: University of Chicago Press.

Diccionario de la Lengua Española. 1992. Madrid: Real Academia Española.

During, Simon, ed. 1994. *The Cultural Studies Reader*. London: Routledge.

Durkheim, Emile. 1965[1912]. *The Elementary Forms of the Religious Life*, trans. J. W. Swain. New York: Random House.

———. 1933[1893]. *The Division of Labor*, trans. George Simpsom. New York: Free Press.

Foucault, Michel. 1978. *The History of Sexuality*, vol. 1. *An Introduction*, trans. Alan Sheridan-Smith. New York: Random House.

Geertz, Clifford. 1973a. "Thick Description: Toward an Interpretive Theory of Culture." In *The Interpretation of Cultures*, 3–30. New York: Basic Books.

———. 1973b. "Religion as a Cultural System." In *The Interpretation of Cultures*, 87–125. New York: Basic Books.

Giddens, Anthony. 1979. *Central Problems in Social Theory: Action, Structure, and Contradiction in Social Analysis*. Berkeley: University of California Press.

Ginsburg, Faye, and Anna Tsing, eds. 1990. *Uncertain Terms: Negotiating Gender in American Culture*. Boston: Beacon.

Hall, Stuart. 1986. "Gramsci's Relevance for the Study of Race and Ethnicity." *Journal of Communication Inquiry* 10(2): 5–27.

Haraway, Donna. 1986. "Situated Knowledges: The Science Question in Feminism and the Privilege of Partial Perspective." *Feminist Studies* 14(3): 575–99.

Hobbes, Thomas. 1978[1642]. *Leviathan*. New York: Liberal Arts.

Limón, José E. 1994. *Dancing with the Devil: Society and Cultural Poetics in Mexican-American South Texas*. Madison: University of Wisconsin Press.

Lugo, Alejandro. 1990. "Cultural Production and Reproduction in Ciudad Juarez, Mexico: Tropes at Play among Maquiladora Workers." *Cultural Anthropology* 5(2): 173–96.

———. 1995. "Fragmented Lives, Assembled Goods: A Study in Maquilas, Culture, and History at the Mexican Borderlands." Ph.D. diss., Stanford University.

———. 1996. "Border Inspections." Paper presented at the annual meeting of the American Anthropological Association, San Francisco, November.

Malinowski, Bronislaw. 1944. *A Scientific Theory of Culture and Other Essays*. Chapel Hill: University of North Carolina Press.

Martín-Rodríguez, Manuel M. 1996. "The Global Border: Transnationalism and Cultural Hybridism in Alejandro Morales's *The Rag Doll Plagues*." In *Alejandro Morales: Fiction Past, Present, Future Perfect*, ed. José Antonio Gurpegui, 86–98. Tempe, Ariz.: Bilingual Review.

Morales, Alejandro. 1996. "Dynamic Identities in Heterotopia." In *Alejandro Morales: Fiction Past, Present, Future Perfect*, ed. José Antonio Gurpegui 14–27. Tempe, Ariz.: Bilingual Review.

Nash, June. 1983. "The Impact of the Changing International Division of Labor on Different Sectors of the Labor Force." In *Women, Men, and the International Division of Labor*, ed. June Nash and María Patricia Fernández-Kelly, 3–38. Albany: State University of New York Press.

Ong, Aihwa. 1995. "Women Out of China: Traveling Tales and Traveling Theories in Postcolonial Feminism." In *Women Writing Culture*, ed. Ruth Behar and Deborah A. Gordon, 350–72. Berkeley: University of California Press.

Ortner, Sherry. 1984. "Theory in Anthropology since the Sixties." *Comparative Studies in Society and History* 26(1): 126–66.

Radcliffe-Brown, A. R. 1952. *Structure and Function in Primitive Society*. New York: Free Press.

Rosaldo, Renato. 1980. *Ilongot Headhunting, 1883–1974: A Study in Society and History*. Stanford, Calif.: Stanford University Press.

———. 1993. *Culture and Truth: The Remaking of Social Analysis*. Boston: Beacon.

———. 1994. "After Objectivism." In *The Cultural Studies Reader*, ed. Simon During, 104–17. London: Routledge.

Sahlins, Marshall. 1981. *Historical Metaphors and Mythical Realities: Structure in the Early History of the Sandwich Islands Kingdom*, Ann Arbor: University of Michigan Press.

———. 1982. "Individual Experience and Cultural Order." In *The Social Sciences: Their Nature and Uses*, ed. William H. Krustel, 35–48. Chicago: University of Chicago Press.

———. 1985. *Islands of History*. Chicago: University of Chicago Press.

Weber, Max. 1958[1920]. *The Protestant Ethic and the Spirit of Capitalism*. New York: Charles Scribner's Sons.

———. 1977[1905]. "'Objectivity' in Social Science and Social Policy." In *Understanding and Social Inquiry*, ed. B. Dallmayr and T. McCarthy, 24–37. Notre Dame, Ind.: University of Notre Dame Press.

Webster's New Collegiate Dictionary, 8th ed. 1974. Springfield, Mass.: G. & C. Merriam.

Williams, Raymond. 1979. *Politics and Letters: Interviews with New Left Review*. London: Schocken.

Willis, Paul. 1977. *Learning to Labor. How Working Class Kids Get Working Class Jobs*. New York: Columbia University Press.

5

Technologies of Identity and the Identity of Technology

Race and the Social Construction of Biometrics

KELLY A. GATES

In the nineties, it was hard to resist the temptation to celebrate the radical potential of the Internet. For postmodernists and other observers alike, one of the Internet's greatest promises lay in its potential to undermine rigid identity categories and enable users to adopt multiple simulated personas. Sherri Turkle's *Life on the Screen: Identity in the Age of the Internet* (1995) explored "dramatic examples of how computer-mediated communication can serve as a place for the construction and reconstruction of identity" (14). Her interview respondents—mostly participants in new Internet communication forums called multiuser domains (MUDs)—seemed to perfectly embody a new disembodied ideal. In the text-based freedom of cyberspace, they were anonymous individuals taking on multiple and disparate identities, each more or less of their own choosing. Internet users, it appeared, could adopt any race, gender, or class background, any sexual orientation or political persuasion, any age, height, weight, or hair color. If, as the famous *New Yorker* cartoon quipped, no one knew you were a dog on the Internet, then the possibilities for social transformation were enormous.

Less ambitiously, the fluid model of identity experienced by participants in MUDs, MOOs,[1] and Internet Relay Chats seemed better suited to life in the global village. In fact, well before the Internet made its dramatic popular debut in the nineties, identity had already been exposed for what it was: not a fixed and stable object, not "an already accomplished fact," but a "'production,' which is never complete, always in process, and always constituted within, not outside, representation" (Hall 1990, 222). Identity in the disembodied world of cyberspace was both a symbol *for* and a symbol *of* identity in real life. As a "space" for articulating already existing practices of identity production, the Internet provided a new way of exposing the futility, if not the violence, of ongoing attempts to establish rigid identity categories. In short, even in the offline world, it made sense to face up to the messiness of identity.

But the social forces working to control identity and shore up categories would not be routed by this unruly new technology. The struggle for the normalization of identity would proceed apace, fueled in part by the intensive private sector drive to know the consumer, and in part by growing fears of Internet anonymity's dark underbelly: hackers, identity thieves, virus programmers, child pornographers, and digital pirates. Alongside the Internet's emergence into the mainstream during the 1990s, and the playful forms of "identity tourism" it enabled (Nakamura 2000), came another technical innovation that presented a different set of promises.[2] Companies with futuristic names like EyeDentify, Visionics, Identix, and Viisage were among those social actors using federal funding and venture capital to develop technological solutions to the problem of "disembodied identities"— a problem that had been around at least as long as humans had names to represent them, but one that seemed to take on a new level of urgency in an increasingly wired world. They called their technologies *biometrics*, not to be confused with the statistical study of biology, a field that had its origins in the late nineteenth century. The new biometrics of the late twentieth century borrowed the old technique of reading identity off the body through scientific measurements, this time using computers to digitize and automate the process. By January 2001, MIT's *Technology Review* named biometrics one of the top ten technologies that would change the world (Stikeman 2001), and the biometrics industry revenues were estimated at U.S.\$196 million for 2000, up nearly 100 percent from U.S.\$100 million in 1999 ("2000 Market Review" 2001).[3]

Biometric technologies are designed to "digitize" the body in order to read it as an identification document. The biometric identification process involves storing digital representations of body parts in databases and distributing them across information networks. They are technologies for fixing identity to the body, combining multiple technologies (e.g., photography, video, statistics, fiber optics, image processing, and computer vision), as well as multiple discourses and institutional practices (e.g., policing, workplace surveillance, consumer profiling, state security). They also represent the convergence of visual forms of surveillance with bureaucratic systems, investing computers and networks with new ways of identifying human beings at key points of interface. The now familiar list of biometric technologies includes digital fingerprinting, hand geometry, iris and retina scanning, and signature, gait, and voice recognition. These technologies are being envisioned and designed for a range of applications, including passenger screening, border control, criminal identification, computer security, and physical access control. Here I focus on facial recognition technology precisely because the "content" of the medium—the image of the human face —carries such social and cultural significance. In addition, this particular biometric technology has come to have considerable sway in the public imagination, and it promises to identify humans "at a distance," without their active interface with an identification system.

In this essay, I examine some of the racialized dimensions of the new identification technologies called biometrics, considering the role of "race" in the social construction of these systems. Critical interrogations of the intersection between racial and technological formation have often focused on questionable claims to objectivity and neutrality made in the name of science and technology, and the white ideology of racelessness that pervades dominant discourses of technological progress. As much critical work on race has demonstrated, the absence of race is virtually always equated with whiteness. This has not prevented proponents of facial recognition and other biometrics from making claims to the technical neutrality of their systems. For example, according to Visionics CEO Joseph Atick, his company's technology, called FaceIt®, "delivers security in a non-discriminatory fashion. FaceIt technology performs matches on the face based on analytical measurements that are independent of race, ethnic origin or religion. It is free of the human prejudices of profiling" (*Terrorism Prevention* 2001). Similar claims to technical neutrality accompanied earlier methods for binding identities to bodies, and such claims tended to disavow the applications to which such techniques were put (most notably eugenics practices), and the extent to which particular conceptions of race and racial categories were "built in" to technical systems.[4] Joseph Atick's claim to technical neutrality is, consciously or not, a response to a long history of dubious efforts on the part of state and other social actors to systematically bind identities to bodies (or specifically faces). Today, those advocating for the institutionalization of new identification technologies must insist on their technical neutrality to counter the charge that they amount to a hi-tech form of racial profiling. Such claims to the technical neutrality of biometrics deserve critical attention.

In addition to the ideology of race neutrality, the problem of *differential access* remains central to discussions of race and technology, with research examining race as well as class, gender, and nation-based differences in access to and proficiency with computer and other technologies. In the United States, the "digital divide" occasionally surfaced as a public policy question during the 1980s and 1990s, and computer companies targeted poor and predominantly nonwhite schools in their educational donations. However, as Jonathan Sterne (2000) found, corporations sought philanthropic endeavors that would complement their commercial goals. Apple, for example, "favored educators who were already plugged into larger professional networks … and who already had some access to computing resources and some basic computer knowledge" (206). This selective giving process perpetuated the existing stratifications in computer access. As Sterne argues, "the legacy of the deep federal cuts in public education over the course of the 1980s and corporations' preference for elite, innovative schools still leaves its mark on computer access and attitudes" (208). Thus while utopian visions of the Internet have painted it as a race-neutral space, Sterne explains, a close look at the institutionalized forms of discrimination that have shaped distribution of computers to schools in the United States demonstrates that racial minorities can be at a distinct disadvantage in terms of Internet access and computer literacy. And while the racial and class-based dimensions of computer access are clearly linked, they should not be conflated: "they operate in 'nonsynchronous' fashion (McCarthy 1998, 66–67), where categories may overlap and emphasize one another, as is often the case in school funding, or they may operate in contradiction, as is apparently the case in families' dispositions toward buying computers" (187).

In what follows I consider the problem of differential access through a different lens, examining the pivotal role that biometrics technologies are taking in the efforts of elite interests to control access to the spaces and resources of value to the digital age. In addition, I consider the ideology of racelessness as it relates to the social construction of facial recognition technology, especially in the post-9/11 context when this fledgling technology was articulated to the U.S. "homeland security" agenda and the identification of the enemy Other.

Biometrics and Differential Access

It is necessary to put the emergence of facial recognition technology and other biometrics in the context of the information revolution taking place during the latter half of the twentieth and into the twenty-first century. As Dan Schiller (1999, 2004) has elaborated, we are living through a transition to an informationalized capitalism, a historical phase-change that commenced during the 1960s and arose out of a systemic economic, social, and political crisis. Profit slowdown and industrial stagnation, along with the legitimation crisis posed by Vietnam and domestic civil rights issues, were among the major problems leading to a recognized need on the part of corporate executives and national politicians in the United States to create new sites of profit and to mollify social unrest (Schiller 2004). According to Schiller (2004), "the central role accorded to information and communications as an economic stimulant was unprecedented," as corporate capital invested in information and communication technology (ICT) development and integrated ICTs into business processes, especially to coordinate dispersed locations (2). As an integral part of the process, telecommunications infrastructure worldwide experienced a top-down overhaul during the 1980s and 1990s to bring it in line with the needs of transnational capital (Schiller 1999). For diversified businesses with dispersed operations, telecommunications provided an indispensable means of coordinating those operations. Widespread decisions to interoperate computer systems were motivated by the interests of corporate capital to spread their reach across the globe and deep into economic, social, and cultural life. Corporate reconstruction around networks has occurred economywide, with the installed based of computers in the United States rising from 5,000 in 1960 to 180 million by 1997 (Schiller 2000, 13). The financial sector took a leading role in this process, significantly increasing their telecommunications operating expenses, linking up their offices transnationally, and installing 165,000 networked automated teller machines in the United States by 1998. Banks were not alone as companies in other sectors integrated networks into activities of production, distribution, marketing, and administration. As Schiller elaborates in his extensive study of this process, U.S. corporate capital spending on information processing and related equipment outpaced factory machinery and mobile equipment by the mid-1980s. U.S. legislators were necessarily onboard; "the U.S. policymaking establishment was determined to grant business users the maximum freedom to explore information technology networks as a private matter" (Schiller 2000, 7).

Along with these sweeping changes in the structure and policy of existing telecommunications infrastructure came proliferating forms of corporate surveillance, including a growing need for automated forms of identification in order to control access to information networks and to identify the millions of individuals whose personal data circulated through those networks. Computerization and the spread of information networks provided both the *possibility* and the *areas of need* for new identification technologies. Identification documents, like passports and driver's licenses, which had always had their shortcomings (especially in terms of their inability to accurately and reliably connect bodies to identities) were seen as increasingly inadequate to the task of identification across networks. The banking, credit card, and telecommunications industries were among those social actors expressing an ongoing interest in technologies that could give them greater control over transactions and information. Not only was identity verification needed at the point-of-transaction, but the intensive private-sector drive to know the consumer meant that each transaction became part of individual records that could be mined and compiled to develop consumer profiles. In addition, employers of all sorts saw the need to monitor and control their employees' access to both computer networks and to the physical space of the workplace. These institutional users, along with state and law enforcement agencies, represented the primary markets for emerging commercial biometric systems.

As Robins and Webster (1999) have argued, new ICTs have been enlisted in the extension and reconfiguration of Fordist principles of scientific management, so that those principles can be applied well beyond the workplace. "Cybernetic capitalism" involves the application of new ICTs toward a new regime of social mobilization, characterized in part by "a heightened capability to routinely monitor labour processes by virtue of access to and control over ICT networks" (p. 115). The individualization of labor (Castells 1998, 72), and the increased capacity to monitor work and productivity rates in "real time," creates an increasingly "flexible" and "disposable" work force.[5] In addition, with the penetration of the home by ICTs, leisure time similarly becomes "increasingly subordinated to the 'labour' of consumption" (Robins and Webster 1999 116). It would be difficult, if not impossible, to achieve this new regime of social mobilization without technologies for automatically fixing identities to bodies across information networks. Techniques for automatically binding identities to bodies are central components in what Oscar Gandy (1993) has termed the "panoptic sort"— "a kind of high-tech, cybernetic triage through which individuals and groups of people are being sorted according to their presumed economic and political value" (2). Gandy sees this sorting process as discriminatory not only on a class basis but especially by race. Supported by new ICTs, "this sorting mechanism cannot help but exacerbate the massive and destructive inequalities that characterize the U.S. political economy as it moves forward into the information age" (Gandy, 2). While the ideology of racelessness persists in biometrics discourse, these technologies in fact can and are being designed and used to secure differential access, in ways deeply tied to institutionalized forms of racial discrimination.

In fact, institutionalized forms of racial discrimination have played a central role in determining the particular applications to which these technologies are put, and the different ways in which they are applied to different populations. Ways in which biometrics have been designed and applied to facilitate forms of differential access are evident in their application to the specific needs and investments of U.S. state agencies in the post–Cold War decade of the 1990s. The National Institute of Justice (NIJ), for example, envisioned facial recognition and other biometrics as applicable to crime control in general, but especially to illegal drug control, an issue that has been inescapably tied to racial formation and inequality in the United States, and a problem that would not go away despite billions of dollars of investment, greatly intensified under the Reagan Administration, to fight the "war on drugs." Thanks in large part to the "war on drugs," the U.S. prison population began a steep upwards climb around 1980, reaching an unprecedented 1,219,014 prisoners by 1991, or 482 incarcerated individuals per 100,000 inhabitants. By February 2000, the U.S. prison population reached an astounding 2 million (Christie 2000). Two-thirds of the people in prison in the United States are now racial or ethnic minorities, and one in every eight black males in their twenties is in prison or jail on any given day (The Sentencing Project 2003). Prisons have been among the early adopters of biometrics, employed to bind inmates' identities to their bodies in order to better manage and control their growing numbers. By 2002, the NIJ had provided $21,291,000 in research and development support to companies and academic research centers developing facial recognition technology, according to a U.S. General Accounting Office (2002) report. In addition, the Defense Counterdrug Technology Development Office (part of the Defense Department) has participated in the testing and evaluation of commercial facial recognition systems, and the agency purchased the Visionics FaceIt facial recognition surveillance system in December 2001.

Expanding use of biometric technologies by state agencies can also be linked to the "welfare reform" agenda of the 1990s. In 1995, the *Wall Street Journal* reported that biometrics systems, "designed to reduce fraud and improve efficiency, offer a relatively painless way to reduce welfare costs at a time when President Clinton and Congress are haggling over how much to cut entitlement programs" (Milbank 1995, B1). New York was among the first states to implement biometrics for entitlement programs, beginning with two rural counties in 1992. By 1995, the state had spent $4.5 million on its biometric system for welfare recipients, and anticipated spending another $8.5 million (Milbank, B1). The 1997 Work Opportunity and Personal Responsibility Act recommended that individual states adopt appropriate technologies for limiting fraud in the welfare systems. Although the Act did not mention biometric technologies specifically, by 1998, in an effort to comply with federal policy, eight states had implemented or started procurement of biometric fingerprint systems for identifying welfare recipients. The "war on drugs" and "welfare reform" programs have had a close cousin: the war on "undocumented" immigrants. Biometric technologies have been positioned as central to the future of border and immigration control programs. During the 1990s, liberalization policies like NAFTA, designed to break down economic barriers, were accompanied by the buildup of border policing along the U.S.–Mexico border. The U.S. Border Patrol more than doubled in size between 1993 and 2000. Peter Andreas (2000a) attributes this sharp escalation in border policing to "the often unintended feedback effects of past policy choices, the political and bureaucratic incentives and rewards for key state actors, and the symbolic and perceptual appeal of escalation regardless of its actual deterrent effect" (4). The buildup of border controls has the significant *symbolic* function of "reaffirming the state's territorial authority" (x). The "success" of state border management depends on the ability of the state to create an image of being *in control* of the border, and border narratives that portray a "loss of control" provoke policy responses that lead to escalated border policing. "In the case of the U.S.–Mexico border," writes Andreas (2000b), "signaling a commitment to the *idea* of deterrence and projecting an *image* of progress toward that goal [have] been *more* politically consequential for state actors than actually *achieving* deterrence" (9).

One of the strategies that the state has employed to project an image of progress toward control of the border, and to manage "the twin policy objectives of *facilitating* cross-border economic exchange [while] *enforcing* border controls" (Andreas 2000b, 4), has been to expand and technologically improve upon the state bureaucratic surveillance apparatus and its application at the border. Part of this effort has involved plans to integrate biometrics into the travel document issuance and border inspection processes. The integration of biometrics into state identification systems for border and immigration control began in the early 1990s with the development of IDENT, the Biometric Fingerprint System of the Immigration and Naturalization Service (INS). IDENT was envisioned to deal with the "revolving door" phenomenon of undocumented entry by workers.

The INS also began to institute biometric systems for identifying legal visitors to the United States during the 1990s. In 1996, the INS commenced the *voluntary* INSPASS hand-scan system for frequent business travelers, and federal legislation made *mandatory* the use of biometrics with non-immigrant temporary visas issued to Mexican citizens. INSPASS, short for INS Passenger Accelerated Service System, was instituted as a voluntary service available to businesspeople traveling to the United States three or more times per year, with citizenship from the United States, Canada, Bermuda, or one of the participating Visa Waiver program countries (mostly Western Europe). In contrast, Mexican citizens have been subject to enrollment in the mandatory Border Crossing Card (BCC) program. In compliance with immigration reform legislation passed in 1996 (ironically following the Oklahoma City bombing by *domestic* militia), mandatory temporary visas, or BCCs, are now issued to eligible Mexican citizens for temporary trips to the United States. The new "laser visas" contain individuals' biographical data, a facial image, two digital fingerprints, and a control number, and have been issued to over 4 million Mexican citizens. In addition to storing the information and images on the card, the U.S. State Department has developed a database of mug shot images of laser visa holders, which was recently used as the test sample in a federally sponsored evaluation of the state-of-the-art in facial recognition technology, the Facial Recognition Vendor Test 2002.

The translation of the body into data for the purposes of identification is a need and a practice peculiar to the digital age, although not without connections to history, and especially to earlier efforts of criminal identification, border and immigration control, and other problems of identification related to the expansion of the modern state, the rise of consumer culture, and the Taylorization of the workplace. The aim of this latest innovation in identification systems is to automate the process of connecting bodies to identities, and to distribute that identified body across computer networks in order to control *access*—access to the benefits of citizenship, to the national territory, to information, to computer networks themselves, to transportation systems, and to specific spaces of consumption, safety, and secrecy. While the technical systems themselves do not wholly determine who has greater ease of access and who has more difficulty in any particular context, it is important to recognize the extent to which these new identification systems are being designed and applied to facilitate discriminatory forms of differential access. As I will elaborate in the next section, the apparent need to apply biometrics to secure forms of differential access greatly intensified in the post-9/11 context, as politicians and industry people called for new deployments of facial recognition technology to identify the "faces of terror."

Biometrics and the Ideology of Racelessness

One of the clearest results of the devastating attacks of 9/11 was a proliferation of discourse concerned with defining the problem of terrorism. The stakes were high in this discursive battle, because the definition of the terrorist threat would provide an image of the enemy Other that would do the important work of constituting the national community in a moment of crisis, thereby helping to restore and secure the legitimacy of the state. At the same time, the prevailing definitions of the problem would play a determining role in the conceptualization of "security solutions" in the form of specific technological systems. In this way, proposed technological solutions to the problem of terrorism offered much more than a practical fix. More importantly, proposals for implementing facial recognition and other security technologies reproduced the *idea* of the security state; they lent themselves to the construction of the state's technological sophistication and capacity for security provision. Three predominant signifiers were employed in the post-9/11 moment to define the terrorist threat: "asymmetric threats," "unidentifiable enemies," and "the face of terror." Each of these signifiers contributed to a particular conceptualization of the problem of terrorism, one that carried a racialized subtext and lent itself to a technocratic framing of the possible solutions, and more specifically, to the construction of facial recognition and other biometrics as technologies of "homeland security."

Soon after the 9/11 terrorist attacks, the Defense Advanced Research Projects Agency (DARPA), the central research and development agency of the Department of Defense, instituted the Information Awareness Office, home to the controversial Total Information Awareness (TIA) program. Now defunded by Congress in response to political opposition, TIA combined a number of existing military research and development projects. One of those projects was "Human Identification at a Distance" (HumanID), conceptualized in the mid-1990s following the bombing of the Khobar Towers U.S. military barracks in Saudi Arabia. The aim of HumanID has been to develop and fuse multiple biometrics into one system, including face, voice, and gait recognition, in order to devise automated systems for identifying specific threatening individuals from a distance; for example, around the perimeter of U.S. military installations. Through HumanID, DARPA provided funding to academic and private-sector developers of facial recognition and other technologies.

HumanID was one of a number of projects conceptualized in the 1990s to address the newly defined problem of "asymmetric threats," a term coined by military researchers to define the insidious post–Cold War adversaries, including guerrilla insurgents, drug smuggling cartels, and other stateless actors, those "loosely organized networks that exploit [Western] society's openness" (Grimes 2003, 28). As the chosen mantra for promoting the new Total Information Awareness system, the concept of "asymmetric threats" was briefly addressed in a promotional video for TIA targeted to industry and state officials. The video, outlining the various research and development projects that were combined to form TIA, was shown as the introduction to the keynote address at the September 2002 Biometrics Consortium Conference, delivered by Dr. Robert L. Popp, then Deputy Director of DARPA's newly formed Information Awareness Office. The text opens with a montage of images and sounds signifying the Cold War, the fall of the Berlin Wall, and the newly defined U.S. security threats of the 1990s and early twenty-first century. The Cold War images—black-and-white photos of suffering peasants and video of Soviet soldiers marching in file—are followed by mug shot images of recognizable terrorist suspects and a characteristic video image of an enormous crowd of Arab men moving rhythmically en masse. The montage is accompanied by the following voice-over narration:

> During the Cold War, the enemy was predictable, identifiable, and consistent. We knew the threats, the targets were clear. But times change. Today, with the demise of the other superpower, America is in a different position: a position of vulnerability. When the enemy strikes, it isn't predictable. It isn't identifiable. It is anything but consistent. Times change. We are in a world of "asymmetrics," and we need transformational solutions. The asymmetric threat is now a reality of global life. How do we detect it? How do we predict it? How do we prevent it? (DARPA, 2002)

This opening sequence encapsulates the post–Cold War identity crisis of the national security state. The text invokes a nostalgic longing for the so-called predictability and consistency of the Cold War, when the enemy was ostensibly well-defined and *identifiable*. This nostalgic idea of an identifiable enemy is used to define a new form of national "vulnerability," the construction of "America" as "vulnerable" precisely because it cannot identify its enemy, literally or symbolically. The inference is that the United States is more vulnerable than ever, that the "asymmetric threats" facing the nation today are even greater than the perpetual threat of nuclear holocaust during the forty-year Cold War. The collapse of the Soviet Union may have eliminated the "symmetric" threat of nuclear warfare with the communist other, but in its place came many smaller villains, ostensibly more difficult to locate, define, and identify. Although it is not difficult to discern problems with this nostalgic orientation to old, reliable, and easily identifiable enemies, the collapse of the Soviet Union is truly a vulnerability for the national security state, which in fact *must* identify ever new, more threatening enemy others in order to legitimate itself. The notion of "asymmetric threats" is a key construction in the effort to legitimize and reproduce an imperial-sized national security apparatus. The United States may no longer have an enemy that can match its military might, according to this message, but it has many small enemies that do not play by the conventional rules of state warfare and thus represent significant threats, disproportionate to their small size and military resources. These new "unidentifiable" and "unpredictable" enemies are constructed as major risks, a construction given considerable leverage by the enormity of the violence on 9/11 along with its procession as simulacra. Of course, the mug shot images of specific faces in this video contradict the notion that the new national threats are "unidentifiable." The visual text, including images of specific faces and groups of ethnically coded people, exemplifies the way in which the problem of "asymmetric threats" is bound symbolically to the stereotype of the Arab terrorist. While the implication is that facial recognition and other technologies can accomplish the truly magical feat of identifying the "unidentifiable" threats to the nation, we are invited to imagine precisely who will be identified.

The identity of "asymmetric," "unidentifiable" threats was defined in part through the metaphor of "the face of terror." In one of its first major efforts to position itself at the center of the public–private security response to 9/11, Visionics Corporation, the leading vendor of facial recognition technology, issued a "white paper" on September 24, 2001, titled "Protecting Civilization from the Faces of Terror: A Primer on the Role Facial Recognition Technology Can Play in Enhancing Airport Security." The boldfaced claim that the technology could "protect civilization" can be read as playful hyperbole only in retrospect; in the immediate aftermath of the attacks it represented a serious statement about the capabilities of both the technology and the company. The "faces of terror" metaphor, obviously used as a means of positioning facial recognition technology as a solution to airport security, also must be understood in the grave climate of the moment. While ostensibly referencing the individualized faces of the 9/11 hijackers as well as potential future terrorists, it had more general connotations as well, signifying an amorphous, racialized, and fetishized enemy other that had penetrated both the national territory and the national imagination. With images of the faces of the hijackers and of Osama bin Laden circulating in the press, the "faces of terror" metaphor invoked specific objects: mug shots and grainy video images of Arab men. It is not surprising or unusual that the facial images stood in for the individuals themselves; we commonly understand the image of the face as a signifier for individual identity. However, the idea that certain faces could be inherently "faces of terror"—that individuals embody terror or evil in their faces—could not help but invoke a paranoid discourse of racialized otherness. Such discourse recuperated the guiding principle of the eighteenth- and nineteenth-century science of physiognomy: that a person's true character could be read from the features of the face, the window to the soul.

The Visionics white paper was not the last use of "the faces of terror" metaphor. In November, *The Washington Post* published an article on facial recognition headlined "In the Face of Terror; Recognition Technology Spreads Quickly" (O'Harrow 2001, E1), and the Technology, Terrorism, and Government Information Subcommittee of the U.S. Senate Judiciary Committee held a hearing on "Biometric Identifiers and the Modern Face of Terror: New Technologies in the Global War on Terrorism" (2001). Like Visionics' use of the "Faces of Terror" metaphor, these references could be interpreted as merely clever turns of phrase, if not for the seriousness of the moment and the extent to which they signaled the very real process of fetishizing *the* terrorist face. The *Washington Post* headline, "In the Face of Terror," employed the metaphor to suggest the act of being faced or confronted with the problem of terror rather than a specific archetype or typology of terrorist faces. Still, read alongside the other references to the "face" or "faces of terror," one could not help but read those connotations into the title, particularly in connection with the reference to rapidly spreading recognition technology; the fetishized notion of the so-called terrorist face readily articulated to facial recognition technology in the post-9/11 context. The shift from the plural "faces of terror" to a singular "face of terror" is also significant. In the title of the Senate hearing, "the Modern Face of Terror" signifies a singular "face of terror" characteristic of the present, like the face of Osama bin Laden or Mohammad Atta, or perhaps a morphed composite face of multiple terrorist faces, reminiscent of the cybergenerated "New Face of America" on the cover of a 1993 Special Issue of *TIME* magazine.

In the fall of 1993, *TIME* published its now famous cover depicting "The New Face of America": a computer generated image of a woman's face, morphed together from the facial images of seven men and seven women of various ethnic and racial backgrounds. The cover, designed to promote a special issue on "How Immigrants Are Shaping the World's First Multicultural Society," predictably generated attention, and has since made its way through pages of cultural analysis. Evelyn Hammonds (1997) saw the cybergenerated Eve as "the representation of the desire to deny kinship and retain masculine power based on the maintenance of racial difference" (120). The notion of race and pure racial types remains deeply embedded in morphology, Hammonds argues, and morphing "is at the center of an old debate about miscegenation and citizenship in the United States" (109). Conveniently substituting the bodyless practice of morphing for the flesh-and-blood reality of miscegenation similarly attracted criticism from Donna Haraway (1997), particularly to the extent that it effaced a bloody history and promoted a problematic sense of unity and sameness.

Berlant (1996) has noted that the rhetoric of "the face" has flourished in discourses of social justice, used to solicit personal identification with larger social problems and thereby produce mass sympathy or political commitment (e.g., "the face of AIDS," "the face of welfare," "the face of poverty," etc.) (435). However, the difficulty with this use of "the face" metaphor, Berlant argues, is its tendency to reduce injustice to something "manageable" at the level of the individual, and to enable "further deferral of considerations that might force structural transformations of public life" (406). While the use of the "face of terror" metaphor aims to produce the opposite effect of personal identification and mass sympathy, instead eliciting mass fear and contempt, it similarly leads to the deferral of structural transformations. At best, it represents a gross oversimplification that strives to make manageable the problem of political violence and national insecurity. At worst, it signals a profoundly racist discourse of fear that generalizes the "terrorist face" across a field of facial images, including but by no means limited to specifically identified individuals. According to Berlant (1996), "The New Face of America" presented on the 1993 *TIME* cover was "cast as an imaginary solution to the problems of immigration, multiculturalism, sexuality, gender, and (trans)national identity that haunt the U.S. present tense" (398). The morphed image was feminine, conventionally pretty, light skinned, and nonthreatening, preparing white America for the new multicultural citizenship norm. The post-9/11 "face of terror" is a similar sort of fetishized object, in reverse. It is an imaginary target for directed attention and hatred, but one that is likewise aimed at preparing mainstream America for new citizenship norms, this time involving intensified state practices of surveillance and identification. Like *TIME*'s fictitious multicultural citizen, "the Modern Face of Terror" is a technologically constructed archetype, and one for which racial categories still deeply matter despite the absence of overtly racist references. Where the former allegedly represented progress toward an assimilated ideal, the latter deeply negated those same ideals of integration. Skillfully glossing over the tension between the individualizing and classifying logics of identification—"the tension between 'identity' as the *self-same*, in an individualizing, subjective sense, and 'identity' as *sameness with another*, in a classifying, objective sense" (Caplan 2001, 51)—"the face of terror" discourse helped to construct terrorism as a problem with a specific technological solution: computerized facial recognition.

Similarly invoking the notion of a cybergenerated archetypical "face of terror," the headline of John Poindexter's September 2003 *New York Times* op-ed piece defending the politically unpopular Total Information Awareness system read simply, "Finding the *Face of Terror* in Data." Although the article did not mention facial recognition specifically, the headline conjured the image of the fetishized, digitized "terrorist face." It also invoked the image of searching for the enemy Other within; that is, identifying the dark face that has contaminated the sanitized multicultural "Face of America." After all, as the "Target: Bin Laden" issue of *TIME* noted, "Top law-enforcement officials believe that associates of the hijackers remain tucked away in American communities.... No one can say how many other terrorist cells may be sleeping near our homes" (Cloud 2001, 51). It is not difficult to read a subtext of incubation and national contamination in the reference to "finding the face of terror in data," along with an implicit effort to posit new information technologies as being capable of purifying the nation of its "enemies within."

Embodying the new insidious threat to the nation, references to "asymmetric threats," "unidentifiable enemies," and "the face of terror" circulated widely in the post-9/11 moment. These signifiers constructed the problem of terrorism in keeping with the "traditional gambit of defining and unifying a national identity through the alienation of others" (Der Derian 1992, 95). At the same time, they did important work for those social actors interested in establishing the necessity of facial recognition and other biometrics, investing the deployment of these technologies with a sense of urgent necessity, and lending to their reification as so-called hi-tech solutions to the problem of terrorism. Along with this particular cultural construction of terrorism as having its source in both individual identities and a generalized, racialized enemy Other, state and private-sector actors formulated solutions in the form of new and improved surveillance systems, ostensibly more advanced and "hi-tech" than existing, antiquated systems. The 9/11 terrorist attacks were widely construed as a failure of state surveillance and identification, a missed opportunity to identify "faces of terror" due to a lack of foresight and especially technological preparedness. The circulation of mug shot images of the hijackers, combined with the discourse of "asymmetric threats," "unidentifiable enemies," and "faces of terror," provided an ideal marketing inroad for providers of facial recognition technology in particular, who seemed to have an immediate solution ready for deployment.

Conclusion

Along with the ideology of race neutrality, the notion of "empowerment" has long pervaded discussions of new technologies, especially information and communications technologies, and computerized facial recognition and biometrics are no exceptions. Reminiscent of the protechnology discourse that can be traced at least as far back as the "rhetoric of the electrical sublime" associated with the telegraph (Carey 1989), the biometrics industry has adopted the discursive strategy of "empowerment." An Identix advertising catchphrase for the FaceIt system reads "Empowering Identification"; another vaguely refers to "Enabling Technologies with Mass Appeal." But what exactly does facial recognition technology "empower" or "enable"? Are individuals empowered when images of their faces are housed in databases and digitized for identity verification? In what sense might that be something called "empowerment"? Who do these technologies "empower" and what do they enable them to do? Who, specifically, is *dis*empowered?

As (real or hypothetical) members of the relatively "access-privileged" classes, perhaps we can be "empowered" by new digital identification and access control technologies. We might use these new security technologies to protect our intellectual property, or the physical spaces where we live and work. And in fact, we might be compelled to use them as responsible, technically skilled, and savvy citizens. As Nikolas Rose (1999) has noted, in the present neoliberal sociopolitical context, "individuals, families, firms, organizations, [and] communities are … being urged by politicians and others to *take upon themselves* the responsibility for the security of their property and their persons" (247). To the extent that we are "responsibilized" or obliged to use access control technologies to secure our identities, information, property, and habitats, they may in fact be "empowering" in a productive sense. They are empowering more or less as cars are empowering, providing drivers with greater speed and mobility, and even the occasional opportunity to drive freely on the open road, while at other times leaving them frozen in gridlock traffic on their way to work so that they can afford their gas, car payments, and insurance. Perhaps access-privileged individuals are "empowered" by biometric identification systems in the sense that they feel more secure and free to be mobile as a result of the tighter security measures. They might be relieved of the constraints on their freedoms imposed by suspicion, fear, and real threats. Rose explains that we have seen a "multiplication of sites where exercise of freedom requires proof of legitimate citizenship," and it is now virtually impossible to participate in everyday life practices "without being prepared to demonstrate identity in ways that inescapably link individuation and control" (240). Among the strategies of governance characteristic of the present, according to Rose, is the "securitization of identity," applying new technologies not for covert purposes or for totalitarian control, but to instill a "kind of prudent relation to the self as a condition for liberty" (243).

Of course, the "securitization of identity," along with the "securitization of habitat" and the fortification of cities, are strategies of inclusion that exist in intimate relation with strategies of exclusion. A fundamental question that follows concerns how distinctions are made between threatening and nonthreatening individuals, those who are access-privileged and those who are access-denied. It is important to envision the encounter with facial recognition technology not only through the lens of the access-privileged classes, but as an array of "non-citizens, failed citizens, anti-citizens" (Rose, 259), including the myriad voiceless subalterns who lack historical subject-positions within a Western framework of representation (Spivak 1988). As a host of border studies scholars have demonstrated, "the migrant border crossers from the South into the North are largely *disempowered* by the denial of cultural and legal citizenship" (Saldívar 2002, 253, italics added). Foregrounding the governmental strategies of exclusion that biometrics facilitate, challenges the discourse of technical neutrality that proponents of biometrics associate with the technologies. To the extent that biometrics are applied to strategies of exclusion as much as inclusion—to governmental problems such as those of controlling who is enrolled in entitlement programs or who is entitled to cross the border from south to north—they embody the social forces producing conditions of differential access from their very conceptualization.

In a technological society, Andrew Barry (2001) argues, specific technologies dominate how problems of politics and government are conceptualized, as well as the kinds of solutions that are adopted. "A technological society is one which takes technical change to be the model of political invention" (Barry 2001, 2). The U.S. response to the September 11 terrorist attacks bears out this observation. In the United States, facial recognition and other biometric technologies were posited as solutions to the problems of security and governance in the post-9/11 context. As technologies for controlling access across networks and providing continuous feedback on the movement and location of identified bodies in space and time, they promised to provide a means for reproducing the existing neoliberal socioeconomic and political order in the face of catastrophic risk and insecurity. New and standardized identification technologies aimed at the body, combined with improved intelligence efforts, more integrated networks of information sharing, and sophisticated techniques of data mining would ostensibly enable the free movement, consumption, and business activity of the "honest majority" (Visionics CEO Joseph Atick's term), while precisely identifying, isolating, and preventing the actions of terrorists—fetishized objects simultaneously "unidentifiable" and readily identified by their characteristic "faces of terror."

Notes

1. MOO stands for MUD, Object Oriented.
2. As Lisa Nakamura (2000) explains, Internet role players in LambdaMOO who chose to perform this type of racial play were almost always white, and the "theatrical fantasy of passing as a form of identity tourism has deep roots in colonial fiction" (714). According to Jonathan Sterne (2000) an online atmosphere of racial voluntarism occurs "where race is seen as something that can simply be chosen or forgotten at will" (196).
3. Andrew Barry (2001) defines "technology" as a "method for achieving a given aim which includes the use of one or more devices, but also the knowledge and skills which make it possible for the devices to be used" (269). A technical device is a "material artefact or immaterial object (such as language or software) which forms part of a technology" (269). I employ the term technology according to Barry's definition, distinguishing it from technical artifacts or devices. However, I sometimes employ the term as a reference to material artifacts or devices in continuity with its common use, a compromise that is necessary to disclose since the aim of this chapter is to problematize the notion that technical artifacts and technological systems are neutral and separable from the social.
4. For an excellent exposition of the way racial bias was "built in" to ostensibly objective scientific research on the links between biology and intelligence, see Stephen Jay Gould (1981/1996).
5. By "individualization of labor," Castells (1998) means "the process by which labor contribution to production is defined specifically for each worker, and for each of his/her contributions, either under the form of self-employment or under individually contracted, largely unregulated, salaried labor ... individualization of labor is the overwhelming practice in the urban informal economy that has become the predominant form of employment in most developing countries, as well as in certain labor markets in advanced economies" (72).

References

2000 Market Review. *Biometric Technology Today* 9: 9–11.

Andreas, P. *Border Games: Policing the U.S.–Mexico Divide.* Ithaca, NY: Cornell University Press, 2000a.

Andreas, P. "Introduction: The Wall after the Wall." In *The Wall around the West: State Borders and Immigration Controls in North America and Europe,* edited by P. Andreas and T. Snyder, 1–14. New York: Rowman and Littlefield, 2000b.

Barry, A. *Political Machines: Governing a Technological Society.* New York: Athlone Press, 2001.

Berlant, L. "The Face of America and the State of Emergency." In *Disciplinarity and Dissent in Cultural Studies,* edited by C. Nelson and D. P. Goankar, 397–440. New York: Routledge, 1996.

Biometric Identifiers and the Modern Face of Terror: New Technologies in the Global War on Terrorism: Hearing before the Technology, Terrorism, and Government Information Subcommittee of the Judiciary Committee, U.S. Senate, 107th Cong. (2001). Retrieved December 3, 2001, from Lexis-Nexis Congressional database.

Boyle, J. *Shamans, Software, and Spleens: Law and the Construction of the Information Society.* Cambridge, MA: Harvard University Press, 1996.

Caplan, J. "'This or That Particular Person'": Protocols of Identification in Nineteenth-Century Europe." In *Documenting Individual Identity,* edited by J. Caplan and J. Torpey, 49–66. Princeton, NJ: Princeton University Press, 2001.

Carey, J. "Technology and Ideology: The Case of the Telegraph." In *Communication as Culture.* 201–30. Boston: Unwin Hyman, 1989.

Castells, M. *The End of the Millenium.* Malden, MA: Blackwell, 1998.

Christie, N. *Crime Control as Industry: Towards Gulags, Western Style.* 3rd ed. New York: Routledge, 2000.

Cloud, J. "The Plot Comes into Focus." *TIME,* October 1, 2001, 50–63.

Defense Advanced Research Projects Agency (Producer). *Information Awareness Office* [Motion picture]. (Video shown by R. L. Popp, September 23, Keynote address: "Total Information Awareness," at the meeting of the Biometrics Consortium, Arlington, VA), 2002.

Der Derian, J. *Antidiplomacy: Spies, Terror, Speed, and War.* Cambridge, MA: Blackwell, 1992.

Gandy, O. *The Panoptic Sort: A Political Economy of Personal Information.* Boulder, CO: Westview, 1993.

Gould, S. J. *The Mismeasure of Man*. Rev. ed. New York: Norton, 1996. (Orig. pub. 1981.)

Grimes, S. "Shared Risk, Shared Rewards." *Intelligent Enterprise*, September 1, 2003, 28. Retrieved November 18, 2003, from Lexis-Nexis Academic database.

Hall, S. "Cultural Identity and Diaspora." In *Identity: Community, Culture, Difference,* edited by J. Rutherford, 222–37. London: Lawrence and Wishart, 1990.

Hammonds, E. M. "New Technologies of Race." In *Processed Lives: Gender and Technology in Everyday Life*, edited by J. Terry and M. Calvert, 107–22. New York: Routledge, 1997.

Haraway, D. *Modest_Witness@Second_Millennium.FemaleMan©_Meets_OncoMouse™: Feminism and Technoscience*. New York: Routledge, 1997.

McCarthy, C. *The Uses of Culture: Education and the Limits of Ethnic Affiliation*. New York: Routledge, 1998.

Milbank, D. "Measuring and Cataloging Body Parts May Help to Weed Out Welfare Cheats." *The Wall Street Journal*, December 4, 1995, B1.

Nakamura, L. "'Where Do You Want to Go Today?' Cybernetic Tourism, the Internet, and Transnationality." In *Race in Cyberspace,* edited by B. E. Kolko, L. Nakamura, and G. B. Rodman, 15–26. New York: Routledge, 2000.

O'Harrow, R., Jr. "In the Face of Terror; Recognition Technology Spreads Quickly." *The Washington Post,* November 1, 2001, p. E1. Retrieved February 15, 2003, from Lexis-Nexis Academic database.

Poindexter, J. M. "Finding the Face of Terror in Data." *The New York Times,* September 10, 2003. Retrieved September 10, 2003, from http://www.nytimes.com.

Robins, K., and F. Webster. *Times of the Technoculture: From the Information Society to the Virtual Life.* New York: Routledge, 1999.

Rose, N. *Powers of Freedom: Reframing Political Thought.* New York: Cambridge University Press, 1999.

Saldívar, J. "On the Bad Edge of *la Frontera*." In *Decolonial Voices*, edited by A. J. Aldama and N. H. Quiñonez, 263–96. Bloomington: Indiana University Press, 2002.

Schiller, D. *Digital Capitalism: Networking the Global Market System*. Cambridge, MA: MIT Press, 1999.

Schiller, D. "Informationalized Capitalism: Retrospect and Prospect." Unpublished manuscript 2004.

Sentencing Project, The. *Racial Disparity, 2003*. Retrieved July 7, 2004, from http://www.sentencingproject.org/issues_07.cfm.

Spivak, G. C. "Can the Subaltern Speak?" In *Marxism and the Interpretation of Culture*, edited by C. Nelson and L. Grossberg, 271–313. Urbana: University of Illinois Press, 1988.

Sterne, J. "The Computer Race Goes to Class: How Computers in Schools Helped Shape the Racial Topography of the Internet." In *Race in Cyberspace*, edited by B. E. Kolko, L. Nakamura, and G. B. Rodman, 191–212. New York: Routledge, 2000.

Stikeman, Alexandra. "The Technology Review Ten: Biometrics." *Technology Review*, January/February 2001. Retrieved December 13, 2001, from http://www.technologyreview.com/magazine/jan01/print_version/tr10_atick.html.

Turkle, S. *Life on the Screen: Identity in the Age of the Internet*. New York: Simon and Schuster, 1995.

U.S. Congress. Senate Subcommittee of the Judiciary Committee. *Terrorism Prevention; Focusing on Biometric Identifiers: Hearing Before the Technology, Terrorism and Government Information Subcommittee of the Judiciary Committee.* 107th Cong. (2001). 1st Session (testimony of Joseph J. Atick). Retrieved December 12, 2001, from Lexis-Nexis Congressional database.

U.S. General Accounting Office. *Federal Funding for Selected Surveillance Technologies* (Publication No. GAO-02-438R), March 14, 2002. Retrieved January 23, 2004, from http://www.gao.gov/new.item/d02438r.pdf.

Visionics Corporation. *Protecting Civilization from the Faces of Terror: A Primer on the Role Facial Recognition Technology Can Play in Enhancing Airport Security*. September 24, 2001. Retrieved October 1, 2001, from http://www.visionics.com/newsroom/downloads/whitepapers/counterterrorism.pdf.

6

States of Insecurity
Cold War Memory, "Global Citizenship" and Its Discontents

LESLIE G. ROMAN

Far from being a thing of the past—safely dead or left aside—Cold War memory appears revitalized and rearticulated in the post-September 11th context of U.S., Canadian, and Western European insecurity—at times, even within the so-called benign public talk of "global citizenship". Its archeology is generative of masculinist, racist, imperialistic, and militaristic nation-state politics and policies. The effects of such processes and policies register in the well-documented cases of "racial profiling" criminalizing, among others, anyone thought to be "Muslim" or people from purportedly "suspect" countries (American Civil Liberties Union, herein, ACLU, 2004; Canadian Council for Refugees, herein, CCR, 2001, 2003a, b, 2004a, b; Grewal, 2003). They also register in the increases in discriminatory visa denials and the selective tracking of international students attending North American universities (CCR, 2004b). In Canada, such Cold War memory has triggered other residual nerves, for example, the WWII internment of Japanese Canadians. In the U.S., such memory has sent shivers down the spines of the survivors of those targeted by the McCarthy era's repression of civil liberties and dissent (Duerksen, 2002; Grewal, 2003; Martin & Shohat, 2002; Sassen, 2003; Somers & Somers-Willett, 2002; Wang, 2002; Weldes, Gusterson, & Duvall, 1999; Willinsky, 2002). How is Cold War memory articulated in the post-Cold War context of globalization, public university talk of "global citizenship", and the displacement of refugees longing for safety and the enforcement of internationally recognized human rights?

Hardly a specter for all whom have been and are its subjects or will be its future subjects, the residual ideology of the Cold War appears in the wake of September 11th to have its own counter-subject(s) and counter-memories of the post-Cold War settlement. The "official we" of North America, a collection of dominant interests (and their consumerist beneficiaries) who already erroneously considered themselves the "secure", if not the "original citizens", got not just as some participants at a recent conference on "global citizenship" at the University of British Columbia called it, a "wake up call",[1] but a profound shake-up call. In the commercial and military centers of the New Empire, the attacks on the World Trade Center and the Pentagon have stirred anxieties and insecurities that had for some time been put aside (or so the "official we" thought) by the neo-liberal and neo-conservative merged promise of transnational and global capitalist commerce bringing about a new post-Cold War "global village". Such had been the promise of globalization from some quarters.

The U.S. media aftershocks of September 11th subjected viewers to numerous nostalgic and at once fear-inspiring references to Pearl Harbor, World Wars I and II, and the Korean War—a time remembered as "clear cut", when the blood spilled was seen as necessary sacrifice for the protection of "national freedoms", "rights", and "national identity" altogether. Undercutting the nostalgia for America's national "righteous times" has been a clear rupture in what Raymond Williams called "the structure of feeling" (1961: 47–81). Media commentators noted that the enemy was "elusive", crossing national borders. Repeated references to transnational "terrorist cells and pods" who used the superhighway sounded the alarms of Cold War memory in resurgence, interrupting the triumph of globalized uses of technology. Yet, what does all of this signify? Paradoxically, could it mean that in the heart of the seemingly impenetrable commercial and military centers of the New Empire, September 11th momentarily allowed some of those super-powered nation-states I call "the excessively entitled" to see themselves as "fragile", "vulnerable", and perhaps even as "interdependent"? There, in the metropolis, was a shadowy reminder of the human costs of *unrecognized*, if not *devalued interdependence*.

Did September 11th transform the world as dominant Euro-American media pronouncements of "state of emergency" declared in its immediate aftermath (Martin & Shohat, 2002; Steinmetz, 2003; Wang, 2002)? Some left and right critics of globalization seemed to join the fervour by debating the idea of September 11th as *the* defining catastrophe for the U.S., its North American trading partner, Canada, and the ever-ready signifier of "freedom-loving Western civilization" (Buchanan, 2002; Kelly, 2003; Hardt, 2001; Steinmetz, 2003; Wang, 2002). Ironically, the fervour itself confirms the moment and political subject and place/space of its catastrophe even as it seeks to question whether and what has changed in conditions of post-Cold War globalized life or imperial rule (Grewal, 2003; Martin & Shohat, 2002; Rizvi, 2003).

As observed by Richard Falk (1993, 1996), the first to coin the phrase "globalization from above and below", dominant conceptions from "above" emphasize discourses of national and global competitiveness, the flow of human capital, "highly skilled workers, efficiency, consumption, and productive citizenship" (1993: 39–40). However, as Taylor, Rizvi, Lingard, and Henry (1997) and others note, other contending but less prevalent conceptions of globalization from "below", consider the flow or the containment of people, the intermingling or suppression of languages, cultures, images and imaginaries (Brysk, 2002; Burbules & Torres, 2000; Crane, Kawaskima & Kawasaki, 2002; Cronin & De Grieff, 2002; Drache & Frose, 2003; Held, 2002; Kellner, 2000). They employ the discourses of civic global responsibility, service to community, respect for the environment, and belonging to a common human community across national borders, among other values.

The phrases "globalization from above and below" and "global citizenship" have all but become slogans. They signal but do not sufficiently trouble their own underlying assumptions, as well as substantive conceptual difficulties. Serious normative considerations, as well as the asymmetrical social processes of making gendered, classed, "racialized", and non-disabled subjects, and displacing or containing of refugees and migrants through increasingly restrictive or punitive immigration policies play an integral but mostly over-looked part (Abu-Laban & Gabriel, 2002; Chang, 2000; Meekosha; 2001; Sharma, 2001, 2002) of discussions invoking these glosses. Moreover, critiques of globalization and sympathetic conceptions "global citizenship" often beg questions of global justice and governance, as well as the role of public university education in the context of harsh global inequalities (Bowden, 2003; Held, 2002; Sassen, 2003; Thompson, 2002).

In this article, I trouble the slippery surfaces of "global citizenship" and the conventional binary wisdom of "globalization from above" and "below", bringing their uses and interested conceptions into sharper relational and comparative scrutiny across policy-making and discursive sites. Such binary oppositions obscure the complexity, that is, the ways active socio-political processes in specific institutions and historical contexts transform and rearticulate public memory. Binary logics also obscure the inter-relations between nation-state consolidation as well as the transnational fluidity that exists in processes of globalization and nation-building. Moreover, they smooth over the contradictory pressures exerted on universities to respond to policy interests of different state, local, and supra-national interests. This article asks how the policy sites of immigration, security, and citizenship from outside universities influence the ways in which a public university in a particular nation-state context takes up or articulates official nation-state discourses of "global citizenship".

In whose interests do dominant discourses of "global citizenship" function, and to what normative ends? This article has several purposes. First, it situates the most recent phase of globalization in Canada within the retrenchment of the social democratic welfare state and the policy nexus of immigration and "anti-terrorist national and transnational security" policies in the wake of September 11, 2001, and their revitalization of Cold War memories, fears, and anxieties. I argue that Canada's contemporary dominant discourses of "global citizenship" articulate neither a radical caesura from, nor simple continuity with, the post-Fordist project of U.S. imperialism or Empire (Hardt & Negri, 2000). I draw in part upon the important work of anti-colonial feminist sociologists, Nandita Sharma (2001, 2002) and Yasmeen Abu-Laban and Christina Gabriel (2002), who demonstrate respectively how these policies further entrench existing gendered, classed, and racialized divisions of migrant work (Sharma 2001, 2002) and undermine gains made in Canadian multicultural policy (Abu-Laban & Gabriel, 2002). The policy nexus of an expanding discourse of globalization permitting particular bodies to flow across borders within retrenched social welfare states converging with the heightened attention to and the force of immigration/security/anti-terrorism policy measures after September 11th might ordinarily escape our attention when discussions of globalization in the university context come up. Yet such a policy context requires critical attention by educators and policy-makers, if we are to respond reflexively to both the specificities of and interconnections among and between the different nation-state and supranational policy contexts for creating differential or hierarchical categories of work, skill, and entitlement to full formal substantive citizenship and enforcement of human rights protections.

Second, building upon recent feminist decolonization scholarship on the efforts to internationalize curricula in the North American university contexts within non-traditional programs of Women's Studies, as well as the sociological work of globalization critics, I provide a textual analysis of the three dominant, as well as one emergent alternative, curricular discourses. While the analysis makes no claims to exhaust the curricular possibilities for framing "globalization" or "global citizenship", it will show these discourses operate in everyday practice, supplementing the broader literature's findings in North America and elsewhere with evidence from one northwestern Pacific university, the University of British Columbia, where I teach.

Third, I employ a method of textual analysis (Hall 1984, 2003; Smith, 1990, 1999) to deconstruct University of British Columbia's efforts to foster "global citizenship". Two moments of textual practice—the University's publicly held public conference on "global citizenship" in the aftermath of September 11th (e.g., http://www.vpacademic.ubc.ca/globalcitizenconf) and its official web page of principles, goals, and strategies for internationalizing the curricula (Goldberg, 2002, n.p. http://www.vpacademic.ubc.international/accessed 12/09/2002) provide evidence for the contested discourses of globalization at stake.[2] This analysis will put flesh on the bones of a theoretical argument about the changing form of the Canadian state within the current socio-political and global context and its impact on educational policy initiatives in one "local" site concerning internationalization and the implications for a range of issues hailed by overly ambitious or inadequate notions of "globalization" and "global citizenship".

Immigration Changes and Global Flows: Managing Labouring Bodies after and before September 11th

In the post-September 11th fall of 2001, the Canadian Government announced a combination of measures designed to deal with border controls, national security, and the new global realities. The first efforts included tightening airport security, freezing the assets of those suspected to have terrorist links, and the appointment of a Cabinet committee to oversee Canada's "anti-terrorist" efforts (Abu-Laban & Gabriel, 2002). Subsequently, the Government introduced an omnibus "anti-terrorism" bill, spending $280 million in technology upgrades and increased border controls (Abu-Laban & Gabriel, 2002; CIC news release, 2001). Among them were an omnibus "anti-terrorism" bill and subsequent bills that profoundly alter the immigration and refugee policy of the prior post-War years. Bill C-11's passage coincided with the introduction of the Government's new "anti-terrorism" measures within the fearful climate in which "security" and border-control have dominated the political national and international imagination. Bill C-11, Sharma (2001) argues, should be read in the context of the Canadian nation-state's efforts to increase both its powers of detention over refugees and its refusal grounds for the inadmissibility of refugees and (im)migrants. Expanded state immigration and security powers have included the elimination of particular appeal processes and the shoring up certain interdiction processes. At the same time, she argues that the Canadian state has decreased its obligations to respect and implement international human rights protections for refugees and (im)migrants (Sharma, 2001).

Yet, as indicated in the prior discussion, drawing in part on Sharma's work (2001) analyzing the NIEAP, Bill C-11 is not an exception but rather part of a long-term strategy that makes certain groups much more vulnerable to experiencing difficulties when they attempt to enter, live, and work in Canada (see for example, CCR, 2001; Sharma, 2001). As Sharma (2001, 2002) well documents, we should not be seduced into thinking that the post-September 11th convergence of such national security, immigration, and globalization discourses is entirely novel. She demonstrates that the establishment of Canada's Non-immigrant Employment Authorization Program (herein, NIEAP) in 1973 legitimized the differential categories of citizen and non-citizen (in this example, the nonimmigrant). Thus, those categorized as migrant workers are rendered to work in "un-free" employment relationships as a condition of entering, residing, and working in Canada (2001: 422–423). As Sharma (2001) shows, since 1971, there have been some significant changes in both the "numbers and percentages of the total number of people entering as either permanent residents or temporary, migrant workers over the period of 1973 to 1993" (2001: 419).[3] According to Sharma, the NIEAP has permitted the Canadian nation-state to shift successfully its immigration policy away from one of permanent (im)migrant settlement, towards increased reliance on a highly vulnerable and flexible temporary workforce. In 1973, for example, she documents that 57% of all people classified as workers "destined" to become part of the Canadian workforce came with permanent residence status (Sharma, 2001: 424)! Yet, by striking contrast, in 1993, of the total number of workers permitted to enter Canada, only 30% received this status, while 70% were only allowed to come in as migrant workers on temporary work authorizations (Sharma, 2001: 424). Given the lack of access to human rights protections, routes to citizenship entitlements, and workers' rights, etc., she terms this permanent state of temporary migratory labor, "indentured work" (2001: 433). While it is accurate to argue, as Sharma so well observes, that the last two decades of Canadian immigration policy have become increasingly restrictive, restrictive border control practices represent less a drop in the number of (im)migrants entering and remaining in Canada than a change in the *manner* in which they cross borders (Sharma, 2001). This reshaping, Sharma shows, has worked to cheapen labor power, as well as to redesign citizenship and entitlement.

Less obvious, though, is the manner in which Bill C-11 reconstitutes existing immigration and refugee policies, streamlining the functioning of the NIEAP, so as to strengthen the "market system" and its correlated industrial policies as part of the incentives of globalization to stimulate capital investment and organize anew a particular kind of flexible and inexpensive labour market in this segment. As non-citizens and non-immigrants, migrant workers can be legally excluded from protection by minimum wage standards, collective bargaining of unions, and the provision of social services and programs, including unemployment benefits, social assistance, old age pensions, and so forth. Of significance, "[m]igrant workers are also unable to change any of their conditions of entry or employment without receiving written permission from an immigration officer" (Sharma, 2001: 423). A closer inspection of the program and its policies show just how vulnerable such workers are, especially in terms of redressing their human rights and working conditions by speaking out. Should workers face reprisals for speaking out or for any reason, leave their stipulated employers, or change their occupations without approval from the Canadian government, they are subject to deportation (Sharma, 2001: 423). Moreover, those stipulated or classified as "migrant workers" cannot apply for permanent residency (or "landed status") and furthermore, can be replaced by different people brought into work and be expelled at will (Sharma, 2001: 424).

Bill C-11, thus, represents a fundamental and, in the view of many, unacceptable shift in the treatment of migrants. As Sharma (2001, 2002) and Abu-Laban and Gabriel (2002) show, Bill C-11 was designed to provide policy and legislative tools to deter the exploitation, "smuggling and trafficking of migrants" and to "punish those who engage in this modern form of slavery" (CIC, Bill C-11, Immigration Refugee and Protection Act, "Overview 12", www.cic.gc.ca/English/). Ironically, they argue, it legitimizes a modern form of indentured work for migrants. In all of these regards, such legislative and policy efforts are significant departures from Canada's earlier post-Keynesian social welfare state social contract in that they rob or deny non-immigrant or migrant workers most of the formal and substantive human, civil, and citizenship rights granted to Canadians as sovereign state citizens.

Abu-Laban & Gabriel (2002) drive this point even further by arguing that while the Canadian state formerly has played a "dominant role in the authorization of permits, it is now proposing to partner with business—both individual sectors and firms—to meet labor market skill shortages" (2002: 80) that Canada ostensibly faces in the global economy. Bill C-11 encourages businesses to apply for temporary work authorizations for its highly skilled employees as part of the drive to provide Canada with "human capital" and "retain its competitive edge in the global economy" by removing the previously time-intensive and bureaucratic barriers to securing temporary work permits for the highly skilled (Abu-Laban & Gabriel, 2002). While Bill C-11 facilitates the hiring of highly skilled temporary workers (the majority of whom are males, with most of those coming from the United States), it has also further entrenched the gendered and racialized hierarchies that define "skilled" versus "unskilled" work. Canadian Immigration and Citizenship treats as unskilled and hence, as exceptions to this new temporary worker policy and program, the work of seasonal workers and live-in care-givers (CIC, 1999; Pratt, 1997, 1999). Notably, seasonal workers are composed mostly of men from Mexico and Jamaica and yet, since the early 1990s, about 80% of the women coming through Canada's Live-in Care-Giver Program consistently have been Filipina women (CIC, 1999; Pratt, 1997, 1999).

Thus, the historical coupling of immigration and security policies on both the national and international levels within the larger processes of globalization bespeaks of larger historically dynamic mediations of the local, national, international, transnational, and the global processes. Dominant discourses of "global citizenship", I argue, register another defining sea change—authoritarian post-Fordism. Far from weakening the Canadian nation-state or jettisoning neo-liberalism, authoritarian post-Fordism mobilizes both, but in a transformed way. It constitutes a supra-juridical state that governs with fewer social services but with more *entrepreneurship* (Hall, 2003) through its racialized and gendered globalization policies. This context, he argues, registers deeper and perhaps previously under-estimated shifts in global capital's assertions, namely: "the right" of capital to manage; the globalization of international markets; and the rise of neo-liberal "free-market" ideas written on the body politic from the 1970s through the 1990s (Hall, 2003). The convergence of neo-liberal globalization policies with "national security" and "anti-terrorist" legislation over-writes evocative fears about "terrorists" and "invading immigrants" on the national body politic. Such policies provide literal and metaphorical transnational, economic, and socio-legal mobility with substantive human rights to those immigrants deemed "highly skilled global citizens". Yet, they also reproduce the exclusions and differential hierarchies of gendered, classed, ableist, and racialized notions of skill, flexible work, and vulnerable or *unobtainable* citizenship for those it deems "non-immigrants" and non-citizens (Abu-Laban & Gabriel, 2000; Chang, 2000; Pratt, 1997, 1999; Sharma, 2001, 2002) to those it deems lacking in such skills. How do the historical coupling of immigration and security policies within globalization policy to supply "highly educated" and "skilled" workers to become part of a mobile, flexible, and competitive global workforce construct particular notions of the "global citizen"? What discourses of "global citizenship" emerge as dominant in North American university contexts over the contested meanings of globalization "from above" and "below"? How might a textual deconstruction of "global citizenship" discourses offer insight into the workings of common sense ideologies in official policy articulation?

Textual Deconstruction and the Dominant Discourses of Globalization

The curricular discourses of globalization in which the internationalization of the university curricula and education takes place, which I describe here, are in part heuristic frameworks and by no means exhaustive of the possible frameworks to emerge in variable contexts. Nevertheless, their lived realization depends not on abstract theoretical or linguistic structures but rather on material practices performed in everyday institutional and non-formal contexts that are historically specific (Hall, 1984, 1989, 2003; Smith, 1990). The two related approaches I take to discursive deconstruction and analysis draw on the work of cultural studies sociologist Stuart Hall (1984, 1988, 2003/4 forthcoming) and feminist standpoint theorist and sociologist of education Dorothy Smith (1990, 1999). Both rely in part on putting into productive tension the theoretical and methodological resources of historical materialism and post-structuralism without subscribing to relativism. Both wish to understand how people articulate subject positions within larger ideological discourses in everyday unequal power relations and material conditions. Foucault's (1980) genealogical method of examining and de-naturalizing the operations of power in particular historical, political, and economic contexts influences but does not over-determine Hall and Smith. As Smith (1990: 144) states, "[w]e cannot find an everyday world beyond the categories without examining the organizational processes that do the work of transposing actual happenings, experiences, goings on, events, [and] states of affairs as actualities into an objectified system of records defining and defined by the jurisdiction and objectives of formal organization". For Smith, "[t]exts" are "constituents of social relations, and hence, by exploring our own knowledge of them, we explicate both our own practices and the segment of the social relations in which those practices are embedded and which they organize" (Smith, 1990: 149). Textual analysis, then, uncovers the ideological practices that produce the everyday practical operations of the social relations of ruling.

Hall, on the other hand, pays close attention to the contradictory elements of ideological articulation of common sense and thereby, a people or public in the restructuring of the welfare state under Thatcherism and more recently, post-Thatcherism through Blair's New Labour (Hall, 2003). Hall shows how New Labour builds on this common sense by combining economic neo-liberalism with a commitment to "active government" (n. p.). New Labour, a la Blair, he argues, breaks from

Thatcherism's common sense by establishing a permanent divide between public and private sector workers. It constructs the former as outdated, lacking in entrepreneurial spirit and skills and requiring "modernization" by private sector workers (Hall, 2003) "Modernization" itself connotes an upbeat ring while its ethos of "managerialism" and "market-fundamentalism" undermine a participatory public and substantive democracy. Instead, Hall shows how New Labour, like Clinton-style neo-liberalism, promotes only the most banal form of liberal democracy and a consumerist conception of "governance" as the new public habitus (Hall, 2003).

As much as Thatcherism articulated a neo-liberal version of classic Conservatism, New Labour delivers what Phillip Bobbit calls the "market state" or, more simply, according to Hall (2003), a "social democratic variant of neo-liberalism". New Labour's hybrid strategies bear some similarities with Clinton's ushering in of globalization policies. Clinton secured his prize second term re-election using words like "choice", "change", and "reform", which became slippery signifiers for nation-state marketization. Such signifiers pull selectively from opposing political repertoires, maintaining a double-address to different publics, according to Hall (2003). Similarly, New Labour, argues Hall, adopts a dominant strategy that focuses on managerial and consumerist governance to promote corporate interests in globalization, while its subordinate strategy belatedly speaks of redistribution, long overdue public investment, and public service "delivery", etc. This double address becomes a "double shuffle" (Hall, 2003). Hall notes suggestively that efforts to promote "diversity" in public education, for example, become entangled with the "double shuffle" as a selection function of an increasingly privatizing market state. This insight holds rich potential for conceptualizing current public university efforts to attract international students or prepare Canadian students to "compete in the new global economy". How do public universities select who will become their "globally competitive" and "highly skilled citizens"? What is the nature of differential forms of "global citizenship"? How do racial, gender, class, dis/ability, and national distinctions enter into the selection process for unequal work? How do various texts and textual practices operationalize and win public consent for such selection processes? How do universities mobilize their understandings of "global citizenship", nation, community, and "us vs. them", in the context of globalization discourses within particular nation-state formations?

Canadian Educators/Learners as Intellectual Tourists, Voyeurs, and Vagabonds

The curricular, policy, and programmatic discourse of intellectual tourism, voyeurism,[4] and vagabondism involve the pedagogical and research strategies well known to and employed by naturalistic ethnographers (Roman, 1991, 1993; Roman & Apple, 1990). However, according to sociologist Zygmunt Bauman (1998, cited in Beilharz, 2001), "tourism" as a boundary-making social practice is not confined to ethnographers; it also taken up by diplomats, commercial travelers, and others, arguably, learners/educators, who, on "special occasions"—

> [n]eed to cross into a territory where they are bound to cause and encounter hermeneutic problems, seek enclaves marked for the use of visitors and the service of functional mediators. Tourist countries, which expect a constant influx of large quantities of "culturally under-trained" visitors, set aside such enclaves and train such mediators in anticipation (cited in Beilharz, 2001: 292).

By intellectual tourism in the curricular and pedagogical context—as opposed to that of naturalistic ethnographic discourse, which I have discussed elsewhere (Roman, 1991, 1993)—I mean the discursive codes and cultural practices to which educators and learners consent when they view their pedagogical and curricular experiences as brief excursions into "other" people's lived cultures. In educational contexts, increasingly globalization has provided the rationale and justification for fundamentally intertwining educational goals with educational experiences that amount to intellectual tourism—whether they involve actual travel to places foreign and unfamiliar or virtual encounters in cyberspace creating similar exchanges with the unfamiliar people, places, and cultures. The discourse of intellectual tourism (which effects voyeurism and vagabondism) aspires to achieve "cultural immersion" for the sake of promoting diversity and understanding through cultural exposure. Often, its rhetoric is based on providing 21st century students with the knowledge seen as necessary to deal with today's complex and increasingly communicative presumed "global village". It is now commonplace to find a proliferation of curricular programs of major public and private universities, as in the case of many distance education programs in which classroom-learning environments are conceived as "special occasions" for virtual educational forays. Thus, they are conducted online to other countries and with ESL students. Less clear is the degree to which such intellectual forays accomplish civic and intercultural understanding (Gross-Stein, 2002).

Explaining the logic of this discursive and material practice, Bauman (1998, cited in Beilharz, 2001) wisely observes that intellectual tourism takes its subjects (in this case, educators and learners) outside their ordinary routines and is premised on a conception of deploying boundaries that render some people, cultures, and countries strange and unfamiliar but subject to tourist exchanges and interchanges. For those touring, such places and people are outside their ordinary range of interactions and routines. Intellectual tourism is not always confined to actual physical and geographical travel as part of the educational experience. For example, Mohanty (2003) incisively critiques the use the curricular perspective she terms the "feminist as tourist model" (2003: 239) or as she admits "less charitably", the "white woman's burden or colonial discourse model" (2003: 239) within feminist academic curricular practices within Women's Studies Programs in the United States. Her important analysis holds several affinities with my own discussion of "intellectual tourism" in naturalistic ethnographic discourse (Roman, 1993) and Bauman's description of contemporary globalization practices (1998, cited in Beilharz, 2001). Mohanty (2003) describes this pedagogical strategy as one involving brief forays by students and faculty through the curricula into non-Euro-American cultures. Feminist pedagogy literature well critiques such "add and stir" approaches (Hase, 2001; Morgan, 1994; Rosenfelt, 1998; Rosser, 1999; Stetz, 1998) and while not the predominant view, they were evidenced in one critical comment made within the context of at least one of the breakout sessions of the "Global Citizenship" Conference at the University of British Columbia (2002, n. p.). The forays of intellectual tourists critique particular sexist practices seen to be inherent in non-Western cultures from an otherwise Eurocentric women's gaze that leaves unquestioned the identities of Euro-American feminists—whether they are students or educators. This "add and stir" (Hase, 2001; Mohanty, 2003) approach might include in the curriculum, for example, topical discussion of genital mutilation in Africa for one day or a week without discussing or critiquing the Western practices of breast implantation plastic or other cosmetic surgeries alongside the practices represented as "non-Western" (e.g., Morgan, 1994). While the two procedures are hardly analogous in their consequences, they nonetheless could bare a little more relational scrutiny as part of curricular discussions (Moodley, 1999, 2003). An introductory Women's Studies course (or course on globalization) might address on a one-off basis such topics as women workers in Nike factories in Indonesia, dowry deaths in India, pre-colonial matriarchies in West Africa or, the patriarchal practices of indigenous groups in a far off land (Hase, 2001; Mohanty, 2003).

Left untouched in such discussions would be the everyday lives and contexts of the women for making sense of their worlds in a larger set of geopolitical relations in which the West and neocolonialism are implicated. Such experiences confirm the sense of cultural (and geographical) difference between the local defined as the Western self and the global constructed as the non-Western global "other". They also confirm both racialized and nationalistic privilege

(Bannerji, 2000, 2003; Hage, 2000; Roman, 1997; Mohanty, 2003; Sharma, 2001, 2002). For example, one of the comments summarized from breakout group number nine at the UBC "Global Citizenship" Conference (University of British Columbia, web page on "Global Citizenship" Conference, 2002, n. p.) recommends that international students attending UBC through its exchange programs "'should give constructive feedback' to international students on *our* Canadian way of life" (2002, n. p.). This example of the discourse illustrates the slide from the aim of mutual intercultural and global understanding to a one-way instruction of international students in the presumed superior normative stance of a purportedly commonly held "Canadian" national cultural identity. As Mohanty (2003), Hage (2000), Bauman (1998), I (Roman, 1997; Roman & Stanley, 1997), and others have variously noted, the local is grounded in nationalist assumptions in which familiar bifurcations between centers and margins are reproduced in Eurocentric if not redemptive terms, that is, with the normative frame of reference still being a particular Euro-American nation-state and Anglo-North American-centric contexts. Such nationalistic binary oppositions reinforce the division between the so-called "international" and the "national" spaces, creating the possibility for particular national spaces to function as legitimated hidden norms. While they exaggerate and reify "difference" as "international", "foreign", "Third World", or "non-Western", educational experiences of intellectual tourism freeze in time and space particular stereotypes of what such differences mean. Of significance, educational and pedagogical experiences conceived of as intellectual tourism are voluntary.[5] They are enacted in the service of acquiring more sensations, whether the intellectual touring takes place in the form of actual travel, an exchange program, or a curricular tour or visit. Increasingly, they are seen as one of the most important and immediate ways to internationalize and globalize curricula (Mohanty, 2003: 240–243).

However, for those trapped in states of class, racialized, and gendered immobility, moving from place to place in global space and time becomes much the experience of being "unwanted vagabonds", argues Bauman (1989, cited in Beilharz, 2001):

The vagabonds are the waste of the world which has dedicated itself to tourist services.... The vagabonds know they won't stay for long, however strongly they wish to, since nowhere they stop are they welcome. The tourists move because they find the world within their reach, *irresistibly attractive; vagabonds move because they find the world within their reach unbearably inhospitable.* The tourists travel because they *want to*; the vagabonds because they have *no other bearable choice* (Beilharz, 2001:292).

If we take seriously Bauman's stark contrast between tourists and vagabonds within globalization, then, globalization must be seen in politicized structural terms as the polarization of the effects and forms of social class mobility within and across differently gendered and racialized diasporas—between differentially mobile or confined social classes. In terms of voyeurism, another crucial discursive element of this discourse, there is looking on both sides of the class polarization but to starkly different ends. Bauman (1998: 90) recounts a story he heard from Agnes Heller, a prominent scholar who told him of her experience of meeting a quintessential intellectual tourist on a flight to a scholarly meeting. The woman, according to Heller, an employee of an international trade firm, was multilingual, speaking five languages and attached to no particular place, owning three different homes in different places. She acted not as community member but rather as an isolated tourist who constantly migrated back and forth among many places, belonging to none. Participating in no particular culture of a place or specific time, hers was a "culture of the absolute present" (1998: 90).

[S]he stays in the same Hilton hotel, eats the same tuna sandwich for lunch, or if she wishes, she can eat Chinese food in Paris and French food in Hong Kong (Bauman, 1998: 90).

Empathetically, Heller adds, speaking of her own identification with the woman's ubiquitous experience such that she and the woman become interchangeable, "Even foreign universities aren't foreign" (1998: 91). Lecture after lecture, one can "expect the same questions in Singapore, Tokyo, Paris or Manchester. They are not foreign places, nor are they homes" (Bauman, 1998: 91). While Heller and her travel companion are rootless, they are not homeless. Voyeurism for intellectual tourists becomes a function and an effect of purported cultural immersion in which the tourists look but do not see, reach out but do not touch and more importantly, are not touched or critically reflexive as a consequence, gaze but do not understand.

Bauman contrasts Jeremy Seabrook's story taken from the ever-resonant book, *The Landscape of Poverty* (1985), of a young woman from a nearby Council Estate. At age 15, she "dyed her hair one day red, the next blonde, then jet black, then teased into Afro kinks, and after that, rat-tails, then plaited, then cropped so that it glistened close to the skull..." (1998: 91).

Her lips were scarlet, then purple, then black. Her face was ghost-white and then peach-coloured, then, bronze as if it were cast on metal. Pursued by dreams of flight, she left home to be with her boyfriend, who was twenty-six....

At eighteen she returned to her mother, with two children.... She sat in the bedroom which she had fled three years earlier; the faded photos of yesterday's pop stars still stared down the walls. She said she felt a hundred years old. She had tried all that life could offer. Nothing else was left (Seabrook, 1985: 59, quoted in Bauman, 1998: 91).

While Bauman argues that virtual space serves both the woman exemplifying the intellectual tourist and the girl who is the vagabond, it removes the sedentary barriers of having an imaginary home for the Heller's travel passenger. Yet, for the young women from the Council Estate, it helps dissolve the barriers of a home that is "stultifying" in its reality. Extending the metaphor, Bauman likens the latter's experience to a form of "postmodern freedom" and that of the former to "postmodern slavery" (1998: 92).

Bauman anticipates and glimpses a more relational understanding and analysis of the effects of globalization and poverty in creating a new form of poverty in which the media can show have-not's what they do not have on a grand scale:

Globalization and localization may be inseparable sides of the same coin, but the two parts of the world population seem to be living on different sides, facing one side only much like people of the Earth see and scan only one hemisphere of the moon. Some inhabit the globe; others are chained to place (Beilharz, 2001: 207).

The unequal and yet relational experiences of globalization and localization highlighted by Bauman (1998; Beilharz, 2001) call upon us to remember the newly created category of migrant temporary workers in Canada. Their mobility or migratory experience constitutes only a form of indentured and vulnerable employment, a status of non-belonging lacking in any of the formal and substantive rights and protections given to Canadian citizens and immigrants under consideration for permanent residency and landed status. Hence, even while being inside the Canadian nation as workers, they remain outside its rights of entitlement, humane treatment, and social enfranchisement. It is in this sense that we must question just whose laboring bodies are free to be mobile and, conversely, whose are contained or more aptly confined in large measure by the new immigration legal realities for being non-immigrant migrants within Canada.

Educators/Learners as Consumers of Multicultural and International Difference: Eating "Our" Way through Globalization?

The dominant discourse of the educator/learner as consumer of multicultural and inter(national) difference frames itself within the conception of education and learning as a commodified process. Within the refashioning and roll back of the post-War re-distributive Keynesnian social welfare state, the marketing and selling of "diversity" becomes commonplace. This discourse off-loads the responsibility of social services previously offered through the public institutions of the state onto the already burdened shoulders of individuals, particularly women and families. The emergent form represents collaboration between the public state institutions and the private sector. "Prime Minister Pierre Trudeau's vision of a "just society" articulates the first public national declaration of how cultural diversity became at once a commodity and pluralist vision that blurred the division between private and public in the direction of greater privatization of public institutions. Heralded for his articulation of the values of collectivity, a pan-Canadian identity, and post-War social ideal of the nation-state as a caring one that protects its vulnerable or "weaker" members, he also put forth the emerging notion of "equality of opportunity"—*not* equality of condition. Pluralism is framed within a Canadian "political tradition" which he casts as "neither completely libertarian nor completely state-dominated" (Trudeau cited in Couture, 1996: 89–90). While asserting the language of equal opportunity, pluralism, bilingualism, a subtle hint of support for collaboration between the government and the private sector peeks through:

> Now, Canada seems to me a land blessed by the gods to pursue a policy of the greatest equality of opportunity. A young country, a rich country, a country with two languages, a pluralist country with its ethnicities and its religions, an immense country with varied geographic regions, a federalist country. Canada had, besides, a political tradition that was neither completely libertarian nor completely state dominated, but was based, rather on the collaboration between government and the private sector and on direct action of the state to protect the weak against the strong, the needy against the wealthy (Couture, 1996: 89–90).

The idea of the sovereign nation and of its redemptive (Roman, 1997; Roman & Stanley, 1997) discourses of saving the purportedly morally inferior or weak nations remains undisturbed because "difference" is still intact as a commodity tied to nation-building and productivist (READ: national and imperial) citizenship, available for purchase by those who can afford it. It measures and demands the comportment of "cultural difference" against the ambivalently and ambiguously disclosed public secret of bilingualism—the norms of Anglo-English and French-speaking cultural practices as universal. Framed as consumers of international and national difference, learners and educators become differentially entitled or disentitled citizen-consumers in a global marketplace in which cultural practices are mere commodities. As consumers of inter(national) difference in the purportedly "free" marketplace, learners and educators are taught that cultural and linguistic practices are to be played up or down, depending on the warrant for particular forms of cultural capital. For example, InfoSys, a computer school and worldwide employer for such work in Bangor, India, has a booming business premised on providing services contracted out from the United States. It sends its student employees to such an accent-reduction program so they may be taught to hide their dialects, inflections, geographic and national locations when they speak to customers in North America. Taken into the classroom, such commodified notions of "difference" de-politicize the differential effects of social, cultural, economic, and political processes and consequences of globalization for particular racial, gender, class, and national groups. The global migrations of people as gendered, racialized, classed, able-bodied or people with disabilities, and nationally-specific are rendered nearly absent or invisible as are the ways in which national labor markets and globalized migrations have become inter-related through processes of globalization.

Educators/Learners as Democratic Civilizers and Nation-builders: Living the Multicultural Fantasy of Neo-colonial Humanism?

A common but perhaps underestimated discourse emerges from a larger neo-colonial humanist redemptive narrative of nation-making, educators/learners as democratic civilizers and nation-builders originates in the disciplinary practices of colonial and orientalist assumptions about knowledge divisions. Within the United States Women's Studies context, Mohanty terms this discourse the "feminist as explorer model" of pedagogy and curricula (2003: 240). Yet, I find as much, if not more, reason, to name and conceptualize the discursive and institutional practices to which this discourse refers explicitly under the rubric of humanist neo-colonial nation-building chiefly because such discursive strategies comport historically with the emergence of Area Studies in universities as Mohanty herself notes. Such divisions are well associated with the opposition of modernist Enlightenment notions of Western disciplines and the rest—non-Western purportedly homogenious "Oriental" and Area Studies (Said, 1979; Bannerji, 2003). Of significance, as far the organization of knowledge about globalization in universities, this discourse often assumes that various Area Studies programs (e.g., Asian Studies) should be the programs or departments responsible for studies of globalization. Long-standing, both before and after the post-War period, it appears in residual and emergent forms that reinforce nationalism and white defensive nationalism in particular (Roman, 1997; Roman & Stanley, 1997; Hase, 2001) and, in this instance, Canadian nationalism and nation-building (Bannerji, 2000). The discourse of educators and learners as democratic civilizers and nation-builders often shows a lack of reflexivity in the curricula about either the roles of the Canadian or the U.S. governments, their corporations, and United States-dominated international institutions in effecting differential, if not destructive, impact on those it seeks to democratize or bring into the space of the "international".

The local and global are blended together to internationalize curricula in a purportedly sensitive fashion (Mohanty, 2003). Consider, for example, the language in the web description of the University of British Columbia's mission statement of its principles and goals for the internationalization of its curricula under the auspices of Associate Vice President International, Michael Goldberg, one of the principal proponents and architects of Universitas 21.[6] On the face of it, this discourse is liberal and benign. In terms of principles, it emphasizes that the University "is part of a network of learning that stretches around the world, and in an increasingly global environment it encourages the development of teaching, learning, and research intended to strengthen British Columbia's and Canada's links to other nations". After introducing the first goal of educating citizens to "think globally" to be obtained by the University "advancing international scholarship and research", the web site commits the University to the strategy of increasing enrolment by international students, encouraging study abroad programs, and inviting faculty and staff exchanges and international events on campus. The web page states:

> … Enrolling a significant number of international students from all parts of the world and sending Canadian students to study abroad are important steps in developing cross-cultural awareness and international understanding, and in helping to lay the groundwork for future social, political, and economic co-operation. We should also strengthen links with the faculty and staff of universities in other countries, and collaborate on academic and administrative programs of mutual interest.

> 2. Expand the study of aboriginal culture and history both in Canada and abroad, and increase the numbers of aboriginal students.

> Our First Nations faculty and students are a *resource* that will enable us to expand the study of aboriginal cultures both regionally and internationally. We should also increase the numbers of aboriginal students, both from Canada and from other parts of the world.

3. Concentrate our international academic and research initiatives in three major areas: Asia-Pacific, the Americas, and Europe.

We should build upon our international liaisons and current research strengths in these areas to complement the advantages offered by our geographical location, which positions us well in relation to Pacific Rim studies and to North-South development.

4. Develop international initiatives promoting the contributions of research universities.

We should draw on our international contacts, such as those offered by Universitas 21 or by the Association of Pacific Rim Universities, to build strategies for increasing academic partnerships with universities in other countries, developing performance benchmarks, and promoting the importance to society of university research (http://www.vpacademic.ubc.international/ accessed 12/09/2002. Emphasis added).

However, what this liberal discourse does not attend to are the powerful inequalities and asymmetrical economic, political, and cultural differences that structure, form the conditions, processes, and effects of globalization. For example, no discussion occurs here of the need to pay critical historical attention to the colonial history of the First Nations peoples in Canada. Instead, First Nations are referred to in the mission statement rather possessively and paternalistically as "[o]urs", only after noting how they are a "resource". Only by way of incidental mention, is the issue of under-representation of First Nations students in a Canadian university discussed with the goal of increasing student representation of Aboriginal students locally and from abroad as part of the effort to internationalize. Here, First Nations students appear to be what Stuart Hall (1996) calls in other contexts, "the floating signifiers" for internationalization, at once the exoticized and newly appreciated "local resource" of a university undergoing globalizing expansion and the erased subjects of a longer genealogical colonial history and ongoing struggle.

Moreover, with respect to the University's third principle to "[c]oncentrate our international academic and research initiatives in three major areas: Asia-Pacific, the Americas, and Europe", the discourse of orientalizing Area Studies hums along well, undisturbed in the overall schema to globalize curricula. This is not simply because particular regions are mentioned as geographical "areas" while others stand as the hidden non-geographical norm. Yet, as antiracist educator Yvonne Brown (2002) notes, nowhere in the present curricular map for knowledge in the 21st century of UBC is the entire continent of Africa or related African Studies courses. Also absent from the equation is the "area" of Canada (never mind, the United States), as having any bearing in the North-South relations, so critical to understanding today's global inequalities (Roman & Stanley, 1997). Thus, this discourse relies on the sometimes polite unspoken but nonetheless orientalist binary distinction between the civilized and the barbaric, sometimes couched in language that makes the "us" and "them" distinctions almost palatable; certainly less obvious (Hase, 2001).

When attempting to capture the significance of global inequalities, this discourse figures the democratic rights and freedoms of Anglo Canadians (or Americans) as either as "natural or meritocratic entitlements". The former means Canadians or Americans are simply inherently born with certain rights and privileges, while the latter suggests they were earned by opposing oppressive others who are thought not to appreciate democracy or freedom (i.e., "we worked hard to defend our freedom"). Hence, courses on the global economy, human rights, gendered violence in war, and so forth are framed as projects of modernist enlightenment and democracy.

Yet, such a discourse strains in times of moral crisis, exposing its orientalizing sentiments. The strains and fissures make it easier to recognize that the fascination with the barbaric or not-quite-civilized is matched by an appalling lack of curiosity about the role of the Canadian government in adopting many of the dicta and preferences of the United States in globalization policies. Noted post-colonial educational scholar John Willinsky (2002) observes in the aftermath of September 11th, how tempting it was for North Americans to share the redemptive hope of and faith in [Western] education with the spotlight focused on the opening the schools in Afghanistan and Pakistan after the United States sent its military troops to Afghanistan to root out terrorists. However, as noted post-colonial philosopher of education Fazal Rizvi (2003) convincingly argues in terms that deepen and extend Willinsky's discussion:

> [D]emocratic reforms are not only necessary in schools in the Islamic world but also in the West, where the goal of the internationalization of the curriculum needs to be viewed more broadly than those commercial modes of practice which enable some Muslim students to buy a Western education. It must include a greater focus on the values of intellectual complexity and openness. Students need to be taught to think and speak with subtlety and depth, to listen to others. They must be taught to become more attentive to global issues and to cultures that they have taught in the past to consider as remote, and disconnected from their everyday life (Rizvi, 2003: 39).

As has been well evidenced and critiqued by feminists interested in pedagogies of decolonization (Alexander and Mohanty, 1997; Bannerji, 2000; Hase, 2001), this discourse of Western neo-colonial nation-making practices, which I have identified as "Western educators and learners as democratic civilizers and nation-builders", tends to be underwritten by nationalist and pro-masculinist ideology. It is gendered in predominantly masculinist terms with (white) men as its protectors and heroes and (white) women as its symbols of national honor, hearth, religion, and cultural home (Yuval-Davis, 2001). Conversely, particular racialized and gendered others from specific "suspect" countries; increasingly fill the popular media imaginary as dangerous, fear-inspiring, and threatening. Especially in times of moral panic, it is a curricular discourse capable of inspiring zealous, narrowly conceived patriotism to country: that is, conceptions of patriotism that fathom only a citizenry who defers or acquiesces to official governmental economic, social, and military policy and *not* one who inquires, peacefully dissents, or loyally protests (Dolby & Burbules, 2002; Grewal, 2003) such policies. This discourse fails to link discussions of the internationalization of education with a critical understanding of both the expressions and sources of deep resentment, divisions, and disparities of wealth and power that exist globally.

All three dominant discourses fail to teach what Rizvi (2003) identifies as the aforementioned habits of a moral imagination and civic responsibility. Such habits must be accompanied by a willingness to participate in communities that extend beyond one's own nation and local spheres to develop what Rizvi (2003: 39) calls after feminist theorist, Benhabib, a critical "global intelligence" (Benhabib, 2002: 253). Rizvi states:

> In democratic education, all assertions must be regarded as provisional, subject to discussion and debate. They [students and educators] must learn to develop a global intelligence that prepares them to participate in the processes of complex cultural negotiations as dialogue partners in a global civilization not only insofar as we make an effort to understand the struggles of others whose idioms and terms may be unfamiliar to us but which, by the same token, are also not so different from similar struggles at other times in our own cultures. Global intelligence requires the development of a moral imagination to view the world through the other's eye, and a commitment to build cultural bridges across regimes of fear and suspicion of others. In the end, it involves a range of values central to democracy: reason, compassion and respect of all human life (Rizvi, 2003: 39. Clarification mine).

Educators/Learners as Relational Genealogists

A fourth curricular alternative conceives of the local and the global not as *fixed* geographic or essen-tialist cultural ways of locating people and their differential lived realities by geography, territory, gender, class, race, nation, or religion. Rather, it conceives of *how* communities of people in specific material, temporal, discursive, and contextual places or ubiquitously mobile places (as the case may be) come to be socially and historically related (or not) to land, place(s), and other people and communities throughout the world. This notion of genealogical relationality is not an abstraction. It depends upon and materializes in real, historically contingent global interactions, and relations between and among nations, non-governmental organizations, international agencies, private multi-and transnational corporations, and voluntary associations. These can and do to varying degrees shift the balance of power towards equitable distribution and use of resources, as well as be held and hold others accountable to democratic will in regulating how power and authority are asserted. Here, the conceptual framework for analyzing this geopolitical process of relationality is what I term the "official and structural registers of voice" (Roman, 2003 a, b) and material and nor-mative interests they signify and effect, in particular *interconnected* local and global relations. The word "inter-connectedness" *should not* be underestimated for providing a basis through which stu-dents and educators can examine in curricular terms *how particular histories and genealogies register (or fail to register) within global networks of power,* whose interests count, and on *whose ethical scale* when comparative models are used. Comparison among and between nations, cultures, and com-munities is *not* so much the objective of this curricular discourse as is *historical genealogical rela-tionality* (Alexander & Mohanty, 1997; Anthias, 2001). This entails teaching educators and students how to pay historical attention to the uneven, contradictory, and conflicting interests of power in the social relations that define the contested legal and sociopolitical meanings of "citizenship". It also entreats educators and learners to revisit the facile equation of transnational migration or mobility across borders with possessing full formal substantive citizenship and human rights.

A shared sense of global belonging across nations is no guarantee of such rights, as we have seen with the current neo-liberal attempts to construct migrant work and workers, and thus, redefine citizenship and take more steps toward a post-social welfare state. For example, this curricular dis-course asks educators and learners to call into question how communities, interests, and voices are constituted in through the differential inclusions and exclusions of nation-state citizenship and contemporary dominant discourses of "global citizenship". It necessitates learning about whose voices are heard (or shut out) of larger public debates. Relational genealogists develop a critical "global intelligence" (Benhabib, 2002: 253) to read how communities are constituted in hierarchical relations of power, particularly in relation to other larger structural interests of national-state gov-ernments, private multi- or transnational corporations, and geo-political dynamics. The relational genealogical curricular discourse treats allegiances to other forms of community and interests of humanity that exceed nation-states as urgently necessary if we are to create a "dialogical civilization which seeks shared elements in our value systems" (Yuval-Davis, 2001: 89) across unequal material and geo-political contexts. Such communities are neither given, nor unitary, but produced through interactions that are dynamic and contested. At the same time, however, much room remains for political community-building across differentially located communities within nation-states.

Normative questions over the relationship (or lack thereof) of substantive formal citizenship and human rights with the desire to belong and the constitution of belonging, membership and social justice are crucial to the substantive formal and informal curricula of this alternative dis-course. This is a framework for curricula that at the very least questions the "nation" as a taken-for-granted category of student understanding, interrogating nationalist myths and grand narratives, as well the exceptionally divisive aspects of nationalism in larger global struggles for equality (Anthias, 2001; Bannerji, 2000; Hase, 2001; Mohanty, 2003; Yuval-Davis, 1997, 2001). Mohanty, for example, emphasizes organizing syllabi around social movement politics that elicit the socio-economic histories of particular communities with the objective of emphasizing the interconnections among and between larger global processes of domination and local/global social struggle and resistance. The topics might include sex work, militarization, human rights, environmentalism, the prison/industrial complex, migrant work in the import-export zones, and movements to challenge partnerships between NGOs and corporations, movements to challenge national borders, etc. The implications are clear. The relational genealogical curricular discourse rejects the token add-on measures of the three dominant curricular discourses I have discussed. Instead, it calls for evaluating all curricula from the standpoint from what Mohanty terms the "one third/two thirds world" (2003: 243) as social relations that share differences and commonalities, inside and outside, and distance and proximity. Here, there is no clear essentialist or binary separation between the "West and the rest", the North and the South, the binaries of "us and them" or post-September official rhetoric of the "clash of the civilized and uncivilized" (Yuval-Davis, 2001, n. p.). Such a framework recognizes that there are the "Souths within the Norths, third worlds within first worlds", and vice versa, and so forth. It allows what Mohanty calls "common differences" (2003: 244) to surface among geographically distant or proximate communities in which presumed cultural differences have been used to separate and divide peoples. The idea of "common differences" (2003: 244) stresses how people may establish what is interconnected, shared or different in their experiences. By hailing commonalities, however, asymmetries should not be forgotten in analyzing the relations of power and allocation of resources. The purpose here is not to over-valorize differences or read universal sameness in the process of making interconnections or to say all differences are commensurate. To do so, would thus, repeat past mistakes. Instead, it is to determine the bases and practice of solidarity. Mohanty's notion of "common differences" (2003: 244) and a "pedagogies of decolonization" evident in the work of Alexander and Mohanty (1997), Anthias (2001), Bannerji (2000), Hase (2001), Yuval-Davis (1997, 2001), and other materialist anti-colonial feminists, provides a promising way to think through curricular justice across the rough terrain of cross-structural, contingent, and historically dynamic processes. Their work models and informs what I mean by a "relational genealogy of curricula".

Provisional Conclusion: Making Alternative Knowledge, Political Communities, and Publics

With the privatization of public institutions of the Canadian nation-state, efforts to internationalize university curricula will likely increase opportunities predominantly for those with the economic and cultural capital to be the traveling elites (Fisher, et al., 2001; Fisher & Rubenson, 1998; Atkinskon-Grossean, House & Fisher, 2001). Yet, the unacknowledged other "two thirds", as Mohanty (2003: 243) puts it, are unlikely to benefit from such efforts (Fisher et al., 2001; Hase, 2001; Sharma, 2001, 2002). The arguments I have made for relational genealogical curricula demonstrate the existence of alternative knowledge and standpoints brought into view by newly burgeoning politicized examples of the interplay between and among alternative knowledge, counter-hegemonic publics, and political communities (Abu-Laban & Gabriel, 2002; Bannerji, 2000, 2003; Byrsk, 2002; Lowe, 2000; Mohanty, 2003; Sharma, 2001). A reading of globalization that transforms neo-liberalism by working within and across transnational and extra-national alliances and solidarities requires a focus on human rights that is not abstract or universalizing. Such a focus does not look exclusively to the territorial legal systems of nation-states, international law, or even non-governmental organizations as the sole arbiters of what human rights can mean in cross-border dialogs and counter-public solidarity work (Lowe, 2000). Feminist decolonization scholar Lisa Lowe (2000), for example, describes the work of the Support Committee Maquilladora Workers in San Diego, California, with assisting the workers around issues of labor, health, safety, and sexual harassment in the workplace. The Maquilladora women workers and not the First World women initiated the cross-border work to provide both groups with the tools and alternative knowledge to "test" the limits of international law. They formed a cross-border coalition that was interested whether Title VII of the United States Civil Rights Act will extend extra-territorially to subjects in the United States plants but outside its national territory. Additionally, they were curious about whether Title VII may be used by women in the United States to publicize sexual abuses in U.S. plants (Lowe, 2000: 88) in order to squeeze U.S. companies to reorganize their workplace conduct in the border factories. They were considering how Title VII might form the basis of complaints against NAFTA, as well as a publicity campaign to critique liberal feminist notions of "sexual harassment" that do not currently recognize the racialized and classed dimensions of the problem. In fact, it may be just such provisional grassroots cross-border alliances and democratic associations that exceed the social imaginaries of nations, thus, offer the greatest hope and ethical consciousness against the present despair of resurgent Cold War memories, grand nationalist narratives, and their exacting human toll.

Postscript: Remembering Cold War after "9/11", Imagining "Global Citizenship"

This essay has revealed how the revitalized false binaries of "good" vs. "evil", "freedom-lovers vs. terrorists", the "civilized vs. the barbaric" peoples/nations, and, so prevalent post-September 11th, draw upon a rich repository of Cold War cultural memory as social amnesia, selective remembrance, political symbols, and evocative language that constitute a nationalist Canadian social imaginary. As I have shown in the discussion of dominant discourses of "global citizenship", such memories constitute a social imaginary that is being harnessed within emergent and residual forms of capitalist and neo-colonial expansionism and exploitation. These forms constitute a supra-juridical post-Fordist Canadian state that requires flexible workers and redesigns Canadian citizenship for a post-social welfare retrenched nation-state in the "new economy". The new realities of globalization come together with some relatively "older" residual forms of capitalist and neo-colonial expansionism and exploitation. Such constructions of public and institutional memory in the wake of September 11th in Canada rely on real material and discursive changes to immigration, security, and citizenship legislation and globalization policy that impact post-secondary public education (Atkinskon-Grossean, House, & Fisher, 2001; HRDC, 2002) They also rely on the hegemonic media constructions that privilege some lives in particular nations over others elsewhere. The terrible, deplorable, and terrifying loss of life and public trauma sustained in the attacks on the World Trade Center and Pentagon have been experienced in other parts of the world at different times and on a similar and greater scale without much notice or coverage on North American and Western European television (Sassen, 2003).

"Global citizenship" is a much contested, if not multivalent, mythologized and substantively questionable concept, given the material power of nation-states to determine formal, juridical and substantive citizenship, civil, and human rights. Its polysemic appeal indicates the objective contradictions of globalization, that the global North's institutions of "open democracy" promoting "free trade", "cultural exchange", and so forth, also sow the seeds of deep division and explosive violence that result from its policies of gross inequality and inhumanity. Naive narratives promoting the idea that the world's people are all equally becoming "transnational border-crossers" or "global citizens" do a disservice to educators and students alike who aim to practice critical "global intelligence" (Benhabib, 2002: 253; Rizvi, 2003) or political literacy (Moodley, 1999). Such narratives (particularly those easily articulated with corporatist or private interests in our public institutions) fail to explain the contradictory social processes at work in producing the unequal consequences of gross global and national inequalities of power and wealth. They do so perilously, in the face of urgent ethnic/racialized and religious fundamentalisms, massive illiteracy, grinding poverty, disease and war, and environmental degradation (Anthias, 2001; Drachen & Frose, 2003).

The official spaces constructed by the current dominant discourses of "globalization" and "global citizenship" occupy a conceptual map bordered by hegemonic social definitions with serious institutional, socio-political, economic, and legal force, and consequences for all students, but particularly for international and First Nations students. Such maps are connected to the policy and governmental practices of other institutions of the nation-state, supranational bodies, and private (trans)national corporations. Thus, it makes sense to examine critically how hierarchical relations of "race", class, gender, dis/ability, and nation become tethered to notions of "highly skilled global citizens" in particular "new economy" globalization, immigration, and educational policies (e.g., Human Resources Department of Canada, 2002). Critically attending the definitional, social and juridical borders of dominant discourses of "global citizenship" both within and outside of public educational institutions that attempt to contain the social groups who must live within them such as (im)migrants, refugees, or citizens is a modest starting point for understanding Canada's role in nation-building for the "new global economy". In the coming years, much more scholarly attention needs to be given to the experiences of the 'new economy's' vulnerable transnational or diasporic workers, including those with enduring temporary employment visas, refugee claimants, refugees, migrants, or workers in the underground economy for whom the possibility of accessing formal advanced post-secondary educations may be economically and/or legally prohibitive. How will their everyday experiences put historical flesh on the abstracted, if not oxymoronic, bones of "global citizenship from above"?

Resistance to the official scripts and market-ready slogans of neo-liberalism appropriated from the "globalization from below" protests means that consent to be ruled within such limited spaces can rarely be guaranteed as secure or absolute. Actual students and educators (and various social movements as evidenced in the protests against the World Trade Organization in Seattle in 1999, the International Monetary Fund and World Bank meeting in Prague in 2000, and the Summit for the Free Trade Agreement of the Americas in Quebec City in 2001) may refuse to take up the scripts given to them. Indeed, examples of creative subversions and refusals may prove to inspire the next generation of empirical and pedagogical/political work on the contested meanings of "global citizenship" as they are taken up in lived cultural practice "from below" and across borders (Kenway & Kelly, 2000). As the example discussed in Lowe's (2000) work on cross-border workers demonstrates some of the most promising forms of transnational resistance have not come from accepting the legal and territorial boundaries of "humanity", democratic participation, or community-identification *within* nationalistic frameworks. Strong radical democratic conceptions of "global citizenship" will necessitate other examples of such grassroots transnational alliances, as well as coalitions of educators and students with critically engaged non-governmental agencies and progressive social movements working for non-U.S.-controlled and dominated participation in multilateral global geo-political institutions. Such radical democratic visions of "global citizenship from below" may be the strongest, if not the only viable, alternative to "globalization and global citizenship" imposed from "above".

Similarly, coming to terms with (and challenging) the role public universities may play in making differentiated "citizens" versus (im)migrants, displaced refugees, workers, and places of non-belonging is an important step in deconstructing, disrupting, and transforming and challenging the role of dominant discourses of "global citizenship". Whether I have been successful in connecting the "post-September 11th fears" and Cold War memories to the larger contemporary structural realities of restrictive immigration policies, their denial of human rights, and the reshaping of Canada's notions of citizenship, work, and skill in relation to one university's dominant discourses of "global citizenship" is entirely open to debate. I would suggest, though, that this middle-range (rather than abstracted or disembodied grand) theory, textual analysis, and praxis are of great urgency for educators and learners to explore and develop as part of global literacy. This has been one such effort to bring into sharper relational and genealogical focus the social relations that make some "highly skilled global citizens", while others are others are constructed as permanent non-members of the Canadian nation-state, and thus, perhaps involuntarily vulnerable.

Notes

Acknowledgements: This paper was sharpened by the generous comments of Nicholas Burbules, Gillian Creese, Jacyntha England, Doug Kellner, Jane Kenway, Kogila Moodley, Fazal Rizvi, Kjell Rubenson, Amy Salmon, Nandita Sharma, and Tim Stanley. Stuart Hall graciously provided a well-timed draft paper cited here. I thank Dawn Butler for editorial production assistance.

1. References to September 11th World Trade Center and Pentagon terrorist attacks, equating them with a "wake up call", for particular dominant sectors of white, Western and American capitalism appear in one of the breakout sessions for the UBC "Global Citizenship" Conference held at UBC (2002). See, e.g., http://www.vpacademic.ubc.ca/globalcitizenconf.
2. This is but one part of other projects of mine deconstructing contested discourses of neo-liberalism and globalization in university spaces and places. For related work, see Roman & Pratt, 2000; and Roman & The Discipline and Place Collective (2000).
3. As Sharma notes (2001), excluded from these figures or the category "migrant worker" are large numbers of people admitted to Canada who stay only for short periods of time and perform work that crosses over national borders and thus cannot be considered to be working as un-free wage labor in the country. In fact, they fall in the category of artists, entrepreneurs, literary or performing arts, sports, recreation and those with "not stated" occupations on their employment authorizations.
4. Elsewhere (Roman, 1991, 1993; Roman & Apple, 1990), I have critiqued intellectual tourism and voyeurism in relation to the naturalistic ethnography and my field work with Punk young women.
5. Mohanty (2003) terms the practices of the exchange program model under a separate rubric of the "feminist as explorer model" (pp. 240–243). For my purposes, however, the term, "intellectual tourism" encompasses such practices.
6. Universitas 21 is a new corporate venture that conjoins Thompson Corporation as partners in selling courses, programs, and degrees to an international audience across seventeen universities in ten countries. By joining U21, UBC agreed to license its university name and crest to U21. For a critique of this privatized venture by several faculty in the Educational Studies Department at UBC, see Fisher et al. (2001). For general critiques, see Fisher & Rubenson, 1998 and Atkinkon-Grossean, House & Fisher, 2001.

References

Abu-Laban, Y. & Gabriel, C. (2002). *Selling Diversity: immigration, multiculturalism, employment equity, and globalization*. New York: Broadview Press.

Alexander, M. J. & Mohanty, C.T. (Eds.). (1997). *Feminist Genealogies, Colonial Legacies, Democratic Futures*. New York/London: Routledge.

American Civil Liberties Union (ACLU). (2004, Feb. 26). Sanctioned bias: racial profiling since 9/11. Washington, D.C. The report is online, see: http://www.aclu.org/SafeandFree/SafeandFree.cfm?ID=15102&c=207.

Anthias, F. (2001). New hybridities, old concepts: the limits of 'culture.' *Ethnic and Racial Studies* 24(4), 619–641.

Bannerji, H. (2000). *The Dark Side of the Nation: essays on multiculturalism, nationalism, and gender*. Toronto: Canadian Scholars' Press.

Bannerji, H. (2003, March/April). The tradition of sociology and the sociology of tradition. *The International Journal of Qualitative Studies in Education 16*(2), 157–178.

Barber, B. R. (2002). Beyond Jihad vs. McWorld. *The Nation 274*(2), 11–18.

Bauman, Z. (1998). *Globalization: human consequences*. New York: Columbia University Press.

Beilharz, P. (Ed.). (2001). *The Bauman Reader*. Oxford: Blackwell Pub. Inc.

Benhabib, S. (2002). Unholy wars. Reclaiming democratic virtues after September 11. In C. Calhoun, C. Price & A. Timmer (Eds.). *Understanding September 11* (pp. 241–253). New York: The New Press.

Bowden, B. (2003). The perils of "global citizenship". *Citizenship Studies 7*(3), 349–362.

Brown, Y. (2002). Lecture given in my graduate seminar for the sociology of education, EDST 570 at the University of British Columbia, Vancouver, B.C., November, 14, 2002.

Buchanan, P. J. (2002). *A Republic, Not an Empire: reclaiming America's destiny*. Washington: D.C: Regnery.

Burbules, N. C. & Torres, C. A. (Eds.). (2000). *Globalization and Education: critical perspectives*. New York: Routledge.

Byrsk, A. (Ed.). (2002). *Globalization and Human Rights*. Berkeley: University of California Press.

Citizenship and Immigration Canada (CIC). (1999). The live-in care-giver program: information for employers and live-in caregivers from abroad. Ottawa: Minister of Public Works and Government Services, Cat. #:CI63-17/1999. Available on the internet, http://cicnet.ci.gc.ca/english/visit/caregi_e.html.

Citizenship and Immigration Canada (CIC). (2001, October). News release available on the internet, http://cicnet.ci.gc.ca/english/press/o10119-pre-html.

Canadian Council for Refugees (CCR). (2001, March 14). New immigration bill reduces newcomer rights. News media release. Montreal: CCR.

Canadian Council for Refugees (CCR). (2003a, Feb.). *Refugees and Security.* (pp. 1–31). Working paper available on-line, Web page, http://www.web.net/~ccr/fronteng.htm.

Canadian Council for Refugees (CCR). (2003b, May 29). Interdiction and refugee protection: bridging the gap. Proceedings for an international workshop on Interdiction and Human Rights of Refugees (pp. 1–31), Ottawa: Canada.

Canadian Council for Refugees (CCR). (2004a). Broadcast e-mail from Janet Dench quoting byline of Sonia Verma, "Our dreams are dust': former terror suspects patch up lives in Pakistan still haunted by their arrest in Canada." *The Toronto Star*, February 8, 2004, sent to CCR list members. Web page, http://www.web.net/~ccr/fronteng.htm.

Canadian Council for Refugees (CCR). (2004b). Broadcast e-mail from Janet Dench, quoting byline of Sean Gordon, "Immigrants denied entry based on Security CSIS Report." *The Ottawa Citizen*, February, 9, 2004, sent to CCR list. Web page, http://www.web.net/~ccr/fronteng.htm.

Chang, G. (2000). *Disposable Domestics: immigrant women workers in the global economy.* With a foreword by M. Abramovitz. Cambridge, MA: South End Press.

Couture, C. (1996). *Paddling with the Current: Pierre Trudeau, Etienne Parent, Liberalism and Nationalism in Canada.* Edmonton: University of Alberta Press.

Crane, D., Kawashima, N. & Kawasaki, K. (Eds.). (2002). *Global Culture: media, arts, policy, and globalization. New York/London: Routledge.*

Cronin, C. & De Grieff, P. (Eds.). (2002). *Global Justice and Transnational Politics: essays on the moral and political challenges of globalization.* Cambridge, MA: MIT Press.

Dolby, N. & Burbules, N. C. (2002). Education and September 11: an introduction. Teachers College Record.org. www.tcrecord.org/Content.Asp? Accessed January 1, 2003.

Drache, D. & Froese, M. (2003, September 9). *The Great Global Poverty Debate: balancing private interests and the public good at the WTO.* Report of York University's Robart's Centre for Canadian Studies. Toronto: York University.

Duerksen, R. (2002). The anti-terrorism law and our civil rights. *Peace Center Press* 17(1), 2–3.

Falk, R. (1993). The making of "global citizenship". In J. Brecher, J. Brown Childs & J. Cutler (Eds.). *Global Visions: beyond the new world order* (pp. 39–50). Montreal: Black Rose Books.

Falk, R. (1996). Revisioning cosmopolitanism. In J. Cohen (Ed.). *For love of country: debating the limits of patriotism: Martha C. Nussbaum and respondents* (pp. 53–60). Boston: Beacon Press.

Fisher, D. et al. (2001, May 10). Say 'no' to commercialization, faculty members urge. In *Letters to the Editor of UBC Reports* (p. 2). Vancouver: University of British Columbia, Public Affairs Office.

Fisher, D. & Rubenson, K. (1998). The changing political economy: the private and public lives of Canadian universities. In J. Currie & J. Newson (Eds.). *Universities and Globalization: critical perspectives* (pp. 77–98). Thousand Oaks, California: Sage Publications, Inc.

Foucault, M. (1980). *Power/knowledge: selected interviews and other writings, 1972–1977.* [C. Gorden, Ed.]. New York: Pantheon Books.

Goldberg, M. (2002). Vice President International's Web page. (http://www.vpacademic.ubc.international/). Accessed December 9, 2002. University of British Columbia, Vancouver, British Columbia.

Grewal, I. (2003). Transnational America: race, gender and citizenship after 9/11. *Social Identities* 9(4), 535–561.

Gross Stein, J. (2002). Building global literacy. Unpublished paper given the Global Citizenship Conference, University of British Columbia, Vancouver, British Columbia.

Hage, G. (2000). *White Nation: fantasies of white supremacy in a multicultural society.* New York: Routledge.

Hall, S. (1984). Thatcherism and the theorists. Paper presented at the conference "Marxism and the Reinterpretation of Culture". University of Illinois-Champaign, Urbana.

Hall, S. (1988). The toad in the garden: Thatcherism among the theorists. In C. Nelson & L. Grossberg (Eds.). *Marxism and the Reinterpretation of Culture* (pp. 35–57). Urbana: University of Illinois-Champaign, Urbana.

Hall, S. (1989). *The Hard Road to Renewal.* London: Verso.

Hall, S. (1996). Race: the floating signifier. Audio-video-taped lecture given at Open University.

Hall, S. (2003). New Labour's double shuffle. *Soundings* 24(1), 10–24.

Hardt, M. & Negri,. A. (2000). *Empire.* Cambridge: Harvard University Press.

Hase, M. (2001). Student resistance and nationalism in the classroom: some reflections on globalizing the curriculum. *Feminist Teacher* 13(2), 90–107.

Held, D. (2002). Violence, law, and justice in a Global Age. In C. Calhoun, P. Price & A. Timmer (Eds.). *Understanding September 11* (pp. 92–105). New York: The New Press.

Human Resources Department of Canada. (2002). Canada's Innovation Strategy: skills and learning for Canadians. A two paper series, including "Knowledge matters: skills and learning for Canadians" and "Achieving excellence: investing in people, knowledge, and opportunity," The Government of Canada papers available on the Web, http://www.hrdc.gc.ca/sp-ps/sl-ca/doc/section3_e.shtml. Last updated December 5, 2002. Accessed November 2003.

Kellner, D. (2000). Globalization and new social movements: lessons for critical theory and pedagogy. In N. C. Burbules & C. A. Torres (Eds.). *Globalization and Education: critical perspectives* (pp. 299–322). New York: Routledge.

Kelly, J. D. (2003). U.S. power after 9/11 and before: if not an empire, then, what? *Public Culture* 15(2), 349–368.

Kenway, J. & Kelly, P. (2000). Local/global labour markets and the restructuring of gender, schooling, and work. In N. Stromquist & K. Monkman (Eds.). *Globalisation and Education: integration and contestation across cultures* (pp. 173–197). Lanham, MD: Rowman & Littlefield.

Lowe, L. (2000, Summer). Toward a critical modernity. *Anglistica A.I.O.N.* 4(1), 69–89.

Martin, R. & Shohat, E. (2002). 911—A public emergency? *Social Text* 20(3), 1–8.

Meekosha, H. (2001, May 29). Australian immigration rejects family. Family Disability Research@Jismcmail.ac.uk. Accessed August 2001.

Moodley, K. (1999). Anti-racism education through political literacy: the case of Canada. In S. May (Ed.). *Critical Multiculturalism: rethinking multicultural and anti-racist education.* (pp. 138–152). London: Philadelphia.

Moodley, K. (2003, January 9). Personal Communication. University of British Columbia, Vancouver, British Columbia.

Mohanty, C. T. (2003). *Feminism without Borders: decolonizing theory, practicing solidarity.* North Carolina: Duke University Press.

Morgan, K. (1994). Women and the knife: cosmetic surgery and the colonization of women's bodies. In A. Jaggar (Ed.). *Living with Contradictions: controversies in feminist social ethics* (pp. 239–256). Boulder: Westview Press.

Pratt, G. (1997). Stereotypes and ambivalence: the construction of domestic workers in Vancouver, British Columbia. *Gender, Place and Culture* 4(2), 159–177.

Pratt, G. (1999). From registered nurse to registered nanny: discursive geographies of Filipina domestic workers in Vancouver, B.C. *Economic Geography* 75(3), 215–232.

Rizvi, F. (2003). Democracy and education after September 11. *Journal of Globalization, Societies and Education* 1(1), 25–40.

Rizvi, F. & Lingard, B. (2000). Globalization and education: complexities and contingencies. *Educational Theory* 50(4), 419–426.

Roman, L. G. (1991). The political significance of other ways of narrating ethnography: a feminist materialist approach. In M. LeCompte, W. Millroy & J. Preissle Goetz (Eds.). *The Handbook of Qualitative Research in Education.* (pp. 556–594). San Diego: Academic Press.

Roman, L. G. (1993). Double exposure: the politics of feminist materialist ethnography. *Educational Theory* 43(3), 279–308.

Roman, L. G. (1997). Denying (White) racial privilege: redemption discourses and the uses of fantasy. In M. Fine, L. Weis, M. Won et al. (Eds.). *Off White: readings on race, power and society* (pp. 270–282). New York: Routledge.

Roman, L. G. (2003a, May/June). Conditions, contexts, and controversies of truth-making: Rigoberta Menchú and the perils of everyday witnessing. *International Journal of Qualitative Studies in Education* 16(3), 275–286.

Roman, L. G. (2003b, May/June). Ghostly evidence: official and structural registers of voice, veracity, avarice, and violence in the Rigoberta Menchú controversy. *International Journal of Qualitative Studies in Education* 16(3), 307–362.

Roman, L. G. & Apple, Michael W. (1990). "Is naturalism a move away from positivism? materialist and feminist approaches to subjectivity in ethnographic research. In E. Eisner & A. Peshkin (Eds.). *Qualitative Inquiry in Education* (pp. 38–73). New York: Teachers College Press.

Roman, L. G. and Stanley, T. (1997). Empires, émigrés and aliens: young peoples' understandings of popular and official racism in Canada. In L. G. Roman & L. Eyre (Eds.). *Dangerous Territories: struggles for difference and equality* (pp. 205–231). New York/London: Routledge.

Roman, L.G. & "The Discipline and Place Collective." (2000). An interdisciplinary group of scholars at the University of British Columbia, including Richard Cavell, Gillian Creese, Sneja Gunew, Penny Gurstein, Becki Ross, Geraldine Pratt, Rose Marie San Juan, and Patricia Vertinsky. "The limits of Liberalism: a conversation with Rey Chow, Lisa Lowe and Renata Salecl." *Anglistica* 4(1), 91–118.

Roman, L.G. & Pratt, G. (2000, Summer). Special Issue Editorial Introduction, "The university as/in contested space", for Special Issue, "Transitions: transnational space and universities in transition". *Anglistica* 4(1), 21–24.

Rosenfelt, D. S. (1998). Editorial: Internationalizing the curriculum: integrating Area Studies, Women's Studies, and Ethnic Studies. (Special Issue). *Women's Studies Quarterly* 26(3-4), 4–16.

Rosser, S. V. (1999). International experiences lead to using postcolonial feminism in the life sciences curriculum. *Women's Studies International Forum* 22, 3–15.

Said, E. (1979). *Orientalism.* New York: Vintage Books.

Sassen, S. (2003, August 21). A universal harm: making criminals of migrants. http://www.opendemocracy.net/debates. article-6-96-1444.jsp#. Accessed August 9, 2003.

Seabrook, J. (1985). *Landscapes of Poverty.* Oxford: Blackwell.

Sharma, N. R. (2002, Spring/Summer). Immigrant and migrant workers in Canada: labor movements, racism and the expansion of globalization. *Canadian Woman Studies Special issue on Women and Globalization* 21/22(4/1), 17–25.

Sharma, N.R. (2001). On being not Canadian: the social organization of "migrant workers" in Canada. *The Canadian Review of Sociology and Anthropology,* 38(4), 415-439.

Smith, D. (1990). *The Conceptual Practices of Power: a feminist sociology of knowledge.* Toronto/Buffalo/London: University of Toronto Press.

Smith, D. (1999). *Writing the Social: critique, theory and investigations.* Toronto/Buffalo/London: University of Toronto Press.

Sommers, P. & Sommers-Willett, S. B. (2002). Collateral damage: faculty free speech in America after 9/11. *Teachers College Record.* www.tcrecord.org/content.asp?Accessed January 1, 2003.

Steinmetz, G. (2003). The state of emergency and the revival of American imperialism: toward an authoritarian post-Fordism. *Public Culture* 15(2), 323–345.

Stetz, M. D. (1998). Globalizing the curriculum: rewards and resistance. *Feminist Teacher* 12(1), 1–11.

Taylor, S., Rizvi, F., Lingard, R. & Henry, M. (Eds.). (1997). *Educational Policy and the Politics of Change.* London: Routledge.

The University of British Columbia. (2002). Global Citizenship Conference, http://www.vpacademic.ubc.ca/globalcitizen-conf. Accessed December 9, 2002.

Thompson, J. (2003). Reasoning and justice in global society. *Global Change, Peace and Security* 15(3), 231–244.

Wang, B. (2002). The Cold War, imperial aesthetics, and area studies. *Social Text* 20(3), 45–65.

Weldes, J.M., Gusterson, I. H. & Duvall, R. (Eds.). (1999). *Cultures of Insecurity: states, communities and the production of danger.* (G. Marcus, Foreward). (Borderlines book series, vol. 14). Minneapolis, MN: University of Minnesota Press.

Williams, R. (1961). *The Long Revolution.* London: Chatto & Windus.

Willinsky, J. (2002, September 3). Hope within the limits of education. *Teachers College Record.* Retrieved January 28, 2003. http://www.tcrecord.org/Content.asp?ContentID-11030.

Yuval-Davis, N. (1997). *Gender and Nation.* London: Sage.

Yuval-Davis, N. (2001). The binary war. http://www.opendemocracy.net/forum/.

7
Whiteness and War

GEORGE LIPSITZ

The question of identity is a question involving the most profound panic—a terror as primary as the nightmare of the mortal fall. An identity is questioned only when it is menaced, or when the mighty begin to fall, or when the wretched begin to rise, or when the stranger enters the gates, never thereafter, to be a stranger; the stranger's presence making you the stranger, less to the stranger than to yourself.

—James Baldwin

In 1982, two unemployed white male auto workers in Detroit attacked Chinese American draftsperson Vincent Chin with a baseball bat, smashed his skull, and beat him to death. Although they denied any racist intent, one of the auto workers remarked during the incident, "It's because of you we're out of work"—apparently thinking that Chin was Japanese and therefore responsible for layoffs in the auto industry caused by competition from cars made in Japan. Neither perpetrator ever served a day in prison for the murder.[1] In 1984, a white male high school teacher pushed Ly Yung Cheung, a pregnant nineteen-year-old Chinese American woman, off a New York City subway platform into the path of a moving train that decapitated her. In his successful plea of not guilty by reason of insanity, the teacher claimed that he suffered from "a phobia of Asian people" that led him to murder Cheung.[2] In 1989, a white man wearing combat fatigues fired more than one hundred rounds of ammunition from an AK-47 assault rifle into a crowd of mostly Asian American children at the Cleveland Elementary School in Stockton, California, killing five children and wounding close to thirty others. Four of the children killed were Cambodian refugees—Ram Chun, Sokhim An, Rathanar Or, and Oeun Lim. The fifth was a Vietnamese American, Tran Thanh Thuy. An investigation by state officials found it "highly probable" that the assailant picked that particular school because of his animosity toward "Southeast Asians," whom the gunman described as people who get "benefits" without having to work.[3] In 1992, a group of white males attending a party in Coral Springs, Florida, beat nineteen-year-old Luyen Phan Nguyen to death when he objected to racial slurs directed at him. At least seven of the men ran after Nguyen as he attempted to flee, shouting "Viet Cong" and hunting him down "like a wounded deer" while bystanders refused to intervene and stop the beating.[4]

Although these incidents sprang from different motivations and circumstances, they share a common core—the identification of Asians in America as foreign enemies, unwelcome and unwanted by white Americans. Hate crimes enact the rage of individual sociopaths, but they also look for justification to patterns of behavior and belief that permeate the rest of society in less extreme form. The logic that legitimated the attacks on Vincent Chin, Ly Yung Cheung, the school children in Stockton, and Luyen Phan Nguyen stemmed from longstanding patterns and practices in the United States. As Lisa Lowe, Yen Le Espiritu, and Gary Okihiro among others have demonstrated repeatedly in their sophisticated research, for more than a century and a half Asian immigrants have met the need for cheap labor by U.S. businesses without receiving recognition as vital contributors to the national economy. Diplomats and corporate officers have obtained access to vital markets and raw materials by integrating Asia into the North American economy, yet through law, labor segmentation, and "scientific" racism, Asians in America have been seen as forever foreign and outside the rewards of white identity.[5]

U.S. wars in Asia over the past five decades have also contributed significantly to this view of Asian Americans and Asians as foreign enemies incapable of being assimilated into a U.S. national identity. Military action against Japan in World War II led to the internment of more than 100,000 Japanese Americans and to the forced sale and seizure of their property. No other group of immigrants and their descendants have been identified with their country of origin in this way, not even German Americans during World War I. The national groups from countries allied with the United States at different moments in these wars—Chinese, Koreans, Filipinos, Japanese, Vietnamese, and Cambodians—have often found themselves identified as undifferentiated "Asians" in the United States and vilified for the actions of governments and nations that they have also opposed. Armed conflicts against Asian enemies in the Philippines, Korea, China, Vietnam, Laos, and Cambodia functioned geopolitically to decide control over markets and raw materials after the demise of European imperialism, to contain China and the Soviet Union, and to determine access to the rim economies of Southeast and Northeast Asia. Yet they functioned culturally to solidify and reinforce a unified U.S. national identity based in part on antagonism toward Asia and Asians.

During the 1980s, Asians accounted for nearly half of all legal immigrants to the United States. More than a million Southeast Asians entered the country as refugees after the war in Vietnam, and between 1970 and 1990 more than 855,000 Filipinos, 600,000 Koreans, and 575,000 Chinese immigrated to the United States. During the same era, the rise of Japanese businesses as competitors with U.S. firms, the painful legacy of the U.S. war in Vietnam, the stagnation of real wages, and increasing class polarization combined to engender intense hostility toward Asia and Asian Americans. As Yen Le Espiritu explains, hostility toward Asian competitors overseas and Asian American immigrants at home functions as components in an interlocking system. "In a time of rising economic powers in Asia, declining economic opportunities in the United States, and growing diversity among America's people," Espiritu observes, "this new Yellow Perilism—the depiction of Asia and Asian Americans as economic and cultural threats to mainstream United States—supplies white Americans with a united identity and provides ideological justification for U.S. isolationist policy toward Asia, increasing restrictions against Asian (and Latino) immigration, and the invisible institutional racism and visible violence against Asians in the United States."[6]

Anti-Asian sentiment in the United States depends upon its necessary correlative—the assumption that true cultural franchise and full citizenship requires a white identity. This violence against Asian Americans stems from the kinds of whiteness created within U.S. culture and mobilized in the nation's political, economic, and social life. The "white" identity conditioned to fear the Asian "menace" owes its origins to the history of anti-Indian, antiblack, and anti-Mexican racism at home as well as to anti-Arab and anti-Latino racisms shaped by military struggles overseas and by condescending cultural stereotypes at home. White racism is a pathology looking for a place to land, sadism in search of a story.

Reginald Horsman's study of nineteenth-century racism and Manifest Destiny explains how presumptions about racial purity and fears of contamination encouraged white Americans who envisioned themselves as Anglo-Saxons to fabricate proof of the inferiority of other groups. Horsman shows how racialized hierarchies on the home front served as impetus for imperial expansion abroad, with the rationalizations originally developed to justify conquest of Native Americans eventually applied to Mexicans and Filipinos. Yet the categories created for racist purposes displayed great instability—at one time or another, depending on immediate interests and goals, Native Americans, blacks, Mexicans, and Asians might be either elevated above the others or labeled the most deficient group of all. Similarly, David Roediger's research shows how the derogatory term "gook" originated among U.S. forces to deride the Nicaraguans fighting with Cesar Augusto Sandino during the U.S. occupation of that nation in the 1920s before it was applied as a racial slur against Koreans, Vietnamese, and even Iraqis in subsequent conflicts.[7]

Yet whiteness never works in isolation; it functions as part of a broader dynamic grid created through intersections of race, gender, class, and sexuality. The way these identities work in concert gives them their true social meaning. The renewal of patriotic rhetoric and display in the United States during and after the Reagan presidency serves as the quintessential example of this intersecting operation. Reagan succeeded in fusing the possessive investment in whiteness with other psychic and material investments—especially in masculinity, patriarchy, and heterosexuality. The intersecting identity he offered gave new meanings to white male patriarchal and heterosexual identities by establishing patriotism as the site where class antagonisms between men could be reconciled in national and patriotic antagonisms against foreign foes and internal enemies. By encoding the possessive investment in whiteness within national narratives of male heroism and patriarchal protection, Reagan and his allies mobilized a crossclass coalition around the premise that the declines in life chances and opportunities in the United States, the stagnation of real wages, the decline of basic services and infrastructure resources, and the increasing social disintegration stemmed not from the policies of big corporations and their neoliberal and neoconservative allies in government, but from the harm done to the nation by the civil rights, antiwar, feminist, and gay liberation movements of the 1960s and 1970s. By representing the national crisis as a crisis of the declining value of white male and heterosexual identity, Reagan and his allies and successors built a countersubversive coalition mobilized around protecting the privileges and prerogatives of the possessive investments in whiteness, in masculinity, in patriarchy, and in heterosexuality.

The murders of Vincent Chin, Ly Yung Cheung, the Southeast Asian school children in Stockton, and Luyen Phan Nguyen become understandable as more than the private and personal crimes of individual criminals when placed in these two contexts: widely shared social beliefs, practices, and images that render Asians as foreign enemies, and the decline of life chances and opportunities in the United States viewed as the result of the defeat in Vietnam and the democratic movements for social change that helped end that war.

The key to the conservative revival that has guided leaders of business and government since the 1970s has been the creation of a countersubversive consensus mobilized around the alleged wounds suffered by straight white men. At the heart of this effort lies an unsolvable contradiction between the economic goals of neoconservatives and neoliberals and the cultural stories they have to tell to win mass support. The advocates of surrendering national sovereignty and self-determination to transnational corporations rely on cultural stories of wounded national pride, of unfair competition from abroad, of subversion from within by feminists and aggrieved racial minorities, of social disintegration attributed not to systematic disinvestment in the United States but to the behavior of immigrants and welfare recipients. Thus we find ourselves saturated with stories extolling American national glory told by internationalists who seek to export jobs and capital overseas while dismantling the institutions offering opportunity and upward mobility to ordinary citizens in the United States.

The seeming paradox of reconfirmed nationalism during the 1991 Gulf War and the globalization of world politics, economics, and culture that emerged in its wake represents two sides of the same coin. For more than twenty years, reassertions of nationalism in the United States have taken place in the context of an ever increasing internationalization of commerce, communication, and culture. Furthermore, some of the most ardent advocates of public patriotism and militant nationalism have been active agents in the internationalization of the economy. Wedded to policies that have weakened the nation's economic and social infrastructures in order to assist multinational corporations with their global ambitions, political and economic leaders have fashioned cultural narratives of nationalism and patriotic excess to obscure and legitimize the drastic changes in national identity engendered by their economic and political decisions. In times of crisis, the illusion that all contradictions and differences would be solved if we would only agree to one kind of culture, one kind of education, one kind of patriotism, one kind of sexuality, and one kind of family can be comforting.

Exploring the dynamics of nationalistic rhetoric and patriotic display during an era of economic and political internationalization can help us understand the role of whiteness as a defining symbolic identity that mobilizes gender and sexual elements in the service of obscuring class polarization. Close study of the patriotic revival of the post-Vietnam era, especially, reveals organic links between discussions of white male identity and the U.S. defeat in the Vietnam War, deindustrialization, changes in gender roles, and the rising emphasis on acquisition, consumption, and display that has characterized the increasingly inegalitarian economy of the postindustrial era. Perhaps most important, analysis of the connections among these events and practices will enable us to see how the whiteness called forth by dominant narratives of "American patriotism" has functioned paradoxically to extend the power of transnational corporations beyond the control of any one nation's politics.

The New Patriotism

In his brilliant analysis of the 1915 D. W. Griffith film *The Birth of a Nation*, Michael Rogin demonstrates the persuasive power of scenarios depicting "the family in jeopardy" for the construction of nationalistic myths. By representing slave emancipation and the radical reforms of the Reconstruction era as threats to the integrity and purity of the white family, Griffith's film fashioned a new narrative of national unity and obligation based on connections between patriotism and patriarchy—between white patriarchal protection of the purity of the white family and the necessity for whites to forget the things that divide them in order to unite against their nonwhite enemies.[8]

The kind of patriotism articulated by neoconservative politics in the United States since the 1970s has successfully updated the formula advanced by Griffith in 1915. It is perhaps best exemplified during ceremonies in 1984 commemorating the fortieth anniversary of the World War II Normandy invasion, when President Ronald Reagan read a letter written to him by the daughter of a veteran who had participated in the 1944 battle. The imagery created by Reagan and his media strategists for this ceremony encapsulates the conflation of whiteness, masculinity, patriarchy, and heterosexuality immanent in the patriotic renewal that revolved around the Reagan presidency. A serious illness had made it impossible for the veteran to attend the anniversary ceremonies himself, but his daughter had promised that she would travel to Normandy in his place and attend the commemoration, visit monuments, and place flowers on the graves of his friends who had been killed in combat. "I'll never forget," she promised him. "Dad, I'll always be proud."

Her father died shortly before the anniversary, but she kept her word and sat in the audience at Omaha Beach as Reagan read her letter to a crowd of veterans and their families. In an image broadcast on network newscasts (and featured repeatedly in an advertisement for the president's reelection campaign that year), tears filled her eyes as the president read her words, his voice quivering with emotion. Media analyst Kathleen Hall Jamieson identifies the imagery encapsulated in that scene as emblematic of the key themes of the Reagan presidency. In one short, sentimental, and cinematic moment, the president depicted military service as a matter of personal pride and private obligation.[9] The drama of a father's military service and a daughter's admiring gratitude reconciled genders and generations (even beyond the grave) through a narrative of patriarchal protection and filial obligation. It offered a kind of immortality to the family by connecting it to the ceremonies of the nation state, and it served the state by locating and legitimating its demands for service and sacrifice within the private realm of family affections. Reagan's rhetoric eclipses the political purposes ostensibly served by the Normandy invasion—defeating fascism, defending democracy, and furthering freedom of speech, freedom of worship, freedom from fear, and freedom from hunger—in his enthusiasm for a story celebrating personal feelings and family ties.

World War II served as a suitable vehicle for patriotic revival in the post-Vietnam era because of the contrasts between the two wars. The United States and its allies secured a clear victory over the Axis powers in the Second World War, the postwar era brought unprecedented prosperity, and the unity forged in the face of wartime emergencies did much to define the nationalism and patriotism of the Cold War era. Yet the deployment of memories about World War II as a "good war" also rested on nostalgia for a preintegration America, when segregation in the military meant that most war heroes were white and de jure and de facto segregation on the home front channeled the fruits and benefits of victory disproportionately to white citizens.

Reagan's rhetoric had enormous appeal in the eighties—at least in part because it connected nostalgia for the whiteness of the pre–civil rights era with the affective power of nationalist narratives rooted in private family obligations and the responsibilities of paternal protection. From the popularity during the Korean War of Lefty Frizell's song "Mom and Dad's Waltz" with its improbable rhyme, "I'd do the chores and fight in wars for my momma and papa," to the government distribution of pin-up photos of blonde and snow-white Betty Grable as a symbol of white womanhood and companionate marriage to soldiers during World War II, to Senator Albert Beveridge's description of U.S. annexation of the Philippines in the 1890s as an "opportunity for all the glorious young manhood of the republic—the most virile, ambitious, impatient, militant manhood the world has ever seen," patriotism has often been constructed in the United States as a matter of a gendered and racialized obligation to paternal protection of the white family.[10]

As Robert Westbrook points out, appeals to private interests as motivations for public obligations in the United States stem from a fundamental contradiction within democratic liberalism as it has emerged in Western capitalist societies. Drawing upon the scholarship of liberal political theorist Michael Walzer, Westbrook explains that liberal states must present themselves as the defenders of private lives, liberty, and happiness. But precisely because they are set up to safeguard the individual, these states have no legitimate way to ask citizens to sacrifice themselves for the government. Lacking the ability to simply command allegiance as absolutist states do, and unable to draw on the desire to defend an active public sphere that might emerge within a broad-based participatory democracy, in Westbrook's view liberal capitalist states must cultivate and appropriate private loyalties and attachments if they are to mobilize their citizens for war.[11]

Westbrook's analysis helps us understand some of the deep-seated emotional appeal of Ronald Reagan's remarks at the Normandy commemoration as well as the political capital they built. Like so much recent scholarly work, it helps us see the connection between the nation and what has come to be called the "imagi-nation."[12] Westbrook captures one aspect of the relationship between citizens and the liberal state quite cogently and convincingly by showing how the state borrows legitimacy and commands obligation by insinuating itself into family and gender roles. But the state also creates those very family and gender roles in a myriad of ways: the state licenses marriages and legislates permissible sexual practices, regulates labor, commerce, and communication, and allocates welfare benefits, housing subsidies, and tax deductions to favor some forms of family life over others. Just as the state uses gender roles and family obligations to compel behavior that serves its interests, powerful private interests also use the state to create, define, and defend gender roles and family forms consistent with their own goals.

In his speech at Omaha Beach, Ronald Reagan not only used the family to serve a certain definition of the state, but he also put the power of the state behind specific definitions of acceptable gender and family roles, with enormous ramifications for the distribution of power, wealth, and life chances among citizens. While clearly colonizing private hopes and fears in the service of the state, Reagan's framing of the Normandy observance also mobilized the affective power of the state to address anxieties in the 1980s about private life, gender roles, jobs, community, and consumption patterns during the president's first term in office.

Reagan's celebration of a daughter's fulfillment of her father's last wish relied on clearly defined gender roles, situating women as dutiful, grateful, and proud. By taking her father's place at the ceremony, the letter writer wins the approval of the president, whose tears and quivering voice add a layer of paternal approval for her actions. The ceremony affirmed the continuity of white male heroism, female spectatorship, and national glory as the answer to anxieties about change, death, and decay. In the context of national politics in 1984, the Normandy observance celebrated gender roles and family forms consistent with Reagan's policies as president. It addressed anxieties about combat raised by Reagan's acceleration of the Cold War and by the deaths of U.S. service personnel in Lebanon and Grenada. It projected a sense of national purpose and continuity in an age of community disintegration engendered by deindustrialization, economic restructuring, and the evisceration of the welfare state. It offered spectacle without sacrifice, a chance for audiences to recommit themselves to the nation without moving beyond personal emotions and private concerns. By fashioning a public spectacle out of private grief, it combined the excitement of action with the security of spectatorship. In a country increasingly committed to consumption and sensual gratification, it presented the nation state as a source of spectacle, producing the most elaborate shows of all. As J. A. Hobson noted a century ago, "Jingoism is merely the lust of the spectator."[13]

Ronald Reagan's success in establishing himself as both president of the United States and as what some critics have jokingly called "the most popular television character of all time" depended in no small measure upon this ability to project reverent patriotism and confident nationalism. In 1980, the last year of the Carter presidency, two media events framed the nation's problems in distinctly racialized forms. Extensive media coverage made the Iranian hostage crisis a symbol of the military and diplomatic weaknesses of the United States (perhaps along with backdoor deals between the Reagan campaign staff and Iranian officials eager to procure the weapons that Reagan eventually did send secretly to that nation). The Iranians released all of their nonwhite captives, a move possibly aimed at building support in nonwhite communities but one that guaranteed the national crisis would be viewed as a crisis for whites. In the same year, the victory of the U.S. hockey team over the Soviet Union in the Olympics received unprecedented publicity as a Cold War triumph, especially since it came in a sport long dominated by the U.S.S.R. and Canada, and because it took place after the Soviet invasion of Afghanistan. Furthermore, although many previous U.S. athletic teams had defeated teams from the Soviet Union, the victory in hockey was achieved by a team composed entirely of white males.

Elected to the presidency in the wake of the Iranian hostage crisis and the U.S. hockey team's victory, Reagan cultivated support for his policies and programs by making himself synonymous with beloved national symbols. Making especially skilled use of mass spectacles like the ceremonies marking the Normandy invasion, the opening of the 1984 Olympics, and the centennial of the Statue of Liberty in 1986, the president guided his constituency into a passionate appreciation for displays of national power and pride. Yet for all of Reagan's skills as a performer and politician, he was more the interpreter than the author of the "new patriotism." Revived nationalistic fervor and public displays of patriotic symbols predated and followed his presidency. Popular support for the Gulf War and for the invasion of Panama, the tumultuous parades for soldiers returning home from Operation Desert Storm (and retroactively veterans of Vietnam and Korea), and the outpouring of films, television programs, and popular songs with nationalistic, militaristic, and heroic themes signal a broad base of support for nationalistic public patriotic celebration and display.

During the 1988 presidential election, for example, George Bush successfully depicted Michael Dukakis as an enemy of the Pledge of Allegiance because the Massachusetts governor supported a court decision exempting Jehovah's Witnesses and other religious objectors from school ceremonies saluting the flag. Dukakis responded, not by delineating the civil libertarian basis for his stance, but by circulating film footage of himself riding in an army tank. In 1992, Bush deflected attention away from his own performance in office with a stream of accusations and insinuations about William Clinton's absence from military service during the Vietnam conflict. For his part, Clinton identified himself with the Cold War rhetoric and actions of President Kennedy, and he selected Vietnam veteran Al Gore as his running mate, perhaps to contrast with Bush's vice-president, Dan Quayle, whose service in the Indiana National Guard had enabled him to avoid service in Vietnam. At the same time, third-party candidate Ross Perot called attention to his own education at the U.S. Naval Academy and to his efforts on behalf of U.S. prisoners of war held in Vietnam through his selection of a navy officer and former prisoner of war, Admiral James Stockdale, as his running mate.

Yet for all of its apparent intensity and fervor, the "new patriotism" often seemed strangely defensive, embattled, and insecure. Even after the collapse of the Soviet Union and the end of the Cold War, a desperate quality permeated the discourse and display of loyalty to the nation's symbols. Only in the rarest of cases did the new patriotism address aspects of national identity that might truly command the love, loyalty, and lives of citizens—the expressive freedoms of speech, press, assembly, and worship guaranteed by the Bill of Rights; the rule of law and the system of checks and balances; and the history of rectifying past injustices as exemplified in the abolitionist and civil rights movements. To the contrary, the covert activities carried on by Oliver North in the Reagan White House, press self-censorship about U.S. military actions in Grenada, Panama, and the Persian Gulf, and popular support for a constitutional amendment to prohibit flag burning, all indicate that (to borrow a phrase from singer and activist Michelle Shocked) many Americans are more upset by people like flag burners who would "wrap themselves in the Constitution to trash the flag" than by those like Oliver North who would "wrap themselves in the flag in order to trash the Constitution." Samuel Johnson called patriotism the "last refuge of a scoundrel," but scoundrels evidently had more patience in his day; in recent years refuge in patriotism has been the first resort of scoundrels of all sorts.

In place of a love for the historical rights and responsibilities of the nation, instead of creating community through inclusive and democratic measures, the new patriotism has emphasized public spectacles of power and private celebrations of success. It does not treat war as a regrettable last resort, but as an important, frequent, and seemingly casual instrument of policy that offers opportunities to display national purpose and resolve. In several instances, spectacle has seemed to serve as an end in itself, out of all proportion to the events it purports to commemorate. For example, after the thirty-six-hour war in Grenada in 1983, six thousand elite U.S. troops were awarded 8,700 combat medals for defeating the local police and a Cuban army construction crew. President

Reagan announced that "our days of weakness are over. Our military forces are back on their feet and standing tall."[14]

When a group of antiwar Vietnam veterans picketed an appearance by actor Sylvester Stallone in Boston in 1985 because they thought his film *Rambo, First Blood: Part II* simplified issues and exploited the war for profit, a group of teenagers waiting to get Stallone's autograph jeered the veterans and pelted them with stones, screaming that Stallone was the "real veteran."[15] Stallone actually spent the Vietnam War as a security guard in a girl's school in Switzerland, but, like Pat Buchanan, Newt Gingrich, Dick Cheney, Phil Gramm, Clarence Thomas, and Rush Limbaugh—all of whom conveniently avoided military service in Vietnam themselves—Stallone established credentials as a "patriot" in the 1980s by retroactively embracing the Vietnam War and ridiculing those who had opposed it.

In contrast to previous periods of patriotic enthusiasm like World War II, when Americans justified military action by stressing citizen action in defense of common interests through their participation in armed forces firmly under civilian control, the patriotism of the last twenty-five years has often focused on the actions of small groups of elite warriors. In popular paramilitary magazines like *Soldier of Fortune*, in motion pictures ranging from *Red Dawn* to *Rambo* to *Missing in Action*, and in covert operations directed from the White House by Oliver North and John Poindexter during the Reagan administration, elite warriors defying legal and political constraints to wage their own personal and political battles have presented themselves as the true patriots.[16]

These men also offer hope for healing the nation's racial wounds. In Hollywood films, precombat racial rivalries disappear when the ordeal by fire builds communion among soldiers from different backgrounds. Rambo's character combines German and Native American ancestry in an identity that allows audiences to root for cowboys and Indians at the same time. Outside of motion pictures, life follows art as Republicans and conservative Democrats revere a man they know little about, General Colin Powell, because his combination of African American identity and military distinction promises a form of cultural unity at no real cost to whites.

Proponents of the new patriotism often cite their efforts as attempts to address the unresolved legacy of the Vietnam War. In their view, antiwar protest during that conflict undermined the welfare of U.S. troops in the field, contributed to the U.S. defeat, and ushered in an era of military and political weakness in the 1970s. Moreover, they claim that Vietnam-era opposition to the war, the military, and the government in general triggered a series of cultural changes with devastating consequences for U.S. society. As William Adams notes, "[I]n the iconography of Reaganism, Vietnam was the protean symbol of all that had gone wrong in American life. Much more than an isolated event or disaster of foreign policy, the war was, and still remains, the great metaphor in the neoconservative lexicon for the 1960s, and thus for the rebellion, disorder, anti-Americanism, and flabbiness that era loosed among us."[17]

Thus, the new patriotism not only seeks to address the issues of war and peace, unity and division, loyalty and dissent left over from Vietnam, but also contains a broader cultural project. While purporting to put Vietnam behind us, it actually tries to go back to Vietnam, to fight the war all over again, this time not only to win the war, but to undo the cultural changes it is thought to have generated. The new patriotism must redemonize the Vietnamese enemy, as in *The Deer Hunter*, and invert the power realities of the war by depicting Americans like Rambo as underequipped, feisty guerrilla fighters battling superior numbers and equipment. Just as former National Endowment for the Humanities director Lynne Cheney called for the replacement of social science textbooks stressing "vacuous concepts" like "the interdependence among people" with textbooks filled with "the magic of myths, fables, and tales of heroes," the rosy new patriotic spectacles ignore the complex causes and consequences of U.S. involvement in Vietnam and celebrate the redeeming virtues of violent acts and heroic stories.[18]

These attempts to put Vietnam behind us began as early as 1976, less than a year after the communist victory in Southeast Asia, when President Ford sent an armed force to rescue thirty-eight U.S. merchant sailors aboard the cargo ship *Mayaguez*. The ship and crew had been seized by the Cambodian navy in the confusion of the Khmer Rouge's ascendance to power in that country. Forty-one U.S. Marines died (and forty-nine were wounded) in an effort to free thirty-eight Americans who had already been let go—the Cambodian government had released the *Mayaguez* crew before the U.S. attack began. Yet Senator Barry Goldwater, among many others, hailed the raid as a boost to America's self-image. "It was wonderful," according to the senator. "It shows we've still got balls in this country."[19]

Ronald Reagan boasted that the invasion of Grenada in 1983 and the bombing of Libya in 1985 proved that the United States "was back and standing tall," while George Bush contended that the U.S. invasion of Panama demonstrated the same point. In the mid to late 1980s, many cities including Chicago and New York held massive parades honoring Vietnam veterans—a decade after the conclusion of that war. On the eve of the Gulf War, Bush contrasted the forth-coming campaign with the Vietnam War where, he claimed, U.S. forces fought with "one hand tied behind their backs"; at the war's conclusion he proudly announced that "we've licked the Vietnam syndrome."[20]

When massive public parades welcomed home the veterans of Operation Desert Storm from the Persian Gulf, new patriots lost no opportunity to draw parallels to previous wars. In an opinion piece in the *Los Angeles Times*, a Vietnam-era veteran confessed his jealousy of the Desert Storm vets and their rousing homecoming receptions. Korean War veterans from New York staged a parade on their own behalf two months after the end of the Persian Gulf War, contrasting the immediate gratitude shown to Desert Storm veterans with their own perceived neglect. "My personal feeling was, God, they got it fast," said the executive director of the New York Korean Veterans Memorial Commission, adding, "Some guy came over to me and said is that the memorial for Desert Storm? I said, 'Do me a favor, walk the other way. We've waited 40 years. Desert Storm can wait a couple of months.'"[21]

Yet, no matter how many times they have been declared dead, the memories of Vietnam—and their impact on U.S. society—have not gone away, and that is as it should be. The deaths of more than fifty thousand Americans and more than two million Vietnamese, Laotians, and Cambodians demand our attention, grief, and sorrow. In a guerrilla war with no fixed fronts, savage punishing warfare took the lives of soldiers and civilians alike. U.S. forces detonated more explosives over Southeast Asia during those years than had been exploded by all nations in the entire previous history of aerial warfare. The devastation wrought by bombs, toxic poisons, napalm, fragmentation grenades, and bullets continues in succeeding generations in all nations affected by the conflict. Small wonder then that an overwhelming majority of respondents to public opinion polls for more than twenty years have continued to affirm that they view U.S. participation in the war to have been not just a tactical error but fundamentally wrong.[22]

The realities of mass destruction and death in Vietnam are not the realities addressed by the new patriotism. There has been no serious confrontation with the real reasons for the U.S. defeat in Vietnam—the unpopularity and corruption of the South Vietnamese government; the claim on Vietnamese nationalism staked by the communists through their years of resistance against the French, the Japanese, and the United States; the pervasive support for the other side among the Vietnamese people that turned the conflict into an antipersonnel war; and our own government's systematic misrepresentation of the true nature of the conflict to the American people.[23] All the subsequent celebrations of militarism, nationalism, and obedience to the state have not salved the still-open wounds of Vietnam.

Perhaps this is not a failure; perhaps evocations of Vietnam have been designed less to address that conflict and its legacy than to encourage Americans to view *all* subsequent problems in U.S.

society exclusively through the lens of the Vietnam War. This strategy not only prevents us from learning the lessons of Vietnam, but even more seriously, it prevents us from coming to grips with quite real current crises—the consequences of deindustrialization and economic restructuring, the demise of whole communities and their institutions, and the social and moral bankruptcy of a market economy that promotes materialism, greed, and selfishness,—that makes every effort to assure the freedom and mobility of capital while relegating human beings to ever more limited life chances and opportunities.

Evocations of powerlessness, humiliation, and social disintegration that the new patriotism ascribes to the Vietnam War perfectly describe what has been happening to U.S. society ever since. They transmit anxieties about social decay through metaphors about threats to the bodies of heterosexual white males, who appear as put-upon victims, and present an economic and social crisis as an unnatural disruption of racial and gender expectations. Since 1973, a combination of deindustrialization, economic restructuring, neoconservative politics, austerity economics, and the transformation of a market *economy* into a privatized market *society* (in which every personal relation is permeated by commodity relations) has revolutionized U.S. society. Stagnation of real wages, automation-generated unemployment, the evisceration of the welfare state, threats to intergenerational upward mobility, privatization of public resources, and polarization by class, race, and gender have altered the nature of individual and collective life in this country. At the same time, the aggrandizement of property rights over human rights has promoted greed, materialism, and narcissism focused on consumer goods, personal pleasure, and immediate gratification.

These changes have created a society in which people cannot participate in the decisions that most affect their lives. Our society no longer offers enough jobs at respectable wages; it discourages work while encouraging speculation, gambling, and profiteering. Entertainment spectacles nurture voyeurism, sadism, and sensationalism while stoking envy, avarice, and resentment. Advertising messages invade and exploit—in a word, colonize—the most intimate areas of desire and imagination for profit, while the power of concentrated wealth pits communities against each other in a competition for declining resources and services. As capital becomes more and more mobile—rapidly circling the globe in search of profitable returns on investments—people become less and less mobile and less and less able to control the ordinary dimensions of their own lives.

In such a society, patriotic spectacles serve an important function: the imagined power and majesty of the nation state compensate for the loss of individual and collective power. As we control our own lives less and less, we look increasingly to images outside ourselves for signs of the power and worth that we have lost. Patriotism and patriarchy both ease the anxieties of powerlessness, humiliation, and social disintegration, offering us identification with the power of the state and larger-than-life heroes, or at least authority figures.

The new patriotism projects back onto the Vietnam War the alienations and indignities generated in the present by our postindustrial market society. We can best understand the social and cultural work performed by the new patriotism only when we understand how the death of industrial America and its replacement by an expanded privatized market society has destabilized individual and collective identity, engendering feelings of displacement and powerlessness that leave people hungry for symbolic representations of the power and purpose they have lost in their everyday lives.

Systematic disinvestment in U.S. cities and manufacturing establishments has forced millions of people to suffer declines in earning and purchasing power, to lose control over the nature, purpose, and pace of their work, wreaking havoc in their lives as citizens and family members. Plant shutdowns have disrupted once stable communities, truncated intergenerational upward mobility, and made speculation, gambling, and fraud more valuable than work. Investments in plant and equipment by U.S. corporations declined from an average of 4 percent of the gross national product between 1966 and 1970 to 3.1 percent from 1971 to 1975, and 2.9 percent from 1976 to 1980.

Unemployment averaged over 7 percent in the United States between 1975 and 1979, a rise from 5.4 percent between 1970 and 1974, and only 3.8 percent from 1965 to 1969. Real median family income, which doubled between 1947 and 1973, fell 6 percent between 1973 and 1980.[24] Despite massive spending on armaments and radical reductions in the tax obligations of corporations and wealthy individuals, capital continues its exodus to more profitable sites of exploitation in other parts of the globe. Thirty-eight million people in the United States lost their jobs in the 1970s as a result of computer-generated automation, plant shutdowns, and cutbacks in municipal and state spending.[25]

At the same time, the emerging postindustrial economy generated sales and service jobs with much lower wages, benefits, and opportunities for advancement than the jobs they replaced. Between 1979 and 1984 more than one-fifth of the newly created full-time jobs paid less than $7,000 per year (in 1984 dollars). For the entire decade, the lowest paying industries accounted for nearly 85 percent of new jobs. By 1987, 40 percent of the work force had no pension plans, and 20 percent had no health insurance. Between 1979 and 1986 the real income of the wealthiest 1 percent of the population increased by 20 percent, while the real income of the poorest 40 percent of the population fell by more than 10 percent. Real discretionary income for the average worker by the early 1980s had fallen 18 percent since 1973. At the same time, housing costs doubled, and the costs of basic necessities increased by 100 percent.[26] Changes in tax codes in the 1980s further penalized working people by making them pay more in the form of payroll taxes, while making investment and property income more valuable than wage income.[27]

By presenting national division during the Vietnam War as the root cause of the diminished sense of self and community experienced by many Americans during the past twenty years, the new patriotism deflects attention and anger away from capital, away from the disastrous consequences of neoconservative economics and politics. But it also makes a decidedly class-based appeal to resentments rooted in the ways that the working class unfairly shouldered the burdens of the war in Vietnam and has unfairly shouldered the burdens of deindustrialization and economic restructuring since. It also makes a decidedly race-based appeal by presenting the white U.S. combatant as the only true victim of the conflict, representing antiwar protesters as women or effete men who chose the well-being of Asian "others" over the survival needs of white American men.

The ground war in Vietnam was a working-class war, but not a white war. Out of a potential pool of 27 million people eligible to serve in the military, only 2.5 million went to Vietnam, according to a recent study by Christian Appy. Eighty percent of those who served came from poor or working-class backgrounds. As one veteran complained, "Where were the sons of all the big shots who supported the war? Not in my platoon. Our guys' people were workers.... If the war was so important, why didn't our leaders put everyone's son in there, why only us?"[28] The sons of the important people backing the war, like the sons of most of the important and unimportant people actively opposing it, did not serve in combat because of their class privileges. When protest demonstrations at home and insubordination, desertions, and low morale at the front made it politically dangerous to continue the war, President Nixon and other leaders chose to buy time for a decent interval, allowing them to withdraw gracefully by trying to turn resentment against the war into resentment against antiwar demonstrators. Richard Nixon realized that the public could be persuaded to hate antiwar demonstrators, especially college students, even more than they hated the war. Military leaders picked up on Nixon's cue, telling soldiers that antiwar demonstrators hated them, blamed them for the war, and actively aided and abetted the enemy. Of course, much of the antiwar movement made it easy for their enemies by all too often displaying elitist and anti-working-class attitudes and by failing to make meaningful alliances with the working-class public, which opposed the war (according to public opinion polls) in even greater numbers than did college students.[29]

The new patriots are certainly correct when they charge that the American people have neglected the needs of returning Vietnam veterans, but they reveal more about their own agendas than about neglect of veterans when they cite the absence of homecoming parades as proof of this maltreatment. The miserable state of Veterans Administrations hospitals, the scarcity of education and job-training opportunities for veterans, and corporate/government refusals to acknowledge or address the consequences to veterans of defoliants like Agent Orange have all demonstrated far more neglect of Vietnam-era veterans than has the absence of parades. Ironically the dishonorable treatment afforded Vietnam veterans has come in no small measure as a direct consequence of the neoconservative attack on the welfare state, which provided extensive social services for previous generations of veterans. Thus, by directing veteran resentment toward antiwar protesters, neoconservatives hide from the consequences of their own policies, from what they have done to social welfare programs, to the social wage in the United States, and to the ability of government to respond to the needs of its citizens.

In addition, the neoconservative new patriots have been extremely selective about which veterans should be given attention. When antiwar veterans attempted to tell their story at the 1971 Winter Soldier hearings, or when they flung their medals onto the steps outside the halls of Congress to protest the continuation of the war that same year, almost none of the individuals and groups angry about the lack of parades did anything about the veterans' concerns. The dangers faced and overcome in Vietnam by Chicano, black, Native American, and Asian American soldiers have not persuaded Anglo Americans to root out racism from the body politic and recognize the ways in which "American" unity is threatened by the differential distribution of power, wealth, and life chances across racial lines. Most important, by ignoring the ways in which social class determined who went to Vietnam, the new patriots evade the degree to which the veterans' station in life has been diminished because they were workers and members of minority groups.

The mostly working-class veterans of the Vietnam War returned to a country in the throes of deindustrialization. They participated in the wave of wildcat strikes resisting speed-up and automation in U.S. factories during the 1960s and 1970s. They played prominent roles in the United Mine Workers strikes and demonstrations protesting black lung and in the Amalgamated Clothing Workers campaigns against brown lung and other industrially caused health hazards. They have been visible among the ranks of the unemployed and the homeless. But their status as workers victimized by neoconservative politics and economics in the 1970s and 1980s is far less useful to the interests of the new patriots than their role as marchers in parades and as symbols of unrewarded male heroism.

The official story disseminated by new patriots and the news media about Vietnam veterans has obscured the connection between deindustrialization and the national welfare since the seventies, but many representations of Vietnam veterans in popular culture have brought it to the surface. Billy Joel's 1982 popular song "Allentown" and Bruce Springsteen's 1984 hit "Born in the USA" both connect the factory shutdowns of the post-1973 period to the unresolved anger of Vietnam veterans at broken promises and frustrated hopes. Joel's "Goodnight Saigon" has become the basis for the climactic moment at his live concert performances; audience members wave lighted matches and cigarette lighters as they sing the song's anthemlike verse, "We said we would all go down together." Similarly, Bobbie Ann Mason's novel *In Country* presents a Kentucky town filled with fast-food restaurants and advertising images, but no meaningful jobs for its disillusioned Vietnam veterans.[30] Unfortunately, even these progressive representations focus solely on U.S. veterans, obscuring the people of Southeast Asia and the war's dire consequences for them. They seem to presume that the psychic damage done to some Americans by the experience of defeat in Southeast Asia outweighs the nightmare visited on Vietnam, Cambodia, and Laos by the war itself. Yet, despite their callousness toward Asian victims of the Vietnam War, these representations call attention to an important unspoken dimension of the war—its class character.

Hollywood films about the Vietnam War have repeatedly drawn on its class character for dramatic tension and narrative coherence. In contrast to films about previous wars, where the experience of combat often leveled social distinctions and built powerful alliances among dissimilar soldiers, Vietnam War films seethe with what one critic called "a steady drone of class resentment." Perhaps expressions of class resentment only "drone" for those who feel they are being resented. For working-class audiences in the 1970s and 1980s, no less than for working-class soldiers in the 1960s and 1970s, expressions of class anger might be long overdue. In these films, draftees and enlisted men hate their officers, soldiers hate college students, and corruption almost always percolates down from the top.[31] For example, the Ukrainian American workers portrayed in *The Deer Hunter* fail in their efforts to protect themselves from surprises either in the dying social world of their hometown in the industrial steel-making city of Clairton, Pennsylvania, or in the equally unpredictable and rapidly disintegrating social world they enter in Vietnam.[32] The combat soldiers in *Hamburger Hill* constantly compare themselves to college students who have escaped military service, while Rambo reserves his greatest rage for the automated technology in his own supervisor's operations headquarters. Lone-wolf commandos in the *Rambo* films, *Missing in Action*, and other action/adventure stories assume underdog status by reversing reality: this time the Americans fight as guerrillas with primitive weapons against foes with vastly superior arms and technology.[33]

Nearly every Hollywood film about the Vietnam war tells its story from the perspective of white males. Yet the disproportionate numbers of African Americans and Latinos on the front lines in the actual war's combat situations complicate the racial politics of Vietnam War films, preventing a simple binary opposition between whites and Asians. Most often, these films depict initial hostilities between distrustful groups of whites and blacks, who then bond through the shared experiences of combat. Asian American soldiers are almost always absent, Latino soldiers appear rarely, but combat in Vietnam becomes a site where masculine bonds between black and white men magically resolve and dissolve racial antagonisms.[34] At the same time, the oppositions that provide dramatic tension in many of these films build upon long established narrative practices of racialized good and evil—especially the motifs of westward expansion with their hostile and "savage" Native Americans whose stealth and ferocity threaten white American troops, and the captivity story that once featured whites captured by Native Americans, reworked for Vietnam War films as a ghostly presence in accounts of U.S. soldiers missing in action or held as prisoners of war by the Vietnamese.

War as the Best Show of All

In spectacles on-screen and off, the new patriotism attempts to channel working-class solidarity into identification with the nation state and the military. To oppose the government and its policies is seen as opposing working-class soldiers in the field. But the class solidarity proclaimed in political and entertainment narratives rarely includes both genders. If there is a crisis for the working class in the Vietnam of the new patriotism, it is a distinctly gendered and racialized crisis for working-class white men only. They often become surrogates for all people in representations of Vietnam, in both politics and entertainment, that use the war to demonstrate and analyze a crisis of masculinity, centered on an alleged erosion of male prestige and power. The exploitation of low-wage women workers in the postwar economy or the burdens imposed on women raising children by the decline or disappearance of the "family wage" in heavy industry rarely appear in films about the Vietnam War and its aftermath.

In a compelling and quite brilliant analysis, Lynda Boose notes the narcissistic and homoerotic qualities of contemporary warrior films. Rather than citizen soldiers, the characters played by Sylvester Stallone and Chuck Norris more closely resemble World Wrestling Federation performers playing out a little boy's fantasy of bodily power and domination over other men. *Iron Eagle,*

Top Gun, and *An Officer and a Gentleman* all revolve around anxious sons and absent fathers. For Boose, these representations reflect arrested development, "a generation stuck in its own boyhood" attempting to recover the father. She notes that in *The Deer Hunter* there are no fathers, only brothers. In that film and many others like it, the idealized nuclear family dies in Vietnam, providing audiences an opportunity to mourn the loss of patriarchal power and privilege produced not only by defeat in Vietnam, but by deindustrialization at home with its decline in real wages for white male breadwinners and the attendant irreversible entry of women into the wage-earning work force. But rather than presenting either the war or deindustrialization as political issues, these films and the national political narrative they support present public issues as personal. In Boose's apt summary: "The political is overwhelmed by the personal and adulthood by regressive desire."[35] But in our society, regressive desire and a preoccupation with the personal are intensely political phenomena—they nurture the combination of desire and fear necessary to our subordination as citizens and consumers. The binary oppositions between males and females reinforced by the Vietnam War narrative of the new patriotism serve broader ends in an integrated system of repression and control.

As Boose, Susan Jeffords, Philip Slater, and others have argued, the glorification of the military in our society has served as a key strategy for forces interested in airing anxieties about feminist and gay/lesbian challenges to traditional gender roles.[36] During the 1980s the core of Ronald Reagan's supporters from the extreme Right viewed patriotism as intimately connected to the restoration of heterosexual male authority. Religious writer Edward Louis Cole complained that in America, "John Wayne has given way to Alan Alda, strength to softness. America once had men," but now it has "pussyfooting pipsqueaks." Similarly, Reverend Tim LaHaye argued that "it has never been so difficult to be a man," because so many women are working outside the home for pay. In Reverend LaHaye's opinion, such women gain "a feeling of independence and self-sufficiency which God did not intend a married woman to have."[37] Yet the solutions offered by the New Christian Right, like the solutions offered by paramilitary culture or consumer society, do not prescribe adult interactions between men and women to determine mutually acceptable gender definitions. Rather, they offer men juvenile fantasies of omnipotence through the unleashing of childish aggression and desire for control over others.

They also encourage the most blatant forms of homophobia and misogyny. By attaching agency and heroism to the identities of heterosexual men and by requiring physical and emotional bonding based on a presumed common identity, the new patriotism seeks to equate social boundaries with natural limits, to present social transgression as biological transgression, and to fuse group loyalty through fear of foreigners. One might think that the desire on the part of previously excluded groups to share the burdens of combat and citizenship would augment rather than diminish one's own service, but the virulent reaction against gays and lesbians in the military or against women in combat reveal that primary attachments to identity politics transcend claims about citizenship and patriotic responsibility among large segments of the new patriots. It should come as no surprise that efforts to include women in combat or to acknowledge the obvious presence of gays and lesbians in the military were perceived as threatening by the new patriots rather than as confirming their values. Radio talk-show host Armstrong Williams, a black neoconservative, summed up much of the Right's anxiety in an October 1996 broadcast, when he explained, "If the feminists and the politically correct people had their way, they would turn our little boys into fairies and queers."[38]

War films and other narratives of military life prove ideal for representing and validating aggressive and regressive male behavior. Psychoanalyst Chaim Shatan observes that basic training can strip recruits of their identities, discouraging their participation in broader communities on or off base. All power is vested in the drill instructors and training leaders. In Shatan's view, "the dissolution of identity is not community, though it can relieve loneliness. Its success is due to the recruit's ability to regress to an earlier stage of development, in which he is again an unseparated appendage of the domain ruled over by the Giant and Giantess, the DIs of the nursery."[39] Rather than teaching independence and responsibility, the social relations and subjectivities glorified by the new patriotism fuse the narcissism of consumer desire with the nascent authoritarianism of the warfare state.

The glorification of masculine authority and conflation of patriotism with patriarchy in the military might make us think of combat films as exemplars of what our culture often calls an oedipal journey into adulthood—a rite of passage through sacrifices that make individuals distinct from others and responsible for their actions. If this were true, the films would help teach discipline, restraint, and responsibility. But the identities encouraged in the military by identification with the group, denials of difference, unquestioning obedience to authorities, and bonding through hatred, anger, and violence conform more closely to what our culture calls preoedipal traits—dissolution of the self into a more powerful entity, unleashing normally repressed behaviors and emotions, and fueling hatred for the subjectivities and desires of other people. Rather than teaching responsibility, the new patriotism stages sadomasochistic spectacles that use revenge motifs to justify unleashing the most primitive and unrestrained brutality, imitating the enemies we claim to fear. To manage the anxieties generated by this regression, the new patriots have to affirm all the more intensely their abstract fidelity to leaders, causes, and entities outside themselves.

The dynamics of militaristic spectacles have a self-perpetuating character. Oedipal and preoedipal identities play upon one another: regression to primitive desires generates an anxious longing for identification with powerful patriarchal authority; systematic submission to superior authority gives rise to anxious feelings of loneliness and isolation, which in turn fuels the desire for even more connection to powerful authorities. In *The Origins of Totalitarianism*, Hannah Arendt suggests that people in putatively democratic societies become ready for totalitarianism when loneliness becomes a routine feature of everyday existence. The combined effects of deindustrialization, economic restructuring, and the oppressive materialism of a market society where things have more value than people feed a sense of isolation and loneliness. Privatization prevents people from active engagement in civic society, from participating in processes that might lead to a healthy sense of self. Militarism becomes one of the few spaces in such a society where a shared sense of purpose, connection to others, and unselfish motivation have a legitimate place.

The denial of the political in combat films and fiction no less than in public patriotic rhetoric connects the new patriotism to the narcissism of consumer desire as the unifying national narrative. The ascendancy of greed and materialism in U.S. society during the 1980s has been widely acknowledged, but the distinctive form this greed assumed in an age of deindustrialization has attracted less attention and analysis. Changes in investment policies and tax codes during the Reagan years accelerated trends favoring consumption over production, leveraged buyouts over productive investments, short-term profits over long-term investment, and love of gain over collective obligations and responsibilities. People at the highest income levels embraced behaviors previously associated with the poor—seeking short-term sensations and pleasures rather than pursuing disciplined long-range investments, programs, or policies. At the macrosocial level, these policies have produced paralyzing levels of public and private debt, squandered the social resources and industrial infrastructure of the nation, and generated long-term costs to individuals and their environments while imposing burdens on future generations. On the microsocial level, they have encouraged the very attitudes displayed most often in adolescent warrior fantasies—regressive desire, narcissistic grandiosity, and anxieties about identity that lead to craving for sensations, distraction, and displays of power.

As president of the United States, no less than in his role as a performer in commercials for General Electric in the 1950s, Ronald Reagan communicated the language of consumer desire with extraordinary skill. He offered more for less, promising that tax cuts would not reduce government revenues because they would stimulate massive economic growth. He claimed that ending government regulation would free the private sector to find market-based solutions to social problems. He told Americans that they could have it all, as in his 1986 State of the Union speech when he announced, "In this land of dreams fulfilled where greater dreams may be imagined, nothing is impossible, no victory is beyond our reach, no glory will ever be too great. So now, it's up to us, all of us, to prepare America for that day when our work will pale before the greatness of America's champions in the 21st century."[40] When this philosophy led the government to accumulate a larger national debt during Reagan's terms in office than had been incurred by all previous presidents combined, when it produced massive unemployment, homelessness, and health hazards, and when it created the preconditions for massive fraud in the savings and loan industry leading to enormous debts that executives from deregulated industries then passed on to consumers, Reagan continued to insist that his policies were working. In their own way they were, not to solve problems and make the nation stronger, but to transform the political system into a branch of the entertainment industry, into an entity seeking scapegoats for social problems rather than solutions to them.

Of course, the severe economic decline experienced by most people in the United States during the 1980s should not be attributed solely to Reagan; it predated and postdated his terms in office. The stagnation of real wages owed much to long-term imbalances in the U.S. economy between the needs of capital and the needs of the majority of the population. But the political culture that Reagan nurtured in the wake of this devastation perfectly complemented the escape from responsibility promoted by a consumer commodity society fixated on instant gratification. Reagan basked in the glow of the glory he attained by invading Grenada, bombing Libya, and identifying himself with the overwhelming U.S. victory at the 1984 Olympics (gained largely because the Soviet Union and other Warsaw Pact nations did not participate). By timing the Libya bombing for maximum exposure on network prime time, he set the stage for the voyeurism of the Gulf War, where news reports often resembled video games or commercials by weapons manufacturers. In return for all of the broken promises and devastated lives of his era, Reagan left the nation with a better-developed taste for spectatorship of the kind described long ago by J. A. Hobson—gloating "over the perils, pains, and slaughter of fellow-men whom he does not know, but whose destruction he desires in a blind and artificially stimulated passion of hatred and revenge."[41]

The new patriotism arises from deeply felt contradictions in U.S. society. It arbitrates anxieties about changes in gender roles, jobs, communities, and collective identity brought on by deindustrialization and economic restructuring. Narratives of national honor take on increased importance as the practices of transnational corporations make the nation state increasingly powerless to advance the interests of its citizens. Private anxieties about isolation, loneliness, and mortality fuel public spectacles of patriotic identification that promise purposeful and unselfish connection to collective and enduring institutions. The new patriotism serves vital purposes for neoconservative economics and politics, providing psychic reparation for the damage done to individuals and groups by the operation of market principles, while at the same time promoting narcissistic desires for pleasure and power that set the stage for ever more majestic public spectacles and demonstrations of military might.

Yet while providing logical responses to the diminution of collective and individual power in an age of deindustrialization, the new patriotism encourages us to evade collective problems and responsibilities rather than to solve them. It interferes with serious public discussion of the world we have lost and the one we are building through deindustrialization and economic restructuring. It promotes male violence and female subordination, builds identification with outside authorities at the expense of personal integrity and responsibility, and inflames desires that can only be quenched by domination over others.

Perhaps most ominously, the new patriotism builds possessive identification with warfare and violence as solutions to personal and political problems. Although aggression is often portrayed as natural in our culture, the elaborate pomp of patriotic ceremonies and rituals may indicate precisely the opposite—that aggression needs to be nurtured and cultivated. It is not easy for humans to kill other humans; one study of the World War II Normandy invasion showed that even among specially trained combat troops, many failed to fire their weapons once the battle started. Nightmares, guilt, and other signs of postcombat stress have plagued veterans of all wars, not just Vietnam. The attention devoted to ceremonial commemoration of past wars may be not so much evidence of how easy it is for people to go to war, but rather how much persuasion, rationalization, and diversion are required to make warfare acceptable.

Unfortunately, elaborate public appeals to honor the memory of slain soldiers only create the preconditions for new generations of corpses. Shatan explains that "ceremonial vengeance" serves to perpetuate rather than resolve the legacy of past wars because it requires repression of the genuine agonies caused by combat. In his eloquent formulation, "unshed tears shed blood," grief and mourning are transformed into scapegoating and fantasies of revenge. Unresolved grief and guilt lead us to inflict our wounds on others; reincarnating yesterday's dead as today's warriors "promises collective rebirth to all who have died for the Corps," but at the price of creating more martyrs whose deaths must be avenged in the future.[42]

Ceremonial celebrations of militarism perpetuate dangerous illusions about warfare. They hide the ambiguous outcome of every conflict, the limited utility of force in resolving conflicts of interest and ideology, and the ways in which the resolution of every war contains the seeds of the next one. But even beyond any practical shortcomings of war as a way of resolving conflicts lies its atrocious immorality. Our nation is not the first (and it will not be the last) to believe that participating in the systematic destruction of other humans will not fundamentally compromise our morality and our humanity, but the weight of the historical record is inescapable. Author and Vietnam War veteran Tim O'Brien counsels that moral lessons cannot be learned from warfare. He tells us that a war story "does not instruct, nor encourage virtue, nor suggest models of proper human behavior." O'Brien asks us to cease believing in the morality of war, advising us that any time we feel uplifted or righteous after reading a war story, we have been made the victim of "a very old and terrible lie."[43]

Of course, this is not to say that nothing of value is ever salvaged from war. Certainly many of the people who have seen combat become ferociously antiwar precisely because they have witnessed the waste and destructiveness of warfare firsthand. In addition, as George Mariscal points out in his important book *Aztlan and Vietnam*, for communities of color in the United States, the Vietnam War (like previous conflicts) sharpened contradictions and accelerated demands for civil rights from soldiers who saw themselves asked to fight and possibly die overseas for freedoms that they did not enjoy at home.[44] At the level of soldiers in the field, lessons about mutuality and interdependence often break down prejudice and parochialism. For these individuals and those they influence, warfare holds meanings that counteract the stories of heroism and glory that dominate combat narratives.

On the level of spectacle, however, war can be the best show of all. During World War I, Randolph Bourne argued that war was "the health of the state"—that nothing furthers the totalitarian projects of centralized power as effectively as warfare. During the Gulf War, Todd Gitlin amended Bourne's formulation, claiming that war is also the health of the networks—and we might add the health of the advertisers, toy makers, film producers, and other merchants of diversion, distraction, and vicarious thrill seeking. Even if only as symbolic compensation, war enables, or at least seems to enable, individuals to negotiate otherwise intolerable contradictions.

The Wages of War

If war remains "the health of the state," it nonetheless does great harm to individuals and groups. Psychoanalyst and cultural critic Joel Kovel reminds us that a false subject needs a false object—people who do not know who they are need demonized enemies in order to define themselves. Hatred of the external enemy does not end when the shooting stops; on the contrary, the spectacles of war and the rituals of ceremonial vengeance promote appetites that need to be sated. It is hardly an accident that with the end of the Cold War the neoconservative lobbyists and public relations specialists in the John M. Olin Foundation, the Heritage Foundation, and the Bradley Foundation, among others who did so much to promote the new patriotism, now collaborate with overtly white supremacist organizations like the Pioneer Fund to publicize the most vulgar and discredited forms of white supremacist thought. In Charles Murray and Richard Herrnstein's *The Bell Curve*, but also in Dinesh D'Souza's *The End of Racism* and in Samuel P. Huntington's "The Clash of Cultures," neoconservatives present people of color at home and abroad as the new enemy to be scape-goated for the lost wages of whiteness. They offer the possessive investment in whiteness as reparation and consolation for the destructive consequences of the economic and political policies demanded by the transnational corporations that pay their salaries and fund their research. Their efforts to portray the victims of racism as the beneficiaries of unearned privileges given to them because of their race hide the history of the possessive investment in whiteness and invert the history of racial politics in the United States. Yet while deficient as history and shamefully indecent as intellectual argument, these public relations campaigns have enjoyed broad success, from attacks on affirmative action to the promotion of hate crimes against people of color.

In a brilliant analysis of the role of anti-immigrant attitudes in contemporary conservatism, Kitty Calavita observes that "balanced budget conservatism" promises wealth, stability, and security to taxpayers and home owners, but creates an economy characterized by uncertain relations between work and reward, the plunder of public resources for private gain, economic uncertainty, and social disintegration. Moral panics, military mobilizations, and nativist attacks on immigrants provide a useful safety valve for the fear, anger, and frustration fostered by the false promises of the "balanced budget" conservatives. Because of the possessive investment in whiteness and its history, people of color easily become the main targets of this meanness masquerading as morality.[45]

U.S. wars in Asia have pitted U.S. combat troops against soldiers and civilians of nearly every eastern Asian nation. The experiences of warfare in Asia and the propaganda attendant to it have had racist consequences for citizens of those nations as well as for Asian immigrants to the United States. Of course, racism against Asians has a long history in the United States that includes disgraceful acts of mob violence, bigoted legislation denying immigrants from that continent opportunities to become citizens or own property, persistent economic exploitation, and the forced internment of more than 100,000 Japanese Americans, most of them citizens. Yet while not new, anti-Asian racism has taken on an especially vicious character in the context of the U.S. defeat in Vietnam and the rise of Asian economies as competitors with the United States. The hate crimes against Asian Americans enumerated at the beginning of this chapter are only a tiny sample of a much broader pattern of criminal behavior directed against people of Asian origin in the United States.[46] At the same time, the conflation of patriotism with whiteness has also had disastrous consequences for racialized immigrant groups from Mexico, Central and South America, the Caribbean, and the West Indies.

Deliberately inflammatory metaphors by politicians and journalists describing undocumented workers as an invading army prepare the public to see immigrants as the enemy. At the same time, antidrug policies that focus on border interdiction rather than on the suppression of demand and supply incentives create a context for actual low-intensity warfare along the border. Government policy and vigilante actions complement one another in bringing the hurts and hatreds of warfare within our own borders. In San Diego, a group of young whites active in their high school's Junior Reserve Officers Training program participated in unofficial and unauthorized nighttime excursions on the border during which they fired air rifles at defenseless immigrants. In 1992 a U.S.

Border Patrol agent fired rounds from an M-16 rifle into a group of undocumented immigrants traveling on foot near Nogales, Arizona, because he thought they were drug couriers. Although one of the immigrants was wounded by the agent's fire, the incident did not become public until three months later when the same agent shot an unarmed Mexican man running away from him in the back two times with an AR-15 rifle. The agent attempted to cover up his crime by dragging his victim some fifty yards out of sight, leaving him to die, then returning later to bury the body. Another agent encountered him in the act and agreed (reportedly at gunpoint) to keep quiet about the shooting, but fifteen hours later he reported the incident to authorities, who charged the first agent with first-degree murder. At his trial six months later, a jury found the agent not guilty on all charges, accepting defense arguments portraying him as a "law officer on the front line of our nation's war on drugs" whose actions were justified because he was operating in a "war zone."[47]

Immigrants detained for border violations in a private jail contracting with the INS in Elizabeth, New Jersey, succeeded in having the facility closed in 1995 because of inhumane conditions and brutality by guards. Some two dozen of the inmates from that facility then found themselves transferred to the Union County Jail in Elizabeth, where guards punched and kicked them, pushed their heads into toilets, and compelled a line of men to take off their clothes, kneel before the guards, and chant "America is Number One."[48] In May 1996, a group of Marines assigned to a secret unit combating drug smuggling along the border shot and killed a teenaged U.S. citizen herding goats near his home. A county grand jury recommended that no charges be filed.[49]

Identities are complex, relational, and intersecting. By disguising the social crises of our time as assaults on white male heterosexual power and privilege, the new patriotism has fanned the flames of white supremacy, homophobia, and anti-immigrant hatred. It has encouraged workers to feel their losses as whites, as men, as heterosexuals, but not as workers or community members. It has channeled resentments against foreigners, immigrants, members of aggrieved racial groups, women, gays and lesbians, college students, and intellectuals—but not against transnational capital and the economic austerity and social disintegration it creates and sustains.

The great scholar W. E. B. Du Bois argued long ago that the United States lost its best chance to be an egalitarian and nonracist society in the years after the Civil War because elites successfully manipulated the class resentments of white workers, directing them away from themselves and toward African Americans, Asian Americans, and Mexicans. White workers endured hardships in exchange for the security of knowing that there would always be a group below them, that there was a floor below which they could not fall. Du Bois called this assurance of privilege "the wages of whiteness," what white workers received instead of the higher economic wages they would have earned had they joined with all other workers in an interracial, classwide alliance. Du Bois quotes a populist white Georgia newspaper editor who identified the fatal flaw in going along with the elites' strategy: "Since at least 1865, we have been holding back the Negro to keep him from getting beyond the white man. Our idea has been that the Negro should be kept poor. But by keeping him poor, we have thrown him into competition with ourselves and have kept ourselves poor."[50]

A century later, the egalitarian promise of the social movements of the 1960s has similarly been betrayed by a version of nationalism and identity politics that hides the attack on wages, hours, working conditions, education, transportation, health care, and housing by encouraging a possessive investment in the contemporary version of the wages of whiteness. By investing their identities in these narratives of the nation that depend on the demonization of others, white Americans only serve the interests of the transnational corporations whose policies are directly responsible for the disintegration of the nation's social and economic infrastructure. Accepting the possessive investment in whiteness as consolation and compensation is a bad deal. It guarantees that whiteness is the only thing whites will ever really own.

Notes

The epigraph is from Baldwin, *The Devil Finds Work*, 93.

1. Yen Le Espiritu, *Asian American Panethnicity: Building Institutions and Identities* (Philadelphia: Temple University Press, 1992), 141–43; see also the film by Renee Tajima and Christine Choy, *Who Killed Vincent Chin?* 1988.
2. Helen Zia, "Violence in our Communities: 'Where Are the Asian Women?'" in *Making More Wives: New Writing by Asian American Women*, ed. Elaine H. Kim, Lilia v. Villaneuva, and Asian Women United of California (Boston: Beacon, 1997), 208.
3. Darrell Y. Hamamoto, *Monitored Peril: Asian Americans and the Politics of TV Representation* (Minneapolis: University of Minnesota Press, 1994), 165; Yen, *Asian American Panethnicity*, 155–56.
4. Hamamoto, *Monitored Peril*, 166–67; Mike Clary, "Rising Toll of Hate Crimes Cited in Slaying," *Los Angeles Times*, October 10, 1992, sec. A.
5. Lowe, *Immigrant Acts*, 6–22; Yen, *Asian American Women and Men*, 9–13; Okihiro, *Margins and Mainstreams*.
6. Espiritu, *Asian American Panethnicity*, 90.
7. Reginald Horsman, *Race and Manifest Destiny: The Origins of American Anglo-Saxonism* (Cambridge: Harvard University Press, 1981); David Roediger, *Toward the Abolition of Whiteness: Essays on Race, Politics, and Working-Class History* (New York: Verso, 1994).
8. Michael Rogin, *Ronald Reagan, the Movie: And Other Stories in Political Demonology* (Berkeley and Los Angeles: University of California Press, 1987).
9. Kathleen Hall Jamieson, *Eloquence in an Electronic Age* (New York: Oxford University Press, 1988), 162, 163.
10. Lefty Frizzell, "Mom and Dad's Waltz," Columbia Records 20837, appears in *Billboard* on August 18, 1951, and stays on the charts for twenty-nine weeks; Joel Whitburn, *Top Country Hits, 1944–1988* (Menomonee, Wis.: Record Research, 1989), 107; Robert Westbrook, "'I Want a Girl Just like the Girl that Married Harry James': American Women and the Problem of Political Obligation in World War II," *American Quarterly* 42, 4 (December 1990): 587–615; Amy Kaplan, "Romancing the Empire: The Embodiment of American Masculinity in the Popular Historical novel of the 1890s," *American Literary History* 2, 4 (Winter 1990): 659–90.
11. Robert Westbrook, "Private Interests and Public Obligations in World War II," in *The Power of Culture: Critical Essays in American History*, ed. Richard Wightman Fox and T. J. Jackson Lears (Chicago: University of Chicago Press, 1993), 195–222.
12. Benedict Anderson, *Imagined Communities* (New York: Verso, 1983).
13. Hobson quoted in Kaplan, "Romancing the Empire," 677.
14. Francis X. Clines, "Military of U.S. 'Standing Tall,' Reagan Asserts," *New York Times*, December 13, 1983.
15. Kevin Bowen, "'Strange Hells': Hollywood in Search of America's Lost War," in *From Hanoi to Hollywood: The Vietnam War in American Film*, ed. Linda Dittmar and Gene Michaud (New Brunswick, N.J.: Rutgers University Press, 1991), 229.
16. James William Gibson, "The Return of Rambo: War and Culture in the Post-Vietnam Era," in *America at Century's End*, ed. Alan Wolfe (Berkeley and Los Angeles: University of California Press, 1991), 389, 390.
17. William Adams, "Screen Wars: The Battle for Vietnam," *Dissent*, Winter 1990, 65.
18. See Lynne Cheney, "Report," in *On Campus* 7, 3 (November 1987): 2, as well as Lynne Cheney, "Report to the President, the Congress, and the American People," *Chronicle of Higher Education* 35, 4 (September 21, 1988): A18–19.
19. It was reported that the *Mayaguez* carried only paper supplies for U.S. troops, but as a container ship its cargo could have included much more sensitive material for surveillance or combat, which may account for the vigorous government reaction to its capture. See Marilyn Young, *The Vietnam Wars, 1945–1990* (New York: HarperCollins, 1991), 301; see also Thomas J. McCormick, *America's Half Century: United States Foreign Policy in the Cold War* (Baltimore: Johns Hopkins University Press, 1989), 178–79.
20. "A Force Reborn," *U.S. News and World Report*, March 18, 1991, 30; Harry G. Summers, Jr., "Putting Vietnam Syndrome to Rest," *Los Angeles Times*, March 2, 1991, sec. A; E. J. Dionne, Jr., "Kicking the 'Vietnam Syndrome,'" *Washington Post*, March 4, 1991, sec. A; Kevin P. Phillips, "The Vietnam Syndrome: Why Is Bush Hurting If There Is No War?" *Los Angeles Times*, November 25, 1990.
21. Robert McKelvey, "Watching Victory Parades, I Confess Some Envy: Vietnam Vets Weren't Feted by Parades," *Los Angeles Times*, June 16, 1991, sec. M; James S. Barron, "A Korean War Parade, Decades Late," *New York Times*, June 26, 1991, sec. B.
22. Young, *The Vietnam Wars*, 314.
23. George C. Herring, *America's Longest War* (New York: Wiley, 1968), George McT. Kahin, *Intervention* (New York: Knopf, 1986), and Stanley Karnow, *Vietnam: A History* (New York: Viking, 1984) present different perspectives on the war, but their cumulative evidence reveals the untenable nature of any hypothesis blaming internal division in the United States for the war's outcome.
24. Thomas Ferguson and Joel Rogers, *Right Turn: The Decline of the Democrats and the Future of American Politics* (New York: Hill and Wang, 1986), 79, 80.
25. Katherine S. Newman, "Uncertain Seas: Cultural Turmoil and the Domestic Economy," in *America at Century's End*, ed. Alan Wolfe (Berkeley and Los Angeles: University of California Press, 1991), 116.
26. Ibid., 116, 117, 121; Chafe, *The Unfinished Journey*, 449.
27. See Michael I. Luger, "Federal Tax Incentives as Industrial and Urban Policy," in *Sunbelt/Snowbelt: Urban Development and Regional Restructuring*, ed. Larry Sawers and William K. Tabb (New York: Oxford University Press, 1984), 201–34.

28. Christian G. Appy, *Working Class War: American Combat Soldiers and Vietnam* (Chapel Hill: University of North Carolina Press, 1993), 6, 11.

29. There were, of course, important exceptions to this pattern. Antiwar activists supported coffeehouses, draft counseling centers, and antiwar newspapers at dozens of military bases. Many local peace coalitions united trade unionists, intellectuals, suburban liberals, students, and poor people, and—especially after 1970—the antiwar counterculture had a substantial working-class presence. But almost nowhere did any of this produce a class-based critique of why the war was fought and who had to fight it. Of course, the antiwar movement emerged as an ad hoc coalition based on college campuses with few other institutional resources. McCarthyism's destruction of the Old Left and the timidity of social democrats left the work of radicalism to politically inexperienced children of the middle class.

30. Billy Joel, "Allentown," Columbia Records 03413, entered *Billboard* charts on November 27, 1982, rose as high as number seventeen, and remained on the charts twenty-two weeks; Bruce Springsteen, "Born in the USA," Columbia Records 04680, entered *Billboard* charts November 10, 1984, rose to number nine, and remained on the charts seventeen weeks; see Joel Whitburn, *Top Pop Singles* (Menomonee Falls, Wis.: Record Research, 1987), 266, 475. Bobbie Ann Mason, *In Country* (New York: Perennial Library, 1985).

31. Adams, "Screen Wars," 71–72.

32. Frank Burke, "Reading Michael Cimino's *The Deer Hunter:* Interpretation as Melting Pot," *Film and Literature Quarterly* 20, 3 (1992): 252–53.

33. Adams, "Screen Wars," 72; Gaylin Studlar and David Dresser, "Never Having to Say You're Sorry: Rambo's Rewriting of the Vietnam War," in *From Hanoi to Hollywood: The Vietnam War in American Film*, ed. Linda Dittmar and Gene Michaud (New Brunswick, N.J.: Rutgers University Press, 1991), 111, 108; Stephen Prince, *Vision of Empire: Political Imagery in Contemporary American Film* (New York: Praeger, 1992), 66, 69.

34. Susan Jeffords, *The Remasculinization of America: Gender and the Vietnam War* (Bloomington and Indianapolis: Indiana University Press, 1989).

35. Lynda Boose, "Techno-Muscularity and the 'Boy Eternal': From the Quagmire to the Gulf," in *The Cultures of United States Imperialism*, ed. Donald Pease and Amy Kaplan (Durham: Duke University Press, 1994), 588–99, 600, 602.

36. Jeffords, *The Remasculinization of America*, 180; Philip Slater, *A Dream Deferred: America's Discontent and the Search for a New Democratic Ideal* (Boston: Beacon, 1991).

37. Cole and LaHaye are quoted in Michael Lienesch, *Redeeming America: Piety and Politics in the New Christian Right* (Chapel Hill: University of North Carolina Press, 1993), 60, 54, 58.

38. "Talk Radio Lowlights," *Extra! Update* (newsletter), December 1996, 2.

39. Chaim F. Shatan, "'Happiness Is a Warm Gun'—Militarized Mourning and Ceremonial Vengeance: Toward a Psychological Theory of Combat and Manhood in America, III," *Vietnam Generation* 3, 4 (1989): 147.

40. Jamieson, *Eloquence in an Electronic Age*, 161.

41. Hobson quoted in Kaplan, "Romancing the Empire," 679.

42. Shatan, 'Happiness Is a Warm Gun,'" 140–41.

43. O'Brien is quoted in Young, *The Vietnam Wars*, 329.

44. George Mariscal, "'Our Kids Don't Have Blue Eyes, but They Go Overseas to Die': Chicanos in Vietnam," paper read at the conference "America and Vietnam: From War to Peace," University of Notre Dame, South Bend, Ind., December 4, 1993.

45. Kitty Calavita, "The New Politics of Immigration: 'Balanced Budget Conservatism' and the Symbolism of Proposition 187," *Social Problems* 43, 3 (August 1996), 284–306.

46. See for example Rita Chaudry Sethi, "Smells Like Racism: A Plan for Mobilizing against Anti-Asian Bias," in *the State of Asian America: Activism and Resistance in the 1990s*, ed. Karen Aguilar-San Juan (Boston: South End, 1994), 235–50.

47. Timothy J. Dunn, *The Militarization of the U.S.-Mexico Border, 1978–1992* (Austin, Center for Mexican American Studies, 1996), 87–89.

48. Mark Dow, "Behind the Razor Wire: Inside INS Detention Centers," *Covert Action Quarterly*, no. 57 (Summer 1996): 35.

49. Jesse Katz, "Marine is Cleared in Texas Border Death," *Los Angeles Times* August 15, 1997 sec. A; Sam Howe Verhovek, "Pentagon Halts Drug Patrols After Border Killing," *The New Times*, July 31, 1997, sec A.

50. W. E. B. Du Bois, *Black Reconstruction in America, 1860–1880* (New York: Touchstone, 1992), 696.

8
The Homeless Citizen

NIKOS PAPASTERGIADIS

Across the world today people are experiencing profound insecurity. In the wake of colonization, globalization, and terror, the citizen is engulfed by fear. People may not be able to define the source of their fears, but ambient fears dominate the political landscape. The enemy is no longer on the other side of a boundary, but possibly beside them in the darkness. This intimacy unsettles comfort or surety. The fear that is generated by being suspended in this no-man's-land has eviscerated the structures of hope. In this state of perpetual trepidation there is a distinct absence in the forms of leadership. Politicians extend their power by stoking the fears of invasion, with the success of political scaremongering depending not only on the accuracy of impending threats but the capacity to express deeper cultural anxieties. This signals a deeper malaise in the recent shifts of the political landscape of the West. As similar trajectories are adopted by all the major parties in the United States, United Kingdom, and Australia, a vacuum has been created in the political heart of the West. The problem is not just the collapse of a clear ideological distinction between the left and the right, nor even the competition for the center, but rather the shameless abandonment of a moral dimension. The new authoritarianism increasingly shaping the political discourse of the West simultaneously demands faith whilst cutting down the institutions within which the citizen can develop a sense of trust. The resulting nervous oscillation between hope and fear has become a constitutive process in the overall social and political landscape. This new authoritarianism, moreover, exacerbates the condition of rootlessness. Uncertainty dominates the field of relations and citizenship is being undermined because people are finding it more and more difficult to identify with their state. The form of ambivalence that prevails today is spread out on an open horizon of homelessness. People's own homes have become a place of alienation. Exile has occurred without the drama of an exit.

This essay examines the emotional register of hope and fear as a way of tackling both the complex shifts in society and the transformation in the modalities of political authority. The emotional register of hope and fear is not to be measured purely as a response to either the pressure of external forces or the reflection of an empirical condition. The nervous oscillation between hope and fear has become a constitutive process in the overall social and political landscape. For those in government the experience of fear is no longer interpreted as a sign of weakness but as a stimulus to vigilance. For the homeless citizen, hope is no longer an abstract sentiment but the ground from which the vision of critique is based. Beyond the predominance of one over the other there is the manifestation of an expanded ambivalence that binds both modes of being and feeling into every aspect of everyday life. The aim of this essay is therefore to examine the ways in which politicians manipulate and amplify the rising fears that exist in the public imaginary. Parallel to this is the attempt to redefine hope, after the collapse of the great ideological structures that sustained the classical ideas of progress, unity, and justice.

My father arrived in Australia in the same year as the 1956 Olympic games. He was proud of his Greek heritage but was quick to adopt Australian citizenship. He always announced with great pride that he was a *new* Australian.[1] It was as if the renewal extended beyond his body and family. After forty-five years he retired from a succession of laboring jobs and enrolled in an English language class for elderly migrants. Every night he did his homework and by morning he had forgotten almost everything. He laughed at his failures and self-administered punishment by rapping his knuckles on his head. He was hoping to learn how to read a newspaper and he was pleased that the government valued even his education.

The institutions of government, like the migrant English class, have the capacity to create new forms of communal engagement and extend the aspirations of people. In the classroom my father felt that for the first time he was being both encouraged and challenged. Citizenship is at its most exquisite juncture when people believe that their actions are positively nurtured and wishes constructively illuminated within the structures of the state. Belonging is affirmed not by the formal rights of political representation or the economic cost benefit analysis but by the feeling of acceptance within the "warm circle" of community.[2] It now seems fanciful, if not nostalgic, to assume that there is a progressive chain that reinforces the links between personal values, communal understandings, state structures, and government policies. Before the end of the year the language school was closed. My father's protest was to no avail. He now learns about disasters in Australia by watching the Greek news on satellite television. In a world of global communication, where are the institutions that create a local sense of belonging? Distance is no longer the telling factor that determines our experience of information. And so the question on the relationship between communication networks and communal understandings can be asked in a different way. What prevents the citizen from feeling at home in his or her own place? The blunt answer is betrayal. The knife of betrayal cuts into the need for belonging. The sharpest form is the dictator who rules by oppression and persecution. There the blade goes directly to the throats of the enemy, and they must either flee or suffer the violence. However, beyond the aggressor, the victim, and the witnesses, there is also a larger community that learns to fear by rumor.

In the West, the knife of betrayal lies hidden. Today the modalities for transmitting rumor are multiple, but everywhere there is evidence of its effects. The consequences of violence flow in more complex and subtle ways and people are experiencing profound insecurity. Citizenship is being undermined because people are finding it more and more difficult to identify with their state. Increasingly there is a shrinking sense of connection or even a withdrawal of any attachment. People may continue to live in their place of birth and maintain their formal rights to citizenship, but at a deeper emotional level, and in many substantive ways, they no longer feel at home. The loss of trust, hope, and belief is so penetrating that it has reached those who thought they were cocooned from the world of suffering. From the most affluent and secure suburb in Melbourne, a citizen writes the following letter to the editor of a daily newspaper:

I look forward to my morning coffee, a cigarette and a browse through the pages of the The Age. I am lucky. I want for little and feel secure. Anxiety, fear and insecurity are not unknown to me, but my personal safety and welfare have never been threatened. And I feel indignation from time to time when I read stories in your paper, yet I am rarely moved sufficiently to overcome my complacency. I can both empathise and sympathise with the plight of others, for a few minutes. In reality, I live in a cocoon called "Middle Australia"—which is a very desirable place to be. Why then am I starting to feel uncomfortable? Is it concern about the property bubble bursting? International terrorism? Iraq and Afghanistan? The Middle East? Asylum seekers? Locking children up in detention centres? The answer is, none of these and all of these.

What makes me feel uncomfortable is that I no longer believe what I am told by the political leaders in this country. I am now questioning the veracity of everything our Prime Minister says, does and stands for. The simple truth is that you can't feel secure when those leading you no longer have credibility.[3]

In an equally privileged part of the world, Austin, Texas, a group of disaffected left-leaning Democrats gathered to discuss the obliqueness of mainstream parties, the moral slide in foreign policy, the threats toward environmental protection, and the decline of civil rights. At the end of all these worthy speeches an anonymous man in the crowd stood up and said: "I agree with a lot of what I've heard and I want to get involved but I'm scared."

Robert Jensen, a journalism professor, who also attended this meeting, recognized that the type of fear that disturbed this man was not the physical threat of reprisal but the insecurity of being seen as "not normal." It is as if the psychological comfort of belonging to the American dream is now incompatible with questioning the "Bush agenda."[4]

On the eve of the 2001 Australian election, I asked my father, whose family supported the communist guerrillas in Greece during the Second World War, whether he would continue to vote for the Australian Labor Party, the current main opposition party whose politics have traditionally been working class and more left of center.

"No!" he replied, and then added, "I vote Greens."

I was surprised by his resoluteness. My father, whose greatest pleasure in life was to chop down a tree and plant concrete, was about to vote for the Greens, a more marginal left wing political group. He was so alienated by the Labor Party's display of political opportunism and moral cowardice during the refugee crisis,[5] where they presented no opposition or alternative to the conservative Liberal government's hardline position, that he felt that he had no other option than to give his vote to a party, led by an openly gay man, who did not hesitate to speak with a clear conscience.

Political Demoralization

My father was not alone in his reevaluation of the Labor Party. Up to 20 percent of traditional Labor voters in inner-city areas of Australia were shifting their preferences to the Greens. It is now estimated that up to a third of voters now vote for alternative candidates to the governing conservative Liberal Party or Labor, or don't vote at all. Guy Rundle argued that Labor "drifted back into a chauvinist style" and was courting the "politics of authoritarian reaction."[6] He argued it was not just the left factions that were being isolated by the convergence between the center and the right, but that moral principles were being abandoned in favor of more expedient political responses to globalization. Disaffection has also spread within the membership of the Liberal Party itself, traditionally conservative in its politics. While the polls showed that the government's policies on refugees were popular, they did not reflect whether people felt at ease with the options. The Prime Minister, John Howard, had scathing attacks launched on him by prominent Liberal Party members, including the former Prime Minister Malcolm Fraser, for the stance the government took. Another former minister Marie Tehan listed the shortcomings of the government's attitude and behavior:

Since the Tampa and the children-overboard saga, many Liberals have been concerned at the Coalition's hardline approach to, and overt political use of, refugees and the issues surrounding them. Whether towing away boats by the navy, excising lands from migration zones, detaining women and children indefinitely in detention centres, awarding only temporary visas to genuine refugees, repatriating refugees or asylum seekers to troubled countries like Afghanistan or Iran, many Liberals have been dismayed by the Government's lack of compassion, lack of truth and openness, lack of fairness, and lack of compliance, in fact or in spirit, with human rights and other international treaties.[7]

Like many other Liberals who have supported refugee advocacy groups, she expressed "disquiet" over the government's policies, but was "assuaged" by the indifference of the Labor Party. Compliance was secured by the absence of an alternative. Members of the Liberal party felt uneasy with the direction of their leadership but they also felt that they had nowhere else to go.

While the Liberal Party dispensed its own liberalism, the Labor Party had forgotten its historical commitment to a social contract. Both major parties were increasingly seeking to govern by capturing the attention of what campaign managers were calling the "aspirationals."[8] This is a group that has been characterized by their efforts to establish personal security through individual financial gains. According to Keith Suter this is a new category of voters who define themselves by their aspiration to a better life "not so much as to who you are now but what you might become."[9] They aspire to greater wealth in order to afford private health cover, elite education, and secure housing. They also have a fear of refugees and welfare recipients, for they represent a burden on the state. They are indifferent to moral issues and regard life as the survival of the fittest. However, there is a deeper disquiet here as well. Aspiration is also marked with insecurity. Individual gain is always threatened by losses in the collective. They know that their own progress upwards could all be in vain, and the fall downwards more brutal once the social safety nets are removed.

There are new risks when the contents of the social contract have been progressively hollowed out and reconfigured to promote an individual's right to flexibility, choice, and consumption. When a party defines its constituents in terms of individual aspirations but fails to map out social values, then it is left with a multiplicity of individualized aspirations but no direction that can connect them together. Where would a party head if it is only seeking to attract the aspirationals? These aspirationals may have clear ideas of their current fears and desires. They are insecure about changes in the workplace and pensions, so they invest in property and take out insurance. In place of having a clear career path, an appreciation of the aging process, and sound awareness of their own place in society, they have financial planners, personal trainers, and life coaches. Being part of the "do it yourself" lifestyle may promote freedom from the strictures that prevail over others, but where is the security that you can survive on "yourself"? Aspirationals are increasingly defined by their detachment and disengagement from collective and social struggles, but this presumed abhorrence of dependency exaggerates the benefits of autonomy and minimizes the risks of self-reliance. Representing the citizen as aspirational may reflect the desire for individuals to get themselves "off the ground," but it also glosses the absence of maps. The journey of the aspirational is not only a solitary one, but heads toward an uncharted terrain. It could be cross-mapped with what Ulrich Beck calls a "life of risk" where all certainties collapse.[10] Trying to imagine a society of aspirationals is like recalling the experiments in Brownian motion. Who knows where the next step or collision will lead?

The disappearance of a political alternative did not occur overnight. Under the moral spotlight of the refugee crisis the two-decade-long ascendance of neoliberalism and new authoritarianism became sharper in its focus. Throughout the Hawke-Keating governments of the 1980s and early 1990s, the Australian Labor party attempted to balance neoliberalism and social democracy. It sought to expand its constituency by embracing the rhetoric of cultural diversity and sexual difference.

However, the national transformation in the policies of social inclusion was underscored by a triumphalist discourse of globalization. It was already presumed that the national foundations of social democracy were sundered. Australian industries and products were no longer internationally competitive and Labor was persuaded that there was no alternative to neoliberal economics. Their reforms revolved around the notion of "reciprocal obligation." They abandoned the universalist principles of social democracy and adopted approaches that rewarded the effort of individuals. Advances in the workplace, education, and culture were welcome insofar as they made Australia competitive in the global marketplace for goods, knowledge,and tourism. Neoliberalism and globalization converged to produce a radical transformation of the social contract. Any form of difference that could be commodified was celebrated. But it was a hollow party. For over a decade they governed on the illusion that free market policies eventually would benefit all sections of Australian society. During this period Australia developed into a society with one of the highest levels of income inequality and experienced the most profound shrinkage in the welfare state.

By the time Howard gained power in 1996, the Australian society and economy had already been subjected to the campaign of modernization that Tony Blair was about to commence in Britain. On the basis of the Australian experience one could already predict that Blair's dual commitment to "Fairness and enterprise. Social justice and economic efficiency together"[11] would always lean to the latter at the expense of the former.

The political discourse that now dominates both the left and the right in the West is based on maintaining global competitiveness and maximizing rewards for individual effort and responsibility. Welfarist and redistributive ideologies that are based on universalist principles are seen as encouraging complacency, dependency, and waste. This aversion to all forms of universalist political thinking has diminished the space for political debate on social justice. Politicians now compete with each other in terms of how they can reconcile different social and cultural groups by stressing their common interest in not only economic gain but also individual prosperity.

Rundle has once again noted the depressing defensiveness and the lack of veracity of the Labor Party's political leadership: "Increasingly they see their job as not to represent the demands of the social elements of the social classes that form their base, but to act as a reality check upon them, to steadily limit their expectations about how much can be changed."[12] Yet the politics of fear are even more profoundly expressed by the government's Liberal party. Today we have entered what Russell Jacoby has called the "era of acquiescence."[13] A utopian vision of the future has disappeared from the political horizon. The options are now confined to maintaining a precarious hold on the status quo or a treacherous slide into the abyss of chaos. Neither of the two mainstream parties is offering an opportunity to believe in a genuine alternative. Antagonism toward the opportunities and the morphing of policy between the traditionally progressive and the conservative parties has created a deep ambivalence. Representatives of the "antipolitics" of the sixties generation have increasingly aligned themselves with the Greens.[14] By expanding their politics beyond ecological issues, they could address issues where values were central and new alternatives explored. However, this optimism that the Greens could offer a "third force" was not shared by all the disaffected. Russell Jacoby echoes these sentiments on a global front:

> [R]adicalism no longer believes in itself. Once upon a time leftists acted as if they could fundamentally reorganize society. Intellectually, the belief fed off a utopian vision of a different society; psychologically, it rested on self-confidence about one's place in history; politically, it depended on the real prospects. Today the vision has faltered, the self-confidence drained away, the possibilities dimmed. Almost everywhere the left contracts, not simply politically but, perhaps more decisively, intellectually.[15]

Shortly after the 2001 elections in Australia I met Stuart Hall. I recounted the story of my father's vote. Stuart Hall is the founding father of cultural studies and one of the most incisive commentators on British politics. Hall was the first to use the term *Thatcherism* and his analysis of the phenomenon helped the British Labour Party toward what he called "the hard road to renewal."[16] This road subsequently turned toward the "third way," and its particular adaptation of neoliberalism left Hall by the wayside. Hall shared my father's sense of political alienation. He agreed that it was now impossible to vote for Labor, but in an even more pessimistic bite, he added that it was almost meaningless to vote for the Greens.

Hall's touch of realism points to the fact that disaffection with the mainstream political parties is not tempered by seeking refuge in a fringe party. A party cannot mount a genuine contest if it lacks a philosophy that can inspire a broader social movement. In what sense was my father at home in the conscience and convictions of the Greens? Clearly he was disgusted by the Liberal position on the refugee crisis and disappointed by Labor's prevarications. He might never vote Labor again. This loss may be strategically countered by voting Green, but will he ever say "I am a Green" in the way he used to say "I am a Labor"?

In an interview on national television at the end of 2003, Howard described Australian society as the most "detribalized" it has ever been in history. It was a peculiar choice of words to convey the collapse of ideological markers between the left and the right in Australian politics. He then added: "I am proud of my own Liberal background," and here he stopped, possibly to bid farewell to his own ideology, or at least to qualify it through a more inclusive political framework, "but I must govern with the national interest in mind."[17] This seemingly patriotic revelation concedes that Howard's philosophical and political principles have been pushed into the background, but then fails to give any indication of the basis for defining the national interest. It determines the priority of the national over any given ideology but it also obscures any possibility for having a dialogue over its representation. How is the national interest now mapped? Has the end of ideology liberated politicians from defining the bases of their own political representation? Is the floating signifier of the national interest, coupled with the social observation that the contemporary forms of political affiliation are now "detribalized," an opportunity for the politician to take flight into the rootless fantasies of vulgar postmodernism?

Howard recognizes that political survival now depends on expressing reassurance, but also avoiding articulating criteria that would make any commitment firm and transparent. He renounces the need to rely on any of the old frameworks and also entrusts his ability to judge the needs of the nation. He dismisses the "tribalism" of his adversaries as outdated, but also refuses to bind his decision making to any binding framework for defining equality. The effect is a silencing in the political. Without a model for defining exchange or determining direction, Howard is free to "move on" and "stay on." His only obligation is to announce rather than to debate. At every instance, Howard has proclaimed that the ethos of governance is based on the particularity of the context. The concept of experience looms large to justify his authority and the transcendence from his own political principles. He grasps every opportunity to expose the risks of trusting others, changes tack when confronted by a challenge, and seizes the chance to reveal the threats from elsewhere. At every juncture there is the heightened fear of destabilization. This shrill note of paranoia is evident in the warning that he repeatedly issues to his followers: "We are only one loss away from oblivion." Howard never declares the form of his protection or how survival can be insured, but he does stress the need for vigilance against the surrounding threats.

This adaptive mode of government appears inevitable and realistic, but it also inspires an ambivalent mode of attachment. No one can ever feel comfortable on this journey. People may give their votes to an opportunist but they do not identify with the method. They seem to have conceded to the power of the conclusions but cannot feel at home in the logic of the argument because the very structure of belonging has been emptied. Richard Golt, writing for *The Guardian*, concludes that the voice of the "angry, disgruntled and disillusioned," will not be heard in the ivory tower of the media but through the silent act of abstaining:

> For 40 years I have belonged to that grouping of the left that regularly resigns from the Labour party over the issue of foreign wars or nuclear weapons, and then is sheepishly cor-ralled back into the fold at election time when faced with the awesome reality of a Tory gov-ernment. Not any more. Four years of New Labour have devalued politics in this country to such an extent that the political system itself is teetering on the verge of illegitimacy. How can it be right to support a system where two ideologically bankrupt parties hold an absolute monopoly of political power?[18]

New Authoritarianism

It is this loss of identity that signals a deeper malaise in the recent shifts of the political landscape. Weak party identification and consensus over foreign policy and neoliberalist policies on privati-zation has created a vacuum in the political heart of the West. The space for political dissent has collapsed as a result of all the major parties, on the left and right, across the United States, United Kingdom, and Australia adopting similar trajectories on the distribution of economic resources and adopting a common response to global terror. After President Bush's "win this war" speech to Congress following September 11, Senate Majority leader Tom Daschle, a Democrat, and Minority Leader Trent Lott, a Republican, strode to a podium where Lott declared, "Tonight, there is no opposition party."[19] In the United States the disillusionment within mainstream poli-tics has favored both the conservative and single-interest groups that can capitalize on voter disaffection. Ani Shivani has argued that the electorate is not necessarily becoming more conser-vative or being converted to say the Green movement, but rather, when they see the political sys-tem being unable to handle complex problems "they vote conservatively" or look for a simple alternative.[20]

The problem is not just the collapse of a clear ideological distinction between the left and the right, nor even the competition for the center, but rather it is the shameless abandonment of a moral dimension. In the war to prevent refugees arriving by boat, and throughout the "war on ter-ror," politicians have brazenly thrown truth overboard. Blair said, "Trust me." Bush warned against the risk of having to wait for the evidence. Howard declared that facts are irrelevant. Logic, proof, and the rule of law were all put on hold. The citizens of the West were asked to have faith as govern-ments rushed in new bills to curtail civil liberties and to expand the power of the police and the secret services.

Prior to the American led invasion of Iraq, Howard and Blair offered a fig leaf to Saddam Hus-sein. He could stay in power and avoid a bloody war if he disarmed his weapons of mass destruc-tion. The war was supposedly all about the WMDs. Then Hans Blix, the chief weapons inspector for the UN, stressed that they had no evidence that Iraq possessed the WMDs. Iraqi officials repeatedly stated that they did not exist. Bush took this as a sign of intransigence and provocation. Two mem-bers of the U.S. Congress summed up the logic that was driving the invasion. In a letter to the CIA, Republican Porter Goss and Democrat Jane Harman argued: "The absence of proof that chemical and biological weapons and their related development programs had been destroyed was consid-ered proof that they continued to exist."[21] All the investigation teams that combed through the remains of Iraqi sites before and after the war failed to produce any empirical evidence of the phan-tom WMDs. Bush, Blair, and Howard offered no explanation for their previous claims that they "knew" about their existence. They tried to comfort the rest of us with the illusion that the world is a safer place with Hussein ousted from power, and without blinking over their tanklike logic they proceeded with the invasion, because, in Blair's words, they had "no reverse gears."

The new authoritarianism that increasingly shapes the political discourse of the West is a paradoxical phenomenon. It demands faith but it also cuts down the institutions within which the citizen can develop a sense of trust. Unlike mere obedience that can be sustained by fear alone, belief is dependent on a combination of logic and art. True political leadership has the capacity, as Paul Kelly suggested, to take us "out of ourselves" and conversely, its absence is experienced as a diminishment of the self and an "extinguishment of hopes that might have been realized."[22] Is there any contemporary politician who enjoys popular support on the basis of either the truthfulness of his or her argument or the sheer beauty of their ideas? Today there are politicians who attract voters by following the lines of opportunity and averting other risks, but who can say that the people have someone in whom they can believe? Never before have these leaders called their troops to war and so many come out in protest. On February 15, 2003, protest marches were launched in almost every major city in the world. From Melbourne to Madrid posters carrying the word *NO* led the way. The placards of "Not in My Name" captured both the frustration and the isolation of the protesters. In London almost a million people marched against the war with Iraq. The composition of the crowd was not confined to the usual radicals but largely drawn from the respectable sectors of "Middle England." These students, middle-class families, and retired generals were dubbed "marching virgins." Most had never protested on the streets before but many felt that Blair's war mongering government was not listening to the people. Only 15 percent of Britons, 22 percent of Australians, 39 percent of Americans, and 25 percent of Spaniards supported a war without UN approval. However, these antiwar rallies had no coherent voice that could articulate an alternative position. The crowd expressed resentment against the alliance that was being formed in the West and also felt frustrated by the lack of an organized political opposition:

> Under his [Blair's] leadership, New Labour has now leapfrogged European Social Democracy and even Gaullism and landed in the lap of the most rightwing forces of the planet, from America's Republican President George Bush to Italian premier Silvio Berluscioni. This result is the most glaring example of the fundamental dislocation between political culture and an isolated political class.[23]

Bush, Blair, and Howard have demonstrated the resoluteness of their convictions, but paradoxically this has not inspired greater levels of unity nor clarified the purpose of power. The emotional register of new authoritarianism within the national sociopolitical landscape is therefore linked to economic and cultural transformations of globalization. The rhetoric of versatility and flexibility is not just the hollow jargon of corporate marketing, just as the apocalyptic "endings" of postmodernism were not merely idle philosophical speculations. Together they represent both the limit of earlier models and an imperative for new modalities. To a generation of workers disciplined into commitment and loyalty, the transformation in the contemporary economic structures is not just an opportunity for mobility but also a risk that includes exposure to new forms of alienations and greater levels of displacement. The foundations of the workplace and the cultural values have both split.

New authoritarianism is not without its own peculiar comfort zones. The exploitation of fears and prejudices has been interpreted as part of the divisive strategy of "wedge politics." Howard and Bush have exposed unresolved hostilities, mobilized embedded stereotypes, and exploited the simmering resentments that surround issues like race, sexuality, and welfare. Wedge politics operates by defining the needs of a minority as a threat to the national interest. It forces the opposition to defend this minority view while promoting the government as the protector of unity and cohesion.

By attacking the rights of refugees, delegitimizing the status of gay people, or dismantling supportive services for the less privileged, these governments also claim to be defending national sovereignty, traditional family values, and ensuring equity in the marketplace. Not only do they hide the violence of their actions but they claim to be assaulted, violated, and manipulated by the unscrupulous demands of minorities. The profound contradiction that wedge politics tries to displace is the ownership of violence and division. While the wedge politicians proclaim the role of defender of national cohesion, they are also spearheading divisive tactics. Their justification that this is a defensive reaction and that they are under siege is a thin cover for their own violence.

Wedge politics shares some of the characteristics of a sporting conquest. It divides support along oversimplified boundaries. It focuses attention in terms of winning and losing. Resolution is defined by an outcome rather than through addressing the need. The fears that are mobilized by contradictory strategies are not the unfortunate effects but the precondition and fuel that support its appeal. The wedge politicians thrive when they speak into the public anger and resentment. Finding a reception in this place they not only manipulate the hostility to cover their own contradictions and smear their opponents, but they also discover energy from the symmetries of their own stride and strut. They begin to feel at home in this world of division and conquest. In all the anxious talk of national unity and the dread in global security there is also a pleasure in feeling embattled and the little thrill of justified retaliation whenever they launch attacks on the weak.

In the late 1990s, the British tabloid press targeted refugees as thieves who were invading the nation. Headlines ranged from punitive instructions by the *Sunday People* to "Clamp em at Calais" to wild exaggerations by the *Daily Star* of "Refugees get flats with Jacuzzis, sunbeds and … a sauna." After September 11, refugees were not only linked with the spread of terrorism, made responsible for sexual diseases and prostitution but, with the discovery of the poison ricin at the home of a refugee, they were constructed as the carrier of a new invisible threat. The *Sun* followed with the ultimate summation of the invasion complex: "Britain is now a Trojan horse for terrorism." In response to this hysteria the government began to incrementally restrict services and welfare, heighten security on new applications, revise the law on asylum and immigration, and finally enforce higher levels of detention and expulsion. Each draconian step by the government gave more credence to the hysteria generated by the media. The overriding impression was that Britain was in the midst of a flood of refugees, with polls revealing that most people believed that over a quarter of the world's refugees had entered the country. In reality, Britain received less that 2 percent of the world's refugees. However, with the Home Office overspending its 2001 immigration budget by £600 million and Home Secretary David Blunkett welcoming the new center-right party in France on the grounds that "we can do business with this government," it is not surprising that people fear and exaggerate the issues of asylum.[24]

In Australia, the voices of new authoritarianism peak on the talkback radio stations. Inside their darkened, muffled studios shock jocks pump out their litany of curses and abuses. Listeners across the country, receiving the message in the dazzling sunlit context of their own background noises, desperately reach for their phone to either join in the national lament or to nationalize their grievances. As the process of call and response rebounds, indignation spirals into vicious circles. Politicians have become increasingly attuned to this mode, where one lament spirals into another, or grievances find focus as they coil into each other. They now enter the frame in a distinctive way, no longer speaking with the detachment of a patrician nor the charged zeal of a guide who has seen a new future. As Bauman has noted, the form of political leadership has been transfigured to meet the aesthetics of the media: "Its principal vehicle is no longer the ethical authority of leaders with their visions, or moral preachers with their homilies. But the example of celebrities in view."[25] Today the politician is neither above nor ahead, but desires the position of being an idol who can appear in the media as if he or she is one among the crowd. They offer assurance by confessing their own experience of insecurity but also sharing their own stories of conquest. They do not argue a position or even express commitments but seduce through the act of sympathy. They claim to share the pain of ordinary people. Sympathy with populist perspectives quickly turns into endorsement of the reasonableness of feeling confused, insecure, and angry. Howard was asked to reflect on the extraordinary claims that Muslims should be asked to remove traditional headdress for fear that they might be possibly used to conceal weapons: He replied, "Obviously."[26] This is one of the ways in which the power of the media has developed a new twist. The heightened levels of interaction, of call and response, have transformed it from a platform for simply transmitting messages into a network for stimulating and producing new messages. As the politicians enter the loop, their scripted speeches have been displaced and a new circuit of immediate and ordinary speech has dominated.

In the name of listening and responding to the fears of ordinary people, new authoritarianism begets new monsters. The monstrous lie that refugees throw their children overboard, and the mythical weapons of mass destruction that were at the fingertips of that monster Saddam Hussein, were an extension of the desire to twist and stretch the fears of ordinary people within the coil of the mass media. These dreams of "monstrous" refugees and terrorist sleepers in the neighborhood have long parted from logic and reason. They are fueled by fear and are expressed in the language of righteous vengeance. In the midst of rage, the politician seeking to be immersed and in union with ordinariness rejects the voice of moderation and mediation, and mobilizes the sentiment of extraordinary "sameness." They are not there to defend inviolable standards nor to lead toward a new destination but to channel the flows of rage toward new targets. As Jennie Bristow argues: "The political elite is so insecure about the distance between itself and the electorate that it does not even dare to argue against the kind of intolerance it professes to despise."[27]

Neoconservatives complain that during the 1990s successive American governments had a holiday from history. Blair's alliance with Bush turned him into "Bliar." Howard earns praise as an opportunist. A caricatured version of morality pervades every political conviction. For instance, note the statement by Tony Blair to the House of Commons on April 29, 1999, where he argued that the expression of regret for collateral damage was the difference between a moral civilization and a barbaric dictatorship. In a similar twist of logic, the Australian Labor party did not oppose Howard's mandatory detention policy for refugees but merely promised that they would exercise it with "compassion." One assumes that "regret" in killing and imprisoning innocent civilians is either the justification for immoral acts or the foundation of a new moral sensibility. In the mouth of today's politician, the traces of morality appear in ever more generalized and abstract terms, while the criteria and standards of judgment collapse and fade from view. With every example of transgression, outrage bellows, but what disappears is the basis for judgment. Without moral markers it becomes impossible to measure the degree of transgression. In the absence of goals, any deviation is like the fall into the abyss.

Bush, Blair, and Howard have seized on the battle with the enemy as a zero-sum game. Danger is represented in absolute terms. Victory is also elevated into salvation. These opportunists have recognized that the absence of standards can inflate peril and dignify defense. Survival is marked between the fear that September 11 was the beginning of a different kind of invasion and the hope in the deterrent effect of an overwhelming exhibition of "forward defensiveness." As Frank Furedi argued: "The resulting impression, in politics and industry but also across society, is that September 11 represents the emergence of threats beyond the capabilities of traditional risk management, beyond existing systems of insurance and beyond our social resilience."[28] It becomes impossible to rank the minor infraction from the total destruction. The representation of the threat is so utterly divorced from tangible characteristics that devastation is possible at every instant and therefore every act of defence is reasonable.

The attacks of September 11 were described by Bush, Blair, and Howard in apocalyptic terms. Terrorism was invoked not only as the weapon of a political adversary but also the means for inciting new forms of cultural clash. Islamic fundamentalism was pitted against Western democracy. Despotic and brutal tyranny loomed over the horizon to threaten the vulnerable and tolerant structures of the open society. Fear was not only concentrated against militant external enemies but also dispersed within the West. Was it loyalty or the bonding of shared fears that were expressed in the headlines of the British press when they announced: "We're all New Yorkers now." The state of generalized anxiety, where disparate fears over crimes, health, and technology conjoined with state sanctions and visible catastrophes, heightened the sense of vulnerability and collapsed the boundary between "us" and "them." Where fear dominates, suspicion proliferates. Terrorists were indistinguishable from citizens. They were already operating as sleepers, ready to strike at any point. The defense against terror was articulated in evangelical terms. The West would "root out evil wherever it lay." As Michael Humphrey noted: "The 'new terrorism' has become a funnel for the more generalised level of anxiety and uncertainty created by the 'risk society' in a globalised world."[29] However, he also added that the demonization of the terrorists' identity would not only help to disperse the fear but also blur the causes of conflict and resentment. The field of operation for this new terrorism is not defined by the capture of key strategic sites or the occupation of a specified territory, but rather it only exists in the imaginary. Violence multiplies as it resonates in the fantasy of the global viewers. The spectacle of the collapse of the WTC was the goal of the terrorist. It was also a spectacle that triggered an upsurge of fear in the American imaginary.

The opportunism that is central to new authoritarianism thus rests with the unshackling of the boundaries of fear in the imaginary. Richard Nixon's observation that "people react to fear not love" has become the guiding principle of contemporary political discourse. Despite the doubling of their life expectancy in the twentieth century, the decline in crime rates throughout the 1990s, and the real improvements in child welfare, Americans are obsessed with the spread of pandemic diseases, convinced that they are at greater risk of violence, and that drug abuse is rampant from early youth. America is in a state of near panic. In California they spend more on prisons than on higher education and across the country they are increasingly cutting social services in order to fund programs that inevitably stoke the fears of crime and disease.[30] After September 11 anxiety levels rose rather than declined when the governments informed their citizens that new defense mechanisms had been installed. The most extreme example was the rush on emergency supplies and the construction of a safe room in the event of biochemical attacks. Such safety plans risked becoming suicide pacts, for had people followed the advice of Tom Ridge, the new head of the Department of Homeland Security, and sealed themselves in a room with plastic sheeting and duct tape, the average family would last just three hours before they suffocated from the lack of oxygen.

As fear was dispersed into every aspect of domestic life, Bush announced that America would go on the offensive and attack any country that was "harboring terrorists." His Deputy Sheriff, Howard, promised to lead the charge in Asia. Debate over the legality of these preemptive strikes was suppressed by the representation of this aggressive defensiveness not only as a necessity but as a virtue. Striking out in defiance, however, failed to produce unity at home. It only bolstered the sense of loss and embattlement. Today there is no clarity in the identity of the enemy and no consensus about the uses of power.

Political discourse, once trapped in this paranoia, is aloof to any reality tests, it elevates itself above the need to measure perceptions against rational benchmarks that may measure the legal entitlements, social equivalences, and cultural correspondences with others. Dialogue disappears. Communication is not only monological but reduced to ever diminishing phrases with monosyllabic syncopations that force the listener to sway in the tick-tocking oscillation between enunciations and promised salvations. A politician like Bush would never dream of writing his own speeches, let alone memorizing them. However, when such politicians read from transcripts they still seek to appear as if they are speaking from the heart. Speechwriters have adjusted their text to suit such a performance. In place of the flowing rhetoric of the patrician and zealous leaders of the past, there is now a procession of short phrases in a staccato rhythm. Note the beat that drums up conviction but also underscores the dread in Howard's address at the dedication of the Australian War Memorial in London:

In mourning our fallen,
in numbers still difficult to comprehend,
we also acknowledge the terrible power
of those forces that would conspire
against such a dream.
History's lesson is that evil will always dwell within the world
— in the past represented by armies rolling across national borders,
in this new century finding form in acts of indiscriminate terrorism inspired by distorted faith.
Such intent can be defeated
by the willingness of decent men and women to put aside the comfort
safety and security of their own lives
to understand that militarism and totalitarianism and terror
are creeping sicknesses that will inevitably spread
if left unchallenged and unchecked,
and by the willingness of nations to stand together
in mutual defence of the common values
which underpin the progression of man. [31]

What is excluded by such oscillating mnemonics and syncopated tonalities? There is at once a decline in the space for connection. The voice moves from one extreme to another as if it could mimic the stiffened dignity of vigilance and reproduce the scar from the severed dialogue with others. The theater of invasion and defense excludes a place of coming together to face the other and witness the complicities and connections that now exist in everyday life. To avoid recognition, in all the shame of self-reflection and mutual extension, the opportunist must always move on. There is no space for historical consciousness that reveals complicity with violence or a cultural understanding of the needs of strangers. In response to the growing pressures for a postcolonial or multicultural perspective on Australian history and culture, Howard expressed indignation. He dismissed the "black arm-band" of history for fear of being blamed for the legacies of the past and resented the inclusion of other cultural values for fear that this would expose the inadequacy of the dominant culture. In response to global terror, Howard's impatience with civil procedures resulted in the extension of his executive powers to bypass the rule of national and international law. Historical facts, cultural values, and legal procedures are all seen as limits that could constrain his need to display decisiveness. To keep things moving, being alert to the new global threats meant being empowered to loosen, multiply, and disperse the categories for evaluation. The new authoritarianism of contemporary politics is not marked by its commitment to fixed hierarchies and standards but by its capacity to reinvent the benchmarks of acceptability in order to secure a normalized aggressivity.

The freedom that the West expects for itself is usually gained at the expense of other people's security. Philosophers have struggled with the balance between the master's control over security and the slave's dream for freedom. At stake is not just the political question of domination but also the moral problems of dependency. Mastering security is a trap that encloses everything within the windowless space of slavery. Open freedom risks leaving everyone without any boundary for negotiation. The freedoms that Bush, Blair, and Howard demand in the marketplace have consequences in the loss of security in the community. The security that they strive for in the global arena is also borne as a loss of freedom at home. They complain that traditional values have been destroyed and yet they refuse to uphold either the saliency of civic rights over political experience, or even value the difference between an economic organization and a cultural institution. Why should everything be the same? Is our society so simple that it can only maintain one benchmark for success? They are convinced that core values need to be preserved but are also willing to change the structures that confer continuity and identity. They seek to reassure by stressing their conviction to fight evil but refrain from defining the moral and legal basis of their own actions. This dissembling exceeds mere spin because there is no pregiven trajectory to their lines of thought. Politicians no longer swerve, they cut and paste. As fear has saturated the political imaginary, it is now impossible to differentiate the theater of dreams and the theater of war. Novalis wrote that "when we dream that we are dreaming, the moment of awakening is at hand." Such a refreshing form of awareness is remote to the prevailing nightmare of competing fictions. In amongst the ruins of ideology there still lies the conviction that renewal springs from the eternal spirit of the nation and the boundless reservoir of self-belief.

The Twin Towers of Globalization

The structures of labor and consumption have been redefined in terms of a new discourse of immediacy. "Just in time" technologies are not just smarter ways of delivering products but reflective of a broader way of thinking about needs and investment. At every level corporations are aiming at achieving "lightness," "fluidity," and "flexibility." This is in contrast to the earlier industrial models of "heaviness," "solidity," and "integrated," self-sufficiency. Industrial architecture demonstrates this transition in stark terms. In the nineteenth century, industrialists built factories to resemble either an impregnable castle or an opulent palazzo. In the late twentieth century, the factory's architectural display was compressed into its temporary modular function. The workers' place in the world, their commitment, security, and ethical frameworks, are also part of this transformation from heavy to light. Terms of employment are increasingly defined in terms of the execution of precise needs. Even personal engagements tumble into the form of a rolling contract, where the mutual expectations within a partnership are confined to specific and time-bound tasks without the guarantee of continuity in the future. The sentiments of attachment and forms of belonging are also being restructured through an aversion to depth, fixity, and finality. The fear of commitment intertwines with the new technologies of flexibility. The desire for mobility reacts against the strictures of domesticity. The personal transformations in "life politics" mirrors the economic changes of post-Fordism. The promises of living life to the max also carry new risks of burnout and isolation. It is the combination of different forms of fear within and between the workplace, family, community, and national security that create a new culture of ambient fear.

Paolo Virno has recognized the centrality of fear and the "ambivalence of disenchantment" in contemporary culture and society. This is not just a negative position of withdrawal or passive resignation, but an agitated state that is mobilized within new personal ways of being in the world and forms of production that combine to advance new structures of domination. The restructuring of home and work is no longer simply defined by a break with the solidity of tradition but an activation of the already fragmented state of traditions and an engagement—a process of putting to work—sentiments, inclinations, and states of mind that have been severed from any form of traditional foundation.[32] The mobilization of the sentiment is therefore not just a response but part of the precondition or mechanism for the advancement of specific socioeconomic practices.

The mutability of economic relations and the fragmentation of cultural values combine to create a sense of uncertainty and insecurity on the horizon. The anxiety is compounded by the unpredictability of both the trajectory and the fallout from the ongoing processes of restructuring. These changes, rather than moving in a linear path, create a cascading pattern, where one slippage tumbles into another. As Virno argues:

> Fears of particular dangers, if only virtual ones, haunt the workday like a mood that cannot be escaped. This fear, however, is transformed into an operational requirement, a special tool for the trade. Insecurity about one's place during periodic innovation, fear of losing recently gained privileges, and anxiety over being "left behind" translate into flexibility, adaptability, and a readiness to reconfigure oneself ... fear is no longer what drives us into submission *before* work, but the active component of that stable instability that marks the internal articulations of the productive process itself.[33]

These displacements create new cleavages along previously unseen fissures and split down unanticipated pathways. Even the survivors live in the fear of the ground beneath and the security of structures above. Things move in turbulent ways. Structures collapse but the lament is not a metaphysical nostalgia for the loss of home. For if homelessness is the norm, and all homes are temporary, to be displaced from one is not the loss of any primal notion of security, but simply the loss of a structure that itself was never defined in terms of its centrality but only for its specific and contingent use value.

The agony of exile has been the subject of countless philosophical meditations and the driving force in literary narratives now sounds like a quaint sentiment of bygone ages. For today, if there is no longer a fixed notion of the home, then the classical sense of exile has also been displaced. Exile occurs in more banal terms, it is no longer on the margin of cultural existence but a constitutive force in the construction of all social relations. As the condition of exile has been brought inside by the process of being at home in the ruins of tradition, there is not a greater sense of repose but a heightened state of fear. The source of fear is no longer located beyond. The monstrous other and the place of dread is within. Fear is not an external force that drives the citizen into submission but an internal force that compels vigilance, competition, and restlessness. It does not come from above or beyond but from the nervousness of not knowing where the threats are but knowing that they exist within intimacy. Being close is being vulnerable to betrayal.

Globalization promised to bring different worlds together. However, with every step toward economic integration and cultural interpenetration, there has been an even steeper slide toward polarization and an entanglement with even more complex forms of differentiation. The gaps within equality and understanding have expanded rather than diminished. The turbulence of these changes in the socioeconomic and cultural landscape has provoked new levels of defensiveness in the political discourse. As the authority of the nation-state has been undermined, politicians have sought to impose greater controls over national institutions. This is evident not only in the dismantling of welfare agencies that serve minority groups but also in the attempt to regulate the media, the universities, the courts, and the museums of the nation. While demanding that these institutions redefine themselves by making themselves competitive with global and corporate organizations, they are also increasingly involved in trying to shape the content of these institutions. Expectations of higher levels of accountability and compliance with government priorities have risen despite the decline in levels of funding. While the executive boards of the national media and museums are increasingly filled by government appointees, the politicians continue to complain of bias and misrepresentation. Why do these governments feel victimized by their own institutions?

Politicians are anxious about these institutions because their new authoritarianism is in conflict with the traditions of truth, knowledge, justice, and beauty. All these traditions rely on complexity and the negotiation with difference for survival. The defenders of these traditions recognize that dogma is death. Today politicians would rather witness a sporting event than attend an exhibition at an art gallery. George Bush is never as happy as he is whilst watching baseball, and feels most at ease in fielding questions on global conflict while preparing to demonstrate his golfing technique. John Howard would gladly swap his position as Prime Minister for the captaincy of the Australian cricket team. Both fail to grasp that in the time of war the meaning of games is far from simple.

Ambivalence Now

In 2003 Martin Flannagan, a Melbourne sportswriter, published a book called *The Game in the Time of War*. It begins by recounting a fabled "bloodbath" between two rival teams. Flannagan describes, with great eloquence, the intense hostility that had preceded the game and the gritty character of the players. Their display of courage, ferocity, and solidarity is portrayed with humor and warmth. However, with even greater poignancy Flannagan also reports that the game was played shortly after the First World War ended. The players, who were exempted from battle, played in front of spectators who had just returned. Throughout the book there are further sporting episodes which Flannagan interprets as lessons on facing fear. Most of all he teaches us that strength comes from a relaxed tenderness toward adversity and the sweetness of balanced poise. The book ends with a scene that he declares was a setup. It recounts the author walking home on the Sabbath having watched a football game with a Jew and a Muslim. On the long journey home they intersperse observations of the game with comments on the hollowness of politicians who speak of courage and sacrifice.

Flannagan did not write about the new world aggression, but he evoked, in the most ordinary of words, how the order of strength holds up hope. His message could not be ridiculed as mere intellectual posturing or dismissed as politically biased. However, it could be ignored if we only spoke of the game in the time of war. Having toured the country and conducted countless interviews, Flannagan returned home depressed, feeling alone and out of place. "Tell us about the game when …," "Was Jack 'Blood' Dyer really that big?" These were the questions that were returned to a book that tried to awaken the dreamers. Flannagan knows that the game is both an escape and a model, it is neither a totality nor a substitute for life. His attention is not confined to the statistics of victory but drawn to register the unspoken qualities of humans in the glimpsing moments when they excel. These rare flashes reveal the warmth of hope and ultimately give faith to the view that the world, irrespective of results, does not revolve around fear and conquest.

During my youth, the experience of going to the movies was dramatically enhanced by the invention of the surround sound system. The tension on screen could spike by a sudden screech or thud that seemingly thumped into you from behind your shoulder. Fear engulfs the citizen in another version of the surround system. The enemy is no longer on the other side of a boundary, but possibly beside you in the darkness. This intimacy unsettles comfort or surety. Ambient fears dominate the political landscape. The fear that is generated by being suspended in a no-man's-land, surrounded by the unpredictability of threat and the unlocatability of opposition, has eviscerated the structures of hope. In this state of perpetual trepidation there is a distinct absence in the forms of leadership. The old patriarch and the zealous ideologues have been replaced by a new mawkish bully. Authority is grasped with nervousness and held tightly while treading between lashing aggressivity and squealing defensiveness. The moral hesitancy that tears every edge of political vision ensures that every promise comes with a disclaimer.

Blaming is a habitual strategy that politicians use to evade responsibility. When fault is discovered blaming is a way of attributing causality to an external party. The practice of blaming is linked to broader strategies of distancing and disavowal. Today the state does not stand as the primary structure for shaping social values. To accept this role would entail a heavy burden of responsibility. As the state recedes from its position of authority it also distances itself from fault. It acquires both inbuilt mechanisms for avoiding blame by outsourcing the delivery of key social services and then accepting secrecy clauses to protect commercial interests. In the rare instances when fault is disclosed, the politicians can either maintain their silence, due to the confidentiality provisions in their contractual arrangement, or if public interest is so inflamed, they can then enter the blame game. In the crisis over the detention of children whose parents were refugees, the Howard government progressively blamed "soft hearted" elites, misguided professional investigators, divisive advocacy groups, representatives from the intermediary state governments, and finally the private company that was responsible for exercising the government contract. Throughout, the circular logic of blaming protected the government from responsibility, and maintained a distance from the issues of care toward innocent children. As the origin of fear becomes more and more diffuse, the recall to blaming is more pervasive. It is no longer a defensive reaction but part of the offensive. Politicians justify their preemptive strike by blaming others for the fear of fears. Bush blames Saddam Hussein for the War on Terror. Howard blames the refugees for the chaos of global migration. New authoritarianism conceals its aggression behind the night cloud of its blaming flack attack.

Complexity is the victim of denial and smearing. The centrality of blaming in new authoritarianism returns us to a meaning that lurks in its etymology. The origin of blaming is linked to the act of blasphemy. Who has the power to slander, to judge others as faulty and inferior? Who has the authority to know of the crime before the evidence and dismiss the plea without examining the facts? To blaspheme and to blame the other not only presumes a level of superiority but also upholds an elevated form of innocence. In what sense is the West, the prime beneficiary from colonization and globalization, the victim of global terror?

What are the means for verification in a context of fear and blaming? How do we distinguish between a false scare and a real alarm? The volume of stories that provoke fear and anxiety is growing in the media. Journalists and politicians are quick to parade anecdotal evidence, adopt selective use of facts, vilify people, and impute monstrous intentions. Alarmism spreads and in parallel the importance of the whistleblower grows. The success of political scaremongering depends not only on the accuracy of impending threats but also on its capacity to express deeper cultural anxieties. The slipperiness of these fears may unfold in a complex and contradictory manner, but their expression allows little room for understanding complexity and contradiction. Bush, Blair, and Howard rhetorically declare a form of resoluteness and steadfastness, but also a desire to "move on" when fault is found and qualify their responsibility from any political liability. A new pathology is evident in this discourse of denialism. Loyalty to the nation demands unity and in this bond difference is not only compressed but the need for open critique is also repressed. The tension between the image of the nation and the voices of its imagined communities has never been so extreme. The world of difference is coming into daily struggle with the notion of sameness. Bush, Blair, and Howard are leaders who represent the last generation, in which the dream of sameness found potency. The stand that they have taken on border protection and the war on terror could also be seen as the final gasp of a social order that is also struggling against the presence of difference within.

The emotional register of ambivalence in contemporary politics has revealed not only the enhanced role of opportunism in leadership but also the uneven feeling of resignation within the community. This ambivalence is heightened by the very effort to push a political philosophy into the background, and by the separation of political judgment from any comprehensible sense of moral totality. It creates a state of belonging in nonbelonging, for it sets up a political life as a series of arbitrary encounters along an unmarked path of chance. Even the joy of improvisation is condemned in advance as adaptation to change is framed by the need to avert risk or defeat fear. Moreover, such a state of unease flattens and abstracts the very places of engagement, allowing no trace or resonance with the possibility that circumstance and context can ever produce a reality that contains delight and wonder.

The experience of ambivalence in the contemporary political landscape is not framed by either the hope in the eventual return to a secure home, or the belief that enlightenment can be found in the journey. The form of ambivalence that prevails today is spread out on an open horizon of homelessness. The ambivalence we feel is an uneasy sense of the nostalgia for the impossible return and a realization that we have embarked on a paradoxical journey. It involves movement without clear points of departure and destination. It is a mixture of slow drift and nervous restlessness. Ambivalence in the current context is not just the inner conflict between desire and dread, but also the confrontation of the contradictions between the personal as political and the increasing separation of the political from the social. Individual responsibilities and opportunities have never been more compelling and the cost of a society of individuals has never been so glaring. This experience of ambivalence has been threaded into the new modes of domination. Precariousness is on the tip of everyone's grip of reality. Politicians have extended their power by stoking the fears of invasion. The threat of redundancy and inbuilt obsolescence ensures higher levels of competitiveness in the workplace. A new dependency is created out of the exaggerated fears of invasion and abandonment. Uncertainty dominates the field of relations. It becomes impossible to make ongoing plans for living and sharing when there is the permanent risk that the Other may terminate his or her obligations. This dread of abandonment stimulates the perverse desire to please the subject who is the very cause of uncertainty. Citizens become trapped inside the fears that politicians inflate. Employees become anxious that their own needs will render them obsolete. They feel increasingly bound to their own slavery while the dreams of mobility proliferate on all screens of everyday life. Their own homes have become a place of alienation. Exile has occurred without the drama of an exit.

The multiplicity of media in the domestic space has collapsed the boundaries between inside and outside, work and respite, private and public. Multiplicity has turned the story of exile into the banal narrative of daily life. Politicians have grasped the anxiety over the loss of the moorings to place and have replied with the promise of choice and the ideal of the nation. Multiplicity has become the name of our modern migration. Surrounded by a near infinity of cultural signs and the contradictions between free choice and loyalty to the nation, political subjectivity has not only become more and more restless but it has also compromised the idea of roots.

It may sound paradoxical to suggest that the nationalism of the new authoritarianism is also exacerbating the condition of rootlessness. However, the idea of connectedness to place was never simply a matter of geography but shaped by what Raymond Williams called the "structures of feeling." It required cultural modes and social institutions for shaping perception. The experience of place and the traditions for emplacement have now been cleaved apart. When Howard chides the mixtures and combinations of multiculturalism as a sign of fake cultural identity and insists that national identity needs to be rerooted in a hollowed out version of the past, there is a desperate plea to block the noise that surrounds the migrant neighborhood and seek refuge in a tiny old refrain that lurks somehow in the background of his family upbringing. Yet this cultural filtering is discordant with his own political agenda. In politics the channelling works to a different rhythm. It is constantly cutting and pasting signs from outside and rejecting the view that everything can be found inside the old home of liberalism. There is a constant process of uprooting and the hallmark of his authority is in his capacity to respond to this ever-changing environment. Howard does not decry the multiplicity of signs in the political, rather he promotes it in order to demonstrate that from amidst all the noise he can still deliver a decisive voice. The excess frames his attention to fear because in itself it becomes another sign of instability and out of the abstracted state of anxiety he can offer isolated examples of threat against which his responses can assumes the mantle of authority.

Howard adapts and morphs with the geopolitical changes, without seeming to move from his own stubbornly singular cultural way of seeing the world. In the Australian media there has been a great deal of attention to the shape of the opposition. Much discussion has been given to the kind of target that the opposition presents. Prior to the refugee crisis and September 11, it was presumed that the opposition party would win if it minimized its own political identity. It was presumed that the prevailing ambivalence would favor the party that presented the smallest target. However, in a crisis, manufactured or otherwise, ambivalence rebounds in the cross-currents of a booming political authority and whirling moral vacuums. The negative strategy of hoping to win by not risking to lose puts citizenship into a coma. The citizens may appear to be asleep but their dreams outflank the alternatives to the mainstream. While the mainstream parties appease the fears of strangers, parasites, and enemies and reassure the populist initiative to exert more force, control, and restrictions on others, the door to extremism becomes wider. The exhaustion of the driving forces within the mainstream parties had been put down to voter apathy. But this explanation of fatigue ignores the counterreaction at its own peril. As Jeremy Seabrook observed in relation to the rise of the far right in Europe: "Apathy is no such thing. It is the sullen silence that covers growing popular disaffection from the 'depoliticised' politics of the perpetual centre; beneath it, deeper political divisions are striving to find expression."[34] Voters are reminded every day that globalization has produced greater economic inequality and social disintegration. The disenfranchisement they see in others becomes a mirror of their own dispossession. Getting tougher on refugees does not make the citizen sleep better at night.

Ambivalence is at the core of the political. My father voted Green not because he belonged to their tradition, nor because of a new willingness to participate in their projects. He was alienated. He chose Green because he still needed to belong and participate in the political. He did not accept the ultimatum of new authoritarianism. He needed to vote for something that was affirmative, even if it was without the full sense of belonging and participation. This ambivalence toward mainstream politics may be a sign of alienation but it is also a signal for resistance. It is the glimmer of hope in the expression of despair by the homeless citizen.

Notes

1. The term *New Australia* was the expression used by the Australian government to describe those migrants who came to Australia from Europe as part of the massive post-World War II immigration program. This program signaled the first major move away from Australia's previous policy on immigration, which was known as the White Australia policy for its focus on keeping Australia as white and British as possible, hence the new migrants being called New Australians.
2. Goran Rosenberg quoted in Zygmunt Bauman, *Community* (Cambridge, U.K.: Polity Press, 2001), 10.
3. Peter Burt, "Why I No Longer Feel Secure," *The Age*, April 11, 2003.
4. Robert Jensen, "Nothing to Fear but Not Being Normal: Letter from America," *Critical Times*, April/May 2001.
5. The refugee crisis refers to the Australian government's reaction to, and treatment of, asylum seekers. Australia has a policy of mandatory detention of asylum seekers, including children, until their claims are processed, with many detained for years. They also instituted a system of granting temporary protection visas (TPVs) for either two or five years for those granted asylum, creating an ambiguous status and thus greater insecurity for refugees. As numbers of asylum seekers arriving in Australia started to increase—to around 2,800 in 2000 (mainly from the Middle East as a result of the situation in Afghanistan and Iraq)— refugees were increasingly demonized by the Australian government, with their arrival presented as a "flood" of "illegal" immigrants posing a possible threat to Australia. The situation reached crisis point with a number of incidents in late 2001. In August, the *MV Tampa*, a Norwegian container ship, rescued a sinking ship of asylum seekers off the Australian coast. When the captain of the *Tampa* attempted to bring them to safety in Australia, the Australian government refused to allow the ship to disembark. The *Tampa* was

stopped by the Australian military and the asylum seekers on board were transported to the Pacific Island of Nauru for detention and the processing of their asylum claims. When the events of September 11 occurred shortly after, the Australian Prime Minister John Howard rationalized his government's militaristic response to the *Tampa* by what he argued was the possible "threat" presented by asylum seekers who might have "terrorist links." The situation then continued to escalate with the October 2001 "children overboard" crisis. This involved another boatload of Middle Eastern asylum seekers, who, the Australian government claimed, had attempted to force the Australian Navy to come to their rescue by throwing their children into the sea. Exacerbating the existing hysteria, the "children overboard" situation resulted in a climax of revulsion toward Middle Eastern refugees. The demonizing of refugees was epitomized by the Prime Minister's comments on radio that "I certainly don't want people of that type in Australia, I really don't." It was later revealed by the media, and admitted by the government, that the claims that the asylum seekers had thrown their children into the sea were false. What actually happened was that their boat had started to sink; all of the asylum seekers had ended up in the water, and were rescued by the Australian Navy. However, despite this revelation, the "othering" of these refugees had already been well established. Victoria Mason, "Strangers within the 'Lucky Country': Arab-Australians after September 11th" *Journal of Comparative Studies of South Asia, Africa and the Middle East*, 24, no. 1 (2004.) I would like to thank Victoria for her research assistance in this article.

6. Guy Rundle, "The Terror Pretext; the ALP and Asylum Seekers," *Arena Magazine*, February–March 2002.
7. Marie Tehan, "Latham's Refugee Policy May Win Over Liberals," *The Age*, December 16, 2003.
8. Robert Corcoran, "Labor—A Better Way," *Arena Magazine*, February–March 2002, 19.
9. Keith Suter "Fear and Loathing on the Campaign Trail," *Contemporary Review*, 280 (January 2002), 18.
10. Ulrich Beck, *World Risk Society*. Cambridge, UK: Polity Press, 1999, 2.
11. Tony Blair, "Speech by the Prime Minister on New Deal." Birmingham International Convention Centre, June 22, 1999. For a detailed analysis on the way conservative policies have been grounded within the principle of modernizing Labor governments, see C. Johnson and F. Tonkiss, "The Third Influence: The Blair Government and Australian Labor," *Policy and Politics*, 30, no. 1 (1999): 5–18.
12. Guy Rundle, "Commonsense and the ALP," *Arena Magazine*, February–March 2002, 21.
13. Russell Jacoby, *The End of Utopia*. New York: Basic Books, 1999, xiii.
14. Bruce Lindsay, "The Greening of Australian Politics," *Arena Magazine*, February–March 2003, 25.
15. Jacoby, *The End of Utopia*, 10.
16. Stuart Hall, *The Hard Road to Renewal*. London: Verso, 1988.
17. "Howard Not Worried by Generational Change," interview with Tony Jones, *Dateline*, ABC (March 12, 2003).
18. Richard Golt, "I Shall Not Vote," *The Guardian*, June 7, 2001.
19. John Nichols, "A Growing Opposition," *The Nation*, September 21, 2001.
20. Ani Shivani, "Conservative Politics in an Era of Dealignment," *CounterPunch*, edited by Alexander Cockburn and Jeffrey St. Clair, January 2, 2003.
21. Quoted in Brian Toohey, "WMD Logic Fails Intelligence Test," *Financial Review*, October 4–5, 2003.
22. Paul Kelly, "Leadership, Today's Missing Ingredient," *The Australian*, November 26, 2003.
23. Gary Younge, "Defiance of Global Will: This War Is Not Only about Iraq, but about Who Runs the World and How to Make Them Accountable to Us," *Guardian*, March 10, 2003.
24. For detailed analysis of the impact of the media on government policy see David Renton, "Examining the Success of the British National Party," *Race and Class* 45, no. 2 (October–December 2003): 75 and Jennie Bristow, "Lunatics about Asylum," *Spiked online*, June 19, 2002.
25. Bauman, *Community*, 66.
26. Quoted by John Pilger, "George Bush's Other Poodle," *New Statesman*, January 20, 2003, 18.
27. Bristow, "Lunatics about Asylum."
28. Frank Furedi, *Refusing to be Terrorised*. London: Global Futures, 2002, 7–8.
29. Michael Humphrey, "Risk, Terrorism and Globalisation," *Australian and New Zealand Institute of Insurance and Financial Journal*, 26, no. 3 (2003): 11.
30. Barry Glassner, *The Culture of Fear*. New York: Basic Books, 1999.
31. Transcript of the Prime Minister, the Hon. John Howard M.P., Address at the Dedication of the Australian War Memorial, Hyde Park Corner, London, November 11, 2003, http://www.pm.gov.au/news/speeches/speech568.html.
32. Paolo Virno, "The Ambivalence of Disenchantment," in *Radical Thought in Italy*, edited by P. Virno and M. Hardt. Minneapolis: University of Minnesota Press, 1996, 15.
33. Ibid., 17.
34. Jeremy Seabrook, "The Shock of the Obvious," *New Internationalist*, April 26, 2002.

9

Taboo Memories and Diasporic Visions:
Columbus, Palestine, and Arab-Jews

ELLA SHOHAT

Dr. Solomon Schechter [Cambridge expert in Hebrew documents a century ago] agreed to look at them, but chiefly out of politeness, for he was still skeptical about the value of the "Egyptian fragments." But it so happened that he was taken completely by surprise. One of the documents immediately caught his interest, and next morning, after examining … he realized that he had stumbled upon a sensational discovery…. the discovery has so excited Schechter that he had already begun thinking of traveling to Cairo to acquire whatever remained of the documents…. Schechter was fortunate that Cromer [the British administrator of Egypt] himself took interest in the success of his mission. The precise details of what transpired between Schechter and British officialdom and the leaders of the Cairo's Jewish community are hazy, but soon enough … they granted him permission to remove everything he wanted from the Geniza [a synagogue chamber where the community books, papers, and documents were kept for centuries], every last paper and parchment, without condition or payment. It has sometimes been suggested that Schechter succeeded so easily in his mission because the custodians of the Synagogue of Ben Ezra had no idea of the real value of the Geniza documents—a species of argument that was widely used in the nineteenth century to justify the acquisition of historical artifacts by colonial powers…. [C]onsidering that there had been an active and lucrative trade in Geniza documents … and impoverished as they were, it is hard to believe that they would willingly have parted with a treasure which was, after all, the last remaining asset left to them by their ancestors. In all likelihood the decision was taken for them by the leaders of their community, and they were left with no alternative but acquiescence. As for those leaders … like the elites of so many other groups in the colonized world, they evidently decided to seize the main chance at a time when the balance of power—the ships and the guns—lay overwhelmingly with England…. Schechter … filled out about thirty sacks and boxes with the materials and with the help of the British embassy in Cairo he shipped them off to Cambridge. A few months later he returned himself—laden … "with spoils of the Egyptians."

—*From Amitav Ghosh*, In an Antique Land[1]

I begin my essay with a quotation from Amitav Ghosh's remarkable account of the emptying out of the Jewish-Egyptian Geniza archive, which by World War I was stripped of all its documents. The contents of the archive were then distributed to Europe and America, with a large part of the documents going into private collections. There is nothing unusual about such a colonial raid of the archive—in this case a very literal archive indeed. What is unusual, however, are the ways the two groups of coreligionists, the European Ashkenazi Jews and the Sephardic Arab-Jews, fell out on opposite sides of the colonial divide. European Jews' closeness to Western powers permitted the dispossession of Arab-Jews, even before the advent of Zionism as a national project.

In this historical episode, the culture of the Egyptian Jewish community was partially "disappeared" through the confiscation of its most sacred documents. At the moment of the Geniza removal, two years after its "discovery" in 1896, Egyptian Jews had been for millennia a symbiotic part of the geocultural landscape of the region. The British Jewish scholars, like their non-Jewish compatriots, cast a similarly imperial gaze at the Egyptian Jews, the very people who produced and sustained the Geniza for almost a thousand years, and whose remarkable achievement these scholars were engaging in appropriating, but whom the scholars describe as "aborigines," "scoundrels," whose religious leaders have the "unpleasant" habit of kissing other men "on the mouth."[2] In a traumatic turn of events, the diasporization of the Geniza anticipated by half a century the exiling of its owners. In the wake of the Israeli-Arab conflict, especially after the British withdrawal from Palestine, and the establishment of the state of Israel in 1948, Arabs and Jews were newly staged as enemy identities. If Ghosh's description vividly captures a moment when Arab-Jews were still seen as simply "Arabs," colonized subjects, with the partition of Palestine, Arab-Jews, in a historical shift, suddenly become simply "Jews."

The historical episode described by Ghosh and its aftermath suggest not only that alliances and oppositions between communities evolve historically, but also that they are narrativized differently according to the schemata and ideologies of the present. As certain strands in a cultural fabric become taboo, this narrativization involves destroying connections that once existed. The process of *constructing* a national historical memory also entails the *destruction* of a different, prior historical memory. The archive of the Geniza was largely written in Judeo-Arabic, a language my generation is the last to speak. Since the dispersal of its people from the Arab world, Judeo-Arab culture has been disdained as a sign of *galut* (diaspora)—a negative term within Euro-Israeli Zionist discourse. The European "discovery" and "rescue" of the Geniza from its producers had displaced a long tradition in which Ashkenazi Jewish religious scholars had corresponded and consulted with the Sephardi religious centers of the Judeo-Islamic world. But since the Enlightenment, Eurocentric norms of scholarship have established typically colonial relations that have taken a heavy toll on the representation of Arab-Jewish history and identity. In this essay, I will attempt to disentangle the complexities of Arab-Jewish identity by unsettling some of the borders erected by almost a century of Zionist and colonial historiography, with its fatal binarisms such as civilization versus savagery, modernity versus tradition, and West versus East.

Toward a Relational Approach to Identity

Recent postcolonial theory has at times shied away from grounding its writings in historical context and cultural specificity. Although innumerable poststructuralist essays elaborate abstract versions of "difference" and "alterity," few offer a communally participatory and politicized knowledge of non-European cultures. At the same time, however, the professionalized study of compartmentalized historical periods and geographic regions (as in Middle East studies and Latin American studies) has often resulted in an overly specific focus that overlooks the interconnectedness of histories, geographies, and cultural identities. In *Unthinking Eurocentrism*, Robert Stam and I argue for a relational approach to multicultural studies that does not segregate historical periods and geographic regions into neatly fenced-off areas of expertise, and that does not speak of communities in isolation, but rather "in relation."[3] Rather than pit a rotating chain of resisting communities against a Western dominant (a strategy that privileges the "West," if only as constant antagonist), we argue for stressing the horizontal and vertical links threading communities and histories together in a conflictual network. Analyzing the overlapping multiplicities of identities and affiliations that link diverse resistant discourses helps us transcend some of the politically debilitating effects of disciplinary and community boundaries.

The kind of connections we have in mind operate on a number of levels. First, it is important to make connections in temporal terms. Although postcolonial studies privilege the imperial era of the nineteenth and twentieth centuries, one might argue for grounding the discussion in a longer history of multiply located colonialisms and resistances, tracing the issues at least as far back as 1492. We propose connections in spatial/geographic terms, placing debates about identity and representation in a broader context that embraces the Americas, Asia, and Africa. We also argue for connections in disciplinary and conceptual terms, forging links between debates usually compartmentalized (at least in the United States): on the one hand, postcolonial theory associated with issues of colonial discourse, imperial imaginary, and national narrations, and, on the other, the diverse "ethnic studies," focusing on issues of "minorities," race, and multiculturalism. The point is to place the often ghettoized discourses about geographies ("here" versus "there") and about time ("now" versus "then") in illuminating dialogue. A relational approach, one that operates at once within, between, and beyond the nation-state framework, calls attention to the conflictual hybrid interplay of communities within and across borders.

My subtitle, "Columbus, Palestine, and Arab-Jews," already juxtaposes disparate entities to underline the ways in which nation-states have imposed a coherent sense of national identity precisely because of their fragile sense of cultural, even geographic, belonging. The formation of the postcolonial nation-state, especially in the wake of colonial partitions, often involved a double process of, on the one hand, joining diverse ethnicities and regions that had been separate under colonialism and, on the other, partitioning regions in a way that forced regional redefinitions (Iraq/Kuwait) or a cross-shuffling of populations (Pakistan/India, Israel/Palestine, in relation to Palestinians and Arab-Jews). Given the "minority"/"majority" battles "from within" and the war waged by border-crossers (refugees, exiles, immigrants) "from without," Eurocentric historiography has had a crucial role in handing out passports to its legitimate races, ethnicities, and nations. And in the words of the Palestinian Mahmoud Darwish's well-known poem, "Passport" ("Joowaz sufr"): "'ar min al ism, min al intima? fi tarba rabit'ha bilyadyn?" ("Stripped of my name, my identity? On a soil I nourished with my own hands?"). The same colonial logic that dismantled Palestine had already dismantled the "Turtle Island" of the Americas. Thus, the first illegal alien, Columbus,[4] remains a celebrated discoverer, while indigenous Mexicans "infiltrate" barbed borders every day to a homeland once theirs, while Native Americans are exiled in their own land.

Here, by way of demonstration of the "relational" method, I will focus on Sephardic Arab-Jewish (known in the Israeli context as Mizrahi) identity as it intersects with other communities and discourses in diverse contexts over time. I will take as a point of departure the 1992 quincentennial commemorations of the expulsions of Sephardic Jews from Spain to argue that any revisionist effort to articulate Arab-Jewish identity in a contemporary context that has posited Arab and Jew as antonyms can only be disentangled through a series of positionings vis-à-vis diverse communities and identities (Arab-Muslim, Arab-Christian, Palestinian, Euro-Israeli, Euro-American Jewish, indigenous American, African-American, Chicano/a), which would challenge the devastating consequences that the Zionist-Orientalist binarism of East versus West, Arab versus Jew has had for Arab-Jews (or Jewish-Arabs). Linking, delinking, and relinking, at once spatial and temporal, thus become part of adversary scholarship working against taboo formulations, policed identities, and censored affiliations.

Staging the Quincentenary

"Your Highnesses completed the war against the Moors," Columbus wrote in a letter addressed to the Spanish throne, "after having chased all the Jews … and sent me to the said regions of India in order to convert the people there to our Holy Faith."[5] In 1492, the defeat of the Muslims and the expulsion of Sephardi Jews from Spain converged with the conquest of what came to be called the New World. Although the celebrations of Columbus's voyages have provoked lively opposition (ranging from multicultural debates about the Eurocentric notion of "discovery" to satirical performances by Native Americans landing in Europe and claiming it as their discovered continent), the Eurocentric framing of the "other 1492" has not been questioned. Apart from some enthusiastic scholastic energy dedicated to the dubious pride in whether Columbus can once and for all be claimed as a (secret) Jew, expulsion events have been navigated within the calm seas of Old World paradigms. Furthermore, the two separate quincentenary commemorations, both taking place in the Americas, Europe, and the Middle East, have seldom acknowledged the historical and discursive linkages between these two constellations of events. To examine the relationship between contemporary discourses about the two "1492s" might therefore illuminate the role that scholarly and popular narratives of history play in nation-building myths and geopolitical alliances.

The Spanish-Christian war against Muslims and Jews was politically, economically, and ideologically linked to the caravels' arrival in Hispaniola. Triumphant over the Muslims, Spain invested in the project of Columbus, whose voyages were partly financed by wealth taken from the defeated Muslims and confiscated from Jews through the Inquisition.[6] The *reconquista's* policies of settling Christians in the newly (re)conquered areas of Spain, as well as the gradual institutionalization of expulsions, conversions, and killings of Muslims and Jews in Christian territories, prepared the grounds for similar *conquista* practices across the Atlantic. Under the marital-political union of Ferdinand (Aragon) and Isabella (Castile), victorious Christian Spain, soon to become an empire, strengthened its sense of nationhood, subjugating indigenous Americans and Africans. Discourses about Muslims and Jews during Spain's continental expansion crossed the Atlantic, arming the conquistadors with a ready-made "us versus them" ideology aimed at the regions of India, but in fact applied first toward the indigenous of the accidentally "discovered" continent. The colonial misrecognition inherent in the name "Indian" underlines the linked imaginaries of the East and West Indies. (Perhaps not coincidentally, Ridley Scott's film *1492: The Conquest of Paradise* [1992] has Orientalist "Ali Baba"-style music accompany the encounter with Caribbean "Indians.") India awaited its colonized turn with the arrival of Vasco da Gama (1498) and the Portuguese conquest of Goa (1510). If, in the fifteenth century, the only European hope for conquering the East—given the Muslim domination of the continental route—was via sailing to the West, the nineteenth-century consolidation of European imperialism in the East was facilitated by Europe's previous self-aggrandizing at the expense of the Americas and Africa. Thanks to its colonization of the Americas and Africa, Europe's modernization was made possible, finally allowing the colonization of North Africa (Maghreb) and the so-called Near East *(mashreq)*. "The Indian Ocean trade, and the Culture that supported it," writes Amitav Ghosh, "had long since been destroyed by European navies. Transcontinental trade was no longer a shared enterprise; the merchant shipping of the high seas was now entirely controlled by the naval powers of Europe."[7]

Although Moorish Spain testifies to syncretic multiculturalism *avant la lettre*, the *reconquista* ideology of *limpieza de sangre*, as an early exercise in European "self-purification," sought to expel, or forcibly convert, Muslims and Jews. The Crusades, which inaugurated "Europe" by reconquering the Mediterranean area, catalyzed Europeans' awareness of their own geocultural identity, and established the principle that wars conducted in the interests of the Holy Church were axiomatically just. The campaigns against Muslims and Jews as well as against other "agents of Satan," heretics, and witches, made available a mammoth apparatus of racism and sexism for recycling in the "new" continents. Anti-Semitism and anti-infidelism provided a conceptual and disciplinary framework that, after being turned against Europe's immediate or internal others, was then projected outward against Europe's distant or external others.[8] Prince Henry ("the Navigator"), the pioneer of Portuguese exploration, had himself been a crusader against the Moors at the battle of Ceuta. Amerigo Vespucci, writing about his voyages, similarly drew on the stock of Jewish and Muslim stereotypes to characterize the savage, the infidel, the indigenous man as a dangerous sexual omnivore and the indigenous woman as a luringly yielding nature.[9] In this sense, the metonymic links between Jews and Muslims—their literal neighboring and their shared histories—are turned into metaphoric and analogical links in relation to the peoples of the Americas.[10] The point is not that there is a complete equivalence between Europe's oppressive relations toward Jews and Muslims and toward indigenous peoples; the point is that European Christian demonology prefigured colonialist racism. Indeed, one can even discern a partial congruency between the phantasmic imagery projected onto the Jewish and Muslim "enemy" and onto the indigenous American and black African "savage," all imaged to various degrees as "blood drinkers," "cannibals," "sorcerers," "devils."[11]

One of the rare contemporary representations that expose ecclesiastical participation in genocidal measures, the Mexican film *El Santo Oficio* (The Holy Office, 1973) features the attempt by the Holy See to spread the Inquisition into the New World. Although the film focuses on the Sephardi *conversos*, it also shows that they are persecuted alongside heretics, witches, and indigenous infidels. Consumed by enthusiastic spectators, their burning at the stake is performed as a public spectacle of discipline and punishment, just as lynching was sometimes consumed as a popular entertainment by some whites in the United States. Screened at a Los Angeles ceremonial opening for a conference (organized by the International Committee–Sepharad '92) dedicated to the quincentennial expulsion of Sephardi Jews, *El Santo Oficio* provoked strong emotions. Its documentation of Sephardic-Jewish rituals practiced in secrecy, and its visual details of torture, rape, and massacre, were not received, however, in the spirit of the linkages I have charted here. The audience, consisting largely of Euro-American, Jewish, and a substantially smaller number of Sephardi-American educators, scholars, and community workers, was eager to consume the narrative evidence of the singular nature of the Jewish experience. To point out the links between the Inquisition and the genocide of the indigenous peoples of the Americas, between the Inquisition and the devastation of African peoples, would be tantamount to a promiscuous intermingling of the sacred with the profane. In the reception following the film, Chicano waiters catered food. The simplistic category of "them" (Spanish Christians), however, stood in remarkably ironic relation to the indigenous faces of the waiters; their presence suggested that the charting of Sephardi *conversos* history must be negotiated in relation to other *conversos*.

The importance of rupturing the boundaries of these histories becomes even clearer in the actual intersection of diverse histories of forced conversions in the Americas. For example, the case of Chicano and Mexican families of part Sephardic-Jewish origins suggests that at times the links are quite literal. Recent research by the Southwest Jewish Archives in the United States points out that Sephardic traditions remain alive in predominantly Roman Catholic Mexican-American families, although the family members are not always conscious of the origins of the rituals. They do not understand why, for example, their grandmothers make unleavened bread called *pan semita*, or Semite bread, and why their rural grandparents in New Mexico or Texas slaughter a lamb in the spring and smear its blood on the doorway. Revealing that some Chicanos and Mexicans are the descendants of secret Jews is a taboo that results in contemporary secrecy even among those who are aware of their ancestry.[12] The issue of forced conversions in the Americas and the consequent cultural syncretism implicates and challenges Jewish as well as Catholic Euro-indigenous institutions. The hybridity of Chicano and Mexican culture, however, does not necessarily facilitate the admission of another complex hybridity, one crossing Jewish-Catholic boundaries.

If the genocide of indigenous Americans and Africans is no more than a bit of historical marginalia, the linked persecutions in Iberia of Sephardi Jews and Muslims, of conversos, and *moriscos*,[13] are also submerged. The quincentennial elision of the Arab-Muslim part of the narrative was especially striking. During the centuries-long *reconquista*, not all Muslims and Jews withdrew with the Arab forces. Those Muslims who remained after the change of rule were known as *mudejars*, deriving from the Arabic *mudajjin*, "permitted to remain," with a suggestion of "tamed," "domesticated."[14] The Spanish Inquisition, institutionalized in 1478, did not pass over the Muslims. Apart from the 1492 expulsion of three million Muslims and three hundred thousand Sephardi Jews, in 1499 mass burnings of Islamic books and forced conversions took place, and in 1502 the Muslims of Granada were given the choice of baptism or exile. In 1525–26, Muslims of other provinces were also given the same choice. In 1566, there was a revival of anti-Muslim legislation, and between 1609 and 1614 came edicts of expulsions. In other words, the same inquisitional measures taken against the Jewish *conversos* who were found to be secretly practicing Judaism were taken against the *moriscos* found to be practicing Islam, measures culminating in edicts of expulsion addressed specifically to Muslims. As a result, many fled to North Africa, where, like Sephardi Jews, they maintained certain aspects of their Hispanicized Arab culture.

This well-documented history[15] found little echo in the events promoted by the International Committee–Sepharad '92, whose major funds came from the United States, Spain, and Israel. Spain, which still has to come to terms with its present-day racist immigration policies toward—among others—Arab North Africans, embraced its "golden age" after centuries of denial, while reserving a regrettable mea culpa only for the official spokespersons of "the Jews." As for all other representatives, including conservative upper-middle-class Zionist Sephardim, the elision of comparative discussions of the Muslim and Jewish (Sephardi) situations in Christian Spain was largely rooted in present-day Middle Eastern politics. The 1992 commemorations entailed a serious present-day battle over the representations of "Jewish identity" in terms of an East-West axis, a battle dating back to the nineteenth-century beginnings of Zionist nationalism.

The Trauma of Dismemberment

Zionist historiography, when it does refer to Islamic-Jewish history, consists of a morbidly selective "tracing the dots" from pogrom to pogrom. (The word *pogrom* itself derives from and is reflective of the Eastern European Jewish experience.)[16] Subordinated to a Eurocentric historiography, most quincentenary events lamented yet another tragic episode in a homogeneous, static history of relentless persecution. Not surprisingly, the screening of *El Santo Oficio* at the expulsion conference elicited such overheard remarks as "You think it's different today? That's also what the Nazis did to us. That's what the Arabs would do if they could." (A curious claim, since the Arab Muslims had a millennium-long opportunity to install an inquisition against Middle Eastern Jews—or against Christian minorities—but never did.) Such common remarks underline the commemorations' role as a stage for demonstrating (Euro-)Israeli nationalism as the only possible logical answer to horrific events in the history of Jews. The inquisition of Sephardi Jews is seen merely as a foreshadowing of the Jewish Holocaust. In this paradigm, the traumas left by Nazi genocidal practices are simplistically projected onto the experiences of Jews in Muslim countries, and onto the Israeli-Palestinian conflict.[17]

My point here is not to idealize the situation of the Jews of Islam, but rather to suggest that Zionist discourse has subsumed Islamic-Jewish history into a Christian-Jewish history, while also undermining comparative studies of Middle Eastern Jews in the context of diverse religious and ethnic minorities in the Middle East and North Africa. On the occasion of the quincentenary, the Zionist perspective privileged Sephardi-Jewish relations with European Christianity over those with Arab

Islam, projecting Eurocentric maps of Christians and Jews as West and Muslims as East, and ignoring the fact that at the time of the expulsion, syncretic Jewish communities were flourishing all over the Islamic Middle East and North Africa. Quincentennial events not only rendered the interrelations between Jewish *conversos* and indigenous *conversos* invisible, but also undermined the Sephardic-Jewish and Muslim cultural symbiosis. The only Muslim country that received some quincentennial attention was Turkey, partly because of Sultan Beyazid II's ordering his governors in 1492 to receive the expelled Jews cordially. But no less important is Turkey's contemporary regional alliances, its national fissured identity between East and West. Unlike Arab Muslim countries, where expelled Sephardim also settled (Morocco, Tunisia, Egypt), Turkey has not participated in the Israeli-Arab conflict, nor in the nonallied embargo that has for decades regionally isolated Israel. Yet, even in the case of Turkey, the quincentennial emphasis was less on Muslim-Jewish relations than on the voyages of refuge, and on the Turkish (national) as opposed to the Ottoman Muslim (religious) shelter, an anachronistic framework given that the national/secular definition of Turkey is a twentieth-century development.

In this rewriting of history, present-day Muslim Arabs are merely one more "one-Jewish" obstacle to the Jewish-Israeli national trajectory. The idea of the unique, common victimization of all Jews at all times provides a crucial underpinning of official Israeli discourse. The notion of uniqueness precludes analogies and metonymies, thus producing a selective reading of "Jewish history," one that hijacks the Jews of Islam from their Judeo-Islamic geography and subordinates it to that of the European Ashkenazi shtetl. This double process entails the performance of commonalities among Jews in the public sphere so as to suggest a homogeneous national past, while silencing any deviant view of a more globalized and historicized narrative that would see Jews not simply through their religious commonalities, but also in relation to their contextual cultures, institutions, and practices. Given this approach, and given the Israeli-Arab conflict, no wonder that the Jews of Islam, and more specifically, Arab-Jews, have posed a challenge to any simplistic definition of Jewish identity, and particularly of the emergent Jewish Euro-Israeli identity.

The selective readings of Middle Eastern history, in other words, make two processes apparent: the rejection of an Arab and Muslim context for Jewish institutions, identity, and history, and their unproblematized subordination into a "universal" Jewish experience. In the Zionist "proof" of a single Jewish experience, there are no parallels or overlapping with other religious and ethnic communities, whether in terms of a Jewish hyphenated and syncretic culture or in terms of linked analogous oppressions. All Jews are defined as closer to each other than to the cultures of which they have been a part. Thus, the religious Jewish aspect of diverse intricated and interwoven Jewish identities has been given primacy, a categorization tantamount to dismembering the identity of a community. Indeed, the Euro-Israeli separation of the "Jewish" part from the "Middle Eastern" part, in the case of Middle Eastern Jews, has resulted in practically dismantling the Jewish communities of the Muslim world, as well as in pressures exerted on Mizrahim (Orientals) to realign their Jewish identity according to Zionist Euro-Israeli paradigms. Since the beginnings of European Zionism, the Jews of Islam have faced, for the first time in their history, the imposed dilemma of choosing between Jewishness and Arabness, in a geopolitical context that perpetuated the equation between Arabness and Middle Easternness and Islam, on the one had, and between Jewishnes and Europeanness and Westerness, on the other.[18]

The master narrative of universal Jewish victimization has been crucial for legitimizing an anomalous nationalist project of "ingathering of the Diaspora from the four corners of the globe," but which can also be defined as forcing displacements of people from such diverse geographies, languages, cultures, and histories, a project through which, in other words, a state created a nation. The claim of universal victimization has also been crucial for the claim that the "Jewish nation" faces a common "historical enemy"—the Muslim Arab—implying a double-edged amnesia with regard to both Judeo-Islamic history and the colonial partition of Palestine. False analogies between the Arabs and Nazis, and in 1992 with inquisitors, becomes not merely a staple of Zionist rhetoric, but also a symptom of a Jewish European nightmare projected onto the structurally distinct political dynamics of the Israeli-Palestinian conflict. In a historical context of Sephardi Jews experiencing an utterly distinct history within the Muslim world than that which haunted the European memories of Ashkenazi Jews, and in a context of the massacres and dispossession of Palestinian people, the conflation of the Muslim Arab with the archetypical (European) oppressors of Jew downplays the colonial-settler history of Euro-Israel itself.

The neat division of Israel as West and Palestine as East ignores some of the fundamental contradictions within Zionist discourse itself.[19] Central to Zionism is the notion of return to origins located in the Middle East.[20] Thus, Zionism often points to its linguistic return to Semitic Hebrew, and to its sustaining of a religious idiom intimately linked with the topography of the Middle East, as a "proof" of the Eastern origins of European Jews—a crucial aspect of the Zionist claim for the land. And although Jews have often been depicted in anti-Semitic discourse as an alien "Eastern" people within the West, the paradox of Israel is that it presumed to "end a diaspora," characterized by Jewish ritualistic nostalgia for the East, only to found a state whose ideological and geopolitical orientation has been almost exclusively toward the West. Theodor Herzl called for a Western-style capitalist-democratic miniature state, to be made possible by the grace of imperial patrons such as England or Germany, whereas David Ben-Gurion formulated his visionary utopia of Israel as that of a "Switzerland of the Middle East." Although European Jews have historically been the victims of anti-Semitic Orientalism, Israel as a state has become the perpetrator of Orientalist attitudes and actions whose consequences have been the dispossession of Palestinians. The ideological roots of Zionism can be traced to the conditions of nineteenth- and early twentieth-century Europe, not only as a reaction against anti-Semitism, but also to the rapid expansion of capitalism and of European empire building. In this sense, Israel has clearly been allied to First World imperialist interests, has deployed Eurocentric-inflected discourse, and has exercised colonialist policies toward the Palestinian land and people.

The question is further complicated by the socialist pretensions, and at times the socialist achievements, of Zionism. In nationalist Zionist discourse, the conflict between the socialist ideology of Zionism and the real praxis of Euro-Jewish colonization in Palestine was resolved through the reassuring thesis that the Arab masses, subjected to feudalism and exploited by their own countrymen, could only benefit from the emanation of Zionist praxis.[21] This presentation embodies the historically positive self-image of Israelis as involved in a noncolonial enterprise, and therefore morally superior in their aspirations. Furthermore, the hegemonic socialist-humanist discourse has hidden the negative dialectics of wealth and poverty between First and Third World Jews behind a mystifying facade of egalitarianism. The Zionist mission of ending the Jewish exile from the "Promised Land" was never the beneficent enterprise portrayed by official discourse, since from the first decade of the twentieth century, Arab-Jews were perceived as a source of cheap labor that could replace the dispossessed Palestinian fellahin.[22] The "Jews in the form of Arabs" thus could prevent any Palestinian declaration that the land belongs to those who work it, and contribute to the Jewish national demographic needs.[23] The Eurocentric projection of Middle Eastern Jews as coming to the "land of milk and honey" from desolate backwaters, from societies lacking all contact with scientific-technological civilization, once again set up an Orientalist rescue trope. Zionist discourse has cultivated the impression that Arab-Jewish culture prior to Zionism was static and passive, and, like the fallow land of Palestine, as suggested by Edward Said, was lying in wait for the impregnating infusion of European dynamism.[24] While presenting Palestine as an empty land to be transformed by Jewish labor, the Zionist "founding fathers" presented Arab-Jews as passive vessels to be shaped by the revivifying spirit of Promethean Zionism.

The Euro-Zionist problematic relation to the question of East and West has generated a deployment of opposing paradigms that often results in hysterical responses to any questioning of its projected "Western identity." Zionism viewed Europe both as ideal ego and as the signifier of ghettos, persecutions, and the Holocaust. Within this perspective, the "Diaspora Jew" was an extraterritorial rootless wanderer, someone living "outside of history." Posited in gendered language as the masculine redeemer of the passive Diaspora Jew, the mythologized sabra simultaneously signified the destruction of the diasporic Jewish entity. The prototypical newly emerging Jew in Palestine—physically strong, with blond hair and blue eyes, healthy-looking and cleansed of all "Jewish inferiority complexes," and a cultivator of the land—was conceived as an antithesis to the Zionist's virtually anti-Semitic image of the "Diaspora Jew." The sabra, which was modeled on the Romantic ideal, largely influenced by the German *Jugendkultur*, generated a culture in which any expression of weakness came to be disdained as *galuti*—that which belongs to the Diaspora. Zionism, in other words, viewed itself as an embodiment of European nationalist ideals to be realized outside of Europe, in the East, and in relation to the pariahs of Europe, the Jews. Thus, the sabra was celebrated as eternal youth devoid of parents, as though born from a spontaneous generation of nature, as in Moshe Shamir's key nationalist novel of the 1948 generation *Bemo Yadav* (In his own hands), which introduces the hero as follows: "Elik was born from the sea." In this paradoxical, idiosyncratic version of the Freudian *Familienroman*, Euro-Zionist parents raised their children to see themselves as historical foundlings worthy of more dignified, romantic, and powerful progenitors. Zionism posited itself as an extension of Europe in the Middle East, carrying its Enlightenment banner of the civilizing mission.

If the West has been viewed ambivalently as the place of oppression to be liberated from, as well as a kind of an object of desire to form a "normal" part of it, the East has also signified a contemporary ambivalence. On the one hand, it is a place associated with "backwardness," "underdevelopment," a land swamped, in the words of 1950s propaganda films, with "mosquitoes, scorpions, and Arabs." On the other hand, the East has symbolized solace, the return to geographic origins, and reunification with biblical history. The obsessive negation of the "Diaspora" that began with the Haskalah (European-Jewish Enlightenment) and the return to the homeland of Zion led, at times, to the exotic affirmation of Arab "primitiveness," as a desirable image to be appropriated by the native-born sabra. The Arab was projected as the incarnation of the ancient, the pre-exiled Jews, the Semitic not yet corrupted by wanderings in exile, and therefore, to a certain extent, as the authentic Jew. This construction of the Arab as presumably preserving archaic ways and rootedness in the land of the Bible, in contrast with the landless ghetto Jew, provoked a qualified identification with the Arab as a desired object of imitation for Zionist youth in Palestine/Israel, and as a reunification with the remnant of the free and proud ancient Hebrew.

This projection, however, coexisted with a simultaneous denial of Palestine. The role of archaeology in Israeli culture, it should be pointed out, has been crucial in disinterring of remnants of the biblical past of Palestine, at times enlisted in the political effort to demonstrate a historical right to the "land of Israel." In dramatic contrast to Jewish archaeology of the text,[25] this idea of physical archaeology as demonstrating a geography of identity carries with it the obverse notion of the physical homeland as text, to be allegorically read, within Zionist hermeneutics, as a "deed to the land." And corollary to this is the notion of historical "strata" within a political geology. The deep stratum, in the literal and the figurative sense, is associated with the Israeli Jews, while the surface level is associated with the Arabs, as a recent "superficial" historical element without millennial "roots." Since the Arabs are seen as "guests" in the land, their presence must be downplayed, much as the surface of the land has at times been "remodeled" to hide or bury remnants of Arab life, and Palestinian villages, in certain instances, have been replaced with Israeli ones, or completely erased. The linguistic, lexical expression of this digging into the land is the toponymic archaeology of place-names. Some Arabic names of villages, it was discovered, were close to or based on the biblical Hebrew names; in some cases, therefore, Arabic names were replaced with old-new Hebrew ones.

Parting Worlds, Subversive Returns

Yet, despite the importance of the idea of Return, it is no less important to see Zionist representation of Palestine in the context of other settlers' narratives. Palestine is linked to the Columbus narrative of the Americas in more ways than it would at first appear. The Columbus narrative prepared the ground for an enthusiastic reception of Zionist discourse within Euro-America. The Israeli-Palestinian conflict as a whole touches, I would argue, on some sensitive historical nerves within "America" itself. As a product of schizophrenic master narratives, colonial-settler state on the one hand, and anticolonial republic on the other, "America" has been subliminally more attuned to the Zionist than to the Palestinian nationalist discourse. Zionist discourse contains a liberatory narrative vis-à-vis Europe that in many ways is pertinent to the Puritans. The New World of the Middle East, like the New World of America, was concerned with creating a New Man. The image of the sabra as a new (Jewish) man evokes the American Adam. The American hero has been celebrated as prelapsarian Adam, as a New Man emancipated from history (i.e., European history), before whom all the world and time lay available, much as the sabra was conceived as the antithesis of the Old World European Jew. In this sense, one might suggest an analogy between the cultural discourse about the innocent national beginning of America and that of Israel. The American Adam and the sabra masculinist archetypes implied not only their status as creators, blessed with the divine prerogative of naming the elements of the scene about them, but also their fundamental innocence. The notions of an American Adam and an Israeli sabra elided a number of crucial facts, notably that there were other civilizations in the Promised Land; that the settlers were not creating "being from nothingness"; and that the settlers, in both cases, had scarcely jettisoned all their Old World cultural baggage, their deeply ingrained Eurocentric attitudes and discourses. Here the gendered metaphor of the "virgin land," present in both Zionist and American pioneer discourses, suggests that the land is implicitly available for defloration and fecundation. Assumed to lack owners, it therefore becomes the property of its "discoverer" and cultivators who transform the wilderness into a garden, those who "make the desert bloom."

In the case of Zionist discourse, the concept of "return to the motherland," as I have pointed out, suggests a double relation to the land, having to do with an ambivalent relation to the "East" as the place of Judaic origins as well as the locus for implementing the "West." The sabra embodied the humanitarian and liberationist project of Zionism, carrying the same banner of the "civilizing mission" that European powers proclaimed during their surge into "found lands." The classical images of sabra pioneers as settlers on the Middle Eastern frontiers, fighting Indian-like Arabs, along with the reverberations of the early American biblical discourse encapsulated in such notions as "Adam," "(New) Canaan," and "Promised Land," have all facilitated the feeling of Israel as an extension of "us"—the U.S. Furthermore, both the United States and Israel fought against British colonialism, while also practicing colonial policies toward the indigenous peoples. Finally, I would argue for a triangular structural analogy by which the Palestinians represent the aboriginal "Indians" of Euro-Israeli discourse, while the Sephardim, as imported cheap labor, constitute the "blacks" of Israel.[26] (Taking their name from the American movement, the Israeli "Black Panthers," for example, sabotaged the myth of the "melting pot" by showing that there was in Israel not one but two Jewish communities—one white, one black.) The manifest Palestinian refusal to play the assigned role of the presumably doomed "Indians" of the transplanted (far) Western narrative has testified to an alternative narrative in whose narration Edward Said has been in the forefront. The story of Sephardim—as the Jewish victims of Zionism—also remains to be heard.[27]

The same historical process that dispossessed Palestinians of their property, lands, and national-political rights was intimately linked to the process that effected the dispossession of Arab-Jews from their property, lands, and rootedness in Arab countries, as well as their uprootedness from that history and culture within Israel itself.[28] But whereas Palestinians have fostered the collective militancy of nostalgia in exile (be it *fil dakhel*, under Israeli occupation, or *fil kharij*, under Syrian, Egyptian, and American passport or on the basis of laissez-passer), Sephardim, trapped in a no-exit situation, have been forbidden to nourish memories of at least partially belonging to the peoples across the river Jordan, across the mountains of Lebanon, and across the Sinai desert and Suez Canal. The pervasive notion of "one people" reunited in their ancient homeland actively disauthorizes any affectionate memory of life before the state of Israel. Quincentennial events luxuriated in the landscapes, sounds, and smells of the lost Andalusian home, but silence muffled an even longer historical imaginary in Cairo, Baghdad, Damascus, and hid an even more recent loss. For centuries, both Muslim and Jewish poets eulogized Andalusia, referring to the keys they persisted in carrying in exile. Yet, in contemporary Palestinian poetry, Andalusia is far from being only a closed chapter of Arab grandeur, for it allegorizes Palestine. In the words of Mahmoud Darwish's poem "Al Kamanjat" ("The Violins"):

> Al kamanjat tabki ma'a al ghjar al dhahibina ila al andalous
> al kamanjat tabki 'ala al 'arab al kharigin min al andalous
> al kamanjat tabki 'ala zaman daib la ya'ood
> al kamanjat tabki 'ala watan daib qad ya'ood.

> (The violins weep with the Gypsies heading for Andalusia
> the violins weep for the Arabs departing Andalusia.
> The violins weep for a lost epoch that will not return
> the violins weep for a lost homeland that could be regained.)

But the parallelism between Andalusia and Palestine stops precisely at the point of reclaiming a Palestinian future.

The 1992 discussions of expulsion brought out the "wandering Jew" motif of the Jews as perennially displaced people. But the Jews of the Middle East and North Africa, for the most part, had stable, "nonwandering" lives in the Islamic world. As splendidly captured in *In an Antique Land*, the Sephardim who have moved within the regions of Asia and Africa, from the Mediterranean to the Indian Ocean, did it more for commercial, religious, or scholarly purposes than for reasons of persecution. Ironically, the major traumatic displacement took place since 1948, when Arab-Jews were uprooted, dispossessed, and dislodged because of the collaboration between Israel and some of the Arab governments under the orchestration of Western colonial powers that termed their solution for the "question of Palestine" as a "population exchange."[29] That no one asked either the Palestinians or the Arab-Jews whether they wished to be exchanged is yet another typical narrative of Third World histories of partition. Sephardim who have managed to leave Israel, often in an (indirect) response to institutionalized racism there, have dislocated themselves yet again, this time to the United States, Europe, and Latin America. In a sudden historical twist, today it is to the Muslim Arab countries of their origins to which most Middle Eastern Jews cannot travel, let alone fantasize a return—the ultimate taboo.[30]

The commonalities between Middle Eastern Jews and Muslims is a thorny reminder of the Middle Eastern/North African character of the majority of Jews in Israel today. Not surprisingly, quincentenary events in Europe, the Middle East, and the Americas centered on the Spanishness of Sephardi culture (largely on Ladino or Judeo-Español language and music), while marginalizing the fact that Jews in Iberia formed part of a larger Judeo-Islamic culture of North Africa, the Middle East, and the European Balkan area of the Ottoman Empire. Major Sephardi texts in philosophy, linguistics, poetry, and medicine were written in Arabic and reflect specific Muslim influences as well as a strong sense of Jewish-Arab cultural identity, seen especially in the development of Judeo-Arab script, used in religious correspondence between Jewish scholars across the regions of Islam, as well as in some specific local Jewish-Arabic dialects.[31] The Jews of Iberia who had come from the East and South of the Mediterranean—some with the Romans, others largely with the Muslims—returned there when they fled the Inquisition. More than 70 percent returned to the Ottoman Empire regions, while the rest went to Western Europe and the Americas.[32] Thus, a historiography that speaks of a pan-Jewish culture is often the same historiography that speaks of "Arab versus Jew" without acknowledging Arab-Jewish existence.

The erasure of the Arab dimension of Sephardim-Mizrahim has been crucial to the Zionist perspective, since the Middle Easternness of Sephardi Jews questions the very definitions and boundaries of the Euro-Israeli national project. Euro-Israel has ended up in a paradoxical situation in which its "Orientals" have had closer cultural and historical links to the presumed enemy—the "Arab"—than to the Ashkenazi Jews with whom they were coaxed and coerced into nationhood. The taboo around the Arabness of Sephardi history and culture is clearly manifested in Israeli academic and media attacks on Sephardi intellectuals who refuse to define themselves simply as Israelis, and who dare to assert their Arabness in the public sphere.[33] The Ashkenazi anxiety around Sephardi-Mizrahi identity (expressed both by right and liberal left) underlines that Sephardi Jews have represented a problematic entity for Euro-Israeli hegemony. Although Zionism collapses the Sephardim and the Ashkenazim into a single people, at the same time the Sephardi difference has destabilized Zionist claims for representing a single Jewish people, premised not only on a common religious background, but also on common nationality. The strong cultural and historical links that Middle Eastern Jews have shared with the Arab Muslim world, stronger in many respects than those they shared with the European Jews, threatened the conception of a homogeneous nation on which European nationalist movements were based. As an integral part of the topography, language, culture, and history of the Middle East, Sephardim have also threatened the Euro-Israeli self-image, which sees itself as a prolongation of Europe, "in" the Middle East but not "of" it. Fearing an encroachment from the East upon the West, the Israeli establishment attempted to repress the Middle Easternness of Sephardic Jews as part of an effort to westernize the Israeli nation and to mark clear borders of identity between Jews as Westerners and Arabs as Easterners. Arabness and Orientalness have been consistently stigmatized as evils to be uprooted, creating a situation where Arab-Jews were urged to see Judaism and Zionism as synonyms, and Jewishness and Arabness as antonyms. Thus, Arab-Jews were prodded to choose between anti-Zionist Arabness and a pro-Zionist Jewishness for the first time in history. Distinguishing the "evil East" (the Muslim Arab) from the "good East" (the Jewish Arab), Israel has taken it upon itself to "cleanse" Arab-Jews of their Arabness and redeem them from their "primal sin" of belonging to the Orient. This conceptualization of East and West has important implications in this age of the "peace process," because it avoids the issue of the majority of the population within Israel being from the Middle East—Palestinians citizens of Israel as well as Mizrahi-Sephardi Jews; for peace as it is defined now does not entail a true democracy in terms of adequate representation of these populations, nor in terms of changing the educational, cultural, and political orientation within the state of Israel.

The leitmotif of Zionist texts was the cry to be a "normal civilized nation," without the presumably myriad "distortions" and forms of pariahdom typical of the *gola* (Diaspora), of the state of being a non-nation-state. The *Ostjuden*, perennially marginalized by Europe, realized their desire of becoming Europe, ironically, in the Middle East, this time on the back of their own *Ostjuden*, the Eastern Jews. The Israeli establishment, therefore, has made systematic efforts to suppress Sephardi-Mizrahi cultural identity. The Zionist establishment, since its early encounter with Palestinian (Sephardi) Jews, has systematically attempted to eradicate the Middle Easternness of those other Jews—for example, by marginalizing these histories in school curricula, and by rendering Mizrahi cultural production and grassroots political activities invisible in the media. Despite its obvious shifts since the partition of Palestine, however, Sephardi popular culture has clearly manifested its vibrant inter-textual dialogue with Arab, Turkish, Iranian, and Indian popular cultures. Oriental-Arabic music produced by Sephardim—at times in collaboration with Israeli Palestinians—is consumed by Palestinians in Israel and across the borders in the Arab world, often without being labeled as originating in Israel. This creativity is partly nourished through an enthusiastic consumption of Jordanian, Lebanese, and Egyptian television programs, films, and Arabic video-music performances, which rupture the Euro-Israeli public sphere in a kind of subliminal transgression of a forbidden nostalgia. In fact, musical groups such as the Moroccan-Israeli Sfatayim (Lips) traveled back to Morocco to produce a music video sung in Moroccan Arabic against the scenery of the cities and villages that Moroccan Jews have left behind, just as Israeli-born Iraqi singers such as Ya'aqub Nishawi sing old and contemporary Iraqi music. This desire for "return of the Diaspora" is ironically underlined by what I would describe as a kind of a reversal of the biblical expression: "By the waters of Zion, where we sat down, and there we wept, when we remembered Babylon."[34]

Arab Muslim historiography, meanwhile, has ironically echoed the logic of Zionist paradigms, looking only superficially into the culture and identity of Arab-Jews both in the Arab world, and, more recently, within Israel. Thus, Ghosh, the visiting Indian anthropologist, notices what is otherwise unnoticeable: that in the Geniza's home country, Egypt,

> nobody took the slightest notice of its dispersal. In some profound sense, the Islamic high culture of Masr [Arabic for Egypt] has never really noticed, never found a place for the parallel history the Geniza represented, and its removal only confirmed a particular vision of the past.... Now it was Masr, which had sustained the Geniza for almost a Millennium, that was left with no traces of its riches: not a single scrap or shred of paper to remind her of the aspect of her past. It was as though the borders that were to divide Palestine several decades later had already been drawn, through time rather than territory, to allocate a choice of Histories.[35]

The amnesia of this recent history in most contemporary Arab culture has fed into a Israeli and Arab refusal of the hybrid, the in-between. Even Israeli Arab-Jews, such as the Iraqi-Israeli writer Samir Naqash, who to this day writes his novels in Arabic, are "rejected" from membership in the Arab geo-cultural region, simply seen as "Israeli." The Jews of Islam thus today exist as part of a historiography in which our relations to the Arab Islamic world exist only in the past tense. Colonial partitions and nationalist ideologies have left little room for the inconvenient "minority" of Arab-Jews. Even the Geniza itself, presumably rescued from obscurity and decay at the hands of our own producers, has been used to support a nationalist narrative in which every text or fragmented document was deciphered for a Zionist transformation "megola le'geula" ("from Diaspora to redemption"). The historiographical work of Euro-Jewish scholars such as S. D. Goitein and E. Strauss might have facilitated the entry of an Indian anthropologist such as Ghosh into the Indian Ocean world of a twelfth-century Tunisian-Jewish trader, Abraham Ben-Yiju, who, unlike Ghosh, traveled in an era when "Europe" did not dominate the channels of scholarship and communication. But the Geniza scholarship was shaped and used within a context of Zionist Enlightenment readings of the otherized Jews of the Levant, the very same Jews whose cultural practices made possible the Geniza scholarship of Western academic institutions. Within these asymmetrical power relations, it is the work of Euro-Jewish scholars that infused the colonized history with national meaning and telos, while, ironically, at the same time, Arab-Jews were being displaced, and in Israel subject to a schooling system where Jewish history textbooks featured barely a single chapter on their history.

Today, Mizrahim inhabit the pages of Euro-Israeli sociological and anthropological accounts as maladjusted criminals and superstitious exotics, firmly detached from Arab history that looms only as deformed vestiges in the lives of Israelis of Asian and African origin. Sociology and anthropology detect such traces of underdevelopment, while national historiography tells the story of the past as a moral tale full of national purpose. Such scholarly bifurcation cannot possibly account for an Arab-Jewish identity that is at once past and present, here and there. Perhaps it is not a coincidence that the author of *In an Antique Land*—a hybrid of anthropology and history—ends up by splitting the subjects of ethnography and historiography, the first focusing on present-day Egyptian Muslims, and the second on past Arab-Jews. Ghosh, at the end of his book, stops his narrative at the very point where the subject of his historiography could have turned into a subject of his ethnography. Anthropological accounts of Ghosh's visits to Egypt are paralleled by his historiographical chronicle of the Judeo-Islamic world through the travels of Ben-Yiju. On Ghosh's final trip to Egypt, Ghosh notices Arab-Jewish pilgrims from Israel coming to Egypt to visit the tomb of the cabalistic mystic Sidi Abu-Hasira, a site holy for both Muslims and Jews, with many similar festivities. Yet, for one reason or another, he ends up never meeting them. Perhaps Ghosh's missed rendezvous, his packing up and leaving Egypt precisely as the Arab-Jews visit Abu-Hasira's holy site, is revelatory of the difficulties of representing a multidiasporic identity, the dangers of border crossing in the war zone. Thus, we Arab-Jews continue to travel in historical narratives as imbricated with a legendary Islamic civilization; but, as the postcolonial story began to unfold over the past decades, we suddenly cease to exist, as though we have reached our final destination—the state of Israel—and nothing more need be said.

In contrast to the negatively connoted term *Orientals* (in the United States), in Israel "Orientals" (Mizrahim) signifies radical politics, evoking a common experience shared by all Asian and African Jews in Israel, despite our different origins. On the part of radical Sephardi movements, it also suggests a resistant discourse that calls for linkages to the East, as opposed to the hegemonic discourse of "we of the West." The names of the 1980s movements East for Peace and the Oriental Front in Israel, Perspectives Judéo-Arabes in Paris, and the World Organization of Jews from Islamic Countries in New York point to the assertion of the historical and future interwovenness with the East. Mizrahim, along with Palestinians within Israel proper (Israeli Palestinians), compose the majority of the citizens of a state that has rigidly imposed an anti-Middle Eastern agenda. In a first-of-its-kind meeting between Mizrahim and Palestine Liberation Organization representatives held at the symbolic site of Toledo, Spain, in 1989, we insisted that a comprehensive peace would mean more than settling political borders, and would require the erasure of the East/West cultural borders between Israel and Palestine, and thus the remapping of national and ethnic-racial identities against the deep scars of colonizing partitions. A critical examination of national histories may thus open a cultural space for working against taboo memories and fostering diasporic visions.

Notes

Parts of this essay have appeared in preliminary form in *Middle East Report* 178 (September–October 1992) and *Third Text* 21 (Winter 1992–93). An earlier version was included in *Cultural Identity and the Gravity of History: On the Work of Edward Said*, ed. Keith Ansell-Pearson, Benita Parry, and Judith Squires (London: Lawrence and Wishart, 1997). I thank Meir Gal, Rachel Jones, and Tikva Parnass for their generosity and help with the images.

1. Amitav Ghosh, *In an Antique Land* (New York: Alfred A. Knopf, 1992), 89–94. Some of my comments here on the book were made in a CUNY Television conversation with Amitav Ghosh in March 1994. The conversation also included Tim Mitchell, and was organized and moderated by Kamala Visweswaran and Parag Amladi.

2. Ibid., 85, 93.

3. I thank Robert Stam for allowing me to use here some "shared territory" from our book *Unthinking Eurocentrism: Multiculturalism and the Media* (London: Routledge, 1994).

4. See, for example, "Green Card" artwork by Inigo Manglano-Ovalle.

5. Quoted in Jean Comby, "1492: Le choc des cultures et l'évagélisation du monde," *Dossiers de l'episcopat français* 14 (October 1990): 14.

6. See Charles Duff, *The Truth about Columbus* (New York: Random House, 1936).

7. Ghosh, *In an Antique Land*, 81.

8. Jan Pieterse makes the more general point that many of the themes of European imperialism traced antecedents to the European and Mediterranean sphere. Thus, the theme of civilization against barbarism was a carryover from Greek and Roman antiquity, the theme of Christianity against pagans was the keynote of European expansion culminating in the Crusades, and the Christian theme of "mission" was fused with "civilization" in the *mission civilisatrice*. See Jan Pieterse, *Empire and Emancipation* (London: Pluto Press, 1990), 240.

9. For details, see Jan Carew, *Fulcrum of Change: Origins of Racism in the Americas and Other Essays* (Trenton, N.J.: Africa World Press, 1988).

10. The indigenous peoples of the Americas similarly were officially protected from massacres by the throne only once they converted to Christianity.

11. The presumed "godlessness" of the indigenous people became a pretext for enslavement and dispossession. Whereas Jews and Muslims were diabolized, the indigenous Americans were accused of devil worship. The brutalities practiced by official Christianity toward Jews and Muslims have to be seen, therefore, on the same continuum as the forced conversions of indigenous peoples of the Americas who, like the Jews and Muslims in Christian Spain, were obliged to feign allegiance to Catholicism.

12. Pat Kossan, "Jewish Roots of Hispanics—Delicate Topic" *Phoenix Gazette*, April 14, 1992, section C.

13. Moors converted to Christianity.

14. Spanish Muslim culture in Christian Spain, like Sephardi-Jewish culture, was expressed in Spanish as well.

15. See, for example, W. Montgomery Watt and Pierre Cachia, *A History of Islamic Spain* (Edinburgh: Edinburgh University Press, 1977); James T. Monroe, *Hispano-Arabic Poetry* (Berkeley: University of California Press, 1974).

16. This picture of an ageless and relentless oppression and humiliation ignores the fact that, on the whole, Jews of Islam—a minority among several other religious and ethnic communities in the Middle East and North Africa—lived relatively comfortably within Arab Muslim society.

17. For a more complex analysis, see, for example, Ilan Halevi, *A History of the Jews: Ancient and Modern* (London: Zed Books, 1987); Maxime Rodinson, *Cult, Ghetto, and State: The Persistence of the Jewish Question* (London: Al Saqi Books, 1983).

18. See Ella Shohat, "Sephardim in Israel: Zionism from the Standpoint of Its Jewish Victims," *Social Text* 19–20 (Fall 1988).

19. For more on the question of East and West in Zionist discourse, see Ella Shohat, *Israeli Cinema: East/West and the Politics of Representation* (Austin: University of Texas Press, 1989).

20. During the early days of Zionism, other "empty" territories were proposed for Jewish settlement; typically, they were located in the colonized world. However, one of Theodor Herzl's famous proposals for settlement—Uganda—created a crisis for the Zionist Congress, known as the Uganda crisis.

21. See Maxime Rodinson, *Israel: A Colonial-Settler State?* trans. David Thorstad (New York: Monad Press, 1973).

22. See Yoseff Meir, *Hatnua haTzionit veYehudei Teman (The Zionist Movement and the Jews of Yemen)* (Tel Aviv: Sifriat Afikim, 1982); G. N. Giladi, *Discord in Zion: Conflict between Ashkenazi and Sephardi Jews in Israel* (London: Scorpion Publishing, 1990).

23. The phrase "Jews in the form of Arabs" was used already during the first decade of the twentieth century by the early engineers (such as Shmuel Yaveneli) of "Aliya" of Jews from the regions of the Ottoman Empire. See Meir, *The Zionist Movement and the Jews of Yemen*.

24. See Edward Said, *The Question of Palestine* (New York: Times Books, 1979).

25. See, for example, Jacques Derrida, "Edmund Jabès and the Question of the Book," in *Writing and Difference*, trans. Alan Bass (Chicago: University of Chicago Press, 1978), 64–78; George Steiner, "Our Homeland, the Text," *Salmagundi* 66 (Winter–Spring 1985): 4–25.

26. In recent years, the term *sh'horim* (blacks) has also applied to the Orthodox religious Ashkenazi codes of dressing. I should point out that the sartorial codes favoring dark colors of centuries-ago Poland were never part of Sephardic-Arabic culture. Since the massive arrival in Israel of Ethiopian Jews in the 1980s, the pejorative term *blacks* or *kushim* has been used against Ethiopian Jews.

27. I specifically address the relationship between the Palestinian and the Sephardi-Mizrahi questions vis-à-vis Zionism in my essay on Sephardi identity in Israel, "Zionism from the Standpoint of Its Jewish Victims," a title referring to Said's essay "Zionism from the Standpoint of Its Victims" (*Social Text* 1 [1979]), also a chapter in Said's *The Question of Palestine*. Both have been republished in *Dangerous Liaisons: Gender, Nation, and Post-colonial Perspectives*, eds. Anne McClintock, Aamir Mufti, and Ella Shohat (Minneapolis: University of Minnesota Press, 1997).

28. Neither Palestinians nor Arab-Jews have been compensated for their lost property.

29. See, for example, Abbas Shiblak, *The Lure of Zion* (London: Al Saki Books, 1986); Gideon Giladi, *Discord in Zion* (London: Scorpion Publishing, 1990).

30. Thus, for example, when the Iraqi-Israeli writer Shimon Ballas wrote the novel *Vehu Aher (And He Is an Other)* (Tel Aviv: Zmora Bitan, 1991), which partially concerned an Iraqi Jew who remained in Iraq after the dislodging of his community and converts to Islam, he was vehemently attacked in a rush to censor the imaginary.

31. Jewish-Arabic language was written in Hebrew script, but the script resembles very little the Ashkenazi Hebrew script that became a lingua franca since the revival of modern Hebrew and its spread through Zionist institutions. Today, Sephardi prayer texts use the common Ashkenazi script, even when the prayer is in Judeo-Arabic, because the Ashkenazi script is better known to most younger-generation Mizrahim.

32. Most cultural expression of Jews in the Arab world, needless to say, was not in Ladino/Español but in Arabic (whether literary Arabic, Judeo Arabic, or other Arabic dialects). It was perhaps this misconception that led Bharathi Mukherjee to have her Iraqi Jewish protagonist, Alfie Judah, in *The Middleman* say that the "form of Spanish" we spoke in "old Baghdad" was "a good preparation for the Southwest" (i.e., of the United States).

33. Such attacks were made, for example, on Shimon Ballas after the publication of his novel *And He Is an Other*, as well as on myself after the Hebrew publication of my book *Israeli Cinema: East/West and the Politics of Representation* (published as *Hakolnoa haIsraeli: Histpria veIdiologia* [Israeli cinema: history and ideology; Tel Aviv: Breirot, 1991]).

34. See Ella Shohat, "Dislocated Identities: Reflections of an Arab-Jew," *Movement Research: Performance Journal* 5 (Fall–Winter 1992).

35. Ghosh, *In an Antique Land*, 95.

10

Contesting Culture
*Identity and Curriculum Dilemmas in the
Age of Globalization, Postcolonialism,
and Multiplicity*

CAMERON McCARTHY, MICHAEL D. GIARDINA,
SUSAN J. HAREWOOD, AND JIN-KYUNG PARK

A single overmastering identity at the core of the academic enterprise, whether that identity be Western, African, or Asian is a confinement, a deprivation. The world is made up of numerous identities interacting, sometimes harmoniously, sometimes antithetically. (Edward Said 1991, 17)

And no race has a monopoly on beauty, on intelligence, on strength... (Aimé Césaire 1983, 77)

Introduction

This essay examines the practical and philosophical challenges posed to twenty-first century curriculum organization and classroom pedagogy by the intensification of the proliferation of difference in contemporary educational settings and in society. In what follows, we draw out and build on the significance of this insight by first discussing the transforming context of culture and identity in late-modern society, a context deeply informed by the logics and processes of globalization now imposing themselves on the educational enterprise inside and outside schools around the globe. Second, we assess the very different ideological assumptions and responses of mainstream (and minority) cultural monologists and postcolonial school critics and artists to this proliferation of difference precipitated by globalization. Third, we draw some conclusions, pointing in the direction of an alternative approach to the topic of difference and curriculum and pedagogical reform.

Globalization and the Transforming Context of Identity

Over a decade ago, Keith Osajima (1992) documented the story of a Chinese-American student's ambivalence toward and discomfort with issues of racial/ethnic identity that she faced in her daily life. She articulated her liminal position this way:

I grew up in a white suburb and my parents are also very Americanized, and spoke mostly English at home, so I don't speak Chinese.... I also grew up trying to identify as much as possible with white people and feeling very inadequate because I would never be like them.... I mean, it's constant conflict with me now. I assume it's going to be for the rest of my life.... you know either being with white Americans and not feeling I'm like them, or going to the Chinese environment, like Chinatown or something, and not feeling like I fit in there. (p. 1; also quoted in McCarthy and Crichlow 1993)

This brief confession of uncertainty over one's own belonging—expressed so poignantly and in such heartfelt language—speaks directly to the questions of culture and identity in the late-capitalist moment, and reveals the utter failure of multiculturalism within the United States to effectively come to grips with the ever-changing face of America. On the heels of twelve years of racial antagonism fueled by the assaultive and exploitative assimilationist rhetoric of the Reagan/Bush era public policy and cultural representation, this young Chinese-American woman, like all her peers, was facing the coming Clinton years already deeply ensconced within an educational setting that viewed the twinned concepts of "culture" and "race" rather statically, as unchanging monochromatic structures of identity. However, she was also standing at the frontier of the Clintonian project of multicultural racial equality, which was presented as a keystone concept to fully realizing the promise of the New Democratic (centrist) country President Bill Clinton was envisioning for the direction of the United States (cf., Klein 2002). But, alas, in contemporary curriculum and educational policy discourses about diversity, hybridity, and multiculturalism, the last decade-plus—like that of Clinton's multiculturalist project—has not lived up to expectations. This is most especially true when we consider the intersection of popular forms of culture to the educational experience, both inside and outside the classroom. And, in fact, the country has seemed to regress under the second Bush (George W.) regime, one whose policy orientation, particularly post 9/11, has been defined by hostility toward the rampant pluralism that the cultural modernization accompanying globalization has proffered. In this context, too, cultural difference has been expressed in educational and social institutions in the form of Balkanization and the exacerbation of racial and ethnic inequalities. Popular culture, like the formal school curriculum, has become a fertile site of these oppositions, a veritable battleground of first world/third world distinctions as social combatants struggle over the boundary lines of group identity and affiliation and the definition of citizenship and trans/national belonging.

But this conflict over culture and identity—of one's own place in the world—is not limited solely to the United States or Great Britain, nor is it adequate to cast it as a phenomenon exclusive to the domain of the West/first world. Given the intensification of diasporic flows of cultural and economic capital, and aided most significantly by deepening patterns of aestheticization in popular culture as foregrounded in advertising (e.g., Nike, Benetton, Tommy Hilfiger) and new forms of electronic mediation (e.g., the Internet, satellite television), the millennial nation-state now comprises an increasingly hybridized population where practices of identity construction are no longer bounded by the physical borders of nation-state formations (Silk 2001; Giardina 2003). Rather, one sees practices favoring "flexibility, mobility, and repositioning in relation to markets, governments, and cultural regimes" (Ong 1999, 6) becoming more and more common and, in some cases, moving toward the established norm. Indeed, as Caglar (1997) argues, an ever-increasing number of people define themselves "in terms of multiple national attachments ... that encompass plural and fluid cultural identities" (169). Evidence of such change abounds. In her book, *Borrowed Identities*, Jennifer Kelly (2003), for example, reveals that Afro-Canadian youth strategically and situationally patch together their identities from an international array of global television, popular music, and technoculture so as to manipulate and maneuver around the constraints of racial hierarchy and experience the benefits of so-called ideal forms of citizenships (see also Ong 1998). We also encounter similar findings in Britain where, according to Gurinder Chadha in her pioneering documentary, *I'm British But* (1989), Asian youth in south London variously identified themselves as "British," "Asian," or "British-Asian," depending upon the given situation. In a further example, at the 2000 Olympic Games in Sydney, Australia both reveled in and revealed the dynamic tensions of hybridity as located in the celebrity of Australian-Aboriginal 400-meters track star Cathy Freeman vis-à-vis fostering a national discussion on race (Bruce and Hallinan 2001).

Throughout the course of these examples, it is the affectively charged realm of the popular that drives, and is likewise driven by, the formative encounters of and with national identity and cultural signification. However, and though pivotal to mainstream curriculum and educational discourses and policies such as multiculturalism, we believe that "culture" has and remains significantly undertheorized. "It" is often treated as a preexistent, unchanging deposit, consisting of a rigidly bounded set of elite or folkloric knowledges, values, experiences, and linguistic practices specific to particular groups. The current cultural studies approach to culture as the production and circulation of meaning in stratified contexts remains inadequate. Instead, we need to think about culture along the lines suggested by Tony Bennett in "Putting Policy into Cultural Studies" (1996) and *The Birth of the Museum* (1995). Following Bennett, culture is understood throughout the course of this essay not so much, or at all, as the distinctive forms of "a whole way of life" in the Raymond Williams sense. Rather, we conceptualize culture as a set of dynamic, productive, and generative material (and immaterial) practices in the regulation of social conduct and social behavior that emphasize personal self-management (i.e., the modification of habits, tastes, and style), political affiliation, and trans/national identity.

Globalizing Pedagogies

Recent large-scale developments are wholly transforming social and cultural life outside and inside schools around the globe. These developments have enormous implications for pedagogical practice and the educational preparation of school youth—yet curriculum thinkers and practitioners have tended to dismiss or ignore them. These developments might be grouped under the term *multiplicity*, brought about by globalization and the rapid advances in electronic media, changing conceptions of self and other, and new explanatory discourses. These developments can be summarized as follows.

First, there is that broad set of processes that has come to be known as "globalization," understood here as the intensified and accelerated movement of people, images, ideas, technologies, and economic and cultural capital across national boundaries. From former U.S. president Bill Clinton's relentless pursuit of "building a bridge to the 21st century" and the passage of the North America Free Trade Agreement (NAFTA) to the activist protesters at the World Trade Organization meetings in Seattle, Washington, and Cancun, Mexico, and the ever-expanding reach of the U.S. war and culture industry, the word *globalization* has become fully ensconced in our everyday vernacular. Whether in the form of Rupert Murdoch's News Corporation—which has the potential to reach 1 billion persons per day via its various cable and satellite television providers—or the ever-expanding worldwide reach of the Internet, it goes without saying that we are living in a time of unheralded interconnectivity. Driven forward by the engines of modern capital reorganization and the correspondingly changed interests, needs, and desires of ordinary people everywhere, globalizing processes are sweeping all corners of the contemporary world. These processes are rapidly shrinking the distance between hitherto far-flung parts of the world (Giddens 1994; Castells 2001; Desai 2002), deepening the implication of both the local in the global and the global in the local, or what Kevin Robins and David Morley, in *Spaces of Identity* (1996), refer to as the "global/local nexus."

While in the last century popular media such as television, film, newspapers, radio, and various genres of pop music had already expanded the range of information, images, and identities available to people, the power of contemporary globalizing processes—fueled by migration and the new technologies of electronic mediation associated with computerization—have exploded the pace of these rapid, expansionary mechanisms and opened the door for new and empowering developments while at the same time reminding us of the gross inequalities that remain unchanged in the contemporary world.

Second, these developments have the potential to stimulate the imaginative work of the broad masses of the people. The expansion of representational technologies means that people now express their senses of past, present, and future—their very destinies and their senses of self—in terms of the new mediascapes dominating late-capitalist life. These new mentalities and self-imaginings are driven forward by an ever-expanding sense of possibility—as well as terror and constraint—as modern humanity cultivates new interests, needs, desires, and fears in the landscape of the new media. These are the "dangerous crossroads" of media culture writ large that George Lipsitz (1994) reminds us of, replete as it is with profound possibilities as well as dangers.

Third, and finally, new critical discourses have been generated, largely outside the field of education, to address the challenges of this new age. New interpretive, interdisciplinary frameworks abound. In the academic realm, these discourses include cultural studies, postmodernism, multiculturalism, and postcolonialism—the latter being the framework that integrates the various disparate elements and threads of this essay. But in the realm of the popular, these interpretive frameworks are often formulated in the language of moral panic, and its obverse, the language of panaceas and quick fixes. Here, we are referring to the panic/panaceas offered by psychic networks, extreme sports, stock options, E-trading, "reality" television, and the like that now dominate commercial advertising and the calculations of both private citizenry and the transnational capitalist enterprise. All of these developments, both critical and panicked, represent the triumph of multiplicity and the lack of clear answers now overtaking our daily lives. And they incite new challenges for the reproduction of increasingly unstable social orders generally and the practices of classroom pedagogy more specifically. Indeed, we are being compelled at every point to reconsider what pedagogy and curriculum practices mean in these circumstances.

Against the tide of these currents of change, however, mainstream educational thinkers—particularly in the United States—have tended to draw down a bright line of distinction between the established school curriculum and the teeming world of multiplicity that flourishes in the everyday lives of youth beyond the school proper. These educators still insist on a project of homogeneity, normalization, and the production of the socially functional citizen. This is true even of contemporary, progressive approaches to curriculum reform (such as multiculturalism) that have sought to bring the problems of multiplicity and difference into a framework of institutional intelligibility and manageability. Thus, proponents of the modern curriculum tend to speak a "technicist discourse," a discourse of experts, professional competence, and boundary maintenance. In these instances, potentially powerful tropes such as "multiculturalism" have become reconfigured "through a proliferation of images and practices into a normalized, non-politically charged discourse that assume[s] that ethnic minority communities [are] homogenous and somehow representative of an authentic and unified culture" (Giardina and Metz 2001, 210). While purporting to be positive, progressive textual artifacts and emancipatory practices subverting the status quo, the majority of these popular iterations commonly wash over and efface the harsh realities witnessed at the ground level of everyday interactions between and among diverse segments of the population generally and the school setting specifically. As a result, while an unthreatening form of multiculturalism has been integrated into the curriculum, more critical discourses—such as Marxism, pragmatism, Frankfurt school critical theory, cultural studies, poststructuralism, and postcolonialism—have been left aside.

Rejecting such monologic projects, we confront the heart of Friedrich Nietzsche's diagnosis of the modern condition, which we think speaks adroitly to contemporary educational and social dilemmas and to the antinomy of center–periphery relations more generally. In his *On the Genealogy of Morals* (1887/1967), Nietzsche insisted that a new ethical framework had come into being in the industrial age that informed all patterns of human exchange in the bureaucratic arrangements of social institutions. He called this moral framework "ressentiment" (resentment), or the practice in which one defines one's identity through the negation of the other. This is a process governed by the strategic alienation of the other in forms of knowledge building, genres of representation, and the deployment of moral, emotional, and affective evaluation and investments. One sees this in operation in the whole contemporary stance in educational institutions toward the topics of difference, multiplicity, and heterogeneity. Moreover, such thinking is revealed most especially in the fratricidal wars taking place on campuses across the country over the question of the canon versus multiculturalism and the traditional disciplines versus alternative forms of knowledge such as cultural studies and postcolonial theory. But these debates do not stop at the hallowed gates of the university, the preparatory classrooms of the high school, or the playgrounds of the elementary school; we also see this antipathy to difference in popular culture and public policy in the United States—a country in which the professional middle-class dwellers of the suburbs have appropriated the radical space of difference onto themselves, occupying the space of social injury, the space of social victim and plaintiff. In so doing, this suburban professional class denies avenues of complaint to its other: the inner-city poor. It projects its suburban worldview out into the social world as the barometer of public policy, displacing issues of inequality and poverty and replacing these with demands for balanced budgets, tax cuts, and greater investments in surveillance and security. All of this is accompanied by a deep-bodied nostalgic investment in Anglo-American cultural form and its European connections.

Of course, this framework of oppositions can be mapped a thousandfold onto third world/first world relations. But, ironically, these developments are taking place at a time when, all over the world, the processes of migration, electronic mediation, and the work of the imagination of the great masses of the people have effected the separation of culture from place (Appadurai 1996); difference has become an abstract value that can be dirempted from specific groups and settings and combined and recombined in ways that allow, for example, clothing designer magnates like Tommy Hilfiger to appropriate elements of hip hop culture and sell these elements back into the inner city itself. Further, the movement of peoples from Latin America, the Caribbean, Asia, Africa, and the Middle East to the United States has had the effect of reworking American culture and its very demographic character from within. In schools throughout California, Texas, and New York, it is now not unusual to encounter classrooms in which the minority child is Anglo-American and where English has been supplanted by Spanish, Armenian, Chinese, Korean, or Ebonics. These vastly transformed circumstances, consequent upon the movement and collision of people, impose new imperatives on curriculum and pedagogy in schooling. But, in our era, we seem evermore to lack the qualities of empathy, the desire for collaboration and cooperation and negotiation, or the magnanimity of spirit to engage with the other as a member of our community or even our species.

The Dominant Paradigm

The dominant approach to the contemporary challenges of multiplicity and difference in schooling—and one increasingly associated with minority practitioners as well—is to think of "culture" and "identity" within the crisis language of imaginary unity, singular origins, singular ancestry, bounded nationality, and so forth. Culture is thus defined as a tightly bounded set of linguistic, aesthetic, and folkloric practices specific to a particular group; group identity is seen as the true self within the collective association—as the fulfillment of a linear connection to an unsullied past and ancestry. The overriding slogans now resonate a discourse of "These are our people"; "We are different from all other groups"; and "These are *our* cultural forms and meaning of style." Thus in the United States, hegemonic Anglocentric school critics such as Arthur Schlesinger, George Will, and William Bennett maintain that the U.S. school curriculum should have a unitary and homogenizing focus around Western Eurocentric culture. Will (1998) makes the point in very direct language:

> Our country is a branch of European civilization … "Eurocentricity" is right, in American curricula and consciousness, because it accords with the facts of history, and we—and Europe—are fortunate for that. The political and the moral legacy of Europe has made the most happy and admirable of nations. Saying that may be indelicate, but it has the merit of being true and the truth should be the core of any curriculum. (Will quoted in McCarthy 1998, 109)

On the other hand, minority school critics such as Afrocentrist scholar Molefi Asante (1993) argue for placing African culture at the heart of the curriculum, maintaining that the curriculum for African Americans should be organized around "solid identities" with Africa as revealed in the Eurocentric/Afrocentric debate over curriculum reform. Both Eurocentric and Afrocentric discourses of cultural monologism rely on the simulation of a pastoral sense of the past in which Europe and Africa are thrown back to the Stone Age and made available to American racial combatants without the noise of their modern tensions, contradictions, and conflicts. The dreaded line of difference is drawn around glittering objects of heritage and secured with the knot of ideological closure. The modern American school has become a playground of this war of simulation, revealing at every turn contending paradigms of knowledge that have become embattled as combatants release the levers of atavism, holding their faces in their hands as the latest volley of absolutism circles in the air. Nowhere is this sense of cultural antagonism more strongly articulated than in debates over the canon versus minority and third world cultural form.

The effect of these ethnocentric projects in the curriculum field has been to create an arbitrary divide between the traditions and cultural forms of the West or the first world and those of indigenous minorities of the United States and third world peoples. This is now foregrounded in the hot button debates taking place in the United States about the merits of the Western canon versus multiculturalism and postcolonial third world cultural form. Curriculum organized around a Eurocentric notion of the canon maintains a monological interpretation of culture and identity. And, further, proponents formulate a curricular approach that is deeply informed by the following kinds of ideological assumptions. First, curricular monologists conceptualize culture and identity as consisting of a clearly demarcated and bounded set of lived and commodified cultural forms and practices specific to particular groups. These practices are defined as forms of some kind of final property and are seen as constituting the totality of group capacity and definition. Second, mainstream theorists motivated by the manipulation of this model of culture and identity propose that curriculum reform should take the form of content addition to the dominant Eurocentric core curriculum, adding selectively from the stock of knowledges and experiences associated with minority groups. Third, monologists suggest that only the members of a given minority group are fully competent to understand the knowledge and the experiences pertinent to that particular group. This often leads to a dangerous tendency to construct as other, as internal enemies, those who are not part of the monologist's preferred group or who do not share his real or imagined ancestry. The other in this context is then targeted for exclusion; the history, knowledge, and culture of such others are consequently perceived as illegitimate, in the Bourdieuian sense, and, often therefore, suppressed.

The Postcolonial Response

The evaluation of the status of postcolonial theory and of the postcolonial imagination in contemporary sociological and commonsense understandings of the dynamics of modern life has assumed a great urgency in the light of the events of 9/11 and their global dimensions. These developments have forced critical scholars in the United States to awake from our methodological slumber regarding the perils of amnesia or disinterest in the facts of U.S. relations to the outside world and to its particular imperialist and possessive investment in the third world in particular. In this sense the work of postcolonial art—that is, literature, painting, and music—has been, to use the language of Jacques Attali (1992), prophetic, anticipatory, and instructive. But what do we mean by postcolonial theory, and what status does such theory have in interrogating the productive relations of popular culture forms? By postcolonial theory, we are referring to the practice or practices of systematic reflection on domination relations produced in the processes of elaboration of colonial/neocolonial relations and encounters between metropolitan countries of the West and the third world. These relations are properly but not exhaustively understood as center–periphery relations in that they have been and continue to be asymmetrical in their organization and character. Postcolonial theorists argue that these relations are overdetermined, many-sided, often reciprocal; that is, that agency flows both ways along the center–periphery divide and in many directions—it is not simply unidirectional. In the postcolonial view, the cultural forms of the third world are *not* simply bastardized texts of the first. Arguing for the model of overdetermined asymmetry and the rethinking of space and geography, postcolonial critics such as Homi Bhabha, Stuart Hall, Edward Said, Gayatri Spivak, Michael Dash, Edouard Glissant, and others refuse both the top-down models of structural integration of the neo-Marxist theorists of cultural imperialism and the cultural diffusion and modernization models that have come out of overwrought ethnographic anthropology and mainstream sociology and political science. All of this raises the status of aesthetics or the work of the imagination in postcolonial rethinking of the center–periphery couplet.[1]

Correlatively, postcolonial artists, writers, and painters such as Nicolas Guillén, Toni Morrison, Michael Ondaatje, Jean Michel Basquiat, Arnaldo Roche-Rabell, and Gordon Bennett have been both precursors to, as well as contemporary participants in, postcolonial theorizing. These critically minded cultural *artistes* scour the flotsam and detritus, the historical ruins generated in colonial relations, reworking and reordering them with the dispassion of what Walter Benjamin, in *The Origins of German Tragic Drama*, calls "melancholy." They foreground the complex nature of the human condition produced in the wake of colonization and its aftermath and the struggles of resistance against colonial and neocolonial domination. And they work against the grain of binary oppositions associated with third world/first world, classical versus vernacular paradigms, always pointing toward themes that underscore a deep sense of community, interdependence, and cultural translation across the minefield of difference. In this sense, then, postcolonial cultural workers have always been ahead of postcolonial critics and criticism, pointing to the fitful, incomplete, reciprocal relations between the colonizer and the colonized. This extraordinary insight about modernity's interment in pre/antimodernity—the corridors or doorways between genres, tradition, and histories, as the Guyanese philosophical novelist Wilson Harris maintains in *Tradition, the Writer, and Society* (1967)—is foregrounded in postcolonial aesthetics, an insight that seemed to be lost on the social sciences until the last few decades with the emergence of poststructural, postmodern, and postcolonial criticism spreading across the disciplines.

Specific to discussions of culture, identity, and curriculum, these aforementioned postcolonial writers and critics point to the limitations of monological and homogenizing approaches, arguing instead that culture and identity are the products of human encounters, the inventories of cross-cultural appropriation and hybridity—not the elaboration of the ancestral essence of particular groups. Within this framework, culture and identity are the moving inventories and registers of association across narrowly drawn boundaries of group distinction. In his very important essay, "Cultural Identity and the Diaspora," Hall (1990) maintains that within any given community, there are several other hidden or alternative communities wrestling to come to the surface, to come face-to-face with the unsuspected horizons and trestles of affiliation across human groups and cultures normally regarded as separable and distinct.

To illustrate this point about cultural hybridity, the Cuban novelist, Alejo Carpentier, tells the story of an intriguing encounter he had while visiting the remote forest community of Turiamo, on the Caribbean coast of Venezuela. Here, the villagers introduced Carpentier to the "poet"—an illiterate Afro-Latin griot who was regarded as the keeper of communal history, the people's poet. In this illiterate, itinerant peasant, Carpentier came face to face with the multiaccented, polyphonic voice of these anthropologically defined "natives." At a late night communal gathering, which Carpentier attended, this Afro-Latin griot, "the Poet," recited for his forest dwellers gathered by the sea extensive passages of eighth-century French epic verse in an indigenous Venezuelan language. Carpentier tells the story this way:

> Let me tell you an anecdote which illustrates the poetic tradition in Latin America. More than twenty years ago, when I was living in Venezuela, my wife and I went to stay in a small fishing village on the Caribbean coast called Turiamo. There were no hotels, no bars, and you get there by crossing kilometers and kilometers of virgin forest. All the inhabitants of the village were black, there were no schools and almost everyone was illiterate. We soon got to know the village people and they told us about the Poet, a person who enjoyed a great deal of prestige there. He hadn't been to the village for about two months and the people missed him. One day he reappeared, bringing news from other areas. He was a colossal African, illiterate and poorly dressed. I told him, I'd like to hear his poetry. "Yes," he replied, "Tonight, by the sea." And that night all the village people, children, old folk, everyone, gathered on the beach to wait for the Poet. He took off his hat with a ritual gesture and, looking out to sea, began in quite acceptable octosyllables to recite the wonderful story of Charlemagne in a version similar to that of the Song of Roland.
>
> That day I understood perhaps for the first time in our America, wrongly named Latin, where an illiterate black descendant of Yorubas could recreate the Song of Roland—in a language richer than Spanish, full of distinctive inflections, accents, expressions and syntax—where wonderful Nahuatl poetry existed long before Alfonso the Wise and San Isidoro's Etymologies, in our America, there were a culture and a theatrical disposition which gave poetry an importance long lost in many countries in Europe. (Carpentier 1985, 160)

The St. Lucian playwright, Derek Walcott (1993), also calls attention to this theme of hybridity. In his 1992 Nobel lecture, "The Antilles: Fragments of Epic Memory," Walcott talks about taking some American friends to a peasant performance of the ancient Hindu epic of Ramayana in a forgotten corner of the Caroni Plain in Trinidad. The name of this tiny village is the happily agreeable, but Anglo-Saxon, "Felicity." The actors carrying out this ritual reenactment are the plain-as-day East Indian villagers spinning this immortal web of memory, of ancientness, and modernity. Here, Walcott is "surprised by sin" at the simple native world unfurling in its utter flamboyance:

Felicity is a village in Trinidad on the edge of the Caroni Plain, the wide central plain that still grows sugar and to which indentured cane cutters were brought after emancipation, so the small population of Felicity is East Indian, and on the afternoon that I visited it with friends from America, all the faces along its road were Indian, which as I hope to show was a moving, beautiful thing, because this Saturday afternoon Ramleela, the epic dramatization of the Hindu epic of Ramayana, was going to be performed, and the costumed actors from the village were assembling on a field strung with different-colored flags, like a new gas station, and beautiful Indian Boys in red and black were aiming arrows haphazardly into the afternoon light. Low blue mountains on the horizon, bright grass, clouds that would gather colour before the light went. Felicity! What a gentle Anglo-Saxon name for an epical memory. (Walcott 1993, 1).

The world on the Caroni Plain integrates the ancient and modern, as Indian peasants, historically displaced as indentured laborers to the Caribbean, create in their daily lives a rememory of their past before modern colonialism. In so doing, they add an extraordinary ritual and threnodic nuance to the folk culture of the Caribbean as a whole. In the art of living, these East Indian peasants triumph over the imposed history of marginalization and the middle-passage history of indentureship.

This vitality of multiple origins and connections informs the theater that Walcott, ultimately, envisions for a Caribbean breaking with European hegemonic norms of representation. He offers a powerful set of tropes for an equally powerful social vision:

In the West Indies, there are all these conditions—the Indian heritage, the Mediterranean, the Lebanese and Chinese…. When these things happen in an island culture a fantastic physical theatre will emerge because the forces that affect that communal search will use physical expression through dance, through the Indian dance and through Chinese dance, through African dance. When these things happen, plus all the cross-fertilization—the normal sociology of the place—then a true and very terrifying West Indian theatre will come. (310)

Both Carpentier's and Walcott's vivid vignettes point us toward the complex flow of humanity across presumptive borders. What these authors highlight is the radical encounter of ancient and modern peoples and Western and indigenous third world cultures in the postcolonial setting, and the unanticipated trestles of affiliation that link up disparate populations. They highlight the difficulty, indeed the futility, of atavistic attempts to maintain group purity. Further, and like so many other postcolonial artists, Carpentier and Walcott challenge the ways the colonial imagination has sought to constrain third world subjects in reductive and simplistic discourses of racial and national origin (McCarthy 1998). It is these simplistic discourses, as Cameron McCarthy and Greg Dimitriadis note in *Reading and Teaching the Postcolonial* (2003), that are consolidated in curricular projects in the West—multicultural and otherwise—projects which have sought to quell the unpredictable noise of dialogue that is the inexorable and interminable state of contemporary identity formation. But these postcolonial artists allow no such easy closure; they challenge us to look to new—and less prefigured—representational practices.

In quoting and combining elements of Western and third world cultural forms, writers such as Walcott are engaged in a radical aesthetics of double coding. But this practice is not limited only to the authorial pen. One also finds this strategy of double coding foregrounded in the work of postcolonial visual artists. By double or triple coding, we are referring to the tendency of the postcolonial artist to mobilize two or more plains or fields of idiomatic reference in any given work, what Wilson Harris calls "the wedding of opposites." The postcolonial artist may therefore quote or combine the vernacular and the classical, the traditional and the modern, the cultural reservoir of images of the East and the West, the first world and the third, the colonial master and the slave.[2]

By way of example, this strategy of double or triple coding is powerfully emphasized in the work of the Australian Aboriginal painter, Gordon Bennett. In his art, Bennett, the son of an Aborigine mother and European father, documents his struggle with the profound personal and political issues historically surrounding identity formation in Australia. Bennett came to art relatively late in life, graduating from art school in 1988, the year Australia celebrated the bicentennial of European settlement. His work registers the attendant tensions and concerns of this historical moment. I would like to foreground here one of his pivotal paintings, *Outsider*. This painting combines methods of Aboriginal pointillism and European perspectival painting to stunning effect. In *Outsider*, Bennett ironically quotes and densely refigures Vincent Van Gogh's *Starry Night* and his *Vincent's Bedroom at Arles*, intensifying and heightening the atmosphere of brusque, startling anxiety that works through Van Gogh's paintings. Bennett's double coding of European and Native traditions exposes an unsettling environment of cultural hegemony. Most importantly, Bennett interposes a new scenario into the settings in Van Gogh's paintings: a decapitated native body stumbling toward a blood-besmirched cradle on which lie two classical Greek heads. Against this backdrop of a reconfigured *Starry Night* and *Vincent's Bedroom at Arles*, the essential ground of Aboriginal and hegemonic Anglo-Australian identities is now populated with trip wire questions located in this motif of hybridity and double vision. The work of hybridity unearths the symbolic violence of Australian history and the brutality of European "discovery" and subjugation of the native. At the same time, through this double coding, Bennett highlights the incompleteness of the modern Aboriginal search for identity. This is sharply underscored in Bennett's use of space. Avoiding the linear arrangement of space of the European colonial oil painting in which the native is clinically separated from the colonizer, Bennett deliberately yokes the colonizer and colonized into the same space, indeed the same body. Boundaries between the European and the Aboriginal are collapsed and antagonistic spaces of colonized and colonizer are folded into each other in a violent and eruptive manner.

Bennett himself uses art as a profound pedagogical tool—one that challenges the histories taught to him from a very young age, including the story that Captain Cook "discovered" Australia as an empty land—*Terra Nullius*. This history stood in powerful contradistinction to the more hybrid reality he lived, though it was a reality maintained and sustained every step of the way by a colonial education system. Bennett stresses the importance of opening up alternative kinds of histories, alternative perspectives on Australian history, in art. He speaks of one self-portrait as a "visual text trying to open up history, to say there are other perspectives that are possible" (*Black Angles*). Yet the power of this work lies not simply in presenting other versions of history. Rather, Bennett opens a space where the very project of constructing history from a single perspective is called into question. Note the constant stress on multiple lines of vision (typically three) in his work. Bennett offers a profound challenge to contemporary educational movements that seek merely to insert "other stories" into already existing curricula in an additive fashion. His project of double coding dominant and dominated motifs, of destabilizing coherent origins, is significantly more powerful and provides more fruitful avenues for those interested in constructing curricula relevant to the complex lives of the disenfranchised.

The work of the postcolonial imagination, then, points toward a larger inventory of associations in the conceptualization of culture and identity than one finds in the educational thought of the cultural monologists. Refusing monologism and ethnocentrism, postcolonial writers such as Edward Said (1993, 2000) suggest that a complex and dynamically relational treatment of culture and identity should deeply inform curriculum in schooling as we enter the new millennium. Curriculum change to address the new challenges of culture and identity and predicated upon the framework suggested by postcolonial theorists operates on the following assumptions. First, post-colonial theorists maintain that the opposition between the Western canon and third world cultural form is illegitimate. They suggest that this opposition is not empirically based, insisting instead that there is a vigorous critique of and dialogue with the West taking place in the literature, music, and paintings of third world artists. Second, postcolonial school critics argue that curricular knowledge should be an interdisciplinary product of heterogenous sources. They maintain that pedagogy in the classroom should be organized around the thesis of the constructed nature of all knowledge. Postcolonial theorists further assert that the accumulation of the latter is not a linear or singular process but one that is best facilitated by an open practice of knowledge production rooted in a plurality of methodologies and strategies of inquiry. Third, postcolonial theorists suggest that the contemporary context of all school knowledge and experiences is profoundly shaped by globalization and the ever-expanding pattern of integration of local realities into more global dynamics and vice versa. The world, they argue, is now more interdependent; contemporary students must be prepared for this kind of changing reality sparked by globalization.

The lines that separate the philosophical and practical approaches of cultural monologists and postcolonial theorists to curriculum formulation about culture and identity are therefore firmly drawn. Monologists see the curriculum as the servant of the core cultural values, knowledges, and experiences of particular groups. They believe that the integrity of these groups is best preserved by curricular recognition of group distinctiveness and specificity. Postcolonial theorists on the other hand argue for the interminable process of cultural integration and coarticulation of majority and minority cultures in the modern world. These theorists see contemporary reality as defined by globalization and the blurring of the boundaries of the cultural and economic distinctions that exist between the inhabitants of industrialized countries of the West and third world people. These social actors of the third world have been for too long now consigned to marginalization in the curriculum formulations of U.S. educators. These developments provide extraordinary challenges and great opportunities for curriculum reform in the contemporary U.S. school context.

Conclusion

The great task confronting teachers and educators as we move into the twenty-first century is to address the radical reconfiguration and cultural rearticulation now taking place in educational and social life. As enumerated at the beginning of this essay, a set of new developments have presented themselves to the modern educator in this new millennium. These developments are foregrounded and driven forward by the logics of globalization, the intensification of the movement and migration of people, the heightened effects of electronic mediation, the proliferation of images, and the everyday work of the imagination of the great masses of the people affecting their sense of the past, the present, and the future.

All these developments have shifted the ground of commonly taken-for-granted stabilities of social constructs such as "culture," "identity," "race," "nation," "state," and so forth. One response, indeed the dominant response to this proliferation of difference and multiplicity, is to suppress the implications for rethinking the ethical, political, and epistemological basis of education by imposing a program of homogeny. This hegemonic approach constitutes a top-down project that attempts to hold the Eurocentric and establishment core of the curriculum in place, inoculating it by simply adding on selective, nonconflictual items from the culture and experiences of minority and subaltern groups. But this monological approach to culture is also to be found in the curricular formulations of some minority school critics as well. Cultural monologists within subaltern groups argue for the simple inversion of the Eurocentric dominance of the curriculum. They maintain that the cultural knowledges and experiences of their specifically embattled minority group—be it

African American, Chicana/o, Asian American—should be foregrounded in a manner that would effectively displace the Eurocentric core of the curriculum, replacing it with a specific minority program of affirmation of cultural heritage.

But these monological approaches to curriculum reform, hegemonic or minority, merely lead us down the path of a cultural illiteracy of the other—an illiteracy that we cannot afford in a world context of deepening globalization and interdependence. We cannot afford a continued blissful ignorance of groups that are different from ours—a practice that is still perpetuated in the dominant school curriculum. As postcolonial theorists suggest, a fundamentally new direction is needed in the approach to culture and identity as we enter the new millennium. This approach must begin with an effort to reject the simplistic economy of the canon versus the third world opposition in education. It must involve a radical rethinking of the linkages of knowledge, culture, and association among people. For instance, as dependency theorists such as Andre Gunder Frank, Samir Amin, and Fernando Enrique Cardoso have pointed out, the links between first world development and third world underdevelopment must be thoroughly explored in the curriculum so that today's school youth might have a fuller understanding of the vital imbrication of industrialized countries like the United States in the underdevelopment of third world countries and of how these relations themselves are transposed onto core–periphery relations within developed countries. Indeed, the events of 9/11 and after have made the examination of center–periphery relations an even more urgent subject for curricular attention.

Thinking in postcolonial terms about the topic of difference and multiplicity in education means thinking relationally and contextually. It means bringing back into educational discourses all the tensions and contradictions that we tend to suppress as we process experience and history into curricular knowledge. It means abandoning the auratic status of concepts such as "culture" and "identity" for a recognition of the vital porosity that exists between and among human groups in the modern world. It means foregrounding the intellectual autonomy of students by incorporating open-mindedness and inquiry that come from letting traditions debate with each other under the rubric that we learn more about ourselves by learning about others. It means ultimately thinking across disciplinary boundaries and the insulation of knowledge—linking the syndical and the pedagogical in the way we do our work.

Notes

1. It is important to note here that the "post" in the postcolonial is not to be understood as a temporal register as in "hereinafter" but as a sign and cultural marker of a spatial challenge and contestation with the occupying powers of the West in the ethical, political, and aesthetic forms of the marginalized. Uneven development between the metropole and periphery plays itself out in aesthetic form, in ways that problematize colonial/postcolonial networks of power relations as well as the Cartesian stability of subjecthood fabricated in and through these relations. The postcolonial imagination in material form—represented by the work of novelists, playwrights, painters, scholars, and musicians—is a product of colonial histories of disruption, forced migration, false imprisonment, and pacification. This "post," as we conceive it, ultimately specifies a coarticulation of colonial and postcolonial histories, not a self-serving separatism and isolationism.
2. Here we differentiate this strategy from the type of double coding that postmodernist critics such as Charles Jencks talk about when defining postmodernism. Instead of foregrounding the collapse of master narratives of individualistic or maverick imagination, we point instead to the collective purposes, the collective history, the visualization of community memory that constitute the central issues at stake within the postcolonial artistic project.

References

Appadurai, A. *Modernity at Large*. Minneapolis: Minnesota Press, 1996.
Asante, M. *Malcolm X as Cultural Hero and Other Afrocentric Ideas*. Trenton, NJ: Africa World Press, 1993.
Attali, J. *Noise: The Political Economy of Music*. Minneapolis: Minnesota Press, 1992.
Bennett, T. *The Birth of the Museum*. New York: Routledge, 1995.

Bennett, T. "Putting Policy into Cultural Studies." In *What Is Cultural Studies*, edited by J. Storey, 307–21. London: Arnold, 1996.

Bruce, T. and C.J. Hallinan. "Cathy Freeman and the Quest for Australian Identity." In *Sport Stars: The Cultural Politics of Sporting Celebrity*, edited by D.L. Andrews and S.J. Jackson, 257–70. London: Routledge, 2001.

Caglar, A.S. "Hyphenated Identities and the Limits of 'Culture.'" In *The Politics of Multiculturalism in the New Europe: Racism, Identity, and Community*, edited by T. Modood and P. Werbner, 169–86. London: Zed Books, 1997.

Carpentier, A. "The Latin American Novel." *New Left Review* 154 (1985): 159–91.

Castells, M. *The Internet Galaxy*. Oxford: Oxford University Press, 2001.

Césaire, A. "Notebook of a Return to the Native Land." In A. Césaire, *Collected Poetry*, translated by C. Eshleman and A. Smith, 77. Berkeley: University of California Press, 1983.

Chada, G. *I'm British But*. London: British Film Institute, 1989.

Desai, M. *Marx's Revenge: The Resurgence of Capitalism and the Death of Statist Socialism*. London: Verso, 2002.

Giardina, M.D. "'Bending It Like Beckham' in the Global Popular: Stylish Hybridity, Performativity, and the Politics of Representation." *Journal of Sport and Social Issues* 27 (2003): 65–82.

Giardina, M.D. and J.L. Metz. "Celebrating Humanity: Olympic Marketing and the Homogenization of Multiculturalism." *International Journal of Sports Marketing and Sponsorship* 3 (2001): 203–23.

Giddens, A. "The Consequences of Modernity." In *Colonial Discourse and Postcolonial Theory*, edited by P. Williams and L. Chrisman, 181–94. New York: Columbia University Press, 1994.

Hall, S. "Cultural Identity and the Diaspora." In *Identity: Community, Culture, Difference*, edited by J. Rutherford, 222–37. London: Lawrence and Wishart, 1990.

Harris, W. *Tradition, the Writer, and Society—Critical Essays*. London: New Beacon, 1967.

Kelly, J. *Borrowed Identities*. New York: Peter Lang, 2003.

Lipsitz, G. *Dangerous Crossroads: Popular Music, Postmodernism and the Poetics of Place*. New York: Verso, 1994.

McCarthy, C. *Uses of Culture: Education and the Limits of Ethnic Affiliation*. New York: Routledge. 1998.

McCarthy, C. and W. Crichlow. "Theories of Identity, Theories of Representation, Theories of Race." In *Race, Identity, and Representation in Education*, edited by C. McCarthy and W. Crichlow, xiii–xxix. New York: Routledge, 1993.

McCarthy, C. and G. Dimitriadis. "Globalizing Pedagogies: Power, Resentment and the Re-Narration of Difference." *World Studies in Education* 1 (2000): 23–9.

Morley, D. and K. Robins. *Spaces of Identity*. New York: Routledge, 1995.

Nietzsche, F. *On the Genealogy of Morals*, translated by W. Kaufmann. New York: Vintage, 1967. (Orig. pub. 1887.)

Ong, A. "Flexible Citizenship among Chinese Cosmopolitans." In *Cosmopolitics: Thinking and Feeling beyond the Nation*, edited by P. Cheah and B. Robbins, 134–62. Minneapolis: University of Minnesota Press, 1998.

Ong, A. *Flexible Citizenship: The Cultural Logics of Transnationality*. Durham: Duke University Press, 1999.

Osajima, K. Rethinking Asian American identity. Unpublished paper, Department of Education, Colgate University, 1992.

Said, E. "Identity, Authority, and Freedom: The Potentate and the Traveler." *Transition* 54 (1991): 4–18.

Said, E. "The Politics of Knowledge." In *Race, Identity and Representation in Education*, edited by C. McCarthy and W. Crichlow, 306–14. New York: Routledge, 1993.

Said, E. *Out of Place*. New York: Knopf, 2000.

Silk, M. "Together We're One?: The 'Place' of Nation in Media Representations of the 1998 Kuala Lumpur Commonwealth Games." *Sociology of Sport Journal* 18 (2001): 277–301.

Walcott, D. *The Antilles: Fragments of Epic Memory*. New York: Farrar, Straus and Giroux, 1993.

Will, G. "Eurocentricity and the School Curricula." *Baton Rouge Morning Advocate*, December 18, 1989, p. 3.

11

Representations of Islam and Education for Justice

FAZAL RIZVI

Introduction

Late one evening, some four weeks after the tragic events of September 11, 2001, I received a telephone call that still haunts me. At the other end of the phone was a man I had never met before. He spoke in a heavy Indian accent, in a voice that was clearly distressed. He had phoned me in desperation because he believed that as an educator who had a Muslim name I might understand his dilemma and might be able to advise him. He told me that he was a devout Muslim who was born in India but had been a citizen of the United States for more than fifteen years. He regarded himself as a loyal American; he was grateful to the United States for the opportunities it had given him; and that is where his two daughters, aged 14 and 12, were born. He was a software engineer who lived in a middle-class suburb where his teenage daughters attended a public school that was known for its cultural diversity and commitment to multiculturalism. The man believed that his teenage daughters were exemplary students, and had always enjoyed school. September 11 changed all this.

Both of his daughters were now reluctant to go to school, and came home unhappy and agitated, often in tears. They told their parents that they were subjected to constant name-calling, even from those who they had regarded as their close friends. They were called "terrorists," and their religion was repeatedly mocked. According to the girls, even the teachers were not sympathetic, expressing stereotypes of Islam, and constantly drawing attention to the fact that the girls were Muslim. Despite this harassment the girls did not want their parents to contact the school to discuss the matter, for the fear of making things worse. Herein lay the man's dilemma. The girls wished to be as invisible as possible but could not be. Their father wanted to raise the issues with the school but felt that in an emotionally charged atmosphere he might not be heard, and might even exacerbate the situation for his daughters. He too wanted to become invisible, not identifiable by his religion. He had already determined that he would not require his daughters to wear the hijab, the Muslim headscarf, and that he would encourage them to relegate their religious expressions to the private domain. Our telephone conversation ended in my advice that he take the risk of contacting the principal and discuss with him the dilemma in precisely the terms he had described it to me. That was the last I heard from him. I still do not know his name.

Coincidently, at a teacher conference a few months later, I had an opportunity to meet the principal of the school I had imagined the man's daughters attended. The principal told me proudly that while he feared and anticipated some incidents of hostility toward Muslim students following September 11, none was reported to him. Proudly, he put it down to the work the school had done to promote the principles of cultural understanding and tolerance. When I told him of the telephone call I had received from a Muslim parent he was genuinely shocked and invoked the possibility himself that, in a political climate suspicious of Islam, some Muslim students and parents might have indeed been silenced. He acknowledged that the broader climate of suspicion in the United States following September 11 remained antagonistic toward all Muslims, despite the U.S. government's rhetoric that the enemy was not the religion but the terrorists who had used Islam for their own warped political ends. The principal realized that the hostility toward Muslims, fueled by the popular media, must have had some impact on his school community; but he remained unclear as to how to help his teachers recognize this impact and how to develop a schoolwide response to it. In the end, he had preferred to wait until an incident occurred at the school before formulating such a policy response; and, as he said, none was reported.

In a sense, the principal's decision is perfectly understandable: why open a Pandora's box of popular prejudices? From another perspective, however, his approach is based on an assumption, which the principal himself recognized, that if an incident does not occur then there is no problem to address. It leaves those who are already affected feeling doubly marginalized. Of course, as has been widely noted, such a problem does exist throughout the United States and must therefore be addressed. But how? In my view, it requires an appropriate form of moral leadership.

In this paper, I would like to discuss some of the conceptual, ethical, and practical issues raised by my vignette. In particular, I want to explore some of the dilemmas that Muslim citizens of the United States have been forced to confront, in light of the popular representations of Islam that have portrayed them as potentially disloyal and dangerous. The discursive terrain within which these representations have been articulated has had the effect of not only silencing American Muslims but also curtailing debates about the relationship between Islam and global terrorism. I argue that schools committed to diversity and justice have a special responsibility for understanding the ways in which this discursive terrain operates in a range of historically and politically specific ways, and to provide forms of moral leadership that challenge current representations of Islam, by developing communication structures that do not shut off particular cultural voices, no matter how controversial.

Teachers and administrators need to find ways of not only uncovering silences that help reproduce misleading and harmful representations of Islam but also of exploring how certain organizational practices perpetuate them. They need to develop pedagogic strategies that enable students to approach diverse religious beliefs and practices with an open mind and respect for others, without falling into the specter of relativism. This task is not easy, but I maintain that it is nonetheless possible to engage critically with other cultural and religious traditions, without belittling them. If this is so then the test of good pedagogy must surely involve opportunities for non-Muslim students to explore Islamic beliefs and practices critically, but in ways that do not offend Muslim students with representations that are implicitly hostile to their faith, and to their sense of themselves as both American and Muslim.

After September 11

The immediate impact of the horrific and tragic events of September 11 was felt around the globe. It is hard to imagine anyone living in the United States who was unaffected in some tangible way. Unused to such horrors on their soil, most Americans found it hard to comprehend the brutality of such wanton acts of destruction and of such disregard for human life. While some tried to understand how this could have happened, others called for justice in the form of punishment and retribution. Within the context of such general anger, the Muslim community in America found itself in an extremely difficult position. While it regarded itself as no less patriotic, abhorred violence, and was as distressed by the events of September 11 as any other community, it was forced to defend its loyalty to America. Within hours of the tragedy, fearing a backlash, national Muslim organizations felt it necessary to issue statements condemning the violence, expressing sympathy for all those directly affected, and reminding the American people that the victims included over 200 Muslims. However, such statements did little to stop an unprecedented rash of anti-Muslim incidents, from low level harassment, ethnic slurs, broken windows, and threatening calls to attacks on mosques and property, and even murders.

Leaders of the American-Arab Anti-Discrimination Committee (ADC) and the Arab American Institute (AAI) reported that there were over 600 incidents of hate crimes directed against Arab Americans within the first week following September 11. Ibrahim Hooper of the Council on American-Islamic Relations (2001) said, "The atmosphere is very tense for Muslims in this country." Fearing violence, some families kept children out of school and a number of mosques and Islamic academies remained closed for more than three months. As reports of hate crimes against Muslims and South Asians rose sharply across the United States, many Muslims, even those who did not practice the religion, felt deeply insecure. Many compared their sense of insecurity to the experiences of the Japanese Americans during the internment camps of the Second World War.

But more broadly, the tragic events of September 11 focused the nation's attention on the role of religion in public life, particularly as many, including many Muslims, turned to religious leaders and houses of worship in search for answers and consolation. According to the Pew Research Center (2002), within the weeks following the terrorist attacks, Americans of all faiths flooded into houses of worship, packing weekend services, and engaging in spontaneous religiosity. According to a poll conducted in mid-November 2001, 78 percent of the American public said the influence of religion on American life was increasing. And while this level of interest in Islam has not been sustained, debates about its role in promoting terrorism have continued to suggest an essential link between Islam and violence. These popular debates have shown how little most Americans know about Islam and Muslims, a religious community that is rapidly growing in the United States, with estimates ranging from 6 to 8 million (U.S. State Department 2003). For their part, scholars of Islam have poured out books and articles on Islam, and many American-Muslim organizations have encouraged educational programs through interfaith services and shared dialogue. They have sought to distinguish between the radical fundamentalism of a few and the faith shared and practiced by over 800 million Muslims around the world. The American government too has encouraged this perspective, with President George W. Bush, on more than one occasion, declaring that "the face of terror is not the true faith of Islam.... Islam is peace. These terrorists don't represent peace. They represent evil and war. When we think of Islam, we think of a faith that brings comfort to a billion people around the world" (reported on the Pew Research Center Website, 2002).

Yet the anti-Muslim rhetoric of some religious leader such as Franklin Graham, who called Islam "evil," and Jerry Vines, the former head of the Southern Baptist Convention, who called the Prophet Mohammad "a demon-possessed pedophile," have undermined the cause of interfaith dialogue and have left many Muslims uncertain about their status in the United States. And while the U.S. government has been careful to distance itself from remarks hostile to Islam, many American Muslims complain that the government has been far too equivocal. Their confidence in the government to defend their civil rights has been shaken by the Department of Justice's aggressive pursuit of Muslims within the United States as suspected terrorists or those who might support some of the goals of Islamic fundamentalism. Many provisions of the Patriot Act have led Muslim organizations to express concerns over racial profiling and other violations of their civil liberties.

In the aftermath of September 11, there has emerged then a new discourse about Islam that is systematically equivocal in that it preaches at once the values of cultural tolerance and respect for others, but constructs the Islamic Other against what Edward Said (1978/1985) has referred to as an "orientalist imaginary." Nowhere is such an imaginary more clearly evident than in the popular Western media, where stereotypes of Islam are employed freely to explain the causes of September 11 in religious rather than political and economic terms. The roots of Islamic fundamentalism are assumed to be located within the metaphysical postulates of Islam. In the popular media, informed and balanced accounts of Islamic traditions are difficult to find, as religious debates within Islam are largely overlooked. In an introduction to a revised edition of his book *Covering Islam*, published after September 11, Edward Said (2002) points out that the focus on Muslims and Islam in the American and Western media has become characterized by an even "more exaggerated stereotyping and belligerent hostility." Indeed, the orientalist ideas that had begun to be discredited have been revived—"ideas which have achieved a startling prominence at a time when racial or religious misrepresentations of every other cultural group are no longer circulated with such impunity" (p. xi–xii). After September 11 in particular, Ahmed (2002) has noted that any expression of Muslim identity has risked the fear of being suspected as a "terrorist." Muslims have felt that Islam itself is under siege. Ahmed (2002, 31) has been careful not to suggest a media conspiracy but seeks rather to explain that "one of the main problems of our time is the preference the media give to the 'exclusivists'— that is, people who are opposed to the values of inclusion and global integration."

Racialization of Islam

Media representations of Muslims and Islam have not however been uniformly negative. Some attempts have been made to understand what has been referred to "Islamism," the attempt by a militant group of Muslims to use selected Islamic notions such a jihad to develop an anti-Western political agenda that rails against a whole range of modernist ideas and practices, including globalization, neoliberalism, and Western popular culture. Islamism views globalization as another form of Western hegemony over Islamic countries and people, and invites Muslims everywhere to return to the dictates of the Sharia law. Such a view is based on an isolationist ideology that imagines dialogue between civilizations to be impossible. The majority of Muslims clearly do not subscribe to this political agenda. However, the superficial and sensationalist manner in which popular media presents controversial topics often privileges these more extreme narratives, making it difficult for audiences to differentiate between other competing political positions subscribed to by Muslims from various different cultural and political traditions. The popular media has increasingly begun to interpret Islam not in religious terms but in terms that are racialized. How is this so?

Recent theoretical work (e.g., Miles 1989; Goldberg 1993; Hall 1996) on its nature and scope suggests that a universal characterization of racism is impossible, and that racist representations and practices are continually changing, being challenged, interrupted, and reconstructed, and that all forms of racism are historically specific. As Stuart Hall (1996, 435) points out, while there are no doubt certain general features to racism, what is "more significant are the ways in which these general features are modified and transformed by the historical specificity of the contexts and environment in which they become active." Discourses of contemporary racism do not represent a coherent set of ideas, but are often contradictory, and often involve conflicting constructions of the Other. Nor do racist discourses necessarily refer to visible color difference or a biological category of race. As Cohen (1988, 14) argues, "racist discourses have never confined themselves to body images. Names and modes of dress, states of mind and living conditions, clothes and customs, every kind of social behaviour and cultural practice have been pressed into service to signify this or that racial essence."

Theorists like Omi and Winant (1986) have used the term *racialization* to refer to the complex processes through which racial designations are established. Thus, particular expressions, policies, practices, and institutions can be said to be racialized if they are predicated on the assumptions of racial differentiations, either biological or cultural, through which particular groups of people are evaluated negatively, or through which hierarchical ordering of groups of people are established. Such evaluations have profound effects on people's everyday experiences and life chances. But practices of racialization are never homogenous or static, but are continually changing, as people attempt to understand major dissonances in their lives, and the events that might affect them, either directly or indirectly, through constructions of difference (Mac an Ghaill 1999). While on some occasions, such constructions involve the creation of new interpretive categories, in other circumstances old discourses persist, often through the use of new ideological forms—new code words that obscure the exercise of power, prejudice, and discrimination.

While such constructions of difference are invariably designed to marginalize and exclude groups of people, it is important to note that the mechanisms of marginalization and exclusion vary considerably, and have historically specific form. They may involve physical violence, political repression, psychological abuse, harassment, paternalism, inequality of access and treatment, legislated inequalities, and so on, but *not in the same way.* Goldberg (1993) has observed that recent constructions of difference have sought to avoid being recognized as racism, masking themselves behind the discourses of nationhood, patriotism, and nationalism. They assume a necessary distance from crude ideas of biological superiority and inferiority and seek to work with an image that is characterized by discourses of national security, social cohesion, and the perceived unassimilable nature of certain cultural groups. Clear differentiations are drawn between "us" and "them," so that those who are not "us" do not "belong here" (Rizvi 1993). In the aftermath of September 11, many Muslims have experienced life the United States in precisely these terms. Representations of Islam have been couched within the broader discourses of national security, social cohesion, and patriotism.

Even before September 11, the rise of anti-Muslim sentiments was widely noted not only in the United States but in Europe as well. Partly in order to overcome the limitations of the black–white dualistic framework for understanding racism, a number of theorists, particularly in Europe, had begun to speak of *Islamophobia*, a term designed to highlight the specificities of contemporary forms of racism directed against Muslims. In a major report, the highly influential Runnymede Trust (1998) in England defines "Islamophobia as dread, hatred and hostility towards Islam and Muslims perpetuated by a series of 'closed views' that imply and attribute negative and derogatory stereotypes and beliefs to Muslims." It argues that Islamophobia is expressed toward Muslims in a range of ways including: negative or patronizing images and references in the media, and in everyday conversations, attacks, abuse and violence on the streets, attacks on mosques and cemeteries, discrimination in employment, and lack of provision, recognition, and respect for Muslims in most public institutions (Allen and Nielsen 2002). It suggests that over recent years, the identifier for prejudice and discrimination is no longer confined to race, color, or nationality but extends also to religion. And along with other forms of racism not based on color and physical appearance (e.g., anti-Gypsy racism and anti-Semitism) it involves ignorance and misinformation, often perpetuated by the media and the educational system. It also involves attributing the same negative qualities to the whole community without differentiation, although these may only be observable in a few members of that community.

Islamophobia is a relatively new word in the English language, but the realities to which it refers have been around in Western societies for many centuries. Indeed, as Miles (1989, 18) points out, the European image of Islam first emerged in the eleventh and twelfth centuries, and involved portraying the Islamic Other as "barbaric, degenerate and tyrannical, and these alleged characteristics were rooted in the character of Islam as a supposedly false and heretic theory." The Prophet

Mohammad was represented as an impostor, whose life was dominated by personal failings of violence and sexuality. It was believed that Islam spread itself throughout the world by means of aggression and war, and that the idea of jihad, the holy war, was one of its constitutive features. Also prominent in this image of Islam was the idea that as a barbaric religion it permitted and encouraged sexual deviance, including polygamy, sodomy, and a general sexual laxity. Miles argues, moreover, that "the equation of Islam with violence was sustained by a clerical agitation that culminated in the eleventh century in what became known in Europe as the Crusades." Also significant in this historical image of Islam was the contention that since Islam and Christianity, East and West, represented two incommensurable discourses, that in both theological and cultural terms, there was no meeting point between Muslim Arabs and Christian Europeans; that Islam was a negation of Christianity; and that Mohammad was Antichrist in alliance with the Devil. In his influential treatise, *Orientalism*, Said (1978/1985, 167) maintains that, within the Western scholarly traditions, the Islamic other was for the most part represented structurally in terms of a dualistic opposition; as backward, inherently cruel, and violent and irrationally sexual, determined to disrupt the European sense of harmony and spirituality.

Some of these ideas have now returned hauntingly to become elements in a new moral panic against Muslim people generally (Majid 2004). First the Islamic Revolution in Iran and the Gulf War and then September 11 and the events surrounding the subsequent wars in Afghanistan and Iraq, have served only to give credence to the views that Islam represents a direct challenge to the Western, and more specifically, American hegemony; and that Islamic fundamentalism constitutes a major threat to the West's construction of itself as liberal and democratic. In so constructing the moral panic, an idealized view of the West has been promoted, which needs to be defended against what Hoogvelt (1997) has referred to "a militant Islamic revival." This revival is considered particularly threatening within the West partly because, as Castles and Miller (1993, 27) point out, rapidly increasing Muslim minorities within countries like United States, Britain, and France "are linked to strong external forces, which appear to question the hegemony of the North and partly because they have a visible and self-confident cultural presence."

Against such representations, Muslims living in the West, in particular, have had to become defensive about their public religious expressions, for the fear of being demonized as an enemy from within. On the other hand, within the majority community, September 11 has given Islamophobia, the fear of Islam, a new legitimacy, as hegemonic regimes within the United States and Great Britain, in particular, have drawn upon and integrated an historical negative imagery of Islam, represented by the crusade and the like, with a more contemporary discourse of the Islamic threat into a refurbished and serviceable patriotism rooted in authoritarian populism (Apple 1993). This has led to the construction in the West of a new racialized discourse of Islam constituted by historical imageries applied to the current conditions of insecurity and moral panic.

Violence, the Veil, and the Clash of Civilizations

This new racialized discourse of Islam increasingly equates Islam with violence, shaped, so it is assumed, by Islam's metaphysical postulates and ethical demands, prescribed by the Muslim holy book, the Quran. In recent years, the idea of jihad has thus come to be associated with Muslim militancy against the West. The main problem with this representation is that in the Quran, the idea of jihad does not have just one essential meaning. It can be translated in several ways, all suggesting struggle of various kinds, such as a personal struggle each individual has against one's own distinctively human weaknesses, including such temptations as greed and pride. In other parts of the Quran, the concept of jihad is used to mean struggle for self-preservation and self-defense, always regulated by a range of ethical principles and sanctions. Such sanctions exclude acts of terror and indiscriminate violence against civilians. The Islamic scholar Barbara Metcalf (2002, 61) has argued that jihad has two meanings: one is the jihad of personal purification and the other of warfare. It is the latter meaning that the militant self-appointed "defenders of the faith" have hijacked, but without any reference to the ethical principles that guide the conduct of war. The fundamentalists have exploited the feelings that many Muslims have of feeling increasingly threatened and marginalized by the forces of global modernization. So the term *jihad* has come to connote an aggressive attitude that is rooted in a reactionary discourse of authenticity and purity that traditional Islam arguably never possessed.

The moderate Muslims have, on the other hand, sought to reclaim the concept of jihad, and provide Muslims everywhere with a more complex but accessible analysis of their feelings of marginalization, of the contemporary processes of globalization, and of more realistic resources of hope than those provided by the fundamentalists. These Muslim intellectuals have attempted to show how jihad has always had a historically specific meaning and that in the present context it must mean struggle for economic development, modernization, and the creation of a democratic civil society. Jihad, they have maintained, is self-destructive if it does not produce economic and social prosperity, and if it is aimed simply at striking nihilistically at a target that in the long run has the power to inflict more harm on Muslims than they can on it. As a leading Egyptian scholar of Islam, An-Naa'm (1990), has argued, there is nothing inconsistent between Islam and the ideas of democracy, freedom, the rule of law, and partnership with the West and indeed capitalism.

Yet, as Bruce Lawrence (1998) has shown, popular representations of Islam in the West have depended on "singularizing Islam and then describing it as both different and violent." He has argued that in popular imagination, Islam is assumed to emanate essentially from those sections of the "Arab" Middle East that are hostile to the West, and those who wish to project an orthodox face of puritanical Islam called Wahabi throughout the global Islamic community. What this view overlooks is the enormous diversity, both cultural and ideological, that spans the Muslim world. So, for example, while less than 25 percent of American Muslims have an Arab background, it is they who have become iconic in the popular imagination of Islam. Almost 3 million African-American Muslims are simply overlooked. What this shows is that Islam is at least as plural as the West, in the regions, races, languages, and cultures it encompasses. Lawrence (1998) argues that especially in the aftermath of the Cold War, Islam has been widely viewed as just "one Islam, the militant, unyielding, violent face of 'Arab' Islam." "Whether one picks up a popular book claiming to represent 'Western cultures and values' under attack from Islam, or lead articles in the The New York Times, such as the recent 'Seeing Green: The Red Menace is Gone. But Here's Islam' the message is the same: Islam is one, and Islam is violent" (Lawrence 1998, 5).

According to this essentialist view, Islam is not only violent toward its others but is also internally violent within its own community, especially toward women. In popular thinking in the West, nothing symbolizes the differences between the Western and the Muslim worlds more than the hijab. Yet, as Robert Young (2002, 80) observes, "few items of clothing throughout history can have been given more meanings and political significances." In the West, the hijab symbolizes the exotic mysteries of the East, on the one hand, and the violence toward women on the other. It is believed to be a symbol of a patriarchal society in which women are subordinated, oppressed, silenced, and subjected arbitrarily to the desires of men. According to Brah (1996, 136), "The veil is the ultimate icon of this fantasmatic field, frustrating the Western gaze by its opaqueness and its apparent dismissal and disregard for its hegemonic forces." In contrast, for many Muslims, including Muslim women, it signifies social status and community respect. As a symbol of cultural and religious identity, many Muslim women have increasingly chosen to cover themselves as a matter of choice. As a result, more Muslim women now wear hijab than ever before, as a symbol of control and defiance.

It is wrong, however, to assume that hijab has a uniform meaning across all Muslim communities. For example, in Iran, the wearing of hijab is mandatory, while the secular legislation in Turkey prohibits wearing of any kind of veil in public institutions such as schools, universities, offices, and even hospitals; and those Turkish women who wear hijab do so as an expression of defiance and resistance. This diversity of approaches is understandable because in the Quran hijab signifies above all calls for modesty and self-control. Yet, in the West, it has become a major signifier of Islamic backwardness, a symbol that exemplifies an almost irrational fear of Islam. So much so that the French government in 2004 sought to ban its use in public institutions, paradoxically forcing more Muslim women back into the private realm, be it a Muslim school or the home. It is clear that the core issue here concerns not the garment itself but the significance that is attached to it. According to Young (2002, 88), ultimately the hijab is a situational issue, and its use can only be understood in terms of its local meanings, which are generated within its own social and political space.

The example of the hijab shows that Islam "cannot be understood except as a major and complex religious system, shaped as much by its own metaphysical postulates and ethical demands as by the circumstances of Muslim politics in the modern world" (Lawrence 1998, 3). To suggest a uniform characterization of Islam is just as impossible as it is to represent the West as essentially monolithic, devoid of internal differences and political struggles. Yet, this is precisely the assumption made by those, like the political scientist Samuel Huntington, orientalist historian Bernard Lewis, and many American political leaders commonly referred to as the neoconservatives, who seem to interpret contemporary global politics in terms of a "clash of civilizations." According to Huntington, the fundamental source of conflict between civilizations in the new world is primarily not ideological or even economic but cultural. He maintains that the

> differences between civilizations are not only real; they are basic. Civilizations are differentiated from each other by history, language, culture, tradition, and, most important, religion. The people of different civilizations have different views on the relations between God and man, the individual and the group, the citizen and the state, parents and children, husband and wife, as well as differing views on the relative importance of rights and responsibilities, liberty, authority, equality and hierarchy. (Huntington 1993, 6)

The problem with this thesis is that it casts the differences between the West and Islam as absolute and constructs them in terms of a range of metaphysical postulates rather than the political conflicts that produce them, through a range of material historical processes. To articulate differences between civilizations in such absolutist terms is to represent the world as polarized in a binary way that runs the risk of increasing levels of conflict. As Nira Yuval-Davis (2001) points out, in times of war, the pressure to conform to binary oppositions, to absorb them not only into our language but also our very thought processes, is considerable. The temptation to divide the world into "civilizations" is especially great: "us" and "them." Not surprisingly, therefore, the clash of civilizations thesis that describes the world as involving two unbridgeable blocs, religiously and culturally, has come to occupy center stage since September 11. As a number of recent commentators, such as Syela Benhabib (2002), have observed, many cultural and political critics in America seem to have accepted the events of September 11 as offering a belated confirmation of Huntington's thesis concerning an unbridgeable cultural divide between Islam and the West.

Closed and Open Views of Islam

From an educational point of view, this culturalization of conflict is as wrong as it is dangerous. It is wrong because while the origins of some disputes are certainly cultural, prolonged conflict is always much more complex, involving factors that are not only cultural but also economic and political. And it is dangerous because it perpetuates some of the popular representations of Islam as radically different, making it difficult if not impossible for people in the West to enter into a realistic and meaningful dialogue with Muslims. To assume the basic tenets of the clash of civilizations thesis is to differentiate one civilization from another in a holistic and abstract manner, with impenetrable borders. But, as Edward Said (2002) and others have pointed out, Huntington has made civilizations into "shut down and sealed off" entities, overlooking the exchange, cross-fertilization, and sharing that has always been responsible for cultural change within all communities, not only as a result of current and countercurrents of trade but also colonialism, and more recently postcolonial migration.

A more serious problem with the clash of civilizations thesis entails, as Modood (2002) points out, the real danger of becoming a self-fulfilling prophecy, precisely at a time when a more complex and open understanding of cultural traditions, exchange, and conflict is most needed. Indeed, the popular suggestion that Islam and Christianity represent two different and separate ways of looking at the world runs the risk of reinforcing the forms of fundamentalism promoted by extremists on both sides of the presumed civilizational divide (Khan 2002). It should be remembered, however, that historically, both Islamic and Western traditions developed in the same part of the world. As a result, they share a common set of legal, religious, and cultural beliefs. Both faiths are monotheistic, and are based on similar religious narratives. Sources of conflict between them are therefore not to be found in their metaphysial postulates but in contesting political constructions of difference.

It is important to remember that, during the Middle Ages, the Judeo-Christian West borrowed heavily and learned a great deal from Muslims, both in the appreciation of arts and the humanities as well as in scientific and technological innovation, just as Muslims had done earlier from Athens and Rome. More recently, colonialism intertwined their cultural and political experiences. And over the past fifty years, migrations from Islamic countries to the West have made Muslims into sizable minorities living in countries such as United States, Britain, and France. The idea of a clash of civilizations thus masks close historical links between the two traditions, creating conditions for both cooperation and conflict. It needs to be recognized that the supposed differences between "civilizations" may in fact be politically constructed. As recent postcolonial theorists (McLeod 2000) have repeatedly argued, differences are produced and reproduced for a wide variety of ideological purposes that often remain hidden from those who repeat the mantras about their distinctive cultural identity and about the impossibilities of cultural translation.

This does not of course mean that there are no major differences between Islam and the West. If this were so then the world would be, as Majid (2003, B11) has suggested, "as monochrome as any corporate franchise." The challenge for educators is "to find ways to uphold their cultural beliefs while leaving room for dialogue with others who seem to be radically different," to teach students how not only to recognize difference but also to understand how representations of difference are historically produced and articulated. Learning about other cultures is never easy, because it often accompanies doubt as to whether we can really understand people who belong to "alien" cultures. But the presence of this doubt does not imply the impossibility of communication across cultures, or indeed of criticism. It simply suggests that while we may disagree and even condemn actions we may not like, we should refrain from assuming that our beliefs are necessarily superior. Teaching about other cultures requires that we seek to engender in students attitudes of humility and open mindedness, and develop in them skills of critical analysis so that they are able to examine popular prejudices, and work against them.

To combat Islamophobia, the Runnymede Trust (1998) has highlighted the importance of developing open views of Islam. Such views regard Islam as diverse, with internal differences, debates, and development, rather than as a monolithic bloc unresponsive to new realities, incapable of modernity. Teaching Islam in such a nuanced way requires recognition of the enormous differences that exist across and among Muslim communities. As we have already noted, enormous variations exist within the population of American Muslims alone. More than 40 percent of American Muslims are people of African descent who regard themselves as both deeply religious and undeniably patriotic. American Muslims thus represent a complex community, characterized by enormous differences across culture, region, gender, and class. To speak therefore of a single Islamic *ummah*, a universal Islamic community, is both mistaken and misleading.

Yet this is precisely what the fundamentalist Muslims do, insisting on the idea of an *ummah* as a universal community based on shared Islamic faith and a strict implementation of its law. But this is a closed hegemonic view of Islam, which demands Muslims everywhere to conform to its Wahibist form. In an ever-shrinking world this is an impossible dream, even if it were desirable. Indeed, while the global movement of people, capital, and cultural ideas emanating from the West may have helped produce a destructive Islamic militancy in many of the parts of the world, it has also led to the emergence of multiple centers of Islam. Within the American Muslim community, there is now considerable debate about the ways in which Islamic principles are best interpreted and practiced. And with developments in communication technologies and increasing levels of literacy, Muslims everywhere are increasingly forced to acknowledge their cultural and social diversity. As Riaz Hasan (2003) has pointed out, "globalization is prompting a critical reformulation of the belief that Islam is not only a religion but also a complete way of life," which is encapsulated in its dictum: "one religion, one culture." Many Muslims around the world now challenge this Wahibist sentiment as they are forced to acknowledge the vast differences in the religious practices of, for example, syncretic Javanese Muslims, who celebrate hybridity, syncreticity, and heterogeneity and Wahibi Muslims, who insist upon an essentialist "authentic" Islamic way of life.

Education for Justice

Within Islam, there is thus an intense struggle between those who view Islam in terms of an "authenticity" and those who regard syncreticity as essential to the development of a modern view of an Islam committed to democracy and justice. If this is so, then educators in the West must embrace a more open view of Islam as not only diverse but also interdependent with other faiths and cultures, having certain shared values and aims, being affected by them and enriching them. Islam, the religion, should not be seen as a source of global concern, but as an actual or potential partner in joint cooperative enterprises and in the solution of shared problems. Islam should be viewed as a genuine religious faith, practiced sincerely by its adherents. This is not to say that we should be constrained from criticizing aspects of Islamic beliefs and practices, but that the views critical of Islam should themselves be subject to exploration and critique, lest they be inaccurate, ill informed, or unfair. Nor should debates and disagreements within Islam be allowed to diminish efforts to combat racist practices of marginalization, discrimination, and exclusion.

However, a commitment to teach about Islam and to debate its key concepts in an open manner cannot occur in a school context in which democratic participation is denied or discouraged; where certain voices are repressed; and where administrative practices prevent the uncovering of voices that feel silenced. One of the problems with the prevailing views of multiculturalism is that while it preaches the need to respect other cultures and religions, it does not deal adequately with the political complexities of difference. It conceptualizes cultural differences in an abstract way, only contingently linked to other forms of inequalities such as class and gender. It celebrates empty universalisms that often inhibit the examination of the broader social relations and structures within schools that produce silences of the kind that the daughters of my telephone caller experienced. In my view, leadership for educational justice requires a better concept of the cultural mechanisms that affect educational participation of students, parents, and teachers alike.

We need to recognize that the discursive structures employed in schools legitimize and perpetuate the existing patterns of power relations. Favored ways of speaking and acting, as well as favored conceptions of knowledge of the Other, are the constitutive elements of such discourse structures, which govern not only student life chances but also such matters as who can speak, about what, and to whom. The dominant discourses of most schools are often marked by defensive, closed boundaries that discourage participation from students and parents alike. Recognition of these factors must lead to the conclusion that unless learning takes place in an organizational context better articulated to the complexities and contradictions of cultural life and to the lived realities of difference, then it will continue to leave many students confused, agitated, silenced, and alienated. What is required then are those forms of moral leadership that appreciate the need for a complex multivoiced approach to educational engagement—which does not assume fixed categories of cultural difference but encourages instead their exploration. We need to develop administrative principles that enable us to search out ways in which current events outside school might have profound effects in silencing students. This must surely require intercultural dialogues that are both democratic and critical (Rizvi 1997).

However, while this democratic aspiration is eminently laudable, it does rest on a paradox that cannot be ignored. While it advocates a contrasting view of educational authority it does not examine the structural conditions within which this authority resides. While it rejects a static, reified view of religion and culture, and views them instead as inherently dynamic, constantly changing in response to emerging ideas, beliefs, and circumstances, and open to negotiations of various kinds, it does not explain the role of the educational leader in establishing the boundaries of dialogue. Moreover, such an approach assumes teachers and educational leaders to be neutral with respect to the ideological voices that are permitted and cultural understandings that are to be negotiated. It assumes that educators are or can somehow be without their own histories, without class, gender, race, and their own political and religious views. As Martin and Mohanty (1986, 208) have pointed out, "The claim to a lack of identity and positionality is itself based on privilege, on the refusal to accept responsibility for one's implication in actual historical and social relations, or a denial that positionalities exist, or that they matter, the denial of one's own personal history and the claim to a total separation from it."

This separation has the consequence of disembodying the educator. It is not possible, however, to live as human subjects outside the framework of one's own history. Educators, like everybody else, come to their roles against the background of an already formed subjectivity, which is linked to different histories of power and powerlessness. They are moreover socially situated actors who are caught up in power relations of gender, ethnicity, and class in ways that are not arbitrary but are historically situated, and may not be entirely understood by them. Their sentiments are no less affected by the wider media representations and the broader political hysterias generated by world events of such magnitude as September 11. The school attended by the daughters of my telephone caller cannot be assumed to be an exception. Its principal and teachers too would have been disturbed by the tragic events of September 11, and would have clearly shared some of the popular views of Islam that have since prevailed.

Is there a way out of this paradox of educational reform, where democratic engagement with other cultures and religions is sought on the one hand and where we cannot simply assume educators to be able to exercise their authority in a neutral manner on the other? Perhaps not, but we can insist that educators critically examine the ways in which they exercise their authority in educational encounters involving issues of diversity, and how their exercise of authority has consequences for particular groups of students. As educators, we need to reexamine again and again particular exercises of authority in their material specificity, in terms of their relation to issues of culture, religion, and difference, in order to determine how they are currently constituted and could be reconstituted.

We cannot deny the existence of authority, but our challenge must be to work with and to work through the contradictions of this authority to create new patterns of pedagogic relations more consistent with the goals of social justice and democratic education. The daughters of my telephone caller needed this kind of courageous moral leadership.

References

Ahmad, A. and H. Donnan, eds. *Islam in the Age of Postmodernity in Islam, Globalization and Postmodernity.* London: Routledge, 1994.

Ahmad, A. *Islam Under Siege.* Cambridge, UK: Polity Press, 2003.

Allen, C. and J. Nielsen. *Summary Report on Islamophobia in the EU after 11 September 2001.* Brussels: European Monitoring Centre on Racism and Xenophobia, 2002.

American-Arab Anti-Discrimination League. http://www.adc.org/.

An-Naa'm, A.A. *Toward an Islamic Reformation: Civil Liberties, Human Rights and International Law.* Syracuse: Syracuse University Press, 1990.

Apple, M. "Constructing the Other: Rightist Constructions of Commonsense." In *Race, Identity and Representation in Education*, edited by C. McCarthy and W. Crichlow, 24–39. New York: Routledge, 1993.

Arab American Institute. http://www.aaiusa.org/.

Benhabib, S. "Unholy Wars. Reclaiming Democratic Virtues after September 11." In *Understanding September 11*, edited by C. Calhoun, P. Price, and A. Timmer, 241–53. New York: The New Press, 2002.

Brah, A. *Cartographies of Diaspora: Contesting Identities.* London: Routledge, 1996.

Castles, S. and M. Miller. *The Age of Migration: International Population Movements in the World.* Oxford: Blackwell, 1993.

Cohen, P. "The Perversions of Inheritance: Studies in the Making of Multiracist Britain." In *Multiracist Britain*, edited by P. Cohen and H. Bains, 3–51. Basingstoke, UK: Macmillan, 1988.

Council on American-Islamic Relations. http://www.cair-net.org/.

Goldberg, D. *Racist Culture: Philosophy and the Politics of Meaning.* Oxford: Blackwell, 1993.

Hall, S. "Gramsci's Relevance for the Study of Race and Ethnicity." In *Stuart Hall: Critical Dialogues in Cultural Studies*, edited by D. Morley and K.-H. Chen, 411–40. London and New York: Routledge, 1996.

Hasan, R. "Globalization's Challenge to Islam." (http://yaleglobal.yale.edu/display.article?id=1417) 2003.

Hoogvelt, A. *Globalization and the Postcolonial World: The New Poltical Economy of Development.* Basingstoke, UK: Macmillan, 1997.

Huntington, S. *The Clash of Civilizations and the Remaking of the World Order.* New York: Simon and Schuster, 1996.

Khan, Muqtedar. "Towards a New Ethic of Civilizational Discourse." In *Blaming Ourselves: September 11 and the Agony of the Left*, edited by I. Salusinszky and G. Melleuish, 95–106. Sydney: Duffy and Snullgrove, 2002.

Lawrence, Bruce. *Shattering the Myth: Islam beyond Violence.* Princeton, NJ: Princeton University Press, 1998.

Mac an Ghaill, M. *Contemporary Racisms and Ethnicities: Social and Cultural Transformations.* Buckingham, UK: Open University Press, 1999.

Majid, A. "Living with Islam." *Chronicle of Higher Education*, March 14, 2003: B10–11.

Majid, A. *Freedom and Orthodoxy: Islam and Difference in the Post-Andalusian Age.* Stanford, CT: Stanford University Press, 2004.

Martin, B. and C. Mohanty. "Feminist Politics: What's Home Got to Do with It." In *Feminist Studies/Critical Studies*, edited by T. deLauretis, 191–212. Bloomington: Indiana University Press, 1986.

McLeod, J. *Beginning Postcolonialism.* Manchester, UK: Manchester University Press, 2000.

Metcalf, B. "Traditionalist Islamic Activism: Deoband, Tablights and Talibs." In *Understanding September 11*, edited by C. Calhoun, P. Price, and A. Trimmer, 35–48. New York: The New Press, 2002.

Miles, R. *Racism.* London and New York: Routledge, 1989.

Modood, T. "Muslims and the Politics of Fear of Multiculturalism in Britain." In *Critical Views of September 11*, edited by E. Hershberg and K.W. Moore, 193–208. New York: The New Press, 2002.

Omi, M. and H. Winant. "On the Theoretical Concept of Race." In *Race, Identity and Representation in Education*, edited by C. McCarthy and W. Crichlow, 3–10. New York: Routledge, 1993.

Pew Research Center. http://pewforum.org/religion-9-11/.

Rizvi, F. "Critical Introduction: Researching Racism and Education." In *Racism and Education*, edited by B. Troyna, 65–78. Buckingham, UK: Open University Press, 1993.

Rizvi, F. "Educational Leadership and the Politics of Difference." *Melbourne Studies in Education*, 38 (1997): 91–102.

Runnymede Trust. *Islamophobia: A Challenge for Us All.* London: The Runnymede Trust, 1998.

Said, E. *Orientalism.* London: Penguin, 1985. (Orig. pub.1978.)

Said, E. *Covering Islam.* Rev. ed. New York: Vintage Books, 2002. (Orig. pub. 1981.)

U.S. Department of State. http://usinfo.state.gov/products/pubs/muslimlife/immigrat.htm, 2003.

Young, R.C. *Postcolonialism: A Very Short Introduction.* Oxford: Oxford University Press, 2003.

Yuval-Davis, N. "The Binary War." http://www.opendemocracy.net/forum/docu (2001).

12

A Note to "Identification with the Aggressor"

DEBORAH P. BRITZMAN

A provocative description that links learning to live to its psychical consequences belongs to Marcia Cavell's (1993) discussion on psychoanalysis and philosophy: "Freud found the source of human neurosis in our long dependency on others and our capacity for symbolization" (1). Neurosis is the name Freud lent to the strange conflicts of longing made from infantile desires and wishes, and defenses against these.[1] Meaning itself is compromised, resisting and missing its own significance. Paradoxically, only with a new symbolization, with the understanding that there is another, can a turning against the self be worked through. Cavell's point is that having to be a child—beginning in dependency and helplessness—matters quite specifically throughout the lifetime of an individual but not because there are developmental milestones to achieve and leave behind. Rather, the child's own theories about development, what will be called throughout this chapter "phantasy,"[2] organize both her or his emotional understanding of conflicts with social milestones *and* those of her or his inner world. Moreover, emotional understanding is not achieved once and for all but rather is affected by the adult's return to the scene of childhood, heightening its meanings, adding reminisces, losses, and the contour of time. Readers should keep in mind both symbolization and dependency as working along the lines of this "logic of the emotion" (Issacs 1952, 89).

One of the most paradoxical emotional ties that belongs to the question of dependency is an ego defense called "identification with the aggressor." For now, it is enough to state that this ego defense is one against anxiety, that it is largely unconscious, and its symbolization is the means to carry emotional states into meaning. To follow this trajectory from inarticulate literalness and anxiety made from dependency to the creative world of metaphor, narrative, and significance is to encounter the question of how inside and outside worlds are formed. It is also to ask, what is internalization? Over the course of this chapter I suggest a need to understand identification with the aggressor from its most prosaic and typical forms for while it emerges from dependent relations—the prototype is a child's identification with her or his parents—as an ego defense its organization turns on loss of love. Its presenting paradox is that the ego will take inside its perceptions of outside threats but in doing so transform both itself and the threat. It is impossible, on this view, to experience dependency and helplessness without trying to symbolize them. Yet attempts to symbolize loss of love incur psychical drama: anxiety, inhibition, and defense become mixed up with the work of thinking, reparation, atonement, and creativity. Identification organizes psychical life and the elusive desire comes as a call to the other. If we are used to considering aggression only in its catastrophic points, we are apt to miss the idea that a mundane psychology of aggression goes hand in hand with conflicts of dependency and symbolization and brings into relief the importance of thinking of the emotional side of representing self/other relations. Later in this essay, readers will meet so common and small an instance of this ego defense that it may seem almost irrelevant to discussions of social breakdown. However, the most irrelevant detail returns us to the significance of what we discard.

We may have many ways to narrate why aggression makes us nervous and why dependency is a vulnerable relation but why should symbolization affect us in this way as well? One reason is that having to narrate a self wavers between wish and defense, between the childhood of the adult and the child's conflicts of love and hate with the parents. Here, symbolization leans upon dependency coloring in the outlines of significance with emotional verve. Another reason has to do with the very qualities of putting things into words and entering into a metaphorical and interpretative world. Finding words, feeling understood and recognized, and thinking deeply with others are all experiences that allow symbolic confidence, a confidence with the sign and with others. Yet this work is slow. So a third reason is captured by Alice Balint (1954), who stressed the frustrations of having to learn when she noticed that the time of education occurs too soon, before the educator or parent can count on understanding, either the understanding of the other or of the self. Learning and its symbolization, on this view, is composed of a radical and original uncertainty and a promise. Not knowing but still needing to respond can make one nervous. Balint may help us remember that mistakes and misunderstandings are not the outside of education, but rather are constitutive of its very possibility. These unintended qualities of learning, more often than not, are disavowed through obsessions with corrections, themselves a defense against the uncertainties of learning. The belatedness that belongs to learning is difficult to express, particularly during times when what is to be learned concerns both histories of woeful disregard and the pleasures of social difference. Balint and Cavell compose very difficult dilemmas for any education that attempts to address the significance and pain of social conflict, misunderstanding, and the breakdown of meaning. They add as well further questions for how we self-represent to others our singularity.

From the clinical fact of dependency and symbolization a further claim on the pressures of symbolization emerge: what distinguishes the human from other forms of life is its need to self-represent, self-theorize, and interpret through symbols, self/other relations (Laplanche 1989; Pontalis 2003).[3] Were it not for dependency, there would be no drive to symbolization. In psychoanalytic terms, however, symbolization is never simply representing more accurately the qualities of objects in the world. Nor is it a problem of decoding what is already there. Instead, symbolization is an emotional experience, a link between affect and idea. It bridges a lifetime of losing and finding and its vulnerability and promise lean upon two precarious resources that are often at odds even as both require construction and interpretation: internal or psychical reality and external or historical reality. The outside world is animated by one's feeling states even as it seems to demand particular feelings from us. But also, feeling states create the internal world. This paradox of relationality plays well in psychoanalytic theories and is useful for understanding some of the constitutive difficulty that inaugurates thinking. Symbolization, too, may entangle the subject with objects it never consciously called upon. It engages and disclaims the subject's psychological events of introjection, or taking in aspects of the world into the self, and projection, or sending out and putting into the other either aspects of the self that are good, or parts felt to be bad. Because these phantasized events or object relations begin within a subject, their magnetizing qualities mean that projection and introjection are also places of identification. The bits and pieces of the self sent out into the world and that seem to come from elsewhere invoke what Melanie Klein (1946/1975) called "projective identification," a kind of identification meant to control the object which is actually a disparaged part of the self but also, "the impulses to control an object from within it stir up the fear of being controlled and persecuted inside it" (11).

How dynamics of introjection and projection relate to symbolization is stated well by the British child analyst Susan Issacs:

They refer to such facts as that ideas, impressions and influences are taken into the self and become part of it; or that aspects of elements of the self are often disowned and attributed to some person or groups of persons, or some part of the external world.... Now these mental mechanisms are intimately related to certain persuasive phantasies. The phantasies of incorporating (devouring, absorbing, etc.) loved and hated objects, persons, into ourselves are amongst the earliest and most deeply unconscious phantasies, fundamentally oral in character since they are psychic representatives of the oral impulses. (1952, 98–99)

Issacs places introjection and projection under the sign of phantasy. These phantasies, a sort of representation of representation, are persuasive and compelling and, in the beginning, emerge from internal aggression and defenses against it.

Aggression, however, does not only equate with destruction. D. W. Winnicott (1989) views positively these beginnings with the suggestion that the infant's ruthlessness and anticoncern—the biting, screaming, and kicking, for example—is not a response to the world but a way to call the world of others or reality into being. Winnicott's very different view of aggression relieves this concept from the weight of moralistic discourses. In doing so, he allows us to notice not just the baby's raw potential to make a place for herself or himself in the world with others, but also turns our attention to a needed relationship made from the other's capacity to tolerate, without being destroyed, the baby's aggression. Here, the question of the baby's intention belongs to its drives. And to think with Winnicott on these matters is to consider intention as a secondary process, attributed only retroactively to actions. Sonia Abadi (2001) describes the paradox Winnicott presents: "For Winnicott it is not recognition of one's destructiveness that leads to the possibility of reparation, but instead constructive and creative experiences that enable recognition of one's own destructiveness.... It is the attitude of the environment toward the child's primary aggressive impulses that marks both the fate of the aggression and the capacity for love and reparation in each individual" (81–82). There are then two kinds of dependency: our dependency on internal processes and our dependency on others. Both must be symbolized in ways that allow the self's capacity to think. We again return to the question of education, now as a container for self/other relations and so as a third space where interest and curiosity (as opposed to retaliation) toward others and with others can be made.[4]

Psychoanalytic debates on symbolization, aggression, and dependency can be understood as a counterdiscourse to such antiinterpretive school-based policies as "zero tolerance," compliance to school authority, and obedience to cultural and normalizing conventions, whether those be of a gender, sexual, or racial nature. They are themselves a symbolization, stressing, too, the difficulty of ever knowing for certain the dynamics it rests upon or even if its resting points invent the very subject of psychoanalysis. Radical uncertainty, however, is required for the claim that psychical life matters and that creativity is possible. Still, epistemological and ontological uncertainty brought to difficult topics can also grate on nerves because if the subject is so unstable in and susceptible to its own unknown, how is it possible to even recognize reality? While cultural, sociological, anthropological, historical, and postcolonial knowledge of self/other relations, for example, have much to say on problems of social breakdown, on the historical reality of inequality and social strife, and continue to be central to conceptualizing the content of antiracist pedagogy, the processes of learning, thinking, and feeling made within history, however, and the work of tying knowledge to significance is just beginning to be explored (Pitt and Britzman 2003). One of the most perplexing problems for any pedagogy that engages the work of representation concerns the status of the external world in our inner world, not from the vantage of attitudinal change or new epistemologist standpoint theories, but from the ways the inner world can even be imagined (Britzman 2003).

Along with many contemporary discussions that address and construct the cultural field of race, representation, and identity through psychoanalytic theory, I do so with some trepidation of being misunderstood. The misunderstanding has to do with the objection that social structures and historical oppression will be either ignored or worse, that the latter will be seen as the grounds of pathology. Anne Anlin Cheng's (2001) study of racial melancholia begins with an insightful deconstruction of the orienting binaries of sociological, epistemological, and theoretical objections to psychoanalytic work: there are worries that the victim will be blamed or seen only as damaged, that focusing on individual psychology wipes away social responsibility and the history of woeful disregard, and that psychological orientations universalize and therefore ignore difference between cultures. Cheng summarizes these objections aptly as "a debate about the assignment of social meaning to psychical processes" (15). Christopher Lane's (1998) understanding of a psychoanalysis of race considers the other side of the assignment; that is, how psychical meanings symbolize social processes. Lane proffers more difficulties to an overreliance on appeals to consciousness and knowledge. I agree with his view that psychoanalysis may be used: "to ruin the myth that psychic enigmas are best explained as racial conflicts, and to critique the assumption that conflicts over the cultural meaning of race can be resolved *without* our tackling or understanding the unconscious" (20). Young-Bruehl (1996) demonstrates a sense of how the unconscious works in her index on the history of social science's grasp of prejudice. She argues that the appeal of prejudice is precisely in its illogical character, taking neurotic, psychotic, narcissistic, and obsessional forms, all of which lean upon unconscious desires. Prejudice is propped up and animated by phantasies of omnipotence and rigid wishes for a "black and white" or concrete and unsymbolic reality. Social prejudices may be indicative of rigid ego defenses and desires for a mastery that shut out uncertainties that are carried in symbolization. To understand these obdurate processes—how hatred of self and others links to resistance to interiority and so to accepting the psychological significance of dependency—requires a working analysis of emotional states and their bonds, seeing these not as pathology, but as a constitutive feature of knowledge, sociality, and subjectivity.

Agencies

Sigmund Freud (1933/1964) described the internal world through its agencies and their functions. His structural model of psychical life split the subject into three: the id, the ego, and the superego (or the it, the me, and the above-me). Respectively, they articulate the conflictive spheres of pleasure, reality, and morality. The content of these spheres varies widely; the range of their intelligibility depends upon culture, accidents, and the history (both imagined and actual) of one's upbringing. Melanie Klein represents the internal world as made from object relations, which refer to constructions of the self's representatives of its relationships with its first others[5] and the premature self's symbolization of the anxieties these early beginnings entail. Phantasy is the representation then, not of actual others but one's feelings about feelings. It is an anxious commentary on the fragility of symbolization and the need for a semblance of meaning before there is something like understanding. On this view, pleasure, reality, and morality emerge from the baby's expelling and taking in parts of its world of others, yet its decisions as to what is good and what is bad pass through and are distorted by the anxiety of dependency. In object relations theory, for example, the superego forms early from a combination of what is desirable about parents but also encompasses their prohibitions and their parental strangeness. Whether one works from Freudian or Kleinian theories, internalization is a complex of phantasies: the unconscious actions of taking in the object transform both the object and the ego.[6]

Regardless of whether one conceptualizes the self as seeking pleasure or as seeking relations, its most unknown motivation is the unconscious. Here is "the logic of emotions" in all its glory. The unconscious knows no time, no negation, and tolerates contradiction. The unconscious may be elegiac and described as the development of development. To understand the work of symbolization from this vantage and its importance for becoming a subject with agency is to speculate on the ways in which the human comes to give up wishful and omnipotent thinking, mourns losses, tolerates new representations, respects the difference between internal and external reality, and grasps, indeed, makes pleasure from, the actuality of others as separate from the self (Hinshelwood 1991).[7] These psychological processes loosen symbolization from identifications, indeed, allow for difference between feeling states and external events, and so gradually ease ego boundaries just enough so that the ego risks learning and change with a measure of confidence that it and the world can survive the evitable mistakes, illusions, and misunderstandings that symbolization with others also carries.

A psychoanalytic narrative of the ego's learning, then, begins within infantile dependency and theorizes the ego's anxious experience of and defenses against the helplessness dependency entails. Here the world matters personally, although not in ways that are predicable. The matter of culture in its most intimate and dematerialized, or introjected, form leaves us with questions as to how culture then becomes psychologically significant, where it loses its import, how it is affected by the psychical reality of individuals and the structures of dependency created from this needed relation. From this susceptibility to self and other, Freud (1926/1959) speculated that the bodily ego is the seat of anxiety but also observes itself and the world, judges reality, and thinks by joining wish, perception, and conception with reality. Linking affect or thing with idea or symbolization is not just the ego's work but its passionate possibility. Here is where the ego may be seen as affected by the outside world it also affects, and in this relation the ego must defend itself against any perception of danger, the key one being the fear of loss of love. Its defenses, however, refract and so distort the danger, as if through a fun house mirror for the purpose of working over anxiety. Imagine, then, such internal actions, or mental gymnastics meant to protect the ego from inevitable loss: identification, turning around upon the self, projecting onto the other one's own intentions and worries, changing ideas into their opposite, undoing what has already happened, isolating idea from affect, denial, splitting into good and bad, repression, idealization, altruism, and identification with the aggressor. These mechanisms affect the very functions of the ego—its cohesiveness, its flexibility, and its curiosity toward the world.

Identification

Many analysts and academics begin with the promise and peril of identification, a special psychical process that allows the ego to attach to others and to take inside the outside world. In educational contexts, there is a keen desire to create ways for individuals to make identifications with others, knowledge, and events in the past. There is a hope that emotional ties to social justice can be made from the study of social devastation (Britzman 2000). There is also a fear that the identifications themselves may impede an awareness of difference and an acknowledgment of what is incommensurable. Implicitly, identification has to do with ego boundaries. Yet because aspects of the ego are unconscious, the journey of one's emotional ties—where they begin, lose their interest, freely associate, or become passionate, for instance—does not rest with conscious choice. Identification is both an ego defense and its first means of becoming. It is also the way the ego splits itself, constituting its own superego. Freud (1926/1964) described the superego as a history of libidinal identifications, "and as a structural relation ... not merely a personification of some such abstractions as that of conscience" (64).

As with many concepts in psychoanalysis, the meanings, functions, and structures of identification and the processes called identification will take readers into the psychoanalytic archive: one will then meet foundational concepts such as introjection, projection, mourning, splitting, and object relations. Identification is not a cognitive, willful process or a result of rhetorical persuasiveness. It is not voluntary as in a conscious choice made from the world of possibilities. Rather identifications say something about one's own internal world and the solutions one needs there. They are a psychical representation for internal impulses and their qualities make this ego process complex. Identifications are partial, a whole object is not taken in; they are contradictory in that two opposing qualities of an object can be incorporated or fused for incorporation; and, they are ambivalent, bestowed with both love and aggression. And if Freud pressed the view that consciousness for the human is the exception, which may be one reason why he was so skeptical about consciousness raising through rational appeal, there also remains his insistence that consciousness, or the ego's capacity to think over instinctual conflict and so reality test, carries with it an ethical responsibility, what Melanie Klein (1937/1975) will call "the urge to make reparation," a desire made to keep the other in mind, to repair what phantasy breaks, and to understand the other's fragility as an other.

Freud's (1933/1964) "New Introductory Lectures" contains a chapter simply titled, "The Internal World." Originally, the ego cannot distinguish itself, and while its boundaries are a developmental achievement, they are never so absolute or settled because ego development takes place through the mechanism of identification: "A portion of the external world has, at least partially, been abandoned as an object and has instead, by identification, been taken into the ego and thus become an integral part of the internal world" (205). In the very process of taking in what is no longer there, in the very awareness of loss and love, and in its passionate and longing perception in the world, from all these positions, psychical agencies are also transformed. But also, the taking in is a libidinal process, meaning that love of the object, in the logic of emotions, sustains our emotional ties to the outside.

So, what portion of the world is taken in since not all losses can be noticed? Here is where identification becomes more complicated because it is tied to a desire that is in excess of socialization and logical processes of thought. We may identify with qualities of others as like the self but also may identify with a wish to have a self like the other. Being and having are two of identity's events. Their representation in the internal world, however, transforms these desires. Even if the external object is destructive, identification is a means to maintain an emotional tie. And identification is also a residue of an emotional tie, however unlikely.

Identification with the Aggressor

The concept of identification with the aggressor has worked its way into social science research and into social and political thought. Readers meet echoes of this term in the writings of Fanon (1963/1986, 51) when he speaks of ego withdrawal and developmental impairment in the colonial Manicheistic, dualistic world.[8] Hints of this concept find its way into W. E. B. Dubois's (1905/1989) idea of "double consciousness"—of watching one's self through the eyes of the other.[9] Another variation motivates Ogbu's (1974) notion of the burden of acting white, where identification wobbles through worries over race betrayal and self-betrayal. In these views, a splitting of the world into good and bad is the consequence of identifying with the aggressor. In the literature on school bullying, the concept of identification with the aggressor is tied to its acting out. Identification with the aggressor takes a detour through the vague concept of "internalized oppression" whether that be internalized homophobia or racism, or whether it refers to the psychological aftereffects of social inequality in the form of inferiority complex and self-hatred. In antiracist pedagogy, identification with the aggressor may be used to explain the persistence of white working class racism. But it can also be the reason and justification for the use of role models to instill new identifications. All these orientations, while suggesting something of the ambivalence and significance of identification, however, may gloss over the psychical dynamics of defense and its effects on the ego's representational qualities. Bracketing the external world for a moment, to try and take in the logic of emotions at play in this defense, asks a great deal of the educator, who must also consider individuals in relation to larger groups and to the tugs of her or his own pedagogical desires and nightmares (Gardner 1994).

We are apt to forget that the psychoanalytic concept of identification with the aggressor describes an ego defense. In the psychoanalytic archive, identification with the aggressor has a rather peculiar and contradictory history, reaching into the problem of unconscious phantasy and projection and forming from the eventual dissolution of the Oedipus Complex.[10] "The aggressor" may be actual or a phantasy. But the identification is with the emotional logic of the relationship. For the child, it may be any figure who represents authority or is felt to be an authority. Again, we meet up with the symbolization of dependency, now in the form of identification with the aggressor. That is, the ego introjects the powerful other and at least in phantasy, can then meet the other as more powerful, indeed, as destroyed! There are, to be sure, actual aggressors, people who hurt, humiliate, and crush the life out of others. But the early groundwork for the conflict between dependency and symbolization does not emerge from this cruel extreme and rather concerns the emotional logic of dependency in everyday lives. The issue here is how educators might consider the spurious nature of identifications as also defying concrete or literal correspondence, causality, or even, explanatory power. Indeed, we can glimpse the radical instability of the ego's mechanisms by taking them through phantasy and the unconscious.

Anna Freud (1936/1966) codified the ego's mechanisms of defense, identifying twelve of them. The problem is not that we have them, for after all, the bodily ego has three partners to placate and experiences danger from each: the external world, and the contrary demands of the id and the super-ego. These three sources of anxiety—anxiety over others, over pleasure and guilt, and over morality—require different strategies of reality testing. In the world, what is tested is the veracity or truth of things, that the objects in our mind can be found again in the world. Our internal world requires the understanding of the adequacy of feelings to internal and external events. The problem is that these mechanisms may distort the nature of the danger and the ego's response to it, whether we are considering *realangst* or the ego's attempt to protect itself from persecuting feelings that emanate from its internal world. The ego is affected by its defenses and the very defense employed may incur more ego anxiety. Anna Freud advises her readers not to get caught up in deciding the origin of the ego's defense in terms of whether they emerge because of external reality or internal reality: "Even when we admit that the ego has not an entirely free hand in devising the defense mechanism which it employs, our study of these mechanisms impress us with the magnitude of its achievement" (175).

One of the last ego defenses Anna Freud (1936/1966) noted was identification with the aggressor. This mechanism is complex, even in its prosaic forms. "The aggressor" for the child is usually an adult who tells the child what to do and in some way limits the child's pleasures, and the child feels passive and persecuted. Father and mother may be felt as the aggressor, ruining the child's omnipotent wishes to be the parent or to have the parent. This defense transforms passivity into activity. Here is Anna Freud's description:

> Even when the external criticism has been introjected, the threat of punishment and the offense committed have not yet been connected up.... The moment the criticism is internalized, the offense is externalized. This means that the mechanism of identification with the aggressor is supplemented by another defensive measure, namely the projection of guilt. (118–119)

At its most brittle, identification with the aggressor is tied to indignation toward others, pointing out others' wrongdoings as a way to expel one's own guilt. Moral anxiety is transported through condemnation of the other's morality. There are strong feelings of paranoia and an incapacity to understand one's own contribution to one's emotional states. The ego and superego are essentially at war and perception charged with projections will be as angry as the internal world of object relations. So splitting into good and bad, feelings of moral superiority or inferiority, and moral anxiety becomes more exaggerated, as would feelings of idealization and disparagement.

Sándor Ferenzi, a colleague of Sigmund Freud, coined the term *identification with the aggressor*.[11] While Anna Freud generalized Ferenczi's term as an inevitable outcome of a child's development toward autonomy from the parent's love, Ferenczi was able to hold in tension internal and external reality and the problem of guilt. He considered a more traumatic defensive function with ties to a confusion of libidinality in terms of the child's emotional state made from the adult's misreading of the child's tenderness as seductive behavior. Ferenczi argued that having to identify with the aggressor emerges from the seeds of a traumatic relation and thus sets the stage for a terrible compliance. His paper, "The Confusion of Tongues between the Adult and the Child"(1933/1988), explored the child's need to love her or his parent, even if the parent's actions upon the child devastate her or him. The child would rather identify with the aggressor than give up on the parent. "It is difficult," writes Ferenczi,

> to imagine the behaviour and the emotions of children after such violence. One would expect the first impulse to be that of reaction, hatred, disgust, and energetic refusal.... *The same anxiety, however, if it reaches a certain maximum compels them to subordinate themselves like automata to the will of the aggressor, to divine each one of his desires and to gratify these; completely oblivious of themselves they identify themselves with the aggressor....* The most important change, produced in the mind of the child by the anxiety-fear-ridden identification with the adult partner, is *introjection of the guilt feelings of the adult* which makes hitherto harmless play appear as a punishable offence. (201–202, italics in original)

Ferenczi's conceptualization of identification with the aggressor highlights specific qualities of introjection made from scenes of abuse. Even if it means the destruction of the ego, for the ego losing love is so catastrophic that it would rather take in the threatening object. Then a network of associations, tinged with guilt, anger, and despair, are turned inward. Here, the identification is with the adult's guilt and the punishment it implies. The child abandons self-defense for identification with the parent.

There is also, however, a less traumatic form, having to do with the child's desire for autonomy and the need to identify with what is more powerful in order to even imagine a future autonomy. This relation may, however, agonize the adult who cannot yet give up the desire to control. In describing this aspect Ferenczi comes very close to a dilemma of education which also puts into place what he calls "an oppressive love" (204):

> Parents and adults, in the same way as we analysts, ought to learn to be constantly aware that behind the submissiveness or even the adoration, just as behind the transference of love, of our children, patients and pupils, there lies hidden an ardent desire to get rid of this oppressive love. If we can help the child, the patient or the pupil to give up the reaction of identification, and to ward off the over-burdening transference, then we may be said to have reached the goal of raising the personality to the highest level. (203–204)

To understand something of its more prosaic qualities from the vantage of the ego who uses this defense, Anna Freud (1936/1966) recounts an example from August Aichhorn's work with children.[12] It has to do with a child making faces at an adult when feeling threatened, which is transformed into making threats.

> On such occasions he made faces which caused the whole class to burst out laughing. The master's view was that either the boy was consciously making fun of him or else the twitching of his face must be due to some kind of tic. His report was at once corroborated, for the boy began to make faces during the consultation, but, when master, pupil, and psychologist were together, the situation was explained. Observing the two attentively, Aichhorn saw the boy's grimaces were simply a caricature of the angry expression of the teacher and that, when he had to face a scolding by the latter, he tried to master his anxiety by involuntarily imitating him. The boy identified himself with the teacher's anger and copied his expression as he spoke, though the imitation was not recognized. Through his grimaces he was assimilating himself to or identifying himself with the dreaded external object. (110)

So many dilemmas are noteworthy here, but for the purposes of the discussion, three will be raised. These dimensions add up to the fact that in the confines of identification with the aggressor, there is no real other to discover, that the "dreaded object" is not yet the other, only the heavy trace of its affect. Before exploring this paradox—that the identification is with anxiety and in the process of identification, passivity is changed to activity—let us trace the various threads. First, identification with the aggressor is with a quality of the aggressor's aggression. In Anna Freud's example, the student identified with the authority's anger. He did not want to become the teacher, only master his anxiety with the dependency with his teacher. Second, the actions of the identification worked to deflect the boy's worries. The boy made his class laugh and sent the teacher on a wild goose chase of gathering the bits of a crumbling class. The teacher is now chasing the grimace. Third, even if the object is dreaded and here, the object is a part object made from the worry over the teacher's retaliatory anger, a relationship will be attempted, now in the form of the boy's relationship to his own feelings. The grimace symbolizes the transformation of passivity into activity. The ego will make a strange alliance with the dreaded external object in such a way that the relationship will repeat the breakdown. There is not yet an other because there is not yet symbolization.

Earlier in this chapter I suggested that identification and projection go hand in hand. I now want to think about another side of this relationship, what Melanie Klein(1946/1975) noted as "projective identification." This is where phantasy takes an unconscious social turn, for in the case of making a face at an authority, there is also an anticipation of what the authority will do next. Others read the grimace and may respond with the force of their own anxiety, attuned, so to say, to the child's notice of a crisis within authority and so with what else the child's anxiety calls forth. The defense that is the grimace, and in a sense, the little private scenario of aggrieved affect, calls forth the other's aggression. It is almost as if the face said, "The dreaded object will retaliate, just as I expect it to!" Thus in projective identification, we can see that while the anxiety may emanate from within, there is also the other it seeks and affects. If we turn to Winnicott's sense of aggression as a way to call others, its fate must depend upon *how* the other responds, not in the technical sense of procedural rules but in the emotional sense of affective bonds. This is another aspect of dependency, where the other's thoughtfulness is a resource for the self.

Now making faces is a rather common occurrence between children and adults in families and in schools. If one confines its meaning only to oppositional defiance, one is likely to miss the communication that is also difficult to receive. The grimace condenses a self-representation, a social representation, and a commentary on the very impossibility of doing just that. Such difficulties return in the very way these funny faces foreclose insight into the difficulty that makes a grimace the response that it is. At worst, we are reduced to making funny faces to each other, a carnival now of trade in insults meant to ruin our dependency upon one another. Stereotypes and manic name calling, for example, work in these destructive ways, defending as they do against interpretation, symbolization, and psychological relationships. When dependency and helplessness are communicated to others there is still the work of others symbolizing the significance of the communication. This is perhaps why Ferenczi thought of identification as a reaction, as organizing what he called "oppressive love," a shadow dependency where there are no chances for either the surprises of an actual self or the reply of an actual other.

Representation, Again

Psychoanalysis is a theory of the meanings and transformations of human suffering. Indeed, Freud attributes to human interiority a particular madness that is both creative and detritus. Something about living makes us nervous, lending longing to the human condition. Interaction with others and symbolizing that significance carries a kernel of this neurosis, not because so many things can go wrong when people get together—although this is also the case—but because our dependency upon the outside world animates phantasies that then structure both our inner world and our perceptions of and wishes for the outside world. We are absolutely affected by what we try to affect. However, if it may then seem obvious to state that psychoanalysis is a depth psychology, less obvious is what this "depth" is made from and how our natality creates from dependency and symbolization something like a self. These observations also raise a further question of what understanding these beginnings can mean for conceptualizations of thoughtful education that takes a psychological approach to understanding aggression.

In an essay that examines the nature of creativity and compliance, Adam Phillips (1998) offers a difficult warning that comes precariously close to the paradox of education: "Psychoanalysis should not be promoting knowledge as a consolation prize for injustice" (50). I take this to mean that however elegant our explanations may be on the designs and structures of our inner world, however much we invest in the healing power of understanding, indeed, of "finding neurosis," knowledge is not to be a substitute for transforming injustice in the social world. Yet thinking, too, is a mode of freedom, a means for mourning, a possibility beyond oppressive love, and an expression of singularity. The capacity to think well about injustice and justice belongs to beginnings and education, which, after all, is a second chance with another beginning. Yet one of the common objections to psychoanalytic views on social destruction and the construction of the human begins with the question: Compared to doing something about the conditions of poverty, social abuse, and civil war, what difference does it make to be able to think within the sophisticated and complex process of psychical life and recognize its capacity for suffering? Must these be our choices? The passage from individual difference and subjectivity to social difference and various modes of subjection is not a maze one travels through to reach an outside. Development is uneven, recursive, and retrospective, dependent upon others and symbolization. The objection that splits, that either one analyzes or is an activist, is not a choice because it may only return us to the question of identification and the illusion that one's identity is the only story in town. The problem, rather, is how will we think about self/other relations in ways that take into account the complexity and creativity of psychical life but also to hold in mind that psychical life is not the afterthought of social history although it is its own afterhistory. As for education, it can be made from understanding its own acts as beyond and even in contradiction to consciousness. This is the space of thinking about thinking, an exploration, however uncertain, of how one feels in the world of others and what knowledge means in this intimacy.

In another study that wonders if freedom and equality are at all compatible with human sociality, Phillips (2002) considers again psychoanalytic knowledge, not in terms of its use value, or application, but as potential space for the work of symbolization: "Psychoanalysis as a treatment and an experience, like democracy as a political process, allows people to speak and to be heard. Indeed it encourages people to give voice to their concerns, to be as difficult as they can be, because it depends upon their so doing" (15). This mode of "doing" is the other side of our capacity to self-represent. Here then is a new dependency now on difficult symbolization. And this act of speaking and listening permits new considerations on how the self makes from things like dependency and symbolization, something like a self and its own funny face.

Notes

1. Freud (1926/1959) distinguished between realistic anxiety and neurotic anxiety but positing the latter as "an unknown danger" and "a lack of an object" (165) animated by an expectation of a repetition of an earlier scene of helplessness. The central feature belongs to infancy: "Thus, the first determinant of anxiety, which the ego itself introduces, is loss of perception of the object (which is equated with loss of the object itself).... Pain is thus the actual reaction to loss of object, while anxiety is the reaction to the danger which that loss entails and, by a further displacement, a reaction to the danger of the loss of the object itself" (170). The danger comes from within.
2. The term *phantasy* connotes unconscious mental processes, pertaining to phantasies with or of a world of objects. The "ph" spelling is used to distinguish itself from "fantasy" that is associated with daydreams or literary genres. Moreover, in the work of Melanie Klein, phantasies are the beginning of thinking over instinctual conflict and so they are not viewed as a binary with reality.
3. Laplanche (1989) describes self-representation as a creative act where, "the representative is 'not constrained by the restrictive demands of the real,' and that its 'essential quality is to bring about the possible' ... [this] concerns the human being's capacity for self-symbolization" (84).
4. While the concept of "third space" can be found in the postcolonial work of Homi Bhabha, it is also a term in object relations theory; a notion of the third space refers to that which is between subjects but also to the analytic setting and the knowledge made there.
5. In everyday language, the term *object* is often conflated with objectification. However, psychoanalytic vocabulary uses it as a technical term meant to connote a representation of the instinct (or a phantasy) and a representation of one's feelings toward actual others that take on the qualities the self projects. Objects, then, are not "the other," although in phantasy they may take on the qualities of others. Objects are internal relationships of self and other. Felt within the self, these are called internal objects. If felt as outside, they are external objects. Originally, the object is bestowed by the self with a motivation before it is known.
6. For a discussion on internalization that considers subjection, see Butler (1997).
7. See R.D. Hinshelwood's (1991) entry "Symbols in the Depressive Position," where he overviews the phases of recognizing a symbol as separate from the original object. This division, indeed, the qualities of difference, is necessary in Kleinian views because in the beginning, phantasy made from anxiety renders meaning terrifying, persecuting, and subject to idealization, splitting, and paranoid reversals. Klein called this early position "the paranoid–schizoid position." If these feelings are to be contained and worked through, the damaging phantasies incur some guilt and then lead to the urge to repair, what Klein saw as the "depressive position."
8. Fanon's (1967/1986) view of psychoanalysis is notoriously difficult in that as a psychiatrist he was more than aware of its techniques and practices. Yet in his passionate exploration of the existential painfulness of racism in colonial contexts and the ways in which the figure of "the Black man" functioned as a phobic object, Fanon also argued passionately against any psychoanalytic generalization on subject formation and sexuality for understanding the predicament of race, even as he himself depended upon some of its concepts. It is only in his discussions of his own clinical practices that one senses his gifts as a psychiatric clinician. See, for example, the chapter "Colonial War and Mental Disorders" in Fanon (1961/1991). For diverse views on the ambivalent status of the psychoanalytic in Fanon and the uses of ambivalence in cultural expression, see Read (1996), Fuss (1995), and Young-Bruehl (1996).
9. For a rich discussion on Du Bois's "double consciousness," and one that traces the ambivalence of split identifications, see Gilroy (1993).
10. The Oedipus Complex refers to a phantasy relation the child makes to her or his parents, where one parent is loved while the other is a rival. Freud believed Oedipal feelings begin around the ages of three to five, and the feelings are the emotional logic of the child. The resolution, if there is one, is that the child introjects the parents, accepting their prohibitions and their love. Now internal, the parents form the nucleus of the superego. The identification with the more powerful parents comes under the category of identification with the aggressor.
11. Sándor Ferenczi (1873–1933) was a Hungarian psychoanalyst and founder of the Budapest school of psychoanalysis.
12. For a unique orientation to working with youth that can be made from a psychoanalytic approach, see Aichhorn (1964).

References

Abadi, Sonia. "Explorations: Losing and Finding Oneself in the Potential Space." In *Squiggles and Spaces*, vol. 1, *Revisiting the Work of D. W. Winnicott*, edited by Mario Bertolini, Andreas Giannakoulas, and Max Hernandez in collaboration with Anthony Molino, 79–87. London: Whurr, 2001.

Aichhorn, August. *Delinquency and Child Guidance: Selected Papers,* edited by Otto Fleischmann, Paul Kramer, and Helen Ross. New York: International Universities Press, 1964.

Balint, Alice. *The Early Years of Life*. New York: Basic Books, 1954.

Britzman, Deborah P. "If the Story Cannot End: Deferred Action, Ambivalence, and Difficult Knowledge." In *Between Hope and Despair: Pedagogy and the Remembrance of Historical Trauma*, edited by Roger Simon, Sharon Rosenberg, and Claudia Eppert, 27–57. Lanham, MD: Rowman and Littlefield, 2000.

Britzman, Deborah P. *After-Education: Anna Freud, Melanie Klein and Psychoanalytic Histories of Learning*. Albany: State University of New York, 2003.

Butler, Judith. *The Psychic Life of Power: Theories in Subjection*. Stanford, CA: Stanford University Press, 1997.

Cavell, Marcia. *The Psychoanalytic Mind: From Freud to Philosophy*. Cambridge, MA: Harvard University Press, 1993.

Cheng, Anne Anlin. *The Melancholy of Race: Psychoanalysis, Assimilation and Hidden Grief*. Oxford: Oxford University Press, 2001.

Du Bois, W. E. B. *The Souls of Black Folk*. New York: Bantam, 1989.

Fanon, Frantz. *Black Skin, White Masks,* translated by Charles Lam Markmann. London: Pluto Press, 1986. (Orig. pub. 1967.)

Fanon, Frantz. *The Wretched of the Earth,* translated by Constance Farrington. New York: Grove Weidenfeld, 1991. (Orig. pub. 1961)

Ferenczi, Sándor. "Confusion of Tongues between Adults and the Child: The Language of Tenderness and Passion" (1933). *Contemporary Psychoanalysis* 24 no. 2 (1988):196–206.

Freud, Anna. *The Ego and the Mechanisms of Defense*. Rev. ed. *The Writings of Anna Freud*, vol. 2. Madison, CT: International Universities Press, 1995. (Orig. pub. 1936/1966.)

Freud, Sigmund. "Inhibitions, Symptoms, and Anxiety." *Standard Edition*, 20: 77–178. London: Hogarth Press, 1959. (Orig. pub. 1926.)

Freud, Sigmund. "New Introductory Lectures on Psycho-Analysis." *Standard Edition*, 22: 3–184. London: Hogarth Press, 1964. (Orig. pub. 1933.)

Fuss, Diana. *The Identification Papers*. New York: Routledge, 1995.

Gardner, M. Robert. *On Trying to Teach: The Mind in Correspondence*. Hillsdale, NJ: Analytic Press, 1994.

Gilroy, Paul. *The Black Atlantic: Modernity and Double Consciousness*. Cambridge, MA: Harvard University Press, 1993.

Hinshelwood, R. D. *A Dictionary of Kleinian Thought*. London: Free Association Books, 1991.

Isaacs, Susan. "The Nature and Function of Phantasy." In *Developments in Psychoanalysis*, edited by Joan Riviere, 67–121. London: Hogarth Press, 1952.

Klein, Melanie. "Love, Guilt, and Reparation." In *Love, Guilt and Reparation and Other Works, 1921–1945,* 344–69. New York: Delacorte Press/Seymour Lawrence, 1975. (Orig. pub. 1937.)

Klein, Melanie. "Notes on Some Schizoid Mechanisms." In *Envy and Gratitude and Other Works 1946–1963,* 1–26. New York: Delacorte Press/Seymour Lawrence, 1975. (Orig. pub. 1946.)

Lane, Christopher, ed. *The Psychoanalysis of Race*. New York: Columbia University Press, 1998.

Laplanche, Jean. *New Foundations for Psychoanalysis*, translated by David Macey. Oxford: Blackwell, 1989.

Ogbu, John. *The Next Generation: An Ethnography of Education in an Urban Neighborhood*. New York: Academic Press, 1974.

Phillips, Adam. *The Beast in the Nursery: On Curiosity and Other Appetites*. New York: Pantheon Books, 1998.

Phillips, Adam. *Equals*. New York: Basic Books, 2002.

Pitt, Alice and Deborah Britzman. "Speculations on Qualities of Difficult Knowledge in Teaching and Learning: An Experiment in Psychoanalytic Research." *International Journal of Qualitative Studies in Education* 16, 6 (2003):755–76.

Pontalis, J.-B. *Windows*, translated by Anne Quinney. Lincoln: University of Nebraska Press, 2003.

Read, Alan, ed. *The Fact of Blackness: Frantz Fanon and Visual Representation*. Seattle: Bay Press, 1996.

Winnicott, D. W. *Playing and Reality*. New York: Routledge, 1989. (Orig. pub. 1971.)

Young-Bruehl, Elizabeth. *The Anatomy of Prejudice*. Cambridge, MA: Harvard University Press, 1996.

Part Two

Contested Identities, Contested Desires:
Racial Experience and Curriculum
Dilemmas in the Twenty-First Century

13

Three Women's Texts and a Critique of Imperialism

GAYATRI CHAKRAVORTY SPIVAK

It should not be possible to read nineteenth-century British literature without remembering that imperialism, understood as England's social mission, was a crucial part of the cultural representation of England to the English. The role of literature in the production of cultural representation should not be ignored. These two obvious "facts" continue to be disregarded in the reading of nineteenth-century British literature. This itself attests to the continuing success of the imperialist project, displaced and dispersed into more modern forms.

If these "facts" were remembered, not only in the study of British literature but in the study of the literatures of the European colonizing cultures of the great age of imperialism, we would produce a narrative, in literary history, of the "worlding" of what is now called "the Third World." To consider the Third World as distant cultures, exploited but with rich intact literary heritages waiting to be recovered, interpreted, and curricularized in English translation, fosters the emergence of "the Third World" as a signifier that allows us to forget that "worlding," even as it expands the empire of the literary discipline.[1]

It seems particularly unfortunate when the emergent perspective of feminist criticism reproduces the axioms of imperialism. A basically isolationist admiration for the literature of the female subject in Europe and Anglo-America establishes the high feminist norm. It is supported and operated by an information-retrieval approach to "Third World" literature which often employs a deliberately "nontheoretical" methodology with self-conscious rectitude.

In this essay, I will attempt to examine the operation of the "worlding" of what is today "the Third World" by what has become a cult text of feminism: *Jane Eyre*.[2] I plot the novel's reach and grasp, and locate its structural motors. I read *Wide Sargasso Sea* as *Jane Eyre*'s reinscription and *Frankenstein* as an analysis—even a deconstruction—of a "worlding" such as *Jane Eyre*'s.[3]

I need hardly mention that the object of my investigation is the printed book, not its "author." To make such a distinction is, of course, to ignore the lessons of deconstruction. A deconstructive critical approach would loosen the binding of the book, undo the opposition between verbal text and the biography of the named subject "Charlotte Brontë," and see the two as each other's "scene of writing." In such a reading, the life that writes itself as "my life" is as much a production in psycho-social space (other names can be found) as the book that is written by the holder of that named life—a book that is then consigned to what *is* most often recognized as genuinely "social": the world of publication and distribution.[4] To touch Brontë's "life" in such a way, however, would be too risky here. We must rather strategically take shelter in an essentialism which, not wishing to lose the important advantages won by U.S. mainstream feminism, will continue to honor the suspect binary oppositions—book and author, individual and history—and start with an assurance of the following sort: my readings here do not seek to undermine the excellence of the individual artist. If even minimally successful, the readings will incite a degree of rage against the imperialist narrativization of history, that it should produce so abject a script for her. I provide these assurances to allow myself some room to situate feminist individualism in its historical determination rather than simply to canonize it as feminism as such.

Sympathetic U.S. feminists have remarked that I do not do justice to Jane Eyre's subjectivity. A word of explanation is perhaps in order. The broad strokes of my presuppositions are that what is at stake, for feminist individualism in the age of imperialism, is precisely the making of human beings, the constitution and "interpellation" of the subject not only as individual but as "individualist."[5] This stake is represented on two registers: childbearing and soul making. The first is domestic-society-through-sexual-reproduction cathected as "companionate love"; the second is the imperialist project cathected as civil-society-through-social-mission. As the female individualist, not-quite/not-male, articulates herself in shifting relationship to what is at stake, the "native female" as such (*within* discourse, *as* a signifier) is excluded from any share in this emerging norm.[6] If we read this account from an isolationist perspective in a "metropolitan" context, we see nothing there but the psychobiography of the militant female subject. In a reading such as mine, in contrast, the effort is to wrench oneself away from the mesmerizing focus of the "subject-constitution" of the female individualist.

To develop further the notion that my stance need not be an accusing one, I will refer to a passage from Roberto Fernández Retamar's "Caliban."[7] José Enrique Rodó had argued in 1900 that the model for the Latin American intellectual in relationship to Europe could be Shakespeare's Ariel.[8] In 1971 Retamar, denying the possibility of an identifiable "Latin American Culture," recast the model as Caliban. Not surprisingly, this powerful exchange still excludes any specific consideration of the civilizations of the Maya, the Aztecs, the Incas, or the smaller nations of what is now called Latin America. Let us note carefully that, at this stage of my argument, this "conversation" between Europe and Latin America (without a specific consideration of the political economy of the "worlding" of the "native") provides a sufficient thematic description of our attempt to confront the ethnocentric and reverse-ethnocentric benevolent double bind (that is, considering the "native" as object for enthusiastic information-retrieval and thus denying its own "worlding") that I sketched in my opening paragraphs.

In a moving passage in "Caliban," Retamar locates both Caliban and Ariel in the postcolonial intellectual:

> There is no real Ariel-Caliban polarity: both are slaves in the hands of Prospero, the foreign magician. But Caliban is the rude and unconquerable master of the island, while Ariel, a creature of the air, although also a child of the isle, is the intellectual.
>
> The deformed Caliban—enslaved, robbed of his island, and taught the language by Prospero—rebukes him thus: "You taught me language, and my profit on't / Is, I know how to curse." ["C," pp. 28, 11]

As we attempt to unlearn our so-called privilege as Ariel and "seek from [a certain] Caliban the honor of a place in his rebellious and glorious ranks," we do not ask that our students and colleagues should emulate us but that they should attend to us ("C," p. 72). If, however, we are driven by a nostalgia for lost origins, we too run the risk of effacing the "native" and stepping forth as "the real Caliban," of forgetting that he is a name in a play, an inaccessible blankness circumscribed by an interpretable text.[9] The stagings of Caliban work alongside the narrativization of history: claiming to *be* Caliban legitimizes the very individualism that we must persistently attempt to undermine from within.

Elizabeth Fox-Genovese, in an article on history and women's history, shows us how to define the historical moment of feminism in the West in terms of female access to individualism.[10] The battle for female individualism plays itself out within the larger theater of the establishment of meritocratic individualism, indexed in the aesthetic field by the ideology of "the creative imagination." Fox-Genovese's presupposition will guide us into the beautifully orchestrated opening of *Jane Eyre*.

It is a scene of the marginalization and privatization of the protagonist: "There was no possibility of taking a walk that day … Out-door exercise was now out of the question. I was glad of it," Brontë writes (*JE*, p. 9). The movement continues as Jane breaks the rules of the appropriate topography of withdrawal. The family at the center withdraws into the sanctioned architectural space of the withdrawing room or drawing room; Jane inserts herself—"I slipped in"—into the margin—"A small breakfast-room *adjoined* the drawing room" (*JE*, p. 9; my emphasis).

The manipulation of the domestic inscription of space within the upwardly mobilizing currents of the eighteenth- and nineteenth-century bourgeoisie in England and France is well known. It seems fitting that the place to which Jane withdraws is not only not the withdrawing room but also not the dining room, the sanctioned place of family meals. Nor is it the library, the appropriate place for reading. The breakfast room "contained a book-case" (*JE*, p. 9). As Rudolph Ackerman wrote in his *Repository* (1823), one of the many manuals of taste in circulation in nineteenth-century England, these low bookcases and stands were designed to "contain all the books that may be desired for a sitting-room without reference to the library."[11] Even in this already triply off-center place, "having drawn the red moreen curtain nearly close, I [Jane] was shrined in double retirement" (*JE*, pp. 9–10).

Here in Jane's self-marginalized uniqueness, the reader becomes her accomplice: the reader and Jane are united—both are reading. Yet Jane still preserves her odd privilege, for she continues never quite doing the proper thing in its proper place. She cares little for reading what is *meant* to be read: the "letter-press." *She* reads the pictures. The power of this singular hermeneutics is precisely that it can make the outside inside. "At intervals, while turning over the leaves of my book, I studied the aspect of that winter afternoon." Under "the clear panes of glass," the rain no longer penetrates, "the drear November day" is rather a one-dimensional "aspect" to be "studied," not decoded like the "letter-press" but, like pictures, deciphered by the unique creative imagination of the marginal individualist (*JE*, p. 10).

Before following the track of this unique imagination, let us consider the suggestion that the progress of *Jane Eyre* can be charted through a sequential arrangement of the family/counter-family dyad. In the novel, we encounter, first, the Reeds as the legal family and Jane, the late Mr. Reed's sister's daughter, as the representative of a near incestuous counter-family; second, the Brocklehursts, who run the school Jane is sent to, as the legal family and Jane, Miss Temple, and Helen Burns as a counter-family that falls short because it is only a community of women; third, Rochester and the mad Mrs. Rochester as the legal family and Jane and Rochester as the illicit counter-family. Other items may be added to the thematic chain in this sequence: Rochester and Céline Varens as structurally functional counter-family; Rochester and Blanche Ingram as dissimulation of legality—and so on. It is during this sequence that Jane is moved from the counter-family to the family-in-law. In the next sequence, it is Jane who restores full family status to the as-yet-incomplete community of siblings, the Riverses. The final sequence of the book is a *community of families*, with Jane, Rochester, and their children at the center.

In terms of the narrative energy of the novel, how is Jane moved from the place of the counter-family to the family-in-law? It is the active ideology of imperialism that provides the discursive field.

(My working definition of "discursive field" must assume the existence of discrete "systems of signs" at hand in the socius, each based on a specific axiomatics. I am identifying these systems as discursive fields. "Imperialism as social mission" generates the possibility of one such axiomatics. How the individual artist taps the discursive field at hand with a sure touch, if not with transhistorical clairvoyance, in order to make the narrative structure move I hope to demonstrate through the following example. It is crucial that we extend our analysis of this example beyond the minimal diagnosis of "racism.")

Let us consider the figure of Bertha Mason, a figure produced by the axiomatics of imperialism. Through Bertha Mason, the white Jamaican Creole, Brontë renders the human/animal frontier as acceptably indeterminate, so that a good greater than the letter of the Law can be broached. Here is the celebrated passage, given in the voice of Jane:

> In the deep shade, at the further end of the room, a figure ran backwards and forwards. What it was, whether beast or human being, one could not ... tell: it grovelled, seemingly, on all fours; it snatched and growled like some strange wild animal: but it was covered with clothing, and a quantity of dark, grizzled hair, wild as a mane, hid its head and face. [*JE*, p. 295]

In a matching passage, given in the voice of Rochester speaking *to* Jane, Brontë presents the imperative for a shift beyond the Law as divine injunction rather than human motive. In the terms of my essay, we might say that this is the register not of mere marriage or sexual reproduction but of Europe and its not-yet-human Other, of soul making. The field of imperial conquest is here inscribed as Hell:

> "One night I had been awakened by her yells ... it was a fiery West Indian night...
> "'This life,' said I at last, 'is hell!—this is the air—those are the sounds of the bottomless pit! I *have a right* to deliver myself from it if I can.... Let me break away, and go home to God!'...
> "A wind fresh from Europe blew over the ocean and rushed through the open casement: the storm broke, streamed, thundered, blazed, and the air grew pure.... It was true Wisdom that consoled me in that hour, and showed me the right path ...
> "The sweet wind from Europe was still whispering in the refreshed leaves, and the Atlantic was thundering in glorious liberty....
> "'Go,' said Hope, 'and live again in Europe.... You have done all that God and Humanity require of you.'" [*JE*, pp. 310–11; my emphasis]

It is the unquestioned ideology of imperialist axiomatics, then, that conditions Jane's move from the counter-family set to the set of the family-in-law. Marxist critics such as Terry Eagleton have seen this only in terms of the ambiguous *class* position of the governess.[12] Sandra Gilbert and Susan Gubar, on the other hand, have seen Bertha Mason only in psychological terms, as Jane's dark double.[13]

I will not enter the critical debates that offer themselves here. Instead, I will develop the suggestion that nineteenth-century feminist individualism could conceive of a "greater" project than access to the closed circle of the nuclear family. This is the project of soul making beyond "mere" sexual reproduction. Here the native "subject" is not almost an animal but rather the object of what might be termed the terrorism of the categorical imperative.

I am using "Kant" in this essay as a metonym for the most flexible ethical moment in the European eighteenth century. Kant words the categorical imperative, conceived as the universal moral law given by pure reason, in this way: "In all creation every thing one chooses and over which one has any power, may be used *merely as means*; man alone, and with him every rational creature, is an *end in himself*." It is thus a moving displacement of Christian ethics from religion to philosophy. As Kant writes: "With this agrees very well the possibility of such a command as: *Love God above everything, and thy neighbor as thyself.* For as a command it requires respect for a law which *commands love* and does not leave it to our own arbitrary choice to make this our principle."[14]

The "categorical" in Kant cannot be adequately represented in determinately grounded action. The dangerous transformative power of philosophy, however, is that its formal subtlety can be travestied in the service of the state. Such a travesty in the case of the categorical imperative can justify the imperialist project by producing the following formula: *make* the heathen into a human so that he can be treated as an end in himself.[15] This project is presented as a sort of tangent in *Jane Eyre*, a tangent that escapes the closed circle of the *narrative* conclusion. The tangent narrative is the story of St. John Rivers, who is granted the important task of concluding the *text*.

At the novel's end, the *allegorical* language of Christian psychobiography—rather than the textually constituted and seemingly *private* grammar of the creative imagination which we noted in the novel's opening—marks the inaccessibility of the imperialist project as such to the nascent "feminist" scenario. The concluding passage of *Jane Eyre* places St. John Rivers within the fold of *Pilgrim's Progress*. Eagleton pays no attention to this but accepts the novel's ideological lexicon, which establishes St. John Rivers' heroism by identifying a life in Calcutta with an unquestioning choice of death. Gilbert and Gubar, by calling *Jane Eyre* "Plain Jane's progress," see the novel as simply replacing the male protagonist with the female. They do not notice the distance between sexual reproduction and soul making, both actualized by the unquestioned idiom of imperialist presuppositions evident in the last part of *Jane Eyre*:

> Firm, faithful, and devoted, full of energy, and zeal, and truth, [St. John Rivers] labours for his race.... His is the sternness of the warrior Greatheart, who guards his pilgrim convoy from the onslaught of Apollyon.... His is the ambition of the high master-spirit[s] ... who stand without fault before the throne of God; who share the last mighty victories of the Lamb; who are called, and chosen, and faithful. [*JE*, p. 455]

Earlier in the novel, St. John Rivers himself justifies the project: "My vocation? My great work? ... My hopes of being numbered in the band who have merged all ambitions in the glorious one of bettering their race—of carrying knowledge into the realms of ignorance—of substituting peace for war—freedom for bondage—religion for superstition—the hope of heaven for the fear of hell?" (*JE*, p. 376). Imperialism and its territorial and subject-constituting project are a violent deconstruction of these oppositions.

When Jean Rhys, born on the Caribbean island of Dominica, read *Jane Eyre* as a child, she was moved by Bertha Mason: "I thought I'd try to write her a life."[16] *Wide Sargasso Sea*, the slim novel published in 1965, at the end of Rhys' long career, is that "life."

I have suggested that Bertha's function in *Jane Eyre* is to render indeterminate the boundary between human and animal and thereby to weaken her entitlement under the spirit if not the letter of the Law. When Rhys rewrites the scene in *Jane Eyre* where Jane hears "a snarling, snatching sound, almost like a dog quarrelling" and then encounters a bleeding Richard Mason (*JE*, p. 210), she keeps Bertha's humanity, indeed her sanity as critic of imperialism, intact. Grace Poole, another character originally in *Jane Eyre*, describes the incident to Bertha in *Wide Sargasso Sea*: "So you don't remember that you attacked this gentleman with a knife? ... I didn't hear all he said except 'I cannot interfere legally between yourself and your husband'. It was when he said 'legally' that you flew at him'" (*WSS*, p. 150). In Rhys' retelling, it is the dissimulation that Bertha discerns in the word "legally"—not an innate bestiality—that prompts her violent *re*action.

In the figure of Antoinette, whom in *Wide Sargasso Sea* Rochester violently renames Bertha, Rhys suggests that so intimate a thing as personal and human identity might be determined by the politics of imperialism. Antoinette, as a white Creole child growing up at the time of emancipation in Jamaica, is caught between the English imperialist and the black native. In recounting Antoinette's development, Rhys reinscribes some thematics of Narcissus.

There are, noticeably, many images of mirroring in the text. I will quote one from the first section. In this passage, Tia is the little black servant girl who is Antoinette's close companion: "We had eaten the same food, slept side by side, bathed in the same river. As I ran, I thought, I will live with Tia and I will be like her.... When I was close I saw the jagged stone in her hand but I did not see her throw it.... We stared at each other, blood on my face, tears on hers. It was as if I saw myself. Like in a looking glass" (*WSS*, p. 38).

A progressive sequence of dreams reinforces this mirror imagery. In its second occurrence, the dream is partially set in a *hortus conclusus*, or "enclosed garden"—Rhys uses the phrase (*WSS*, p. 50)—a Romance rewriting of the Narcissus topos as the place of encounter with Love.[17] In the enclosed garden, Antoinette encounters not Love but a strange threatening voice that says merely "in here," inviting her into a prison which masquerades as the legalization of love (*WSS*, p. 50).

In Ovid's *Metamorphoses*, Narcissus' madness is disclosed when he recognizes his Other as his self: "Iste ego sum."[18] Rhys makes Antoinette see her *self* as her Other, Brontë's Bertha. In the last section of *Wide Sargasso Sea*, Antoinette acts out *Jane Eyre's* conclusion and recognizes herself as the so-called ghost in Thornfield Hall: "I went into the hall again with the tall candle in my hand. It was then that I saw her—the ghost. The woman with streaming hair. She was surrounded by a gilt frame but I knew her" (*WSS*, p. 154). The gilt frame encloses a mirror: as Narcissus' pool reflects the selfed Other, so this "pool" reflects the Othered self. Here the dream sequence ends, with an invocation of none other than Tia, the Other that could not be selfed, because the fracture of imperialism rather than the Ovidian pool intervened. (I will return to this difficult point.) "That was the third time I had my dream, and it ended.... I called 'Tia' and jumped and woke" (*WSS*, p. 155). It is now, at the very end of the book, that Antoinette/Bertha can say: "Now at last I know why I was brought here and what I have to do" (*WSS*, pp. 155–56). We can read this as her having been brought into the England of Brontë's novel: "This cardboard house"—a book between cardboard covers—"where I walk at night is not England" (*WSS*, p. 148). In this fictive England, she must play out her role, act out the transformation of her "self" into that fictive Other, set fire to the house and kill herself, so that Jane Eyre can become the feminist individualist heroine of British fiction. I must read this as an allegory of the general epistemic violence of imperialism, the construction of a self-immolating colonial subject for the glorification of the social mission of the colonizer. At least Rhys sees to it that the woman from the colonies is not sacrificed as an insane animal for her sister's consolidation.

Critics have remarked that *Wide Sargasso Sea* treats the Rochester character with understanding and sympathy.[19] Indeed, he narrates the entire middle section of the book. Rhys makes it clear that he is a victim of the patriarchal inheritance law of entailment rather than of a father's natural preference for the firstborn: in *Wide Sargasso Sea*, Rochester's situation is clearly that of a younger son dispatched to the colonies to buy an heiress. If in the case of Antoinette and her identity, Rhys utilizes the thematics of Narcissus, in the case of Rochester and his patrimony, she touches on the thematics of Oedipus. (In this she has her finger on our "historical moment." If, in the nineteenth century, subject-constitution is represented as childbearing and soul making, in the twentieth century psychoanalysis allows the West to plot the itinerary of the subject from Narcissus [the "imaginary"] to Oedipus [the "symbolic"]. This subject, however, is the normative male subject. In Rhys' reinscription of these themes, divided between the female and the male protagonist, feminism and a critique of imperialism become complicit.)

In place of the "wind from Europe" scene, Rhys substitutes the scenario of a suppressed letter to a father, a letter which would be the "correct" explanation of the tragedy of the book.[20] "I thought about the letter which should have been written to England a week ago. Dear Father …" (*WSS*, p. 57). This is the first instance: the letter not written. Shortly afterward:

Dear Father. The thirty thousand pounds have been paid to me without question or condition. No provision made for her (that must be seen to)…. I will never be a disgrace to you or to my dear brother the son you love. No begging letters, no mean requests. None of the furtive shabby manoeuvres of a younger son. I have sold my soul or you have sold it, and after all is it such a bad bargain? The girl is thought to be beautiful, she is beautiful. And yet … [*WSS*, p. 59]

This is the second instance: the letter not sent. The formal letter is uninteresting; I will quote only a part of it:

Dear Father, we have arrived from Jamaica after an uncomfortable few days. This little estate in the Windward Islands is part of the family property and Antoinette is much attached to it…. All is well and has gone according to your plans and wishes. I dealt of course with Richard Mason…. He seemed to become attached to me and trusted me completely. This place is very beautiful but my illness has left me too exhausted to appreciate it fully. I will write again in a few days' time. [*WSS*, p. 63]

And so on.

Rhys' version of the Oedipal exchange is ironic, not a closed circle. We cannot know if the letter actually reaches its destination. "I wondered how they got their letters posted," the Rochester figure muses. "I folded mine and put it into a drawer of the desk…. There are blanks in my mind that cannot be filled up" (*WSS*, p. 64). It is as if the text presses us to note the analogy between letter and mind.

Rhys denies to Brontë's Rochester the one thing that is supposed to be secured in the Oedipal relay: the Name of the Father, or the patronymic. In *Wide Sargasso Sea*, the character corresponding to Rochester has no name. His writing of the final version of the letter to his father is supervised, in fact, by an image of the *loss* of the patronymic: "There was a crude bookshelf made of three shingles strung together over the desk and I looked at the books, Byron's poems, novels by Sir Walter Scott, *Confessions of an Opium Eater* … and on the last shelf, *Life and Letters of* … The rest was eaten away" (*WSS*, p. 63).

Wide Sargasso Sea marks with uncanny clarity the limits of its own discourse in Christophine, Antoinette's black nurse. We may perhaps surmise the distance between *Jane Eyre* and *Wide Sargasso Sea* by remarking that Christophine's unfinished story is the tangent to the latter narrative, as St. John Rivers' story is to the former. Christophine is not a native of Jamaica; she is from Martinique. Taxonomically, she belongs to the category of the good servant rather than that of the pure native. But within these borders, Rhys creates a powerfully suggestive figure.

Christophine is the first interpreter and named speaking subject in the text. "The Jamaican ladies had never approved of my mother, 'because she pretty like pretty self' Christophine said," we read in the book's opening paragraph (*WSS*, p. 15). I have taught this book five times, once in France, once to students who had worked on the book with the well-known Caribbean novelist Wilson Harris, and once at a prestigious institute where the majority of the students were faculty from other universities. It is part of the political argument I am making that all these students blithely stepped over this paragraph without asking or knowing what Christophine's patois, so-called incorrect English, might mean.

Christophine is, of course, a commodified person. "'She was your father's wedding present to me'" explains Antoinette's mother, "'one of his presents'" (*WSS*, p. 18). Yet Rhys assigns her some crucial functions in the text. It is Christophine who judges that black ritual practices are culture-specific and cannot be used by whites as cheap remedies for social evils, such as Rochester's lack of love for Antoinette. Most important, it is Christophine alone whom Rhys allows to offer a hard analysis of Rochester's actions, to challenge him in a face-to-face encounter. The entire extended passage is worthy of comment. I quote a brief extract:

> "She is Creole girl, and she have the sun in her. Tell the truth now. She don't come to your house in this place England they tell me about, she don't come to your beautiful house to beg you to marry with her. No, it's you come all the long way to her house—it's you beg her to marry. And she love you and she give you all she have. Now you say you don't love her and you break her up. What you do with her money, eh?" [And then Rochester, the white man, comments silently to himself] Her voice was still quiet but with a hiss in it when she said "money." [*WSS*, p. 130]

Her analysis is powerful enough for the white man to be afraid: "I no longer felt dazed, tired, half hypnotized, but alert and wary, ready to defend myself" (*WSS*, p. 130).

Rhys does not, however, romanticize individual heroics on the part of the oppressed. When the Man refers to the forces of Law and Order, Christophine recognizes their power. This exposure of civil inequality is emphasized by the fact that, just before the Man's successful threat, Christophine had invoked the emancipation of slaves in Jamaica by proclaiming: "No chain gang, no tread machine, no dark jail either. This is free country and I am free woman" (*WSS*, p. 131).

As I mentioned above, Christophine is tangential to this narrative. She cannot be contained by a novel which rewrites a canonical English text within the European novelistic tradition in the interest of the white Creole rather than the native. No perspective *critical* of imperialism can turn the Other into a self, because the project of imperialism has always already historically refracted what might have been the absolutely Other into a domesticated Other that consolidates the imperialist self.[21] The Caliban of Retamar, caught between Europe and Latin America, reflects this predicament. We can read Rhys' reinscription of Narcissus as a thematization of the same problematic.

Of course, we cannot know Jean Rhys' feelings in the matter. We can, however, look at the scene of Christophine's inscription in the text. Immediately after the exchange between her and the Man, well before the conclusion, she is simply driven out of the story, with neither narrative nor characterological explanation or justice. "'Read and write I don't know. Other things I know.' She walked away without looking back" (*WSS*, p. 133).

Indeed, if Rhys rewrites the madwoman's attack on the Man by underlining of the misuse of "legality," she cannot deal with the passage that corresponds to St. John Rivers' own justification of his martyrdom, for it has been displaced into the current idiom of modernization and development. Attempts to construct the "Third World Woman" as a signifier remind us that the hegemonic definition of literature is itself caught within the history of imperialism. A full literary reinscription cannot easily flourish in the imperialist fracture or discontinuity, covered over by an alien legal system masquerading as Law as such, an alien ideology established as only Truth, and a set of human sciences busy establishing the "native" as self-consolidating Other.

In the Indian case at least, it would be difficult to find an ideological clue to the planned epistemic violence of imperialism merely by rearranging curricula or syllabi within existing norms of literary pedagogy. For a later period of imperialism—when the constituted colonial subject has firmly taken hold—straightforward experiments of comparison can be undertaken, say, between the functionally witless India of *Mrs. Dalloway*, on the one hand, and literary texts produced in India in the 1920s, on the other. But the first half of the nineteenth century resists questioning through literature or literary criticism in the narrow sense, because both are implicated in the project of producing Ariel. To reopen the fracture without succumbing to a nostalgia for lost origins, the literary critic must turn to the archives of imperial governance.

In conclusion, I shall look briefly at Mary Shelley's *Frankenstein*, a text of nascent feminism that remains cryptic, I think, simply because it does not speak the language of feminist individualism which we have come to hail as the language of high feminism within English literature. It is interesting that Barbara Johnson's brief study tries to rescue this recalcitrant text for the service of feminist autobiography.[22] Alternatively, George Levine reads *Frankenstein* in the context of the creative imagination and the nature of the hero. He sees the novel as a book about its own writing and about writing itself, a Romantic allegory of reading within which Jane Eyre as unself-conscious critic would fit quite nicely.[23]

I propose to take *Frankenstein* out of this arena and focus on it in terms of that sense of English cultural identity which I invoked at the opening of this essay. Within that focus we are obliged to admit that, although *Frankenstein* is ostensibly about the origin and evolution of man in society, it does not deploy the axiomatics of imperialism.

Let me say at once that there is plenty of incidental imperialist sentiment in *Frankenstein*. My point, within the argument of this essay, is that the discursive field of imperialism does not produce unquestioned ideological correlatives for the narrative structuring of the book. The discourse of imperialism surfaces in a curiously powerful way in Shelley's novel, and I will later discuss the moment at which it emerges.

Frankenstein is not a battleground of male and female individualism articulated in terms of sexual reproduction (family and female) and social subject-production (race and male). That binary opposition is undone in Victor Frankenstein's laboratory—an artificial womb where both projects are undertaken simultaneously, though the terms are never openly spelled out. Frankenstein's apparent antagonist is God himself as Maker of Man, but his real competitor is also woman as the maker of children. It is not just that his dream of the death of mother and bride and the actual death of his bride are associated with the visit of his monstrous homoerotic "son" to his bed. On a much more overt level, the monster is a bodied "corpse," unnatural because bereft of a determinable childhood: "No father had watched my infant days, no mother had blessed me with smiles and caresses; or if they had, all my past was now a blot, a blind vacancy in which I distinguished nothing" (*F*, pp. 57, 115). It is Frankenstein's own ambiguous and miscued understanding of the real motive for the monster's vengefulness that reveals his own competition with woman as maker:

> I created a rational creature and was bound towards him to assure, as far as was in my power, his happiness and well-being. This was my duty, but there was another still paramount to that. My duties towards the beings of my own species had greater claims to my attention because they included a greater proportion of happiness or misery. Urged by this view, I refused, and I did right in refusing, to create a companion for the first creature. [*F*, p. 206]

It is impossible not to notice the accents of transgression inflecting Frankenstein's demolition of his experiment to create the future Eve. Even in the laboratory, the woman-in-the-making is not a bodied corpse but "a human being." The (il)logic of the metaphor bestows on her a prior existence which Frankenstein aborts, rather than an anterior death which he reembodies: "The remains of the half-finished creature, whom I had destroyed, lay scattered on the floor, and I almost felt as if I had mangled the living flesh of a human being" (*F*, p. 163).

In Shelley's view, man's hubris as soul maker both usurps the place of God and attempts—vainly—to sublate woman's physiological prerogative.[24] Indeed, indulging a Freudian fantasy here, I could urge that, if to give and withhold to/from the mother a phallus is *the* male fetish, then to give and withhold to/from the man a womb might be the female fetish.[25] The icon of the sublimated womb in man is surely his productive brain, the box in the head.

In the judgment of classical psychoanalysis, the phallic mother exists only by virtue of the castration-anxious son; in *Frankenstein's* judgment, the hysteric father (Victor Frankenstein gifted with his laboratory—the womb of theoretical reason) cannot produce a daughter. Here the language of racism—the dark side of imperialism understood as social mission—combines with the hysteria of masculism into the idiom of (the withdrawal of) sexual reproduction rather than subject-constitution. The roles of masculine and feminine individualists are hence reversed and displaced. Frankenstein cannot produce a "daughter" because "she might become ten thousand times more malignant than her mate ... [and because] one of the first results of those sympathies for which the demon thirsted would be children, and a race of devils would be propagated upon the earth who might make the very existence of the species of man a condition precarious and full of terror" (*F*, p. 158). This particular narrative strand also launches a thoroughgoing critique of the eighteenth-century European discourses on the origin of society through (Western Christian) man. Should I mention that, much like Jean-Jacques Rousseau's remark in his *Confessions*, Frankenstein declares himself to be "by birth a Genevese" (*F*, p. 31)?

In this overly didactic text, Shelley's point is that social engineering should not be based on pure, theoretical, or natural-scientific reason alone, which is her implicit critique of the utilitarian vision of an engineered society. To this end, she presents in the first part of her deliberately schematic story three characters, childhood friends, who seem to represent Kant's three-part conception of the human subject: Victor Frankenstein, the forces of theoretical reason or "natural philosophy"; Henry Clerval, the forces of practical reason or "the moral relations of things"; and Elizabeth Lavenza, that aesthetic judgment—"the aerial creation of the poets"—which, according to Kant, is "a suitable mediating link connecting the realm of the concept of nature and that of the concept of freedom ... (which) promotes ... *moral* feeling" (*F*, pp. 37, 36).[26]

This three-part subject does not operate harmoniously in *Frankenstein*. That Henry Clerval, associated as he is with practical reason, should have as his "design ... to visit India, in the belief that he had in his knowledge of its various languages, and in the views he had taken of its society, the means of materially assisting the progress of European colonization and trade" is proof of this, as well as part of the incidental imperialist sentiment that I speak of above (*F*, pp. 151–52). I should perhaps point out that the language here is entrepreneurial rather than missionary:

> He came to the university with the design of making himself complete master of the Oriental languages, as thus he should open a field for the plan of life he had marked out for himself. Resolved to pursue no inglorious career, he turned his eyes towards the East as affording scope for his spirit of enterprise. The Persian, Arabic, and Sanskrit languages engaged his attention. [*F*, pp. 66–67]

But it is of course Victor Frankenstein, with his strange itinerary of obsession with natural philosophy, who offers the strongest demonstration that the multiple perspectives of the three-part Kantian subject cannot co-operate harmoniously. Frankenstein creates a putative human subject out of natural philosophy alone. According to his own miscued summation:

"In a fit of enthusiastic madness I created a rational creature" (*F*, p. 206). It is not at all farfetched to say that Kant's categorical imperative can most easily be mistaken for the hypothetical imperative—a command to ground in cognitive comprehension what can be apprehended only by moral will—by putting natural philosophy in the place of practical reason.

I should hasten to add here that just as readings such as this one do not necessarily accuse Charlotte Brontë the named individual of harboring imperialist sentiments, so also they do not necessarily commend Mary Shelley the named individual for writing a successful Kantian allegory. The most I can say is that it is possible to read these texts, within the frame of imperialism and the Kantian ethical moment, in a politically useful way. Such an approach presupposes that a "disinterested" reading attempts to render transparent the interests of the hegemonic readership. (Other "political" readings—for instance, that the monster is the nascent working class—can also be advanced.)

Frankenstein is built in the established epistolary tradition of multiple frames. At the heart of the multiple frames, the narrative of the monster (as reported by Frankenstein to Robert Walton, who then recounts it in a letter to his sister) is of his almost learning, clandestinely, to be human. It is invariably noticed that the monster reads *Paradise Lost* as true history. What is not so often noticed is that he also reads Plutarch's *Lives*, "the histories of the first founders of the ancient republics," which he compares to "the patriarchal lives of my protectors" (*F*, pp. 123, 124). And his *education* comes through "Volney's *Ruins of Empires*," which purported to be a prefiguration of the French Revolution, published after the event and after the author had rounded off his theory with practice (*F*, p. 113). It is an attempt at an enlightened universal secular, rather than a Eurocentric Christian, history, written from the perspective of a narrator "from below," somewhat like the attempts of Eric Wolf or Peter Worsley in our own time.[27]

This Caliban's education in (universal secular) humanity takes place through the monster's eavesdropping on the instruction of an Ariel—Safie, the Christianized "Arabian" to whom "a residence in Turkey was abhorrent" (*F*, p. 121). In depicting Safie, Shelley uses some commonplaces of eighteenth-century liberalism that are shared by many today: Safie's Muslim father was a victim of (bad) Christian religious prejudice and yet was himself a wily and ungrateful man not as morally refined as her (good) Christian mother. Having tasted the emancipation of woman, Safie could not go home. The confusion between "Turk" and "Arab" has its counterpart in present-day confusion about Turkey and Iran as "Middle Eastern" but not "Arab."

Although we are a far cry here from the unexamined and covert axiomatics of imperialism in *Jane Eyre*, we will gain nothing by celebrating the time-bound pieties that Shelley, as the daughter of two antievangelicals, produces. It is more interesting for us that Shelley differentiates the Other, works at the Caliban/Ariel distinction, and *cannot* make the monster identical with the proper recipient of these lessons. Although he had "heard of the discovery of the American hemisphere and *wept with Safie* over the helpless fate of its original inhabitants," Safie cannot reciprocate his attachment. When she first catches sight of him, "Safie, unable to attend to her friend [Agatha], rushed out of the cottage" (*F*, pp. 114 [my emphasis], 129).

In the taxonomy of characters, the Muslim-Christian Safie belongs with Rhys' Antoinette/Bertha. And indeed, like Christophine the good servant, the subject created by the fiat of natural philosophy is the tangential unresolved moment in *Frankenstein*. The simple suggestion that the monster is human inside but monstrous outside and only provoked into vengefulness is clearly not enough to bear the burden of so great a historical dilemma.

At one moment, in fact, Shelley's Frankenstein does try to tame the monster, to humanize him by bringing him within the circuit of the Law. He "repair[s] to a criminal judge in the town and ... relate[s his] history briefly but with firmness"—the first and disinterested version of the narrative of Frankenstein—"marking the dates with accuracy and never deviating into invective or exclamation.... When I had concluded my narration I said, 'This is the being whom I accuse and for whose seizure and punishment I call upon you to exert your whole power. It is your duty as a magistrate'" (*F*, pp. 189, 190). The sheer social reasonableness of the mundane voice of Shelley's "Genevan magistrate" reminds us that the absolutely Other cannot be selfed, that the monster has "properties" which will not be contained by "proper" measures:

"I will exert myself [he says], and if it is in my power to seize the monster, be assured that he shall suffer punishment proportionate to his crimes. But I fear, from what you have yourself described to be his properties, that this will prove impracticable; and thus, while every proper measure is pursued, you should make up your mind to disappointment." [*F*, p. 190]

In the end, as is obvious to most readers, distinctions of human individuality themselves seem to fall away from the novel. Monster, Frankenstein, and Walton seem to become each others' relays. Frankenstein's story comes to an end in death; Walton concludes his own story within the frame of his function as letter writer. In the *narrative* conclusion, he is the natural philosopher who learns from Frankenstein's example. At the end of the *text*, the monster, having confessed his guilt toward his maker and ostensibly intending to immolate himself, is borne away on an ice raft. We do not see the conflagration of his funeral pile—the self-immolation is not consummated in the text: he too cannot be contained by the text. In terms of narrative logic, he is "lost in darkness and distance" (*F*, p. 211)—these are the last words of the novel—into an existential temporality that is coherent with neither the territorializing individual imagination (as in the opening of *Jane Eyre*) nor the authoritative scenario of Christian psychobiography (as at the end of Brontë's work). The very relationship between sexual reproduction and social subject-production—the dynamic nineteenth-century topos of feminism-in-imperialism—remains problematic within the limits of Shelley's text and, paradoxically, constitutes its strength.

Earlier, I offered a reading of woman as womb holder in *Frankenstein*. I would now suggest that there is a framing woman in the book who is neither tangential, nor encircled, nor yet encircling. "Mrs. Saville," "excellent Margaret," "beloved Sister" are her address and kinship inscriptions (*F*, pp. 15, 17, 22). She is the occasion, though not the protagonist, of the novel. She is the feminine *subject* rather than the female individualist: she is the irreducible *recipient*-function of the letters that constitute *Frankenstein*. I have commented on the singular appropriative hermeneutics of the reader reading with Jane in the opening pages of *Jane Eyre*. Here the reader must read with Margaret Saville in the crucial sense that she must *intercept* the recipient-function, read the letters *as* recipient, in order for the novel to exist.[28] Margaret Saville does not respond to close the text as frame. The frame is thus simultaneously not a frame, and the monster can step "beyond the text" and be "lost in darkness." Within the allegory of our reading, the place of both the English lady and the unnamable monster are left open by this great flawed text. It is satisfying for a postcolonial reader to consider this a noble resolution for a nineteenth-century English novel. This is all the more striking because, on the anecdotal level, Shelley herself abundantly "identifies" with Victor Frankenstein.[29]

I must myself close with an idea that I cannot establish within the limits of this essay. Earlier I contended that *Wide Sargasso Sea* is necessarily bound by the reach of the European novel. I suggested that, in contradistinction, to reopen the epistemic fracture of imperialism without succumbing to a nostalgia for lost origins, the critic must turn to the archives of imperialist governance. I have not turned to those archives in these pages. In my current work, by way of a modest and inexpert "reading" of "archives," I try to extend, outside of the reach of the European novelistic tradition, the most powerful suggestion in *Wide Sargasso Sea*: that *Jane Eyre* can be read as the orchestration and staging of the self-immolation of Bertha Mason as "good wife." The power of that suggestion remains unclear if we remain insufficiently knowledgeable about the history of the legal manipulation of widow-sacrifice in the entitlement of the British government in India. I would hope that an informed critique of imperialism, granted some attention from readers in the First World, will at least expand the frontiers of the politics of reading.

Notes

1. My notion of the "worlding of a world" upon what must be assumed to be uninscribed earth is a vulgarization of Martin Heidegger's idea; see "The Origin of the Work of Art," *Poetry, Language, Thought*, trans. Albert Hofstadter (New York, 1977), pp. 17–87.

2. See Charlotte Brontë, *Jane Eyre* (New York, 1960); all further references to this work, abbreviated *JE*, will be included in the text.

3. See Jean Rhys, *Wide Sargasso Sea* (Harmondsworth, 1966); all further references to this work, abbreviated *WSS*, will be included in the text. And see Mary Shelley, *Frankenstein; or, The Modern Prometheus* (New York, 1965); all further references to this work, abbreviated *F*, will be included in the text.

4. I have tried to do this in my essay "Unmaking and Making in *To the Lighthouse*," in *Women and Language in Literature and Society*, ed. Sally McConnell-Ginet, Ruth Borker, and Nelly Furman (New York, 1980), pp. 310–27.

5. As always, I take my formula from Louis Althusser, "Ideology and Ideological State Apparatuses (Notes towards an Investigation)," *"Lenin and Philosophy" and Other Essays*, trans. Ben Brewster (New York, 1971), pp. 127–86. For an acute differentiation between the individual and individualism, see V. N. Vološinov, *Marxism and the Philosophy of Language*, trans. Ladislav Matejka and I. R. Titunik, *Studies in Language*, vol. 1 (New York, 1973), pp. 93–94 and 152–53. For a "straight" analysis of the roots and ramifications of English "individualism," see C. B. MacPherson, *The Political Theory of Possessive Individualism: Hobbes to Locke* (Oxford, 1962). I am grateful to Jonathan Rée for bringing this book to my attention and for giving a careful reading of all but the very end of the present essay.

6. I am constructing an analogy with Homi Bhabha's powerful notion of "not-quite/not-white" in his "Of Mimicry and Man: The Ambiguity of Colonial Discourse," *October* 28 (Spring 1984): 132. I should also add that I use the word "native" here in reaction to the term "Third World Woman." It cannot, of course, apply with equal historical justice to both the West Indian and the Indian contexts nor to contexts of imperialism by transportation.

7. See Roberto Fernández Retamar, "Caliban: Notes towards a Discussion of Culture in Our America," trans. Lynn Garafola, David Arthur McMurray, and Robert Márquez, *Massachusetts Review* 15 (Winter–Spring 1974): 7–72; all further references to this work, abbreviated "C," will be included in the text.

8. See José Enrique Rodó, *Ariel*, ed. Gordon Brotherston (Cambridge, 1967).

9. For an elaboration of "an inaccessible blankness circumscribed by an interpretable text," see my "Can the Subaltern Speak?" *Marxist Interpretations of Culture*, ed. Cary Nelson (Urbana, Ill., forthcoming).

10. See Elisabeth Fox-Genovese, "Placing Women's History in History," *New Left Review* 133 (May–June 1982): 5–29.

11. Rudolph Ackerman, *The Repository of Arts, Literature, Commerce, Manufactures, Fashions, and Politics*, (London, 1823), p. 310.

12. See Terry Eagleton, *Myths of Power: A Marxist Study of the Brontës* (London, 1975); this is one of the general presuppositions of his book.

13. See Sandra M. Gilbert and Susan Gubar, *The Madwoman in the Attic: The Woman Writer and the Nineteenth-Century Literary Imagination* (New Haven, Conn., 1979), pp. 360–62.

14. Immanuel Kant, *The Critique of Pure Reason, the Critique of Practical Reason and Other Ethical Treatises, the Critique of Judgement*, trans. J. M. D. Meiklejohn et al. (Chicago, 1952), pp. 328, 326.

15. I have tried to justify the reduction of sociohistorical problems to formulas or propositions in my essay "Can the Subaltern Speak?" The "travesty" I speak of does not befall the Kantian ethic in its purity as an accident but rather exists within its lineaments as a possible supplement. On the register of the human being as child rather than heathen, my formula can be found, for example, in "What Is Enlightenment?" in Kant, *"Foundations of the Metaphysics of Morals," "What Is Enlightenment?" and a Passage from "The Metaphysics of Morals,"* trans. and ed. Lewis White Beck (Chicago, 1950). I have profited from discussing Kant with Jonathan Rée.

16. Jean Rhys, in an interview with Elizabeth Vreeland, quoted in Nancy Harrison, *An Introduction to the Writing Practice of Jean Rhys: The Novel as Women's Text* (Rutherford, N.J., forthcoming). This is an excellent, detailed study of Rhys.

17. See Louise Vinge, *The Narcissus Theme in Western European Literature Up to the Early Nineteenth Century*, trans. Robert Dewsnap et al. (Lund, 1967), chap. 5.

18. For a detailed study of this text, see John Brenkman, "Narcissus in the Text," *Georgia Review* 30 (Summer 1976): 293–327.

19. See, e.g., Thomas F. Staley, *Jean Rhys: A Critical Study* (Austin, Tex. 1979), pp. 108–16; it is interesting to note Staley's masculist discomfort with this and his consequent dissatisfaction with Rhys' novel.

20. I have tried to relate castration and suppressed letters in my "The Letter as Cutting Edge," in *Literature and Psychoanalysis; The Question of Reading: Otherwise*, ed. Shoshana Felman (New Haven, Conn., 1981), pp. 208–26.

21. This is the main argument of my "Can the Subaltern Speak?"

22. See Barbara Johnson, "My Monster/My Self," *Diacritics* 12 (Summer 1982): 2–10.

23. See George Levine, *The Realistic Imagination: English Fiction from Frankenstein to Lady Chatterley* (Chicago, 1981), pp. 23–35.

24. Consult the publications of the Feminist International Network for the best overview of the current debate on reproductive technology.

25. For the male fetish, see Sigmund Freud, "Fetishism," *The Standard Edition of the Complete Psychological Works of Sigmund Freud*, ed. and trans. James Strachey et al., 24 vols. (London, 1953–74), 21:152–57. For a more "serious" Freudian study of *Frankenstein*, see Mary Jacobus, "Is There a Woman in This Text?" *New Literary History* 14 (Autumn 1982): 117–41. My "fantasy" would of course be disproved by the "fact" that it is more difficult for a woman to assume the position of fetishist than for a man; see Mary Ann Doane, "Film and the Masquerade: Theorising the Female Spectator," *Screen* 23 (Sept.–Oct. 1982); 74–87.

26. Kant, *Critique of Judgement*, trans. J. H. Bernard (New York, 1951), p. 39.

27. See [Constantin François Chasseboeuf de Volney], *The Ruins; or, Meditations on the Revolutions of Empires*, trans. pub. (London, 1811). Johannes Fabian has shown us the manipulation of time in "new" secular histories of a similar kind; see *Time and the Other: How Anthropology Makes Its Object* (New York, 1983). See also Eric R. Wolf, *Europe and the People without History* (Berkeley and Los Angeles, 1982), and Peter Worsley, *The Third World*, 2d ed. (Chicago, 1973); I am grateful to Dennis Dworkin for bringing the latter book to my attention. The most striking ignoring of the monster's education through Volney is in Gilbert's otherwise brilliant "Horror's Twin: Mary Shelley's Monstrous Eve," *Feminist Studies* 4 (June 1980): 48–73. Gilbert's essay reflects the absence of race-determinations in a certain sort of feminism. Her present work has most convincingly filled in this gap; see, e.g., her recent piece on H. Rider Haggard's *She* ("Rider Haggard's Heart of Darkness," *Partisan Review* 50, no. 3 [1983]: 444–53).

28. "A letter is always and *a priori* intercepted, … the 'subjects' are neither the senders nor the receivers of messages.… The letter is constituted … by its interception" (Jacques Derrida, "Discussion," after Claude Rabant, "Il n'a aucune chance de l'entendre," in *Affranchissement: Du transfert et de la lettre*, ed. René Major [Paris, 1981], p. 106; my translation). Margaret Saville is not made to appropriate the reader's "subject" into the signature of her own "individuality."

29. The most striking "internal evidence" is the admission in the "Author's Introduction" that, after dreaming of the yet-unnamed Victor Frankenstein figure and being terrified (through, yet not quite through, him) by the monster in a scene she later reproduced in Frankenstein's story, Shelley began her tale "on the morrow … with the words 'It was on a dreary night of November'" (*F*, p. xi). Those are the opening words of chapter 5 of the finished book, where Frankenstein begins to recount the actual making of his monster (see *F*, p. 56).

14
One Living Female Child
The Education of a Sirdar's Daughter in Canada

RISHMA DUNLOP

I hear them behind me in another continent

across the Indian Ocean

crossing the floors, soft sweep of sandals

in my mother's country. I was born there four

decades ago at 2am. My birth certificate reads

One Living Female Child.

Today my passport reads Nationality: Canadian.

Questions of race, culture, identity, and representation are entangled with immigrant memories, shaped by gender, class, education, sociohistoric, and economic factors and the unstable notion of "home." Ultimately, it is my work as a writer that enables what poet Meena Alexander calls "a dwelling at the edge of the world." This sensuous location is a transnational borderland shimmering with the rhythms and tongues of multiple languages: Punjabi, French, English, Spanish, colored also by Sanskrit, Latin, Italian. Canada is physical geography, my home. India is my birthplace, my origin, the original homeland of my parents and ancestors. The study of diasporic identity opens up a multitude of paradoxes, shifting identities, and intellectual challenges. Diasporic identity shifts into a home I share with other writers from multiple homelands. Within our community of shared artistic practice is a shelter of words, not reliant on national, political, ethnic, or other allegiances and categorizations. Home is in our poems, the identity of the writer shared as a way of speaking to the other, across immense global and diasporic group differences, a way of speaking that has the potential to transcend what separates us. This writing is a push against the existing order of things, speech that makes possible new understandings of human differences, writing against the grain of history. Writing against the grain of dualistic polarities enables understandings of global cultures and identities in the twenty-first century at a time when physical, social, and conceptual borders can be challenged and sometimes dismantled.

The reality of where we live and the dislocations of vast populations make the phenomenon of diaspora a commonplace in our time. In the imagining and constitution of diasporic identities and communities, it is critical to include the categories of ethnicity and nation, along with gender, class, religion, and language. In her article "Two Ways to Belong in America," Bharati Mukherjee writes: "This is a tale of two sisters from Calcutta, Mira and Bharati, who have lived in the United States for some thirty-five years, but who find themselves on different sides in the current debate over the status of immigrants. I am an American citizen and she is not…. She is here to maintain an identity, not to transform it…. The price that the immigrant willingly pays, and that the exile avoids, is the trauma of self-transformation" (1996, 3).

Mukherjee embraces a monolithic Americanness, regardless of ethnicity and class, frequently comparing her discouraging and sometimes hostile experiences in Canada to what she sees as a more "immigrant-friendly" United States. In the Preface to her collection of stories, *Darkness*, she writes: "Indianness is now a metaphor, a particular way of partially comprehending the world"(1985). Though the characters in *Darkness* are or were "Indian," most of these stories explore notions of fractured identities, discarded languages, and the will to bond oneself to a new community against the ever-present fear of failure and betrayal. Mukherjee embraces being "American"—not Indian and American, not hyphenated. Furthermore, she wants to be recognized as "an American writer" in the tradition of American writers.

Another Indian American writer, Meena Alexander, allies herself with the voices of other minority writers, particularly Asian Americans. She acknowledges her past and links her present and past history as a South Asian American to that of other ethnic groups in the United States: "The present for me is the present of 'multiple anchorages,' " she notes in her essay "Is There an Asian American Aesthetic?" "It is these multiple anchorages that an ethnicity of Asian American provides for me, learning from Japanese Americans, Chinese Americans, African Americans, Indian Americans, and everyone jostling, shifting and sliding the symbols that come out of my own mind." In the same essay, she considers the "aesthetics of dislocation" as one component of an Asian American aesthetic; "the other is that we have all come under the sign of America. In India, no one would ask me if I were Asian American or Asian. Here we are part of a minority, and the vision of being 'unselved' comes into our consciousness. It is from this consciousness that I create my work of art"(1992).

As a Canadian writer of Indian origin, I find myself embracing both Bharati Mukherjee and Meena Alexander's visions of the diasporic writer's consciousness. I write from that unhyphenated consciousness that Mukherjee speaks of, as well as the unselved consciousness that Alexander claims. The diasporic individual frequently has a double consciousness, caught between "here" and "there," a privileged knowledge and perspective that is aligned with postmodernity and globalization. For the writer, the initial dual or paradoxical nature of diasporic consciousness moves the mind beyond dualism into a multiple consciousness, cognizant of multilocalities.

*　*　*

My story begins many years ago in India. I am born on October 19, 1956, in a nursing home, in Poona, India, a city close to what is now called Mumbai, then called Bombay. In Poona, my mother tends to her infant daughter. Her maidservant brings her tea and fresh flowers for her hair every morning.

My mother is a teacher, the daughter of a landowner, a farmer of Jat roots. She is a young woman who fought against tradition to get a higher education after attending convent school in Sialkote, Lahore (now in Pakistan), where she was taught by British nuns. She went to Lady McLaughlin High School where half the teachers were British and the principal was Mrs. White. She was in grade 9 when violence and border wars erupted between India and Pakistan, resulting in Partition. Her family escaped across the Pakistan border in the middle of the night taking only the possessions they could carry. She got her bachelor of arts at Government College, Ludhiana and then convinced

her father to let her go to Teachers College in Simla. She married my father only after several years
of a career of her own as an elementary school teacher. My father was the son of a Supreme Court
judge, university educated with a Ph.D. in biochemistry. My father courted my mother, coming to
her school to take photos of his nephew who was in her class; this resulted in a correspondence of
love letters and family negotiations to arrange their marriage.

Ancestors

I hear them behind me in another continent
                     across the Indian Ocean
crossing the floors, soft sweep of sandals
in my mother's country. I was born there four
decades ago at 2 am. My birth certificate reads
One Living Female Child.

Today my passport reads Nationality: Canadian.

My mother's land is still there
scooters and rickshaws navigating through crowded streets
full of billboards for Bollywood films,
dreamscapes of floating lotus ponds
lush public gardens, the smells of decay and sweet jasmine,
still the bustling bazaars and stinking alleyways,
cities like Victorian London among palm trees and banyans,
the rivers marking the routes of cranes and egrets

The ancestors are still there, with the last remnants of the
                           British Raj
drinking chai scented with cardamom
old women in desert white saris,
turbaned sirdars,

the young women with amber skin, hair and brows as black
as crows wings, eyes of lionesses in heat,
dressed in silks of delirious hues, violent pinks,
                  bangles and anklets clinking

they wander through foreign rooms
          in the last daylight of the century
painting their eyes
brush of sandalwood across the collarbone

Somewhere out of them, alive or dead I have sprung

yet no one seems to recognize me.

No one.

*   *   *

In 1958, Canada is recruiting scientists through the National Research Council and my father is offered a postdoctoral fellowship to conduct research in Ottawa for the NRC. We set out for Canada, an adventure my parents expected to last for two years. In the beginnings of immigrant memory, I travel across the world with my parents, the Sirdar's daughter in my tiny frocks, in my red smocked dress, riding camels in Egypt, double-decker buses in London. In Rome, the nuns and priests bless me, call me little Madonna. In Canada, the old photographs catch the scenes, freeze frames of Kodachrome moments.

In my parents' bedroom
the bureau holds the gifts my father gave my mother,
lingerie drawers of lace and silk, peignoir sets of filmy chiffon,
bottles of perfume *Chanel No.5*, *Miss Dior*, *Je Reviens*.

Silver-framed photographs on the nightstand,
lives stilled in sepia and Kodachrome.
There we are, the three of us on Parliament Hill among
tulips, my mother in her red sari, red shoes, red handbag,
my father with his turban, me in my British duffle coat with
the pointed hood, blue like the one Paddington bear wore.

Another snapshot.
My father teaching me to skate on Rideau Canal,
to lie in fresh powder and make snow angels.

In this one I am walking with my mother
in the Gatineau Hills in the flame of maple trees.
We are dressed to match our new country,
my mother in orange printed sari
me in my orange frock sashed at my waist.

A handtinted photo. My mother in her 50's bathing suit,
posing in front of the rounded curves of our blue Ford.
Coke bottles cooling in the sand, lined up along the shoreline.

There is my mother in her sari in front of Niagara Falls.
In another shot the three of us are standing under the falls
in our shiny yellow slickers.

I am the only child then. I am home in Canada and beloved.

* * *

After our two years in Ottawa, my father is offered a job with Ayerst Pharmaceuticals in Montreal. We move to Beaconsfield on the West Island. Beaconsfield is a white Anglophone community.

I speak Hindi and Punjabi and English. Soon I learn French. Gradually after my two sisters are born, English becomes the main language of my home and I start to lose my Indian languages.

In Beaconsfield, our difference is marked as we are the only Indian family. My mother is an exotic bird, her fashionable Western clothes, brilliant saris, her radiant smile.

My turbaned, bearded father has his share of encounters with landlords who tell him to go back to where he came from.

I notice my father's difference through other children's eyes. One Christmas season, we are downtown and a little boy on the street asks his mother if my father is Santa Claus.

We celebrate Christmas in Canada—the parts my father finds magical. In my memory he stands for hours with his little girls in front of Ogilvy's department store on St. Catherine's Street. Ogilvy's wrapped their customer's purchases in green tartan boxes and bags and they had a bagpiper and a tearoom in those years. Ogilvy's is renowned for their amazing Christmas displays, complete with moving elves and toy making scenes. The year I am remembering there is a Santa's village display. We stand holding our father's hands in the bitter cold, our breath frosting the air, watching the elves hammering and packing Santa's bag with toys, loading it onto the sleigh with sauntering reindeer, red-nosed Rudolph in the lead. We write letters to Santa Claus, letters my father takes and mails to the North Pole. My father fed our dreams and wishes and belief in imagination. He gave us magic.

* * *

I inherit my love of reading from my mother. First the vestiges of a British colonial education ... Enid Blyton, Kipling, Wordsworth's daffodils.... *A Child's Garden of Verses, The Arabian Nights, Grimm's Fairy Tales, Little Red Riding Hood,* Rapunzel letting down her hair ...

First Lessons: Postcolonial

Every morning my mother would
part my hair down the middle, plait
it into long braids reaching down to
my waist. I would walk with the other
neighbourhood kids to the elementary
school, absent-minded, my face always
in a book, reading as I walked, dressed like
the other girls in dark navy tunics, white blouses,
novitiate-like collars.

Those days, my knees were always scraped
and skinned from roller-skating on the concrete
slopes of Avondale Road, my skate-keys around
my neck, flying, weightless
my father continuously swabbing my cuts with
hydrogen peroxide, scabs peeking out over the
tops of my white kneesocks, my Oxford shoes.

In the classroom, we stood at attention
spines stiffened to the strains of singing
God Save the Queen to the Union Jack
recited The Lord's Prayer
hallowed be thy name, learned lessons
from a Gideon's bible.

In geography and history lessons the
teacher would unroll the giant map of
the world from the ceiling, use her
wooden pointer to show us the countries
of the Empire, the slow spread of a faded
red stain that marked them, soft burgundy
like the colour of my father's turbans.
*Ancient history. Crisp whites of cricket
matches at officers' clubs. Afternoon tea
in the pavilion.*

Decades later I can reconstruct the
story, move past the pink glow,
excavate the hollows of history.

I know now that if that surface was scratched
the pointer would fly along the contours of
the parchment world, across the Himalayas,
through emerald coils of steaming rivers.
Under my fingernails, the scents of spices
and teas, the silk phrasings of my mother's
saris, the stench of imperial legacy, blood
spilled from swords on proper khaki uniforms

lanced through the bodies of Sikh soldiers at
the frontlines of her Majesty's British Army.

But our teacher never said. *Remember this.*

* * *

The 1960s. Only as I look back now do I see the gaps in history. What is never taught. Silences of the colonial and the postcolonial. My mother and father's survival of the Partition of India. My mother's escape in the middle of the night with her family. The bloody violence and inhumane killings on the trains crossing the borders. Trains arriving full of dead bodies. The senseless brutality of religious warfare and ethnic hatred. The loss of a beloved home located on the other side of the Pakistan border.

Only as an adult do I learn of the vastly different immigration experiences in Canada. Of the Punjabi Sikhs who built the lumber industry in British Columbia, of the shameful silences in Canada's immigration history—the Komagata Maru incident. Of the waves of farming communities, of poverty, racism, tales of empire and colonialism. In white Anglophone Quebec in the 1960s, these are unspoken stories, absent histories, effaced.

These questions of history, of hybrid realizations, of constructing new maps, new geographies are borne out in South Asian writers' imaginative works. In Jhumpa Lahiri's story, "When Mr. Pirzada Came to Dine," the birth of Bangladesh and the history of the Partition of India and Pakistan are seen from ten-year-old Lilia's point of view. For the U.S.-born child, this is a foreign history. While her father is frustrated about what his daughter learns about the world in school, her assimilated mother is defensive: "Lilia has plenty to learn at school. We live here now, she was born here" (1999, 26). Her father categorically says of Partition, "We were sliced up," the passive voice indicating that the majority of the population had no say over this traumatic event (25). Lahiri sets the story during the struggle for Bangladesh's independence from Pakistan. Dacca-based Mr. Pirzada, visiting the United States, is suddenly cut off by the war from news about his wife and seven daughters at home. The daily news is hardly adequate and full of stereotypes disconnected from people's actual lives.

Mr. Pirzada seems to be living in limbo, his watch set eleven hours ahead to reflect the local time in Dacca. With a child's sensitivity, Lilia tunes into his anxiety about the fate of his family and shares the daily ritual of meals carefully prepared by her Bengali mother (who remains tied to homeland tastes and uses the precise kind of mustard oil needed for the fish or the particular kinds of chili peppers). Still, "no one at school talked about the war followed so faithfully in my living room. We continued to study the American Revolution and learned about the injustices of taxation without representation and memorized passages from the Declaration of Independence" (Lahiri 32–33). Lilia discovers what Meena Alexander (1992) describes accurately as the burden "of carrying our histories within us since they are not visible in the world around us."

At school, when Lilia takes the initiative to look up a book on Pakistan, she is reprimanded: "Is this book a part of your report, Lilia?.... Then I see no reason to consult it"(Lahiri 1999, 33). The reality at home is radically different, as the family tries to be supportive of Mr. Pirzada, awaiting "the birth of a nation on the other side of the world" (34). The whole drama unfolding in the subcontinent—the war for independence, poets and intellectuals killed, refugees flooding into India, and then war declared between India and Pakistan backed by the two superpowers—leaves most Americans untouched. Much of this history remains "a remote mystery with haphazard clues" for the young child who feels the anxiety that her parents share with Mr. Pirzada (40). "Most of all I remember the three of them operating during that time as if they were a single person, sharing a single meal, a single body, single silence, and a single fear"(41). At last Mr. Pirzada is able to return to Dacca and reunite with his family. A new nation is created, and new maps must be made, as the local people redraw the old colonially imposed boundary. As Lilia recalls: "Every now and then I studied the map above my father's desk and pictured Mr. Pirzada on that small patch of yellow, perspiring heavily I imagined in one of his suits, searching for his family. Of course, the map was outdated by then" (41).

Lahiri's stories capture the humanity of ordinary people, struggling with "traditions," arranged marriage, food preparation, helping the destitute, people who take diasporic leaps to create new lives even as they keep hold on the small details of their culture—eating with their fingers, enjoying a specific regional pickle, speaking native languages, being dutiful. While Lahiri's characters remain self-consciously aware of their ethnicity, they participate in this U.S. culture through their intimate relationships, married, single, raising children, driving that extra mile to get an absolutely necessary ingredient for a favorite recipe. Even as their ethnicity as South Asian Americans is performed in daily life, they work towards a hybrid realization of their subjectivity as Asians and as Americans.

*   *   *

My Mother's Lost Places

My teachers and the women in the
neighbourhood would admire the crimson
blooms on my mother's Kashmiri shawls,
exotic, intricate embroideries on the finest
wool the colour of nightfall.

I know they could never imagine,
as I have only just begun to imagine,
my mother's lost places,
laughter in summer houses, wild monkeys
at the hill stations of her youth, peacocks,
the heady profusions of flowers and fruit,
jasmine and roses, custard-apples and
guavas. They could not imagine her with
braids and proper Catholic uniform at the
convent school under the stern eyes of nuns
with their Bride of Christ wedding rings
who taught them all their subjects including
domestic skills such as the tatting of lace and
embroidery stitching. They could not taste the
sweetness of Sanskrit poetry, or the star-flung
nights of Persian ghazals.

In Canada, my mother's young life gets frozen into
the icy winters of my childhood, new stories spun
in English on skating rinks, tobogganing hills and
ski slopes. A new wife, a new mother, she reads
Ladies Home Journal, learns to bake me birthday
cakes and gingerbread houses, wears Western clothes,
pedal pushers and sheath dresses and high heels, sews
me party frocks with sashes bowed in the back.

*   *   *

My mother was a Girl Guide in India. The colonial influences of Lord and Lady Baden Powell are felt globally. I too am enrolled in Girl Guides to become a good Canadian citizen, a capable girl.

The Education of Girls

We learn to recite the Girl Guide promise:

I promise, on my honour, to do my best:
To do my duty to God, the Queen, and my country,
To help other people at all times,
To obey the Guide Law.

We learn the language of semaphore, how to
build campfires and lean-tos and latrines.
We earn badges, pitch tents, learn how to use an axe and chop wood,
how to tie knots, learn first aid and how to survive in the
wilderness. We Learn to *Be Prepared* and to *Lend a Hand*.

We learn the Guide Law.

A Guide is obedient. You obey orders given you by those
in authority, willingly and quickly. Learn to understand that
orders are given for a reason, and must be carried out without question.

A Guide smiles and sings even under difficulty. You are
cheerful and willing even when things seem to be going wrong.

A Guide is pure in thought, word and deed. You look for
what is beautiful and good in everything, and try to become strong
enough to discard the ugly and unpleasant.

We become capable girls, soldiers in our uniforms, with our
companies and patrols and salutes. We learn to build nations and
at the close of the day, we sing Taps, the soldiers' bugle call to
extinguish the lights.

Day is done, gone the sun
From the hills, from the lake
From the sky
All is well, safely rest
God is nigh.

And our mothers kept house, did the laundry and
the cooking and the ironing, drove us to Brownies
and Girl Guides, did volunteer work, refinished furniture,
watched *The Edge of Night* and *Another World*
took antidepressants when their lives did
not resemble the glamorous adventures of Rachel
and Mac Corey, had hysterectomies at 40.

At the close of every day, they had supper ready when
their husbands returned from the city, fresh and slick,
briefcases in hand, polished shoes tapping them home past
manicured lawns along the asphalt driveways.

*   *   *

My mother knits us ski sweaters, heavy cable knits that I wear to the local skating rink and to the ski hills. My father learns to ski, a rare sight on the hills of the Eastern Townships, St. Sauveur, Mont Tremblant, his turban and ski goggles, among a sea of white faces in Montreal winters. The newspaper photographs him, writes a story on the Sikh skier in Canada—the new Canadian. Every Saturday morning in winter, he drives me to catch the bus to my ski lessons, picks me up at the end of the day at the Beaconsfield Shopping Centre.

*   *   *

A curious mix, my cultural education. I am not raised on Indian dance or music. Chamber music concerts, ballets. Every Christmas, my mother sews velvet dresses for us, takes us to see *The Nutcracker* at Place des Arts. And every year those unforgettable ballet classes. The stern Miss Damrol's ballet classes, our pristine white tunics, powder blue sashes, pink tights, at the school gym or Stewart Hall, bodies stiff at the barre, our hair in tight buns at the napes of our necks. I can hear Miss Damrol's voice, clipped and British: "Eyes forward young ladies, chin up, stomachs in, bottoms tucked, *plié*, *port de bras*, first position, second position, hold it."
And then there were other forms of dancing.

Slow Dancing: Beaconsfield 1973

Parents away for the weekend
we are in a house like all the others,
freshly painted trim and gabled windows,
brass-numbered door and neatly pruned hedges,
and the basement recreation room is overflowing
with us, sweet sixteens, bodies clutched together in sweat in
the cigarette smoke and beer, slow dancing to Chicago's *Color
My World* and Led Zeppelin's *Stairway to Heaven.*

My girlfriends and I wear angora sweaters our mothers
bought for us in the soft pastel shades of infants: fingernail
pink, baby blue, pale yellow, and cream. We wear drugstore
scents named for innocence and fruit: *Love's Baby Soft, Love's Fresh
Lemon*, or the more sophisticated *Eau de Love* or Revlon's *Charlie.*

For years we have danced in ballet studios, spinning, dreaming our mothers'
dreams of Sugar Plum Fairies, our rose tight confections, pink slippers twirling
pas de deux, jetés, pirouetting our taut muscles until our toes bled. But tonight
we dance in our tight blue Levis, our mothers' voices fading as Eric Clapton's
electric guitar shivers our spines, the music claiming us and we spill out
under the streetlamps, dancing across equators into the earth's light.

On the streets of suburbia, this is the beginning of hunger.
It catches me by surprise, exploding like a kiss.

*   *   *

Teenagehood. My black hair, olive skin, nontypical features. By Indian standards I am fair, a whiteness about me. I speak fluent French and English. In Quebec I am taken for every nationality, Italian, French, Arab, Egyptian. "Where are you from?" becomes a repeated refrain.

On our first trip to India with my family, this confusion about identity is mirrored by Bollywood billboards. The actresses have dyed their hair reddish brown and their skin is light. In Indian magazines, Lakme cosmetic creams are advertised, claiming to make the skin fair and light. Lakme sells Fairever Fairness Cream. The ad reads: "NOW YOU CAN CHANGE THE FUTURE! Look fairer, feel more beautiful than ever, with new FAIREVER!… Change the way you look, and face the world with new confidence! Contains no bleach. Suitable for all skin types."

Lakme also sells Fair and Lovely Fairness Cream and Fairever Mantra Fairness Cream, which is lauded in their ads for being "India's fairness secret, a fairness cream that combines the power of diverse fairness ingredients to make your skin visibly fairer, naturally." Other feminine beauty ads market skin bleaches to make the skin fair. My relatives call me beautiful, fair. They call my dark-skinned younger sister *kali*—dark, black, less marriageable, less marketable. I feel the guilt of this difference even then at six-teen, a growing consciousness of an orientation in the education of girls and women that perpetuates a within-culture racism aimed at women's beauty, a woundedness that moves beyond immigrant identity.

Back in Canada, my girlfriends Colleen, Debbie, Lorrie, and I still baste ourselves in baby oil at the Beaconsfield Swimming Pool, seeking Coppertone tans, the white lines at the edges of our bathing suits the beginning of a sensuous existence of teenage girls.

Sometimes my sister and I dream of being blonde and blue-eyed like the models in *Seventeen* magazine.

My sister is the first child from Anglophone Beaconsfield to attend French school. My parents thought it would be the best way for her to learn French. One day, my sister comes home from French school, weeping inconsolably. The French kids call her "nigger."

In the most elemental of ways, through my sister's life at school, we are confronted with racism and with our first demonstration of Francophone Quebec fundamentalist belief in the notion of "*pure laine.*" The term *pure laine* ("old stock," literally "pure wool"), is sometimes taken to be synonymous with Québécois. This term refers to someone whose ancestry is almost entirely Québécois. As with any ethnicity in a multicultural country such as Canada, few people can accurately claim to be *pure laine.* The idea of *pure laine* has been at the root of some heated polemic battles about ethnicity, culture, and belonging in recent years in Quebec; many find the idea and its linking with Québécois identity and culture to be racist, and belief in the identity of French origins with the Québécois is by no means universal.

Family Life

In the 1960s they called it *Health Education*
on our report cards. Today they call the subject
Family Life.

At our school, girls are separated from
boys, gathered in the school gymnasium.
The nurse distributes pamphlets about
life cycles and Kotex. There is something
pristine and sanitized about it, the glossy
brochures with the beautiful fresh-faced
girl, her blonde hair swept back with pink
satin ribbon. We know we will soon become
her, young women leading Breck girl lives.

We learn our lessons well, believe we can
hold on to our well-groomed dreams.

It takes us years before we realize how many
things will make us bleed, how easy
for the world to rip us to pieces.

*　　*　　*

We did not attend a *Gurudwara*, a Sikh temple, on a regular basis—only if there was a wedding or special occasion. My father did not believe in organized religion. But he was a spiritual man who lived his life according to humanist principles. So in sixties fashion, my parents took us to a Unitarian church in Pointe Claire. In 1967, the minister was Fred Cappuccino. With his wife Bonnie, they had two birth children and five adopted children from around the world. I remember Annie from Vietnam and Mohammed from Bangladesh. The church was a lively community, one that perpetuated a Buddhist belief in humans as sacred and that this sacredness was not reliant on an external force.

Fred and Bonnie Cappuccino now live in Maxville, in eastern Ontario, where they run an organization called Child Haven International. Their family grew to include twenty-one adopted children, some disabled or of mixed "race" from Third World countries.

*   *   *

At Beaconsfield High School, I am on the debating team, the Reach for the Top quiz show team, a bit of a geek but still popular in a way that enables me to have a sense of a secret identity. My mother's refrain at this time of my life is: "Don't talk so much, a girl should be more reserved." She wanted me to excel at everything, be strong but reserved, articulate but quiet....

She wanted me to have a profession she could define—lawyer, doctor, teacher, engineer—something that had a label. I never imagined I would become a poet, but years later she gives me a tiny notebook she had saved. I had written it when I was twelve—descriptive, flowery nature poems, full of allusions to classical myth. I had titled the notebook *Poems* by Rishma Singh.

Meanwhile my life was absorbed by books. I spent hours in the Beaconsfield Public Library and eventually got a part-time job there. I read every moment I could steal from the day, and late into the night under covers by flashlight, even though my mother said I would go blind. I finished entire novels in a day. I loved books, devoured them, eating up the words until ink spilled from my mouth. I lived the lives of fictional characters, walking around in my daily life in an absent-minded haze. I read while getting dressed, eating meals, walking to school. Books were my talismans, reading a form of faith.

Little Red

First stories, fragments of colonial texts,
Enid Blyton, Noddy's Adventures, Kipling's Jungle Book
Wordsworth's daffodils
stories full of words like pram, lorry, Wellingtons, nappies.

Then worlds of fairies and witches
Rapunzel letting down her hair from the tower,
princesses and ogres.

The story she loved best was Little Red Riding Hood.
As a young child she learned all the words
                              by heart.
In the storybook her parents read to her,
Little Red is always saved by the woodcutter.

Years later, when she knows the real ending, the Perrault
one where the wolf waits for her in bed, and Little Red takes off
her clothes, lies down beside him and he gobbles her up

                                         it is no surprise.

She is still the red cloaked one, using her words as incantations
against the wolf at the door, the wolf who comes again and again

                                   on nights black as doctrine.

There is no other story, no other text.

                              *   *   *

Reading Wonder Woman

The comic book heroes I loved best
                       were the mutants and freaks.
Spiderman and Batman, Aquaman who was half-fish.

And then there was Wonder Woman. She was glorious,
descended from the Amazons of Greek myth. She had
fabulous breasts, a tiara, a magic lasso and belt, red boots,
as well as those bulletproof wristbands worn by the
Amazons to remind them of the folly of submitting to men's domination.
If a man could bind an Amazon's wrists, she lost all her powers.

In early stories she captures
spies, Third World War Promoters,
sends them to imprisonment on Venus
where they are forced to wear
Venus Girdles of Magnetic Gold to
tame them into peaceful life.
In another story, she defeats the
evil Fausta, Nazi Wonder Woman
in "Wanted by Hitler, Dead or Alive."

Wonder Woman was beautiful and powerful as a hero,
understated and reserved in her secret identity as Diana Prince,
the secretary in her smart-chick glasses.

She taught me radical truth.
The geek, the hybrid mutant is a treasure,
so easily misunderstood in real life
a secret identity is necessary. Hold it close.
Protect your wrists.
Put on your red boots step into fire.

*   *   *

Reading Ladies Home Journal

Reading my mother's magazines
Ladies Home Journal and *Miss Chatelaine*
pictures of women with cinch-waist dresses,
bouffant hairdos. They ride in convertibles
headscarves keeping every hair in place.

These women are so happy with their pink and aqua
kitchen appliances. In one ad for Scott toilet paper,
the woman wears an evening gown in the exact
pastel blue of the toilet paper and Kleenex tissue.

These women use Yardley Lavender and Cashmere Bouquet
talcum powder. They buy new davenports and credenzas. Pictured
in exotic landscapes in their underwear, they dream in their Maidenform
bras and girdles that promise to set them free.

The ad I like best is for the black lace corset called a Merry Widow.
Under the sedate hairdo and perfect makeup of the model, her Max Factor
red lips whisper *It's simply wicked what it does for you. Care to be daring, darling?*

*   *   *

Girl Detective Chronicles

Long after my mother thought I was asleep,
late into the night, I would read under the
covers with a flashlight.

How I loved them, the stories about the
girl detectives, reading and recording the
world in notebooks—Harriet the Spy
the ones who solved crimes with their
wits, their brains, their All-American good looks.

I drove that blue roadster with Nancy
Drew, dated Ned, looked lovely and charming
and desirable at college football games.

And how I dreamed of being Cherry Ames, student
nurse, with her stylish cap and uniform, her black
hair and rosy cheeks, her boyfriends and her adventures.

And when I grew up, I became them, Nancy and Cherry.
I cut off my long black braids, styled my hair into a bob.

I became the girl detective, the nurse, capable of building
nations and soothing the hearts of men
for awhile.

*　*　*

On the autumn football fields at Beaconsfield High School, the cheerleaders chanted and jumped, their pleated miniskirts flipped into the air, flurries of thighs gleaming. Anything seemed possible, for such young bodies, in such a place and time. I would watch and remain reading my books under the trees, losing myself in imaginary worlds, in the tomes of *War and Peace* and *Dr. Zhivago*, dreaming of dancing in evening gowns and elbow-length gloves. Books about revolution excited me, seduced me. I tried to reimagine the heroines, their perpetual tragedies. Emma Bovary, Anna Karenina. Anna flinging her body into the locomotive steam, her red purse on the tracks. I tried to read them and write them differently, give them different endings, new destinies. I wanted them to stay alive, to breathe, to be plump with blood and desire, to believe that anything is possible.

Reading Anna Karenina

The volume of Tolstoy thumbs her open.
She tries to keep the heroine alive.

Outside the library windows
ragged moths beat against the streetlamps.
She feels the heat of locomotive steam
rising from the stacks, weeps when she
sees Anna's red purse on the tracks.

She closes the book with stunned hands
as if she had touched the hem of a final
morning, a sense of that going into it alone.
She begins to think she will not be carried
unscarred, untorn into any heaven. Wants
someone to hold her while she burns.

*   *   *

In Chitra Divakaruni's short story "Leaving Yuba City," a second-generation daughter leaves home. The cultural gulf between daughter and parents is so wide that she has to make an escape in the middle of the night and has to face the question: in which language would she leave a note to her parents? "The words, the language. How can she write in English to her parents who have never spoken to her in anything but Punjabi, who will have to have someone translate the lines and curves, the bewildering black slashes she has left behind?"(1993, 39). She hopes that later, as she learns to make her own space in the world, she will be able to communicate more openly with her parents: "Maybe the words will come to her … halting but clear, in the language of her parents, the language that she carries with her, for it is hers too, no matter where she goes"(40).

In Divakaruni's poem, "Yuba City School," a mother struggles with the knowledge that her son is being racially harassed in school. The mother feels helpless because she is not fluent enough in English to argue with the teacher: "My few English phrases," she thinks. "She [the teacher] will pluck them from me, nail shut my lips"(121). Through a few deft phrases, Divakaruni evokes fear and cultural impasse.

*   *   *

The late 1960s. Lived to soundtracks of Jimi Hendrix, Janice Joplin, Gracie Slick and Jefferson Airplane, the Rolling Stones. These were rebel years when my parents waited up for me at night, smelled my breath for traces of alcohol. My mother would run her hands across my back to make sure I was wearing a bra. She would check the length of my skirts as I left the house. I wore min-skirts, rolled up the waistbands after I left home to make them even shorter.... I wore hotpants and fishnets. My mother stopped smiling in these years—told me I should be modest and show no cleavage.

Prom night was a pale pink gown with rosebuds, corsage, dance at the airport Hilton, drinking what we thought were sophisticated drinks—Pink Ladies, Gin Fizzes, Tia Marias with milk, and then watching the sunrise on Mount Royal....

*   *   *

At eighteen, I left Beaconsfield to study literature, languages, and translation at university. I meet Jim, a young man from New Brunswick. I am in love.

By this time, the dialogues between me and my mother went something like this:

Sound of the phone ringing/answering machine: "Hi, I can't come to the phone right now. Leave a message." Beep of answering machine.

My mother's voice on the answering machine: "Beta, we can never reach you. You're never home. Are you studying? Call us back." Tone at end of mother's message. Click, hanging up of phone.

Sound of phone ringing: "Hi, I can't come to the phone right now. Leave a message." Beep of answering machine.

Mother's voice: "Beta, what are you doing? Your uncle has sent letters from India. Some eligible men, London-*Angreji* educated, who want to marry and come to Canada. One is an engineer and one a doctor—good families and good-looking boys.

(Mother gives a big sigh, exasperated tsk, tsk sound).

"You are becoming too Western. You should remember your culture.
Love you. Stay in touch. Call us. It would be good to hear from you."

Tone at end of message. Sound of tape rewinding.

*   *   *

I come home for the summer after my first year at university. It is the time of the 1980 referendum in Quebec. My neighborhood has been vandalized. I am shocked by the stop signs with the word STOP slashed out with black paint, the word ARRET written over top. We are confronted with the notion of "pure" ethnicity again: *pure-laine*. Everywhere, there is a war of language on our neighborhood signs. *Langue, ma langue*; in French *language* and *tongue* are the same word. I always thought French and English were my languages, *mes langues*, my tongues, the tongues of home.

My mother finds my birth control pills, calls me a prostitute.

I move into an apartment with Jim. My parents are beside themselves with worry.

After several years of living together I phone home:

R: "Mom, Jim and I want to get married. We want a civil ceremony."

Mother: "Well, if you want to do that, your father and I will not be there."

My mother refuses to meet Jim. She talks to him on the phone after some coaxing and never physically meets him until the wedding. J and I decide we will have the wedding my parents want. They can send photos to the relatives in India and make everyone happy. We have a Sikh wedding and a United Church wedding. The day of the wedding, I realize I can't dress myself. My aunts have to wrap and fold and drape my sari around my body.

My wedding sari is not the usual bridal red. I have rebelled against the red, brocade-encrusted, heavy wedding saris. My sari is pale peach-pink, a shot silk like dawn with a deep purple and gold brocade border. I wear a pale mauve orchid in my hair. In traditional ceremonies, the groom rides in on a white horse but we dispensed with this custom. Jim wears a turban and my mother begins to love him a little.

The *Anand Karaj*, the Sikh wedding ceremony, begins with the sound of chanted prayers in a language I do not understand. I am laden with gold—a *rani-haar*-necklace around my throat, my hands painted in henna designs, the bridal *mehndi*-head covered and suitably bowed, the Sirdar's daughter walking around the holy book. To signify our union and the giving away of the bride, my father places one end of a scarf in my hand and the other in Jim's hands. The *Adi Granth*, the holy book, is opened and *Lavan*, the marriage prayers, are read. During each of the four stanzas, we walk around the holy book. Still holding our ends of the scarf, we circle around the book four times. I am guided by men—my groom, my father, my cousin, my uncle—as if I could not find my own way. We are seated for final prayers and then given Kara Parshad, a holy sweet to share with the congregation.

We sign the official register, Jim takes off his turban and we are married again in a Christian ceremony, double-ringed, the look of relief on my mother-in-law's face as she hears the English vows she understands.

We leave the church, walking out into the sunshine as friends and relatives place garlands of flowers around our necks, to bless us and congratulate us. We are showered with rose petals.

At the end of the day, I look over at Jim, my sisters, mother, father, everyone dancing at the reception, all beloved, all strangers.

*   *   *

2004. I am now a university professor of language and literature, a poet. Poetry becomes my migrant home, lit with the many languages that are part of me, a sensuous land, a transnational borderland. Although I write in English, I also write through the rhythms of other languages, French, Punjabi, Hindi, Spanish, Latin, the strut and play of words shimmering with the rhythms and sounds of lines that permit a sense of home even through dislocation.

For many years, I felt distant, foreign from the culture of my *desh* or homeland of my birth. My home is Canada, my tangled identity is hybrid. My two daughters are hybrid mixes, born of my Indian and their father's Scottish-Canadian heritage.

Every Sikh girl is named *Kaur*, meaning *princess*; it is her name along with her other given names.

Princess Stories

When I was young my father called me *Princess*.
And princess stories were the ones I loved most,
especially the one about Sleeping Beauty. Her
name was sometimes Briar Rose or Aurora. The
story of the beautiful princess who pricked her
finger on the spindle of a spinning wheel, falling
under the spell of the witch who had been shunned
at her christening.

The curse of a girlchild's birth.

She slept along with the kingdom for a hundred years
until she is rescued by a handsome prince who hacked
through the dense tangle of thorns and wild rose bushes.
The curse lifted with love, his kiss on her lips,
awakening the world.

While my daughters are young, I read them princess stories
The Paper Bag Princess, The Princess and the Motorcycle.
Tales of strong, independent princesses of wit and courage and
intellect who do not depend on princes.

Still, as I watch my girls, young women now, I am filled
with longing, something that mourns the loss of belief
that a beloved would hack through forests of thorns into
waking.

* * *

Jhumpa Lahiri writes of the post-1965 generation of immigrants who embark on the psychological and sociocultural journey of becoming "American" and their attempts to adopt an Asian American identity. Her collections of stories frequently present an ethnoglobal vision that transcends narrow nationalism, but celebrates an ethnic heritage along with evoking an exemplary universalist humanism.

In the title story of the Pulitzer Prize-winning *Interpreter of Maladies*, the Das family returns to India from the United States. While crossing national borders they are forced to recognize their own dual identities—more American in clothing, speech, body language than Indian, though ethnically marked.

Indian North Americans are also described in India as NRIs—Nonresident Indians. Although India does not allow dual nationality, the label of nonresident is a way to retain close emotional ties; even as American citizens, they are still identified as "Indian." As Inderpal Grewal notes, the Indian government nurtures the ties to home because they want to entice NRI financial investments to India; this NRI population is not interested in forming coalitions with other people of color in the United States, and most are uncritical of the U.S. "ideology of 'democracy' and 'freedom'" (Grewal 1993, 226).

The Das family embark with cameras on a journey to see the famous Sun Temple at Konarack. They want to learn from the ethnic heritage that is not part of their everyday geography in the United States. Lahiri sensitively captures the image of this native-returned-as-tourist in the portrayal of Mrs. Das, whose interest in the local guide/driver, Mr. Kapasi, is interpreted quite differently by the foreign-returned and by the native. The driver, Mr. Kapasi, who works as a doctor's assistant, one who describes the various maladies of patients to the doctor to help him to prescribe medicines, is called "the interpreter of maladies." He regards this as "a job like any other"; to Mrs. Das it is "so romantic" and "full of responsibility" (Lahiri 1999, 50). He finds "nothing noble in interpreting peoples' maladies" (51). He works with the doctor in "a stale little infirmary where Mr. Kapasi's smartly tailored clothes clung to him in the heat, in spite of the blackened blades of a ceiling fan churning over their heads"(52).

Lahiri's representations, on one level, acknowledge the ethnic and national in descriptions of Mr. Kapasi and his modest work, as well as in Mrs. Das's return to nativism. She can romanticize his job and make it sound grander than it is from her outsider's perspective. Lahiri recreates national identity via ethnicized codes of communication, both spoken and unspoken; culturally defined signals are misinterpreted by Mr. Kapasi, who regards Mrs. Das as both native and U.S.-stamped. Of course, he does not have her privileges of travel, or of picking and choosing from different cultures—a kind of global entitlement that she and her family have acquired by living in the United States.

When Mrs. Das casually asks for Mr. Kapasi's address—something that tourists do when they take photographs and "promise" to send them back—he overinterprets the request as signifying real interest in him and his work. Lahiri subtly weaves in the sexual attraction that he experiences. "He began to check his reflection in the rear-view mirror as he drove, feeling grateful that he had chosen the gray suit that morning and not the brown one.... He glanced at the strawberry between her breasts, and the golden brown hollow in her throat.... He could smell a scent on her skin, like a mixture of whiskey and rosewater. He worried suddenly that she could smell his perspiration" (53–55).

He fantasizes that since she has asked for his address, they will correspond regularly and he will tell her many more stories of the maladies that he interpreted. He is already anticipating the letter as he calculates how long it would take to get one after their return to the United States. "In its own way, this correspondence would fulfill his dream, of serving as an interpreter between nations" (59). He dreams of crossing national boundaries in his imagination, serving as a kind of cultural ambassador representing his nation to the U.S.-bred and Indian-looking Mrs. Das.

As he continues to fantasize and the sexual innuendoes mushroom, and as the others wander off, Mrs. Das offers a startling revelation: that her son's father is not Mr. Das. Mr. Kapasi is shocked, but tries to keep his composure. Why tell him? She had kept this secret for eight years and was hoping that his job as an interpreter of maladies would help her to feel better, that he would be able to suggest a remedy. Perhaps one reason for this revelation is that Mrs. Das is looking for a spiritual, mystical India with healing powers, and sees the interpreter as a vehicle sent to her for that purpose.

Lahiri resolves the story beautifully. The mother's guilt and pain is somehow transferred to the innocent son, who has wandered off alone and is attacked by a pack of monkeys. Bleeding and crying, he needs to be carried back to the car. As Mrs. Das tries to comfort him and reaches into her bag, the piece of paper on which she had scribbled Mr. Kapasi's address floats away. Her revelation of sexual infidelity to someone who shares her ethnicity but is divided from her in every other way, especially in class privilege, is a reminder that the gap dividing them is more significant than their common ethnicity.

Some stories in the collection unfold in the United States, while others travel back to India through their characters' imaginations and histories or are set in India with the ever-present West looming in the wings. There are women who have affairs, men who leave their wives, women who chose careers over family, nontraditional women and men. Lahiri's characters demonstrate the diversity of the South Asian American community with their various languages, religions, and regional food cultures. Their daily lives in this diasporic location unfold as they struggle and dream, argue and entertain. These portrayals broaden the representations of Indian Americans, abandoning any fixed notion of North American Indian culture.

* * *

Reading Amy Lowell

Summer and I have returned to the town where
                    I was a young wife
where we raised our daughters.
The name of the place means *a place to live forever.*
Mythology and daily life. Legends of sea serpents,
ghosts of horses lost swimming in from the island, tangled with
slow pitch tournaments, ball players and Winnebago campers,
tourists on the beaches and lunching at wineries.

Today I am marking freshman English papers in the backyard.
The air is sweet and fugitive. In the garden, wild strew of roses,
pink blooms amidst the silver foliage of planted pathways
                  fragrance spilling from their thorn beds
the morning stillness stung by the
screeching of Steller's jays and flocks of crows
              singing a crude chorale.

In the distance, the sound of ducks landing on the swimming pool,
                              splashing and flapping their wings.
My daughters laugh and I am struck by that particular radiance
                    again and again how the laughter of girls
                              cuts through blue air.

How did I come to this place
                    the professor circling sentence fragments,
the occasional leap of the heart when a student writes a beautiful phrase.
My student has written an essay on Amy Lowell.
And suddenly I am transported, back to 1972 at Beaconsfield High
in Mr. Whitman's North American Literature class,
                              yes that was his name.

Fifteen years old, sitting in those straight-backed wooden chairs,
          my legs cramped under the tiny desk with my huge Norton anthology
                    open at Amy Lowell's "Patterns."
There have been so many words I have committed to heart. This poem was one of them.
I could taste this poetry, feel the rhythms of it beating in my eyelids.
For the first time, reading Amy Lowell,
          I understood that burnt cadence of sense,
                    the quickstep of syllables in my throat.

I wrote an essay on Amy Lowell's "Patterns"
something about the Imagist movement, the poet's use of figurative
                              language and form
in a consideration of how societal expectations may
                    inhibit a woman's actions in society.

Mr. Whitman gave me an A on my essay.

I promptly forgot what I knew about patterns
                    in the wisdom of my sixteenth year.

I must have known then, something about the effect of patterns,
knowing Lowell's narrator, the feel of her corset, her pink and silver
brocade gown, how she grieves for her dead lover
                    how a heavy-booted lover would have loosened
                    the stays of her stiff correct brocade
in the pink and silver garden
                              the bruise and swoon of it.

I, too am a rare
Pattern.

In dreams I see the husband of my girlhood
                              my pink and silver time
his arms around me like a familiar blanket.
He is holding something out to me, places it in my palm
                    a scroll, a tablet, some lost history inscribed
                                        unreadable.

And centuries pass and we are still *gorgeously arrayed*
                              trousseaus of pink and silver
mouths stuffed with bone china
pink and silver, boned and stayed

Christ! What are patterns for?

At sixteen I used to mouth the words
                              swords springing from the repetitions
from the ribs of consonants.

Today, in my forty-sixth year, I reread the poem and the body flies apart,
remembering how a grown woman can brush back her hair in moonlight
watch her husband and daughters inside her house as if in a dream.

Remembering days when the woman wakes up and she understands her skin

doesn't fit her anymore

What she does inside that skin leaves

her outside her house in long nights of crickets

singing and the lake whispering.

Sometimes, she longs to be like characters in a novel or a poem,

the relief of flatness on paper.

The heart is literate.

It wants to read the pages it has unfurled.

It wants the grip of roses on love-ridden afternoons,

the ordinary of tv, chair, table, plate, sneakers

entangled through a sky of blood tracery swept innocent by rain.

I want conversation that is like the stripped truth of the poem,

the way I felt when I first read Amy Lowell's "Patterns."

Over the years I wondered what kind of shelter

I could make with words.

I search for the color of home in the extravagance of reading.

I am looking for it still.

This town is not a place for introspection. Such beauty.

The lake, the blue air, the sun, all defy me

to find some fault in this horizon.

Over the years I weaned my babies, got ready to walk

into the pink and silver light.

*   *   *

I have learned the stories of my students of Indian heritage, the immensely different immigrant stories of struggle, hardship, racism, and class. I have come to know the huge divides of race, ethnicity, class, gender, economy, and education that mark these differences within cultures.

A dwelling at the edge of the world, this home. The hold of a loved place cannot be taken for granted and the making of a home and locality, given the shifting worlds we inhabit, might be understood as an art of negativity-praise songs for what remains when the taken-for-grantedness of things falls away.

The question of language always haunts me, brings me back to a memory of a lover who wanted to know about my childhood, my childhood language. He wanted to know my father's words, called me *beta*, little one, child, my father's name for me, as he stroked my hair back from my forehead. And in these moments, I realized how much of this language was deeply connected to a place of soul for me. Punjabi—there is still something beloved about this tongue. Some sense of home, like the poem, a shelter we make of words.

Language uses are a significant part of diasporic experience. In a poem entitled "Language," Amita Vasudeva recreates the levels of ignorance about Asian languages and cultures in U.S. society: Can you speak Mexican…. No I am from India….Can you speak Hindu?" (1993, 119). Such ignorance compounds a second generation's conflict about learning mother-tongues that are not heard in mainstream culture. Yet those languages, especially those mother-tongues, cling to them, stuck almost like a second skin that cannot be shed.

*   *   *

May 25, 1990. My father dies young. He is sixty-two years old. My mother and father have many plans for his retirement in a few years, travels around the world. My mother now works at the Beaconsfield Public Library. He leaves my mother cooking dinner. He goes to the Pointe Claire Tennis Club for a game of tennis with a close friend. A blood clot finds its way into his heart, and he dies instantly there on the red earth courts.

My mother gets a call from the Lakeshore General Hospital. Life is never quite the same. We mourn, we gleam.

I find myself remembering my childhood lullaby, the one my father sang to me each night at bedtime, stroking my hair back from my forehead. My father's voice: "*Soja beta*, sleep little one. Sleep child." The Hindi and Punjabi words, my childhood tongues, lost languages to me now.

At the funeral, it's all I can think about, this lullaby, the childhood words, as I have returned home. My sisters and I have shed our Western clothes and are dressed in the brilliant silk saris my father would have loved. Mine is blue like the lake near our childhood home, the blue of Lake St. Louis in Beaconsfield on the West Island of Montreal.

I know the gleam and smell of the polished

leather of his shoes, buffed every morning

        before he left for work.

I press my face into the crisp white cotton of his shirts,

brush my cheek against his jackets,

sweaters still warm with him.

I touch my teeth to the metal of his watch, his cufflinks.

I can hear his voice reading fairytales, singing

Harry Belafonte's "Jamaica Farewell"

But I'm sad to say I'm on my way
Won't be back for many a day
My heart is down, my head is turning around
I had to leave a little girl in Kingston town

I hear him singing Punjabi and Hindi ghazals, lullabies

Soja Rajkumari, soja,
Soja meethe sapne aayen
Soja pyari Rajkumari

Sleep, princess, sleep
Sleep with sweet dreams
Sleep beloved princess

In the hush, I am cradled by the sound of him,
 voice lifting me like birdsong through the pyre.

In my mother's house I enter silence,
wear it as a dress, my father's ashes acrid
in my throat. I remember the days of savage
adoration, child for father, father for child, when
I was tiny enough to stick to his trousers like a burr.
His sudden vanishing a brute sledgehammer blow.

(Excerpt from "Soja")

*   *   *

Longing for homes left behind may be intense for first-generation immigrants who seek a community to belong to. A form of culture shock occurs when you live as a citizen in a country for a long time, over forty years and still, when someone asks you where you are from and the name of your religion and your first thought is *I don't know*. In becoming diasporic, we need to keep in mind the political parameters of home, community, and nation, as analyzed usefully in Chandra Mohanty's essay, "Defining Genealogies: Feminist Reflections on Being South Asian in North America":

What is home? The place I was born? Where I grew up? Where I live and work as an adult? Where I locate my community—my people? Who are "my people"? Is home a geographical space, a historical space, an emotional sensory space? Home is always so crucial to immigrants and migrants.... I am convinced that this question—how one understands and defines home—is a profoundly political one.... Political solidarity and a sense of family could be melded together imaginatively to create a strategic space I could call "home" (1993, 352).

The notion of home and ethnoglobal vision is also explored in the poetry of Agha Shahid Ali, whose recent death leaves a profound gap in the South Asian American literary tradition. His deep and abiding love for his homeland of Kashmir gave the world ways of imaginatively "finding" home while living away from it. Ethnically grounded and simultaneously embracing a vast humanity, the narrator in the opening poem of *The Half-Inch Himalayas* startlingly touches his home in a picture postcard. The complex notion of home is constructed through the power of the imagination and through language, through writing home. "Kashmir shrinks into my mailbox/My home a neat four by six inches./I always loved neatness. Now I hold/The half-inch Himalayas in my hand./This is home. And this is the closest/I'll ever come to home" (Ali 1987)

* * *

In my life as a Sirdar's daughter in Canada, my immigrant journey has proven to be vastly different from immigrant memories of many other immigrants. Canada has allowed me an existence of hybridity, shaped by my individual experiences and all the factors of class, gender, education, and circumstance in my life. My work as a writer is driven by the desire to write against such locations as Britain where hybridity has not historically been allowed, where racism has provided the impetus for diasporic individuals to maintain strong ties with their homelands and encouraged them to shape selves and identities that are rooted in their ethnicities. But the writer in me refuses to choose. As Salman Rushdie writes:

But I, too, have ropes around my neck, I have them to this day, pulling me this way and that, East and West, the nooses tightening, commanding, *choose, choose.*

I buck, I snort, I whinny, I rear, I kick. Ropes, I do not choose between you. Lassoes, lariats, I choose neither of you, and both. Do you hear? I refuse to choose. (1996, 211)

* * *

And everywhere I travel in life there is still this—

A small girl in her red smocked dress

Her father clasps her hand in his, teaches her

to recognize the convulsive beauty of things ... (Dunlop 2004, 7)

In my memory and in my writing home, I am in Beaconsfield again. Kissing my father's forehead before we let him go to the crematorium. How the return home can be treacherous, unstable in its imaginings and remembrances. Ultimately, immigrants and others in the world we call home must invent a history of shared space in which to dwell. And I, in my blue sari, help my mother and my sisters to spread my father's ashes on the waters of the lake he loved, in the place we called home.

Acknowledgments

Unless otherwise noted, poems by Rishma Dunlop in this chapter are excerpts from *Reading Like a Girl*. The chapter opening poem and the poem "Ancestors" are from *Red Silk: An Anthology of South Asian Women Poets*. The lines cited from the lullaby "Soja RajKumari, Soja" in my poem "Soja" are from the song written by Kundan Lal Saigal, originally performed in the 1940 Bollywood film *Zindagi*. Lines from Harry Belafonte's song "Jamaica Farewell" in the poem "Soja" are from *Calypso*, RCA recording, 1956, LPM-1248.

References

Alexander, Meena. "Is There an Asian American Aesthetic?" *SAMAR* (South Asian Magazine for Action and Reflection) 1: (Winter 1992): 26–27.

Ali, Agha Shahid. *The Half-Inch Himalayas*. Middletown, CT: Wesleyan University Press, 1987.

Divakaruni, Chitra. "Leaving Yuba City," *Our Feet Walk the Sky: Women of the South Asian Diaspora*, edited by the Women of South Asian Descent Collective, 38–40. San Francisco: Aunt Lute Books, 1993.

Dunlop, Rishma. *Reading Like a Girl*. Windsor, ON: Black Moss Press, 2004.

Dunlop, Rishma and Priscila Uppal. *Red Silk: An Anthology of South Asian Canadian Women Poets*. Toronto, Mansfield Press, 2004.

Grewal, Inderpal. "Reading and Writing the South Asian Diaspora: Feminism and Nationalism in North America." *Our Feet Walk the Sky*, edited by the Women of South Asian Descent Collective, 226–236. San Francisco: Aunt Lute Books, 1993.

Lahiri, Jhumpa. *The Interpreter of Maladies: Stories*. Boston: Houghton Mifflin, 1999.

Mohanty, Chandra. "Defining Genealogies: Feminist Reflections on Being South Asian in North America." *Our Feet Walk the Sky: Women of the South Asian Diaspora*, edited by the Women of South Asian Descent Collective, 351–358. San Francisco: Aunt Lute Books, 1993.

Mukherjee, Bharati. *Darkness*. Markham, ON and New York: Penguin, 1985.

Mukherjee, Bharati. "Two Ways to Belong in America." *The New York Times*, September 22, 1996.

Rushdie, Salman. *East, West*. Toronto: Vintage, 1996.

Vasudeva, Amita. "Can You Talk Mexican?" *Our Feet Walk the Sky: Women of the South Asian Diaspora*, edited by the Women of South Asian Descent Collective, San Francisco: Aunt Lute Books, 1993.

15
The Unwelcome Child
Elizabeth Eckford and Hannah Arendt

VICKY LEBEAU

Little Rock, Arkansas, 4th September 1957. It's a warm Wednesday morning, between eight and nine o'clock. A young black girl, walking towards the imposing front of Central High School, is about to enter into the visual history of the civil rights movement (Figure 1). She is Elizabeth Eckford, fifteen years old, one of the 'Little Rock Nine': nine black students—six girls, three boys—at the centre of the campaign to end the segregation of public schooling in the United States. Eckford has been told to go into the school by the front entrance, but it is blocked by what radio and television broadcasts have been describing as the 'large crowd' gathering at the school (Bates 1966). That crowd—'Hundreds of Little Rock citizens', as one broadcaster puts it—is supplemented by the National Guard, called in by Orval Faubus, Governor of Arkansas. 'Faubus calls National Guard to Keep School Segregated', ran the headline in the *Arkansas Gazette* on Tuesday, 3rd September—a headline that contributed to the NAACP's decision to postpone for one more day the black students' entry to Central High School. There had been late-night telephone calls to families, arranging a safe meeting-point for the students on the following morning. 'Perhaps we would be accompanied by several ministers', Melba Beals recalls in her account of the campaign to integrate Central High; 'some of them would be white' (Beals 1994: 41). Elizabeth Eckford's family had no telephone; she did not receive the call.

The photographs of Elizabeth Eckford's encounter with the segregationists—the Arkansas National Guard, the hundreds of white men, women and children lining the streets around the school—gave vivid, and painful, form to the struggle for legal equality at the heart of the civil rights movement through the 1950s and 1960s. For Will Counts, whose images helped to define the national and international response to Little Rock, the 'crisis began as National Guardsmen allowed a white student to pass through their line while Elizabeth Eckford was directed away' (Counts 1999: 36). Counts's photographs—almost, at times, a type of cinema: using the then new Nikon S2, Counts was able to shoot thirty-six exposures without reloading film—track Eckford's attempts to pass through the guards and, then, with the protestors closing in around her, to escape the hostile crowd. 'The law is white', wrote Richard Wright, in 1941, in response to another photograph: the body of a lynched black man (Wright 1947: 44). That 'white law'—the law of 'separate but equal'

Fig. 1 Elizabeth Eckford is heckled as she walks away from Little Rock's Central High on 4th September 1957.

announced in *Plessy v. Ferguson* in 1896, the law of 'Judge Lynch' in its most perverse manifestation—is there in the images of the mob at Eckford's heels, 'clustered about my friend's head like bouquets of grotesque flowers', as Beals recalls it (Beals 1994: 83). 'The women were shouting, "Get her! Lynch her!"' Benjamin Fine, an editor on *The New York Times*, reported to NAACP activist, Daisy Bates (Bates 1966: 405). 'They came closer, shouting, "No nigger bitch is going to get in our school. Get out of here!"' Eckford herself told Bates. 'I turned back to the guards but their faces told me I wouldn't get help from them' (ibid.: 408–9). It was a devastating blow. 'I kept thinking that the guards would protect me', Eckford insists, as if unable to believe that that loss of distinction between protector and persecutor is part of the horror of what is happening to her on the steps of Central High (ibid.). Raising their bayonets to block her access to the school, the soldiers drove Eckford back into the crowd. 'Not one of those white adults attempted to rescue Elizabeth', Beals concludes her version of the story. 'The hulking soldiers continued to observe her peril like spectators enjoying a sport' (Beals 1994: 50).

It's a stark moment, one that carries the threat of unchecked violence against the body, and spirit, of a black child. On the one hand, the presence of the Arkansas National Guard proclaims the state of emergency, a suspension of normal law and order (Faubus's conviction that 'it will not be possible to restore or maintain order and protect the lives and property of the citizens if forcible integration is carried out' [ibid: 38]). On the other hand, what Counts has captured is an image of *unequal protection before the laws*, one that puts into question the democratic and integrationist ideal symbolised by *Brown v. Board of Education of Topeka*, the Supreme Court decision, handed down on 17th May 1954, that paved the way for desegregation of public education in Little Rock: 'Segregation of white and Negro children in the public schools of a State solely on the basis of race, pursuant to state laws permitting or requiring such segregation, denies to Negro children the equal protection of the laws guaranteed by the Fourteenth Amendment—even though the physical and other "tangible" factors of white and Negro schools may be equal'.[1] As a vision of the law in conflict with itself (the National Guard is at once symbol of resistance to black civil rights and of state resistance to the Supreme Court), Counts's photographs of Elizabeth Eckford bring into focus its failure to deliver equal *protection* to a black child—*protection*, that is, over and above the appeals to *equality* (equal justice or substantive equality) that, as Robin West argues in her recent study of progressive constitutionalism, have dominated the conflicted interpretations of the equal protection clause (West 1994: 29–30). What is distinctive to the Fourteenth Amendment, West suggests, is the 'idea that the state must and should promise each citizen protection against the violence of others if it is truly to be a constitutional state under the rule of law'—promise and protection whose breach is at the heart of the crisis of Little Rock (ibid.: 30).

That breach, I want to suggest, comes right to the fore in one of the most controversial discussions of Little Rock: Hannah Arendt's 'Reflections on Little Rock', published in *Dissent* in 1959. Originally commissioned for *Commentary*, publication of the article was delayed for months, Arendt explains in her 'Preliminary Remarks', 'because of the controversial nature of my reflections'—a controversy, generated by Arendt's refusal to give unqualified support to the struggle for integration in schools, closely associated with media images of Little Rock (Arendt 1959: 45). 'No one', Arendt insists, 'will find it easy to forget the photograph reproduced in newspapers and magazines throughout the country, showing a Negro girl, accompanied by a white friend of her father, walking away from school, persecuted and followed into bodily proximity by a jeering and grimacing mob of youngsters' (ibid.: 50). Arendt gives no further details of the photograph that she has in mind, but her description of its narrative movement—the impression of following a young black girl from one frame to another, of accompanying her from within the crowd—indicate Counts's sequential images of Elizabeth Eckford, the public imagination to which such documents make their appeal, or, more strongly, that they help to form. 'The press photograph', as Roland Barthes puts it, 'is a message'—one that aims both to elicit, and to structure, a response (Barthes 1977: 7). 'Elizabeth Eckford's trials', as Mary L. Dudziak points out, 'appeared on front pages around the world', while Melba Beals recalls a 'pitiful closeup photograph of Elizabeth' accompanying an advertisement paid for by a white man from Arkansas: 'If you live in Arkansas, study this picture and know shame. When hate is unleashed and bigotry finds a voice, God help us all' (Dudziak 2000: 119; Beals 1994: 83).

It's a familiar idea of the documentary photograph as a representation bound to the worlds of feeling—shame, anger, fear, pity—and politics, or, perhaps, to the possibilities for political feeling.[2] In her writings on Little Rock, Arendt grapples with that possibility, offering her readers a remarkable insight into the political and affective life of an image that staked its claim to a place in the public discourses on racism and civil rights. Arendt's tone is at once angry, impatient and empathetic, as if the image of Eckford is engraved on her mind, stalling the work of forgetting its pain ('no-one will find it easy to forget'). 'The girl, obviously, was asked to be a hero', Arendt continues, '—that is, something neither her absent father nor the equally absent representatives of the NAACP felt called upon to be' (Arendt 1959: 50). It's a harsh, and hasty, judgement. 'Miss A.', writes Melvin Tumin, one of her most bitter respondents in the bitter debate that followed, 'obviously knows little or nothing about what actually happened in Little Rock' (Tumin 1959: 70).[3] By all accounts, the black students' parents and families had been told to stay away from the school—'It will be easier to protect the children if adults aren't there', as School Superintendent Virgil Blossom had put it—while the NAACP had attempted to accompany a group of integrating students into Central High by another entrance (Beals 1994: 41; Bates 1966). This is a type of factual truth (in Arendt's own terms, the most politically relevant form of truth) not reflected in her initial response to Little Rock ('She has', as Ralph Ellison comments in interview with Robert Penn Warren in 1964, 'absolutely no conception of what goes on in the minds of Negro parents when they send their kids through those lines of hostile people'); it's a truth vulnerable to Arendt's apparent preoccupation with the idea of a child who has lost the protection of home and community, a child exposed too soon to the world (Arendt 1993: 232; Penn Warren 1965: 342). Looking at the images from Little Rock, Arendt turns *that* child into the subject of her story, investing a brief, but tantalising, narrative which remarks (appears to be driven by) a felt absence of the black family and community, of black and white citizens prepared to act as adults—or, more strongly, as heroes. To put the point another way: her obscure reference to that 'white friend' of Elizabeth Eckford's father (not mentioned in other accounts of Eckford's ordeal) suggests the force of Arendt's own desire to find the hero, the 'strong man', somewhere in this story; that is, her imaginative projection into Counts's photograph.[4] 'The sorry fact was', Arendt concludes, 'that the town's law-abiding citizens left the streets to the mob, that neither white nor black citizens felt it their duty to see the Negro children safely to school' (Arendt 1959: 49).

The pressure of that 'fact' agitates through Arendt's response to the sense of loneliness, and abandonment, carried by the figure of Elizabeth Eckford—a response that, in both 'Reflections on Little Rock' and 'A Reply to Critics', published in a subsequent issue of *Dissent*, casts the crisis of Little Rock as a crisis of childhood. 'Have we now come to the point', Arendt wonders, 'where it is the children who are being asked to change or improve the world?' (ibid.: 50). As various commentators have pointed out, that question depends on Arendt's fine, and contentious, distinctions between the private, the social and the political spheres, on her idea of the school as an institution there to support the child's move from home and family to the public life of the world.[5] 'Children are first of all part of family and home', she writes in 'Reflections on Little Rock', 'and this means that they are, or should be, brought up in that atmosphere of idiosyncratic exclusiveness which alone makes a home a home, strong and secure enough to shield its young against the demands of the social and the responsibilities of the political realm' (ibid.: 55). Home as security, social as demand (the realm of free association, legitimate discrimination), politics as responsibility: the distribution of terms is decisive to Arendt's interpretation of the predicament of Little Rock as one in which children are asked to bear the political, and properly adult, burden of desegregation—to become, as Elisabeth Young-Bruehl puts it, 'the avant-garde of integration' (Young-Bruehl 1982: 311).

Writing to protect her idea of the child, writing, too, to protect her idea of society, Arendt's reflections on Little Rock lend themselves all too easily to that 'cry of protest' (to borrow Martin Luther King's phrasing) against the use of children in civil rights actions. 'Where had these writers been', King wonders in *Why We Can't Wait* in 1963, '… during the centuries when our segregated social system had been misusing and abusing Negro children?' (King 2000: 86). That question echoes Ellison's well-known response to Arendt, his sense that, in her criticisms of the black community, she has failed to grasp the everyday 'terrors of social life' for black men, women and children, the 'ideal of sacrifice' to which such terrors give rise (Penn Warren 1965: 342). In fact, on reading his interview with Penn Warren, Arendt would acknowledge the cogency of Ellison's criticism, her own sense of being 'somehow wrong' about Little Rock, the challenge of its 'stark violence' to her ways of thinking about the conditions of being human in the modern world (Arendt 1965). 'You are entirely right', she writes to Ellison on 29th July 1965, 'it is precisely this "ideal of sacrifice" which I didn't understand'—a forthright concession that begins to refract Arendt's insistence on the child's right to protection from home and community through the difference of being a black child (ibid.). In this case, as Ellison indicates, the best form of protection may well be pain: 'the child is expected to face the terror and contain his fear and anger precisely because he is a Negro American … It is a harsh requirement, but if he fails this basic test, his life will be even harsher' (Penn Warren 1965: 343).

It's a conclusion that begins to take the measure of the distortion introduced into Arendt's concepts, her idea of childhood, by the fact of racism in the United States. 'But, of course', wrote Nella Larsen in 1929, reflecting on one 'passing' mother's complex response to the threat of giving birth to a black baby, 'nobody wants a dark child'—a not-wanting reflected, in all its obviousness, by the lurid vision of miscegenation at the heart of segregationist resistance to the presence of black children in 'white' schools: 'What Race Mixers Are Planning for Us' was the topic addressed at one nighttime rally organised by the Central High Mothers' League at the beginning of 1958 (Larsen 1989: 168; Beals 1994: 234). That vision, in turn, recalls Arendt's (again controversial) critique of liberal unwillingness to confront the fundamental threat to sexuality and sexual freedom—that is, in Arendt's terms, to basic human rights—carried by the legal sanction of state interference in the domain of private life in the South. Why, she asks, is the campaign to end both legal and social segregation of education silent on the 'most outrageous law of Southern states': namely, the laws in 29 of the 49 states which criminalised intermarriage and miscegenation (Arendt 1959: 49)? On this topic, Arendt's critics were at once pragmatic and dismissive. 'We must carefully distinguish what it is possible to obtain *now*', warned David Spitz, while Sidney Hook, in a letter published in *Dissent* in March 1959, described Arendt's 'extreme positions ... that Negroes should give priority to agitation for equality in the bedroom rather than to equality in education' (Spitz 1960: 64; Hook 1959: 203). Unperturbed, Arendt refused to give way. Little Rock, she insisted in 'A Reply to Critics', may be nothing more—and, one might add, nothing less—than an attempt to 'avoid the real issue': 'All parties concerned knew very well that nothing was being achieved under the pretext that something was being done' (Arendt 1959a: 181).

The fact that, by 1964, just 1.2% of black children in the South were attending 'white' schools—the *Brown II* decision for desegregation 'with all deliberate speed' openly flouted by 'all deliberate delay', as Davis and Graham put it—lends some purchase to Arendt's sense that what is happening in Little Rock is a displacement of the struggle for the rights of sexuality onto a campaign for the rights of black children to a desegregated education (the Supreme Court did not rule on the constitutionality of laws against miscegenation until the mid-1960s) (Davis and Graham 1995: 125). Comparing the reluctance of American liberals to confront the issue of the marriage laws in the Southern states to the 'earlier reluctance of the founders of the Republic to follow Jefferson's advice and abolish the crime of slavery', Arendt runs the debate on schooling and segregation—debate stymied, on her view, by the 'routine repetition of liberal clichés'—into a consideration of the rights of black and white adults to desire one another, to establish the private realm of the home, to 'insert a new world into the existing world' (as she describes the birth of the lovers' child in *The Human Condition* in 1958) (Arendt 1959a: 180; 1959: 45; 1959b: 218). To push the point, if the displacement of sexuality represents a failure (however pragmatic, however necessary) of political vision, it also begins to bring into focus the black child as figure of the unwanted—a figure shadowing *both* the laws against inter-racial marriage *and* the more or less virulent resistance to integrated schooling across the Southern States.[6] In this sense, distinct from a liberal protest, Arendt's commitment to the rights of sexuality and sexual desire, including the right to want a 'dark child', catches her writing up into an attempt to find a language adequate to the pain that she begins to identify in the photographs of Elizabeth Eckford. 'My first question', she recalls at the beginning of 'A Reply to Critics', describing again the impact of media images from Little Rock, 'was: what would I do if I were a Negro mother? The answer: under no circumstances would I expose my child to conditions which made it appear as though it wanted to push its way into a group where it was not wanted' (Arendt 1959a: 179).

A strange moment, this, with Arendt attempting to counter the charge that, in making a distinction between the *legal* segregation of education (to which she is clearly opposed) and the *social* custom of segregation in schools, she has failed to grasp the importance of education to the struggle for black equality. For Arendt, by contrast, what the photographs of Elizabeth Eckford reveal is what the campaign for civil rights has refused to grasp: as a *social fact* segregation bears on the concept not of rights but of unwantedness—a 'typically social predicament', Arendt explains, and one harder to bear than its political counterpart, outright persecution (ibid). Arendt's adherence to that distinction between public and social life would continue to beleaguer her readers ('I have always asked myself', acknowledged Mary McCarthy, one of Arendt's closest friends, in 1972: '"What is somebody supposed to do on the public stage, in the public space, if he does not concern himself with the social?"' [McCarthy cited in Bernstein 1985: 250]). But, outrageous though it was to some of her critics, Arendt's distinctive response—her wish to make a distinction—is also intuitive, echoing a theme that runs through various accounts of Little Rock. Melba Beals, for example, recalls comments from family and friends, as well as opponents, on her decision to try to integrate Central High: 'I don't know why you'd want to go where you're not wanted'; 'None of this would be necessary if you'd stayed out of that white school where you're not wanted'; 'He asked me what did I expect when I came to a place where I knew I wasn't welcome' (Beals 1994: 38; 70; 246).

The callousness of the question exposes the cruelty of the dilemma: the situation of being unwanted is not open to change, or challenge, by the one cast out; on the contrary, the very wish to challenge those who fail to welcome you appears to put you at fault. In other words, what Arendt is struggling to identify, and to address, is a form of anguish that cannot find expression in the (political) language of rights and right reason, of equality and representation. Its domain is more fundamental, more natal, because what is coming under attack is 'whatever we happen to be by the accident of birth' (Arendt 1959a: 179). This is not a burden, Arendt insists, to be borne by a child—as if, to push the point, protection due to a child is always protection against the accident of having been born.

'Children who are received in a harsh and unloving way', writes Sándor Ferenczi in 1929, reflecting on the idea of the 'unwelcome child', 'die easily and willingly' (Ferenczi 1999: 271). Read alongside Arendt's reflections on Counts's images of the destructiveness of Southern white racism, it's an unsettling claim, one that may bring us closer to the demand—at once affective and political—carried by, transferred by, the photographs of Elizabeth Eckford. Refusing to give way on her distinction between legal and social discrimination—the idea of unwantedness she derives from that distinction—Arendt brings into focus the 'terrors of social life' (to borrow Ellison's phrase again) in a racist culture, the terrors that Counts's photographs help to reveal: racist hatred as an attack that aims at the black child's right to be born, at his or her right to *be*. It is an attack that draws Arendt into the work of representative thinking, *of revealing herself representing to herself not the actual but the possible viewpoints of others*: black mother, black child (and, later, white mother, white child). Arendt has been criticised for her presumption at this moment in her 'Reply', for her racist assumption, as Meili Steele puts it, of a 'common world that is in good enough shape to articulate and draw together her own position and that of black mothers' (Steele 2002: 187). Certainly, if that assumption is there, Arendt herself is about to expose it (her immediate identification, for example, between equality of opportunity in education and an 'affair of social climbing') (Arendt 1959a: 180).[7] But there may be more at issue for Arendt, for her readers, when she offers us this brief glimpse into what happens when she allows her imagination to 'go visiting', when she uses her imagination—uses her *mind*—in an attempt to respond to that image of attack on a black child (Arendt 1982: 43). Arendt, as Julia Kristeva points out, was often accused of being 'unsympathetic', 'callous', in her writings on public and political events (Little Rock, the Eichmann trial, are Kristeva's first examples) (Kristeva 2001: 114). Breaching liberal consensus on the evils of segregation, both 'Reflections on Little Rock' and 'A Reply to Critics' leave Arendt vulnerable to such a charge—at the same time as they open up a space for *thinking* on the cusp between feeling and politics, between empathy and the struggle for political change. At issue is the process of representation crucial to Arendt's understanding of political thought: 'I form an opinion by considering a given issue from different viewpoints', she writes in 'Truth and Politics' in 1967, 'by making present to my mind the standpoints of those who are absent; that is, I represent them' (Arendt 1993: 241).

Identification, empathy—the attempt to be or to feel like somebody else (Arendt's phrasing)—are absolutely essential to that act of representation, but they do not exhaust it; that is, representation is not exhausted by empathy. As Carolyn J. Dean suggests, the notion that 'we are currently "numb" and inured to suffering is by now commonplace', an indifference, an 'emotional "death"', intimately associated with the ubiquity of the image—even, perhaps especially, the image of a child in pain (Dean 2003: 111; 88).[8] 'The power of *images* of children', writes Lesley Caldwell in her recent introduction to *The Elusive Child*, 'inscribes the indignation and helplessness of the adult world … the response of the helpless and *not* responsible adult faced with devastation produced by other adults' (Caldwell is commenting specifically on the insistent use of children in representations of violent conflict) (Caldwell 2002: 7; 8). Helplessness, irresponsibility: it is as if the spectator is overwhelmed by her own capacity for identification with and as a child, by a proximity that moves her to distress, certainly, but also towards passivity ('a sort of passive, somewhat simplistic acknowledgement of resignation at the failures of society', as Caldwell puts it [ibid.: 8]). By contrast, 'being and thinking in my own identity where actually I am not' is how Arendt formulates the political aim of representation: not blind submission to the thoughts and feelings of others (in which one subjectivity is displaced by another, in which the self is lost in the image) but an opening of the mind, of the 'I', to what, and who, it is not (Arendt 1993: 241). It is difficult to think, to imagine, such an opening. But it may be that Arendt's commitment to the possibility of being and thinking 'where I am not', her demonstration of that commitment in her 'Reflections on Little Rock', provide one possible model for the work of sustaining thought, sustaining imagination, in the face of pain.

Notes

1. One of the most significant decisions in the history of the civil rights movement, *Brown v. Board of Education*, 347 U.S. 483 (1954) brought the 'hearts and minds' of black children (its well-known appeal to modern 'psychological knowledge') into contact with the equal protection clause of the Fourteenth Amendment (the legal basis for its decision). Struggling to find a form of law able to respond to the less 'tangible' effects of segregation, *Brown v. Board of Education* appears to extend the reach of the Fourteenth Amendment, its guarantee of equal protection before the laws, into the realm of psychic and affective life. The key sentence comes towards the end of Chief Justice Warren's statement of the Court's opinion: 'To separate them [children in grade and high schools] from others of similar age and qualifications solely because of their race generates a feeling of inferiority as to their status in the community that may affect their hearts and minds in a way unlikely ever to be undone.' The text of *Brown v. Board of Education* is available at http://caselaw.lp.findlaw

2. On the concept of political feeling—crucial to recent rereadings of Kant's *Critique of Judgement*—see see Meyler (2000). In a review of Anthony Cascardi's *Consequences of Enlightenment* (Cambridge UP: 1999), Meyler notes that, in her *Lectures on Kant's Political Philosophy* (1970), Arendt 'attempted to derive a Kantian account of the political from the *Critique of Judgement*'—an account of politics that, as Meyler suggests, may be inseparable from the figure of the spectator as bearer of aesthetic and moral feeling (Meyler 2000: 26; 34). It's a topic that exceeds the scope, and competence, of this paper, but Arendt's attention to the *image* of Elizabeth Eckford could be read as a contribution to discussions of Kant's legacy to contemporary understanding of the complex ties between politics and spectatorship, taste and feeling. For further discussion see: Lyotard 1991; Nussbaum 1995; Kristeva 2001; Shell 2002).

3. In her 'A Reply to Critics', Arendt describes Tumin as having 'put himself outside the scope of discussion and discourse through the tone he adopted in his rebuttal' (Arendt 1959a: 179). The debate with David Spitz, Sidney Hook and various correspondents can be followed through the Winter and Spring issues of *Dissent* (1959).

4. That projection can be read alongside Arendt's later comments on the human 'instinct of submission' in *On Violence*: 'If we would trust our own experiences in these matters, we should know that the instinct of submission, an ardent desire to obey and be ruled by some strong man, is at least as prominent in human psychology as the will to power' (Arendt 1970: 39). Peg Birmingham comments briefly on this passage in the course of a discussion of Arendt's implicit acknowledgement of the 'alchemy between fear and authority, at the heart of the human psyche' and the potential for dialogue between Arendt's 'politics of natality' and Julia Kristeva's concept of abjection (Birmingham 2003: 92).

5. See Bohman (1996) for a summary of this debate.

6. In this context, it is worth noting the experience of six-year-old Ruby Bridges who, in 1960, became the first African American child to desegregate an elementary school, in New Orleans. For over a year, she was educated in a 'class of one' as white parents boycotted the school and all but one teacher refused to teach a black child. See Morris (2001) for a detailed account of the struggle for desegregation in Arlington, Virginia.

7. Young-Bruehl suggests that Arendt's Jewishness is decisive to her interpretation of what happens in Little Rock, her response to Eckford—and, in particular, her comments on the black mother and child. For further discussion see Young-Bruehl (1982) and Steele (2002).
8. Certainly, Counts's photographs of Elizabeth Eckford have been routinely invoked to symbolise the violence, and hatred, of cultural life. In this sense, the image *works*, its transfer to new people, to new places, evidence of its capacity to secure the innocence and helplessness of childhood. 'TEARS OF INNOCENT CHILDREN; MOB HURLS STONES AT FOUR-YEAR-OLDS AS THEY START SCHOOL IN CITY OF HATE' was the headline to *The Mirror*'s report on sectarian violence against Catholic schoolchildren in September 2001—a report that began with an immediate association between the four-year-old children confronting the mob in Ardoyne and Eckford's ordeal in Arkansas. Deidre Tynan and Ted Oliver sustain that comparison throughout their report: 'But in scenes reminiscent of Alabama in America's deep south 40 years ago, a path through centuries of bigotry, decades of violence and months of rising tension had to be cleared to allow children to reach their desks for the first time' (*The Mirror*, Tuesday, 4th September 2001, pp. 4–5).

References

Arendt, H. (1959) 'Reflections on Little Rock', *Dissent* vol. 6 (issue 1): 45–56.
————. (1959a) 'A Reply to Critics', *Dissent* vol. 6 (issue 2): 179–181.
————.(1959b) *The Human Condition*. New York: Doubleday Anchor Books.
————.(1965) Hannah Arendt to Ralph Ellison, 29th July 1965, The Hannah Arendt Papers at the Library of Congress; available via http://memory.loc.gov/ammem/arendthtml/arendthome.html.
————.(1970) *On Violence*. San Diego and New York: Harcourt Brace & Company.
————.(1982) *Lectures on Kant's Political Philosophy*. Brighton: Harvester Press.
————.(1993) 'Truth and Politics' (first published 1967), in *Between Past and Future: Eight Exercises in Political Thought*, pp. 227–264. Harmondsworth: Penguin.
Barthes, R. (1977) 'The Photographic Message', in S. Heath (ed.) *Image—Music –Text*, pp. 15–31. London: Fontana.
Bates, D. (1966) *The Long Shadow of Little Rock*. New York: McKay.
Beals, M. (1994) *Warriors Don't Cry*. New York and London: Washington Square Press.
Bernstein, R. (1985) *Philosophical Profiles: Essays in a Pragmatic Mode*. Philadelphia: U. of Pennsylvania.
Birmingham, P. (2003) 'Holes of Oblivion: The Banality of Radical Evil', *Hypatia* vol. 18 (issue 1): 80–103.
Bohman, J. (1996) 'The Moral Costs of Political Pluralism: The Dilemmas of Difference and Equality in Arendt's "Reflections on Little Rock", in L. May and J. Kohn (eds.) *Hannah Arendt: Twenty Years Later*, pp. 53–80. London: MIT Press.
Caldwell, L. (ed.) (2002) *The Elusive Child*. London and New York: Karnac.
Counts, W. (1999) *A Life is More than a Moment: The Desegregation of Little Rock's Central High*. Indiana: Indiana UP.
Davis, A. and Graham, B. (1995) *The Supreme Court, Race and Civil Rights*. Thousand Oaks: Sage 1995.
Dean, C. J. (2003) 'Empathy, Pornography, and Suffering', *differences: A Journal of Feminist Cultural Studies* vol. 14 (issue 1): 88–124.
Dudziak, M. L. (2000) *Cold War Civil Rights: Race and the Image of American Democracy*. NJ: Princeton UP.
Ferenczi, S. (1999) 'The Unwelcome Child and His Death Drive', in J. Borossa (ed.) *Sándor Ferenczi: Selected Writings*, pp. 269–274. Harmondsworth: Penguin.
Hook, S. (1959) 'Hannah Arendt's Reflections' (Letters), *Dissent* vol. 6 (issue 2): 203.
Hopkinson, A. (2001) 'Obituary: Will Counts: Photographer who captured an enduring image of America's civil rights struggle in his home town', *The Guardian*, October 16: 24.
King, M. L. (2000) *Why We Can't Wait*. New York: Harper.
Kristeva, J. (2001) *Hannah Arendt*. New York: Columbia UP.
Larsen, N. (1989) *Quicksand and Passing*. London: Serpent's Tail.
Lyotard, J.-F. (1991) '*Sensus communis*: The Subject in *statu nascendi*', in E. Cadava et al. (eds.) *Who Comes After the Subject?*, pp. 217–235. New York and London: Routledge.
Meyler, B. (2000) 'What is Political Feeling?', *diacritics* vol. 30 (issue 2): 25–42.
Morris, McGrath J. (2001) 'A Chink in the Armor: The Black-Led Struggle for School Desegregation in Arlington, Virginia, and the End of Massive Resistance', *The Journal of Policy History*, vol. 13 (issue 3): 329–366.
Nussbaum, M. C. (1995) *Poetic Justice: The Literary Imagination and Public Life*. Boston: Beacon Press.
Penn Warren, R. (1965) *Who Speaks for the Negro?* New York: Random House.
Shell, S. (2002) 'Kant as Propagator: Reflections on *Observations on the Feeling of the Beautiful and Sublime*', in *Eighteenth-Century Studies*, vol. 35 (issue 3): 455–468.
Spitz D. (1959) 'Politics and the Realms of Being', *Dissent* vol. 6 (issue 1): 56–65.
Steele, M. (2002) 'Arendt versus Ellison on Little Rock: The Role of Language in Political Judgment', *Constellations* vol. 9 (issue 2): 184–205.
Tumin, M. (1959) 'Pie in the Sky …', *Dissent* vol. 6 (issue 1): 65–71.
West, R. (1994) *Progressive Constitutionalism: Reconstructing the Fourteenth Amendment*. Durham: Duke UP.
Wright, R. (1947) *Twelve Million Black Voices: A Folk History of the Negro in the United States of America*. London: Lindsay Drummond.
Young-Bruehl, E. (1982) *Hannah Arendt: For Love of the World*. Newhaven and London: Yale UP.

16
How White Teachers Construct Race

CHRISTINE E. SLEETER

In the education literature one finds frequent reference to the fact that the teaching population in the U.S. is becoming increasingly white while the student population becomes increasingly racially diverse. Over the last two decades, a lively discourse has emerged that examines and critiques how white teachers think about race (e.g., Berlak and Moyenda, 2001; Obidah and Teel, 2001; McIntyre, 1997). To attempt to bridge the gap between white teachers and students of color, teacher education programs have added coursework, field experiences, and other activities.

At the same time, the standards-based reform movement is rapidly silencing these discussions. For example, in California, the state has conceptualized teacher education as preparing teachers to deliver state-mandated content to all students; its new standards continually repeat the phrase "state adopted content standards," while having virtually deleted the concepts "multicultural," "culturally relevant," and "bilingual." In January 2004, I attempted an ERIC search for journal articles using the keywords "no child left behind" and "race." Ninety-five articles surfaced from the keywords "no child left behind," and 4617 from the keyword "race." However, none surfaced when both terms were entered. Inadequate though policies and practices addressing race in education might have been ten years ago, the standards-based reform movement has shifted discussion away from race, except when disaggregating student test scores.

In this chapter I argue that race matters because teachers to bring to the classroom interpretations of students and their communities, and their location within a hierarchical society, that are informed heavily by assumptions about race and ethnicity. I locate this chapter within a body of literature that examines how schools reproduce structures of inequality and oppression and that advocates schools undergoing fundamental restructuring for all students (see, for example, Banks and Banks, 2004; Cummins, 1996; Nieto, 1992; Macedo and Bartolomé, 1999; Oakes and Lipton, 1999; Sleeter and Grant, 2003). I will argue that teachers bring to the profession perspectives about what race means, by examining perspectives of teachers of European descent. I will show how a predominantly white teaching force in a racist and multicultural society is not good for anyone, if we wish to have schools reverse rather than reproduce racism.

Theoretical Perspectives about Racism

To "solve" racism by educating whites is to locate racism mainly in biased individual actions, which in turn are assumed to stem from ideas and assumptions in people's heads: prejudiced attitudes, stereotypes, and lack of information about people of color. A psychological view of racism assumes that if we can change what is in the heads of white people, they in turn will create significant changes in institutions. Viewing racism as prejudice and misperception assumes "that racist attitudes are very rarely rational. Even in those cases where the attitudes are regarded as rational, they are not considered to be in the interests of the person expressing them" (Wellman, 1977, p. 14). With more information, white people will abandon racist ideas and behaviors and (presumably) work to eliminate racism.

Educational approaches to addressing racism usually adopt this theoretical perspective. However, educators who try to teach white people about racism usually experience tenacious resistance. Results of studies of preservice and in-service education about multicultural teaching report mixed findings, at best. While some studies find white students' attitudes to improve somewhat immediately after receiving instruction, other studies do not find an improvement. Further, the research has not investigated the extent to which attitude change persists or improves classroom teaching (e.g., Bondy, Schmitz, and Johnson, 1993; Haberman and Post, 1992; Martin and Koppelman, 1991; McDiarmid, 1992).

By contrast, a structural analysis views racism not as misperception but as a structural arrangement among racial groups. Racist institutions, according to Frederickson, are controlled by whites, who restrict the access of nonwhites to "power and privileges" (1981, p. 240), in order to retain and regulate "a reservoir of cheap and coercible labor for the rest of the country" (p. 245). While a psychological analysis of racism focuses on what is in people's heads and asks how to change it, a structural analysis focuses on distribution of power and wealth across groups and on how those of European ancestry attempt to retain supremacy while groups of color try to challenge it. A structural analysis assumes that how white people view race rests on their vested interest in justifying their power and privileges. White people's common sense understandings of race "are ideological defenses of the interests and privileges that stem from white people's position in a structure based in part on racial inequality" (Wellman, 1977, p. 37).

A structural analysis of racism suggests that education will not produce less racist institutions as long as white people control them. As Beverly Gordon has argued, expecting white educators to reconstruct racist institutions ignores the fact that they face

> the sticky dilemma of attempting to educate the masses in a way that allows them accessibility to high status knowledge and places them on an equal footing to compete. Most assuredly in time, they will compete with our children and ostensibly with us for a share of the power and the reallocation of resources. And while most people do have good intentions, when our social status is threatened, we tend to become even more conservative in order to protect our material gains. (1985, p. 37)

In what follows, I will discuss data from a study of a staff development program to illustrate how white teachers process education about race. I will argue that it is important to educate white people as well as people of color about racism, but not with the assumption that white people on their own will then reconstruct racist institutions. As a white teacher educator, I do not believe most of us will do that. After discussing how white teachers construct race, I will then attempt to refocus discussion about the implications of the "whitening" of the teaching force and the role of teacher education.

A Study of Teachers

In 1987 a colleague and I secured funding to offer what became a voluntary two-year staff development project for thirty teachers in schools in which at least one-third of the students were from low-income or racial minority (mostly African American or Latino) families. Twenty-six of the teachers were Euro American, three were African American, and one was Mexican American. They taught in grade levels ranging from preschool through high school (most taught grades one–six); seven taught special education, two taught English as a second language, and the rest taught in the general education program.

The teachers attended nine all-day staff development sessions during the first year of the study and five sessions during the second year. The sessions were conducted by a series of outside consultants and addressed a variety of topics such as demographic changes, culture and learning style, curriculum, working with parents, and cooperative learning. My main role was to conduct classroom observations and interviews with the teachers over the two-year period to find out what they were learning, what sense they were making of the sessions, and how they were relating the material to their teaching and their understanding of their students. The staff development sessions, research methods, and findings are described in detail elsewhere (Sleeter, 1992).

The teachers taught in two contiguous school districts located in two small cities in the Rust Belt that had developed as industrial manufacturing centers. Both cities—New Denmark and Gelegenheit (pseudonyms)—were established in the mid-1880s, when "Old Immigrants" from northern and western Europe and the British Isles, as well as Yankees from New England, came to the area to better their lives, in the process pushing Native people off the land. In the early 1900s a second wave of "New Immigrants" from southern and eastern Europe were encouraged to come to the area to work as industrial laborers. Throughout most of the 1900s descendants of the second wave of immigrants engaged in various forms of conflict with descendants of "Old Immigrants"; for example, they unionized; they combated prejudice and disdain in the community; and they created community organizations to resist attempts to "Americanize" them (Buenker, 1976; 1977). Many teachers in the community were descendants of both waves of immigrants and could draw on their own family histories to understand how mobility is achieved in the U.S.

Although small numbers of African Americans and Mexican Americans had lived in the communities since the 1800s, these groups did not begin to grow significantly until the 1960s. By the late 1980s New Denmark's population was about eighteen percent African American and eight percent Latino, and Gelegenheit's was about six percent African American and six percent Latino, both minority groups growing much more rapidly than the white population. To most residents, African Americans and Mexican Americans were simply the latest (and not too welcome) newcomers in a series of immigrant groups and would have to engage in the same process of self-help, assimilation, and perseverance that previous groups had experienced.

New Denmark School District had instituted a school desegregation plan in the mid-1970s, accompanied by a series of multicultural education workshops; Gelegenheit School District had not begun to do this. On various indicators, African American and Latino students were experiencing large problems in the schools. For example, in New Denmark a series of newspaper articles (published after the conclusion of this study) reported that white students in one of the cities received a progressively disproportionate share of the "A" grades, from eighty-seven percent in the sixth grade to ninety-one percent in the twelfth (students in the district were sixty-nine percent white). By then, "the percentage of Hispanic and Black students who received four or more D's and F's remained above sixty percent. For majority [white] students, that rate was thirty percent" (Taylor, 1990, p. 5A). However, neither district engaged in much open discussion about this kind of racial problem, even after the series of articles was published.

As is currently the case, the dominant discourse around race during the late 1980s was quite conservative. Nationally the media stressed the United States' loss of undisputed world hegemony. Schools were blamed for being too lax and spreading a "rising tide of mediocrity" (National Commission on Excellence in Education, 1983). News magazines and news programs discussed the most recent immigrants, suggesting that racial and cultural diversity posed new problems for the U.S.; most of the discussion centered around trying to identify what we have in common in order to promote national unity (see, for example, Henry, 1990). The media frequently connected African Americans and Latinos with social problems that many whites regarded as the result of moral depravity: drug use, teen pregnancy, and unemployment. Asian Americans were hailed as the "model minority," portrayed as achieving success in the U.S. through hard work and family cohesiveness (Suzuki and Lou, 1989), following the same route to success that many whites believed their ancestors had followed. Most school reforms that were discussed emphasized raising standards and requiring students to work harder, and the "at risk" discourse emerged to describe those who were falling behind (who were mainly children of color and children from low-income backgrounds). In New Denmark and Gelegenheit School Districts, problems students of color faced in schools were generally conceptualized through a cultural-deficiency perspective in which the main causes of their difficulties were located in their homes and communities (such as parental attitudes, gang influence, and "deficient" language skills), and supplementary programs were provided to remedy presumed deficiencies.

As Wellman (1977) remarked, a paradox of white consciousness is the ability not to see what is very salient: visible markers of social categories that privilege people of European ancestry. Racial boundaries and racial privileges, highly visible and ubiquitous in the U.S., were becoming increasingly so in New Denmark and Gelegenheit. One had only to turn on the TV or drive through the community to see people of European ancestry dominating mainstream institutions and the most desirable resources, while people of non-European ancestries were clustered into the least desirable spaces and rendered through media as either invisible, or satisfied with or deserving of their lot. White people usually seek to explain persistent racial inequality in a way that does not implicate white society. Following, I will focus on how the twenty-six white teachers viewed race.

Race = European Ethnicity

Most of the white teachers in the program interpreted race and multicultural education through the European ethnic experience. As Michael Omi and Howard Winant explain,

> ethnicity theory assigned to blacks and other racial minority groups the roles which earlier generations of European immigrants had played in the great waves of the "Atlantic migration" of the nineteenth and early twentieth centuries. (1986, p. 20)

Ethnicity theory holds that the social system is open and that individual mobility can be attained through hard work. Over time, ethnic ancestry will disappear as a determinant of life chances.

Equating race with European ethnicity provided white teachers with a way to explain mobility in U.S. institutions. A few made direct reference to their own ethnic backgrounds; for example, a daughter of Italian immigrants commented,

> One of my pet peeves, that I know if you want to work, you can work.... I know what my father did when he was in need, ... and we didn't have the free lunches and we didn't have the clothes that other kids wore. (Teacher interview, Dec. 15, 1987)

I asked twenty-two of the white teachers about their fathers' occupations: four fathers had held jobs that normally require college education, two had owned small businesses, and the other sixteen had worked as laborers of various sorts. The teachers had attained upward mobility by earning college degrees and becoming teachers; their own families' life experiences had taught them that mobility is attainable, but not necessarily easy.

Ethnicity theory denies the significance of visible, physiological marks of ancestry and of the history of colonization and harsh subjugation that Europeans and Euro Americans extended over other peoples (Omi and Winant, 1986; Ringer and Lawless, 1989). In so doing it denies white social institutions any complicity in the subordinate status of people of color. White teachers of students of color need some way of understanding why people of color have not done as well as whites have. Teachers generally like their students—including their students of color—and wish to help them. How do white teachers explain racial inequality without either demeaning their students or questioning their own privileges? I observed two strategies: denial of race altogether, and defining students of color as "immigrants."

Denying the Salience of Race

What's the big hang-up, I really don't see this color until we start talking about it, you know. I see children as having differences, maybe they can't write their numbers or they can't do this or they can't do that, I don't see the color until we start talking multicultural. Then, oh yes, that's right, he's this and she's that. (Teacher interview, May 16, 1988)

I really believe that elementary teachers feel that kids are kids…. People would say, "Well, what's your minority breakdown?" And teachers would really have a rough time saying, you know, it was like asking how many of your kids are wearing glasses. (Teacher interview, December 15, 1987)

Rios (1992) asked sixteen teachers in an inner-city high school to think aloud about twelve classroom scenes and then analyzed their responses in terms of the salience of three scene characteristics: student gender, student race, and type of action (instructional, disciplinary, and personal). Student race was the only statistically significant characteristic; student gender and type of action were not. Yet, white teachers commonly insist that they are "color-blind": that they see children as children and do not see race (Lewis, 2001).

Many of the twenty-six white teachers began the program with a "color-blind" perspective, and throughout the two years, seven steadfastly maintained it; by the second year, these teachers' attendance at sessions dwindled because of the program's focus on race. What does it mean to construct an interpretation of race that denies it?

People do not deny seeing what they actually do not see. Rather, they profess to be color-blind when trying to suppress negative images they attach to people of color, given the significance of color in the U.S., the dominant ideology of equal opportunity, and the relationship between race and observable measures of success. Many of the white teachers associated people of color—and particularly African Americans and Latinos—with dysfunctional families and communities, and lack of ability and motivation. Several expressed these associations rather freely in discussions of their students and their parents; for example:

I have a very close family,… [my husband and I] have been very strong disciplinarians and we encourage the work ethic…. I realize how foolish and presumptuous [it is] to think all these kids are coming from the same thing…. Just to have a totally helter-skelter house where there is nothing regular and the people who are your parent figures come and go.... (Teacher interview, May 16, 1988)

All these blacks, they're coming to school late every day. Well, nobody takes care of these children, you know, they have to get up and everything like that. (Teacher interview, December 7, 1988)

For the most part, teachers took for granted that the U.S. social structure is fairly open (after all, they "made it"). Some reacted angrily to suggestions that it is not.

The three ladies up there telling us about their experiences as multicultural people in an all-white class and so on, how they interpreted things, and how it stuck with them today,... I couldn't understand why they ... couldn't understand now that most of those kinds of days are gone.... These are things they are hanging on to years ago. I don't think it is that way any more. (Teacher interview, February 23, 1988)

Most of the white teachers did not focus directly on the distribution of resources across groups or the ideology of equal opportunity. Instead they conceptualized racism as the unfair application of (probably) accurate generalizations about groups to individuals, in a way that biases one's treatment of them. Individuals should be able to succeed or fail on their own merit and should not be held back by "deficiencies" of their race as a whole. As long as a teacher does not know for certain which students will be held back by "cultural deficiencies," it is best to treat them as if one did not see their skin color. Therefore, in an effort not to be racist themselves and to treat all children equally, many white teachers try to suppress what they understand about people of color, which leads them to try not to "see" color.

Trying not to see what is obvious (color) and to suppress the negative and stereotypical imagery with which one is bombarded requires considerable psychological energy. Education about race conflicts with many white teachers' strategies of denial, compounding the psychological energy they must expend to continue being "blind" to color. Many simply avoid such discussions or staff development programs. Some of the teachers who participated in this two-year program did so with ambivalence and resented the attention given in sessions to African Americans and Latinos:

I've had a lot on multicultural, you know, I taught in an inner-city school, and we had a lot about habits of the Hispanic, habits of the blacks, so probably that's kind of redoing it. (Teacher interview, March 24, 1988)

To me, all of the speakers were slanted for blacks or Hispanics only, and I think that's an injustice.... Get Indian children, get their views as to what they feel about American playgrounds and classrooms. (Teacher interview, May 18, 1988)

The teachers perceived staff development on multicultural education as useful if it gave them new information about groups they did not already "know all about," or if it reaffirmed what they were doing in the classroom. However, since they believed they already understood African Americans and Latinos, and since constant and direct attention to these groups surfaced their own negative associations (and possibly guilt), some of the white teachers stopped coming.

Using Culture to Ease the Process of Assimilation

Most of the white teachers who participated in the staff development sessions, and who did not vigorously assert a "color-blind" stance, believed that some degree of mutual cultural adaptation between the school and immigrant and minority communities would ease the transition of students into the dominant culture. While they did not view the dominant culture or its institutions as a problem, they recognized that cultural differences can interfere with the successful transition from one cultural context to another and sought adaptations in their own routines that might facilitate the process for some of their students. As one teacher put it,

> At least we can make a dent in the problem by the methods that we're using in teaching and like changing the style a little bit and trying to adapt to the students, rather than expecting them to make the swing and adapt to the way that we're teaching. (Teacher interview, May 18, 1989)

Several of the staff development sessions provided material from which teachers drew for adaptations, such as two sessions on culture and cognitive style, two sessions on parent involvement, and a session on cooperative learning. Teachers came away from these sessions with a variety of insights about cultural compatibility. Some began to reinterpret students' behavior as cultural rather than as simply "wrong."

> It kind of answers some questions as to why do I have certain students who can't seem to stay in their seats and pay attention.... And why I have some that are a little bit more, you know, quiet and withdrawn.... It doesn't always help me to know exactly what to do with them, but at least I have a little better understanding. (Teacher interview, May 17, 1988)

Several teachers added to their repertoire additional strategies for communicating with parents, such as sending or telephoning home positive messages or translating messages into Spanish. A few stopped insisting that students look them in the eye. Many teachers were intrigued by the possibility that students might enjoy and learn more from cooperative learning than from whole-class or individual teaching strategies.

> I remember the first time that I heard that different kinds of different cultures learned in different ways, it made me remember and think about how some of my kids would be reacting in class sometimes, you know, where they would be helping each other and a couple of instances where kids may have just been helping each other instead of copying. I concluded that they were copying, or cheating. (Teacher interview, February 28, 1988)

Increased use of cooperative learning was the greatest observable impact the staff development program had on the teachers' classroom behavior. By the end of the two-year period about half had begun to use this method. And as we found out in the classroom observations, the proportion of teaching time in which children engaged in cooperative learning and other group work had jumped from eleven to thirteen percent in the first observations to thirty percent in the last. Teachers attributed their interest in cooperative learning to its connection with learning style, the fact that colleagues in their buildings had been trained in it and could provide help, students' positive reactions to it, and their perception that cooperative learning can be broken down into steps to master. Several teachers also liked the fact that cooperative learning could be incorporated into the form and structure of their teaching without changing other things too much.

   These kinds of adaptations do have considerable value, reducing the stress students of color must deal with when the culture of the classroom conflicts with their home culture, and building on strengths and preferences students have for learning. The teachers appear to have accepted the validity of such adaptations because they fit within ethnicity theory, according to which "newcomers" face difficulties due to cultural differences and these difficulties can be eased during the process of transition. I should emphasize that several of the staff development facilitators were African Americans who did not adhere to ethnicity theory and did not regard changes in school process as temporary bridges to ease cultural assimilation. Nevertheless, the facilitators focused on presenting useful strategies, and this had some success in that teachers picked up strategies.

But on a keeper level, most of the teachers retained a tacit assumption that a racial achievement gap is normal. An African American facilitator explicitly voiced her commitment to promoting high achievement among students of color. However, in none of the sessions was there rigorous discussion of what should constitute high achievement. In an interview, when I asked a teacher to compare the achievement of her school with that of a predominantly white suburban school, she interpreted my question as changing the subject from multicultural education to something else (and said, of course, the achievement in her school was lower, what else would one expect?). Subsequent to this study my attempts to get groups of white teachers in New Denmark and Gelegenheit schools to define exactly what should constitute a standard for high achievement in inner-city schools became an interesting study in avoidance behavior. Teachers said, for example, that success is different for different children, that existing measures of achievement are biased and therefore do not count, or that it is irrelevant how they define achievement because their efforts will be undone by the homes or the next teacher students have. Relatively few white teachers argue that inner-city students can and should be achieving at the same levels as white suburban students, a pattern that is consistently found in studies of schools (e.g., Anyon, 1981; Fine, 1991; Grant and Sleeter, 1996).

Schools are one of the main gatekeepers in the allocation of social resources. I suspect that most white teachers are at once unsure how much communities of color (and poor white communities) value education, fearful that well-educated African American, Latino, and Native American students might launch a bold critique of white institutions and white people, and aware that parity in achievement across groups would threaten advantages white people and their children currently enjoy. But few teachers will admit to these fears, and they may not even be conscious of them. Instead, many try to implement strategies that might reduce failure and make the system of schooling work more smoothly, and regard support for these actions as evidence that they are not racist. From the perspective of ethnicity theory, such actions help those on the bottom to gain mobility in an open system. From the perspective of a theory of racial oppression, however, such actions serve mainly to mask the oppressiveness of the education system.

Culture as Symbolic of Family and Individual Differences

Using interviews, Richard Alba (1990) investigated the symbolic meaning white Americans attached to ethnicity in the 1980s. He was interested in why Euro Americans continued to express interest in ethnicity despite the belief that ethnicity in the U.S. no longer structures life chances to any significant degree. What he found describes very well the meanings with which many white teachers infuse multicultural education when they try to work with it in the classroom. Alba argued that Euro Americans view participation in ethnic identity as an individual choice. Euro Americans stress the commonality of ethnic immigrant histories and value expressions of ethnicity that can be shared across ethnic lines: food was the most widespread expression mentioned; holidays, festivals, and related activities were also mentioned. Many whites equated ethnicity with private family history, rather than a group's collective experience. Whites rarely connected ethnicity with social structures, such as neighborhood, friendship group, occupation, or political organizations.

The symbolic meaning Euro Americans attach to ethnicity upholds the ideology of individuality and mobility through hard work within an open system, and the myth that everyone came to the U.S. in search of a better life. It attempts to place all groups on an equal status in which ethnicity is a solely private and voluntary matter. In so doing, this meaning averts a structural analysis of racism and inequality in contemporary U.S. society, implicitly reaffirming the superior position of Euro Americans.

If white teachers wish to regard race and ethnicity in a positive manner, and try to reduce tensions among students in multiracial schools, the Euro American ethnic experience provides a repertoire of concepts to use, focusing on customs a group brought from the "old" country. About half of the white teachers in my study encoded Alba's symbolic expressions of ethnicity into lessons they occasionally added to the "regular" curriculum. Essentially these lessons tried to teach students that one should be proud of family and individual differences and not stereotype others negatively.

Some teachers taught lessons oriented around family heritage. Typically such lessons began with a discussion of where (what country) their families came from, and what customs the family has retained.

> We are talking a lot about their heritage and they have gone back and found all these neat things that are going on in their families, and now they've started bringing in recipes because we're going to make a recipe book from some recipes that have been handed down in their families. (Teacher interview, May 16, 1988)

Several white teachers incorporated food, music, and holidays from different countries into their teaching, although these lessons tended to retain a Eurocentric bias. For example, a music teacher developed a "Children Around the World" concert that was very creative but included more countries from Europe than from any other continent and represented Africa in terms of animals and Tarzan whoops. Some teachers developed lessons comparing the customs of different groups. For example, an English teacher concluded the discussion of a story about a Puerto Rican family with a comparison of customs in New York with those in Puerto Rico, and an ESL teacher had immigrant students compare customs for celebrating holidays in their countries with customs for celebrating Christmas in the U.S. Even Native American experiences were interpreted within the ethnicity paradigm. For example, a fifth-grade teacher taught a social studies lesson about how Indians immigrated over the land bridge from Asia, and later in the year her students read a story about the dancer Maria Tallchief's success in ballet and retention of her Indian name because of pride in her ancestry.

Prejudice and stereotyping were the focus of a few lessons I observed, in which teachers tried to teach students not to apply generalizations incorrectly to other individuals and groups. For example, one teacher had students consider how labels can hurt and limit options. Another taught an extensive unit about prejudice, focusing on the Holocaust and *The Diary of Anne Frank*. Several teachers taught lessons about individual differences and self-concepts, connecting these loosely with race and ethnicity. For example, an elementary teacher had students create personal coats of arms that expressed various positive images about themselves and their families. Another teacher created a classroom flower in which each petal included the name of a student and positive words other students had written about her/him. Role models were another theme of several lessons and classroom decorations. Several teachers occasionally put up posters of famous African Americans or other Americans of color, and their textbooks occasionally featured stories about famous Americans of color.

At times African American students resisted participating in lessons about ethnic origins, and this puzzled the teachers. For example, a teacher who taught a lesson about family heritage remarked that,

> I only have three black students in my room and they have not gone back further than Mississippi, and it's been, no way are they going to go back further.... The one little boy said, "We

didn't come from Africa," that was the first thing he said when we started from where our ancestors came. (Teacher interview, May 16, 1988)

When another teacher began a lesson with a discussion of where students' ancestors came from, she was similarly surprised that no African American students located their ancestry in Africa. During the two-year staff development project, none of the teachers connected such responses with the celebration of Europe and silence about Africa that the school curriculum maintains, or with the media's depiction of Europe as industrialized and "developed" and Africa as "underdeveloped" and "primitive."

I regarded many of the lessons described above as positive experiences for students, and some of them (such as the unit on the Holocaust) very worthwhile. I would critique this body of lessons mainly on the basis of their huge silences and collective implications. By omission they implied that race no longer structures access to resources, and that race is significant only in terms of customs in which anyone can participate. Lessons added token representations of Americans of color (mainly by adding personal knowledge about the students in the classroom) to a curriculum that heavily favored Europe and Euro Americans, without reconstructing students' interpretations of the histories of Americans of color, or their knowledge of Africa, contemporary Latin America, or the pre-Columbian Americas. Even depictions of role models, by focusing on an individual's achievements and ignoring her or his difficulties in attaining them, can suggest that the system is open equally to anyone who will try.

Thus, Americans of color were lumped with immigrants. "Whiteness" was taken as the norm, as natural. When teachers told me about "multicultural lessons" or "multicultural bulletin boards," what they usually drew my attention to were the flat representations of people of color that had been added; multidimensional representations of whiteness throughout the school were treated as a neutral background not requiring comment. In a discussion of Rosaldo's (1989) concept of "cultural stripping," McLaren critiqued whites' naturalization of their identities: "Being white is an entitlement, not to preferred racial attributes, but to a raceless subjectivity. That is, being white becomes the invisible norm for how the dominant culture measures its own civility" (1991, p. 244). Whites so internalize their own power and taken-for-granted superiority that they resist self-questioning. Whites appropriate the idea of culture to mean "sub-categories of whiteness (Irishness, Jewishness, Britishness)" (Dyer, 1988, p. 46), which can be fleshed out in personal subjective meanings or residual expressions of life in other countries and other times. This provides a "positive" as well as nonthreatening template to apply to discussions of race.

Beginnings of Analyses of White-Supremacist Institutions

None of the white teachers constructed a strong critique of white-supremacist institutions during the two-year period, but three of the twenty-six (as well as all four teachers of color) expressed insights that would lead in that direction. One white special education teacher, who had described racism as an attitudinal problem early in the study, began to draw connections between racism and the structure of special education.

[I'm] seeing basically how our system is set up, the value system our whole society is set up on. And it makes me feel like we are here because of a lot of suffering. (Teacher interview, May 19, 1988)

Later in a paper she wrote, "Many cultures and governmental systems have been established on the idea that some people were meant to rule and live in luxury and some were meant to serve and live in poverty and suffering." I did not see her translate these insights into her teaching practice, however, and she dropped the program after the first year.

A second white teacher developed similar insights, locating the beginning of her awareness of racism earlier when teaching in a predominantly black school in a university town, when she realized that the town tried very hard to ignore the existence of the school and its needs. Part of her job as a preschool teacher involved working with parents, and she gradually began to identify with them. After the conclusion of this study she became angry about the district's apparent disinterest in programs for low-income and minority parents, and she began talking about organizing the parents to speak out.

A third white teacher taught several social studies lessons for high school special education students about civil rights and labor issues. I observed her teach a lesson about civil disobedience, focusing on the 1960s; the lesson included ideas such as freedom riders, Black Muslims, lunch counter sit-ins, and racial riots in Detroit and Watts.

Why did these three teachers begin to focus their attention on various aspects of racism and institutional discrimination rather than cultural customs and individual differences? Two taught special education and one taught in a state-funded preschool program; all three occupied positions in the school structure that served populations that schools marginalize, where they found themselves waging battles on behalf of their students against conservative bureaucracies and, often, resistant colleagues. In the last interview, when I asked teachers how much power they believed those who participated in the staff development program had to change the school system, two of these three were the only teachers to discuss organizing and exerting pressure; the others all advocated individual solutions. I would suggest that their experience working in marginalized programs, coupled with participation in the staff development program, helped to politicize frustrations they were experiencing.

Conclusion

The staff development program spanned two years. I have not organized this chapter sequentially because I did not see most white teachers construct a qualitatively new understanding of race over the two-year period. Instead, I saw them select information and teaching strategies to add to a framework for understanding race that they took for granted, which they had constructed over their lifetimes from their position as white people in a racist society.

White people are aware of the efforts they and their families and friends have made to better themselves, and they are aware of the problems they encounter in everyday life. It is in their interest to assume that the problems they face are not unique and that the efforts all people make pay off according to the same rules. "Given the racial and class organization of American society, there is only so much people can 'see.' Positions they occupy in these structures limit the range of their thinking. The situation places barriers on their imaginations and restricts the possibilities of their vision" (Wellman, 1977, p. 235). Spending most of their time with other white people, whites do not see much of the realities of the lives of people of color nor encounter their viewpoints in any depth. Nor do they really want to, since those viewpoints would challenge practices and beliefs that benefit white people.

Faced with the paradox of liking and helping students of color while explaining away the subordination of people of color and adhering to social systems that benefit themselves and their own children, the white teachers I studied responded in patterned ways. Many simply refused to "see" color. Others searched for "positive" associations with race by drawing on the European ethnic experience, which points toward petrified vestiges of immigrant culture that add texture to the fabric of everyday life. Discussing race or multiculturalism meant discussing "them," not the social structure. The staff development program provided material they could draw from, it did not reconstruct their basic interpretation of race.

I write this paper as a Euro American who has struggled with my own understanding of race and who for years has been in the process of learning how to teach white educators about race. It is possible for a white person's understanding of race to undergo marked transformation; I experienced a reconstruction of my own understanding over a period of years, and I know other whites who have done so also. As a teacher educator, I continually seek points of access into how Euro American students view the world. But at the same time, while I believe whites are educable, I have gained appreciation for the strength of our resistance to change. My own color gives me a degree of comfort, privilege, and insulation that serves me in ways I continue to take for granted.

At the same time that discussions of racism are being diluted in the rush to align curricula to new standards and raise achievement scores, the U.S. is engaging in increasingly violent forms of imperialism globally. Imperialism, as Williams (1991) defines it, consists of "the use and abuse, and ignoring, of other people for one's own welfare and convenience" (p. 72). The U.S. gained its territory through violent imperialist expansion. In the last few decades, the form of imperialism shifted from military conquest to economic absorption, as transnational corporations subsumed local economies of nations globally. Although the U.S. never stopped engaging in military strikes against smaller countries, the events of September 11, 2001, seem to have legitimated military conquest of nations of color in the minds of many U.S. citizens. Strong majorities of the public in the predominantly white U.S., Britain, and Australia supported military attack against Iraq, for example, while strong majorities of the public in many other countries around the world condemned the attack (Pew Research Center, 2003). U.S. citizens, and mainly white citizens, seem to be using many the same assumptions discussed in this chapter, to claim entitlement to name realities of people of color globally.

On September 12, 2001, teachers in one of my graduate courses wrestled with the concept of globalization in an open discussion, followed by an email discussion. In general, the international teachers and teachers of color could view the attack against the U.S. from perspectives of people outside the U.S., particularly people of color. In an email discussion, two of the teachers of color wrote:

> How much of how we have behaved in the world community is related to our culture of power and how much of this response is related to the culture of the powerlessness?
>
> P.S. I better be careful to not say this too loudly as there are so many U.S. flags flying all around me.
>
> In looking back at U.S. policies and issues and how we throw our might around for economic gains (although we never say that … its always in the name of democracy and freedom). When the horrific events in Tianamen Square happened, all the U.S. did was voice symbolic support, but that was it. Nothing to be gained, I suppose, by supporting democracy there.

A white teacher voiced the reaction of several other white teachers when she wrote:

> Looking at this time of horror in America within the scope of culture and power is very unsettling to me. Maybe the bottom line is that I am not ready to examine it this closely. I find myself turning a deaf ear when someone gives a negative opinion that we had it coming, and I find myself walking away from that source.

But another white teacher, who had lived for a year in Jordan, was able to take a different perspective. Although she, like the teachers of color, was horrified by the attack, she was also deeply concerned about U.S. use of power globally:

> The longer I spent there, the more I understood that their past experience had taught them to be suspicious of foreigners. Many had lost loved ones in the Six Days War and other skirmishes. They felt that most Americans sided with the Israelis and were not about to take any chances. I visited the Palestinian Refugee Camps and saw first-hand how these displaced people lived in cardboard and tin structures, no plumbing, sewage running down the dirt streets. I taught Palestinian refugee children who had lost parents in the war. I began to understand why distrust ran so high.

It is in her reflection on living in someone else's space, and viewing the dominant white society from someone else's point of view, that we see a way to address whiteness in education.

First, I advocate strongly working to reverse policies that propel mainly white people into the teaching profession, such as the use of the entrance exams, lengthening teacher education programs, and other means of defining standards in ways that penalize rather than reward strengths and resources that teachers of color could bring. This is not to say that white people should not be teachers, but rather that schools and classrooms need to be populated by teachers who bring the different points of view of differently racialized life experiences. Educators of color are much more likely to bring life experiences and viewpoints that critique white supremacy than are white teachers and to engage in activities that challenge various forms of racism (Foster, 1990; Ladson-Billings and Henry, 1990; Su, 1996). They are also less likely to "marginalize minority intellectual discourse" (Gordon, 1990, p. 103). Although peoples of color express a wide range of analyses of racism, the strongest critiques of racism tend to come from communities of color. In my own experience I have found much richer discussions of anti-racist teaching to emerge from multiracial groups, in which whites are present but in the minority, than from predominantly white groups.

Second, white people need to learn about racism and imperialism, as well as about the historic experiences and creative works of diverse non-European groups, and about the wide range of implications for schooling. Lived experience across racial boundaries seems to have the strongest impact on helping whites see another point of view, as quotations by some of the white teachers in this chapter illustrate. For example, structured immersion experiences in which a white person spends at least a month in a community of color, coupled with instruction about racism and the history and culture of that group, and opportunity to get to know adult members of the group personally, can propel serious reexamination of his or her perspective. Education for white teachers should aim to encourage them to work collectively with local communities of color and to construct an ongoing process of learning from and connecting with people of color.

Conceptualized as a form of political organizing, education may be a powerful vehicle to confront racism. An educator qua organizer must directly confront the vested interest white people have in maintaining the status quo, force them to grapple with the ethics of privilege, and refuse to allow them to rest comfortably in apolitical interpretations of race, globalization, and multicultural teaching.

References

Alba, R. D. (1990). *Ethnic identity: The transformation of white America*. New Haven: Yale UP.

Anyon, J. (1981). Social class and school knowledge. *Curriculum Inquiry*, 11, 3–41.

Banks, J. A. & Banks, C. M. (eds.). (2004). *Multicultural education: Issues and perspectives*, 5th ed. New York: Wiley.

Berlak, A. Y. & Moyenda, S. (2001). *Taking it personally*. Philadelphia: Temple University Press.

Bondy, E., Schmitz, S. & Johnson, M. 1993. The impact of coursework and fieldwork on student teachers' reported beliefs about teaching poor and minority students. *Action in Teacher Education* 15 (2): 55–62.

Buenker, J. D. (1976). Immigration and ethnic groups. In J. A. Newenschwander (ed.), *Kenosha County in the 20th century* (pp. 1–50). Kenosha, WI: Kenosha County Bicentennial.

Buenker, J. D. (1977). The immigrant heritage. In N. C. Burkel (ed.), *Racine: Growth and change in a Wisconsin county* (pp. 69–136). Racine, WI: Racine County Board of Supervisors.

Cummins, J. (1996). *Negotiating identities: Education for empowerment in a diverse society.* Ontario, CA: California Association for Bilingual Education.

Dyer, R. (1988). White. *Screen* 29, 44–64.

Fine, M. (1991). *Framing dropouts: Note on the politics of an urban high school.* Albany: SUNY Press.

Foster, M. (1990). The politics of race: Through the eyes of African American teachers. *Journal of Education*, 172 (3), 123–141.

Frederickson, G. M. (1981). *White supremacy: A comparative study in American and South African history.* New York: Oxford UP.

Gordon, B. M. (1985). Teaching teachers: "Nation at risk" and the issue of knowledge in teacher education. *The Urban Review* 17, 33–46.

Gordon, B. M. (1990). The necessity of African-American epistemology for educational theory and practice. *Journal of Education* 172 (3), 88–106.

Grant, C. & Sleeter, C. E. (1996). *After the school bell rings.* London: Falmer Press.

Haberman, M. & Post, L. (1992). Does direct experience change education students' perceptions of low-income minority children? *The Midwestern Educational Researcher* 5 (2), 29–31.

Henry, W. A., III. (1990, April 9). Beyond the melting pot. *Time* pp. 28–31.

Ladson-Billings, G. & Henry, A. (1990). Blurring the borders: Voices of African liberatory pedagogy in the United States and Canada. *Journal of Education* 172 (2), 72–88.

Lewis, A. E. (2001). There is no "race" in the schoolyard: Color-blind ideology in an (almost) all-white school. *American Educational Research Journal* 38 (4): 781–811.

Macedo, D. & Bartolomé, L. I. (1999). *Dancing with bigotry.* New York: St. Martin's Press.

Martin, R. & Koppelman, K. (1991). The impact of a human relations/multicultural education course on the attitudes of prospective teachers. *Journal of Intergroup Relations* 18 (1): 16–27.

McDiarmid, G. W. (1992). What to do about differences? A study of multicultural education for teacher trainees in the Los Angeles Unified School District. *Journal of Teacher Education* 43 (2): 83–93.

McIntyre, A. (1997). *Making meaning of whiteness.* Albany, NY: SUNY Press.

McLaren, P. (1991). Decentering culture: Postmodernism, resistance, and critical pedagogy. In N. B. Wyner (ed.), *Current perspectives on the culture of schools* (pp. 232–257). Boston: Brookline.

National Commission on Excellence in Education. (1983). *A nation at risk.* Washington, DC: U.S. Government Printing Office.

Nieto, S. (1992). *Affirming diversity: The sociopolitical/context of multicultural education.* New York: Longman.

Oakes, J. & Lipton, M. (1999). *Teaching to change the world.* Boston: McGraw-Hill.

Obidah, J. E. & Teel, K. M. (2001). *Because of the kids.* New York: Teachers College Press.

Omi, M. & Winant, H. (1986). *Racial formation in the United States: From the 1960s to the 1980s.* New York: Routledge.

Pew Research Center for the People and the Press. (2003). *Views of a changing world.* Washington, D.C.: Author.

Ringer, B. B. & Lawless, E. R. (1989). *Race-ethnicity and society.* London: Routledge.

Rios, F. A. (1992). Teachers' implicit theories of multicultural classrooms. Doctoral dissertation, University of Wisconsin.

Rosaldo. R. (1989). *Culture and truth: The remaking of social analysis.* Boston: Beacon.

Sleeter, C. E. (1992). *Keepers of the American Dream: A study of staff development and multicultural education.* London: Falmer.

Sleeter, C. E. & Grant, C. A. (2003). *Making choices for multicultural education: Five approaches to race, class, and gender,* 4th ed. New York: Wiley.

Su, Z. (1996). Why teach: Profiles and entry perspectives of minority students as becoming teachers. *Journal of Research and Development in Education* 29 (3): 117–133.

Suzuki, B. H. & Lou, R. (1989). Asian Americans as the "model minority": Outdoing whites? or media hype? *Change* 21 (6), 13–19.

Taylor, B. (1990, April 22). Grade gap grows as students advance through Unified. *Racine Journal Times*, pp. 4A–5A.

Wellman, D. T. (1977). *Portraits of white racism.* Cambridge: Cambridge UP.

Williams, W. A. (1991). Empire as a way of life. *Radical History Review* 50: 71–102.

17

What Puts the "Culture" in "Multiculturalism"?

An Analysis of Culture, Government, and the Politics of Mexican Identity

MARY K. COFFEY

The word *culture* suffuses the discourse on multiculturalism. Much multicultural pedagogy and theory uncritically fetishizes the field of culture, thus partaking in what Steve Fuller has characterized as *hyperculturism* (Fuller 2000, 15–19). Yet even within the multiculturalism literature that eschews these facile positions, culture, a critical category itself, often remains un-interrogated. The "dominant culture," "hegemonic culture," "subaltern cultures," "critical culture," these are just a few of the terms invoked within this literature to examine the historical construction of privilege and difference, the maintenance of power and prejudice, or the quest for resistance and critique. As a crucial term embedded within the rubric under analysis in this volume, "culture" begs a similar rigorous consideration. Perhaps this lack of attention is due to the seeming self-evidence of culture; we all think we know what we are talking about when we use or read the word. However, culture is not simply an empirical phenomenon, and the commonsense approach to it as though it were obscures its relation to value, epistemological pursuits, and subject-formation, all significant concerns for multiculturalism. The lack of a critical genealogical approach to the very term at stake within multiculturalism is my concern in this essay.

The examination of culture and government that follows is drawn from my work on the national culture project in postrevolutionary Mexico. Through an analysis of the imbrication of cultural projects and governmental concerns in the Mexican context, I will elaborate upon a theory of culture and power drawn from Foucault that takes into consideration the relationship between the production of knowledge, subject-formation, and social regulation. In so doing, I want to move away from an emphasis within academia to treat culture as a reflection of truth or conversely as an obstacle to truth in order to understand its constitutive role in the production of truth.

What Is Culture?

What is culture? Two common definitions circulate within and without academia. The first defines culture as an aesthetic phenomenon, restricting it to the intellectual and creative activity of the so-called "best and brightest" of any given society. The second definition emanates from anthropology and describes, in the words of Raymond Williams, a "particular way of life, whether of a people, a period, or a group" (Williams 1976, 80). The latter is tacit within the discourse on multiculturalism, yet most discussions employ both intermittently. There is, however, a third definition of culture coming into currency that has yet to be explicitly addressed in these discussions. Introduced by Tony Bennett in his work on cultural policy and the museum, this third definition is informed by Foucault's late work on governmentality (Bennett 1995). Accordingly, it conceptualizes the interstices of knowledge and power as they impact upon the subject through a concern with individual conduct as a problematic of rule. He writes:

> Culture is more cogently conceived … when thought of as a historically specific set of institutionally embedded relations of government in which the forms of thought and conduct of extended populations are targeted for transformation—in part via the extension through the social body of the forms, techniques, and regimens of aesthetic and intellectual culture. (Bennett 1992, 26)

Culture, thus defined, is voided of an a priori empiricism as its constitutive relation to power is made manifest. Through the processes of social management, culture is crafted as both the object and instrument of government. This is not to say, however, that the objects and practices designated as "culture" don't exist (as caricatures of linguistic determinism would have it), but rather it signals a shift in analysis that emphasizes the ways that cultural practices are taken up by the apparatuses of knowledge and power and constituted as such. It is through this process that specialized and everyday practices are coded as "culture" and thereby designated as a category of value and made *useful* to a host of governing projects.

What Is Government?

In his essay on "governmentality" Michel Foucault traces the historical shift from autarchy to the modern state and argues that the weakening of divine rule occasioned the rise of doctrines on *how* to rule (see Foucault 1991; Gordon 1991). This epochal shift marks the emergence of liberalism, signaled by a change in the ends of government, from the accumulation of power and the rule of territory to the investment of the population with power and a concern with governing things and the relations between them. Rather than seeking to merely legitimate rule (as the divine sovereign did), modern forms of social and political organization are concerned with techniques of government, that is, with meditating on how best to rule. This concern with "things and the relations between them" is manifested in a deep concern for the population now conceived through the discourses of economics and social science as productive potential. On this point Foucault writes:

> The population now represents more the end of government than the power of the sovereign; the population is the subject of needs, of aspirations, but it is also the object in the hands of government, aware, vis-à-vis the government, of what it wants, but ignorant of what is being done to it. (Foucault 1991,100)

Governing then is concerned with "conducting conduct" and it is carried out through diverse institutions and agencies. Despite the tendency to associate government with the state, the logic of "governmentality" is manifested in both state and private initiatives, and some have argued that this behooves us to rethink theoretical models of state power that presume the absolute sovereignty of the state (Abrams 1988, 58–89; Coffey 2003, 207–42; Corrigan and Sayer 1985; Sayer 1994, 367–77). As Andrew Barry, Thomas Osborne, and Nikolas Rose (1996) submit, the very category of the state may be a consequence of the rise of liberalism and the attempts to theorize the possibilities of freedom. Given this genealogy of government, they suggest (along with Foucault) that we turn our attention from the state as the center of government, to the multiple sites of government, such as schools, festivals, museums, mass media, and civil associations (1–17).

Foucault's term, *governmental*, refers, in part, to the problematics of rule. Yet it also refers to the dimension of experience, the ways in which humans have reflected on the conduct of themselves and others and realized that thought through governing practices (Rose 1996, 41). Governmentality is therefore a political rationality, that has a moral concern for what is proper, an epistemological character in that it is concerned with elaborating authoritative accounts of the objects of government, and styles or genres of expertise that make what is to be governed thinkable (42). Government in this sense refers to the myriad "authorities of truth" that impact the way in which we establish true and false accounts of who we are and what we should become (Dean 1996, 211). Most important to this concept of government is the way in which questions of being, personal conduct, and identity come to be linked to questions of politics, authority, and government (210).

We return then to Bennett's assertion that culture be understood as both the object and instrument of government. "Culture," he argues, is government's object "insofar as the term refers to the morals, manners, and ways of life of subordinate social strata" (Bennett 1992, 26). In other words, when government is conceived of as a concern for conduct, the anthropological definition of culture is employed as the target of social initiatives and regulation. Similarly, culture is configured as an instrument of government, "insofar as it is culture in its more restricted sense—the domain of artistic and intellectual activities—that is to supply the means of a governmental intervention into the regulation of culture as the domain of morals, manners, codes of conduct, etc." (26). When examined this way, culture, as a category of population or production, is produced rather than given. Furthermore the attendant values that accrue to either sense are also mobilized by their function within a particular set of social relations. In Bennett's work the public museum provides an example of these social processes, for it is in the museum, as a space of rational recreation, that material objects and practices are codified as representative culture while they are employed as instruments of enlightenment. My point here is to call attention to the relations of power that generate these designations and to suggest that we think of the discourses and policies of multiculturalism through this rubric.

What Is Power?

The invocation of power begs further qualification and discussion about the relations between culture and power. At its most uncritical moments, the discourse on culture operates according to a "reflection" theory in which culture merely mirrors, for better or worse, the broader society. Questions of power are thereby rendered moot because representation is understood as a closed circle of correspondence between the object or practice and the "real world." Conversely, a more critical camp theorizes this relationship through tropes of mediation. Here culture is often characterized as a false representation that obscures the true workings of power in the social body. Marx's concept of ideology, particularly as articulated by Althusser, and Gramsci's hegemony are the two most prevalent and deep-seated formulations of culture as mediation for power sectors. Within the former, power is seated within a ruling class that seeks to subjugate the working class through an "ideological apparatus" that employs culture to mask the "real" operations of class privilege (Althusser 1971). Gramsci provides a more nuanced view of the relationship between culture and power, modifying the rigidity of Marx's paradigm with the notion of a "hegemonic process." In this formulation, subjugation is not the product of a false consciousness constructed and maintained through the ideological deployment of culture, rather it is a process that attempts to "transform society" through the creation of a consensus of values and goals, with culture as its primary agent (see Gramsci 1971; Laclau and Mouffe 1985). While this nuanced model continues to be very productive, it often takes culture as a given rather than viewing it as something that has been institutionally and discursively constituted. While the former account of power attributes a purely negative value to culture, as a thing to be manipulated, the latter allows for the possibility of negotiation between different power sectors for consent, and as such culture assumes a positive potential as a site for the struggle over meaning.

Gramsci's formulation has been most useful within an academic multiculturalism that limits its analysis to representation and reading resistance within particular texts. However, as Bennett has argued, this emphasis on textual analysis obscures "the programmatic, institutional, and governmental conditions in which cultural practices are inscribed." These conditions, he writes, "have a substantive priority over the semiotic properties of such practices.... [They establish] in any particular set of circumstances, the regions of person or citizen formation to which specific types of cultural practice are connected and the manner in which, as part of developed technologies, they function to achieve specific kinds of effects" (1992, 28). Rather than seek insight into the operations of power in representation, Bennett suggests we concern ourselves instead with how cultural practices are inscribed in relations of power. In this respect, his approach differs from ideological and hegemonic formulations of culture and power. Marxian formulations treat power as a kind of property that can be seized, as an attribute of domination, and ultimately as localized predominantly in the state and its institutions. As such, power shows itself through the violence of repression and the coercion of propaganda or ideology. In opposition to this model, I am arguing that power is a relation between forces, whether dominant or dominated, that it is exercised through techniques rather than possessed, and that it is productive first and foremost (see Foucault 1972, 1984, 1985, 1995). As Gilles Deleuze states, following Foucault, "power produces reality before it represses [and] it produces 'truth' before it ideologizes or masks" (Deleuze 1988, 28–9).

In the following discussion of the evolution of national culture in postrevolutionary Mexico, I am concerned neither with the processes of hegemony nor with locating culture within the realm of ideology. Rather than analyzing this history through what Foucault has called an "economy of untruth," I trace the production of certain "truths" about the nation and its origins. By eschewing ideology and hegemony, I am not, however, ignoring power. Rather, I understand power to be part of the production of truth, not merely its repression. So, rather than trying to resuscitate what certain cultural products meant prior to their distortion at the hands of one dominating power or another, I explore the epistemological character of culture in order to examine how it functions within governmental apparatuses, like educational projects and public museums. This has implications for multiculturalism, both as a deconstruction of origins and national identity (two of the privileged terms operating within the *hyperculturalist* camp) and as an illustration of how to use governmentality to analyze the relation between culture and power at a given historical juncture. Furthermore, the Mexican example offers an interesting parallel to the corporatist multiculturalism currently evident in the "managing of difference" within universities and other institutional sites. Like this contemporary phenomenon, the Mexican national culture project instrumentalized hybridity in an array of assimilationist projects aimed at social management. That hybridity and assimilation can be seen to work hand in hand in Mexico may not be an aberration, specific to this particular case, but rather a fundamental problem confronting multiculturalism at the governmental level.

Postrevolutionary Mexico: A Case Study in Governmental Culture

Public culture is one "authority of truth" and in this paper, I focus on two of its sites: Diego Rivera's murals at the Ministry of Public Education, in which he inaugurated a nationalized visual vocabulary that asserted indigenous "types" and geographic elements as the essential icons of the Mexican nation; and the National Anthropology Museum, in which the creative production and practices of indigenous populations have been crafted into a national cultural trust, a legacy that is employed to discipline the population into a functional and cohesive citizenry. This embrace of indigenous culture is referred to as to "official *indigenismo*," which David Bradding describes as the contradictory "insistence on the native roots of the Mexican people" and a simultaneous "affirmation of the necessity of modernity" evident in Mexico's cultural projects (Bradding 1988, 89). However, I argue that the employment of folkloric expression for the assimilation of Indian communities into the urban Hispanized population is not contradictory but rather part of the disciplinary logic of modernizing nationalism.

Diagnosing the National Body

At the close of the Mexican Revolution (c. 1917), national discourse focused on the problem of a historically contentious population comprised of "degenerate" indigenes, a large stratum of mestizos (people of mixed racial heritage), and a minority of pure Spanish descent known as creoles. As a discourse framed by the psychological and historical conditions of postcoloniality, Mexican nationalism seized upon the mestizo as the actual and metaphorical "Mexican." In *La Raza Cósmica*, a pseudoscientific treatise on the future promise of "his people," José Vasconcelos elevated racial miscegenation to a transcendent eugenic principle. Arguing that a "mixture of races accomplished through the laws of social well-being, sympathy, and beauty" will lead to a *cosmic race*, "infinitely superior to all that have previously existed," Vasconcelos converted racial impurity from a sign of shame into one of pride (Vasconcelos 1979, 31). "We in America," he concludes, "shall arrive, before any other part of the world, at the creation of a new race fashioned out of the treasures of the previous ones" (40).

Yet despite his celebration of *mestizaje*, Vasconcelos lamented the "race problem," stating, "Whether we like it or not the mestizo is the dominant element of the Latin American continent" (Vasconcelos 1926b, 92). He continues:

> From our local point of view in Mexico, I have started to preach the gospel of the mestizo by trying to impress on the minds of the new race a consciousness of their mission as builders of entirely new concepts of life. But if the mixed race is going to be able to do anything at all, it is first necessary to give it moral strength and faith in its own ability. (95)

Vasconcelos reasoned that the lack of "moral strength" and "faith" he detected in the mestizo was a result of his Indian blood. The Indian, he argued, is a "lower breed" without hope who "reproduces madly" and languishes in a state of degradation (100). This was not merely a problem for the disenfranchised native, but more significantly a problem for the nation. Conceived as a mestizo nation, the intransigence of one part of the body politic was a detriment to the progress of the whole.

As the native "element" emerged as the sign of difference around which a new *mestizo* identity could be elaborated, the perceived "backwardness" of the living and breathing Indian persisted, a reminder of the repercussions of conquest and colonization and a perennial sign of Mexico's lack. Consequently, postrevolutionary national discourse is obsessed with the "Indian Question."[1] In 1917, Mexican anthropologist Manuel Gamio founded the Department of Anthropology, specifically to address this question. Its program, he explained, was to study the racial characteristics, material and intellectual culture, language and dialects, economic situation, and environmental and biological conditions of the regional populations of present and past Mexico. Through this, Gamio insisted that his program would then be able to establish "official institutions" to "stimulate physical,

ellectual, moral and economic development of the people" with the ultimate goal of "cultural
usion, linguistic unification and economic equilibrium" (Gamio 1926, 173). Concluding a lecture
entitled "Incorporating the Indian into the National Population," Gamio stated emphatically that:

> It is unquestionably urgent, most urgent, to investigate the indigenous population of Mexico
> scientifically, for until this is done thoroughly, social contacts cannot be normalized and ori-
> ented authoritatively, a thing by all means desirable since it requires convergent racial, cul-
> tural, and spiritual fusion to secure unification of tongue and equilibrium of economic
> interests. This, and only this, can place the Mexican nation as a nation, upon a solid, logical,
> consistent, and permanent base. (127)

In accordance with this sentiment, the Ministry of Public Education (SEP) was founded in 1921,
immediately after the military struggles of the revolution subsided (1910–1920). José Vasconcelos
was appointed its director and it was his messianic vision that shaped its activities. In his biography
he states explicitly that the project of the SEP was "fivefold," with the promotion and development
of schools, libraries, and the fine arts as its "essential" parts and "bringing the Indian into the current of Spanish culture and … literacy to the masses" its "auxiliary activities" (Vasconcelos 1963,
157). For him, "ignorance" was a "plague" that afflicted the modern native population, and education was the "redemptive" agent of their inclusion within the Mexican nation. This desire to redeem
Mexico's indigenous populations under-girded his interest in developing a national culture. This
project was merely one front of a broad educative mission, and Vasconcelos often compared his role
as Minister of Education with that of the Spanish priests who converted the inhabitants of New
Spain to Christianity. As such the national culture project needs to be understood as a disciplinary
initiative that employed education and the arts as techniques of government to reorganize the conduct of targeted populations.

Under Vasconcelos's leadership of the SEP he commissioned Mexican artists to paint large
murals on public buildings, thus inaugurating the "Mexican Mural Renaissance" as a new category
of national culture. By employing Mexican artists to beautify the walls of the city, Vasconcelos
sought to aggrandize the nation and enhance the lives of its citizens. For him, culture was an
instrument of enlightenment, and his aesthetic theories are quite explicit on this point. In 1923 Rivera convinced Vasconcelos to give over the courtyard walls of the SEP's administration building to
himself and a number of his contemporaries for murals. While working on them from 1923 to
1928, Rivera evolved the visual vocabulary, style, and themes that would come to be recognized as
the stock iconography of the Mexican school of painting. However, while Vasconcelos envisioned
neoclassical allegories of national virtue and humanist values, the artists in his employ were catalyzed by the Communist Party, which prompted a more radical iconography. This marriage of art
and politics produced a new aesthetic commitment to the "values of the Mexican Revolution"
rather than the abstractions of a "Cosmic Race." Nonetheless, we should not presume that the diagnostic discourses of the "Mexican problem" nor the governmental aims of "official *indigenismo*"
were overcome or ignored, rather, as will become clear, the frescos of mural artists helped to make
Mexican society and its population thinkable, and therefore, governable.

Site 1: Diego Rivera's SEP Murals

Rivera's SEP murals explicitly display a political conviction to a militant socialism inflected by the
values of *Zapatismo*. He writes in his autobiography that in these murals he wanted to "reflect the
social life of Mexico as I saw it, and through my vision of the truth to show the masses the outline of
the future" (Rivera and March 1960, 79). His desire to reveal the "truth" to the "masses" in order to
benefit the "future" recalls the disciplinary rhetoric of Vasconcelos and Gamio, and it finds its first

visual articulation in these paintings. Rivera asserts the Indian as the essence of the body politic but reverses the moral hierarchy attributed to race in most of the diagnostic literature discussed earlier. However, by narrating a progressive movement from rural and agrarian idyll to an urban and proletarian future, Rivera's murals invoke indigenous culture largely in the name of socialism.

Recognizing the different ways the Indian was perceived and positioned within the social projects of public education, artistic representation, and anthropological study reveals that these projects were less concerned with outright repression and more concerned with governance. Each of these projects manifested a deep (albeit paternal) concern for Mexico's indigenous populations, and through the development of expertise, their agents sought to affect the conduct of Mexico's indigenous populations so as to convert them into national citizens. By emphasizing the reiteration of certain statements across the fields of social knowledge, I want to call attention to the diffuse nature of government and demonstrate that sites often located outside of or even in opposition to the state do in fact participate in the processes of social governance.

The subject matter of Rivera's cycle is divided into two categories, the courts of labor and fiestas, which correspond to the two, three-floor courtyards of the SEP. The three floors of the court of labor are decorated with murals dedicated to the industrial and agricultural labors of the Mexican people, intellectual work, and portraits of revolutionary heroes. The first-floor murals reflect the values of *Zapatismo* through images of Indians and campesinos working the land and others of the exploitation of these figures by corrupt *hacendados* or dangerous working conditions. Panels such as *The Liberation of the Peon* (1923) depict the rescue of a mistreated Indian by revolutionary soldiers, who are again visible in *The New School* (1923) overseeing the education of peasants. Each of these images is set in vast landscapes that reference the rich and diverse topography of the country and call to mind the revolutionary slogan of Zapata, "Tierra y Libertad" ("Land and Liberty"). Furthermore, paintings of volcanoes, magueys, and cacti, as well as identifiable architectural landscapes such as the hillsides of stacked housing typical in Guanajuato, begin to elaborate an allegorical topography infused with political values. Likewise, panels dealing with industrial labor symbolically reinforce the theme of exploitation. For example, in *Entry into the Mines* (1923) the mineshaft has been rendered in the guise of a skull, effectively equating this dangerous work with death.[2] These images of cruel labor are contrasted with idyllic portraits of Tehuanas dying cloth and artisans making and decorating pottery, clearly a contrast between pre-Hispanic communitarian modes of production and colonial and postcolonial forms of class exploitation and labor for the purposes of wealth and export.

The court of fiestas illustrates popular religious and political festivals and revolutionary *corridos* (songs). On the first floor, amid panels describing indigenous and popular festivals, Rivera has placed three large murals representing agrarian reform, May day, and the popular market. The latter is represented as a modern equivalent to the ancient Aztec market (the *Tianguis)* for which it is titled. The physical disbursement of these three panels produces an equation between each event. These murals are the central focus and therefore the visual anchors of the three painted courtyard walls. Thus an equation between popular traditions, the revolution (represented here by the agrarian platform of *Zapatismo*), and socialism is reinforced visually as well as through the literal procession of the viewer through the space. Rivera's ideological position is clear in these panels, where masses of soldiers, farmers, and factory workers are depicted as unified culturally by ancient traditions and politically by the promise of socialism. Throughout the SEP cycle the spatial distribution of individual mural paintings builds a progressive narrative that is elaborated and communicated as much through representation as it is through the physical movement of the visitor around the building's courtyard. The movement from the revolution toward a proletarian society is conveyed throughout, but it is best illustrated through the narrative convention of *corridos* on the third floor and the physical climb up the stairwell corridor. In both of these spaces representations of indigenous peoples help to legitimize Rivera's vision of past and future Mexico.

The equation between the values of the Mexican revolution and socialism is even more evident in the third-floor panels, which are connected by a painted red ribbon upon which agrarian and proletarian songs are printed. These panels contrast bourgeois values with socialist ones by lampooning figures like J. D. Rockefeller and lionizing the communist worker and the revolutionary soldier. For example, *Wall Street Banquet* (1928) depicts wealthy Manhattanites dining on champagne and ticker-tape. *Our Bread* (1928), on the other hand, portrays a humble table presided over by a worker in blue overalls wearing the red star of communism and a Tehuana who proffers a basket of indigenous fruits. At the table individuals gathered from across Mexico's racial and social classes sit while a soldier and farmer stand nearby. The entire scene is set in front of a factoryscape, a motif that references the (vulgar) Marxist belief that technology would hasten the destruction of capitalist society and thereby bring about social equality.

The third-floor images are introduced by *The Distribution of Arms* (1928), a painting that prophesies the proletarian revolution in its imagery as well as through the proletarian song that frames it and whose slogans structure the vignettes that follow. The opening lines, "Así será la Revolución Proletaria" ("And so the Proletarian Revolution will be"), place the event in the future as each subsequent image describes how the struggle will proceed. At the culmination of this song a revolutionary *corrido* begins, rendered in the same red ribbon. The similarity in iconography between the text and images of each illustrated song articulates the Mexican revolution to a prophesied proletarian revolution and asserts that one follows logically from the other. Here a highly factionalized civil war born out of a subjugated people's collective sense of injustice is equated with the political organization of the international communist movement. Conversely, the authenticity of the local event naturalizes an imported political agenda by asserting that both are structured by the same popular cultural values.[3]

The dynamic between space and representation is best captured in the stairway at the SEP, which is painted from the ground up with a symbolic landscape of social evolution that is conveyed through geological change and the sociocultural development of "peoples" from "premodern society" to proletarian social order (Wolfe 1939, 181–196). These panels make explicit the structure of the SEP murals as a whole. There is a general "progression" throughout as one moves from ground floor to the upper balconies, with the Indian symbolizing an essential yet primitive past and the communist worker representing a unified future. The staircase images are both topographic and ethnographic as they depict a progression from "subterranean waters" through tropical lands, high plateau, and finally, snow-capped mountains. Inhabiting these Mexican landscapes are native types from Mexico's past and present. The mixing together of past and contemporary indigenous populations suggests continuity between Mexico's pre-Columbian past and postrevolutionary present. Nonetheless, there is a subtle chronological progression that commutes this cycle to a history lesson as well. The early panels are mythologized marinescapes that, while inhabited by modern technologies, give no indication of an abusive relationship between man, machine, or land. However, as one moves up from sea level, into the tropics of Tehuantepec, the image of a sugar hacienda appears, complete with lazy boss and exploited labor. The locals are gradually clothed, which suggests the encroachment of "civilization" along with conquest and colonization. The revolution is clearly alluded to in a burial image that recalls Courbet's realist painting *A Burial at Ornans* (1849), as well as Rivera's depictions of slain heroes in his Chapingo murals. Finally, with the passing of the revolution, Rivera represents the overcoming of exploitation with an image of cowering figures depicting the church, capital, and a corrupt military being struck down by a red thunderbolt, a symbol of the proletariat. In the upper right-hand corner, a new socialist society is represented with a trinity of soldier, worker, and farmer united.

The final image, at the top of this historical narrative, shows Rivera, the artist, depicted as a technical worker along with the stone-cutter and architect.

Rivera's SEP murals equate the people and the land literally and figuratively and thereby conform to one of the most recurrent strategies for naturalizing the psychic sense of community promoted in national rhetoric. This mural, dedicated to the Mexican people, their labors, and their celebrations, asserts that the nation is founded in the native soil and its native populations. However, both ultimately undergo changes as industrialization and Marxist social organization assimilate the disparate populace into a collective, proletarian working force and exploit the natural values of the land toward that end. By advocating this change in his imagery, Rivera issues the same tacit mandate to the Mexican "masses" that Gamio endeavored to do in *Forjando Patria* (his multivolume study of the Valley of Teotihuacán, collectively titled *Forging a Fatherland*) and that Vasconcelos promoted through his educational policies. Native peoples and their practices are addressed as the essential "Mexicans" all the while they are being asked to express their citizenship within the new nation by assimilating socially and adapting to new collective values.

Disciplining a National Citizenry

By representing the Mexican nation through an equation between racial types and landscapes, Rivera's SEP murals present a visual counterpart to the literature on Mexican nationalism at the time. For example, in an essay entitled "Similarity and Contrast," Vasconcelos details at length the topographical variety of Mexico and then equates this "land of contrasts" with its various peoples and their characteristics (Vasconcelos 1926a, 3–43). The equation between indigenous groups and their natural environment was also a component of Gamio's massive research into Teotihuacán. As part of this discursive context, Rivera's murals illustrate the prevailing logic of early-twentieth-century nationalism, both in his reliance upon essentialist traits such as "race" and "climate" as well as his enthusiasm about the potential for social control through harnessing these "physical" determinants toward a greater social good, future development, and proper "citizenship." Vasconcelos argues that Mexico is a "nation of contrast" with a history that is "a series of layers composed of materials that do not mix," a "social condition" that is characterized by a "compound of races that have not yet become thoroughly combined," and where a mere "glance at our physical structure will only add to the puzzle of the Mexican problem" (5–7). He speculates that "perhaps the reason of the social contrast lies in the varied physical, temperamental, and historical factors that intervene in the making of our soul" (7).

The crafting of the "Mexican soul" was the explicit project of postrevolutionary cultural nationalism. The "will to nation" expressed in this literature came to fruition with the concept of *mestizaje*, simultaneously producing and circumscribing the sphere of the "indigenous" as an object of study, regulation, and representation. The emergent school of Mexican anthropology sought to know indigenous groups, while governmental programs endeavored to inculcate this disenfranchised population into the newly "imagined community" of mestizo nationhood. Furthermore, national culture seized upon the Indian as an object of representation and a producer of "authentic" Mexican art. The institutional relationship between these fields of practice functioned together to produce powerful popular truths about the nation, its heritage, and the conditions of citizenship.

Rivera's SEP murals offer a folkloric appreciation of indigenous life in the name of an advancing modernization. While he asserts that the social organization of proletarian culture is based upon the communitarian social organization of pre-Hispanic Mexico, his depiction of modern Mexico is as a mestizo nation in which racial and social distinctions no longer matter. In short, his is a vision of assimilation in the name of social development as well and as such a visual corollary of the disciplinary rhetoric of nationalism found in the writings of Vasconcelos and Gamio. All three provide arguments for proper citizenship that rely upon the "natural" racial and territorial markers of a "nation of contrasts." While Rivera's vision of *mestizaje* is cultural rather than racial (as Vasconcelos's was), the underlying principle of achieving a proper balance between the desirable traits of different racial and social sectors was based upon discriminate and selective criteria in the service of a modernizing national project.[4]

Problematizing the Nation

Foucault's notion of "problematization" helps to bring together the discourse on nationalism, governmental initiatives in the fields of education and anthropology, and the artistic project of muralism. In a 1984 interview with François Ewald, Foucault discusses the relationship between "problematization" and truth. He states:

> Problematization doesn't mean representation of a pre-existing object, nor the creation by discourse of an object that doesn't exist. It is the totality of discursive or non-discursive practices that introduces something into the play of true and false and constitutes it as an object for thought (whether in the form of moral reflection, scientific knowledge, political analysis, etc.). (Foucault 1990, 257)

In postrevolutionary Mexico, the "truth" of the nation is problematized and a new set of "objects" are offered up to thought. Within the discursive and nondiscursive practices discussed thus far, the Indian helps to focus questions regarding appropriate being or conduct and political reason or rule. The contemporary Indian is an object of study and therefore knowledge, an object of moral reflection, an object of representation, and an object of government. The problematization of Mexico-as-nation produced statements of truth about the Indian: that in the contemporary period the Indian existed in a degraded state that mandated intervention; that his culture was essential to the nation and the only proper expression of difference; that she was in need of welfare; that he was the historical agent of national becoming; that she had to assimilate to some new form of collective or community. The personal conduct of the Indian became essential to the question of rule and representation, and these truths structured the ways in which the Indian and nation could subsequently be thought about. The struggle over the nation was therefore a struggle over the Indian. The allegiance of indigenous peoples was sought while they were simultaneously subjectified as "the Indigenous" through governing practices that ranged from anthropological scrutiny to institutional representation.

What is significant here is that the problematization and production of Mexico's varied Indian populations as "the Indigenous" occurred across a variety of discursive sites. Furthermore, culture needs to be understood as one of these sites of production. More importantly, these different sites were not all organized from a single perspective, but rather each was pursuing this problem from a different vantage point and with differing agendas. The socialist politics and anticlericalism of Rivera was in direct opposition to the elitism and Catholicism of Vasconcelos, so much so that the latter rescinded his support upon his resignation from the SEP in 1924. Gamio and his team of anthropologists were interested in preserving and studying indigenous culture under the sign of "pure science." The articulation of these many projects through the national culture project over a number of years, and across many institutional sites, is important to understand lest we fall into too simplistic an understanding of either culture or the processes of government. While regularities occurred across these discourses, it was the resonance between them that established the aforementioned truths about Mexico's indigenous populations.

Site 2: The National Anthropology Museum

Indigenous populations were conceived as a "problem population." The national culture project delimited a range of practices as distinctive culture and employed them in governing projects. Through the museum these populations were objectified as the targets of government even while their daily practices were instrumentalized within the institutions dedicated to the nation's pre-Hispanic origins. I want to turn briefly from the early national culture project to the new National Anthropology Museum, inaugurated in 1964, in order examine the museum as a technique of government in which the subjectification of the Mexican through the deployment of indigenous culture has been most evident and powerful. Here the museum is understood as a complex social space of representation and regulation, an instrument of modern government whose raison d'être lies in its civilizing capacity, its ability to improve morals and, more importantly, to shape the conduct of its public.

As the most visited museum in the country, the National Anthropology Museum has come to embody "Mexicaness." Its success has been attributed to its sophisticated spatial organization and to its displays, which assert that national culture has its origins in the Indigenous sectors of the Mexican population. However, as Néstor García Canclini has argued, it does this by marking the limits of the ethnic through a separation of ancient and contemporary cultures (García Canclini 1995). This separation is enacted by a distinction between anthropology (housed on the first floor) and ethnography (located on the second), and within the museum, the former is given much greater emphasis. The museum's collections are distributed across two floors of galleries that form a rectangle around an open patio. While patrons are free to enter each gallery from this patio, there is a clearly marked place to begin their experience in an introductory hall that explicates the museum's mission and articulates its objects to and through the science of anthropology or the study of "man." In his statement about the "origins, aims and achievements" of this museum, Ignacio Bernal, director of the National Institute of Anthropology and History (INAH) in the 1960s, makes explicit the significance of the science of anthropology to the Mexican nation. He writes:

> The diverse indigenous cultures of Mexico, both those which flourished in prehistoric times and those which have persisted until the present day, present anthropology with a vast field for study while providing museums with rich and valuable materials for display.... Keeping this in mind, those who planned the new National Museum of Anthropology decided to include an initiatory hall that would justify the Museum's name and at the same time present a universal framework into which the Mexican cultures could be fitted in space and time, as well as allowing visitors to compare their cultural contributions with those of other peoples. (Bernal 1968, 14).

This introductory hall, designed to pay homage to the science that organizes and explains "man's origins," along with the final hall of the ethnographic section entitled "Modern Autochthonous Mexico," were intended to frame the viewers' experience of the museum. While the introductory hall prepared the viewer to understand the objects in subsequent galleries as both national in content and universal in significance, the final hall punctuated their experience with an invitation to utilize their new knowledge by becoming proper modern citizens. This last hall presented, in the words of Bernal, a "synthesis of the process of social and cultural change taking place in Mexico today" (193). The synthesizing processes of modern Mexico were represented through a photo mosaic in which photographs of various ethnic groups were montaged into a progressively unified and modernized image of the national populace. Bernal explains that this image calls for the "participation of the native peoples, through which the National Indigenist Institute is trying to integrate the various ethnic groups into Mexican national life" (93).[5] Functioning as bookends to the museum experience, these halls convert the viewer's progress through the exhibitions into an evolutionary performance that begins in a glorified indigenous past and looks to a unified or mestizo future. This "ritual of citizenship" implies that the synthetic vision of the nation's future is the fulfillment of a promise embodied in the culture of the nation's past. At once historicized and patriotic, it places the viewer in an evolutionary relationship to the cultures and peoples on display. Finally, it asks them to recognize themselves in the indigenous past but to participate in a synthetic future.

The museum was planned to glorify and educate. Therefore, each room was organized to present easily understood lessons. A report published in 1961 outlines the museum's overt mission, its organization, and the scientific means by which its efficacy should be tested and ensured. Arguing that museum exhibitions "from the didactic point of view only have value with respect to the educative function they perform in relation to the public," the authors of the report suggest a preliminary study of the "general characteristics" of the public in order to fashion viewer surveys aimed at quantifying the "educative influence" of its exhibitions (Salgado and Sánchez Bueno 1961, 1). So at the planning stage this museum was organized with a political pedagogy in mind. As one of the only public museums in the country to receive its own building designed specifically to facilitate its didactic message, the National Anthropology Museum is a unique but paradigmatic public museum in postrevolutionary Mexico. More than a mere representation of the nation, its ritualized space deploys cultural objects in order to produce an identification between its visitors and an indigenized Mexican nation. As Néstor García Canclini eloquently explains, "The watchword that governs this ritual is 'become what you are'" (García Canclini 1995, 135). We might argue that this message has different meanings for different audiences. For the indigenous visitor, the museum encourages Mexicanization; for the nonindigenous visitor, it encourages indigenization. But for both, the ritual space has been orchestrated to craft a relationship between indigenous culture and peoples and the citizenry of the modern nation-state.

Culture and Subjectification

The use of culture in postrevolutionary Mexico is a "pursuit of the popular"—a desire to name, know, and create the "people" as well as to proscribe the modes of their conduct. In this sense the "people" are a "representational effect" of cultural texts as well as a "knowledge effect" of investigations and regulations of the population (Miller 1998, 250). The pursuit of this "fictional" entity on the part of multiple agencies is part of the cultural revolution that established artistic practice as a ritual of citizenship and part of governmental programs concerned with popular conduct. As Toby Miller argues, through government, "living and breathing subjects who act in the everyday become objects of contemplation and intervention" (251). And the museum is an important site for establishing a relationship between the national collective and the individual citizen. The museum, Miller argues, "seeks to attract newcomers and to draw reactions that will be taken into the exterior world through a temporary, voluntary enclosure of the visitors that combines information and entertainment, instruction and diversion" (235).

Miller's attention to the relationship between institution, knowledge, and subject formation brings out the disciplinary component of subjectivity and identity that Foucault began to delimit in his late work. According to this definition subjectivity does not designate an autonomous self-knowledge or a socially constructed automation, rather it indexes a relationship to the self brought into being by processes of subjectification "through which individuals are able, are obliged, to recognize themselves as subjects" (Foucault 1985, 4). In "The Subject and Power," Foucault reminds us that there are two meanings to the word "subject: subject to someone else by control and dependence; and tied to [one's] own identity by a conscience or self-knowledge" (Foucault 1984, 420). In both senses, the individual does not escape the forces of power and knowledge, but rather the truth of his or her individuality is produced at the interstices of both. Culture, as we have seen, is a technique of government and consequently one of the instruments of subjectification by which the individual is called upon or obliged to recognize themselves through particular formations of identity. Identity must be understood as a category produced through disciplinary and governmental initiatives that impinge upon the individual and not as a naturalized category of being. This formulation of the subject helps to highlight the subjugation and regulation that proceeds through the production and naturalization of racial, ethnic, national, and sexual identities. Furthermore, by analyzing the role culture plays in these formations, we can attend to the problematic effects of identity politics (the tendency to essentialize and naturalize) as they emerge within the emancipatory projects of multicultural education.

In Mexico's national culture project, "culture" was produced and disseminated across the axes of regulatory bodies, patrimony legislation, and institutions. Neither muralism nor pre-Hispanic artifacts are unproblematically national culture. Their production as such is inextricably linked to the governmental project of public education and the epistemological pursuits of anthropology, philosophy, and the diagnostic literature on the "Mexican problem." Furthermore, the instrumentalization of this culture of difference within spaces devoted to national consolidation demonstrates the extent to which we must look at how culture functions within broader contexts. Rather than treating culture as a self-evident product to be reviled as ideology or resuscitated through critical reading practices, an analysis of the very constitution of "culture," its uses within governmental spaces, whether state supported or not, and its articulations to other discursive fields, will reveal the complexities of this phenomenon.

By calling attention to the intrication of culture with governmental and disciplinary processes I endeavor to demonstrate that power is a constitutive component of culture, not merely an impositional force that arrives after the fact. Ultimately it behooves us not to try to determine what culture is, in its essence, but rather to ask how it is produced as a category (whether aesthetic or "life world") and how it functions in particular institutional or policy contexts. This attention to culture and government can only augment the "insurgent multiculturalism" that Henry Giroux describes as a "pedagogical terrain in which relations of power and racialized identities become paramount as part of the language of critique and possibility" (Giroux 1997, 235). Continuing, he writes:

> This suggests challenging the narratives of national identity, culture, and ethnicity as part of a pedagogical effort to provide dominant groups with the knowledge and histories to examine, acknowledge, and unlearn their own privilege. (236)

In Giroux's formulation, multiculturalism is not merely the celebration of marginalized identities and their essentialized cultural production; it is a strategy for understanding the emergence of privilege and its conditions of production.

In conclusion, I want to suggest that to understand privilege, we need to understand government as a set of diffuse techniques exercised in and through myriad locations, practices, and authorities. With that in mind we need to ask what are the relations between multiculturalism as a critical pedagogy and the processes of government implicit in the educational context? How are the concepts of culture employed in multicultural discourse linked up with other forms of expertise, and what are the effects of these articulations? Finally, I am arguing that understanding culture as a technique of government helps to make intelligible the strategies by which we are governed, and consequently this provides the possibility for the contestation of those strategies. My analysis of national culture in Mexico is a description of how a particular national (or ethnic when viewed within the U.S. context) culture was produced, but it also points to a theory of subjectification that takes into account the production of knowledge and its relation to governmental power. This in turn provides a perspective on the mechanics of privilege, but it also demonstrates the need to retheorize resistance through governmentality.

Notes

This essay is a revised version of one originally published in Ram Mahalingam and Cameron McCarthy, eds. *Multicultural Curriculums: New Directions for Social Theory, Practice, and Policy* (New York and London: Routledge, 2000). I would like to thank the Tinker Foundation and the Center for Latin American and Caribbean Studies at the University of Illinois for sponsoring two research trips to Mexico. This research enabled and informed my arguments regarding the Mexican national culture project in what follows.

1. While I have emphasized Vasconcelos and Gamio here, the diagnostic quality evident in these examples pervades the intellectual discourse of this period regardless of genre or subject-matter. For other prominent examples see Antonio Caso, *La existencia como económia y caridad* (Mexico Editorial Porrua, 1916) for a philosophical argument; Alberto J. Pani, *Hygiene in Mexico* (New York and London: G. P. Putnam's Sons, 1917); the Knickerbocker Press for a discussion of social policy and problems; and Pedro Henriquez Ureña, *Plenitud de América, ensayos escogidos* (Buenos Aires: del Giudice Peña, 1952) for essays on Mexico's "new culture." These are just three examples of many that reflect the variety of this discourse.

2. For this iconographic detail I am indebted to an anonymous guard who was working at the SEP in 1997 when I first saw and photographed these murals. He asked why I was taking pictures and upon learning that I studied Mexican Muralism engaged me in a very nuanced discussion of the iconography of this particular panel. I have to admit that before our talk I had never noticed the skull; furthermore, it has not been a standard iconographic identification within the literature on this mural. To my knowledge Leonard Folgarait is the first to have written about it in his 1998 publication, *Mural Painting and Social Revolution in Mexico, 1920–1940* (Cambridge, UK: Cambridge University Press). This anecdote, while it can't be held up as representative of the acuity of the general public, makes clear that for some Mexicans this art speaks volumes.

3. This strategy is not exclusive to Rivera; in fact the belief that the communitarian values of Mexico's pre-Hispanic and contemporary indigenous cultures were evidence of proto-socialist organization was common in postrevolutionary intellectual circles. In particular, the Zapotecs from the Isthmus of Tehuantepec were discussed in this way. See, for example, Miguel Covarrubias, *Mexico South: The Isthmus of Tehuantepec* (New York: Alfred A. Knopf, 1946/1967).

4. Rivera's "cultural *mestizaje*" is made all the more explicit in *Portrait of Mexico*, a book written by his biographer and friend, the socialist Bertram Wolfe, and illustrated by the artist. In this collaborative text, they present a history of Mexico from pre-Hispanic times to the present, but preface this with their own diagnostic take on the "Mexican problem." Establishing a homology between the "land of many tierras" and its diverse populations, they too lament the difficulty of unifying a population that in its cultural variety mirrors the incommensurability of Mexico's many regions. While they value this diversity, they insist that it is rapidly becoming a thing of the past due to Mexico's transition into a nation-state and its incorporation into the global economy. They argue that the inevitability of this transition necessitates that the process be guided by the appropriate interests, namely their socialist agenda. To this end, they make recommendations throughout about how to help Mexico's native populations preserve what is "worthwhile" in their traditions while simultaneously incorporating them "into a free union of peoples on the basis of a common national, and ultimately international economy." It is clear throughout this book that, as usual, it is the preindustrial native that needs to brought into modernity, through governmental support, and that those aspects of their communal life that hinder modernization must be eliminated (Wolfe 1937).

5. It is important to note that like many museums, the National Anthropology Museum has undergone renovations since it opened in 1964. Increasingly the museum's displays are changing in response to criticism from Mexican intellectuals and international initiatives within museology. The ethnographic installations are currently being reorganized to more accurately reflect the hybridity of contemporary indigenous life. This is being accomplished through the inclusion of modern appliances and technologies, such as computers, in displays of domestic life. Furthermore, the struggle for self-definition, most fervently asserted by present-day Mayans, is acknowledged in text panels and photographs that undermine the vision of unified nationalism presented throughout the institution. Most significant, perhaps, has been the removal of the final hall. It has been replaced by a temporary exhibition space. Nonetheless, while some of the most egregious offenses have been eliminated, the progressive and developmental narrative of the installations as a whole remains intact.

References

Abrams, Philip. "Notes on the Difficulty of Studying the State." *Journal of Historical Sociology* 1, no. 1 (1988): 58–89.

Althusser, Louis. "Ideology and Ideological State Apparatuses." In *Lenin and Philosophy and Other Essays*, 121–73, translated by B. Brewster. New York: Monthly Review, 1971.

Alvarez, Sonia E., Evelina Dagnino, and Arturo Escobar, eds. *Cultures of Politics/Politics of Cultures: Re-visioning Latin American Social Movements.* Boulder, CO: Westview Press, 1998.

Barry, Andrew, Thomas Osborne, and Nikolas Rose, eds. "Introduction." *Foucault and Political Reason: Liberalism, Neo-Liberalism and Rationalities of Government*, 1–36. Chicago: University of Chicago Press, 1996.

Bennett, Tony. "Putting Policy into Cultural Studies." In *Cultural Studies*, edited by Lawrence Grossberg, Cary Nelson, and Paula Treichler, 23–37. London, New York: Routledge, 1992.

Bennett, Tony. *The Birth of the Museum: History, Theory, Politics.* London, New York: Routledge, 1995.

Bernal, Ignacio. *The Mexican National Museum of Anthropology.* London: Thames and Hudson, 1968.

Bradding, David A. "Manuel Gamio and Official Indigenismo in Mexico." *Bulletin of Latin American Research* 7 no. 1 (1988): 75–90.

Coffey, Mary K. "From Nation to Community: Museums and the Reconfiguration of Mexican Society under Neo-Liberalism." In *Foucault, Cultural Studies, and Governmentality*, edited by Jack Z. Bratich, Jeremy Packer, and Cameron McCarthy, 197–42. New York: SUNY Press, 2003.

Corrigan, Phillip and Derek Sayer. *The Great Arch: English State Formation as Cultural Revolution*. Oxford: Basil Blackwell, 1985.

Dean, Mitchell. "Foucault, Government and the Enfolding of Authority." In *Foucault and Political Reason: Liberalism, Neo-Liberalism and Rationalities of Government*, edited by Andrew Barry, Thomas Osborne, and Nikolas Rose, 209–29. Chicago: University of Chicago Press, 1996.

Deleuze, Gilles. *Foucault*, translated by Seán Hand. Minneapolis and London: University of Minnesota Press, 1988.

Foucault, Michel. "Truth and Power." In *Power/Knowledge: Selected Interviews and Other Writings, 1972–1977*, edited by Colin Gordon, 109–33. New York: Pantheon Books, 1972.

Foucault, Michel. "The Subject and Power." In *Art after Modernism: Rethinking Representation*, edited by Brian Wallis, 427–32. New York: The New Museum of Contemporary Art/ Boston: David R. Godine, 1984.

Foucault, Michel. *The Use of Pleasure*, translated by R. Hurley. New York: Random House, 1985.

Foucault, Michel. "The Concern for Truth." In *Politics, Philosophy, Culture: Interviews and Other Writings, 1977–1984*, edited by Lawrence D. Kritzman, 255–67. New York, London: Routledge, 1990.

Foucault, Michel. "Governmentality." In *The Foucault Effect: Studies in Governmentality*, edited by Graham Burchell, Colin Gordon, and Peter Miller, 87–104. Chicago: University of Chicago Press, 1991.

Foucault, Michel. *Discipline and Punish: The Birth of the Prison*, translated by Alan Sheridan. New York: Vintage, 1995.

Fuller, Steve. "Social Epistemology as a Critical Philosophy of Multiculturalism." In *Multicultural Curriculum: New Directions for Social Theory, Practice, and Policy*, edited by Ram Mahalingam and Cameron McCarthy, 15–36. New York, London: Routledge, 2000.

Gamio, Manuel. "Incorporating the Indian into Mexican Society." In *Aspects of Mexican Civilization: Lectures on the Harris Foundation*, edited by Manuel Gamio and José Vasconcelos, 105–29. Chicago: University of Chicago, 1926.

García Canclini, Néstor. *Hybrid Cultures: Strategies for Entering and Leaving Modernity*, translated by Christopher L. Chiappari and Silvia L. López. Minneapolis: University of Minnesota Press, 1995.

Giroux, Henry A. *Pedagogy and the Politics of Hope: Theory, Culture, and Schooling*. Boulder, CO: Westview Press, 1997.

Gordon, Colin. "Governmental Rationality: An Introduction." In *The Foucault Effect: Studies in Governmentality*, edited by Graham Burchell, Colin Gordon, and Peter Miller, 1–52. Chicago: University of Chicago Press, 1991.

Gramsci, Antonio. *Selections from the Prison Notebooks*, translated by Q. Hoare and G. N. Smith. London: Lawrence and Wishart, 1971.

Laclau, Ernesto and Mouffe, Chantal. *Hegemony and Socialist Strategy: Towards a Radical Democratic Politics*. London: Verso, 1985.

Miller, Toby. *Technologies of Truth*. Minneapolis and London: University of Minnesota Press, 1998.

Rivera, Diego, with Gladys March. *My Art, My Life*. New York: Dover, 1960.

Rose, Nikolas. "Governing 'Advanced' Liberal Democracies." In *Foucault and Political Reason: Liberalism, Neo-Liberalism and Rationalities of Government*, edited by Andrew Barry, Thomas Osborne, and Nikolas Rose, 37–64. Chicago: University of Chicago Press, 1996.

Salgado, Irma M. and M. C. Sánchez Bueno. "Estudio Preliminar de las Características generales del público." In *Consejo de Planeación e Instalación del Museo Nacional de Antropología. Informe general de las labores desarrolladas durante, del 1° de enero al 31 de diciembre de 1961*, edited by Luis Aveleyra and Ignacio Marquina, 2–20. México: INAH, CAPFLE, SEP, 1961.

Sayer, Derek. "Everyday Forms of State Formation: Some Dissident Remarks on 'Hegemony.'" In *Everyday Forms of State Formation: Revolution and the Negotiation of Rule in Modern Mexico*, edited by Gilbert M. Joseph and Daniel Nugent, 367–77. Durham, NC, and London: Duke University Press, 1994.

Vasconcelos, José. "Similarity and Contrast." In *Aspects of Mexican Civilization: Lectures on the Harris Foundation*, edited by Manuel Gamio and José Vasconcelos, 105–29. Chicago: University of Chicago, 1926a.

Vasconcelos, José. "The Race Problem in Latin America." In *Aspects of Mexican Civilization: Lectures on the Harris Foundation*, edited by Manuel Gamio and José Vasconcelos, 75–104. Chicago: University of Chicago, 1926b.

Vasconcelos, José. *A Mexican Ulysses: An Autobiography*, translated by W. Rex Crawford. Bloomington: Indiana University Press, 1963.

Vasconcelos, José. *The Cosmic Race: A Bilingual Edition*, translated by Didier T. Jaén. Baltimore and London: Johns Hopkins University Press, 1979.

Williams, Raymond. *Keywords*. London: Fontana, 1976.

Wolfe, Bertram D. *Portrait of Mexico*. New York: Covici, Friede, 1937.

Wolfe, Bertram D. *Diego Rivera: His Life and Times*. New York, London: Alfred A. Knopf, 1939.

18

How to Be Good

The NFL, Corporate Philanthropy, and the Racialization of Generosity

SAMANTHA KING

Get on board, do your business around the country. Fly and enjoy America's great destination spots. Go down to Disney World in Florida. Take your families and enjoy life the way we want it to be enjoyed.

—George W. Bush
September 27, 2001

Many ask, what can I do to help in our fight. The answer is simple. All of us can become a September the 11th volunteer by making a commitment to service in our own communities.

—George W. Bush
November 8, 2001

Oftentimes, when I speak around the nation, I talk about the great strength of the nation that lies in the hearts and souls of our citizens. I was using military terms at times even before the war began. I talked about Armies of Compassion. I truly believe that's one of the wonderful strengths of America, that we've got armies of compassion all across our country.

—George W. Bush
November 20, 2001

In the wake of the events of September 11, 2001, the National Football League made a multimillion dollar commitment to New York City to help promote tourism and convention business by providing free network television and radio promotional time. The league also donated $500,000 to the city's September 11th commemoration and established the NFL Disaster Relief Fund, which was created to help with the redevelopment of Lower Manhattan. One year later, in September 2002, the NFL launched its new season with the inaugural "Kickoff Live"—a glitzy, star-studded music and football festival held in Times Square. According to league publicity materials, the Kickoff was designed as "a tribute to the American spirit, the resiliency of New Yorkers, and the fact that post-9/11, New York City remains one of the premier tourist destinations in the world" (www.nfl.com). The event drew approximately 500,000 attendees and was covered by 120 media outlets worldwide.

The Kickoff and the philanthropic projects it was used to promote fit perfectly within the framework of dominant responses to the terrorist attacks. While the Bush administration made plans for a military reaction, "ordinary" Americans were told that they could best help the nation to recover from this tragedy by doing two things: consuming and volunteering. In this context, the NFL fundraising campaign and the events surrounding it, offered an accessible and efficient vehicle through which citizens could fulfill both expectations at once, either as consumers of football who donated money to the NFL fund (giving money was a frequently cited example of the types of "volunteerism" in which Americans could engage), or as tourists to New York City. Like so many recently created cogs in the machinery of philanthropic production in the United States, the NFL campaigns encouraged people to do good for others at the same time that they went about their everyday practices of consumption. The initiatives also provided the NFL with an opportunity to market itself as a good corporate citizen through an alternative to their long-running partnership with the United Way.

Although the United States has long been characterized by a strong "voluntary" or "nonprofit" sector, with close ties to large corporations and prominent businesspeople, the deployment of philanthropic initiatives as central components of corporate marketing strategies is a fairly recent development. The struggle to maintain and increase market share in sectors like professional sport drives businesses to constantly seek new and improved ways to win consumer loyalty. Cause-related marketing campaigns have proved among the most popular of these strategies because they are thought to fulfill the heightened desire of consumers to be more generous and civic-minded in their everyday lives.

Alongside these developments, the rise of neoliberalism as the dominant organizing principle of government and the economy in the past two decades has brought with it a renewed interest in philanthropic practice. Public–private initiatives and individual and corporate giving are promoted under this regime as morally and economically viable means through which to respond to social needs. In this context, George Bush's Armies of Compassion initiative—which among other things would signal a major departure from constitutional policy and federal practice by allowing government appropriations and tax benefits for church-based services—builds on the work done by the three previous administrations to devolve responsibility for the poor and disadvantaged to private agencies, both non- and for-profit. In the development of strategic corporate philanthropy programs and an intensified governmental interest in private giving, we see how business strategy and political ideology—and, for that matter business ideology and political strategy—have interacted in the production of techniques designed to encourage private giving, in lieu of the state's role in mitigating the social effects of capitalism.

Not surprisingly, this conjuncture of social forces goes unacknowledged when proponents of philanthropic citizenship claim, as they repeatedly do, that it is a universal and inclusive category, external to the realm of politics and free of the socially divisive forces of race, class, and gender. Nobody, they argue, can be opposed to ordinary folks doing good deeds for one another; philanthropic citizenship is something that we can all support and participate in regardless of our social location or political leanings.

In contrast to this line of thought, the essay argues that such renderings rely on the erasure of power relations that undergird charitable works and the deeply racialized and gendered deployment of philanthropic practice as an ideal of citizenship. The charitable activities that are now a compulsory component of any professional athlete's job description offer a fertile site for exploring this claim. The big three professional sports leagues in the United States draw largely and disproportionately on populations of color, particularly African-American men from poor and working-class backgrounds with limited opportunities for economic security and self-expression, for their pool of laborers. Since the system of exploitative practices and social inequalities on which these organizations rely go largely unacknowledged in popular discourse, professional sport operates as a powerful ideological site for the promotion of the idea that upward mobility is attainable by those who are willing to work hard enough for it. In this context, during the 1980s and 1990s, professional sports leagues and celebrity athletes became particularly potent weapons in racialized struggles over poverty, welfare, and responsibility.

The implication of the professional sport industry in the devolution of social welfare provision from the state to individuals and the private sector was clearly illustrated in NBA's and NFL's cosponsorship of the 1997 President's Summit on America's Future, the extravaganza at which Colin Powell and Bill Clinton launched their campaign to "make volunteerism part of the definition of citizenship" in the wake of welfare reform (Clinton in Hall and Nichols 1997, A12). The more precise goal of the summit was to provide two million underprivileged youth with "five fundamental resources" by the year 2000: mentors, adequate health care, after-school programs, job skills, and the opportunity to do volunteer work. Thus, the underprivileged youth who were to be the beneficiaries of the newly invigorated individual and corporate generosity that was to emerge from the summit were also to be trained as volunteers. In an era in which "neither the government nor the private sector can adequately address the needs of the nation's 15 million disadvantaged children," these children were to learn how to give as well as to receive, to become a generation of adults who are not dependent (Clinton in Hall and Nichols 1997, A12). Exactly *who* these children were was made clear by the armies of students shipped in from inner-city Philadelphia public schools. In media coverage of the opening ceremonies, row upon row of black youth served as a backdrop to appearances by Powell, Clinton, and the other public figures—among them George Bush Sr., Nancy Reagan, Gerald Ford, Oprah Winfrey, and John Travolta—who came to applaud this new approach to welfare management.

In line with this new approach, the NFL's philanthropic programming, which is the particular focus of this essay, is explicitly conceptualized as a tool for building and measuring character among its players who are understood to be engaged in a constant struggle to stay out of trouble and to leave behind the "culture of dependence" in which they are said to have been raised. The league's initiatives, in other words, are designed not simply as public relations ploys, or strategies to distribute services to others, but as tools by which to shape citizens who are both self-responsible and able to take care of others. All of this takes place, as we shall see, in a discursive formation that is saturated with race logic, but because of the ways in which popular conceptions of welfare were so thoroughly racialized during the 1980s and 1990s, rarely needs to name race as such.

Reaganomics, Race, and the Rise of Strategic Philanthropy

The devastating impact of deindustrialization and global integration on poor and working class people in the United States over the past 30 years has been well documented in scholarly research (Bluestone and Harrison 1982; Harvey 1989). The response of the Reagan, Bush, and Clinton administrations to increased poverty wrought by elevated unemployment and the replacement of millions of full-time permanent jobs with low-paying temporary positions should be no less familiar. With considerable assistance from the mass media, these governments engineered a national fantasy by which the effects of economic and social conditions (poverty and welfare "dependency") were blamed on individual inadequacies or failings and, especially in the case of the Republican administrations, the breakdown of the nuclear family. Notwithstanding the fact that the majority of welfare recipients are white, not black, the alleged lack of self-responsibility among America's poor was made visible in public discourse through the bodies of black women. As Valerie Hartouni writes (1997):

> Within Reagan's America, the always black, always urban, supposedly lazy welfare-dependent single mother or "welfare queen" functioned as a condensed symbol deployed to "explain" not only the deeper pathology in black family life, but the destruction of the American way of life. (86)

This fear of threat and decay was heightened through an intensification of the war on drugs, the discursive terrain through which out-of-control criminality and violence were inscribed on the bodies of young, most often black, males. Thus, black women and men became the most visible and widely circulated signs of urban decay, moral breakdown, addiction, and crime during this period, signs that concealed the socioeconomic conditions of late-capitalism and their disproportionate effect on working class, black Americans (hooks 1990, 1992; Reeves and Campbell 1994; West 1990; Williams 1991).

It was within this broad context, and as part of his strategy to make state provision of welfare a thing of the past, that Reagan created, in 1981, the Task Force on Private Sector Initiatives to encourage private sector activity in social programs and increase nongovernmental sources of support for nonprofits. "Volunteerism," Reagan declared, "is an essential part of our plan to give government back to the people. I believe the people are anxious for this responsibility.... We can show the world how to construct a social system more humane, more compassionate, and more effective in meeting its members' needs than any ever known" (Reagan 1981, 1085). Concurrently, the administration introduced incentives by reducing corporate taxes and increasing the limits on charitable deductions for corporations from 5 to 10 percent of taxable income.

At the same time that the nonprofit sector was called upon to partner with corporations to develop private-sector alternatives to public welfare—which was said to stifle "the volunteer impulse of private citizens and private business"—the nonprofit sector saw its budget reduced significantly and its client rolls increase as a result of the administration's cuts in welfare spending and an ongoing recession (Denton, U.S. Senate, 1982, November 8, 2). These cuts, combined with the considerable public attention focused on private-sector initiatives prompted by the launching of the Task Force, coincided to produce a substantial increase in the number of requests on the part of nonprofits for aid from corporations.

Over 75 percent of the executives surveyed for a 1981 Conference Board report said that requests for aid from nonprofits had jumped substantially, with some reporting a 300 percent increase (Muirhead 1999). Although these changes appear to have had an impact on corporate giving in the short term (i.e., until 1987 and the onset of the recession), there was no significant increase in contributions favoring human services. In other words, the increased level of corporate contributions facilitated by Reagan's tax cuts and incentives (which anyway fell far short of the estimated $29 billion needed to "bridge the gap") did not flow to those areas of provision—economic development, hunger relief, or job training, for instance—most affected by cuts in expenditure (Grønberg and Smith 1999; Muirhead 1999; Salamon and Abramson 1982; Zetlin 1990).

Large corporations such as AT&T and leading business organizations such as the Business Roundtable linked their support for the Reagan tax and spending cuts to increases in corporate philanthropy (Levy and Oviatt 1989; O'Connell 1983; Shannon 1991). If business was serious "in seeking to stem over-dependence on government," the Roundtable contested, it had to "increase its level of commitment" to the nonprofit sector (O'Connell 1983, 386). However, when the cuts were actually instituted, business leaders did not express enthusiasm or intent to fill the gap set out by administration strategists (Muirhead 1999, 35). Executives claimed that although their contributions had tripled between 1976 and 1985 from $1.5 billion to $4.5 billion, the $29 billion gap left by Reagan's cuts was too large for corporations to realistically close (Muirhead 1999). Corporate leaders were said to "resent the transfer of the social burden and responsibility to the private sector," and one unnamed "Public Affairs Vice President" told the Roundtable, "Our company supported [President Reagan] because we believed in the elimination of a number of these programs. Naturally, we're not too enthused about continuing the programs and shifting the burden to the corporate sector" (quoted in Muirhead 1999, 36).

The Reagan administration's cuts in social services coincided with a spate of deregulation-induced corporate mergers, restructuring, and downsizing that had begun in the late 1970s. In this context, corporate contributions became the focus of managers who were seeking to gain efficiency in an increasingly competitive marketplace. In the words of James P. Shannon (1996), a corporate philanthropy consultant and recognized proponent of the shift to strategic philanthropy, these changes "put the current managers of corporate philanthropy on notice that henceforth their departments would be evaluated by management against the same standards of performance, efficiency, production, and achievement as all other departments in their companies" (ix). As pressure increased for efficiency and restraint in corporate contributions, some programs disappeared, while in others staff began to look for ways to make philanthropic activities assist with profit making. For instance, when Kodak's community relations and contributions program faced a decrease in its budget, its staff strove to make "community relations a strategic resource in gaining revenue for the company" (Muirhead 1999, 41). Kodak's new strategy involved partnerships between the contributions department and other units of the business so that these units learned "the value of investing in urban markets," "promote business-to-business relationships—not just philanthropic ones—with nonprofits," "leverage contributions to enhance sales opportunities," and "make grants that enhance global access" (Muirhead 1999, 41). Thus, Kodak's philanthropic and profit-making functions have become inextricably intertwined, as philanthropy is viewed as a possible route to gaining access to new markets at home and abroad, finding new partners with whom to do business, and enhancing sales.

Kodak's shift toward strategic philanthropy is typical of corporate America's move to "treat donations like investments" and thus to "expect some return from them"—a move that simultaneously represents a turn away from the understanding of philanthropy as a more straightforward obligation of corporate citizenship (Dienhart 1988, 64). By the 1990s, management guru Peter Drucker's (1984) argument that altruism cannot be the criterion by which corporate giving is evaluated had become a guiding assumption of contributions programs as businesses discharged their social responsibilities by converting them into self-interest.

In practice, the shift toward strategic philanthropy has meant that most large corporations have undertaken at least some of the following changes in their approach to philanthropy and community relations:

- Use of a narrow theme (e.g., environmental protection, breast cancer) to maximize impact of giving and align contributions with business goals and brand characteristics
- Support of programs that target beneficiaries who are or could become customers
- Integration of giving program with marketing, public affairs, and government relations departments
- Formation of partnerships with community groups, local governments, and other companies who share a common interest in a particular concern (e.g., former president Clinton's drive to build "empowerment zones" in economically depressed communities through business, government, and nonprofit partnerships)
- Development of volunteer programs with awards, matching gifts, paid volunteer time, or other incentives to encourage employees to "serve their communities"
- Utilization of already existing company resources to enable noncash forms of contributions
- Use of public relations campaigns that highlight company activities

- Increased emphasis on the measurement of program results
- Instigation of global volunteering or grant-making programs that emphasize and attain a "worldwide" presence

Thus, in the last two decades of the twentieth century, the philosophy and practice of corporate philanthropy had undergone rapid transformation. While there were instances in which corporations made financial contributions without reference to their markets or overall strategic plans, most large corporations employed a business-driven approach to contributions as they sought to attach "value," "strategic vision," and "mission" to their charitable activities. This business-driven approach is known as "strategic philanthropy" and requires that every dollar given must mesh with the company's markets or employees and work as part of their overall strategic plans.

The Branding of Ethics: A History of Cause-Related Marketing

Cause-related marketing (CRM) is one of the most prominent strategies to emerge from this conjuncture. Carol Cone, founder and CEO of Cone Communications, a firm that earns more than $4 million per year promoting CRM, explains the turn to CRM as follows: "No one wants to compete on the basis of price or innovation. Everyone can cut prices, and with today's technology any innovation can be copied within ninety days" (quoted in Davidson 1997, 37). Instead, companies and brands associate themselves with a cause as a means to build the reputation of a brand, increase profit, develop employee loyalty to the company, and add to their reputation as good corporate citizens (Alperson 1995; Davidson 1997; Foley 1998; Graham 1994; Muirhead 1999; Mullen 1997; Stark 1999).

Unlike traditional charity promotions in which a company simply donated money to a cause or sponsored a range of unrelated charities without a coherent strategy, CRM seeks to ensure that the brand and the cause share the same "territory" in a "living, altruistic partnership for mutual benefit" (Pringle and Thompson 1999, 3). Since the mid-1990s, CRM has evolved from what were mostly short-term commitments from corporations to their chosen causes—that is, a one- or two-month promotion with a charitable organization, at the end of which the corporation donated a portion of its profits—to major, long-term commitments to an issue through an alliance that links the company or brand name with the issue in the consumer's mind. According to marketing professionals, the short-term approach is gradually giving way to the long-term approach as the former has come to be seen as opportunistic and therefore possibly harmful to a company's image. In addition, short-term promotions are not thought to shore up the association between the brand and the cause for consumers, and thus fail to "build the brand" in the desired manner (Arnott 1994; Pringle and Thompson 1999).

Marketing experts frequently refer to CRM as a means to "cut through the clutter" caused by increasing competition between manufacturers, the power of multiple retailers, technological advances, fragmentation of media audiences, and the increase in the sheer volume of commercial communications directed at the market (Pringle and Thompson 1999,12). Hence, CRM is understood as a "filter," a way to attract the attention and loyalty of the consumer, who is understood to be increasingly adept at reading marketing messages and dissecting the meaning and symbolism of any particular commercial or advertisement (Pringle and Thompson 1999).

Marketing professionals are explicit in their belief that CRM should be first and foremost a strategy for selling products, rather than an altruistic activity. Writing in the *Harvard Business Review*, Jerry Welsh, the president of Welsh Marketing Associates, expresses his concern that some CRM campaigns do not give consumers a good reason to remember the company or brand "at the end of the day":

Cause related marketing was meant to be marketing, not philanthropy. Otherwise we would know it as "marketing related philanthropy" or something to that effect. The practice was aptly named, however, to describe an innovative and socially useful way to augment the power of more traditional marketing, promotion, and public relations efforts. (Walsh 1999, 24)

A report of the Conference Board even suggested that the very idea of corporate philanthropy might be questionable in the light of the rise of CRM and other aspects of strategic philanthropy:

[T]he appropriateness of the term "philanthropy" to describe corporate giving is being debated. As companies are increasingly driven to analyze the return they're getting for their donations, the process is becoming one of financially sound goodwill. (Alperson 1995, 10)

While marketing professionals are usually explicit about the profit motive behind these campaigns, they often explain the emergence of CRM as a reflection of a shift in consumer attitudes. In this vein, Bill Laberis, editor of *Computerworld* magazine, said of contemporary American consumers, "They want something to believe in, whether it's family, a set of values, or some passion they can pursue.... [It's a] kind of spirituality" (Stark 1999, 20). Meanwhile, Robert Eckert, Kraft Foods president/CEO, told the annual meeting of the Association of National Advertisers, "Consumers are yearning to connect to people and things that will give meaning to their lives" (Stark 1999, 20). Such claims are frequently accompanied by reference to market research by companies such as Cone Communications, which suggests that consumers are more likely to select a brand if it is associated with a cause they care about (Davidson 1997; Pringle and Thompson 1999; Stark 1999). Thus, while CRM is, on the one hand, a response to consumer desires as these desires are constituted through market research techniques, it is, on the other hand, a tool for *incorporating* heightened consumer interest in corporate ethics in a context in which "people are asking more and more questions about the role of commercial organizations in society and are looking for demonstrations of good corporate citizenship" (Pringle and Thompson 1999, xxi–xxii).

Real Men Wear Pink: The National Football League's Breast Cancer Campaign[1]

During the past decade, breast cancer has become a, if not *the*, favorite charitable cause for corporations seeking to attract female consumers through upbeat and optimistic CRM campaigns. In April 1999, the National Football League joined the likes of Avon, BMW, Bristol Myers Squibb, Estée Lauder, Ford Motor Company, General Electric, General Motors, J. C. Penney, Kelloggs, and Lee Jeans, when it became the latest business to form a partnership with a breast cancer foundation, in this case signing on as a national sponsor of the Susan G. Komen Breast Cancer Foundation's Race for the Cure. This arrangement—which partnered a professional sports league that is the epitome of a racialized, black hypermasculinity with a nonprofit that is the epitome of a pink-ribbon, invisibly racialized, white hyperfemininity—brought with it an immediate guarantee of product differentiation and recognition.

The announcement of the new partnership coincided with an ongoing effort on the part of the league to show, in the words of *Detroit News* writer Becky Yerak, "that it's in touch with its feminine side" (2000, B1). Yerak continued: "New advertising and marketing campaigns by the National Football League ... have begun muting the usual machismo and shaping pitches more to women, children and even men who aren't necessarily hardcore fans of the weekend showcase of alpha males" (B1). This new approach to marketing was created, in part, in response to a survey that found 40 percent of the NFL's weekly television viewers are women and, of those 45 million, "20 million call themselves avid fans" (B1). Hoping to maintain this market and to capture the interest of new fans, the NFL turned to breast cancer, an already tried and tested focus for a CRM campaign. DeAnn Forbes, owner of a "female-owned" advertising agency that has a contract with the Detroit Lions, offered this interpretation of the NFL's approach:

> People are tired of seeing a guy in a uniform and another guy in a uniform. Human interest is what'll bring a broader audience…. Whether it's the average fan or novice, they want to know what drives these players. The only way you can really feel connected is to see them, hear them, know them. (Yerak 2000, B3)

In a press release announcing the deal, Nancy Brinker of the Komen Foundation and Sara Levinson of the NFL described their new partnership as an opportunity to spread the message of early detection to the league's huge fan base, which includes more than 68 million women (NFL 1999). The sponsorship deal included a promise by the NFL to enhance marketing and "grassroots" support of the Komen Race for the Cure series. Grassroots activities were to include appearances by players and their families at race events, national television advertising, breast cancer detection information affixed to all "NFL for Her" merchandise, and race signups at NFL Workshops for Women (NFL 1999).

Beginning in October 1999, to coincide with Breast Cancer Awareness Month, the NFL aired a selection of six different TV spots featuring NFL players to "help raise awareness and encourage fans to join in the fight against breast cancer" (NFL 1999). The spots played during NFL games and primetime and daytime programming on ABC, CBS, ESPN, and Fox. Each spot was tagged with a logo bearing the NFL shield wrapped around a pink ribbon, and a phone number that provided information about Race for the Cure events. The footage for the spots was filmed in July 1999 at the Race for the Cure in Aspen, Colorado, a week before the opening of NFL training camps.

Five of the six spots featured a different, high-profile player—Tony Gonzalez, tight end with the Kansas City Chiefs, Jamal Anderson, then running back with the Atlanta Falcons, Hardy Nickerson, then linebacker of the Tampa Bay Buccaneers, Kordell Stewart, then quarterback for the Pittsburgh Steelers, and Jason Sehorn, then defensive back of the New York Giants—describing their experiences as volunteers at the Race. Each of the commercials was visually similar: hundreds of white, middle-aged women (along with smaller numbers of white men and children), decked out in pink and white athletic apparel, walking and jogging along the tree-lined streets of Aspen. Interspersed with these images was footage of the featured players (four of whom are the only people of color visible in the commercials), erecting banners and signs, handing out water to participants as they run by, shaking hands with the men, holding hands with the children, and hugging the women.

In each commercial, the players described their appreciation and admiration for the courage and pride of the survivors. These voice-overs were accompanied by long, lingering closeup shots of the faces of individual women. Jamal Anderson said, "There's nothing like the look of the survivor. And you look into their eyes and you can't help but be overwhelmed." "Man, these people are the true warriors," Tony Gonzales declared. "Man, they're out there struggling with life and death. It's just … it's an inspiration for me." As the players expressed their admiration for the survivors, they also described how their experiences at the Race inspired them to "do more" for the cause. Gonzalez said it is something he might "wanna do in the future," while Anderson suggested that their participation "might help make next year's race bigger" and that it "hopefully raised the awareness of what the Komen Foundation was trying to do."

In tone and style—the sentimental, personal narratives, the soft focus shots, the pink and white color scheme, the uplifting music—the NFL campaign was in many ways a typical breast cancer-related marketing effort. While the significance of the campaign lay partly in its capacity for attracting new consumers, we cannot reduce its significance, or that of CRM in general, to the production of new markets. Nor can we begin to understand its implications simply by undertaking a close textual reading of the commercials. Indeed, what makes it a particularly interesting site for analysis is that it condensed a range of issues related to the gender and racial politics of philanthropy. In order to highlight these issues and read the campaign contextually, I want to take a brief detour through debates about what has come to be known as the "character issue" in the NFL; that is, the alleged propensity of NFL players to criminality, and concomitant debates among officials, coaches, and media critics about how best to screen out "undesirable characters" when recruiting new players to join the league.

Real Men Have Character: Crime and Punishment in the NFL

Public discussions about the world of professional basketball and football have long been a site for the expression of cultural anxieties about race, crime, and violence. Cheryl Cole (1996) argues that during the 1980s and 1990s, popular knowledges about the inner-city, urban problems, and black masculinity were produced and rendered visible through the categories of "sport" and "gangs," where sport appeared as the locus of "conventional values" such as a healthy lifestyle, productivity, and discipline, and gangs as the site for those "behaviors" that were thought to threaten such values—out-of-control violence, insatiable consumerism, and a refusal to take proper and meaningful employment. In turn, such behaviors were deemed responsible for the devastation and "disorder" of America's inner cities. The sport–gang dyad, while ensuring that the values articulated to both sport and gangs remain unquestioned, does not guarantee black athletes an escape from the discourse of racism. For the sport–gang dyad also works as a normalizing lens *within* the world of sport: the criminalization and pathologization of black masculinity is so deeply inscribed and so utterly pervasive as to make black athletes, like all black men, always already potential criminals. Hence, the mass media presents the American public with a constant flow of stories detailing the lives of professional athletes who have been unable to abandon the modes of conduct allegedly instilled in them from a young age. Sports author Jeff Benedict made this point explicit when he claimed in an interview with *Sport* that "you can take the boy out of the inner city but you can't take the inner city out of the boy" (quoted in Keteyian 1998, 33).

Although the alleged propensity of athletes to criminal behavior has been established in the public imagination for some time, since 1996 there has been a proliferation of discourse on the "character issue." When Lawrence Phillips, a player known for his "past bad behavior," was drafted by the St. Louis Rams in 1996 and subsequently arrested on a number of occasions for a variety of offenses (all the subject of intense media coverage), NFL team owners introduced a violent-crime policy by which players arrested for such crimes would be subject to therapy, fines, suspension, or banishment depending on the type of crime committed and the verdict reached by the courts (Attner 1997, S2; Freeman 2000a). The Phillips "fiasco" (Attner's term) was followed, in 1998, by the publication of Jeff Benedict and Don Yaeger's *Pros and Cons: The Criminals Who Play in the NFL*, "the most highly anticipated sports book of the year" (Keteyian 1998, 32). Benedict and Yaeger's "explosive exposé" purported to reveal the "shocking percentage" of NFL players who have been formally charged with committing a serious crime, such as rape, domestic violence, assault, battery, and DUI (Keteyian 1998, 32). Responding to charges by NFL officials that the book would "unfavorably serve to perpetuate stereotypes" and "may, in fact, have been racist," coauthor Benedict told *Sport* magazine that the fact that "so many athletic offenders are black is not a function of race, but rather of the rising recruitment of poorly prepared young men, the majority of whom are black, whose social backgrounds are rife with problems" (Keteyian 1998, 33).

Under headlines such as "NFL: National Felons League" (Baker 2000, A18), "N.F.L. and Union Weigh Player's Violent Acts" (Freeman 2000a, 8), "Despite Lip Service, Team Can't Keep from

Drafting Questionable Characters" (Duncan 2000, C4), "A Dubious Cast of Characters" (Myers 2000, 64), "Tests of Character" (Hruby 2000, 28), "Stains from the Police Blotter Leave NFL Embarrassed" (Freeman 2000b, 8: 1), "Off Field Violence May Stain NFL Image" (Smith 2000, 1), the media set about trying to explain this "unfathomable" set of circumstances and to seek solutions to the "character issue." The theories proffered as explanations ranged from the violent nature of the sport, to the dangers and temptations of women (the "evil that lurks in skirts" according to Diane Shah of the *Chicago Sun-Times*, 2000, 113), to the background or "environment" from which the players originate, to their upbringing in female-headed, "welfare" families.

Among the most high profile solutions to the character issue was the NFL's annual Rookie Symposium, which was first held in 1996, the year of the "Phillips fiasco." Every NFL draftee is required to attend and failure to do so results in a $10,000 fine. Attendees are not allowed to leave the premises without permission, have guests, or drink alcohol. Racially coded accessories such as pagers, do-rags, bandanas, and sunglasses must be left at home. According to a 2002 *New York Times Magazine* article by Stephen Dubner, "The NFL is trying to breed the thug life out of any Rookie so inclined" (2002, 24). For fourteen hours each day, the players learn about the possible "pitfalls" that await them as they launch their professional careers. As they are instructed in the art of how to avoid bar fights, drug stings, sexually transmitted diseases, paternity suits, and domestic violence charges, they are also taught basic financial management skills and alerted to the importance of participating in philanthropic activities.

The philosophy behind the Symposium is thoroughly embedded in the culture of poverty approach to social problems and the conceptions of racialized sexuality upon which it rests: Players are both infantilized and emasculated (they are taught how to put on condoms with the aid of bananas distributed by young women on the NFL staff) and understood as and encouraged to be hypermasculine and hypersexual (they are told by one speaker to "keep a stable of women" to avoid undue complications). Women appear only as scheming money grabbers: Troupes of actors perform scenarios including one in which a player decides to tell his live-in girlfriend to leave the house, but then finds out that she has already met with a lawyer and that they have been cohabitating long enough to be considered legally married. Former friends from home are also to be avoided. Richard Seymour, a rookie the previous year who returned in 2002 to share his experiences, told the participants: "Now that you're in the NFL, everybody's going to say they be there for you. But all they're going to be for me is leeches" (Dubner 2002, 24). The league also seeks to "scare the Rookies into lawfulness" (Dubner 2002, 26) with appearances by former players who have either been in trouble in the past and have turned their lives around or who are currently in prison. Milt Ahlerich, a former FBI assistant director who is now the NFL's security chief, expressed what seems to be a generally cautious approach to the potential outcomes of the event, when he told the *New York Times Magazine* that the Symposium is a "tone-setting device.... But we will not save all souls here, and it's hard to measure the souls that were saved" (26).

As one of their central strategies for "saving souls," the league now places a greater emphasis on "character-building" practices such as volunteerism. In addition to espousing the importance of voluntary work at the Rookie Symposium, the NFL has proposed "dealing" with the character issue by emphasizing, through mass media campaigns, "the positive deeds players do in the community." The focus on media image would give some credence to skeptics who dismiss player volunteerism programs as simply PR, and it would be hard to deny that this is a central motivation on the part of the league. But I also want to suggest that the importance of professional athletes' participation in philanthropy is understood to go beyond its public relations potential. For instance, as the media scrutinized Ray Lewis's "character," they also looked to his record of philanthropic activities to strengthen their assessments. In an extended analysis of the Lewis case, Jarret Bell asks if we should understand Lewis as a "Saint or Thug?" and turns to Lewis's "involvement in the community" to explore his character (Bell 2000, 1C):

> Lewis is considered a "go-to" guy by the Raven's staff because of his generosity with time and money for needy causes. He routinely visits children in hospitals, and he became active with the Police Athletic League in Baltimore. He once purchased 250 tickets for underprivileged kids to attend a Washington Bullets (now Wizards) game, and he hosted a bowling tournament to aid needy kids. And Lewis once matched the team's $23, 000 contribution to a food drive. (Bell 2000, 1C)

"But," Bell continues, making explicit the apparent disjuncture between a propensity toward volunteering and a propensity toward crime, "Lewis has also been the focus of police interest" (2000, 1C).

Following Lewis's and Rae Carruth's respective arrests, the NFL draft became the focus for further discussion of the character issue. In the runup to the draft, league general managers "talked endlessly about picking players with character" (Goldman 2000) and when the New York Jets drafted "three players with rap sheets" (Myers 2000, 64), critics expressed their skepticism (Battista 2000; Duncan 2000; Myers 2000). Alongside details of these players' "troubled ways" (Battista 2000, D7), critics drew attention to new draftees who scored highly on character tests and articulated their scores to their realizing the importance of volunteerism: LaVar Arrington, who was drafted by the Redskins, "spoke about responsibility and character," and Chris Samuels, also picked by the Redskins, "visited with inner city kids in Brooklyn during his stay in New York" (Myers 2000, 64). Unlike officials at the New York Jets, Arrington and Samuels "get it," claimed Gary Myers of the *New York Daily News* (2000, 64). And what do they get, we might ask? That "character counts," according to Myers.[2]

Building "Proper" Citizens: The Pedagogy of Volunteerism and the Racialization of Generosity

The Real Men Wear Pink campaign, then, is part of a discursive formation in which a player's character is judged, at least in part, on the basis of his involvement in volunteerism, and in which participation in volunteerism is articulated to good character and understood, like race, to be predictive of a player's propensity to crime. The character problem in the NFL, if we remember, was also blamed on the absence of a father figure in the players' childhoods. While anxieties about absent fathers are most obviously anxieties about the disintegration of the disciplinary mechanisms of the heteronormative nuclear family, these anxieties are linked, in important ways, to contemporary discourse on volunteerism and philanthropy. Like the youth who were the target of the President's Summit on America's future, many NFL players have grown up in households headed by a "welfare mother" and have thus, it is implied, been deprived of "generous" and "independent" role models. Thus, an embedded message of discourse on the character issue is that these men, like the youth at the Philadelphia summit, must be trained as volunteers in order that they might avoid the life choices taken by their implied and figurative parents, the "welfare queen" and the absent father.

Thus, in the context both of contemporary discourse on volunteerism and responsibility and the debate about character in the NFL, Real Men Wear Pink might best be read as an advertisement for the promise of personal, private philanthropy in the postwelfare, neoliberal era. In its positioning of black men who are drawn disproportionately from poor and working-class communities in the role of the privileged purveyors of goods to the "less fortunate," the campaign also performed a set of erasures about race, class, and privilege in the contemporary United States. These erasures were exacerbated by the fact that the narratives and images that constitute the debate about character, as well as those that comprised the breast cancer campaign, were so thoroughly racialized, even as they were characterized by a complete absence of references to "race," race relations, or racial inequalities, an absence that reflects the color-blind constraints of popular culture in the present moment.

The players who appeared in these commercials, and whose participation in philanthropic activity is the stuff of an endless stream of press releases, are the exemplars of "good character," where the latter is defined by a willingness to embrace bourgeois, humanistic values such as the need to perform organized, charitable works. The particular form of compassionate culture that the campaign represented and for which the "American people" are currently supposed to strive is one in which acts of organized volunteerism signify both concern for others and self-responsibility and fulfillment. However, this is most definitely not a culture that recognizes as (American) generosity, the informal networks of support and care upon which poor, urban, and rural communities often depend.

While the commercials offered a model for the ideal practitioner of American generosity, they also gave shape to an idealized recipient. Unlike the welfare mother who is so prominent in the NFL character debates, the breast cancer survivors we saw in Real Men Wear Pink and in discourse on breast cancer more broadly are the embodiment of a middle class, heteronormative, nationally sanctioned womanhood. As survivors, they are ordained with an inherent wisdom and morality. Through their participation in the Race they are at once recipients and purveyors of charity and bearers of the moral worth bound up with healthy discipline. Moreover, these women appear as beacons of hope who through their individual courage, strength, and vitality have elicited an outpouring of American generosity, a continued supply of which will ensure the fight against beast cancer remains an unqualified success.

War Games: Sport and the Militarization of Everyday Life

When market concerns drive philanthropic practice, chosen causes come and go. The NFL partnership with the Komen Foundation lasted two years, and was regarded as a successful initiative by both parties. The league has now moved on. It continues its thirty-year-long collaboration with the United Way, and a range of community outreach and volunteer recognition initiatives under its umbrella program "Join the Team." It has also shifted the emphasis of its post-9/11 community outreach activities away from disaster relief, urban regeneration, and economic recovery to patriotic and militaristic projects, some of which have been carried out in collaboration with the Bush administration.

Most prominently, in September 2003, the league staged the second Kickoff Live. This time the event took place on the National Mall in Washington, DC, in front of a crowd that included 25,000 troops shipped in for the event by the Department of Defense. Publicity materials noted that the purpose of this "new tradition" was to "celebrate the resilient and indomitable spirit of America" (www.nfl.com). Earlier in the week, NFL Commissioner Paul Tagliabue and other representatives of the league met with President Bush, Vice President Dick Cheney, Secretary of State Colin Powell, and National Security Advisor Condoleezza Rice in the Oval Office. During the meeting, Bush was presented with the official Kickoff ball inscribed with the words, "The first football of the 2003 season, presented to President George W. Bush, with deep appreciation" (www.nfl.com).

NFL players have also made numerous trips to visit injured soldiers both within the United States and at air bases in Germany. The league pledged to donate football equipment to all teams associated with the military, and the NFL is working in partnership with the government on "Operation Tribute to Freedom," a program designed to "reinforce the bond between the citizen and the military" and to "help Americans express their support for the troops who are returning from operations in Iraq and Afghanistan, and who continue to fight in the ongoing effort toward victory in the global war on terrorism" (www.nfl.com).

As Gamal Abdul-Shehid (2002) has argued, athletes and soldiers of color (mostly male) play a key role, ironically, in the reproduction of U.S. hegemony and dominant ideological values at home and abroad. Black men, in particular, are overrepresented in both the military and professional sport, institutions that are crucial to the assertion and maintenance of the political, cultural, and economic supremacy of the United States. They fight wars on behalf of our leaders, literally in the case of soldiers, and figuratively in the case of athletes whose labor in international competition is central to the reproduction of U.S. national identity. At the same time, the prominence of men of color in these fields masquerades as evidence of the egalitarian character of U.S. society, rather than an effect of highly limited opportunities for upward mobility in a racialized, capitalist social formation. As Abdul-Shehid further suggests, the adoration reserved for athletes coexists alongside widespread fear and loathing on the part of the white population toward African-American men outside the realm of sport, a state of mind that is most violently manifested in the mass incarceration of African-American men over the past two decades.

When NFL players pay visits to soldiers wounded in Iraq as part of the league's philanthropic programming, these ironies and contradictions play out in ways that are particularly troubling. Washington Redskin Rocky Cartwright's description of a visit to the Walter Reed Army Medical Center is typical of media stories about this programming: "Some of these guys are younger than me, and that's something that really stays with you. They are fighting for this country and you've really got to appreciate everything they do" (www.nfl.com). Jason Taylor of the Miami Dolphins speaks in similar terms:

> It is a different world. It's kind of gratifying but, at the same time, sort of sad. Gratifying to know that we had so many good people fighting the war for us. And sad to see how many of them were injured. There were a lot of 18- and 19-year-old kids who put it all on the line. I'm not ashamed to say I cried a few times meeting some of them and hearing some of the stories. (ESPN.com)

While the moving words of both players draw attention to injured soldiers—in itself a disruption given the Bush administration-ordered blackout of such coverage—these narratives make invisible the exploitative relations that undergird participation in professional sport and military service. That is, by positioning the players as ingratiated to, and thus fundamentally different from, those who have served overseas, the shared histories and social location of these two groups of laborers gets erased. At the same time, these stories work in conjunction with hegemonic discourse on the occupation of Iraq to completely expunge the dramatic and violent effect of the war on its people.

Under the far-right administration of George W. Bush, the call for national spiritual and material prosperity based on charitable works and voluntary financial commitments has intensified. It has become closely entangled with demands for citizens to display patriotism and support for war. Despite the rhetoric of Bush and others, the question of how to be good is, of course, not so easily answered. For when we understand conceptions of good, and of evil, to be socially constituted within complex grids of power relations, it is possible to see how even the most seemingly innocent and straightforward acts of philanthropy have the potential to bring about harmful effects, both for the practitioners and recipients of generosity.

Notes

1. The press release announcing the deal was titled "Real Men Wear Pink." The relationship between the NFL and the Komen Foundation ended in 2001. An NFL official told me that both parties were refocusing their marketing efforts, although it was possible that the relationship might be resumed in the future.
2. Lewis was subsequently acquitted, and Carruth found guilty of conspiracy to commit murder, shooting into an occupied vehicle, and using an instrument to destroy an unborn child.

References

Alperson, M. *Corporate Giving Strategies that Add Business Value.* New York: The Conference Board, 1995.

Arnott, N. "Marketing with a Passion." *Sales and Marketing Management* 146 (1994): 64–71.

Attner, P. "Prospects or Suspects?" *Sporting News* 211, no. 16 (1994): S2–S6.

Baker, K. "There's Not Much the NFL Can Do." *Sporting News* 224, no. 9 (1994): 35.

Battista, J. "N.F.L. Draft: Troubled Pasts Don't Worry Jets." *The New York Times*, April 17, 2000.

Bell, J. "Friend's Come to Lewis' Defense." *USA Today*, May 15, 2000.

Bluestone, B. and B. Harrison. *The Deindustrialization of America: Plant Closings, Community Abandonment, and the Dismantling of Basic Industry.* New York: Basic Books, 1982.

Boris, E. "The Nonprofit Sector in the 1990s." In *Philanthropy and the Nonprofit Sector in a Changing America*, edited by Charles T. Clotfelter and T. Ehrlich, 1–33. Bloomington: Indiana University Press, 1999.

Cole, C. "American Jordan: P.L.A.Y., Consensus and Punishment." *Sociology of Sport Journal* 13 (1996): 366–97.

Davidson, J. "Cancer Sells." *Working Woman*, May 1997, 36–39.

DeFord, F. "Violent Athletes." *Morning Edition.* National Public Radio, February 16, 2000.

Dienhart, J. "Charitable Investments: A Strategy for Improving the Business Environment." *Journal of Business Ethics* 7 (1988): 63.

Drucker, P. "The New Meaning of Corporate Social Responsibility." *California Management Review* 26 (1984): 59.

Dubner, S. "Life is a Contact Sport." *New York Times Magazine*, April 18, 2000.

Duncan, J. "Despite Lip Service, Teams Can't Keep from Drafting Questionable Characters." *The Times-Picayune*, April 23, 2000.

Freeman, M. "N.F.L. and Union Weigh Player's Violent Acts." *The New York Times*, March 26, 2000a.

Freeman, M. "Stains from the Police Blotter Leave N.F.L. Embarrassed." *The New York Times*, January 9, 2000b.

Foley, J. "Picking a Philanthropic Partner." *Marketing Magazine*, September 7, 1998, 16.

Goldman, T. "Jury Selection to Begin Today in the Murder Trial of Pro Football's Ray Lewis." *Morning Edition.* National Public Radio, 2000.

Graham, J. "'Doing Good' Is Good and Bad for Business." *Supervision* (July 1994): 11–13.

Gronberg, K. A. and S. Smith. "Nonprofit Organizations and Public Policies in the Delivery of Human Services." In *Philanthropy and the Nonprofit Sector in a Changing America*, edited by Charles T. Clotfelter and Thomas Erlich, 139–71. Bloomington: Indiana University Press, 1999.

Hall, M. and B. Nichols. "Clinton: Citizenship Means Giving." *USA Today*, April 25, 1997.

Harvey, D. *The Condition of Postmodernity: An Inquiry into the Origins of Cultural Change.* Oxford: Basil Blackwell, 1989.

Himmelstein, J. "Corporate Philanthropy and Business Power." In *Corporate Philanthropy at the Crossroads,* edited by D. Burlingame and D. Young, 144–57. Bloomington: Indiana University Press, 1996.

hooks, b. *Yearning: Race, Gender, and Cultural Politics.* Toronto: Between-the-Lines, 1990.

hooks, b. *Black Looks: Race and Representation.* Boston: South End Press, 1992.

Hruby, P. "Test of Character." *Insight on the News* 16 (May 1, 2000): 28–29

Keteyian, A. "Crime Season: An Explosive New Book Attacks." *Sport*, October 1998, 32.

Levy, R. and F. Oviatt. "Corporate Philanthropy." In *Experts in Action: Inside Public Relations*, edited by C. Burger, 126–38. White Plains, NY: Longman, 1989.

Muirhead, S. *Corporate Contributions: The View from 50 Years.* New York: The Conference Board, 1999.

Mullen, J. "Performance-Based Corporate Philanthropy: How 'Giving' Smart Can Further Corporate Goals." *Public Relations Quarterly* 42 (1997): 8.

Myers, G. "A Dubious Cast of Characters." *New York Daily News*, April 17, 2000.

National Football League, "Real Men Wear Pink: NFL Encourages Women and Men to Join the Fight against Breast Cancer," press release, October 10, 1999.

O'Connell, B. *America's Voluntary Spirit: A Book of Readings.* New York: The Foundation Center, 1983.

Pringle, H. and M. Thompson. *Brand Spirit: How Cause-Related Marketing Builds Brands.* New York: John Wiley, 1999.

Reagan, R. "Remarks at the Annual Meeting of the National Alliance of Business." *Weekly Compilation of Presidential Documents* 17 (October 5, 1981): 1081–1086.

Reeves, J. and Campbell, R. *Cracked Coverage: Television News, the Anti-Cocaine Crusade, and the Reagan Legacy.* Durham, NC: Duke University Press, 1994.

Rose, N. *Powers of Freedom: Reframing Political Thought.* Cambridge, UK: Cambridge University Press, 1990.

Salamon, L. and A. Abramson. *The Federal Budget and the Non-Profit Sector.* Washington, DC: Urban Institute Press, 1982.

Shah, D. "Leagues Try to Protect, Educate Players." *Chicago Sun-Times*, May 7, 2000.

Shannon, J. *The Corporate Contributions Handbook.* San Francisco: Jossey-Bass, 1991.

Shannon, J. "Foreword." In *Corporate Philanthropy at the Crossroads*, edited by D. Burlingame and D. Young, ix–xi. Bloomington: Indiana University Press, 1996.

Shehid, G.-A. "Muhammad Ali: America's B Side." *Journal of Sport and Social Issues* 26 (2002): 317–325.

Smith, K. "Off-Field Violence May Stain NFL Image." *The Tampa Tribune*, May 15, 2000.

Stark, M. "Brand AID: Case Effective." *Brandweek* 40 (1999): 20–22.

U.S. Congress. Senate. *Promoting the General Welfare: Public and private poverty initiatives. Hearing before the Subcommittee on Aging, Family, and Human Services of the Committee on Labor and Human Resources.* 97th Cong. 2nd sess. Washington, DC: U.S. Government Printing Office, 1982.

Walsh, J. "Good Cause, Good Business." *Harvard Business Review* 21 (1999): 24.

Williams, P. *Alchemy of Race and Rights.* Cambridge: Harvard University Press, 1991.

Yankey, J. A. "Corporate Support of Nonprofit Organizations." In *Corporate Philanthropy at the Crossroads*, edited by D. F. Burlingame and D. Young. Bloomington: Indiana University Press, 1996.

Yerak, B. "Lions Share Market with Women: Alpha Males Move Over." *The Detroit News*, January 7, 2000.

Zietlin, M. "Companies Find Profit in Corporate Philanthropy." *Management Review* 79 (1990): 10.

19

Transnationalism, Transcitizenship, and the Implications for the "New World Order"

LUIS MIRÓN, ANTONIA DARDER, AND JONATHAN XAVIER INDA

Transcitizenship

The avant-garde video, *The Sixth Section*, is a startling example of what Smith has aptly character-ized as "transnational urbanism" (M. P. Smith 2001). Here filmmaker and cyberartist Alex Rivera vividly documents the formation and successes of Grupo Unión, a Mexican community develop-ment organization in Newburgh, New York. Grupo Unión represents one of over 3,000 such orga-nizations in the United States, groups that have in one fashion or another apparently exploited the inexpensive labor market, and abundance of service and other relatively low paying jobs, to estab-lish new economic residence while maintaining close family ties with their home in Mexico.[1]

What makes this group both extraordinary and representative of a larger social movement is the political effect it has created on economic development and on politicians in its home town, and its collective solidarity with similar organizations in the United States. Filmmaker Rivera calls the group's political capacity "transnational organizing." These political–economic impacts, moreover, are genuinely transnational in process in that the effects of its community organizing are felt both in the United States, the northern empire, and Mexico, its putative southern periphery neighbor. Such transnational urbanism, we argue and demonstrate below, flies in the theoretical face of struc-turally oriented social theorists who universally state that poor immigrant citizens lack the capacity to effectively resist the deleterious forces of global capital (Harvey 1989); global capitalism is totaliz-ing in its denial of agency. We counter below that such a unidimensional view of the processes of globalization rests on empirically questionable as well as conceptually flawed models of citizenship.

This essay explores new notions of citizenship, ideas that are grounded in what Renato Rosaldo (1994) conceptualizes as cultural citizenship. The essay expands upon Rosaldo's perspective to situ-ate new notions of citizenship in the contemporary global context. Here we advance the argument that the politics of social movements, or what Michael Peter Smith illuminates as a "transnational urbanism," may now conceptually shape the contours of the new discourses of citizenship in this postmodern historicized moment. Rather than displace the meaning of place, the processes of glo-balization and transnationalism propel local actors through their vast social networks to fully engage in the politics of place making. These dual processes—globalization and transnational urbanism (Smith 2001)—potentially better define the meanings for cultural citizenship as well as the implications for the recent military assaults on its constitution. In brief, this conceptual fusion points toward a notion of what we are calling "transcitizenship," whose parameters we sketch in the conclusion of this essay.

The essay will proceed along three fronts: (1) We outline Rosaldo's and Smith's conceptual framework. (2) We borrow from empirical data collected from interviews with a study of "transnational migrants" (Miron, Inda, and Aguirre 1998) in California to illustrate the theoretical utility of the categories of transnational urbanism in particular. (3) We normatively and conceptually argue for a notion of "transcitizenship." This notion is conceptually derived from Rosaldo's and Smith's complementary frameworks. Yet at the same time we remain acutely cognizant of how recent events make this notion, like other theories that embed assumptions of political agency, fragile. Finally we end the essay with observations on post-9/11 wherein we are witnessing a possible return to military imperialism as an institutional marker for the enforcement of anachronistic and foreseeable new hegemonic models of citizenship in liberal democratic societies (McDonough and Feinberg 2003).

Cultural Citizenship

One of the major problems with the nativism (Delgado 1999), and its corresponding politics of citizenship, is that it operates under the assumption that we still live in a world in which the nation-state can properly be bounded and, by extension, in which the only meaningful form of community is one localized within those boundaries. But this world simply does not exist (which is not to say that the nation-state has become irrelevant). As we have seen, the global restructuring since the mid-1970s has involved such a transformation of the economy that capital is able to flow across national boundaries with relative ease. This same restructuring has been responsible for the major demographic transformation not only of the United States but of other nations of the West. Thus the world has witnessed what has variously been called the peripheralization of the core or the implosion of the third world into the first (Sassen 1982; Rosaldo 1988). In other words, the nations of the West, of which the United States is one example, have been "invaded," to use a popular metaphor, by peoples from non-Western or third world countries, so that you now have Algerians in France, Moroccans and Dominicans in Spain, Senegalese in Italy, and folks from just about everywhere in the United States. But the crucial thing about these migrants is that, quite unlike what the traditional literature on immigration suggests (Handlin 1973), they have not uprooted themselves, leaving behind their homeland and facing the often painful process of incorporation into a new national culture; instead, in part because the facilitation of two-way traffic, both physical and metaphorical, made possible by modern technologies of transport and communication (the Internet, telephone, television, airplanes, fax machines, etc.), they have been able to forge multistranded ties that link together their society of settlement and origin. These immigrants, then, as Glick Schiller, Basch, and Szanton Blanc (1995) suggest, are best understood as transmigrants: "Transmigrants are immigrants whose daily lives depend on multiple and constant interconnections across international borders and whose public identities are configured in relationship to more than one nation-state" (1995, 48). What we are witnessing, then, through these transmigrants, is a world in which significant social ties are no longer simply confined within the boundaries of a single territorial national space. This means that we have to think of citizenship in slightly different terms when it comes to (many) contemporary immigrants. Citizenship must be thought of in terms of the strategies migrants use to navigate transnational spaces.

We propose, then, to speak of *cultural citizenship*. Here we loosely follow Katharyne Mitchell (1997). For Mitchell, "although immigrants may become legal citizens through a prescribed, state-regulated path, immigrants become *cultural* citizens only through a reflexive set of formative and locally constructed processes" (1997, 229). In other words, immigrants become cultural citizens, at least in part, through their acculturation to national traditions, giving them the cultural capital necessary to maneuver within the space bounded by such conventions. We say "at least in part" because in the era of transnational flows cultural citizenship involves not only acculturation to local (read national) traditions but to global compacts as well: "In order to function effectively in an interconnected yet locally mediated global economy, the global subject must be attuned to the nuances of a particular locale as well as to the transnational flows characteristic of late capitalism" (Mitchell 1997, 229). This means that while it may be important for immigrants to acquire some form of legal status in the countries in which they have settled, which gives them access to the protection and benefits of the welfare state, it is just as important for them to acquire, even if minimally, the cultural skills necessary for them to navigate this national space. They can even acquire such cultural competencies without legal citizenship. Moreover, since many of them live lives that cut across national boundaries, it is also important for them to maintain a cultural repertoire essential for them to maneuver in this transnational space. In other words, because the space in which they live is not just national, to only acculturate to national traditions, as the nativisms of the 1990s and early twenty-first century would have immigrants do, simply will not suffice. Below we will examine how immigrants, specifically newly arrived Latino immigrants in public schools in California, strive to become cultural citizens of such transnational spaces. In doing so they embody cultural practices of transnational urbanism. With respect to everyday cultural practices, the question of language is crucial because the students we worked with emphasize the importance of becoming polyglot cultural citizens, allowing them to move in spaces that transcend the nation. What we are working with here, then, is a notion of citizenship that goes beyond legalistic definitions to encompass the more informal aspects of how people integrate into their environments, so that legal citizenship is not the end, nor even the beginning, of numerous, active local mediations over the terms of the local-transnational integration of people (Mitchell 1997).

The members of El Grupo Unión exercise their newly negotiated civic entitlements by establishing hybrid cultural identities in upstate New York. When in possession of legal documents permitting them to work as low wage earners in the United States, these immigrants exploit the state apparatus (see below) by holding a form of dual citizenship as citizens of Mexico and legal residents of the United States. Although structurally oriented globalization theorists may reasonably argue that performing menial jobs such as waiting on tables and driving taxis help to reproduce the totalizing effects of capital, such view is theoretically unsophisticated. This is so because from the perspective of the members of these organizations, their economic status as U.S. workers pushes the Mexican state to be more responsive—and less corrupt—to communities, and their extra earnings support their families rather than U.S. corporations. In short we need a new theoretical paradigm to highlight the complexities of transnationalism, a theory that is more sensitive to cultural forces and politics on the ground. We turn now to the work of Michael Peter Smith.

Transnational Citizenship

In numerous writings Smith (among other works see 2001, 1998, 1995, 1992) has theorized on the processes of globalization and transnationalism. Smith is particularly interested in the vast networks of social movements, networks, kin groups, and panethnic identities to recover the sense of human and political agency. This he conceptualizes as "transnational urbanism" or social networks in migration from below (4). His principal aim in doing so is to strike a conceptual balance to what he sees as the totalizing discourses of the global economy (Castells 1998, 1996; Harvey 1989), one that he aptly characterizes as global economism, or "transanational capital from above" (Guarnizo and Smith 1998, 3). Smith views the theoretical and practical results of this conceptualization as producing a cultural reductionism, which (dis)"connects macro-economic and geopolitical transformations (from) the micro networks of social action that people create, move in, and act upon in their daily lives" (2001, 6).

Smith's innovative theoretical alternative is anchored in agency-oriented social theory, which encapsulates the following conceptual and practical dimensions. These dimensions of agency, moreover, are embedded in a metatheoretical framework of social construction; that is, the structures of and processes of capitalism (globalization) are invented, challenged, and potentially transformed by actors.

First, social theorists describe and interpret the world largely in terms of how they perceive reality. Smith believes that social scientists view the world as they perceive themselves. Second, the social structures that shape the actions of human agents and the actors themselves are both "socially constructed understandings of how the world works" (8). Third, direct observation of social and cultural practices, including the texts of urban theorists, is needed to arrive at a deeper understanding of social reality. Finally, deconstruction is not an end in itself. It is a tool of praxis that ultimately leads to "a new discursive space for social inquiry." In short Smith seeks to plow conceptual ground to give new meaning to the everyday practices of social actors, most especially those transnational migrants and citizens exercising agency from below. In a nutshell, these processes Smith conceives as transnational urbanism, in effect processes that point to how migrant-citizens negotiate hybridity in transnational urban spaces (McCarthy and Crichlow 1993, esp. 45).

Transcitizens in the United States

In a 1998 study, Mirón, Inda, and Aguirre found that newly arrived Mexican immigrants[2] to California who enrolled in public schools, witnessing a resurgence of nativism (Chavez 1997) and anti-immigration policies, all strongly desired to learn English. The interview data revealed that these new immigrant students felt that learning English was an economic necessity in their newly adopted country and a key to future upward mobility. For instance, Julio noted: "Knowing [English] gives you the upper edge. For example, one can improve the overall quality of life, have a better job, earn higher wages, fit in socially in any kind of situation, well there's so much more." (Mirón, Inda, and Aguirre 1998, 671). At the same time, all of the students interviewed in the small sample expressed the need to retain their native Spanish language. They were typical of the majority of Mexican families who maintained an acute sense of nationalism even as parents enrolled their children in previously white dominated school districts such as Orange County, California. Immigrants from Mexico and other Latin American nations in this study, aided by policies that eased dual citizenship yet restricted by a backlash against waves of Latino immigration in California and other states, occupied new social and political spaces. They partly comprised global flows that more readily permitted movement between nations. They were cultural citizens (Rosaldo 1994), who navigated somewhat independently of legal requirements, yet some of them were "illegals," who were painfully reminded of their vulnerability that limited their freedoms.

In the bulk of this article we provide detailed analytical commentary on this ethnographic study of transnational urbanism. We use the empirical data and interpretation of the research findings as a kind of social text that can aid in the deconstruction and, hence, "concretization" (Dhillion 1994) of the abstract structural forces of globalization, as well as in the construction of a vision of praxis in light of world events such as 9/11 and the war in Iraq. First we locate the processes of globalization on the grounds of locality, in the burgeoning demographic shifts occurring in the United States, specifically California.

The U.S. Context of Transnational Urbanism

Since the mid-1970s, California has witnessed a major demographic transformation, going from predominantly white and U.S.-born to increasingly Latino and foreign-born (see below). One of the symptoms of this transformation has been the flourishing of nativism during the 1990s, producing a climate that has been distinctly hostile toward immigrants. Much of this hostility stems from the perception that immigrants threaten the integrity of the American nation because they are culturally different. This is clearly the case with the current antipathy toward the use of non-English languages, a sentiment that springs largely from the fear that linguistic difference is fragmenting the United States. The solution (one of them anyway) was the elimination of bilingual education from California classrooms. At least such was the aim of Proposition 227 ("English for the Children"), a grassroots initiative that came before the voters of California in June 1998. The implicit promise of this initiative is to remove those language barriers that prevent the proper assimilation of immigrants into our common American culture and keep our nation disunited (One Nation/One California 1998).

With this hostile climate as a political context, this article will focus on how new Latino immigrant students in Santa Ana, California, attempt to make social and cultural spaces for themselves.[3] We argue that one of their strategies is to become cultural citizens of transnational spaces. This means that rather than simply acculturating to the dominant traditions of the United States, as the nativism of the 1990s would have it, these students strive to acquire the cultural capital necessary to maneuver across national spaces, across those spaces that connect the United States and their homelands. In this respect, the question of language becomes crucial: it is only through becoming polyglots that they can better navigate in spaces that transcend the nation. As polyglot cultural citizens, these students would be better able to form bonds of belonging across national terrains, allowing them to take advantage of opportunities, market or otherwise, wherever they become available. Thus their lives and future aspirations would not be confined to just one national space. What we are working with here, then, is a notion of citizenship that goes beyond legalistic definitions to encompass the more informal aspects of how people are integrated into their cultural milieus, in this case milieus that are not confined to just one national space. We begin our discussion with a closer look at the recent demographic developments in the United States and the nativist climate in California, a climate some have dubbed the *new* nativism (Chavez 1997; Sanchez 1997).

The closing years of the twentieth century marked an epochal transformation in the nature of U.S. society and the nations of the West in general. Nowhere is this more obvious than in the demographic transformations since the 1960s and 1970s. Since the late 1960s, immigration patterns to the United States have changed in at least two important ways.[4] First, there has been a significant increase in the overall annual entry levels: from about 400,000 a year in the 1970s to 600,000 a year in the 1980s to about 800,000 a year in the 1990s (Westphal 1998, 13). As a consequence, the foreign-born population of the United States now stands at over 25 million, which means that roughly one out of every ten residents was born abroad, making it the nation's highest proportion since before World War II (Westphal 1998, 13). And second, there has been a marked shift in the regional composition of migration flows: In 1940, approximately 70 percent of all immigrants entering the United States came from Europe, while in 1992 most of them came from either Asia (37%) or Latin American/Caribbean (44%), Europe accounting for only 15 percent of the immigration pie (*Time* 1994, 15). Given these two changes, the United States has become increasingly racially and ethnically diverse. This has been particularly true for those states in which the latest waves of immigrants tend to cluster, these being California, New York, Illinois, New Jersey, Florida, and Texas, which together receive about three quarters of all new immigrants (Sassen 1989).[5] And it has been even more true for certain large metropolitan areas, such as New York, Los Angeles, San Francisco, Chicago, Houston, and Miami, where immigrants and their children make up a notably higher proportion of the population than they do of the U.S. total (Sassen 1989). Many U.S. cities have thus been transformed from primarily European-American metropolises into meeting places for a wide rage of peoples from all over the world, zones that showcase the juxtaposition of different societies, modes of life, and social practices.

This demographic transformation has been most marked in California, which has the highest percentage of foreign-born residents of any state in the nation. It is estimated that about one fourth of the state's 33 million inhabitants was born outside of the United States (about 2 million of these foreigners are undocumented immigrants). California also leads all other states in the number of new legal immigrants who settle within its borders each year, which is calculated to be anywhere from 200,000 to 300,000 (Garcia y Griego and Martin 1997). In addition, it is estimated that roughly 105,000 Mexicans have settled illegally in the United States each year since 1990 (del Olmo 1997, M5), a good number of these undoubtedly in California. It is suggested by some researchers that the immigrant population of California will only continue to grow into the next century (Garcia y Griego and Martin 1997).

Transnational Urbanism in Motion

We noted above that the world today is no longer simply organized, if it ever was, along national parameters, emphasizing that immigrants often inhabit transnational spaces. Such a world is nowhere more apparent than in the case of Latino immigrants residing in the United States. For example, Roger Rouse argues that migrants between rural Mexico and the United States after World War II, and specially after the mid-60s, have developed sociospatial arrangements that question the received ways of viewing migration as a one-way movement from one set of social relationships to another, thus obliging us to map an alternative cartography of social space:

> [I]t has become inadequate to see Aguilillan migration as a movement between distinct communities, understood as the loci of distinct sets of social relationships. Today, Aguilillans find that their most important kin and friends are as likely to be living hundreds or thousands of miles away as immediately around them. More significantly, they are often able to maintain these spatially extended relationships as actively and effectively as the ties that link them to their neighbors. In this regard, growing access to the telephone has been particularly significant, allowing people not just to keep in touch periodically but to contribute to decision making and participate in familial events even from a considerable distance. (1991, 13)

In short, "through the continuous circulation of people, money, goods, and information," separate places effectively become a single community—one spread across a variety of sites, something Rouse refers to as a "transnational migrant circuit" (1991, 13). This facilitates the formation of pan-ethnicities and, ultimately, may culminate in what we call here the possibilities of "transcitizenship" (see below). Thus this cultural circuit—this circuit that cuts across national boundaries—rather than any particular local, becomes the site where the lives of Aguilillans take place. This being the case, Rouse deduces that the older possibilities of assimilation to a single national order are being subverted, so that it becomes "difficult to delimit a singular national identity (a politically bounded subject) and a continuous history, and the claims of politicians to speak authoritatively on behalf of this imagined community [the imagined community that is the nation] and its purported interests become increasingly hollow" (1991, 17, parenthetical comment ours). The upshot of this, then, is not simply that significant social ties are no longer just confined within the boundaries of a single territorial national space, but that as a result of such ties we are witnessing a new generation of migrants who escape, to some extent, the impress of the nation to shape their identity (Kearney 1991). In short these migrants enter, and may occupy, transnational urban spaces. We assert that these spaces are both cultural and political. And since they escape such impression, the nation of settlement, for example, is placed in somewhat of a bind because it is not really able to turn the cultural differences it encounters into homogeneous identity. In other words, the nation, the Western nation really, is unable to turn its territorially defined space into a culturally homogeneous community. All this suggests, then, that while immigrants may reside in the United States, the land of their birth is not simply left behind, but brought into a network of attachments of which the "homeland" and the United States form two nodes. In other words, the processes of transnational urbanism have aided migrants to form multilocale attachments that stretch across national boundaries. The attachments form the contours of hybrid, multiple cultural identities (Dhillon 1994, 39–51).

Locating the Places of Transcitizenship

Santa Ana, California, can be seen as one such locale, forming part of a multitude of transnational networks. Santa Ana, a community of 300,000 residents, is little known outside of southern California. Situated in northern Orange County, a sprawling suburb of nearly three million people located forty miles south of Los Angeles, it is unique in a number of ways, especially in the profound demographic changes it has undergone since 1970. During that period, the percentage of Latinos in Orange County has grown from 8 percent of the total population to 27 percent. In Santa Ana these numbers are more dramatic: 69 percent of the population is Latino, and more than half are foreign born, mostly from Mexico. Dubbed by the 1990 U.S. Census as one of the most impoverished cities in the entire nation, Santa Ana has also been designated as one of two "youth capitals" in the country, second only to a small town near El Paso, Texas. According to the census, in one square mile of the city alone there live approximately 26,000 youth, ages 18 and under, many of whom are undocumented residents. In effect, Santa Ana has become a young Latino city; people come here from communities all over Mexico and other parts of Latin America, reinventing themselves along with the city. As a consequence of such migrations, Santa Ana has been transformed from a strictly national space to what may be called a translocality (Appadurai 1996). Generally speaking, a translocality belongs in one sense to particular nation-states because it occupies their territorially defined spaces, but at the same time, because it is traversed by a multitude of processes—transnational urbanism in particular—that is, since it forms a node in a multitude of transnational circuits that connect it elsewhere beyond the nation, a translocality also transcends, to some extent, the nation-state. In other words, a translocality is a space of which the nation-state is not in complete command, weaving together, as it does, various "circulating" populations with various kinds of "locals" (Appadurai 1996, 192). As Smith notes (2001), agency flourishes in these social spaces and within the lived experiences of plural local communities.

It is in this space, this translocality, that the lives of thousands of immigrant students take place.[6] It is a space of flows, a node in multifarious transnational migrant circuits. It is also a space, however, entwined with vehement attacks on bilingual education. Orange County is at the forefront in the state, if not the nation, of the English-only grassroots movement discussed earlier. This movement's principal aims are: (1) to eliminate all bilingual education in California; (2) to institutionalize English immersion programs (in elementary school, programs that would force foreign-born and native-born students who speak little English to "sink" or "swim" using English as the language of instruction); (3) and finally, to deny, in pedagogical practice, Mexicans and other immigrants access to their culture by prohibiting instruction and conversation in Spanish or the mother tongue. So Santa Ana is caught at the crossroads of those national processes that attempt to regulate the conduct of subjects in the interests of the nation-state and those transnational ones that prevent this regulation from fully taking place. It is at such crossroads that we attempt to understand the experience of newly arrived immigrants in public schools.

The Voices on the Ground of Transnational Urbanism

In the summer of 1997, we conducted ethnographic interviews with twelve students from two high schools in the Santa Ana Unified School District.[7] The students represented in this study are self-selected rather than randomly sampled. They were all enrolled in a summer language assistance program for newly arrived immigrants. We found students who were willing to participate by explaining the project to them and asking for volunteers. All of the interviews were conducted in Spanish at the two schools.[8] All of them were also audiotaped. Of the twelve students, seven were males while five were females; ten were from Mexico, one from Colombia, and another from Bolivia; five had been in the United States for more than a year, but less than three, while the others had been here anywhere from one to six months; and most of them, with a couple of exceptions, were from working-class backgrounds. In conducting these interviews, we were out to collect what might be called life narratives—"narratively shaped fragments of more comprehensive life stories" (Ginsburg 1989, 153). We felt that through these life narratives—or migrant stories, because they are about the migrant experience—through these self-representations, we might be able to attend closely to the ways in which Latino immigrant students talked about themselves and their lives, to how they articulated notions of who they were and where they belonged, and thus we could potentially put into circulation, or disseminate, narratives that called into question, to some extent, those projects, such as Proposition 227, that aimed to transform people into strictly national subjects. These life stories, then, are about bringing forth the voice of the student, meaning voice in both a personal and political sense.

According to Mark Bauerlein:

> In its personal reference, "voice" signifies those responses and expressions unique to every human psyche. This voice comes from the self, from the memories, feelings, and beliefs residing in a core of personal identity.... It is a particular subject's vision of the world, her outlook on things, her elemental registration of what happens. In voice one finds personalized effects of cultural processes, political systems, and social events, limited but authentic evidence of historical reality.... In its political reference, "voice" signifies not a personal position, but a political position. To have a voice in this sense means to have political meaning, to be admitted to the political marketplace. Voice represents an opinion, not an experience. (1997, 132–133)

But, of course, the personal and the political are not always separable. The opinion voice carries often stems from personal experience, in which case this experience has political inflection. This is so with the voices of the immigrant students we interviewed. Their voices are personal in the sense that they express the truth of their experience. But they are also political in the sense that they swim, to some extent, even if the students are not conscious of it, against the tide of political opinion in California, particularly when it comes to the question of language. Thus what we present is the personal experience of the immigrant, an experience that is politically inflected.

English for the Children

One thing that is very clear in reviewing the migrant stories we collected is that all of the students think it is important to learn English. They realize that English is not only the dominant language in the United States, but that it is also the leading language in the world (for science, technology, and international business). As such, English is the language of social and economic opportunity. Moreover, these students also regard English as medium for communicating with the wider U.S. society, and thus for maneuvering in social and cultural spaces outside the Latino immigrant community. On the surface, then, it appears that these students accept one basic emphasis of such movements as Proposition 227 (also known as "English for the Children"), this being the need for everyone residing in the United States to learn English. But, as we will argue, things are not so simple. Before we do this, however, we would like to illustrate just how important English is for these students. Here we profile four of them, selectively presenting tidbits of their immigrant stories.

Profile 1. Julio's story began with his pronouncement *"Soy fugitivo, ya no soy legal, se me venció mi pasaporte."* (I'm a fugitive, no longer legal, my passport expired.) Equipped with a three-month visitor's passport, seventeen-year-old Julio, an only child, arrived in Santa Ana approximately six months ago from Morelos, Mexico, where he had recently completed his second semester of *prepa*, the Mexican equivalent of the sophomore year in high school. His mother, a single parent, stayed behind working long, hard hours as owner of a *tortillería* to ensure that Julio's education is guaranteed, preferably in the United States. Julio currently lives with his maternal aunt and her three children in Santa Ana. Although he would prefer to hold a part-time job to earn spending money, his aunt is adamant about his real job, learning English.

By all standards in Mexico, Julio and his mother were economically stable. Compared to other immigrant students, he received an above-average, consistent education. This is evident by Julio's mannerisms, his speech, his ability for critical reflection, and the way in which he articulates his thoughts. He is committed to staying in California, albeit illegally, at least until he gets his prize: a high school diploma.

Julio loves the English language. "Knowing it gives you the upper edge," he notes, speaking authoritatively. "For example," he continues, "one can improve the overall quality of life, have a better job, earn higher wages, fit in socially in any kind of situation, well, there's so much more." Then with a wide, sheepish grin he admits innocently, "My girlfriend and I love to speak English around her parents and my aunt because they don't understand, so you see, there are so many advantages!"

Other than through taking English classes, Julio feels that watching movies is the best way to learn English as well as American culture. Julio is excited about having been declared a "program major" at his high school, which will guide him into the type of postsecondary programs necessary to pursue his field of study. Already astute in navigating Spanglish, Julio declares, *"Me dieron un estudio de public service."* A loose translation is that he is certain that his placement in a public service program major will help him pursue a career in law or law enforcement here or in Mexico.

Julio sees no barriers to his goals because as he puts it, *"A la escuela no le importa que sea ilegal. Aquí me dan mi educación, sea como sea. La escuela nos toman en cuenta."* (It doesn't matter to the school that I am illegal. Here they give me my education, regardless of who I am. The school pays attention to us. Teachers care for us.)

Julio sums up his assessment by stating that he wants his children to be proud of him and to be able to say their father is a successful professional. He is convinced that there are no barriers at his school to prevent this: the major barrier at the time of the interviews was then governor Pete Wilson. It was and is Wilson and other anti-immigrant politicians, of course, who arouse public sentiment against Julio and others like him.

Profile 2. "¡Un día les voy a enseñar mi acta de nacimiento!" (One day I'm going to show my birth certificate to my classmates!) Javier's inability to speak English belies his American citizenship. In sharp contrast to Julio, fourteen-year-old Javier, a ninth grader who was born in Chicago, Illinois, knows little English. At age six his family returned to Mexico, where they remained until four months ago when they made their way to Santa Ana. "Podía hablar bien con mis hermanos." (I could speak well with my brothers.) Javier remembers a time before leaving for Mexico when he spoke English with his brothers. "Llegué a México y casi no hablaba español" (I arrived in Mexico hardly speaking Spanish.) Recalling his arrival in Mexico knowing little Spanish, he points out the irony of finding himself in the same situation, this time in his place of birth, not knowing English. "¡Se me olvidó todo!" He laments that he forgot it all.

Javier's educational background has been inconsistent. He missed his entire eighth grade year due to a disciplinary expulsion from his Mexican school. His family has a history of traversing between Chicago, the home of his maternal grandparents, and Mexico, the birthplace of his parents. Typical of many immigrant families, Javier and two of his siblings were born in the United States, while two others were born in Mexico.

His immediate goal is to learn English, following the lead of his two older brothers who have excelled in their studies here. He thinks that he too can be successful if he tries hard "hechándole muchas ganas" (putting forth much effort). Although he finds English difficult to learn, he points out that it is not because immigrants are *flojos* (lazy) like Americans would believe, but because one gets desperate, "no se les pega el inglés y se desesperan y tiran el inglés, entonces prefieren trabajar." (English is so difficult that sometimes it just doesn't stick and they lose patience. Many immigrants just give up and go to work.) This feeling is familiar to Javier, who after two hours per week of English instruction found it too difficult. The exasperating challenge of learning English contributed to his acting out in class, from which he was ultimately expelled. He will not fail this time, he assures us.

Javier turns wistful as he describes his father's work in a factory where years of exposure to fiberglass have harmed his health, "Lo está dañando mucho." (It is causing him much harm.) He vows to have a different type of job, one that requires working with his mind, "Yo quiero trabajar con mi mente, quiero ser un maestro de historia." (I want to work with my mind, become a history teacher.) Working with his mind, becoming a history teacher, Javier reasons, is safer and more rewarding. Javier recognizes that he needs to learn English not only because it is necessary, but as he points out, because one can have a better job.

Profile 3. Fourteen-year-old Galia, like Javier, is a legal resident. In Santa Ana since April, Galia was quick to point out that in Bolivia she was far more advanced educationally. In fact she was ready to enter the ninth grade in March, the beginning of the school year in Bolivia, but instead moved to Santa Ana. Because of her inability to speak English, she was placed in the eighth grade in a Santa Ana intermediate school from which she graduated in June. Galia will be a ninth grader in September. She speaks with the wisdom of a sage, articulate beyond her years, witty and very positive about her role in life. While telling her story, she freely dispensed opinions about everything from the educational system to the types of students it serves, whom she finds "un poco extraño." (a bit strange.)

In addition to her struggle to learn the English language, Galia finds herself immersed in an environment where culture, food, dress, and customs differ remarkably from her more privileged environment in Bolivia. The challenge to learn English is compounded by the need to learn what she calls *español Chicano*, a perplexing mix of English and Spanish, formal as well as slang. "El primer día y el segundo sufría mucho porque decía ¡¿Qué quiere decir eso?!" Galia recalls how she suffered those first few days of school constantly asking, "What does that mean!?" Now she prides herself in having learned many of the expressions and being able to talk *como los mexicanos* (like

Mexicans) at school and in the larger society, while reverting to formal Spanish with family and friends. Her desire to speak English like *los americanos* (Americans) remains her foremost goal.

Although Galia feels that the greatest barrier to living in the United States is not being able to speak English, she admits that her school does the best to make immigrant students feel accepted by teaching them English and including them in many other ways. *"Siempre me han dado la palabra ... me dan de vale."* (They've always given me a voice; they value me.) She feels compassion for immigrants, both legal, and illegal who come to theUnited States. *"Vienen a sufrir mucho por el inglés."* (How they suffer because of English.)

Enthusiastic about her future prospects in the United States and how advantaged she will be by learning English, Galia nevertheless recognizes the great sacrifices her parents have made so that she and her sister may learn English. Her father, a former university librarian and a part-time tailor in Bolivia, is now a legal resident, having lived in California with other relatives for the past fifteen years. Galia claims he learned English by being in California so long. Exhausted after working twelve-hour days and double shifts cleaning hotel rooms, he nevertheless found time to indulge his passion for books at the Santa Ana Public Library. Galia recounts how her father methodically planned his family's arrival in Santa Ana—where they would live, work, attend school. Since their arrival, the library has been like a second home, so much so that at times Galia tires of it. But her father persists, *"Tienen que ir a averigüar."* (You must go and investigate.) In the end, Galia proudly describes her report on Rhode Island that could not have been prepared so well without library research.

Galia's major concern is for her mother, once a professional secretary who also taught on a substitute basis, and now cleans hotel rooms with her husband. Eloquently, she describes her mother's predicament: *"Aquí es mucho esfuerzo en la vida. Hay que trabajar, hay que esforzarse demasiado porque hay veces mi mamá llega cansadísima del trabajo.... Es muy difícil para ella, muy difícil porque ella no esta acostumbrada...."* (Life is such a struggle here. One must work, put forth so much effort because my mother comes home so tired.... It is difficult for her, so difficult because she is not used to it....) Reflecting on her parents' situation, Galia achingly wonders out loud, *"Si tú vienes de otro país y eres profesional, no te toman mucho en cuenta ¿verdad?"* (If you come from another country as a professional, you aren't really given much due, are you?) This accurate but painful assessment reflects a similar sentiment of most immigrants—without English one is nothing.

Profile 4. An aspiring nurse, Adriana, a painfully shy fifteen-year-old ninth grader from Guadalajara, Mexico, is constantly aware of her limited English skills. In stark contrast to the more sophisticated Julio and Galia, Adriana represents the overwhelmingly typical immigrant student from Mexico. Her educational background is weak, she is poor, and, along with her family, she is struggling to find her place in the United States. In spite of her desire to learn English, she exudes an uncertainty about reaching that goal, not due to lack of *ganas*, desire, but for the simple reason of economics.

Fearful that we were *la migra* (immigration officials), Adriana was initially hesitant in telling her story. Once we had convinced her otherwise, she shared a humbling story of the immigrant's life. Adriana immigrated to Santa Ana with her three sisters and mother three months ago. Back in Mexico, she and her family heard nothing but the wonders of life in *el norte* from her aunt. But now, she and her family find that same life a double-edged sword. With surprising candor and a touch of embarrassment, Adriana explained the paradox: *"La familia de mi mamá le decía que podíamos estar mejor que allá pero no estamos bien. Entonces en una parte se me parece mejor aquí y en otras no. La primera porque aquí aprendo más con el inglés y la otra porque no estamos bien por falta del dinero.... Alla teníamos casa propia y aquí no."* (My mother's family told us we would be better off here than in Mexico, but we are not. So on the one hand it is better here, but on the other it isn't.... One because here I can learn English, but we are not well for lack of money.... There we had our own home and here we do not.") Herein lies the conflict of the typical immigrant: to learn English or to survive.

Adriana notes wryly that her experience in crossing the border alone should have been an indication of the struggles that lie ahead. Although her mother and sisters all crossed the border with other relatives' birth certificates, she was hidden in the car. Adriana remembered feeling nervous, but not fearful. She admits harboring a secret desire of being found out and returned to her home in Guadalajara. And forego learning English, we asked? She responded, "*Es que no hay como la tierra de uno.*" (There is nothing like one's own country.) Her illegal status is a source of deep consternation, embarrassment, and fear. She is haunted daily by the fear of being exposed and returned to Mexico—"*Diario estás con el miedo de que te agarre la migra*" (Every day you fear that *la migra* will get you.) Laughing nervously, she affirms her fear of *la migra*, "*Y eso pensaba cuando ustedes vinieron al salón.*" (This is what I thought when you came to my classroom.) In other words, she thought that we were INS agents.

Adriana's biggest disappointment is her aunt who made appealing promises about receiving an education in United States. Adriana found out none too soon that her aunt's primary motive for wanting them to come to Santa Ana was to put them to work. Soon, she explains, they became a burden, but not before her older sister succumbed to the aunt's wishes. Now that her eighteen-year-old sister is married, has a child, and works in a factory, Adriana is more convinced of the need to learn English and to attend college.

But Adriana is finding that learning English is not so easy. Of course, anyone can learn, she believes; that is not the difficult part. It is the social barriers that make learning English such a challenge. She describes her insecurity and internal conflict about speaking both English and Spanish, worried that if she speaks Spanish in front of her English-speaking counterparts they will call her a *mojada* (wetback). Yet, she is very self-conscious about speaking in English.

In final exasperation Adriana asks rhetorically, "Why all the controversy over illegal immigrants?" After all, she insists, "*La educación es para todos, no importa la posición social. He visto muchos americanos que según ellos quieren estudiar pero no les hechan ganas y nada más vienen a calentar la banca.*" (Education is for all, no matter their social status. I've seen so many Americans who say they want to study, but they don't try, they just come to keep the seat warm.) In summarizing her story, Adriana explains her ongoing ritual of trying to lessen the guilt she feels due to her illegal status. She justifies it this way: "*Pues es una obligación de venir a la escuela y aprender y yo quiero aprender.*" (Well, it's an obligation to attend school and to learn, and I want to learn.) Furthermore, even though she is illegal, Adriana states that she has the right to study, go out with family and friends, and even venture as far south as San Diego without getting caught and returned to Mexico. With a distant look in her eyes, Adriana ends her story with assurance, "*Sí, voy a aprender el inglés y lograr un futuro mejor porque no toda la vida vamos a seguir siempre con que hay, no tenemos que comer.*" (Yes, I'm going to learn English and have a better future because we can't continue all our life with ... oh, we have nothing to eat.)

It is quite clear from these immigrant narratives, not to mention those not presented here, that the students we worked with place a lot of faith in English as a mechanism for economic betterment. We understand this desire as a potential form of transcitizenship, in the sense that, on the one hand, it is part of their acculturation to the traditions of the U.S. state, thus giving them, at least to some extent, the cultural currency necessary to maneuver within this national space. On the other hand as the linguistic choices (Dhillon 1994) of the students we interviewed indicate, these acculturations are not confined to a single nation, whether "real" or "imaginary." Rather we want to argue that these linguistic practices, the choices of language, constitute a form of citizenship that can be acquired, in this case, without the sanctions of legal citizenship. Below we lay out the conceptual parameters of transcitizenship that ironically carry for previously marginalized, and militarily threatened, immigrants the affording of legal citizenship in the hoped-for liberal democratic state.

Although in this particular case, because these students are enrolled in public schools, it does require a radically more inclusive definition of citizenship such that there is a disjunction between its form and its substance, thus permitting even the undocumented to receive some benefits of the welfare state. In other words, one can become a cultural citizen, that is, culturally enfranchised, regardless of one's legal status: all one has to do is acquire competency, at least to some degree, in the dominant cultural traditions of the host nation. If these immigrants have such a zeal to learn English, then it appears that they agree with the "English for the Children" movement, for they too talk about English as "being the language of economic opportunity," one that allows immigrants "to fully participate in the American Dream of economic and social advancement" (Unz and Tuchman 1998). But this is as far as the agreement goes, at least with the students we worked with.

As we noted earlier, "English for the Children," as well as other citizenship movements we have characterized as nativist, work under the assumption that the United States can properly be bounded, stopping any unwanted influences at its borders. So the role of these nativisms is essentially to regulate the conduct of subjects in the interests of ensuring security and prosperity of the nation-state. In doing so, they seek to eliminate the use of Spanish for fear that it is fragmenting the American nation. But many immigrants don't live in a such a neatly bounded world. As we have seen, the global restructuring since the 1970s has made it possible for immigrants to remain tied to the homeland as never before. As such, they often become part of transnational circuits of which the home and host countries form two nodes. And even if particular immigrants are not closely tied to the homeland, when they live in a place such as Santa Ana, which forms a node in a multitude of transnational networks, they can't help but become embroiled in such circuits. In other words, since Santa Ana is a translocality, a space at once in and beyond the nation, a space continuously traversed by an array of transnational flows, all those who reside there, regardless of their actual ties to an elsewhere, effectively become transnationalized. If this is the case, then it may not be in the best interest of these immigrants to fully acculturate to the dominant culture of United States. In other words, since the space that they occupy is not just national, to only acculturate to national traditions, as "English for the Children" would have immigrants do, simply will not be sufficient. What they have to do, instead, is acquire the cultural repertoire necessary to maneuver in a transnational space. Practically this means that in order to be cultural citizens of such a translocality as Santa Ana, as well as of those spaces to which it is connected outside the United States, immigrants must maintain their use of Spanish, thus becoming polyglot cultural citizens.

This is precisely what the students we interviewed are striving to be, for not only is English important to them, but Spanish is as well. This is clear in the following statements from some of the students:

Adriana: "I'm going to try my best to learn English, but I can't cease from speaking Spanish because I've always spoken it. It is important to maintain Spanish ... because there are times when a friend visits who does not understand English, so I have to speak with him in Spanish. The same is true in some stores or other places [where business is conducted in Spanish]. I can write and read Spanish well. It is important to be bilingual here as in Mexico because in Guadalajara [where she is from] there are jobs in the airport and in large hotels who need bilinguals ..."

Javier: "It is important to be bilingual because here almost all the elderly people [of Latino origin] don't speak English. So if one speaks only English, those who speak Spanish won't understand, and if one only speaks Spanish then ..."

Bertha (age: fifteen; birthplace: Gazuphitlan, Mexico): "It is important to maintain Spanish because I can be bilingual here as in Mexico, because in Mexico there are also places where English is spoken, so I can be a bilingual nurse [in either place]."

Maria (age: fourteen; birthplace: Guadalajara, Mexico): "Yes, it's important if I speak both languages because I can get a better job because I can speak in Spanish to those people who don't speak English and … being bilingual is very important in Mexico as well because over there, who are tourists or whatever, [who speak only English] and one must communicate with them."

Implicit in these statements are two recognitions. The first is that they live in a translocality. This means that they live in a space that, at any given time, will be occupied not only by people who are not acculturated to the norms of the United States, but also by beings who are strictly national subjects. Thus, it behooves these students to maintain their use of Spanish while at the same time learning English. This allows them to form bonds with a multiplicity of subjects, whether national or not. It also gives them an advantage in the marketplace because they can occupy more than one cultural niche at the same time. The second recognition is that they don't have to confine their lives and future aspirations to living in just one national space. In other words, because these students, at least some them, are tied to networks that link the United States to their homelands, they see themselves as operating across national borders. In this case, being bilingual is even more advantageous, making it possible for them to move back and forth with relative ease, as well as allowing them the flexibility to take advantage of job opportunities wherever they may become available. The upshot here, then, is that in order for these students to achieve some form of cultural citizenship it is not enough for them to simply acculturate to the dominant norms of the United States. This is so because they do not live in a space that is strictly national, but one that cuts across and reaches across other terrains. So, in order for these immigrants to best navigate this space, they must be attuned to both their local and transnational integration.

The Material Discourses of Transnational Urbanism

The narratives we have related towards the end of this paper speak to the issues and problems that face Spanish language students within the context of the current immigration debate. More than a social indicator, our students recognize that the English language is the defining characteristic of a global, economic society. They are painfully aware that, unfortunate as it may be, people draw conclusions about how others use language to communicate, and if they cannot use the dominant language, they are not valued. In other words, there is a lot of pressure from the dominant society for immigrants to learn English. So on the face of it, it does not appear that our students' wishes to learn English necessarily contradict the goals of grassroots "English only" movements. Unfortunately, such movements advocate the use of English while denigrating languages such as Spanish. It is as if the "national community," suggests Rosaldo, "imagines that language is a finite good—one citizen, one language, no more, no less. The notion of the monolingual citizen implies a hydraulic model in which the more Spanish one speaks, the less English, and vice versa" (1994, 403). The students we interviewed, given that their formative years were spent in Spanish language environments, will be unlikely to discard their mother tongue. For them, knowing both languages is even a plus. Javier, for example, believes that the ability to speak both English and Spanish will enhance his opportunities of employment in both Mexico and the United States. If they all manage to learn English, while retaining the mother tongue, it will lead to the formation of polyglot citizens, which seems to be Javier's ideal. Such citizens work with "another linguistic economy, one where language is an expandable good, not a finite one. In certain cases, the more Spanish one speaks, the better one's knowledge of English, and vice versa" (Rosaldo 1994, 403).

The upshot of all this is that, by claiming the right to learn English, the students we interviewed are striving for cultural citizenship. It is part of their struggle to enfranchise themselves. It is part of their search for social and cultural space in America. As such, they are claiming the right to be different, to be polyglot citizens, without compromising their right to belong. Unfortunately, the dominant society views such difference as a threat. We would suggest, instead, that a polyglot citizen should be seen as a benefit to the United States. If the current economic globalization of the world continues apace, where nations are each day more and more interconnected, it is just such polyglot citizens who are going to give the United States the competitive edge. It would behoove us all to see language as an expandable good.

Conclusion

What is happening in the United States and Mexico with regard to transnational citizens is relevant to other places of the world.[9] Just as bilingualism marks the citizenship practices of transnational migrants, so does the desire of Iraqis, Afghanistans, and Canadians for self-governance give rise to potential resistance toward the "new world order." The key contextual differences are that whereas in California, the new nativism is expressed in oppressive statewide propositions (187, 209), in the Middle East, apparently religious intolerance expresses itself in military violence and insurgent assassinations. Innocent citizens and soldiers die almost daily. The stakes are obviously higher. The Bush administration's metaphor of the war against terror is more than merely a rhetorical device. This global image apparently justifies the use of military force, occupation of territory, and even regime change and rule by an imperial power. How should we view these vastly different, yet globally parallel, local phenomena?

From the traditions of social theory informing the conceptualization and the cultural practices and lived experience of citizenship, the relationship between state and nation needs reexamining. As Smith argues (2001), the conflation of state with nation, which is taken for granted, needs practical deconstruction and empirical testing in relation to social movements on the ground, specifically in relation to transnational urban citizens. Specifically the concept of the nation must be decoupled from the concept of the state in order to account empirically for Rosado's and Smith's theoretical innovations. We have attempted to do this with our interpretation of the life stories of transcitizens moving back and forth between Latin America and Santa Ana, California. Stated more abstractly, by anchoring the notion of transcitizenship within the cultural practices of the nation, rather than the state, theorists may now map new, hybrid cultural identities onto new administrative structures; for example, NAFTA and the new Iraqi Governing Council and constitution.

The theoretical implications of privileging the nation as opposed to the state in the practices of citizenship are first, that the cultural practices are embedded in pluralistic models of nation, which in the context of liberal democratic societies (McDonough and Feinberg 2003), embrace multiple ethnicities, religions, and nationalisms. Second, as citizens occupy transnational spaces owing to the processes and structures of globalization, they develop an increased capacity for agency; that is, they are both unintended effects and agents of a capitalism gone global. Finally, as the nation becomes decoupled from the state apparatus, transcitizens may impose new demands for entitlements such as new legal status, the right to possess a driver's license, and retroactive legal status allowing them to continue to work and send money home despite the oppression of the new nativism.

These are the broad strokes of a heuristic category we would like to see empirically investigated in other social contexts. At the very least we expect that social theory and ethnographic studies of transnational urbanism can be immediately launched with an eye to a culturally and historically grounded everyday understanding of civic and economic life in the new world order.

Notes

1. The members of this upstate New York organization migrated from Soquerón, Mexico. One of the members of the group routinely travels home to Mexico to work on community development projects the organziation has funded for his home town, for example, a new baseball stadium.
2. At the time of this study the Mexican government had instituted provisions for dual citizenship so that Mexicans who migrated back and forth from the U.S. to work would not lose their citizenship in Mexico.
3. In this study we define "newly arrived" immigrants as those who have resided in the country for one year or less.
4. These demographic transformations have a lot to do with the changing nature of the U.S. economy. As industrial production has moved overseas, to take advantage of wage differentials, the traditional U.S. manufacturing base has deteriorated and been partly replaced by a downgraded manufacturing sector, one characterized by an increasing supply of poorly paid, semiskilled, or unskilled production jobs. The economy has also become more service oriented. Financial and other specialized service firms have thus replaced manufacturing as the leading economic sectors. This new core economic base of highly specialized services has tended to polarize labor demand into high-skill and low-skill categories. The upshot of all this, then, is that these changes in the economy, particularly the creation of low-skill jobs, have created the conditions for the absorption of vast numbers of workers. For a longer exposition of these economic transformations see Kitty Calavita (1996) and Saskia Sassen (1988, 1995).
5. Of these states, California is demographically the most important: in 1990, it alone accounted for one-third of all immigrants in the United States, up from one-fourth in 1980 (Rumbaut 1996, 32).
6. Like most school districts throughout the country, Santa Ana Unified provides mostly transitional forms of bilingual education, with the goal of having 1.4 million limited English speakers in the state quickly assimilate into English and U.S. culture. See Anderson (1997, A16).
7. The sample we are using is rather small. But given our informal interaction with other students, as well our experience in working with Mexican immigrants more generally, we feel that the information we gathered is representative of a much larger grouping.
8. The actual interviews were conducted by JoAnn Aguirre and Lewis Bratcher, both of whom are doctoral students at the University of California at Irvine. They are both bilingual.
9. In Iraq, for example, citizens and residents in an emerging liberal state both resist and seeek to transform the U.S./U.K. efforts to define their ethnic and religious identities in universal terms as citizens of the new world order.

References

Aguirre, J. K. and L. Bratcher. *Student Interviews.* Irvine, CA: The Center for Collaborative Research in Education, University of California, July 29, August 4, 1997.
Anderson, N. "Testing the Limits of Bilingual Education." *Los Angeles Times,* August 8, 1997.
Appadurai, A. *Modernity at Large: Cultural Dimensions of Globalization.* Minneapolis: University of Minnesota Press, 1996.
Bauerlein, M. *Literary Criticism: An Autopsy.* Philadelphia: University of Pennsylvania Press, 1997.
Buchanan, P. "What Will America Be in 2050?" *Los Angeles Times,* October 28, 1994.
Calavita, K. "The New Politics of Immigration: 'Balanced-Budget Conservatism' and the Symbolism of Proposition 187." *Social Problems* 43 (1996): 284–305.
Castells, M. *The Rise of the Network Society.* Oxford, U.K.: Blackwell, 1996.
Castells, M. *End of Millennium.* Oxford, UK: Blackwell, 1998.
Chavez, L. R. "Immigration Reform and Nativism: The Nationalist Response to the Transnational Challenge." In *Immigrants Out! The New Nativism and the Anti-Immigrant Impulse in the United States,* edited by J. F. Perea, 61–77. New York and London: New York University Press, 1997.
Citizens for Legal Immigration/Save Our State. *Proposition 187: The "Save Our State" Initiative: The Questions and the Answers.* Pamphlet, n.d.
Crawford, J. *Hold Your Tongue: Bilingualism and the Politics of "English Only."* Reading, MA: Addison-Wesley, 1992.
Delgado, R. "Citizenship." In *Race, Identity, and Citizenship: A Reader,* edited by R. D. Torres, L. F. Milton, and J. Inda, 247–52. Oxford, U.K.: Blackwell, 1999.
del Olmo, F. "End Border Hysteria and Move On." *Los Angeles Times,* September 14, 1997.
Dhillon, P. *Multiple Identities: A Phenomenology of Multicultural Communication.* New York: Peter Lang, 1994.
Garcia y Griego, M. and P. Martin. *Immigration and Integration in the Post-187 Era.* Report for the California Policy Seminar, 1998.
Ginsburg, F. D. *Contested Lives: The Abortion Debate in an American Community.* Berkeley: University of California Press, 1989.
Glick Schiller, N., L. Basch, and C. Szanton Blanc. "From Immigrant to Transmigrant: Theorizing Transnational Migration." *Anthropological Quarterly* 68 (1995): 48–63.
Handlin, O. *The Uprooted.* 2nd ed. Boston: Little, Brown, 1973.

Harvey, D. *The Condition of Postmodernity*. Oxford, U.K.: Blackwell, 1989.

Holston, J. and A. Appadurai. "Cities and Citizenship." *Public Culture* 8 (1996): 187–204.

Inda, J. X. "Matter Out of Place: Mexican Immigrants, National Terrains." PhD dissertation. University of California, Berkeley, 1997.

Kearney, M. "Borders and Boundaries of State and Self at the End of Empire." *Journal of Historical Sociology* 4 (1991): 52–74.

Kymlicka, W. and W. Norman. "Return of the Citizen: A Survey of Recent Work on Citizenship Theory." In *Theorizing Citizenship*, edited by R. Beiner, 283–322. Albany: State University of New York Press, 1995.

McCarthy, C. and W. Crichlow, eds. *Race, Identity and Representation in Education*. New York: Routledge. First edition, 1993.

McDonough, K. and W. Feinberg. *Citizenship and Education: Teaching for Cosmopolitan Values and Collective Identities*. Oxford: Oxford University Press, 2003.

Mirón, L. F., J. Inda, and J. Aguirre. (1998). "Transnational Migrants, Cultural Citizenship and the Politics of Language in California. *Educational Policy* 12, 6 (1998): 659–681.

Mitchell, K. "Transnational Subjects: Constituting the Cultural Citizen in the Era of Pacific Rim Capital." In *Ungrounded Empires: The Cultural Politics of Modern Chinese Transnationalism,* edited by A. Ong and D. M. Nonini, 228–56. New York: Routledge, 1997.

Muller, T. "Nativism in the Mid-1990s: Why Now?" In *Immigrants Out! The New Nativism and the Anti-Immigrant Impulse in the United States*, edited by J. F. Perea, 105–18. New York and London: New York University Press, 1997.

One Nation/One Children. www.onenation.org/aboutonoc.html. Retrieved July 27, 1998.

Ong, A. "On the Edge of Empires: Flexible Citizenship among Chinese in Diaspora." *Positions* 1 (1993), 745–778.

Rosaldo, R. "Ideology, Place, and People without Culture." *Cultural Anthropology* 3 (1988): 77–87.

Rosaldo, R. "Cultural Citizenship and Educational Democracy." *Cultural Anthropology* 9 (1994): 402–11.

Rouse, R. "Mexican Migration and the Social Space of Postmodernism." *Diaspora* 1 (1991): 8–23.

Rumbaut, R. G. "Origins and Destinies: Immigration, Race, and Ethnicity in Contemporary America." In *Origins and Destinies: Immigration, Race, and Ethnicity in America*, edited by S. Pedraza and R. G. Rumbaut, 21–240. Belmont, CA: Wadsworth, 1996.

Sanchez, G. J. "Face the Nation: Race, Immigration, and the Rise of Nativism in Late Twentieth Century America." *International Migration Review* 31 (1997): 1009–30.

Sassen, S. "Recomposition and Peripheralization at the Core." *Contemporary Marxism* 5 (1982): 88–100.

Sassen, S. *The Mobility of Labor and Capital*. Cambridge, UK: Cambridge University Press, 1988.

Sassen, S. "America's Immigration 'Problem.'" *World Policy Journal* 6 (1989): 811–32.

Sassen, S. "Migration to the United States." In *A Place in the World? Places, Cultures and Globalization*, edited by D. Massey and P. Jess, 40–42. Oxford: Oxford University Press, 1995.

Sassen, S. *Globalization and Its Discontents: Selected Essays 1984–1998*. New York: New Press, 1998.

Smith, M. P. "Postmodernism, Urban Ethnography, and the New Social Space of Ethnic Identity." *Theory and Society* 21 (1992): 493–531.

Smith, M. P. "Putting Race in Its Place." In *The Bubbling Cauldron: Race, Ethnicity and the Urban Crisis*, edited by M. P. Smith and J. R. Feagin, 3–27. Minneapolis: University of Minnesota Press, 1995.

Smith, M. P. *Transnational Urbanism: Locating Globalism*. Malden, MA: Blackwell, 2001.

Smith, M. P. and L. E. Guarnizo. *Transnationalism from Below*. New Brunswick, NJ: Transaction, 1998.

Time. "The Numbers Game." *Time* (Fall 1993): 14–15.

Unz, R. K. and G. M. Tuchman. "The Unz Initiative." http://www.catesol.org/unztext.html (Retrieved July 22, 1998).

Westphal, D. "Foreign Language Population of U.S. Surges." *The Orange County Register*, April 9, 1998.

Young, I. M. "Polity and Group Difference: A Critique of the Ideal of Universal Citizenship." *Ethics* 99 (1989): 250–74.

20

Geographies of Latinidad
Deployments of Radical Hybridity in the Mainstream

ANGHARAD N. VALDIVIA

In February 2003, the U.S. Census announced that, ahead of projected statistics, Latina/os composed the largest minority group in the country, barely passing the former most numerous minority, African Americans. Moreover, whereas U.S. Latina/os were formerly thought to be concentrated in the tricoastal regions of the Southwest, Florida, and the Northeast, with Mexican Americans, Cuban Americans, and Puerto Ricans in those respective regions, the Census fleshed out a widespread geographic swath of populations, with the fastest growing regions being the Midwest and the South. Geographically speaking, Latina/os are all over the United States. Indeed, as most contemporary Latina/o studies scholars would argue, it is impossible, not to mention inadvisable and undemocratic, to reduce the location of Latina/os to one national space because both borders and bodies move in response to geopolitical forces. Transnational movement, of bodies and cultural forms, characterizes the Latina/o population. In fact, Latina/o studies scholars warn that the political dangers and social and cultural difficulties that confront Latina/os also confront the rest of the U.S. and global populations. As such Latina/os are imperative to study not just because of our numbers and long-standing contributions to the history and culture of the United States, but also because we are, in a sense, a metaphor for or a window to the ravages of globalization and the erosion of democratic rights and citizen status, which are being daily attacked by transnational processes of global capital and which serve to deny Latinos and others "full societal membership" (Rocco 2004, 4).

Latina/os challenge commonsense and theoretical notions of race and ethnicity. Often referred to as the "brown race," Latina/os supposedly fall somewhere between white Eurocentric and black Afrocentric racial categories. The muddled ethnoracial space signified by brownness means, among other things, impurity and contamination in relation to the pure poles of blackness and whiteness. However, the lack of purity within Latina/os, rather than establishing us as different, reveals that the simplicity of easily distinguishable ethnoracial categories is but a fiction that certainly does not apply to Latina/os but also does not apply to whites or blacks (McCarthy 1998). Just as Adrian Piper's insightful academic and performance art work has long been challenging the fantasy of racial purity within the biracial mapping of the United States, now the whole category of Latina/os underscores the hybridity that exists within all populations. Furthermore, hybridity has to be contextualized and studied so as to provide a useful way to study blending of cultures and bodies rather than a careless way to celebrate globalization in the way done by neoliberal cheerleaders. As such applying hybridity to the study of Latina/os shows the spaces for intervention as well as the possible displacements and erasures generated by the hybrid geographies of Latinidad.

This essay explores the concept of hybridity and applies it to the study of contemporary Latina/os. In particular, it seeks to complement documented demographic and political evidence of increased Latina/o presence to representations in the mainstream media. The study maps out the many ways that hybridity as a concept is strategically deployed in a range of contemporary media, with strong tendencies to resolve tensions by settling for syncretism. Despite undeniable increases in representation of Latina/os, representational analysis and findings are examined in terms of the gains in visibility against the costs, displacements, and erasures within that visibility. In turn these costs are borne by Latina/o bodies despite the popularity of Latina/o cultural forms.

Hybridity

While some Latina/os are brown, they are also white and black as well as all other colors that signify different ethnoracial traces. The facile allocation of roots to Latin America serves to foreground the radically hybrid traces of the U.S. Latina/o population. Latin America is not the site of a brown cosmic race of certain origin. The definition of Latina/o brownness as a combination of American indigenous blood with Spanish white blood is the most common. However, this assumes homogeneity within the indigenous tribes as well as within the Spanish, neither of which is historically tenable. Dating back to the days of New Spain in the sixteenth century, the Spanish developed elaborate classification schemes or casta tablets to account for the extensive *mestizage* occurring in the colonies (Klor de Alva 1996). These attempts to categorize ethnoracial mixing included all four major racial groups now existing in the United States: white, black, Asian, and native. *Criollo, mestizo, mulato, indio, chino,* and so on, were some of the many possible permutations of the hybridity resulting from a mixture of different populations. While some debate whether the term *chino* referred to Chinese, as it does today, or to a mixture of native, black, and Spanish in the sixteenth century, the fact remains that America's colonizers imported Asian slave populations as well as Africans. Moreover, as Menocal (2002) reminds us, Spain, at the time of its westward expansion, was the site of a multicultural, multireligious, and racially diverse population that included Jewish, Moorish, and Christian components. The year the Spanish began their effort to reach the Indies and ended up in the Americas, 1492, coincided with the decision of the Catholic King Ferdinand and Queen Isabella to fortify their nation-state along religious lines and to expel both the Jewish and Moorish populations, many of whom headed to the "New World" as well (Shohat, chapter 9 in this volume). Thus from the outset of the European colonization of the Americas, the colonizers were of mixed and diverse religious, geographic, and racial heritage. Given that other European nations, including Portugal, Germany, Italy, England, and the Netherlands, joined in the effort to colonize the "New World" or have provided continued waves of migrants through the present, the fiction of the purity and whiteness of the European descent is easily debatable. The fact is, Latina/os as a population group are radically hybrid (Valdivia 2003a, 2004), forcing us to recognize the hybridity within Latina/os as well as within the entire population.

Hybridity is not a new term or concept. Although its original use in the seventeenth century was as a biological term, much of the resistance to it stems precisely from its racist social applications. Hybrid agricultural plants, for example, are not only more resistant to disease but are also infertile. However, when applied to populations in the eighteenth century, hybridity was often "invoked by those hostile to racial difference" (Labanyi 2000, 56), usually in conjunction with the term *miscegenation,* which connoted unwanted, and often illegal, reproduction between white women and men of color. This concern was all the more intense in a historical period marked by colonial expansion that brought many previously separate populations in contact with each other (Young 1995). Miscegenation was precluded in some settings so as to preserve both purity and colonial authority, and in others it was encouraged so as to improve, westernize, and whiten the local population in a positivist quest for racial breeding. Of course the latter strategy always simultaneously generated fears of the tipping point where the native blood, stock, and bodies would outnumber the racial purity of the white colonizer. Such fears of contamination, dilution, and disappearance of the pure white subject have continued to the present day, and are central to understanding the contemporary sociopolitical situation wherein Latina/os have become the largest U.S. minority, with some demographic projections showing us becoming the majority sometime in this century. In addition, these fears demonstrate the endurance of a biologically and anthropologically untenable belief in purity.

Contemporary scholars continue to contribute to this language of cultural tension, collision, mixture, erasure, and displacement. Thus Mary Louise Pratt uses "zones of contact"; Gloria Anzaldúa speaks of "nepantla"; Homi Bhabha writes of "mimicry" and a "third space"; and Nestor García Canclini uses "hybrid cultures." Whereas its application to population and cultural form is undeniable, there are still many who caution against the wholesale adoption of the concept of hybridity. Foremost among concerns is the depoliticizing potential of accepting that there is an inevitable mixture and hybridity in everything and that if everything and everyone is hybrid then there is no theoretical validity to the term. Sommer (1996) worries that the deployment of hybridity duplicates national unity movements that seek to rewrite the violent and uneasy history of many Latin American nations. Others worry that concepts such as hybridity, mestizage, syncretism, miscegenation, and assimilation are being used carelessly and interchangeably, flattening historical, geographical, and cultural specificity. Shohat warns that a "celebration of syncretism and hybridity per se, if not articulated in conjunction with questions of hegemony and neocolonial power relations, runs the risk of appearing to sanctify the *fait accompli* of colonial violence" (1992, 109). The concept is foremost a rejection of essentialist notions, either of gender or of ethnicity and race, as well as an acknowledgment that there is no purity to be found either at the level of culture, the body, blood, or DNA.

It is precisely in the spirit of specificity that Nestor García Canclini writes *Hybrid Cultures* (1995) as a way to theorize, from an anthropological perspective, the tensions in the interaction between Latin America and the United States, between tradition and modernity. Yet Renato Rosaldo, in his foreword to the book, cautions against using hybridity as lying between two zones of purity, tradition and modernity. Rather he prefers treating hybridity as something that pervades all, much like Paul Gilroy's approach in *There Ain't No Black in the Union Jack* (1987). Still Canclini, Rosaldo, and Gilroy acknowledge the unequal and contradictory forms that hybridity takes in different settings. Canclini and Rosaldo also focus on the Latina/o population as a hybrid with their hybrid cultural forms. Yet again Rosaldo reminds us, as do Coco Fusco (1995, 1998) and Alejandro Lugo (2000), that it is far easier for cultural forms to cross borders than it is for human beings, for whom hybridity is often a wrenching lived experience.

As a way to explore the tensions associated with the mixture of two or more cultures and fleshing out the difference between hybridity and syncretism, Levine (2001) applies Naficy's (1993) work on Iranian television in Los Angeles to issues of Latina/o media throughout the United States. According to Naficy, syncretism is more stable than hybridity because the former is "an impregnation of one culture with the content of another (or multiple others) to create a third culture," whereas in hybridity "two (or more) cultures blend and shift in an indeterminate array of positions, sometimes displaying the features of one culture more prominently than another" (Levine 2001,

34). The former is less ambivalent and potentially longer lasting than the latter, which is less comfortable and less able to express the boundaries of a community. The marketplace seeks to resolve the unstable and tension-filled situation of hybridity through the construction of a syncretic identity, which can in turn be marketed as a commodified style. Yet the lived experience of Latina/o bodies remains a hybrid one full of ambivalence, tension, and pain despite celebratory and messianic messages of the joys and pressures of globalization. Whereas music, food, and style may cross borders unchecked, bodies are continuously inspected, even after legal and successful border crossings, as Latina/os remain the eternal outsiders within the U.S. political psyche and system. To some hybridity might suggest a playful space, where one can try on different identities. Indeed studies of contemporary ethnicity (Dávila 2001; Halter 2000; Moorti 2003) suggest that hybrid traces are very useful for commodification purposes and the marketing of ethnicity. Any resistance to the syncretic paradigm registers a mere style change within hegemonic popular culture. Thus the body remains suspect while cultural forms can always be co-opted in the never-ending search for the new fashion or style.

The concept of hybridity is extremely useful to communications scholars for a number of reasons, yet remains to be fully utilized by our interdiscipline (Kraidy 1999, 2002; Murphy and Kraidy 2003). Kraidy (2002, 317) proposes that we foreground this concept, as it "needs to be understood as a communicative practice constitutive of, and constituted by, sociopolitical and economic arrangements" that are "complex, processual, and dynamic." Beyond its merely descriptive uses, hybridity also opens up the space for the study of cultural negotiations, conflicts, and struggles against the backdrop of contemporary globalization (Shome and Hegde, 2002a, 2002b) wherein an increasing percentage of the global population is simultaneously becoming geographically displaced and endlessly commodified.

This is the contemporary geographical situation of Latina/os in the United States and the cultural aspects of being Latina/o—Latinidad. Latina/os encourage us, indeed force us, to acknowledge the fact that not only is the United States composed of a heterogeneous population, but that this population is neither binarily black and white nor is it easily identifiable by commonsense markers of race and ethnicity such as skin color, hair texture, food and music preferences, religion, and national origin. In sum Latinidad makes it absolutely essential that we theoretically consider and face up to the inescapable hybridity of both bodies and cultural form (Aparicio and Jaquez 2003; *Communication Review* 2004). As Jorge Duany has said of salsa so can we say of Latinos: we are a hybrid of hybrids and as such challenge any simple narratives of race and ethnicity that would have separate and easily identifiable groups.

Geography and Democracy

Given that Latina/os as a hybrid lot reside not only all over the United States national space but also overflow its borders, Latina/os also reveal the inadequacy of concepts of geographically bound populations that can be said to have direct correspondence to a political system that grants them both membership and citizenship. Rocco (2004) proposes that not only was the dated formulation of correspondence between nation, location, and citizenship never a universalist one but also it is in sore need of revision, especially when it comes to granting democratic rights to huge sectors of the global population. With his case study focusing on Latina/os in particular, Rocco exposes the fact that there are many instances of nation-states acknowledging a need to revise the sovereignty and separateness of nation-states for the economic sake of transnational capital, with NAFTA and MERCOSUR as two major examples. Yet the same has not been done to acknowledge the transnational, regionally dispersed needs of groups of people. "Institutional change has occurred to facilitate the operations of transnational corporations, but not in response to the changes in the broader sectors of society" (17).

Issues of cultural citizenship become all the more relevant given that the Latina/o population is not only growing proportionately to other ethnic groups, and in absolute terms, but it is also increasingly diverse (Oboler 2004). Although it is getting more difficult to generalize across the Latina/o population, one thing that remains true is the contested belonging of the entire Latina/o population regardless of difference. Even though the processes of racialization and exclusion from the U.S. body politic have not been the same, as a group, Latina/os have been racialized and excluded and treated as a different ethnic group from African Americans (Aparicio 2003; Rocco 2004). Despite very real class, racial, religious, national origin, and many other differences, the majority of Latino groups have been categorized within a preexisting racialized cultural imaginary produced, limited, and modified by the dominant cultural institutional apparatus such as the media, legal, and educational spheres (Rocco, 10). For instance, inability to deal with whiteness within Latinidad (Rios-Bustamante 1992; Valdivia and Curry 1998) has generated suspicion of white and blonde border crossers. In the case of Rene Cardona, she was treated suspiciously as a white Cuban immigrant. In the case of Xuxa, her blonde bombshell persona befuddled U.S. television producers used to brown narratives of Latinidad. In the case of Cameron Diaz, Hollywood's top-earning actress in mid-2004, her Latinidad is erased or ignored by nearly all accounts in the mainstream.

The short digression into Latina/o whiteness serves to highlight the two alternatives apparently available even to those Latinas who fall within accepted racial norms of belonging, inclusion, and therefore eventual citizenship: continued inspection and suspicion in the case of acknowledged Latinidad or nearly total erasure of Latinidad in the case of acceptance within the mainstream. As such the mass media and other means of mainstream popular culture serve as powerful pedagogical tools on the location of Latina/os within the U.S. national imaginary and body politic (Cortés 1992; López 1991). The enduring trope that Latina/os belong somewhere outside of national boundaries has implications in terms of political enfranchisement and the everyday lived experience of belonging. Especially since 9/11, when brown bodies have become the object of a politics of surveillance that more often than not ignores civil rights and liberties, Latina/os face increased inspection and exclusion. As the U.S. security state sets about reducing, limiting, and dismantling the hard-won rights of minorities, Latina/o studies scholarship seeks to reinsert themes of democracy and social justice at the center of any political or academic discussion (Bonilla and Villegas 2003).

Theoretically and conceptually, just as there is diversity within Latina/os, there is not unanimity among Latina/o studies scholars. In fact, there is no agreement on whether to move forward under the umbrella category of Latinidad or to preserve the specificity of Chicano, Boricua, and Cuban-American studies. There is also an immense diversity in theoretical and methodological terms. Social scientific, political, economic, and qualitative approaches explore a wide range of topics spanning nearly all contemporary disciplines and interdisciplines. Given that Latina/o studies would not exist were it nor for a sensitivity to ethnoracial issues, one of the enduring and foregrounded debates remains the relative importance of issues of race vis-à-vis class, gender, sexuality, and other vectors of difference. For example, drawing on and expanding their introduction to the *Latino Studies Reader* (1998), Darder and Torres (2003) assert the need to return to a scholarship and activism based on class analysis and struggle—the basic tenet of a Marxian analysis infused with historical specificity. In response, Lugones and Price (2003), echoing many other Latina/o studies scholars such as Oboler (1995) and the legions of us who focus on the intersecting issues of ethnicity, class, sexuality, and gender, maintain that acknowledgment of the inseparability of race, class, and gender is precisely the strength of Latina/o studies, whose most important contribution has been to provide "alternative cultural/conceptual systems to those of European modernity" (331).

However, the disagreement is not so much over whether class is more important than race, ethnicity, sexuality, or gender, but rather over a mistrust of critical cultural scholarship within ethnic studies. Being part of the contemporary U.S. academic and theoretical context, it is not surprising that Latina/o studies inherits the suspicion between cultural studies and political economy brought to the fore of mainstream news by the 1996 Sokal affair,[1] and that continues to permeate a number of disciplines and interdisciplines.

In a sense Darder and Torres (1998, 2003), and to a certain extent Cabán (1998), reveal a suspicion of cultural studies as a form of textual analysis or literary analysis that seems more intent on establishing academic and theoretical credentials than in pursuing social justice goals (Noriega 1992). The "real" of politics and economics is juxtaposed to the textual or literary analyses of cultural forms. However, the two complement each other and are inextricably intertwined. One major way to explore their inextricability is through representational analysis of Latina/os in the mainstream media.

Hybridity in Contemporary Representations

The increased representations of Latina/os is both a response to Latina/o communities' demands for inclusion as well as an effort on the part of governmental and marketing institutions to reach, account for, organize, and profit from this newly created ethnic category. The demographic increase is real, so is the increased spending power, and so are concerted marketing campaigns that seek to appeal to Latina/os. These are all documented and numerically verifiable processes. In fact, they are so documented that both governmental and marketing institutions have to reconcile their strategies with the undeniable presence of hybridity. Hybridity represents a challenge to the government, both in the sense that it has to acknowledge diversity and in the sense that it has to figure out a politically acceptable way in which to categorize people so as to divvy up resources. That is because, for marketing apparatuses, which are absolutely central to the operation of mainstream for-profit media, the challenge is how to extend appeal to these newly acknowledged ethnics without losing the white consumers. Latina/os represent a welcome addition precisely because of our hybridity and ambiguity.

Representational analysis is the necessary half of the realist strategy of counting and measuring. Rather than dismissing textual analysis as a selling out strategy in the name of academic advancement, the representational terrain extends our analysis about what is valuable in our culture. Representations speak to our fears and desires as a culture. As well, what is missing from representations is often a sign of that which we desire to extirpate or marginalize. What is foregrounded speaks to issues of power rather than actual numerical or mimetic correspondences and therefore, once more, is an invaluable complement to political economic analysis. The fact that hybridity is beginning to appear much more often in our mainstream media is very much related to documentable findings of an increasingly hybrid population and the untenability of a bipolar spectrum of racial purity. In fact ethnic ambiguity is a most useful strategy because it has the potential of speaking to different segments of the audience with one economical image or set of images.

There are at least four possible strategies of representing hybridity, and in all four of these Latina/os are very useful. The first strategy is one of morphing. Both Michael Jackson's *Black and White* music video as well as *Time* magazine's (1993) cover of Eve are examples of visual attempts to express the dynamic hybridity that composes contemporary human beings. Given that morphed images are likely to include a range of skin tones, the paradigmatic Latina/o brownness can, in fact, sign in for global hybridity. A second strategy for expressing hybridity is the visual shattered[2] image; that is, disjointed, almost broken mirror-type pieces of different images loosely pieced together to form an uneasy whole. This is an almost psychoanalytic version of morphing, or one could say that morphing is to syncretism and shattering is to hybridity: one is comfortable and stable while the other is shifting and dynamic. Ella Shohat's "ethnicities in relation" approach (1994) posits ethnicities, especially as represented in film and other mass media, as dynamic and unstable, gaining meaning only in terms of the representation of other ethnicities within a given textual context. Latina/os, of course, can be examined in this relational framework, gaining meaning by virtue of their supposed location as an in-between ethnicity, not white yet not black.

A third representational strategy for hybridity is the palette. Some of these palettes represent distinct ethnoracial positions in the human spectrum, while others spill into the fourth representational strategy, which is ambiguity. Prior to the palette approach, of course, there was the homogeneous representation of whiteness. This was followed by a bipolar representation of white and blackness, usually with more numerous whites in the foreground and less numerous blacks in the background (Seiter 1993). Today, we have specific ethnicity palettes, such as the one found in some American Girl catalogs that go from Native American Kaya, the "adventurous" one on the left, all the way to Anglo Molly, the "imaginative" one on the right, with Hispanic Josefina the "hopeful" one and African American Addy the "courageous" one falling somewhere in between. Such a palette is rather unusual, both in its ethnoracial specificity as well as in its extension of the multicultural spectrum to include not only African Americans but Hispanics and Native Americans as well: only the Asian Americans are missing. Nonetheless, the in between ethnics could be nearly interchangeable were it not for the overly stereotypic clothing, hairdos, and settings which only relationally mark their difference despite their similar brownness.

The more usual palette is found in ads such as the one for Gap underwear, which begins on the left with a headless black model and moves to the white model at the right, with ambiguously ethnic models in the middle. Another image from American Girl eerily duplicates the Gap ad, beginning to the left with an African American girl and ending on the right with an Anglo girl. Magalogs such as Tommy Hilfiger are also including multiple instances of ambiguous palettes. These palettes are also present in audiovisual media such as *Barney*, which always has a group of children friends with a couple of ambiguous ethnics, to *That Seventies Show*, which includes the character Fez, who is an ambiguous ethnic but unambiguously ethnic. We are never sure whether he is Latino, Indian, or Arab, but we are always sure he is ethnic because he is different in language, dress, and other behaviors. Once again, ambiguity is desirable because it appeals to a range of different ethnicities. Indeed, if the representation is brown but not too brown it has the potential of appealing to all, because it could be a tanned white, everything in between, and a light black. Ambiguity is by far the most common representation of hybridity in mainstream media, and this maps out onto representations of Latina/os as well.

Latina/os are increasingly represented in contemporary mainstream media, and the lessons from hybridity serve to include certain Latina/os and exclude others, as well as some non-Latina/os. Whereas there is an extensive history of representations of Latina/os in the mass media, contemporary representations bear out the tendencies toward representing hybridity through ambiguity. The demographic and spending power growth of Latina/os has not gone unnoticed by mainstream media. Additionally the hipness of Latinidad in a culture where ethnicity becomes another commodity makes the representation of Latina/os much more prominent. However, the tendency to represent this highly diverse and hybrid group in mostly undifferentiated terms has implications in relation to omissions of certain portions of this umbrella category. Thus we have all sorts of recent mainstream examples of Latina/os in the media. Ranging from prime time television, such as *The George Lopez Show* and *American Family* on PBS, to children's television with *Lucha Libre* and *Dora the Explorer* to girl culture, including books and toys, such as Josefina from the American Girl series and all the synergistic products in the Dora the Explorer line, to magazines such as *People en Español* and *Latina,* to a slew of Hollywood and indie movies such as *Chasing Papi* (2003), *Real Women Have Curves* (2002), *Girlfight* (2000), *Tortilla Soup* (2001), *A Day without a Mexican* (2004), and some of the Jennifer Lopez vehicles, including *Selena* (1997) and *Maid in Manhattan* (2002), nearly all of these instances include unambiguous, mostly light brown Latina/os.

Another type of Latina/o representation involves a subtle Latinidad. Here we have to apply a concept from queer studies to Latina/o studies. "Gay-dar," the ability to discern signifiers of queerness among those in the know, which are imperceptible to the general audience, can be termed *Latino-radar*. Latino-radar is necessary to identify subtle Latina/os in a range of popular culture. In teen pics such as *Blue Crush* (2002) and *Josie and the Pussy Cats* (2001), two Latinas, Michelle Rodriguez and Rosario Dawson, respectively, play one third of a trio. In *Blue Crush*, three young hotel maids survive on the edge of solvency in order to fulfill their dream of becoming big-time surfers. In *Josie,* a young threesome survives on the edge of solvency hoping to make it big in the music industry. In both of these movies the Latinas play supporting roles, as the more Anglo coded protagonist achieves her dream. Both characters are ever so subtly Latinas that only those looking for Latinidad would find it, but since they are both Afro Latinas (albeit light ones) they are brown enough that one could interpret them as light African Americans.

A similar thing happens on television. On Disney Channel's defunct (yet still popular in reruns) *Lizzie McGuire*, Miranda, the best friend, is subtly Latina. Other than because she has brown in relation to Lizzie's platinum blonde hair, we know she is Latina because toward the end of the series and in the feature length movie *Lizzie McGuire* (2003), she disappears under the guise of visiting her grandmother in Mexico City. Thus she simultaneously reiterates two tropes of Latinidad, the supporting actor category and the eternal outsider or recent immigrant status. Other television shows with subtle Latinidad include the children's *Dragon Tales*, wherein Emmy and Max, the protagonists, would be totally imperceptible Latina/os were it not for the fact that every once in a while their mother makes an appearance in the disembodied form of a Spanish accented voice-over. Moreover, one of the dragons, named Quetzal, also speaks with a heavy Spanish accent. Spanish-accented English is yet another trope of Latinidad within mainstream media. As with the girls in the above-mentioned movies, were it not for these subtle and scarce signs, we would not know they were Latina/os.

Subtle Latinidad and ambiguity is also part of Jennifer Lopez's meteoric rise to stardom (Molina Guzman and Valdivia 2004). Whereas Salma Hayek's accent anchors her as different, Lopez's accentless English and light brownness make her a more pliable signifier, of both ethnicity and whiteness. As the advertising campaign for her second perfume *Still* demonstrates, Jennifer can be represented light enough so as to parody or mimic Marilyn Monroe, the epitome of white femininity and of the Hollywood blonde. In many of the Jennifer Lopez films one has to work very hard to figure out her character's supposed ethnicity, which is precisely the beauty of her ambiguity.

Ethnic ambiguity and the ethnic palette have reached their profit peak in the ethnic urban dolls, Bratz and Flavas. Both toy lines, with combined 2003 sales of over a billion dollars, span a range of possibilities, all of them falling in that middle ethnic register, somewhere between white and black. There is no purity pole in these toy lines. For example, a white doll might have very kinky hair. Or a dark-skinned doll might have nearly blonde straight hair. All of these dolls are undeniably hybrid and ethnic. However, as with the Gap and American Girl layouts, while whiteness remains, and the ethnic ambiguity, retaining identifiable components of Latinidad such as hoop earrings and the like, occupies the middle ground, blackness recedes to the left of the page/screen and it becomes decidedly lighter.

Discussion

There is a changing face of ethnicity in the mainstream media, one that acknowledges hybridity and includes an expanded range of ethnic possibilities. However, as with so much representational change, an increase in representation does not necessarily mean more progressive approaches to ethnicity. At this point it is very helpful to return to one of the major issues in representational analysis—namely, what is missing from this picture? In the representation of hybridity through Latinidad and ambiguity is there a corresponding exclusion? Of whom? The answer is twofold: the exclusion occurs both within Latinidad and without it.

The four types of hybridity within the media—morphing, fragmentation, palette, and ambiguity—bear out the acknowledgment, even by marketing apparatuses, that we can neither think of the United States as a white nor as a binary black and white bipolar nation. Central in this acknowledgment are the newly constructed ethnoracial categories of Latina/os. To get to this point in the analysis we have to incorporate both the documented evidence of demographic growth, political mobilization, and marketing appeals as well as the conceptual hybridity that challenges both mainstream narratives of race and conceptions of Latinidad from within and without.

Within Latinidad the foregrounding of the light Latina excludes both the light and dark members of this constructed ethnic category. White Latina/os are suspect both within Latinidad and within Anglo whiteness. The options are blending in, a return to assimilation within hegemonic culture, or an uneasy location within Latinidad. Black Latina/os are "too black to be Latina/o" both within and without Latinidad (Katerí Hernández 2003). Afro Latinos report being treated as outsiders within the African American community, especially if they have a Spanish accent, and are not considered authentic Latinos by Latina/os invested in the politics of brownness. More extensively, the inclusion of Latina/os and ambiguous ethnics within mainstream representational strategies pushes blackness to the left of the picture, sometimes beheaded; lightens them so as to be indistinguishable from brownness; or pushes them out altogether. In fact representing Latina/os (i.e., light brown Latina/os) allows marketers, media producers, and advertisers to once again displace and erase blackness, something that reveals the enduring racism in mainstream U.S. culture. Not only are black Latinos displaced and erased from both Latinidad and blackness, but all blacks are displaced and erased from mainstream culture in general. In fact preliminary research suggests that numerical analysis will bear this out.[3]

The light brown ambiguous emphasis within Latinidad, the same tendencies that partly account for Jennifer Lopez's tremendous mainstream success, also displace and erase another segment of the population, Mexican Americans. Given that this is the largest segment of the U.S. Latina/o population, this is no small feat. Whereas Mexican Americans were previously racialized after the Treaty of Guadalupe-Hidalgo, despite their former status as whites (Haney Lopez 1996), by the twenty-first century, Mexican Americans no longer sign in for white. They are inescapably ethnic. Yet within Latinidad, wherein Arlene Dávila (2001) discerns competing discourses of Latinidad and Elana Levine (2001) attempts to differentiate between the hybrid and the syncretic, Mexican Americans compose the traditional discourse of Latinidad that refuses assimilation and blending. They are neither represented as hybrid nor syncretic since they are seen outside of any blend. On the other hand, Puerto Ricans stand in for the syncretic modern discourse because they are represented as the ambiguous hybrids, whose ambiguity can sometimes be linked to Latinidad through tropicalist tropes (Aparicio and Chávez-Silverman 1997) but is nevertheless more comfortable. After all, ambiguity can be interpreted as the implied "we" of mainstream media, the white Anglo subject, only with a little bit of added hipness. As beneficiaries of "hybridized, manipulated identities, they live the relative benefits of relative exploitation" (Zimmerman 2003, 116). The recent ascendance of this new discourse of Latinidad and of the ambiguous Latina/os serves to displace and erase Mexican Americans from within Latinidad (Valdivia 2003b). More research in political, church, and educational institutions—to name a few—will be necessary to explore whether this displacement is pervasive.[4]

Hybridity as a concept allows us to study the complex diversity of the population and its representation. If we are to understand the possibilities and drawbacks of the deployment of hybridity in the mainstream, we have to move beyond any given constructed ethnoracial category into its relational signification with other categories. Latina/os make it absolutely imperative that we proceed this way, as there is unavoidable seepage into other categories of identity. The gains for individual Latina/o actors or cultural creators, as well as the increased media space we occupy as Latina/os, has to be weighed against the displacement and erasure of both Mexicans and blackness that representation of Latina/os, especially through ambiguity, allows. Foregrounding brownness simultaneously includes some Latina/os and excludes others. The capitalist preference for syncretic comfort is achieved at great cost, which once more reiterates the old effort to leave out the bulk of the people, not just Latina/os but the bulk of the global population from representation, both symbolic and political, despite some real and symbolic gains.

Notes

1. In 1996, *Social Text* published an essay suggesting a link between quantum mechanics and post-modernism by Alan Sokal, a physicist at New York University. On the day of publication Sokal stated in *Lingua Franca* that the article had in fact been a hoax.
2. I owe John Nerone gratitude for helping me come up with this term.
3. Both Victoria Ozokwelu and Tanika Ely conducted McNair research projects that bore out this finding.
4. Anecdotal reports from Catholic church parishes in Southern California as told to this author suggest that this is very much the case.

References

Anzaldúa, G. *Borderlands/La Frontera: The New Mestiza*. San Francisco: Aunt Lute Books, 1987.
Aparicio, F. A. "Jennifer as Selena: Rethinking Latinidad in Media and Popular Culture." *Latino Studies* 1 (2003): 3.
Aparicio, F. R. and S. Chávez-Silverman, eds. *Tropicalizations: Transcultural Representations of Latinidad*. Hanover, CT: University Press of New England, 1997.
Aparicio, F. A. and C. F. Jáquez, with M. E. Cepeda, eds. *Musical Migrations: Transnationalism and Cultural Hybridity in Latina/o America*, vol. 1. London: Palgrave, 2003.
Bhabha, H.K. *The Location of Culture*. London and New York: Routledge, 1994.
Bonilla, F. and J. Villegas. "Reflections on Latino Research after 9/11." *Latino Studies* 1 (2003): 208–10.
Cabán, P. "The New Synthesis of Latin American and Latino Studies." In *Borderless Borders: U.S. Latinos, Latin Americans, and the Paradox of Interdependence*, edited by F. Bonilla, E. Meléndez, R. Morales, and M. Torres, 195–216. Philadelphia: Temple University Press, 1998.
Cepeda, M. E. "Shakira as the Idealized, Transnational Citizen: A Case Study of *Colombianidad* in Transition." *Latino Studies* 1 (2003): 211–32.
Communication Review. Special Issue on "Latina/o Studies in Communication," edited by Angharad N. Valdivia, 7, 3 (2004).
Cortés, C. E. "Who Is María? What Is Juan? Dilemmas of Analyzing the Chicano Image in U.S. Feature Films." In *Chicanos and Film: Essays on Chicano Representation and Resistance*, edited by Chon Noriega, 74–93. New York: Garland, 1992.
Darder, A. and R. Torres, eds. *The Latino Studies Reader*. London: Blackwell, 1998.
Darder, A. and R. Torres. "Mapping Latino Studies: Critical Reflections on Class and Social Theory." *Latino Studies* 1 (2003): 303–24.
Dávila, A. *Latinos Inc.: The Marketing and Making of a People*. Berkeley: University of California Press, 2001.
Fusco, C. *English Is Broken Here: Notes on Cultural Fusion in the Americas*. New York: New Press, 1995.
Fusco, C. "We Wear the Mask." In *Talking Visions: Multicultural Feminism in a Transnational Age*, edited by E. Shohat, 113–18. New York: New Museum of Contemporary Art and the MIT Press, 1998.
García Canclini, N. *Hybrid Cultures: Strategies for Entering and Leaving Modernity*. Minneapolis: University of Minnesota Press, 1995.
Gilroy, P. *There Ain't No Black in the Union Jack*. Chicago: University of Chicago Press, 1987.
Halter, M. *Shopping for Identity: The Marketing of Ethnicity*. New York: Schocken Books, 2000.
Haney López, I. F. *White by Law: The Legal Construction of Race*. New York: New York University Press, 1996.
Katerí Hernández, T. "'Too Black to Be Latino/a': Blackness and Blacks as Foreigners in Latino Studies." *Latino Studies* 1 (2003): 152–59.
Klor de Alva, J. J. "Mestizaje from New Spain to Aztlán: On the Control and Classification of Collective Identities." In *New World Orders: Casta Paintings and Colonial Latin America*, edited by Ilona Katzew, 58–71. New York: Americas Society, 1996.
Kraidy, M. M. "The Global, the Local, and the Hybrid: A Native Ethnography of Glocalization." *Critical Studies in Mass Communication* 16 (1999): 456–76.
Kraidy, M. M. "Hybridity in Cultural Globalization." *Communication Theory* 12 (2002): 316–39.
Lbanyi, J. "Miscegenation, Nation Formation and Cross-Racial Identifications in the Early Francoist Folkloric Film Musical." In *Hybridity and Its Discontents: Politics, Science, Culture*, edited by A. Brah and A. E. Coombes, 56–71. London: Routledge, 2000.

Levine, E. "Constructing a Market, Constructing an Ethnicity: U.S. Spanish-Language Media and the Formation of a Syncretic Latino/a Identity." *Studies in Latin American Popular Culture* 20 (2001): 33–50.

López, A. M. "Are all Latins from Manhattan?: Hollywood, Ethnography, and Cultural Colonialism." In *Unspeakable Images: Ethnicity and the American Cinema*, edited by L. D. Friedman, 404–24. Urbana: University of Illinois Press, 1991.

Lugo, A. "Theorizing Border Inspections." *Cultural Dynamics* 12 (2000): 353–73.

Lugones, M. and J. Price. "The Inseparability of Race, Class, and Gender in Latino Studies." *Latino Studies* 1 (2003): 329–32.

McCarthy, C. *The Uses of Culture: Education and the Limits of Ethnic Affiliation.* New York: Routledge, 1998.

Menocal, M. R. *The Ornament of the World: How Muslims, Jews, and Christians Created a Culture of Tolerance in Medieval Spain.* Boston: Little, Brown, 2002.

Molina Guzman, I. and A. N. Valdivia. "Brain, Brow or Bootie: Iconic Latinas in Contemporary Popular Culture." *Communication Review* 7 (2004): 2.

Moorti, S. "Out of India: Fashion Culture and the Marketing of Ethnic Style." In *The Blackwell Companion to Media Studies*, edited by A. N. Valdivia, 293–308. London: Blackwell, 2003.

Murphy, P. D. and M. M. Kraidy. "International Communication, Ethnography, and the Challenge of Globalization." *Communication Theory* 13 (2003): 304–23.

Naficy, H. *The Making of Exile Cultures: Iranian Television in Los Angeles.* Minneapolis: University of Minnesota Press, 1993.

Noriega, C. "Introduction: Chicanos and Film." In *Chicanos and Film: Essays on Chicano Representation and Resistance*, edited by Chon Noriega. New York: Garland, 1992.

Oboler, S. *Ethnic Labels, Latino Lives: Identity and the Politics of (Re)presentation in the United States.* Minneapolis: University of Minnesota Press, 1995.

Oboler, S. "¡Sí se puede! The Caravan of Citizenship." *Latino Studies* 2 (2004): 1–3.

Pratt, M. L. *Imperial Eyes: Travel Writing and Transculturation.* New York: Routledge, 1992.

Rios-Bustamente, A. J., M. Bravo, and H. Ayala. *Latino Hollywood.* New York: The Cinema Guild, 1996.

Rocco, R. "Transforming Citizenship: Membership, Strategies of Containment, and the Public Sphere in Latino Communities." *Latino Studies* 2 (2004): 4–25.

Rosaldo, R. "Foreword." In *Hybrid Cultures: Strategies for Entering and Leaving Modernity*, edited by N. García Canclini, xi–xvii. Minneapolis: University of Minnesota Press, 1995.

Seiter, E. *Sold Separately: Children and Parents in Consumer Culture.* New Brunswick: Rutgers University Press, 1993.

Shohat, E. "Notes on the 'Post-Colonial.'" *Social Text* 31/32 (1992): 99–113.

Shohat, E. "Ethnicities-in-Relation: Toward a Multicultural Reading of American Cinema." In *Unspeakable Images: Ethnicity and the American Cinema*, edited by L. D. Friedman. Urbana: University of Illinois Press, 1994.

Shome, R. and R. S. Hegde. "Culture, Communication, and the Challenge of Globalization." *Critical Studies in Media Communication* 19, 2 (2002a): 172–89.

Shome, R. and R. S. Hegde. "Postcolonial Approaches to Communication: Charting the Terrain, Engaging the Intersections." *Communication Theory* 12, 3 (2002b): 249–70.

Sommer, D. "The Places of History: Regionalism Revisited in Latin America." *Modern Language Quarterly* 57 (1996): 119–27.

Time. "The New Face of America: How Immigrants Are Shaping the First Multicultural Society." *Time* special issue 142, no. 21 (Fall 1993).

Valdivia, A. N. "Radical Hybridity: Latina/os as the Paradigmatic Transnational Post-Subculture." In *The Post-Subcultures Reader*, edited by D. Muggleton and R. Weinzier, 151–65. London: Berg, 2003a.

Valdivia, A. N. "Salsa as Popular Culture: Ethnic Audiences Constructing an Identity." In *Media Studies Companion*, edited by A. N. Valdivia, 399–418. Oxford: Blackwell, 2003b.

Valdivia, A. N. "Latinas as Radical Hybrid: Transnationally Gendered Traces in Mainstream Media." *Global Media Journal* 2 (2004): 4. (http://lass.calumet.purdue.edu/cca/gmj/refereed.htm)

Valdivia, A. N. and R. Curry. "Xuxa at the Borders of Global Television." *Camera Obscura* 38 (1998): 31–58.

Young, R. J. C. *Colonial Desire: Hybridity in Theory, Culture and Race.* London: Routledge, 1995.

Zimmerman, M. "Erasure, Imposition and Crossover of Puerto Ricans and Chicanos in IS Film and Music Culture." *Latino Studies* 1 (2003): 115–22.

Part Three

Racial Affiliation, Racial Resentment, Racialized Citizenship: State and Educational Policy Dilemmas in the Twenty-First Century

21

Governmentality and the Sociology of Education
Media, Educational Policy, and the Politics of Resentment

CAMERON McCARTHY AND GREG DIMITRIADIS

Introduction

As Arjun Appadurai (1996) has argued, social reproduction and integration have been inextricably complicated by the multiple contemporary pressures of globalization. New and unpredictable flows of people, money, technology, media images, and ideologies are spreading out across the globe in often highly disjunctive ways. These developments must be understood both individually and in tandem. Indeed, these dynamics come together in radically different ways in different social sites and locales, inextricably complicating the idea that one can—ultimately—separate the local from the global. As James Clifford (1997) has stressed, the idea of the nation-state itself has come into question as a helpful construct for thinking about social reproduction. The nation-state, he argues, is a fiction of the powerful, often overlaid on top of the heterogeneity of everyday practices. Social networks, cultural resources, and institutions all play important roles in people's lives, in ways that exceed the predictive powers of those invested in the stability and the relevance of the nation-state.

All this has had important implications for education, for educational processes are at the very heart of social and economic reproduction, a point that has been made by numerous educational theorists and researchers operating in the field commonly called "the sociology of education" (Apple, 1979; 1982; Arnot, 1981; Bernstein, 1977; 1990; Bourdieu & Passeron, 1977; Whitty, 1985). Though often differing on questions of structure and agency, this work has traditionally been concerned with how class, race, and gender reproduce themselves across generations by way of pedagogical texts and institutions, often serving to maintain the normative underpinnings of the nation-state. Yet, with the conceptual status of the state itself increasingly thrown into doubt, new questions and complexities emerge here.

Most importantly, researchers and theorists can no longer assume that schools can be studied as isolated and autonomous structures, nor can one simply assume a priori the imperatives of a bounded state. The interconnectedness of local and global forces has, again, posed new questions for those attempting to talk about social and cultural reproduction. In key example, popular culture is coming to play an increasingly important part in the lives of the young (see, e.g., Steinberg & Kincheloe, 1997), complicating questions about cultural reproduction and the curriculum. Yet, popular culture itself is clearly very much a part of a global entertainment industry, with multiple international connections between capital and points of production, distribution, advertising, and so forth. Texts and tropes circulate widely and are coming to reflect a material and cultural hybridity that does not fit neatly into pre-existing modes of nationalist thinking and planning. We now live at the nexus of multiple "power geometries," unpredictable and transnational lines of connection between local and global forces (Massey, 1994).

The responses to these tensions have been varied. Some critics have called for more sober interrogations of the state and its power. Andy Green (1997), most notably, has argued that the nation-state will remain a relevant construct for thinking about the role of education in this age of globalization, that the state will continue to serve it Durkheimian functions. Hence, he argues, state educational planners should be more prescriptive about planning their public education systems, that common curricula can foster some semblance of social cohesion and can be wedded to the imperatives of industry. His work, by and large, assumes that the state will continue to exert its power. Others, however, have taken a more explicitly anti-state stance. Indeed, Green posits his work in counter-distinction to the work of critical pedagogues like Henry Giroux who have been, he argues, too quick to assume that the state is no longer a relevant construct. These critics, he maintains, argue for the importance of locally negotiated curriculum, for the dismissal of any notion of a "common" public in this age of intense globalization and ethnicization. According to Green, these critics have abdicated any investment in the state at all.

Both responses—the unified and unifying permanent state of Green and the post-state society of Giroux—we feel are inadequate, as neither is a compelling model of the state to draw on in these challenging political times. For functionalists and comparativists like Green, the state is a monolithic entity that is a reality forevermore. For critical pedagogues like Giroux, the state can simply be wished away in the ecstasy of the local embrace. What is missing here is a model of the state that is sensitive to both its durability and its permeability, a model that can account for the massive interconnections between local and global forces and different material and discursive sites. We argue here that Michel Foucault's notion of "governmentality" proves helpful in addressing these concerns, providing a fruitful avenue of inquiry for those in education today. And, we argue as well that the related discursive practice of resentment or the mobilization and deployment of affect is a vital element of governmentality, a vital response within the state and the body politic and across social institutions to the challenges of multiplicity and diversity and instability precipitated by globalization.

Offering a new direction for thinking about state reproduction, Foucault argued that the "state" should not be seen as immutable, nor as a reified entity. The "state" is a result of multiple—though very real and very powerful—discursive practices taking place across a range of sites. Elaborating on Foucault's claims, Nikolas Rose writes that:

> The "power of the State" is a resultant, not a cause, an outcome of the composing and assembling of actors, flows, buildings, relations of authority into relatively durable associations mobilized, to a greater or lesser extent, towards the achievement of particular objectives by common means. This is not a matter of the domination of a "network" by "the State" but rather a matter of *translation*. The translation of political programmes articulated in rather general terms—national efficiency, democracy, equality, enterprise—into ways of seeking to exercise authority over persons, places and activities in specific locales and practices. The translation of thought and action from a "centre of calculation" into a diversity of locales dispersed across a territory—translation in the sense of a movement from one place to another. Through a multitude of such mobile relays, relations are established between those who are spatially and temporally separated, and between events and decisions in spheres that none the less retain their formal autonomy. (1996, p. 43)

Hence, the "state" and its power derives from various "relatively durable" associations of "persons, places, and activities" which take place across and between specific local sites and in interaction with particular global settings. These associations gel together around specific modalities such as "efficiency, democracy, equality [and] enterprise" which tend to operate in specific though unpredictable ways (p. 43). This is not the stuff of top-down state planning, but rather, indexes the ways that these discursive constructions come to infuse themselves in institutions as such, orchestrating cohesion and elaborating affect, sensibility, feeling, and association in complex ways. The goal of educational theorists here is to map out relations between specific sites, and the ways these constructs translate between and across these sites. Contemporary educational theorists, however, have not interrogated these kinds of interconnections and interrelations as clearly as they might, tending, instead, to take less relational and more formal and instrumental approaches. As such, much of this work is limited in its effectivity, its ability to address the mutual imbrication of the various sites that inform educational practice today. Much of this work fails to engage with a power that does not simply prohibit or repress, a power that is dispersed, that circulates—a power that does not exist outside relations but produces relations (Foucault, 1980). Indeed, the locus of power struggles in the modern society is not now to be found pure and simple in the classic sites of state politics, including in labor-capital arm wrestling, or bulldozing actions of civil rights and union-based political actors and their detractors. Modern power struggles are also to be located in the deeply contested arena of the popular, the domain of struggles over social conduct, popular commitments, anxieties and desires, and ultimately the disciplining of populations (Miller, 1998).

Yet, work on popular culture and education has tended not to engage with such notions of power, assuming instead that popular culture can be looked at as an autonomous set of affectively invested texts that exert repressive power on young people. Two approaches, as David Buckingham (1996) makes clear, tend to dominate here. First, critical pedagogues like Henry Giroux and Douglas Kellner argue that media and popular culture play important roles in young people's lives and must be explored as a kind of alternative "lived" curriculum. Yet, as with much curriculum history and theory, textual analysis has reigned supreme here, much of which simply demonstrates how these texts reproduce dominant cultural imperatives, assuming high levels of predictability from text to subject. Second, theorists of "media literacy" such as Len Masterman (1990) have stressed the ways young people can be taught to resist these seemingly deleterious effects of contemporary media cultures. This has tended to be, as David Buckingham (1996) writes, a "*defensive*" position, one that attempts "to inoculate students against or protect them from what are assumed to be the negative effects of the media" (p. 644). Both approaches assume that popular culture is a site of oppression for the young.

Missing, however, is a sense of how different sites—e.g., popular culture, educational policy, classroom practices—mutually inform each other in ways that help reproduce contingent state imperatives. Missing, as well, is a sense of how the local and the global are entirely interrelated in the "relatively durable" associations between these sites. Investigating these seemingly common sense connections, we argue, is a first step towards a more fruitful approach to popular culture, education, and state power.

Taking Foucault's notion of "governmentality" as a starting point, we will interrogate one of its forms of elaboration, a complex of technologies of truth, a set of discursive practices that operates across multiple contemporary sites. This can be summarized in Friederich Nietzsche's term "resentment." Resentment is understood here as the deployment of moral evaluation in political life—a technology of truth that is generated within the reciprocal relationship between the state and the body politic. As an expression of governmentality, resentment performs the ideological and discursive work of managing the complexities and challenges of diversity and multiplicity and social, cultural, and economic change generated by globalization. Resentment is directly linked to governmentality in the sense that resentment is deeply imbricated in the techniques and processes of self-management and the self-regulation of modern populations. This is what Foucault (1980) describes as "rule at a distance." These practices of self-management shift accountability and responsibility for the welfare of the poor and disadvantaged, for example, from a centripetal state to its capillary systems extended in the body politic.

These developments do not displace the state, neither do they herald its ultimate demise. They, instead, help to re-constitute the state as a de-centered system of networks—one in which everyday practices in social institutions such as education and in popular culture help to broker contemporary change. In this sense, we seek to disabuse readers of the notion of the state as a unitary material object. The notion of a centralized state is, in our view, an ideological construct—a project of legitimation (Coffey, 1999). As Philip Corrigan and Derek Sayer (1985) argue, "the repertoire of activities and institutions conventionally identified as the 'state' are cultural forms" and regulations (p. 3). They further maintain that:

> Out of the vast range of human social capacities—possible way in which social life could be lived—state activities more or less forcibly "encourage" some whilst suppressing others ... this has cumulative and enormous cultural consequences for how people identify (in many cases, have to identify) themselves and their "place" in the world. (1985, p. 84)

The link between the state as legitimized administrative apparatuses and the state as one of the crucial sites of the production of identities in the body politic leads us to the wide-open spaces of the public sphere in which civic order is built from discourses that manage the needs, interests and desires generated by and within the socially combatant populations that make up society. These discourses are increasingly overtaken by the language and practice of resentment. Like "efficiency, democracy, equality [and] enterprise," resentment is informing many and different sites today, and is, as such, an important way to think about the relations and associations between what happens in school, what happens in the media, and how public policy is being informed. We cannot, following Foucault, think about these things separately anymore. Power operates in multiple and discursive ways, in ways that must be understood with a flexible set of tools. As such, this article is both methodological and substantive. We both want to suggest a new direction for the sociology of education as well as to deconstruct "resentment" as a powerful way that education is being formed and reformed and, as such, open a space to resist it.

Resentment, Popular Culture, and Educational Practice

A key insight to be gleaned from Foucault and his notion of "governmentality" is that educational institutions are always in synch with popular culture in terms of strategies of incorporation and mobilization of racial identities. And thus the vast field of meaning making is opened up in which the tasks of educating about group differences, the management of diversity, and so forth, have been absorbed within an ever-expanding arena of simulation generated by and through electronic mediation. Television, film, radio, and the Internet are now the most powerful sites for educating about difference and the production of resentment. We live in a time when "pseudo-events" fomented in media-driven representations have usurped any relic of reality beyond that which is staged or performed, driving, it is crucial to note, incredibly deep and perhaps permanent wedges of difference, between the world of the suburban dweller and his or her inner-city counterpart. Daniel Boorstin writes, "We have used our wealth, our literacy, our technology, and our progress, to create a thicket of unreality which stands between us and the facts of life" (Boorstin, 1975, p. 3). These Durkheimian "facts of life"—notions of what, for example, black people are like, what Latinos are like—are invented and reinvented in the media, in popular magazines, in newspapers and in television, music, and popular film. As critics such as Len Masterman (1990) point out, by the end of his or her teenage years, the average student will have spent more time watching television than he or she would have spent in school. In the United States, it is increasingly television and film that educates American youth about race, as evidenced by the so-called "hood" or "reality" films of the early nineties (McCarthy, 1998).

Because reality itself has been redefined by and through media cultures, it is increasingly difficult to separate what happens in the realm of the popular from what happens in schools. Both are in synch in terms of cultural reproduction. We therefore want to take the subject of diversity, knowledge, and power to a place that is normally considered outside the circuit of the education field itself, to the end point and margin of education, to the terrain of popular culture and its pedagogies of wish fulfillment and desire. In so doing, we want to shift attention from the multiculturalist complaint over current modes of teaching and curriculum, per se, to the broader issue of the cultural reproduction of difference and the coordination of racial identities, foregrounding the connections between the production and reproduction of popular cultural form and the operation of power in daily life. We see resentment as a powerful organizing trope here, one that operates across multiple sites.

In his *On the Genealogy of Morals* (1967), Friedrich Nietzsche conceptualized resentment as the specific practice of identity displacement in which the social actor consolidates his identity by a complete disavowal of the merits and existence of his social other. Here, one becomes "good" by constructing the "other" as evil. Nietzsche writes, "Picture 'the enemy' as the man of ressentiment conceives him—and here precisely is his deed, his creation: he has conceived 'the evil enemy,' '*the Evil One*,' and this in fact is his basic concept, from which he then evolves, as an afterthought and pendant, a 'good one'—himself!" (p. 39). A sense of self, thus, is only possible through an annihilation or emptying out of the other. Indeed, while all processes of identity-construction are relational, processes of resentment are explicitly nihilistic and reactive. The world is conceived of as "hostile" and all one's energies are directed "outward" towards the annihilation of the other. Hence, one's identity becomes pure, good, and coherent. These practices of ethnocentric consolidation and cultural exceptionalism—evident on a global scale—now characterize much of the tug-of-war over educational reform and multiculturalism—and the stakes could not be any higher, for all parties involved.

Indeed, these discourses now dominate the public–popular sphere and involve the critical process of the re-narration of social identities in a time of ever-widening economic and cultural anxiety with clear implications for education. These discourses help to manage feelings of uncertainty and to articulate and mobilize needs, desires, and interests in these complicated times. Resentment enters normatively into the space of social realignments, corporate downsizing, and state disinvestment in public works. This is a space in which the state increasingly sheds itself of social welfarism, thereby allowing or even encouraging the reinterpretation and rearticulation of issues of inequality as matters of individual will, volunteerism, and community goal orientation and moral fibre. The problem of inequality has been reassigned as a problem of individual and group success or failure in navigating the shoals of contemporary life. In what follows, we will briefly look at the mise-en-scene of these resentment discourses or technologies of truth associated with the tug-of-war of racial and cultural strife in the educational life of a divided society—the United States. We will limit our discussion to three such discourses.

Origin and Nation

First, we would like to call attention to the *discourse of origin and nation* as revealed, for example, in the Eurocentric/Afrocentric debate over curriculum reform in the U.S. Discourses of racial origins rely on the simulation of a pastoral sense of the past in which Europe and Africa are available to American racial combatants without the noise of their modern tensions, contradictions, and conflicts. For Eurocentric combatants such as William Bennett (1994) or George Will (1989), Europe and America are a self-evident and transcendent cultural unity. For Afrocentric combatants, Africa and the diaspora are one "solid identity," to use the language of Molefi Asante (1993). Proponents of Eurocentrism and Afrocentrism are themselves proxies for larger impulses and desires for stability among the middle classes in American society in a time of constantly changing demographic and economic realities. The immigrants are coming! Jobs are slipping overseas into the third world! Discourses of Eurocentrism and Afrocentrism travel in a time warp to an age when the gods stalked the earth.

This discourse of origin and nation is foregrounded in a spate of recent ads by multinational corporations such as IBM, United, American Airlines, MCI, and General Electric (GE). These ads both feed on and provide fictive solutions to the racial anxieties of the age. They effectively appropriate multicultural symbols and redeploy them in a broad project of coordination and consolidation of corporate citizenship and consumer affiliation. The marriage of art and economy, as Stuart Ewen (1988) so-defines advertising in his *All Consuming Images*, is now commingled with the exigencies of ethnic identity and nation. One moment, the semiotic subject of advertising is a free American citizen abroad in the open seas sailing up and down the Atlantic or the translucent aquamarine waters of the Caribbean sea. In another, the free American citizen is transported to the pastoral life of the unspoiled, undulating landscape of medieval Europe. Both implicate a burgeoning consumer culture undergirded by the triumph of consumer capitalism on a global scale.

Hence, there is the GE "We Bring Good Things to Life" ad (which is shown quite regularly on CNN and ABC) in which GE is portrayed as a latter day Joan of Arc fighting the good fight of American entrepreneurship overseas, bringing electricity to one Japanese town. In the ad, GE breaks through the cabalism of foreign language, bureaucracy, and unethical rules in Japan to procure the goal of the big sell. The American nation can rest in peace as the Japanese nation succumbs to superior US technology.

On the terms of its present trajectory, multiculturalism can be properly diagnosed as one such discourse of resentment, a discourse that attempts to manage the extraordinary tensions and contradictions existing in modern life that have invaded social institutions including the school. At the heart of its achievement, multiculturalism has succeeded in freezing to the point of petrification its central object: "culture." Within the managerial language of the university, culture has become a useful discourse of containment, a narrow discourse of ascriptive property in which particular groups are granted their nationalist histories, their knowledges, and alas, their experts. Cultural competence then becomes powerfully deployed to blunt the pain of resource scarcity and to inoculate the hegemonic knowledge paradigms in the university from the daylight of subjugated knowledges and practices.

This discourse of racial origin as it is infused in multiculturalism provides imaginary solutions to groups and individuals who refuse the radical hybridity that is the historically evolved reality of the United States and other major Western metropolitan societies. The dreaded line of difference is drawn around glittering objects of heritage and secured with the knot of ideological closure. The university itself has become a playground of the war of simulation. Contending paradigms of knowledge are embattled as combatants release the levers of atavism holding their faces in their hands as the latest volley of absolutism circles in the air. In this sense, multicultural education is articulated to popular culture in ways which implicate broader cultural imperatives. Hence, critical pedagogues like Steinberg and Kincheloe (1997) are correct to note the ways popular texts and their complex pleasures and pedagogies are elided from dominant classroom culture today, an insight underscored by an important body of work in cultural studies and education (see, e.g., Giroux,

1996). In this sense, school life is largely divorced from the realities of the popular. However, in another and equally important sense, schools are, in fact, entirely implicated in the kinds of market logics and imperatives so intrinsic to popular culture. Movements for "school choice," for example, index the ways schools are accommodating, not contesting, dominant discourses of consumer capitalism. These discourses are implicated at all levels of the educational process—from decisions about policy and administration to the situated realities of the classroom. As such, Ruth Vinz calls attention to the "shopping mall" approach to multicultural education so prevalent today, giving a most compelling (hypothetical) example:

> On Monday of a given week, students begin their unit on Native Americans. They learn that Native Americans lived in teepees, used tomahawks to scalp white folks, wore headdresses, and danced together around a fire before eating their meal of blue corn and buffalo meat. By Wednesday of the same week, literature is added as an important cultural artifact; therefore, one or two poems (sometimes including Longfellow's "Hiawatha") represent tribal life of the past and present. By Friday, students take a trip to The Museum of the American Indian with its unsurpassed collection of artifacts and carry home their own renditions of teepees, tomahawks, or headdresses that they made during their art period. (Vinz, in press)

The following week, she notes, students might continue their virtual tour of the globe, moving to, for example, Latin American cultures—i.e., "During the second week, students study Latinos...." As Vinz makes clear, dominant approaches to multicultural education evidence a kind of market logic, putting multiple and fabricated cultural products at the fingertips of students to consume in very superficial ways. This "we are the world" approach to education elides the complexity and tension of the emerging global reality, making it one more product for consumers to consume in simple and simply unproductive ways. This is one example of how media culture is in synch with educational practice and policy. Recall the GE ad mentioned earlier.

Popular Memory, History, and Nostalgia

Second, there is *the discourse of popular memory, history, and nostalgia*. This kind of discourse is clearly evident in much contemporary curriculum proposals, proposals that attempt to use education policy as a key site to re-suture an historical, social cohesion inextricably called into question by the multiple pressures of globalization. This attempt to rewrite the cultural landscape is evidenced in all manner of educational practice—from hiring decisions to curricula construction to textbook selection—all of which help call students into a kind of common heritage narrated from a middle-class bourgeois perspective. Of course, Right-wing educators like William Bennett, Dinesh D'Souza, and George Will have been quite explicit about their efforts to narrate US history from a Eurocentric position—a project that has been roundly criticized by historians of oppressed groups, including African Americans (e.g., Lerone Bennett), Asian Americans (e.g., Ronald Takaki), the working class (e.g., Howard Zinn), and women (e.g., Alice Echols), all of whom have attempted to narrate a kind of non-dominant historical knowledge.

This is common well-documented knowledge, a debate that has been raging for several years and culminated around the "PC (Politically Correct) Wars" of the early nineties. Less often discussed, however, is the role of popular media in buttressing these narratives with all the force of common sense. Indeed, this discourse suffuses the films of the last decade or so. Films such as *Dances with Wolves* (1990), *Bonfire of the Vanities* (1990), *Grand Canyon* (1993), *Falling Down* (1993), *Forrest Gump* (1994), *A Time to Kill* (1996), *The Fan* (1997), *Armageddon* (1998), and *Saving Private Ryan* (1998) foreground a white middle-class protagonist who appropriates the subject position of the persecuted social victim at the mercy of myriad forces—from "wild" black youth in

Los Angeles (in *Grand Canyon*), to Asian store owners who do not speak English well (in *Falling Down*), to a black baseball player, living the too-good life in a moment of corporate downsizing (in *The Fan*). All hearken back to the "good old days" when the rules were few and exceedingly simple for now-persecuted white men.

These films are seeped in nostalgia, enmeshed in the project of re-writing history from the perspective of bourgeois anxieties and the feelings of resentment which often drive them. This project is realized perhaps most forcefully in the wildly successful *Forrest Gump*. A special-effects masterwork, this film literally interpolates actor Tom Hanks into actual and re-created historical footage of key events in US history, re-narrating the latter part of the twentieth-century in ways that blur the line between fact and fiction. Here, the peripatetic Gump steals the spotlight from the civil rights movement, the Vietnam War protesters, the feminist movement, and so forth. Public history is overwhelmed by personal consumerism and wish fulfillment. Individual needs, interests, and fantasies replace collective struggle, and the narrative ground of America's contemporary history is rewritten from the point of view of the disadvantaged white middle class.

This nostalgia for the good old days is associated with a set of discourses that recode white middle-class identity as the identity of the oppressed. The professional middle-class suburban dweller has appropriated the radical space of difference, the space of social injury, of social victim—denying avenues of social complaint to the inner-city poor and their immigrant counterparts. The suburbs and their gated communities have become the new barometers of public policy as pro-suburban discourses now displace issues of poverty and inequality, replacing these issues with demands for tax cuts, crime control, and the greater surveillance and incarceration of minority youth. All of this is accompanied by a deeply nostalgic investment in Anglo-American cultural form and its European antecedents.

These shifting currents of association are quintessentially represented in Joel Schumaker's *Falling Down* (1993). The film features a white suburban male protagonist, D-fens, who enters the inner city to settle moral scores with the socially depraved minority poor. D-fens is the prosecuting agent of resentment. He has a very expansive sense of the social other—a vision that embraces Latinos who are gangbangers, Asian store owners who are portrayed as compulsively unscrupulous, and African Americans who are plain low-life and losers.

What is fascinating about a film like *Falling Down* is that it is centered around a proto-normative, anomic protagonist, who as James might put it, is "out there." He is the purveyor of what Jacques Lacan in his "mirror stage ..." essay calls "paranoiac alienation" (Lacan, 1977, p. 5). In this sense, D-fens' character is very closely based on real life characters whose paranoia leads them to office massacres and school murders. We learn, for example, D-fens is a disgruntled laid off white-collar employee—a former technician who worked for many years at a military plant. Displaced as a result of the changing economy of the new world order—displaced by the proliferation of different peoples who are now flooding Los Angeles in pursuit of the increasingly illusive American dream—D-fens is a semiotic prototype of a paranoid single white male who is frustrated by failure in the job site and in personal relations with women. He is the kind of individual we are encouraged to believe a displaced middle-class person might become. As Joel Schumaker, the film director, explains:

> It's the kind of story you see on the six o'clock news, about the nice guy who has worked at the post office for twenty years and then one day guns down his co-workers and kills his family. It's terrifying because there's the sense that someone in the human tribe went over the wall. It could happen to us. (Morgan, 1993)

D-fens is the postcivil rights scourge of affirmative action and reverse discrimination. Nostalgic films like *Falling Down* promote a new kind of social didacticism—one that seeks to expose the depravity of a social system that coddles the slackers and criminal elements among society's minority poor and working class. These films also offer individual agency and determination as the way forward in winning back our communities and society.

Individual Enterprise, Volunteerism, and the Conversationalization of Public Life

Finally, we wish to call attention to resentment discourses facilitating a redirection of whole areas of governmental responsibility and public life towards *individual enterprise and volunteerism and a general pattern of the conversationalizing of public discourse*. First, we will discuss that aspect of the individualization of public life that manifests itself in the promotion of new forms of corporate and state-supported volunteerism. This generalized pattern of individualization of social and political problems generally affects the young. White youth growing up in the 1980s and 1990s in the age of Reagan/Bush regimes—the age of junk bonds, the ruthless pursuit of self-interest, and the icy abandonment of racial minorities—have within the last few years developed a deep sense of a lack of fulfillment that manifests itself in a lost of faith and a crisis of identity (Popkewitz, 1998). This has led to at least two developments within the drama of race relations in the US. On the one hand, there is the increasing declaration of victim status by the white middle classes as we saw in the discourse of popular memory and the rise of nostalgia films such as *Falling Down* (1993) and *Forrest Gump* (1994). This deployment of hostile moral evaluation targets immigrants and minorities for containment and restriction. It is also expressed in public policy, for example, in Proposition 227 (the anti-immigrant, "English Only," initiative passed by a 2 to 1 majority of California voters).

On the other hand, there has been in some quarters among the young an outpouring of a new idealism that serves to reconstruct new millennium youth identities. This new idealism propounds a form of volunteerism that rearticulates the 1960s notion of service overseas as represented by, for example, the Peace Corps, to a sense of rescue mission at home now needed in our times. This form of volunteerism is linked to a sense of national mission and patriotism that seeks to boost America's economic fortunes in the rough and tumble of global capitalism. This idealism feeds on state and business neo-liberal agendas aimed at universalizing the principle of enterprise, bringing entrepreneurial initiative to the inner city, and redirecting inner-city problems away from the public purse and back into the community through a discourse of self-help and volunteerism. This is a form of altruistic resentment. A condescension to help those you fear on your own terms, for your own peace of mind.

This sense of service is deeply racialized. While in the 1960s the target of this idealism was the dispossessed in the Third World, the new found idealism at the dawning of the twenty-first century targets the black and Hispanic minority poor of America's inner cities, who are seen as the tragic ballast weighing down the forward motion of the ship of state. This type of idealism is now being encouraged by the state and corporate interests as a new form of volunteerism and communalism. For instance, corporate organizations such as Nike have promoted the initiative known as P.L.A.Y. or Participate in the Lives of America's Youth, using sport as a vehicle to promote a cleanup of the inner city. Similar initiatives have been promoted by the Bush and Clinton administrations such as The Points of Light Foundation, America's Promise, Americorps—the latter gives young people tuition relief and a stipend in return for volunteering in some area of public need (e.g., working inner-city community centers, old people homes, and so forth).

Perhaps the best example, and certainly one of the most publicized of these volunteeristic projects, is the alternative teacher certification organization, "Teach for America" (TFA). A study of TFA tells us more about the ideological, even psychological, needs of today's middle-class white and minority youth than it does about the underclass to whom the project is targeted. TFA is the 1990s brainchild of a Princeton graduate out of Texas, who dreamed up the idea of a youth service corps of teachers comprising the best and the brightest, interestingly, non-education majors of the top white and black universities in the country. TFA depends on heavy infusions of money from corporate sources interested in a "partnership" with the inner city. And executives from America's leading companies such as IBM, XEROX, and Union Carbide sit on the TFA's executive board. The selected students or corps members are taken on a fast-track to their social rescue goals. In batches starting at 500 and increasing by 500 every year, these corp members are put through a "highly intensive Summer Institute"—in reality an 8 week program that hacks the 4/5 year preservice preparation of teacher education departments down to the barest of essentials. After they have been given their survival tool kit to teach in the urban and rural classroom, these youngsters are placed in classrooms of the most needy school districts across the country, from New York to Los Angeles to New Orleans and rural Mississippi in the South.

For this analysis, we look at Teach For America recruitment literature, one of its main policy documents and its application form for prospective recruits. What is interesting about these documents is their use of the language of resentment. There is a complex of discourses that informs the TFA project as illustrated in its anti-intellectual, deregulation, anti-bureaucracy themes, its media produced images of the sense of threat and danger that the inner city represents, and further, the projection in this TFA literature of the corps member as a special species of green-beret educator. The latter, given his/her intellectual capacity and social pedigree, is armed (sui generis) with the antidote for minority underachievement in the urban and the rural classroom. TFA's thinly disguised objective is to expose the bankruptcy and incompetence of teachers and the system of education preparation and certification that is now centered in the university. Themes of social efficiency and curriculum essentialism that led to the displacement of educators in the post-Sputnik curriculum reform movement of the late 1950s and early 1960s now percolate through TFA's policy discourse. What we want to do very briefly is to take a look at the construction of identity and the other in the literature and TFA's manuals.

For instance, on the front cover of TFA's recruitment brochure entitled "America Needs Both of You" (1994) the object of the mission appears, a black inner-city female student, shot in extreme close up, next to a locker, number "136," outside the urban classroom. Half of the sixth grader's face is completely shadowed, the other half is in light. What we can see inscribed on this child's face is the play of contradictory attributes that are imputed to the inner-city child by TFA. She is the embodiment of rebellion, helplessness, and abandonment. She is standing next to her locker because she has been presumably expelled from the classroom by her real teacher whom we never see. Just above her head and just to the right of the locker, is the classroom door, number "104." It is closed, shut. The "America Needs You" caption which runs underneath this photo interpellates or addresses the corps member. The latter's role is to open the door and let the child back in. The corps member will replace the teacher in this abandoned classroom. To underscore the call to patriotic duty and service, the brochure is done on white card stock and the text is printed in red and blue. Service to inner city is therefore service to country.

Later on page three of the brochure, under the subheading "America Needs You," Teach For America sketches the nature of the educational problem and the task at hand:

Foremost among the factors that threaten America's future is the state of the public school system. Consider the following statistics:

- on average, 3,600 students drop out each school day.
- students in the United States consistently score below those of almost all other industrialized nations in math and science.
- 75% of 17-year-olds are unable write an adequate analytic essay.
- 1/3 of the U.S. population is functionally or marginally illiterate.

This challenge calls for attention and commitment of the nation's best minds. It calls in particular for an increase in the quality and quantity of teachers. Too few teachers come from the top ranks of academic achievers. Some inner-city and rural areas have trouble attracting teachers. (TFA, 1994, p. 3).

These statistics are then further interpreted more elaborately in TFA's literature directed at helping the TFA recruiter prepare for her interview with prospective corps member recruits who will compete for one of the limited corps member slots. One of the most interesting questions in the interview format is the following:

Let's ... pretend that I'm one of your students, named [use your name] and we're going to act out a scene. So, don't tell me what you would do, just do it. Don't tell me what you would say, just say it. I'm going to take out a knife [your pen] in a non-threatening manner. School rules prohibit knives in the building, but some teachers look the other way. Begin. (TFA, 1994, p. 22)

As this passage from the interview format indicates, TFA reproduces the sense of danger that the inner-city school has been branded with in the popular media. Interestingly, this sense of danger is recoded in the TFA discourse. It is reproduced in a new way—the danger and the threat of the inner city is now associated with a sense of high-minded pleasure, a re-energized and re-vivified sense of mission that in turn marks off the fortunate middle-class corps member from the object of her duty: the "at-risk" inner-city child.

TFA offers an activist program of intervention in the inner city that again illustrates the extent to which the terms of public discourse have been redirected towards the idea of universalization of entrepreneurial spirit and individual initiative. TFA offers its model of the school as an enterprise zone. Within this framework, the inner-city school is both feared and loved. It is a site of altruistic resentment—a critical site in the battle to save the nation's poor from self-destruction and ultimately to preserve America's place in the New World Order of globalization. In this high moment of de-intellectualization, teacher education programs in the University are linked to the general educational bureaucracy as targets of moral and affective reform in the world of globalization that is dawning. Inner-city schools, TFA has figured, need emancipatory corporate values. The inner-city child needs moral renovation in order to be made ready for a capitalist future as part of the international reserve army of labor. Resentment discourses that foreground the new volunteerism make social anxieties manageable through the process of marketing the other as a site of intervention and consumerist change.

These resentment discourses also have a conversationalizing dimension as we pointed at the beginning of this section—the new medium for rendering the difficult problems of political and social life accessible and amenable to individual agency and wish fulfillment. From the television and radio talk shows of Oprah Winfrey and Jenny Jones to the rap music of Tupac Shakur to pseudo-academic books like *The Bell Curve*, *The Hot Zone*, and *The Coming Plague*, to self-improvement texts like *Don't Sweat the Small Stuff ... and It's All Small Stuff*, these examples from popular culture all psychologize and seemingly internalize complex social problems, managing the intense feelings of anxiety so much a part of contemporary cultural life. Television talk shows, for example, reduce complex social phenomena to mere personality conflicts between guests, encouraging them to air their differences before staging some kind of denouement or resolution. Histories of oppression are thus put aside as guests argue in and through the details of their private lives, mediated, as they often are, by so-called experts. Racial harmony becomes a relative's acceptance of a "bi-racial" child. Sexual parity is reduced to a spouse publicly rejecting an adulterous partner. Psychologistic explanations for social phenomena reign supreme, and are supported by a burgeoning literature of self-improvement texts, texts which posit poor self-esteem as the preeminent societal ill today. These popular texts and media programs are pivotal in what Deborah Tannen calls *The Argument Culture* (1998) in which the private is the political, and politics is war by other means.

The increasing importance of conversationalizing discourses has had clear influences on school practice. We are thinking here, specifically, of that most important and universally embraced of current educational reforms—the effort to bring computer technology into every classroom. Communication itself, it is important to note, has come to be the dominant trope for much of these reform efforts in schools. We recall here the AT&T "reach out and touch someone" ad campaign which so infused the popular imagination several years ago, a campaign that opened a discursive space for many of its future efforts. Indeed, as one us of discussed elsewhere, AT&T recently sponsored a program entitled "Learning Circles," a program which sought to bring (first as gift, then as commodity) computers into classrooms to encourage "problem solving" between different groups (Dimitriadis & Kamberelis, 1997). Importantly, this technology was supposed to wipe away all social and cultural barriers (after all, no one knows what you look like) and promote uninhibited conversation across geographic and cultural sties. This was a seeming good in-and-of itself and is a clear example of how tropes of media culture—tropes of resentment—can serve to dictate educational policy on the right and left.

In short, then, resentment discourses that emphasize the individualization and the conversationalization of public life facilitate the further penetration of global capital into the undercapitalized sections of society. Much educational policy has become complicit with this project of normalizing the problems of poverty and inequality as the objects of the management of diversity and the individual wish fulfillment of the inner-city other.

Educational Policy and the Pedagogy of Resentment

The notion of "governmentality," particularly its expression in the discourses of resentment, it is important to note, allows us to make these kind of connections—connections between public policy, educational practice, and the work of popular media forms. While educational theorists and practitioners have tended to look at these realms as autonomous, as we have stressed throughout and will show now, they cannot be looked at separately. We now turn to questions of policy.

Educational policies dictated by resentment have had, in point of fact, very real material effects on the dispossessed, those quickly losing the (albeit meager) benefits of affirmative action (e.g., California's Proposition 209), bilingual education (e.g., California's Proposition 227—the so-called "English for the Children" initiative), and need-based financial aid. The idea of high-quality (public) education as the great potential equalizer—a good in and of itself—is now being lost to the bitter resentments at the heart of contemporary culture, lost to petty market logics and the free-standing subject-positions so enabled by them. The pressures of globalization—for example, new patterns of immigration, the proliferation of media images, or the ravages of de-industrialization—have been met here and elsewhere by calls for the weakest kinds of self-serving "diversity." This diversity, as noted, is encouraged by a consumer capitalism that is entirely linked to the imperatives of resentment explored throughout. In a particularly stark example of this process, Martin Luther King Jr's revolutionary dream of the day when his "four little children will … live in a nation where they will not be judged by the color of their skin, but by the content of their character," has been appropriated by right-wing commentators like Shelby Steele (1990) to contest the advances of affirmative action.

How the discourse of resentment has (explicitly) propelled the conservative agenda here is fairly obvious. A new and seemingly beleaguered middle class is looking to recapture its once unquestioned privilege by advocating "color blind" hiring and acceptance policies (in the case of affirmative action) while forging a seemingly unified—and, of course, white Anglo—cultural identity through restrictive language policies (in the case of bilingual education). Indeed, the consolidation of seamless and coherent subjects so at the heart of contemporary cultural media flows (as explored above) has enabled and encouraged the overwhelming public support and passage of bills like California's Propositions 209 and 227. These evidence the popular feelings of resentment that Michelle Fine and Lois Weis (1998) so powerfully document among white working-class men in *The Unknown City*.

Yet, these resentments run deep and operate on numerous levels with respect to the efforts of modern Americans to manage the contradictions and material constraints of everyday life. These tensions are being foregrounded as the logic of globalization impacts the local, and greater diversity within the US urban centers has begun to strain resources and access to education, health care, and so forth. Hence, the tensions now erupting between African Americans and Latinos vis-à-vis many such bills. In a recent *Time* magazine article entitled "The Next Big Divide," the author explores burgeoning conflicts between African Americans and Latinos in Palo Alto over bilingual education, noting that these disputes

> arise in part from frustration over how to spend the dwindling pot of cash in low-income districts. But they also reflect a jostling for power, as blacks who labored hard to earn a place in central offices, on school boards and in classrooms confront a Latino population eager to grab a share of these positions (Ratnesar, 1997, p. 1)

It has been suggested, in fact, that efforts to institute "ebonics" (Black English) as a second language in Oakland, California, was prompted by competition for shrinking funds traditionally allotted to bilingual (Spanish) programs. Resentment, spawned by increasing competition for decreasing resources, is key to unraveling the complexities of these struggles, for, as Joel Schumaker tells us, its power transcends both race and class lines.

Perhaps more importantly, however, the discourse of resentment is also informing more seemingly liberal responses to these issues and bills as well. The importance of public education in equalizing the profound injustices of contemporary American society is increasingly downplayed in favor of discourses about self-interest and the rigid feelings of resentment which under-gird them. Affirmative action, thus, is a good because education will keep dangerous minorities off of "our streets" by subjecting them to a life-time of "civilizing" education, crafting them into good subjects for global cultural capitalism. Further, the story goes, affirmative action really helps middle-class women more than blacks or Latinos, so it should—quite naturally—remain in place.

These discourses inform the debate on bilingual education, as well, a debate that has similarly collapsed liberal and conservative voices and opinions. Indeed, bilingual education, many argue, should be supported (only) because it will prepare young people for an increasingly polyglot global cultural economy, hence keeping immigrants and minorities off of public assistance, allowing them to compete in an increasingly diverse (in the sense developed above) global community. Cultural arguments are also elided from within these positions, for, as many so eagerly stress, bilingual education really helps immigrants learn English and become assimilated faster—a bottom-line supported by an ever-present spate of quantitative studies.

Market logics are all-pervasive here and are deeply informed by self-interest and resentment. These forces have shown themselves most clearly in recent decisions to provide less need-based financial aid for higher education to the poor, apportioning the savings to attract more so-called qualified middle-class students (Bronner, 1998). Competition for the "best" students—seemingly without regard for race, class, and gender—has become a mantra for those wishing to further destroy educational access for the dispossessed. Indeed, why, many argue, should poor minorities take precious spots away from the more qualified wealthy? The resentment of the elite has now come full circle, especially and most ironically, in this moment of unmatched economic wealth. As Jerome Karabel, professor of sociology at UC Berkeley (the site of key roll-backs in affirmative action), comments, "College endowments are at historically unprecedented heights, so the number of need-blind institutions should be increasing rather than decreasing" (p. 16). As we all know, these are not lean, mean times for everybody. We also live in an era of unbridled wealth, won in large measure for the elite through, in part, divide and conquer strategies and the triumph of resentment and its ability to dictate public policy.

Conclusion

Resentment, in sum, is produced at the level of the popular, at the level of the textual. Yet, its implications run deep, across myriad contexts, including in public policy which is increasingly defined by the logics of resentment. Thus, those of us on the left, those wishing to help keep the promise of public education a real one, must question the terms on which we fight these battles. We must question if our responses will further reproduce a discourse with such devastating and wholly regressive implications. As Foucault reminds us, we must choose what discourses we want to engage in, the "games of truth" we want to play. Indeed, what will be our responses to the burgeoning trend of eliminating need-based financial aid policies? What game will we play? And towards what end?

Such questions are crucial and pressing, as this moment is replete with both possibility as well as danger. This period of intense globalization and multinational capital is witness to the ushering in of the multicultural age—an age in which the empire has struck back, and first world exploitation of the third world has so depressed these areas that there has been a steady stream of immigrants from the periphery seeking better futures in the metropolitan centers. With the rapid growth of the indigenous minority population in the US, there is now a formidable cultural presence of diversity in every sphere of cultural life. Clearly, as Appadurai reminds us, social reproduction and integration have been inextricably complicated by globalization and the new and unpredictable flows of peoples as well as money, technology, media images, and ideologies it has enabled (Appadurai, 1996). All these dynamics, he stresses, must be understood individually and in tandem if we are to understand the emerging cultural landscape and its imbrication in a multifaceted global reality. Foucault's notion of "governmentality," as we have stressed throughout, provides us with a way to address these concerns, an important critical tool to begin to deconstruct these seemingly immutable and all-pervasive forces operating, as they do, in numerous social, cultural, and material sites.

Indeed, if this is an era of the post, it is also an era of difference—and the challenge of this era of difference is the challenge of living in a world of incompleteness, discontinuity, and multiplicity. It requires generating a mythology of social interaction that goes beyond the model of resentment which seems so securely in place in these times. It means that we must take seriously the implications of the best intuition in the Nietzschean critique of resentment as the process of identity formation that thrives on the negation of the other—the dominant response from those facing a new and complex global and local reality. The challenge is to embrace a politics that calls on the moral resources of all who are opposed to the power block and its emerging global contours.

This age of difference thus poses new, though difficult, tactical and strategic challenges to critical and subaltern intellectuals as well as activists. A strategy that seeks to address these new challenges and openings must involve as a first condition a recognition that our differences of race, gender, and nation are merely the starting points for new solidarities and new alliances, not the terminal stations for depositing our agency and identities or the extinguishing of hope and possibility. Such a strategy might help us to better understand the issue of diversity in schooling and its linkages to the problems of social integration and public policy in modern life. Such a strategy might allow us to "produce" new discourses as well, especially and most importantly in this highly fraught and exceedingly fragile moment of historical complexity.

References

Appadurai, A. (1996) *Modernity at Large: cultural dimensions of globalization* (Minneapolis: Minnesota).

Apple, M. (1979) *Ideology and Curriculum* (London: Routledge).

Apple, M. (Ed.) (1982) *Cultural and Economic Reproduction in Education* (London: Routledge).

Arnot, M. (1981) Culture and political economy: dual perspectives in the sociology of women's education, *Educational Analysis*, 3, pp. 97–116.

Asante, M. (1993) *Malcolm X as Cultural Hero and Other Afrocentric Essays* (Trenton: Africa World Press).

Bennett, W. (1994) *The Book of Virtues* (New York: Simon and Schuster).

Bernstein, B. (1977) *Class, Codes and Control*, vol. 3 (London: Routledge).

Bernstein, B. (1990) *The Structuring of Pedagogic Discourse: class, codes, and control* (London: Routledge).

Boorstin, D. (1975) *The Image: a guide to pseudo-events in America* (New York: Atheneum).

Bourdieu, P. & Passeron, J.-C. (1977) *Reproduction in Education, Society and Culture* (London: Sage).

Bronner, E. (1998, June 21) Universities giving less financial aid on basis of need, *The New York Times*, p. A1+.

Buckingham, D. (1996) Critical pedagogy and media education: a theory in search of a practice, *Journal of Curriculum Studies*, 28, pp. 627–650.

Clifford, J. (1997) *Routes: travel and translation in the late twentieth century* (Cambridge: Harvard University Press).

Coffey, M. (1999) The State of Culture: institutional patrimony in post-revolutionary Mexico (Unpublished Ph.D. Dissertation, Department of Art and Design, University of Illinois at Urbana-Champaign).

Corrigan, P. & Sayer, D. (1985) *The Great Arch: English state formation as cultural revolution* (Oxford: Blackwell).

Dimitriadis, G. & Kamberelis, G. (1997) Shifting terrains: mapping education within a global landscape, *The Annals of the American Academy of Political and Social Science*, 551, pp. 137–150.

Ewen, S. (1988) *All Consuming Images: the politics of style in contemporary culture* (New York: Basic Books).

Fine, M. & Weis, L. (1998) *The Unknown City: lives of poor and working-class young adults* (Boston: Beacon Press).

Foucault, M. (1980) *Power/Knowledge: selected interviews and other writings, 1972–1977* (New York: Pantheon).

Foucault, M. (1991) Governmentality, in: G. Burchell, C. Gordon, & P. Miller (Eds.), *The Foucault Effect: studies in governmentality* (Chicago: University of Chicago).

Giroux, H. (1996) *Fugitive Cultures: race, violence, and youth* (London: Routledge).

Green, A. (1997) *Education, Globalization and the Nation State* (London: Macmillan Press).

Lacan, J. (1977) The mirror stage as formative of the function of the eye, in: *Ecrits* (New York: Norton).

McCarthy, C. (1998) *The Uses of Culture: education and the limits of ethnic affiliation* (New York: Routledge).

Massey, D. (1994) *Space, Place, and Gender* (Minneapolis: University of Minneapolis Press).

Masterman, L. (1990) *Teaching the Media* (New York: Routledge).

Miller, T. (1998) *Technologies of Truth: cultural citizenship and the popular media* (Minneapolis: Minnesota Press).

Morgan, S. (1993, March) Coastal Disturbances, *Mirabella*, p. 46.

Nietzsche, F. (1967) *On the Genealogy of Morals* (New York: Vintage).

Popkewitz, T. (1998) *Struggling for the Soul: the politics of schooling and the construction of the teachers* (New York: Teachers College Press).

Ratnesar, R. (1997, December 1) The Next Big Divide?, *Time*, p. 52.

Rose, N. (1996). Governing "advanced" liberal democracies, in: N. Rose (Ed.) *Foucault and Political Reason: liberalism, neo-liberalism and rationalities of government* (Chicago: University of Chicago Press).

Steele, S. (1990) *Content of Our Character: a new vision of race in America* (New York: St. Martins Press).

Steinberg, S. & Kincheloe, J. (Eds.) (1997) *Kinderculture: The corporate construction of youth* (Boulder: Westview Press).

Tanner, D. (1998) *The Argument Culture: moving from debate to dialogue* (New York: Random House).

Teach For America (1994) *America Needs Both of You* (New York: Teach For America).

Teach For America (1994) *Teach For America—Recruitment Manual* (New York: Teach For America).

Vinz, R. (1999) Learning from the blues: beyond essentialist readings of cultural texts, in: C. McCarthy, et al. (Eds.) *Sound Identities* (New York: Peter Lang).

Will, G. (1989, December 18) Eurocentricity and the school curriculum, *Baton Rouge Morning Advocate*, p. 3.

Whitty, G. (1985) *Sociology and School Knowledge: curriculum theory, research and politics* (London: Methuen).

22
Patriotism, Democracy, and the Hidden Effects of Race

MICHAEL W. APPLE

Introduction

For a considerable number of years, my arguments have centered on the complex ways in which ideology works in education. As I have documented, issues of power are at the very core of our understanding (and *mis*-understanding) of the realities of curriculum, pedagogy, and evaluation, and about who gets helped and hurt by our commonsense assumptions about education. Common sense is complicated. As I have documented at much greater length elsewhere,[1] it has contradictory impulses and contains elements of both "good sense" and "bad sense." This means that the ways in which ideological tensions are worked out and the ways in which hegemonic relations are constituted, reconstituted, and challenged will themselves be quite complex and will change given new historical realities.

We are living in one of those times when new historical realities are being created before our very eyes. Relations of dominance and subordination are being reconstituted in truly major ways. The horrific events surrounding 9/11, the creation of a new version of a national security state, the withering of long-fought-for protections of crucial civil liberties that some of the political leaders of such a state say it "requires," the invasion of Iraq without UN sanction and against the will of the majority of nations, the continued stifling of dissent and criticism of what have clearly been errors of immense proportion, the building of what seems all too much like an arrogant American empire, and the list could go on—all of these things have come together in powerful ways. It is not an overstatement to point out the very real parallels between what is happening today and the McCarthyism that was discredited years ago. And all of these things are having major effects on how we think about the relationship between culture and power, about who is inside and outside of "our" community, about what we should teach and learn in schools, and the cultural apparatus in general, to prepare ourselves for understanding the lives and realities so many people are now facing nationally and internationally. Indeed, some of the ideological positions now circulating so widely could have been said just as easily by the historical, and all too often racist nativist, figures—Thorndike, Bobbit, Charters, Snedden—who were among the founders of the dominant models we employ to create and evaluate curricula.[2] As we are witnessing, revolutions can be conservative. They can go backwards.

After decades of struggle, many gains were made by critically oriented teachers, community activists, and members of oppressed and dispossessed groups. Such progress was hard won. Granted it was often halting; and sometimes the gains represented compromises with dominant groups that were taken back during the period of economic and ideological attack on the public sphere by neoliberal and neoconservative forces that we have been living under for too long a time. But, spaces for counterhegemonic work were opened up and the gains in education and other parts of society were real.[3] Yet dominant groups have used the current crisis to attempt to turn back the clock. A number of the conservative forces many of us have criticized for years have returned powerfully. They have returned not only because of the economic, political, cultural, and social capital that they possess, although that has played a large part in their resurgence. Nor is the only reason their very clever Gramscian understanding that to win in the state you must win in civil society. Nor is this return only due to their strategy of redefining the meanings of key ideological concepts that organize our common sense such as democracy and citizenship.[4]

Each and every one of these elements is crucial of course. But sometimes dominance returns not because of clever plans, but because of historical events that are "accidental," that are not predictable. But dominant groups are able to bring large groups of people under their leadership because they have already prepared the ideological ground for our understanding of these events and have helped create what Raymond Williams called "structures of feeling" that make it harder to withstand the neoliberal and neoconservative elements that have slowly but effectively become integral parts of our common sense.[5] Thus, even when it is not planned, hegemonic meanings and the differential power relations that they legitimate may get reconstituted in damaging ways. This chapter takes the catastrophic horror of 9/11 as an example of how this may happen. It demonstrates as well how even when it is not overtly on the minds of dominant groups, the effects of 9/11 will have powerful effects on the politics of race in education at a local level.

After 9/11

The volume of material that has been published on the September 11 tragedy has been extensive. While some of it has been filled with an uncritical acceptance of official views on the subject, a good deal of it has been considerably more nuanced and self-critical about the role that the United States may have played in helping to generate the conditions that led to the kinds of despair that might make some people believe that such action could be a "legitimate" response to U.S. hegemony. I do not think that there is any way to justify the acts of 9/11. But I do think that they cannot be understood in isolation from the international and national contexts out of which they arose. I will leave an exploration of the international context to others.[6]

In this chapter, I want to do something else, to bring ideology up to date so to speak. I wish to focus on the most local of levels: the complicated ways in which 9/11 was experienced phenomenologically by teachers such as myself, and the little known effects it had on pedagogy and on the urge to have schools participate in a complicated set of patriotic discourses and practices that swept over the United States in the wake of the disaster. Given this focus, parts of my analysis will need to be personal. I do this not because I think that I have any better purchase on reality than the reader, but because all of us may be better able to understand the lived effects of 9/11 and its participation in complex ongoing ideological transformations by exploring what it meant to identifiable social actors like myself. Thus, I start at the personal level, but my aim is to participate in a collective project in which people from many different social locations and positions tell the stories of what 9/11 meant, and continues to mean, for their lives and educational practices.

I then discuss the impact of 9/11 on the politics of the local, on the school board in Madison, WI where I live. Here, we shall see that the politics of "patriotism" made it much more difficult for schools at all levels to engage in social criticism or even meaningful dialogue about U.S. policies and economic power. As we shall also see, 9/11 had powerful and worrisome effects that are often hidden in our rush to use schools for "patriotic" purposes in much the same ways as the more repressive parts of the Americanization project acted during previous decades of U.S. history.

Horror and Hollywood

"Damn. Who could be calling now?" My annoyance was palpable. This was one of the increasingly rare mornings that I had been able to carve out uninterrupted time to devote myself to serious writing. I ran from my computer to the phone, hoping not to lose the line of thought I was struggling with. The call was from one of my most politically active students.

"Michael, do you have your TV on? Put it on *now, quickly*! The World Trade Center is *collapsing*. It's unbelievable. We're in for a new McCarthyism! What do you think we should *do*!"

I put the TV on. You'll forgive me, but the first words out of my mouth were "Holy shit!" I sat. I watched. But this was decidedly not passive watching. Mesmerized is exactly the wrong word here. As the buildings collapsed, my mind was filled with an entire universe of competing and contradictory emotions and meanings. This wasn't the O.J. slow-motion caravan. Nor was it like my experience of being a young teacher when Kennedy was assassinated. Then, I was giving a spelling test at the time the shooting was announced over the school's loudspeaker. I kept giving the test, too shocked to do anything else. Yes, like the Kennedy experience there now was the intense shock of the surreally slow-motion plane, of the collapsing towers, and worst of all of people jumping out of buildings. But I had changed and so had the cultural assemblage around which one made interpretive sense of what was happening.

At nearly exactly the same time as I felt immense horror at the World Trade Center disaster, something else kept entering into the lenses with which I saw the images on the screen. The key word here is exactly that—*screen*. It seemed almost unreal. The explosions weren't large enough or dramatic enough to seem "real." It was as if I expected Bruce Willis to come running out of the collapsing buildings after a fireball of gargantuan proportions lit up the sky. The fireball was "too small." The scene of the plane as it headed for the second tower—a scene broadcast over and over and over again, as if there was something of a perverse politics of pleasure at work—was too undramatic, too "unemotional" (as if it needed a musical crescendo to tell us of the impending tragedy). The only word I can use to describe that part of this welter of meanings and emotions was that even though I had prided myself on being critically conscious of the ways that our dominant commodified cultural forms worked, I too had been *Hollywoodized*. The horror of death meets The Towering Inferno. But the falling bodies always brought me back to reality. It was *that* sight that brought the carnage back home.

Like many people, I am certain, I sat and watched for hours. Interviews, screaming people running away, running toward, but always running, or seeking cover. Another plane—this one missing. What was its target? Then came the news that the Pentagon was hit. This created an even more complex set of interpretations and readings. Why did I have even more complicated emotions now? I had marched on the Pentagon against the Vietnam War. I had been tear-gassed there. It was the seat of American military might and power. For one fleeting moment I felt that somehow it almost *deserved* to be a target. And yet, real people were killed there, real people who worked there not only out of choice but because, in a U.S. economy that was what is best called military Keynesianism (use government funding to prop up the economy, but by channeling huge amounts of that money into military related enterprises), the Pentagon and similar sites were where many of the jobs *were*.

Then, by that night and throughout the days and nights that followed, the ruling pundits took charge of the public expression of what were the legitimate interpretations of the disaster. The visual construction of authority on the screen and the spoken texts themselves will provide critical media analysts with enough data to once again demonstrate how power is performed in public, how the combination of somber setting, the voices of righteousness, and the tropes of patriotism and vengeance all work together to create a mighty call not for justice but for vengeance.[7] (This is one of the reasons that I and many others joined forces to create the "Justice not Vengeance" movement in towns and cities throughout the nation.)

In understanding this, I try to remember that the media not only help us construct the nature of the problems we face, but they are powerful mobilizing tools. And everywhere one turns after 9/11 there are voices in the media saying the same thing. Dissident voices are not totally silent, but the shock has affected them as well; and their messages are muted. We are at war. Terrorists are here. Freedom has taken a horrible blow. But God is on our side. We cannot afford the luxury of worrying about civil liberties. Lenient policies toward immigrants, the defunding and depowering of the FBI and the CIA, our diminished military strength, all of these and so much more were nearly the only official response. There must be one unitary reply: Track "them" down in all places at all costs. Find their supporters wherever they may be, especially if they are here. Any questions about *why* so many people in so many nations might have been mistrustful of, indeed sometimes hated, the United States, is seen as nearly unpatriotic; they could not be tolerated at this time. Oh, these questions might be worth asking, but after "we" had destroyed the threat to our very way of life that international terrorism represented. Of course, even asking the question "Why do they hate us?" is itself part of the problem. At the same time, I also realize that by constructing the binary of "we/ they," the very nature of the question establishes center–periphery relations that are fully implicated in the production of a reactionary and often racist common sense. Good/bad terms have always dominated the American political landscape, especially in terms of international relations.

How can we interpret this? Speaking very generally, large parts of the American public have little patience with the complexities of international relations and even less knowledge of U.S. complicity in supporting and arming dictatorial regimes; nor does it have a developed and nuanced understanding of U.S. domination of the world economy, of the negative effects of globalization, of the environmental effects of its wasteful energy policies and practices, and so much more, despite the nearly heroic efforts of critics of U.S. international policy such as Noam Chomsky.[8] This speaks to the reality of the selective tradition in official knowledge and in the world beyond our borders that the news portrays. Even when there have been gains in the school curriculum—environmental awareness provides a useful example[9]—these have been either adopted in their safest forms[9] or they fail to internationalize their discussions. Recycling bottles and cans is "good"; connections between profligate consumption of a disproportionate share of the world's resources and our daily behavior are nearly invisible in schools or the mainstream media. In this regard, it is helpful to know that the majority of nonbusiness vehicles purchased in the United States are now pickup trucks, minivans, and sport utility vehicles (to say nothing of the Hummer!)—a guarantee that energy conservation will be a discourse unmoored in the daily practices of the U.S. consumer and an even further guarantee that the relationship between U.S. economic and military strategies and the defense of markets and, say, oil resources, will be generally interpreted as a fight to protect the "American Way of Life" at all costs.

I mention all this because it is important to place what happened in the wake of September 11 in a context of the "American" psyche and of dominant American self-understandings of the role the United States plays in the world.[10] In the domestic events surrounding September 11, *we* had now become the world's oppressed. The (always relatively weak) recognition of the realities of the Palestinians or the poor in what we arrogantly call "the third world" were now evacuated. Almost immediately, there were a multitude of instances throughout the nation of people who "looked Arabic" being threatened and harassed on the street, in schools, and in their places of business. Less well known, but in my mind of great importance, because they show the complexities of people's ethical commitments in the face-to-face relations of daily life, were the repeated instances of solidarity, including university and community demonstrations of support for Islamic students, friends, and community members. Yet these moments of solidarity, though significant, could not totally make up for such things as Islamic, Punjabi, Sikh, and other students in high schools and at universities being threatened with "retaliation" and in the case of some Punjabi secondary school students being threatened with rape as an act of "revenge" for September 11. This documents the connections between some elements of national identity and forms of masculinity, a relationship that cries out for serious analysis.[11]

At the universities, some teachers ignored the horror, perhaps for much the same reason that I as a young teacher in 1963 had dealt with the Kennedy assassination by simply resorting to normality as a defense against paralysis. In other classes, days were spent in discussions of the events. Sadness, disbelief, and shock were registered. But just as often, anger and a resurgent patriotism came to the fore. Any critical analysis of the events and of their roots in the hopelessness, denial of dignity, and despair of oppressed peoples—as I and number of my colleagues put forward in our classes and seminars—had to be done extremely cautiously, not only because of the emotionally and politically charged environment, even at a progressive university like my own, but also because many of us were not totally immune from some of the same feelings of anger and horror. Even for progressive educators, the events of September 11 worked off of the contradictory elements of good and bad sense we too carried within us and threatened to pull us in directions that, in other times, would have seemed to be simplistic and even jingoistic. But at least for me and the vast majority of my colleagues and graduate students, the elements of good sense won out.

Given these elements of good sense, it was clear that pedagogical work needed to be done. But this wasn't a simple issue, because a constant question, and tension, was always on my mind. How could one condemn the murderous events, give one's students a historical and political framework that put these events in their larger critical context, and provide a serious forum where disagreement and debate could fruitfully go on so that a politics of marginalization didn't occur in the classes—and at the same time not be seen as somehow justifying the attacks, which under no circumstances could be justifiable? While I had very strong feelings about the need to use this as a time both to enable students to reflect on the horrible human tragedy we had just witnessed and to show the effects of U.S. global economic, political, and cultural policies, I also had strong "teacherly" dispositions that this was also *not* the time to engage in a pedagogy of imposition. One could not come across as saying to students or the public, "Your understandings are simply wrong; your feelings of threat and anger are selfish; any voicing of these emotions and understandings won't be acceptable." This would be among the most counterproductive pedagogies imaginable. Not only would it confirm the already just-near-the-surface perceptions among many people that somehow the left is unpatriotic, but such a pedagogy also could push people into rightist positions, in much the same way as I had argued in my own work about why people "became right."[12] This required a very strategic sense of how to speak and act both in my teaching and in my appearances on national media.

Take my teaching as a major example. I wanted my students to fully appreciate the fact that the U.S.-led embargo of Iraq had caused the death of thousands upon thousands of children each year that it had been in place. I wanted them to understand how U.S. policies in the Middle East and in Afghanistan itself had helped create truly murderous consequences. However, unless their feelings and understandings were voiced and taken seriously, the result could be exactly the opposite of what any decent teacher wants. Instead of a more complicated understanding of the lives of people who are among the most oppressed in the world—often as a result of Western and Northern economic and political policies[13]—students could be led to reject any critical contextual understanding largely because the pedagogical politics seemed arrogant. In my experiences both as an activist and a scholar, this has happened more often than some theorists of "critical pedagogy" would like to admit.[14] None of us are perfect teachers, and I am certain that I made more than a few wrong moves in my attempts to structure the discussions in my classes so that they were open and critical at the same time. But, I was impressed with the willingness of the vast majority of students to reexamine their anger, to put themselves in the place of the oppressed, to take their more critical and nuanced understandings and put them into action.

Indeed, one of the things that was striking was the fact that a coalition of students in my classes was formed to engage in concrete actions in their own schools and communities, as well as in the university, to interrupt the growing anti-Islamic and jingoistic dynamics that were present even in progressive areas such as Madison and the University of Wisconsin. This activism was extended later on to create widespread protests against the federal government's and university's imposition of a fee on all foreign students that would be used to cover the costs of their own surveillance "to protect our security." At this writing the fee has been temporarily withdrawn, at least at Wisconsin. Thus, activist coalitions that work against the increasing loss of civil liberties of foreign students and of permanent residents and citizens in the United States have lasted and have continued to engage in mobilizations in important ways. Defending our nation is important; but if we lose the reason this nation should in fact *be* defended, and hence become a very different nation in the process, then the enemies of what is best called "thick" rather than "thin" democracy have won—and we will have lost our ethical and political souls in the meantime.

This politics of interruption became even more important, because these complicated pedagogical issues and the contradictory emotions and politics that were produced in the aftermath of 9/11 were felt well beyond the walls of the university classroom. At times, they also had the effect of radically transforming the politics of governance of schooling at a local level in communities throughout the United States. One example from Madison can serve as a powerful reminder of the hidden effects of the circulation of discourses of patriotism and "threat" as they move from the media into our daily lives.

Patriotism, the Flag, and the Control of Schools

On an autumn evening that hinted at the coming of cooler weather, more than 1,200 persons packed the auditorium where the Madison Board of Education had called a special meeting. Flags were everywhere, in hands, on lapels, pasted on jackets. The old and trite phrase that "you could cut the tension with a knife" seemed oddly appropriate here. The tension was somehow *physical*; it could literally be felt, almost like an electrical current that coursed through your body. And for some people present at the hearing, the figures behind the front table deserved exactly that. They needed to be electrically shocked, indeed were almost deserving of something like the electric chair.

Months before the 9/11 disaster, the seeds of this conflict had been planted in what were seemingly innocuous ways. Smuggled into the state budget bill was a bit of mischief by conservative legislators seeking to gain some arguing points for the next election. There was a section in the budget authorization bill that required that students in all publicly funded schools publicly recite "The Pledge of Allegiance" or that schools play or sing the "The Star Spangled Banner," a national anthem that is a strikingly militaristic song with the added benefit of being nearly impossible for most people—and certainly most children—to sing. Even though the legislation allowed for "nonparticipation," given the long and inglorious history of legislation of this kind in the United States, there was a clear implication that such lack of participation was frowned upon. This was something of a time bomb just waiting to explode. And it did.

In the midst of the growing patriotic fervor following 9/11, the Madison, Wisconsin School Board voted to follow the law in the most minimalist way possible. For some board members, the law seemed to be the wrong way to teach patriotism. Rote memorization was not the best approach if one actually wanted to provide the conditions for the growth of thoughtful citizenship. For others, the law was clearly a political ploy by conservative legislators to try to gain more support among right-wing voters in an upcoming election that was felt to be a close call. And for other board members, there were a number of principles at stake. The state should not intervene in the content of local school board decisions of this type. Further, not only had the new law not been subject to close public scrutiny and serious debate, but it threatened the cherished (at least in theory) Constitutional right of freedom of dissent. For all of these reasons, a majority of people on the school board voted not to mandate the reciting of the Pledge or the singing of the anthem in the Madison public schools.[15]

Within hours, the furor over their decision reached a boiling point. The media made it their major story. Prominent headlines in a local conservative newspaper stated such things as "School Board Bans Pledge of Allegiance," even though the board had actually complied with the formal letter of the law, and even though the board had indeed held public hearings prior to its actions where many people had objected both to the law and to the saying of the Pledge and the singing of the anthem. Conservative politicians and spokespersons, colonizing the space of fear and horror over the destruction of the World Trade Center, quickly mobilized. "This could not be tolerated." It was not only unpatriotic, but it was disrespectful both to the women and men who died in the disaster and to our military overseas. To those being mobilized, it also was a signal that the board was out of touch with "real" Americans, one more instance of elite control of schools that ignored the wishes of the "silent majority" of "freedom loving" and patriotic Americans.

At the meeting of the school board approximately 50 percent of the speakers from the audience supported the board's original decision to require neither the Pledge nor the singing of the anthem, a fact that was deeply buried in the news accounts that consistently highlighted the conservative mobilization against the board. This in part was because the voices of those who supported the board's vote were often drowned out by the members of the audience who opposed it. A cacophony of hisses, boos, chants, and phrases reminiscent of earlier periods of "red-baiting" greeted each speaker who spoke in favor of the board's actions. Meanwhile, those who spoke out against the board were greeted with applause and loud cheers. (It almost sounded like an Olympics event in which the chant of "U.S.A., U.S.A." could be heard.)

Throughout it all, the board members tried to remain civil and not respond to what were at times quite personal attacks on their patriotism. In many ways, the hours upon hours of the meeting and the intense conflicts that ensued could be interpreted as an example of democracy in action. In part, such an interpretation is undoubtedly correct. Yet, the harshness of the language, the theater of patriotic symbols, the echoes of war fever, all of this added up to a politics of intimidation as well. Having said this, there was also a sense of genuine expression pain and hurt, a recognition that "ordinary Americans" had been killed and that schools had to recognize the deaths as having occurred among "people like ourselves."

The populist notes being struck here are crucial, since hegemonic alliances can *only* succeed when they connect with the elements of "good sense" of the people.[16] Popular worries over one's children and the schools they attend, in a time of radical corporate downsizing and capital flight, worries about social stability and cultural traditions that are constantly being subverted by the commodifying processes and logics of capital, and so much more—all this allows conservative groups to suture these concerns into their own antipublic agenda. Thus, rampant and fearful conservatism and uncritical patriotism are not the only dynamics at work in this situation, even though the overt issue was about the Pledge and the anthem. None of this could have happened without the growing fear of one's children's future and over the nature of an unstable paid labor market, and especially without the decades-long ideological project in which the right had engaged to make so many people believe that "big government" was the source of the social, cultural, and economic problems we face.[17]

Yet, there were more conjunctural reasons for this response as well. It is always wise to remember that while the state of Wisconsin was the home of much of the most progressive legislation and of significant parts of the democratic socialist tradition in the United States, it also was the home of Senator Joseph McCarthy—yes, the figure for whom McCarthyism is named. Thus, behind the populist and social democratic impulses that have had such a long history here, there lies another kind of populism. This one is what, following Stuart Hall,[18] I have called "authoritarian populism," a retrogressive assemblage of values that embodies visions of "the people" that has been just as apt to be nationalistic, anti-immigrant, anticosmopolitan, anticommunist, promilitary, and very conservative in terms of religious values.[19] In times of crisis, these tendencies can come to the fore. And they did, with a vengeance.

Of course, we cannot understand any of this unless we understand the long history of the struggles over the very meaning of freedom and citizenship in the United States.[20] For all of the protagonists in the school board controversy, what was at stake was "freedom." For some, it was the danger of international terrorism destroying our "free" way of life. Nothing must interfere with the defense of "American freedom" and schools were on the front lines in this defense. For others, such freedom was in essence meaningless if it meant that citizens couldn't act on their freedoms, especially in times of crisis. Silencing dissent, imposing forms of compulsory patriotism, these acts were the very antithesis of freedom. A hidden curriculum of compulsory patriotism would, in essence, do exactly this.

This documents an important point. Concepts such as freedom are sliding signifiers. They have no fixed meaning, but are part of a contested terrain in which different visions of democracy exist on a social field of power in which there are unequal resources to influence the publicly accepted definitions of key words. In the words of one of the wisest historians of such concepts:

> The very universality of the language of freedom camouflages a host of divergent connotations and applications. It is pointless to attempt to identify a single "real" meaning against which others are to be judged. Rather than freedom as a fixed category or predetermined concept, ... it [is] an "essentially contested concept," one that by its very nature is the subject of disagreement. Use of such a concept automatically presupposes an ongoing dialogue with other, competing meanings.[21]

The realization of how concepts such as democracy and freedom act as sliding signifiers and can be mobilized by varying groups with varying agendas, returns us to a point I made earlier, the ideological project in which the economic and cultural right have engaged. We need to understand that widely successful effects of what Roger Dale and I have called "conservative modernization" have been exactly that—widely successful.[22] We are witnessing—living through is a better phrase—a social/pedagogic project to change our common sense, to radically transform our assumptions about the role of "liberal elites," of government and the economy, about what are "appropriate" values, the role of religion in public affairs, gender and sexuality, "race," and a host of other crucial areas. Democracy has been transformed from a political concept to an economic one. Collective senses of freedom that were once much more widespread (although we need to be careful not to romanticize this) have been largely replaced by individualistic notions of democracy as simply "consumer choice." While this has had major effects on the power of labor unions and on other kinds of important collective social movements, it also has created other hidden needs and desires besides those of the rational economic actor who makes calculated individual decisions in a market.[23] I think that these needs and desires have also played a profound role in the mobilization of the seemingly rightist sentiment I have been describing.

Underneath the creation of the unattached individualism of the market is an almost unconscious desire for community. However, community formation can take many forms, both progressive and retrogressive. At the time of 9/11, both came to the fore. The school board's decision threatened the "imagined community" of the nation, at the same time as the nation actually seemed to be under physical threat.[24] It also provided a stimulus for the formation of a "real" community, an organization to "win back" the space of schooling for patriotism. The defense of freedom is sutured into the project of defending the nation, which is sutured into a local project of forming a (rightist) counterhegemonic community to contest the antipatriotic and ideologically motivated decisions by urban liberal elites. Thus, the need to "be with others," itself a hidden effect of the asocial relations of advanced capitalism, has elements of good and bad sense within it. Under specific historical circumstances these elements of good sense can be mobilized in support of a vision of democracy that is inherently undemocratic in its actual effects on those people in a community who wish to uphold a vision of freedom that not only legitimates dissidence but provides space for its expression.[25]

In saying this, do not read me as being totally opposed to ideas of nation or of the building of imagined communities. In my mind, however, social criticism is the ultimate act of patriotism. As I say in *Official Knowledge*, rigorous criticism of a nation's policies demonstrates a commitment to the nation itself. It says that one demands action on the principles that are supposedly part of the founding narratives of a nation and that are employed in the legitimation of its construction of particular kinds of polities. It signifies that "I/we live here" and that this is indeed our country and our flag as well. No national narrative that excludes the rich history of dissent as a constitutive part of the nation can ever be considered legitimate. Thus, in claiming that the board had acted in an unpatriotic manner, the flag-waving crowd and the partly still inchoate movement that stood behind it in my mind was itself engaged in a truly unpatriotic act, one that showed that the national narrative of freedom and justice was subject to constant "renegotiation" and struggle over its very meaning.[26] The 9/11 tragedy provided the conditions for such struggles at a local level, not only in the classrooms at universities such as my own but in the ordinary ways we govern our schools.

Compulsory Patriotism and the Hidden Effects of Race

In Madison, even with the forces arrayed against it, the threat to call a special election to oust the board members who voted against the mandatory Pledge and singing stalled. In fact, the recall campaign failed by a wide margin. The conservative organizers were not able to get anywhere near the number of votes needed to force a new election. This is a crucial element in any appraisal of the lasting effects of 9/11. In the face of resurgent uncritical patriotism and anger, in the face of calls for an enhanced national security state and for schools to be part of the first line of defense, at the local level in many communities wiser heads, ones with a more substantive vision of democracy, prevailed. Yet, this is not the end of this particular story. The pressure from the right did have an effect. The board left it up to each individual school to decide if and how they would enforce the mandated patriotism. This decision defused the controversy in a way that has a long history in the United States. Local decisions will prevail; but there is no guarantee that the decisions at each local school will uphold a vision of thick democracy that welcomes dissent as itself a form of patriotic commitment.

Still, the issues surrounding thick democracy at a local level do not end with the question of whether dissent is welcome or not. To document why we must go further, I need to point to other crucial dynamics that were at work and that were the unforeseen results of this controversy. When the recall campaign failed, conservatives rededicated themselves to winning the next school board election. Two of the seats of people who had been among the majority of members who had originally taken the controversial decision were to be contested. Here, too, the conservatives failed and both seats were taken by progressives. This again seems as if our story had a relatively happy ending. Yet, simply leaving the story there would miss one of the most important hidden effects of the September 11/Pledge connection. Instead, what I shall now describe shows something very different—that often the effects of seeming victories against rightist mobilization must themselves be understood as complicated and as occurring along multiple dynamics of power.

Because of the tensions, controversies, and personal attacks that developed out of the board's deliberations, one of the members who had voted for the board's minimalist response resigned right before the closing date for registering as a candidate for the next election. That member, an African American who had been on the board for a number of years, was "worn out" by the controversy. In essence, while it is trite to say so, it became the straw that broke the camel's back. It had taken so much energy and time to fight the battles over funding cuts, over the development of programs that were aimed specifically at Madison's growing population of children of color, over all those things that make being one of the few "minority" members of a school board so fulfilling and frustrating, that the emotional labor and time commitments involved in the compulsory patriotism conflict and in its aftermath created an almost unbearable situation for him. Even though a progressive "write-in" candidate did win the seat that had been vacated, a cogent voice, one representing communities of color in the community, had been lost.

This points to a crucial set of unintended results. The legislation smuggled into the budget bill had echoes of dynamics that were very different from those overtly involved in the conflict over the Pledge, but these echoes still were profound in their effects. In the context of 9/11, this seemingly "inconsequential" piece of legislation not only created the seeds of very real conflicts and conservative mobilizations; but through a long chain of events, it also led to the loss of a hard-won gain. An articulate African-American elected board member who had fought for social justice in the district could take it no more. In the conjunctural and unpredictable events both of and after the horror of 9/11, a bit of "mischief" in which Republican legislators sought to protect their right flank, rebounds back on the realities of differential power at the local level. Obviously, race was not necessarily as much on the minds of the legislators who placed that piece of legislation into the budget bill as it had been on the minds of some of the more overtly racist educators and legislators in the earlier periods of U.S. history I have analyzed elsewhere.[27] However, the effects to which it led ultimately were, profoundly, raced at the level of local governance.

I want to stress the importance of these effects. In any real situation there are multiple relations of power and an entire and sometimes contradictory assemblage of hegemonic and counterhegemonic relations. Because of this, any serious understanding of the actual results of September 11 on education needs to widen its gaze beyond what we usually look for. As I have shown, in the aftermath of 9/11 the politicization of local school governance occurred in ways that were quite powerful. Yet, without an understanding of "other" kinds of politics, in this case race, we would miss one of the most important results of the struggle over the meaning of "freedom" in this site. September 11 has had even broader effects than we recognize. This should not surprise us. As Charles Mills has argued, a "racial contract" underlies much of what we take for granted in this society.[28] Thus, race is often the "absent presence" behind our everyday assumptions and everyday interactions. What happened in Madison demonstrates the very close connections that exist between what we would ordinarily think is not about race and the manner in which the racialized and racializing dynamics in this society come into play in constitutive ways.

Conclusion

In the account I have given in the second half of this chapter, it is unclear who really won or lost here. But one thing is clear: No analysis of the effects of 9/11 on schools can go on without an understanding of the ways in which the global is dynamically linked to the local. Such an analysis must more fully understand the larger ideological work and history of the neoliberal and neoconservative project and its effects on the discourses that circulate and become common sense in our society. No analysis can afford to ignore the contradictory needs and contradictions that this project has created. And given the power of "race" in this society, any serious understanding must constantly examine the ways in which racial dynamics get played out on fields of power that don't seem to be overtly about that on first glance.

Oh, and one last thing, a complete analysis would require that we look at the effects of the commodified products of popular cultural forms of entertainment that each of us use to "see" the momentous events taking place all around us. Critical cultural analysts have taught us many things. Yes, we participate in guilty pleasures. (How else to explain my framing of the disastrous events of 9/11 in terms of Hollywood images?) And, yes, we can read any cultural form and content in dominant, negotiated, and oppositional ways. But, it might be wise to remember that—at least in the case of the ways in which Michael W. Apple experienced the horrors of the planes and buildings and bodies on 9/11—all three went on at the same time.

Thus, I want to argue that educators—whether teaching a university class or participating in local school board decision making—must first recognize our own contradictory responses to the events of September 11 and to its ongoing aftermath. We must also understand that these responses, although partly understandable in the context of tragic events, may create dynamics that have long-lasting consequences, including ones that are not visible (at least to members of dominant groups) at the time. And many of these consequences may themselves undercut the very democracy we believe that we are upholding and defending. This more complicated political understanding may well be a first step in finding appropriate and socially critical pedagogic strategies to work within our classes and communities to interrupt the larger hegemonic projects—including the redefinition of democracy as "patriotic fervor"—that we will continue to face in the future.

Acknowledgments

I would like to thank James A. Beane and Amy Stuart Wells for their comments and assistance on the material used in this chapter.

Notes

1. See Michael W. Apple, *Official Knowledge*, 2nd ed. (New York: Routledge, 2000), Michael W. Apple, *Educating the "Right" Way: Markets, Standards, God, and Inequality* (New York: RoutledgeFalmer, 2001), and Michael W. Apple et al., *The State and the Politics of Knowledge* (New York: Routledge, 2003).
2. Michael W. Apple, *Ideology and Curriculum*, 3rd ed. (New York: RoutledgeFalmer, 2004).
3. See Michael W. Apple and James A. Beane, eds. *Democratic Schools* (Alexandria, VA: Association for Supervision and Curriculum Development, 1995), Apple, *Educating the "Right" Way*, and Apple et al., *The State and the Politics of Knowledge*.
4. Ibid.
5. Raymond Williams, *Marxism and Literature* (Oxford: Oxford University Press, 1977).
6. See, for example, Noam Chomsky, *9-11* (New York: Seven Stories Press, 2002).
7. For how critical media analysis might interrogate such representations, see Apple, *Official Knowledge*.
8. Noam Chomsky, *Profit Over People* (New York: Seven Stories Press, 1999).
9. See the discussion of needs and needs discourses in Nancy Fraser, *Unruly Practices* (Minneapolis: University of Minnesota Press, 1989).

10. Even though I have used this word before in my text, I have put the word *American* in quotation marks for a social purpose in this sentence because it speaks to the reality I wish to comment on at this point in my discussion. *All* of North, Central, and South America are equally part of the Americas. However, the United States (and much of the world) takes for granted that the term refers to the United States. The very language we use is a marker of imperial pasts and presents. See Edward Said, *Orientalism* (New York: Pantheon, 1978) for one of the early but still very cogent analyses of this.

11. Marcus Weaver-Hightower, "The Gender of Terror and Heroes?" *Teachers College Record*, online, August 2002.

12. Michael W. Apple, *Cultural Politics and Education* (New York: Teachers College Press, 1996). See also Apple et al., *The State and the Politics of Knowledge*.

13. William Greider, *One World, Ready or Not* (New York: Simon and Schuster, 1997).

14. This is one of the reasons that, even though parts of the points may have been based on only a limited reading of parts of the critical pedagogical traditions, I have some sympathy with a number of the arguments made in Carmen Luke and Jenny Gore, *Feminisms and Critical Pedagogy* (New York: Routledge, 1992)—and not a lot of sympathy for the defensive overreactions to it on the part of a number of writers on "critical pedagogy." Political/educational projects, if they are to be both democratic and effective, are always collective. This requires a welcoming of serious and engaged criticism, even when one may not agree with all of it.

15. The reality was actually a bit more complicated than such a simple act of prohibition. The Madison School Board *did* actually comply with the law by having the music of the anthem played over the loudspeaker. Thus, if a school was determined to, say, have the anthem, only an instrumental version was to be played. This would eliminate the more warlike words that accompanied the music. Some members of the board felt that in a time of tragedy in which so many innocent lives had been lost, the last thing that students and schools needed were lyrics that supported some glorified militarism. The solution was a compromise: play an instrumental version of the anthem. This, too, led to some interesting and partly counterhegemonic responses. At one school, a famous Jimi Hendrix rendition of "The Star Spangled Banner" was played over the loudspeaker system. This version—dissonant and raucous—was part of the antiwar tradition of music during the Vietnam-era protests. This raised even more anger on the part of the "patriots" who were already so incensed about the Board's vote.

16. See Apple, *Cultural Politics and Education* and Apple, *Educating the "Right" Way*.

17. Ibid. See also Michael B. Katz, *The Price of Citizenship* (New York: Metropolitan Books, 2001).

18. Stuart Hall, "Popular Democratic vs. Authoritarian Populism," in *Marxism and Democracy,* ed. Alan Hunt (London: Lawrence and Wishart, 1980).

19. Apple, *Educating the "Right" Way*.

20. Eric Foner, *The Story of American Freedom* (New York: Norton, 1998).

21. Ibid. xiv.

22. See Apple, *Educating the "Right" Way* and Roger Dale, "The Thatcherite Project in Education," *Critical Social Policy* 9:4–19.

23. See Apple, *Official Knowledge*, Apple, *Educating the "Right" Way*, and Linda Kintz, *Between Jesus and the Market* (Durham, NC: Duke University Press, 1997).

24. Benedict Anderson, *Imagined Communities* (New York: Verso, 1991).

25. Of course, the conservative groups that mobilized against the board's initial decision would claim that they were exercising dissent, that their members were also engaged in democratic action. This is true as far as it goes. However, if one's dissent supports repression and inequality, and if one's dissent labels other people's actions in favor of their own constitutional rights as "unpatriotic," then this is certainly not based on a vision of "thick" democracy. I would hold that its self-understanding is less than satisfactory.

26. In this regard, it is important to know that the Pledge of Allegiance itself has *always* been contested. It's words are the following: "I pledge allegiance to the flag of the United States of America, and to the republic for which it stands, one Nation, under God, with liberty and justice for all." Yet, the phrase "under God" was added during the midst of the McCarthy period in the early 1950s as part of the battle against "Godless communists." Even the phrase "to the flag of the United States of America" is a late addition. The Pledge was originally written by a well-known socialist and at first only contained the words "I pledge allegiance to the flag." In the 1920s, a conservative women's group, the Daughters of the American Republic, successfully lobbied to have the words *of the United States of America* added as part of an anti-immigrant campaign. They were deeply fearful that immigrants might be pledging to another nation's flag and, hence, might actually be using the pledge to express seditious thoughts.

27. See Apple, *Ideology and Curriculum*. Furthermore, and more currently, as I have argued in *Educating the "Right" Way*, race and the politics of "whiteness" have played a significant role in the historical development of neoliberal, neoconservative, and authoritarian populist anger at the state and in the development of their proposals for school reform.

28. Charles Mills, *The Racial Contract* (Ithaca, NY: Cornell University Press, 1997).

23

Cultural Studies, the War against Kids, and the Re-becoming of U.S. Modernity

LAWRENCE GROSSBERG

The War against Kids

This essay begins with the conditions of children and childhood, adolescents and youth in the contemporary U.S. context. In part, this represents an effort on my part to continue to meet my obligations to a group of people and a culture that I have written about for almost thirty years and, in part, built a career upon, even as I find it more difficult to write about youth culture.[1]

I want to suggest that there is, in the United States today, a war on youth, a war against youth.[2] I use the term *kids* whenever possible to refer both to children and adolescents, that is, to people under the age of eighteen (accepting the rather arbitrary definition of our cultures), because I think it is the term that people under eighteen are most likely to use for themselves, and because it does not have the complex connotations of children, adolescents, or youth. I will argue that, economically, politically, and culturally, the situation of kids in the United States is intolerable and unforgivable, especially given the supposed "advanced" status of the nation, and its economic wealth. But it is not just the fact of the state of kids that has to be questioned, but also the fact that this intolerable situation is tolerated, not only by politicians but also by the general population. And this demands that we consider the changing discourses within which kids are constructed and placed into the maps of everyday life in our society. I want to suggest that kids are increasingly delegitimated, that is, denied any significant place within the collective geography of life in the United States (this might enable us to understand better why and how kids are constructing their own discursive geography of everyday life). By talking about kids, I don't mean to privilege this axis over other—racial, ethnic, gendered, or sexual—axes of difference. Well, actually, for the sake of this argument, I do. While, on each of these axes, we are witnessing rearticulated and reinvigorated attacks, I do believe that there is something new about the attack on kids, especially because it is so little addressed either in public or intellectual life. I recognize that the category of kids is a highly differentiated population, fractured by many lines of difference, and that different fractions are likely to experience the conditions in significantly different ways, but I want to focus nevertheless on a certain commonality of their condition.

Consider the state of kids in the United States in the 1990s, keeping in mind that this was supposed to be the moment of the great "American economic miracle" and that the conditions have

349

remained relatively stable or worse in the current decade. It is also important to keep in mind that, to a large extent, public discourse in the United States is dominated by a very strong appeal to family values. Let's begin with the economic situation. Consider these statistics regarding kids in the United States:[3] 33 percent will be poor at some time in their childhood; 25 percent of all children are born poor; approximately 20 percent of America's children are currently living in poverty. This is compared, for example, with 13.5 percent in Canada, and 2.7 percent in Sweden. These figures are based upon a definition of poverty as $16,600 for a family of four. Now, anyone who has any economic experience in the United States realizes that's absurd. Even the Census Bureau has recently had to raise the bar to $19,500. And various economists and sociologists, working on the definition of a living wage, have placed the bar somewhere between $22,000 and $28,000. At these levels, obviously, the various childhood poverty rates would increase significantly, perhaps higher than 33 percent. Imagine that—the wealthiest nation in the world allows over one third of its children to live in poverty. For the entire decade of the 1990s the child poverty rate was consistently at least 50 percent higher than the poverty rate for the entire population. At the moment, even at the current bar, 10 percent of America's children live in extreme poverty, defined as less than half of the poverty level. And just in case you think it's getting better, in 1998 that number increased by 400,000. Almost 15 percent of America's kids have no health insurance, and thanks to President Clinton and his welfare reform, 207 million children have been added to that number since 1992.[4] Forty percent of the people living in poverty in the United States are kids.

In fact, kids are the fastest growing and largest portion of the population of homeless in America, with an average age of nine years old. If you look at the kids living in poverty, just to challenge any preconceptions, 60 percent are white, 33 percent live in suburbia, 33 percent live in families with married parents, 66 percent live in families in which at least one parent works full time. In fact, economically and statistically speaking, the United States is at the bottom of the list for the advanced industrial world in terms of kids' economic and health situation. Again, I don't mean to deny that the war on kids is linked in complex ways to the restructuration of racial and ethnic relations in the United States, as authors like Jonathon Kozol and Henry Giroux have so powerfully argued, but too often this argument is made against a background assumption that the rest of the kids are being treated all right. And they are not—albeit perhaps not in such visibly egregious ways.

Second, kids in the United States are suffering from what can only be called an epidemic of violence. The U.S. infant mortality rate is higher than that of any industrialized nation in the world. More importantly, 75 percent of all the violent deaths (including homicide, suicide, and firearms related deaths) of children in the industrialized world occur in the United States. The suicide rate for kids under the age of fourteen is double the rate for the rest of the industrialized world. More troubling about this epidemic is the recent moral panic about youth violence and crimes. We often hear about how much violent crime there is among kids and the news coverage of "youth violence" has increased sharply over the past decades even though, actually, the rate itself has been declining sharply for almost a decade. We are rarely told that the increase in the violent crime rate among kids during the 1980s (65% since 1980) is actually less than the increase in the violent crime rate for adults between the ages of thirty and thirty-five. But there seems to be no panic about thirty-year-olds committing crimes.

In fact, according to a study by the Centers for Disease Control and Prevention, the number of violent assaults, weapon possessions, and even just plain fights among high school students is down dramatically in the United States. One might well ask, following this result, since the media and politicians were quick to attack rap music and heavy metal for having contributed to violence, should we not expect them now to congratulate and thank such music for the decline in violence?

And while it is hard to get statistics, it appears that, for every violent and sexual offense committed by a kid, there are three such crimes committed by adults against kids. I want to emphasize this!

What we read about is kid on kid violence (of which Columbine is now the prime example), but for every instance in which a kid attacks or kills another kid in the United States, approximately three kids are attacked or killed by adults. Adults commit 75 percent of the murders of youth in America.

Anyone listening to the rhetoric of the war on drugs would think that kids are the major population of drug users. But there is no evidence—except the arrest and conviction rates—to support such a conclusion. Consider the panic around unwed teenage mothers, and yet no one in the media or politics seems interested in asking how they got pregnant? Somewhere between 400,000 and 500,000 kids are confirmed victims of sexual and violence abuse every year by adults in the United States. Sixty-two percent of all the rape victims in the United States are under eighteen. There is some evidence, although it is spotty (because it is apparently not collected), that suggests that a frighteningly high percentage of teenage pregnancies are the result of sexual relations (whether voluntary or involuntary) with an adult. It is also interesting how little adult violence against kids is covered. Mike Males, in *The Scapegoat Generation,* has in fact documented a remarkable tendency throughout the decade of the 1990s for the media to falsify data about kids.[5] The teen suicide rate, he argues, was exaggerated because it was used to legitimate the mass commitment of teenagers to psychiatric hospitals on rather vague diagnoses such as "alienation," based on their music listening habits and dress habits. The annual birth rate of unwed teen mothers, he argues, was exaggerated to legitimate the attack on welfare. And the number of teenage drug deaths has been exaggerated to fuel passions for the war on drugs.

What is most troubling is the lack of outrage that these figures, facts, and trends provoke. This lack of outrage seems to demand that we agree with Henry Giroux that "American society exudes a deep-rooted hostility and chilling indifference toward youth."[6] How could we begin to confront or even understand the charge that we live in a child-hating world? Notice that we do not even have a word for such a relation.

Many of these trends began in the 1980s; for example, cuts in the federal government's contribution to education; popular backlashes against local taxes and bond issues to support education (so that we spend significantly less, adjusted for inflation, per student than we did in previous decades); the panicked rhetoric of the failure of public education; the increasing incarceration of children both in prisons and mental institutions; the systematic withdrawal of the civil liberties of youth, many of which were gained in the 1960s. Many universities are returning, in practice if not in letter, to acting in loco parentis, invoking their obligation to inform parents about students' behavior, and schools at all levels are increasingly involved with the regulation of students' everyday lives. Higher education is increasingly being restricted to the upper-middle classes. Despite our panicked response to youth's growing sexuality, we have stood by and witnessed the sexualization of youth in the media and corporate culture. We have witnessed, as many critics have pointed out, the extraordinary and, in my opinion, unforgivable commercialization and commodification of youth. In fact, amazingly, the United States—we—are selling, or perhaps we already have sold, our children to advertisers, to private business, to corporate capitalism.

While these trends began in the 1980s, I think they took a definite—a darker and more absurd—turn in the 1990s. As scholarship and public education gave way to student loans and vouchers, we are producing a generation of people who are condemned to live in debt. In most states in the United States, at sixteen today, you cannot get your ears pierced without the permission of your parents, you cannot get a tattoo, and you cannot buy cigarettes. In fact, people under sixteen cannot go to the Mall of America in Minnesota (the largest shopping mall in the country) after 6 PM on Friday or Saturday without a parent. But, you can be tried and jailed as an adult, and that is happening to more and more kids. And in a growing number of states, you can be put to death. Think of that: you can't get your ears pierced, but you can be put to death. We could talk about the kids in prison, or the kids being involuntarily locked up in psychiatric institutions. We could talk about the way zero tolerance is being used to try to produce a generation of compliant, bored, and boring kids, and we could talk about the fact that if that doesn't work, millions of kids are being given psychoactive drugs that have never been tested or approved for their use with children and adolescents.

Increasingly, every moment of kids' lives is being monitored and disciplined. Total and nonstop surveillance is becoming the acceptable disciplinary matrix for youth. Schools increasingly impose regulations about every aspect of kids' everyday lives, their cultural and consumer choices, their forms of identification and relationships. Schools regulate hair color and impose dress codes. One school district has banned black armbands. The AMA and the American Association of Pediatrics have called upon doctors and parents to monitor kids' media taste and exposure, as if these were somehow symptoms that can be reliably correlated to psychology and behavior.[7] Yet, despite the fact that we know that such correlations are unreliable, even the courts seem to be increasingly willing to accept such evidence, especially for judicial commitment procedures. If you like the wrong music, that itself serves as evidence that you are in need of incarceration. More and more schools have imposed random and involuntary drug testing. And some schools, as a way to get around the few remaining court restrictions on such testing, test hair follicles, despite the fact that drug experts almost unanimously agree that it is unreliable. In 1999, a fourteen-year-old girl in Pennsylvania was suspended when she said in class, after Columbine, that she understood how someone who was teased mercilessly could snap. And a boy in Wilmington, North Carolina, was jailed for three days for writing onto his school's computers a screensaver that said, "The end is near." It is also interesting to observe the increasing legitimization of demonstrations of public impatience with and even hostility toward children, not only by individuals, but by service industries as well.

One of my favorite stories involved the fact that some years ago, a number of school districts banned Pokemon cards from schools, but it was the arguments given to defend the prohibition that really interested me.[8] The justification was not that Pokemon causes violent behavior (although trading cards has apparently resulted in some fights). Rather, the two major arguments seem to have been that it is fun, and that it is commercial. So one principal from Wisconsin said, "Whoever came up with this marketing strategy is a genius. The excitement, the intensity of it. I wish children would be that focused on mathematics." He or she banned Pokemon because it is a distraction. Or, to put it another way, it is fun, or play. Yet children have always had their fads, their games, their collectibles, which they brought to school to display, and to play with—whether Davy Crockett caps, or hoola hoops, or baseball cards. But now, apparently, such distractions have to be regulated and disciplined. But the justification given by the superintendent of a school district in Massachusetts was even more disturbing and hypocritical: "The financial dimension is what distinguishes the Pokemon craze from earlier kids' frenzies over marbles, yo-yos, or even Beanie Babies." The hypocrisy emerges from the fact that this same superintendent had approved a deal giving Coca-Cola exclusive control of the soft-drink market and allowing vending machines into the schools. Who has commercialized children's culture? And who has commercialized the everyday life of children, even within the space of schooling?

The question is what has changed between the 1980s and 1990s? The answer will take us into the realms of generations and culture. In the 1980s, the discussion of kids, insofar as it occupied public attention, was largely a discussion of Generation X. That generation is comparatively small, with a total population of 55 million people. When it became the object of media scrutiny, the image of the generation was defined by twenty-somethings. In general, Generation X was characterized as consisting of bored, unmotivated slackers who felt entitled to everything, who whined a lot, who wanted to be entertained rather than educated, who were increasingly conservative—all of this clearly defined in opposition to the "good" baby boomers, who have constructed themselves as somehow radical in their youth and reasonable in their adulthood (although Mike Males [1996], in his work on the war against kids, has argued that the baby boomers are the real bad guys in U.S. society).

The other major discourse about kids was part of an active public (and sometimes popular) culture that constructed and celebrated youth as innocent: from Steven Spielberg movies to the Parents Music Resource Center, childhood was always in danger of being corrupted, perhaps even of disappearing, as a result of either popular culture or the decline of the family (but never as a result of adults or capitalism). This discourse continued into the 1990s and early twenty-first century, although it is increasingly carried to such an extreme as to infantilize youth, taking away any sense of its own agency and possibility. For example, according to a *USA Today* headline story in 1998, "Struggling to Raise Good Kids in Toxic Times,"[9] nine out of ten Americans say it is harder to raise kids to be good people than it was twenty years ago. And two in three Americans say parents are doing a bad job. They blame it on something that *USA Today* calls "a culture gone toxic," which seems to reference the growing presence of computers, advertising, commercialism, and so forth in children's lives, with no recognition of where such things come from. Similarly, the 1999 report of the Judiciary Committee on Children, Violence, and the Media (chaired by Orrin Hatch)[10] claims that "television alone is responsible for 10% of youth violence." I have no idea how anyone could calculate that but I suppose that, if true, we might hypothesize that the Bible is responsible for much of the remaining 90%. According to the report, "the existing research shows beyond a doubt that media violence is linked to youth violence." The report quotes one unnamed expert—one should always take note of nameless experts—claiming that "to argue against it, this link, is like arguing against gravity." So those of us who are "experts" in media violence who would say that the evidence certainly does not say that are obviously fools because we're arguing against gravity. And of course, the report reiterates the requisite claim that a preference for heavy metal music is "a significant marker for alienation, substance abuse, psychiatric disorders, suicide, sex role stereotyping, and risk-taking behavior during adolescence."

I want to make two claims about the discourses of kids in the 1980s. First, both major strands of the argument (Generation X, and innocent kids in jeopardy) were cultural arguments about the "proper" construction and behavior of kids, the proper way to be young. Hence, the distance between these two strands was measured in cultural terms, as an argument about culture, and the regulation of cultural consumption. On the one hand, what was at stake was a project, largely orchestrated by new conservatives and neoconservatives, of rescuing the moral fabric of the nation. It was an attempt to roll back, in the name of innocent childhood, the changes that had been brought about in American society by and since the 1960s, changes that were linked with the civil rights movement, with feminism, with gay liberation, with drug use, with popular culture. On the other hand, it was an attempt to both celebrate the youthful rebellion of the 1960s, while legitimating the generational abandonment of those very ideals in the 1980s.

Second, in an earlier book on the United States in the 1980s, I wrote:

Youth itself has become a battlefield on which the current generation of adolescents, baby boomers, parents and corporate media interests are fighting for control of its meanings, investments and powers, fighting to articulate and thereby construct its experiences, identities, practices, discourses and social differences. "Youth" encompasses a fractious and often contradictory set of social formations, defined not only by the proliferation of postwar generations but also by the attenuation of the relation between age and youth ... in favor of youth as an affective identity stitched onto a generational history. Youth today is caught in the contradiction between those who experience the powerlessness of their age ... and the generations of baby boomers who have attached the category of youth to their life trajectory, in part by redefining it as an attitude (You're only as old as you feel). For the baby boomers, youth is something to be held on to by cultural and physical effort.[11]

That is, in the 1980s, the baby boomers, a generation that grew up defining itself by its youthfulness, was struggling to hold onto its sense of itself as "young." Despite the fact that the very meaning of youth is, as it were, defined by the fact that you don't have to work to stay young, a generation invested itself in physical, cultural, and psychological work designed to accomplish just that. This made a generational conflict almost inevitable, as the baby boomers attempted to establish the culture of their own youth as the very definition of youth. Thus, Generation X was constantly being judged, not merely as somehow inadequate, but more importantly, as inadequately young. There were constant statements made against Generation X, suggesting that its members were old before their time, that they were boring, without any sense of style, or passion for resistance.

But that struggle over youth ended somewhere in the 1990s, and in one important sense, the baby boomers lost. The baby boomers now lead the charge of "the aging of America." Hence, not only have Social Security and Medicare taken on an unprecedented public and political importance, but many of the standard practices of these programs (including how they are financed, and their relation to other budgetary needs) are challenged in the interests of the baby boom generation. One might say that even though they lost the battle over youth, the baby boomers still seem to have won the battle to maintain their social dominance. Nevertheless, I do not think that the baby boomers have taken their loss well. At the very least, they have gone along (if not becoming an active antagonist) with what I have described as the war against kids.

Having said this, I don't want to reduce this war to the trivial claim that we are witnessing a natural "panic" over youth as a result of the aging of the baby boomers. On those rare occasions when one finds comments on the state of kids, it is particularly discouraging to realize how easy it is for someone to claim that "what is frustrating about the current crusade to rein in teenagers is that it seems so, well, adolescent. The high-decibel concern about wayward youth is full of defensive bluster and muddle-headed ambivalence and it is strikingly lacking in realism."[12] It does not seem adolescent, I would argue, to the kids who have to suffer its consequences. I want to reject such an appeal to the naturalized psychology of biological aging as it were, not only because it trivializes the war, but also because I am reluctant to blame the baby boomers directly, or to assume that they are the primary agents responsible for the war. To say that they have often gone along with it, or even that some fractions have helped to give it shape and reality, does not enable us to assign intentionality or blame. I don't think that the war against youth is the project of or belongs to the baby boomers. Rather, I think it is a question of how certain generational tendencies and commitments and concerns are articulated to larger social projects and directions.

I think we do need to ask why this war on kids is happening because the fact that we can offer no explanation for it means that it makes no sense, and I think that is largely responsible for why the very fact is so easily ignored or denied. That is, we still have to keep on asking, whose project it is and for what purpose? But in the end, I do not think we will find a simple answer for I do not think the answer will appear under the sign of blame—the media, the baby boomers, the Christian right, capitalists.

But before we can even address such questions, I want to identify two changes. The object of attack has changed and in this sense at least, the above quote is correct to point out that it is now the children of the baby boom who are the focus. It is no longer twenty-year-old Generation Xers that are of concern in the media. It is the so-called millennial generation, who are living in a state in which the government spent significantly more on their parents than it has on them. It is Generation Y, born after 1980. The focus now is on a generation of teenagers. As *Macleans* magazine put it, "for the first time since the 1960s kid culture is back; kid culture is king."[13] In 1992, the teen population of the United States grew by 70,000, ending a fifteen-year decline. This new baby boom is expected to exceed the postwar baby boom in both size (77 million) and duration. Between 2006 and 2010, it is estimated that there will be 35 million teenagers in the United States, which is more than were ever present during their parents' baby boom.

As the object of this attack has changed, so has the rhetoric of this attack, and it is this change in the way kids are described that is particularly disturbing. Consider again the Judiciary Committee report that I cited earlier: "Behind the facade of our material comfort, we find a national tragedy. America's children are killing and harming each other. As Colorado's governor, Bill Owens, lamented in the wake of the Columbine High School massacre, a 'virus' is loose within our culture. And that virus is killing our culture." In fact, although neither Governor Owens nor Senator Hatch, whose committee wrote the report, admits it, the virus is the children themselves.

Henry Giroux has observed that

children have become our lowest national priority. The crisis of youth does not simply reflect the loss of social vision, the ongoing corporatization of the public space and the erosion of democratic life, it also suggests the degree to which children have been othered across a wide range of ideological positions, unworthy of serious analysis as an oppressed group or posited as no longer *at risk* but *the risk* to democratic public life.[14]

Mike Males seconds Giroux's claim that kids are increasingly othered, arguing that the media and public "employ the same stereotypes once openly applied to unpopular racial and ethnic groups. Kids are violent, reckless, hypersexed, welfare draining, obnoxious, and ignorant."[15] Or again, as Giroux puts it, "kids are portrayed either as over-the-edge violent sociopaths or vulgar brainless pleasure seekers."[16]

We are moving from a concern that "we are not doing a good job of raising our children ... that kids are not being taught what they need to know to grow up to be decent human beings,"[17] to "people are confounded by the world children inhabit,"[18] to blaming kids themselves. In 1967, *Time* declared "youth" to be the Man of the Year. Can you imagine that happening now? Instead it has become common for youth to be seen as a threat to the existing social order, and for kids to be blamed for the problems they experience (much as other "minorities" are).

These rhetorics have been extending their reach and power for the past two decades. *Newsweek* (May 10, 1998) claimed "white suburban youth have a dark side," and continued, "youth culture in general represents the *Lord of the Flies* on a vast national scale."[19] And in an article in *George* (June 1996) entitled "Kids Are Ruining America," Brett Easton Ellis, an icon of the 1980s Generation X, wrote: "Teens are running roughshod over this country—murdering, raping, gambling away the nation's future—and we have the bills for counseling and prison to prove it. Sure not all kids are bad—but collectively, they're getting worse. Why should we blame ourselves?" And *Education Week* (June 5, 1996) had a front-page story that said, "Teen culture is impeding school reform."

In order to pull this off, increasingly, kids are represented as somehow essentially different, as mysterious freaks of nature. *The Los Angeles Times* (December 9, 1993) headline read: "Who Are Our Children? One day they are innocent. The next they may try to blow your head off." This makes kids into the horror character of Freddie. It was bad enough when Freddie was next door. Now, he is inside your kid's bedroom. It's not the babysitter who's the threat anymore, it's the kid who's going to kill the babysitter and then come down the stairs to kill you. Lizzy Borden has become the new norm of America's children. This may explain the growing frequency of appeals, concerns, and rhetorics that are encapsulated in the August 1999 *U.S. News and World Report* cover story, "Inside the Teen Brain. The Reason for Your Kid's Quirky Behavior Is in His Head."[20] It is okay that they do not seem to perform according to our expectations of civil and civilized behavior and it is okay that we have basically screwed them over because, well, they are a different species. Somehow their brains are qualitatively different than human brains, and therefore all their weird behavior is understandable while, at the same time, we are relieved of some of the burden of our responsibility to them. Kids are no longer innocents who have to be protected, long the dominant view of childhood in the United States in the twentieth century. Nor are they small adults who can be held responsible (but must also be given the benefits). Rather, they are another species, some kind of animal, and we are failing to civilize, to domesticate, them.

Hegemony and Modernity

There is a mystery here: how do we make sense of this state of affairs? And how do we make sense of the fact that there is so little discussion (or shame) around the issue either within the media or the academy? When it is acknowledged, it is usually attributed to capitalism (same old, same old) or to racism (given the changing racial and ethnic profile of the American population) or to the desire of the postwar baby boom to hide its own sins behind the shadow of Generation Y or to the Christian right's antifeminist agenda..

Is there a conspiracy against kids? Let me admit at the outset that I do not see any contradiction between believing in conspiracies and cultural studies, but what saves cultural studies from falling into a conspiracy theory is the recognition that there are always many conspiracies. Conspiracies may work with each other, or against each other, or they may, at least for a while, appear to operate independently of each other. But the end result is that what is produced in the end cannot be conceptualized as the outcome of any one conspiracy. People do make history, but that does not mean that they are in control of the history they make. The only thing guaranteed by the complexity of human relations is contingency, that there are no guarantees.

How do we then proceed? How do we understand the possibility and the significance of the "war on kids"? Not surprisingly, I approach the problem by bringing it into the sphere of cultural studies, In particular, I want to turn to a body of work, including *Policing the Crisis, There Ain't No Black in the Union Jack, The Empire Strikes Back, The Hard Road to Renewal, The Politics of Thatcherism, New Times Old Enemies,* and *New Times,* that began by linking racism not only to the problematic of identity and difference (antiessentialism), but also to the rise of the political and economic right ("Thatcherism"). This extraordinary corpus is, in my opinion, the best exemplar of the project of British cultural studies, for in it we can see the crucial mark of cultural studies: its commitment to relationality (and hence its analytic practice of contextuality and articulation); its grounding in discursivity and constructionism; its effort to forge an antireductionist politics by affirming contingency and complexity (rather than leaving them to a closing caveat), and its faith that a better knowledge of what is happening does make a difference; and its desire to put that knowledge in the service of the project of making the world a better place, by opening new possibilities for struggle and change.

Policing the Crisis and the work that circulated around it and followed in its path is usually read (often by those involved with the project—many of whom, I should add, are my teachers and friends) as an expression of a certain theoretical moment in the history of the Centre for Contemporary Cultural Studies, the moment of a Gramscian reading of Althusser, but a Gramsci that had already been reread through Althusser.

This work offered a unique and productive reading of Gramsci's notions of hegemony and the war of positions—as a social struggle that is mobile and dispersed across a range of different sites, where each struggle is defined strategically, built on a temporary articulation of discourses and alliances, and seeking not agreement or consensus but the consent to leadership—as opposed to a war of maneuvers (a model that Gilroy would later describe as "encampment"—two great armies facing each other across the battlefield, each seeking to absorb the other, to make the other into a sort of copy of itself). Thatcherism was the hegemonic victory of a specific alliance, the accomplishment of a certain temporary settlement or balance in a field of forces, which transformed the social field (and common sense) on which any future struggles would have to be fought. The system of compromises enforced by the rule of a hegemonic bloc is a strategic construction of one moment in a set of shifting struggles that is, at least in its public and intentional presence, driven by a constantly renegotiated set of compromises between desires, fractions, and visions of what are loosely called neoliberalism and neoconservatism on the one hand, and labor capitalists and certain social democrats on the other. Thatcherism then was identified as a series of struggles, each complexly articulated as discursive, ideological, economic, institutional, governmental. In each struggle, the hegemonic bloc attempts to win for itself a position of leadership.

Oddly, this work is not as widely influential or visible as one might expect, especially in the United States, and much of its unique and important contribution is overlooked. The central concept of hegemony has been taken up, but too often, people ignore the specific theory of hegemony offered here, as a particular kind of political struggle, not a universal one, and therefore, the presence of a hegemonic struggle is not guaranteed. The work on Thatcherism also demonstrated that cultural studies was not necessarily about popular culture. Instead, the analysis of Thatcherism demonstrated that power (and hence, critical work) needed to enter into and negotiate with "the popular," understood as the everyday modes of address, the logics of calculation, and the structures of emotional and affective experience through which people construct and recognize moral authority, the legitimacy of value claims, and the machineries of personal and collective choice. In this turn, this corpus foreshadowed the (re)turn of a focus on (a significantly transformed) "political economy." "Cultural studies," at least as embodied in this work, did not appear to be, in the first instance, about culture at all, in the narrow sense of expressive culture, although it centrally continued to address the effects of discourse and the discursivity of social reality. It was a turn to what I might call political and economic culture, and the discursivity of political and economic struggles.

This work returned in new and striking ways to one of the fundamental theoretical dilemmas of cultural studies: the problem of totality and determination. Raymond Williams had defined an impossible task for cultural studies, commonly repeated as "describing all the relations among all the elements in a whole way of life." The analysis of "Thatcherism" required these writers to find a way of talking about the complexity of a social formation or, more accurately, the complexity of a social formation in process. How does one construct a totality that is yet the site of explicit and implicit, intended and unintended, struggles, forces, transformations, and most importantly, determinations, even if one recognizes the need to always talk from one (set of) position(s) within that formation, within the struggles and transformations? This body of work moved through the Althusseran description of the "teeth gritting harmony" of the social formation as a "structure in dominance," defined by a hierarchy among relatively distinct levels (each with its own kind of practice), each in its own relatively autonomous spaces (leading to, among other things, a search for the specificity of each level that inevitably pulls one from a radical contextualism into some kind of transcendentalism). I do not want to suggest that the solution to these problems lies somewhere hidden in these works, and I certainly do not want to suggest that I have the solution. But I do think this work brought cultural studies back to the possibility of a new political economy on the one hand, and the problematic of the totality on the other. What connects these two is, to some extent, the problem of determination (and articulation?) itself.

Finally, I think this work made a significant analytic advance, on top of all that I have mentioned. It moved cultural studies from a simple contextualism to a notion of conjunctural analysis. A conjuncture is not simply a slice of space-time or a period; it is a moment defined by an accumulation or condensation of a number of contradictions. It is the result of an articulation of different currents or circumstances. Thus, Hall describes it as "the complex historically specific terrain of a crisis which affects—but in uneven ways—a specific national-social formation as a whole."[21] Conjunctural analysis places a greater burden on the analyst, according to Gramsci, to get the balance between the old and the new, the organic and the conjunctural, right! But it also requires, somewhat circularly and in retrospect, that one decide the limits of the conjuncture. This strikes me as an analytic problem that can only be solved by a political interrogation, and by prying apart the contradiction, and identifying the forces, working, on the ground as it were, to disrupt one settlement of the social formation, and to push in any number of competing directions.

I want to see the war against kids as a conjunctural problem, but I do not think that the analysis can assume—and certainly those involved in the project of analyzing Thatcherism would never have thought so—that it is a hegemonic struggle. In fact, I think that we are confronting something like a struggle between those (liberals and to some extent, leftists) who think they are waging a hegemonic struggle, and those (significant fractions of the new right) who are trying to invent, not only a new social formation, but a new political culture as well, one built not on compromise but on fanaticism.

At the same time, I also think that conjunctural analysis must recognize that often, the settlement is accomplished behind the back of those struggling over the field of the social formation. In this instance, hegemony is inadequate to either analyze or respond to the complexly changing balance in the field of forces or, more conventionally, to the vectors and restructurings that are potentially changing the very fabric of power and experience.

Puzzling about the continuities and discontinuities of the past twenty-five years, we might take a hint from Tony Blair's constant claim to be "modernizing" England, and at the same time, the U.S. new right's sometimes explicit opposition to commonsensical, taken for granted assumptions of "Atlantic modernity." So rather than starting with the assumption that what is at stake in the contemporary struggles is the postwar consensus (e.g., liberalism, or Fordism, or the corporate compromise), I want to see what happens if we assume that the stake is the nineteenth- and twentieth-century crystallization of modernity as it came to be lived in the United States and elsewhere. I propose to see the sweeping transformation of U.S. society that defined the last quarter of the twentieth century, a transformation, even a revolution, that apparently enabled neoliberals and neoconservatives to work together in some unnamed common cause, as a potential revolution on a grand scale, a second secular reformation, as the sociologist Zygmunt Bauman describes it.[22] The Nobel Prize-winning economist Paul Krugman put it this way:

> Ever since the election of Ronald Reagan, right-wing radicals have insisted that they started a revolution in America. They are half right. If by a revolution, we mean a change in politics, economics, and society that is so large as to transform the character of the nation, then there is indeed a revolution in progress. The radical right did not make this revolution, although it has done its best to help it along. If anything, we might say that the revolution created the new right. But whatever the cause, it has become urgent that we appreciate the depth and significance of this new American revolution and try to stop it before it becomes irreversible.[23]

Krugman's point is one that I have tried to make for some years: You cannot fight what you don't understand. That is why intellectual work, why theory, does matter. But even if you don't want to fight it, I would suggest that it is good to stop and reflect upon what is happening, because history has a way of breaking free of our intentions, and the effects of our actions, our struggles, and even our conspiracies usually have little resemblance to the original aims. The present revolution is the product of the articulation of many distinct and heterogeneous struggles in a variety of domains across social life, and the result is, I believe, the dismantling of the liberal subject and the deconstruction of modern society as it came to be defined in the North Atlantic through the articulation of forms of capitalism, democracy and civil society, the nation-state, colonialism, and history. Is this anyone's intention? I don't know. Is there a clear and common vision of what lies beyond the revolution? I doubt it. But I do believe that across a wide range of domains, neoliberals and neoconservatives are operating on the assumption that the current problems facing our society are the inevitable result of the unresolved contradictions of the modern articulation, the articulation of the modern. And I do believe that the shifting alliances and projects of the new right are, for the most part, occupying the position of rule and leadership in this hegemonic struggle. I can describe the contemporary struggle over hegemony then as the *unbecoming* (to use a term from Eric Michaels) and the rebecoming of modernity or, more mundanely, as a radical intensification of the continuous and ongoing rearticulation of modernity within specific spaces.

As an aside, it is important to recognize that the rebecoming of the modern both inaugurates and demands profound theoretical and political challenges and productivity: around questions of the effectivity and materiality of culture; around questions of the forms and mechanisms of individuation, subjectification, identification, and belonging (collectivity); around questions of agency, and the organization and productivity of power; and around questions of time and space (and the very nature of contexts).

Hegemony and Modernity in the United States

The mystery of the war on kids can now be readdressed in terms of the place of this war in the larger struggle over modernity: why would the struggle to change U.S. society spill over into or even involve a war against kids? In order to make this move, from the specific war against kids to the broader revolution, I will have to point quickly to some of the other pieces of the puzzle, some of the other sites of struggle and some of the other specific wars that are being waged.

The first site I want to point to is the state as an institutional apparatus and the construction, often intentionally, of a crisis of politics. There is, on the part of some actors, an explicit desire not merely to reduce the state apparatus back to its laissez faire existence, but to completely eradicate the state. (This seems to be the strategy behind the enormous tax cuts that characterized the Reagan and now the Bush Jr. administrations.) The other side of this struggle might be understood as an attack on citizenship itself as a structure of modern subjectification and identification. These seem to be carried out through a dual strategy: on the one hand, to construct a disinvestment from state politics, and on the other hand, to create the image of an apathetic and cynical population. As to the first, state politics is receding as a viable and active site at which the individual invests and inserts him- or herself into public life. Much of this can be traced to the growing capitalization of politics, the changing role of the media in politics, and the disparity between public commitments and political actions. It is not necessary to ask whether this has all come about intentionally or accidentally to recognize that somehow, the resulting abandonment of citizenship is in some way a desired and desirable (for some) effect. To use an analogy, if one ran an advertising campaign for a particular product for twenty-five years, and the result was not only a decline in the sales on one's own product but also of the generic commodity itself, one would, rationally, change one's advertising behavior. Since the only demonstrable effect of political discourses over the past twenty-five years has been a disinvestment from state politics, and there is no sign that the institutional actors want to change the discourse, its effects must be, in some way, compatible with some desired outcomes or project.

There are many explanations for this. Some people argue that it is an intentional strategy of the political parties to transfer the control of the government from the people to corporations, through the financial manipulation of elections. Some people argue that it is an expression of a more general postmodern cynicism. Some people argue that it is the lack of public community (often blaming that absence on the 1960s). Some people argue it is because we are all too scared and insecure to get involved in politics. Some people argue it's because we think economics and technology have replaced politics. A *Forbes* magazine ad shows a multiracial, multiethnic group of people carrying red banners with icons of their national currency. And the headline reads, "Capitalists of the World

Unite." Capital has replaced the political struggle to overthrow capital. And some people argue that the lack of political will is the consequence of the collapse of civil society and the destruction of the civil sphere.

The second aspect of the struggle over the state involves the claim, widely disseminated and widely believed, that people have become apathetic and cynical about the possibility of political activism, involvement, and change. The bottom line to which most people would accede is the fact of a general loss of faith in political action. As one reporter put it (October 19, 1997),

> How come nobody's marching on Washington these days? Where are the banners and barricades? The President poses for picture with any foreigner who will give him soft money. The gap between rich and poor is bigger than it's been since the days of the robber barons. Children are being neglected by their parents and short-changed by their government. Yet, nobody seems to care. Where's the outrage in America?"[24]

The eminent historian Lawrence Goodwyn of Duke University talks about "the depth of resignation [which he distinguishes from apathy, the former depending on a sense of powerlessness] that pervades broad sections of the American middle class and working poor. It is a weariness that in some cases borders on despair and, for such people, it tends to be immobilizing."[25] Yet I think it can be demonstrated that there is at least as much activism today as there has been at any time since the 1960s, and perhaps even more than during that tumultuous decade, for such activism is no longer limited to any sociologically identifiable audience, or to any single set of issues (especially if we include right-wing activism).

I want to suggest that the struggle that is taking place here is precisely an attempt to make the general population cynical, to "disappear" politics as it were. There is something of a conspiracy, which can use and articulate itself to all of the above accounts, because its aim is to make politics disappear by, in part, producing cynicism in the population. Politicians no longer hide their financial scaffolding, nor do they disguise the fact that they are running advertising campaigns. Campaign slogans are derived not out of any principled commitments but through perception analyzers that measure the autonomic nervous system's response to stimuli, without any consideration of the meaning of a slogan because, as one researcher admitted, meaning just gets in the way when you are seeking a purely emotive response. And on the other side, politicians can ignore the public will (claiming to be doing the right thing for once) when it is obvious that they are serving another agenda, defined by some constituencies they cannot afford to alienate. But what is most telling is that we don't need to hide such things anymore because, I would suggest, they are less involved in constructing a political identity or constituency than in producing the disappearance, the evacuation, of politics. As the sociologist Zygmunt Bauman put it: "If freedom has been won, how does it come about that the human ability to imagine a better world and to do something to make it better is not among the trophies of victory? And what sort of freedom is it that discourages imagination and tolerates the impotence of free people in matters which concern them all."[26]

Of course, one has then to ask, why? Why would any government want to make its population cynical? The most obvious answer is so that it can maintain power without having to confront a constant series of challenges and resistances. And while I think that is certainly true, I am also convinced that there is more at stake. The answer, I think, has to do with an attempt to challenge what we can call, following Michael J. Sandel, the modern political economy of citizenship.[27] That we exist as citizens, that citizenship is one of the absolutely crucial pillars of our individuality and subjectivity, is one of the cornerstones of modern society as it was constructed in the north Atlantic during the eighteenth and nineteenth centuries. That is, one of the crucial essential elements of our individuality is our relationship to the state and to the existence of a civil sphere defined outside the influence of the state (although the state has an obligation to support its existence) and to some extent, the economy. We are defined by our existence as citizens. It is as citizens that we have rights. It is as citizens that we have a (national) identity. It is as citizens that we have historical agency. It is as citizens that we are defined by our obligations to the state. And it is as citizens that we claim the protection of certain spheres of life (for at least certain fractions of the population) from the operation of at least some kinds of power.

Thomas Mann once wrote that "in our time, the question of man's destiny presents itself no longer in religious terms but in political terms."[28] The question of destiny, of the future, is central to the construction of modern citizenship. It is crucial to both the modern state and the modern citizen that the present is defined by its trajectory into a future. Both history and the citizen are necessarily incomplete, realized only in an always deferred future. This is why the concept of time as progress is so central to the modern construction of both the social and the individual. That faith in progress, of course, is embodied in the notion of the American Dream and ultimately in the celebration of childhood in the United States in the twenty-first century. But it rests upon the prior and more basic assumption of what I might call liberal modernity that there is a predictable if not controllable relationship between the present and the future. It is the belief in the connection between what we do in the present and what will happen in the future, even if what happens is not what we expected or wanted, that defines, I believe, that formation of modernity that is currently under attack and in the process of being transformed.

The second site of struggle I want to point to involves the economies in all their complexity. Let me get two things out of the way. First, the claims for an "economic miracle," or even for "the new economy," are discourses that need to be subjected to the same criticism as any other political claim. In fact, it is obvious that this miracle, this new economy, for most people, looks a lot like a disaster, a lot like the old economy. One needs, for example, to look at the increasingly unequal distribution of wealth, and to the question of why people are willing to believe there is a boom when in fact the evidence of the real economic lives of the majority of people suggests something very different. Between 1947 and 1979, family income in America increased fairly evenly across all income levels in this country; between 1977 and 1998, between 66 and 75 percent of U.S. families saw a real decrease in income despite a huge increase in dual-income families and a real increase in the number of hours people in the work. So many families, even with dual incomes, and working longer hours, are still making less money than the equivalent family twenty years earlier. Ninety percent of all the increase in wealth that has been generated since the early 1980s has gone to the richest 1 percent of American households. That 1 percent saw an increase in their yearly income of 120 percent a year and they take home as much after-tax income as the bottom 100 million of the American population. The net worth of the median family in the United States has declined. For the bottom 40 percent of America, it's declined by 80 percent since the early 1980s. The net worth of the bottom 50 percent of the American population equals the net worth of Bill Gates. One report actually suggests that by taxing the richest 225 people, 4 percent of their wealth would provide enough money to feed, clothe, house, school, and provide medical care to the entire population of the world.[29] For the past twenty years, we have been moving away from a middle-class society, the society of the American dream.

Second, while the discourse of "economics" has gained a popular visibility and authority it has not had for some time, it is also not a description of reality or even of policy for that matter. We do not have a neoliberal economy nor a government committed to neoliberalism. There are most certainly elements of neoliberalism in our economy and in government policies (especially when it comes to how other less well off nation-states are supposed to act). Why is this important? Because people seem to be willing to believe that we live in a society in which all values have been reduced to the single calculus of economic values. I have no doubt that there are economists and businesspeople who might hope for such a society, and that there are policies that, if they went unchallenged, might lead to such a conclusion. But I do not see any evidence that U.S. society (at least as it is lived by many people) has abandoned any and all values except economic worth.

There are, obviously, many more things to be said about the transformation of capitalism over the past decades. We might begin by noting the shifting relations and struggles among the various structures and forms of capitalism (and even noncapitalist markets and forms of exploitation), including new financial capital, older speculative capital, mercantile capital, pre-Fordist, and Fordist industrial capital. One could talk about the move away from mass production and consumption to "post-Fordist" or flexible systems of production and accumulation, about the growth of information technologies, and service economies, about the globalization of the market system, and the growth of transnational corporations. Certainly, one of most interesting features of the present economy is that many economists, including Alan Greenspan, the most powerful economist in the world, admit that they just don't understand it. I want to talk about a different aspect of the economic miracle since the early 1980s—namely, the growing importance and power of finance capital. I do not mean to suggest that it is all that is happening or that it can stand in, synecdochally as it were, for everything taking place in capitalism. Nevertheless, it is worth noting that most of the wealth produced since the early 1980s has been built on finance capital and not on labor or commodity production. It is money producing more money. It is built on consumption and credit and not labor and production.[30]

One needs to link the transformations in the production and productivity of capital to the rhetoric of the free market (as opposed to the reality of the economy, which is clearly operating to eliminate competition). Most importantly, we seem to be living in an economy that encourages seriously high unemployment (consider the prison population or the chronically unemployed) and the proliferation of poverty waged jobs. While both of these can be understood as the continuation of long traditions of the exploitation of labor, they may also suggest that something else is going on because they also contradict the direction of capitalism over the past century and the very notion of a consumer economy, especially when connected to the changing nature of the labor market and the changing distribution and forms of labor, including the shift into low-paying, insecure service jobs. Evidence for this might be found in the emergence of discourses and practices, which are less about exploiting labor or terrorizing it with the threat of unemployment, than about actually decreasing necessary labor to a point heretofore unimaginable. One can now begin to imagine advanced capitalist societies with heretofore unimaginably low levels of employment. In fact in the German magazine *Der Spiegel*, two leading European economists speculate that it should be possible to supply all of the economically necessary labor with only 20 percent of the labor force.[31] That would mean an 80 percent unemployment rate in the world. It is one thing to increase profits by cutting labor costs (either through relative or absolute exploitation and the production of surplus value). But it is something else to erase labor itself, as if simply cutting the absolute cost of labor, often by simply disinvesting in or cutting back on production, were sufficient to increase profits. Yet there is a sense in which it is sufficient, at least in this increasingly monetarized and credit economy, even though it means giving up the connection to commodity production.

The economic miracles of high tech companies, from Amazon.com (which has yet to make a profit despite increasing sales) to Red Hat, reveal something about the paradoxical nature of this economic boom. Despite investor's claims, the evidence suggests that there is an inverse correlation between the growth of the stock market in recent decades and the growing corporate debt burdens (produced through takeovers, stock buybacks, increased payments to shareholders, etc.) on the one hand, and actual level of investment in productivity on the other.[32] In fact, there has been almost no significant increase in investment in the productive infrastructure. Much of the profits of the stock market since the early 1980s have resulted from companies buying back their own stock or selling stock in order to purchase other companies. But the infrastructure, the economic basis on which kids today are going to have to build an economics for a society thirty years from now, has not seen any significant investment. There is here a kind of disinvestment in the future; it is as if capitalism no longer cares about making a profit that it can reinvest into the future of capitalism but rather cares only about generating enormous short-term profit for a very small percentage of the population, obviously returning in some ways to older, pre-twentieth-century models. But I think there is even more at stake.

How is it possible for capitalism to challenge the very centrality and status of labor, to challenge its sacred place as the agency of the production of value? Some economists explain this by arguing that while the production of value in industrial capital depended upon the objectification of labor power, the production of value in the new financial markets is made possible by the objectification of risk itself. But I would take this a step further, to argue that the key figure in understanding how the financial markets are being used in the war against modernity is Hayek, who subjectifies the production of value in capitalism. The production of value, according to Hayek, is not made possible by the objectification of risk, but by its subjectification in the figure of the entrepreneur. Hence, it is possible to imagine the circuit of expanding capital without the mediation of labor power.[33]

I think that by placing finance capital at the center, this economy is attempting, however impossible we may think it is, to negate, or at least amend and partially retreat from, the assumption of labor as the source of value. That is, we are witnessing a very real and radical devaluation of labor. If labor is the primary limit on profitability (and the accumulation of wealth), both as variable capital cost and as the major source of demand in modern economies, neoliberalism seems to propose a simple answer: eliminate labor from the equation by making labor into a fixed capital cost (as it were) and by tying demand to credit rather than wages. What is at stake here is creating a space within which the value (and perhaps even the necessity) of labor can be radically challenged. It is accomplishing this through—and I have no doubts that this is intentional—a radical reconfiguration of the capitalist production of wealth. Thus, I believe that the revalorization and subsequent privileging of money and of a monetary economy (but in a different form from previous formations) is being articulated to (although it is unclear that this has to be the case) a devalorization and a devaluation of labor and labor power as the source of value and, hence, of wealth.

Not coincidentally, like citizenship, labor was also one of the pillars on which modern individuality and subjectivity were constructed in north Atlantic modernity in the nineteenth and twentieth centuries. In fact, one could argue that it was precisely because of the need to construct the labor subject, as one who would sell his or her own labor power on the market, that modern capitalism had to link itself to the project of the modern nation and the production of citizenship. These two modes of individualization, labor and citizenship, define two of the pillars of the modern individual.

There are other sites of struggle, all intimately connected with Atlantic modernity, that one can point to as sites of active struggle since around 1980, including the family, the boundaries of the public and private, and other structures of social and cultural identity. And of course, culture itself has become a major site of struggle, and the very nature and terrain of culture (including media culture) have been transformed as a result. A major part of those struggles involve struggles over education (where students are increasingly talked about as consumers and treated as commodities) and even more threatening, struggles over the very nature of the production and authority of knowledge itself. Here the battle involves not only particular institutions and practices, but also the very legitimacy of (secular) knowledge, especially its ability to speak with moral authority and into policy debates.[34]

Now, finally, I want to return to the war against kids, and I want to ask how it might be articulated or connected to these two other struggles. How might we imagine the war against kids to be connected to attacks on two of the foundational structures of modern individuality and subjectivity? This question takes me back to the image that I cited at the beginning, that we are witnessing a second reformation. The reformation of Europe involved the construction of what is commonly called modernity, the construction of the citizen worker, the construction of the modern nation-state, the organization of space according to principles of coloniality and urbanism, the rationalization of production (and eventually consumption), and the reorganization of culture according to principles of secularism and, to a lesser extent, science. Here's my conspiracy theory: I think that there are forces at work—economic, political, cultural, and just as importantly, religious—that are trying to reinvent modernity, trying to put in place a different kind of social, politica,l and economic organization, and trying in the process to redefine our sense of individuality and of the individual's relationship to the forces that produce his or her life and reality. Of course, there is no guarantee that any one conspiracy, any one vision of the coming modernity, will succeed, for there are always other things happening, other projects being offered, other conspiracies being organized. Alliances are forged and then fall apart, giving way to new ones and new compromises. Nevertheless, it may be helpful to imagine that certain fractions of and forces within capitalism, political conservatism, and religious antisecularism were trying to imagine their way out of a series of compromises that were made centuries ago: what if capitalism had not linked itself to democracy, the valorization of labor, and the subordination of religious faith and morality?

Putting Kids in Their Place

What does it mean to suggest that kids have become the enemy of these broad struggles to radically transform modernity? Kids are being subjected to forms of economic, political, legal, penal, medical, and rhetorical attack. They are also being subjected to new forms of biopolitics, discipline, and governmentality. But they are also being subjected to systems of confinement, regulation, and abuse that evidence a retreat from precisely those forms of power—biopolitics, discipline, and governmentality—that Foucault claims characterize modernity.

Where do kids fit into this story of the rebecoming of modernity? After all, there does seem something odd about placing them into this narrative. There is something troubling about politicizing youth. The traditional (modern) discourse of youth inevitably and necessarily places youth outside of and distinct from the realm of politics, as if youth were in a natural state outside the social. It is as if kids have to be protected from the degradation that politics brings because kids are always "becoming social." As Lee Edelman puts it, regarding discussions of children, it's as if the issue of childhood has only one side. After all, who could be (and what would it even mean to be) against children? "Childhood is so uncontested, because so uncontroversial, a cultural value"[35] in our society. No politician would stand up and say, "I'm against children." And yet, kids are used all the time to justify what politicians (society, and even individuals) are doing: we are doing it for the kids. And yet I think the actions and rhetorics of our society, and our politicians, do precisely say that we are against kids. But still we seem unable or unwilling to politicize the issue beyond the acceptable boundaries, which keep politics away from kids. Even such passionate defenders of kids as Jonathan Kozol and Marian Wright Edelman seem unable to say that there might be a political struggle over kids themselves. Kozol, for example, sees it largely as a racial issue (leaving in place what I think is the illusion that the rest of the kids are all right). And even then, he can attribute the declining investment in education to popular sentiments against taxes, but he cannot take the argument further, to point out that such popular resistance to taxes has been politically organized and is connected to much larger political struggles, and to particular political agendas. And he cannot look for the connection, so that he leaves the impression that most people who oppose taxes would change their minds if only they realized that the money was going to kids, except for the fact of the problematic politics of racism.

The key to understanding what is at stake in the war on kids, and hence, to understanding its place in the struggle over modernity, lies I believe in recognizing that kids—the embodiments of the categories of children and youth (as these were shaped and transformed largely at the turn of the twentieth century) are closely linked to another cornerstone of the construction of liberal modernity and of the modern liberal individual. I have already suggested that it involves a particular construction of and investment in time and specifically, in the relation of the present and the future. It involves a particular construction of history, the construction of a sense of belonging built on a faith in the ability to imagine and invest in the future. It involves the assumption that there is a trajectory leading from the past into a future.

While many scholars have noted the importance of a particular sense of time in modernity, the role that childhood and youth (and a certain notion of the family) came to serve in this particular economy of time, especially in the United States, has been less frequently noted. In U.S. society in the twentieth century, more so than any other culture in the world, kids became the privileged sign and embodiment of the future. Youth became the trope of the universal faith in futurity. The baby boomers, of course, more than any generation embodied it. This was the generation that was in a sense to bring history to an end because it would realize the American Dream. Children became, in fact, a kind of symbolic guarantee that America still had a future, that it still believed in a future, and that it was crucial to America to invest its faith in that future. In fact, they took it one step further because their connection to the future seemed to guarantee the truth of liberal modernity's occasional faith in progress.

I want to suggest that it is that faith in the future, embodied in the very modern construction of childhood and youth over the past century, that investment in kids and in the ability of kids to embody that commitment to a future, that is being contested in the war being waged against them. The war against kids is a war against youth's ability to embody the very necessity of a commitment to a future, and to guarantee the connection of the present and the future. This is different than Gill's conservative efforts to explain the crisis of the family by the collapse of the faith in progress, or in a particular future insofar as it entails certain kinds of political and economic visions of the American Dream.[36] The war on youth is about erasing the future as a burden on the present. Or better, it is about changing the very mode by which the future functions, for the future is itself necessary to the possibility of an individualizing identity built on labor and citizenship. The rejection of kids as the core of our common national and social identity is, at the same time, a rejection of the future as an affective investment. Increasingly, the future is defined as either indistinguishable from the present[37] (and therefore as the servant of the present rather than vice versa), or apocalyptically (as radically other than the present, without any continuity). To put it simply, the claim that we are no longer responsible to/for our children (because they no longer deserve it) "signifies," if you will, that the present is no longer responsible to the future. On the contrary, in the reimagined modernity, the future is to be held responsible to the present.

We may be witnessing the attempt to reinvent the individual and the relationship of individuality to the forces that produce reality and are producing our collective futures, and the emergence of a new and distinct mode of individualization and (as)sociation. This "revolution" involves economic, political, ideological, social, theoretical, cultural, and media vectors, all together, and their multiple articulations. It is what brings together new conservative, neoconservative, and neoliberal groups, and sometimes other constituencies, however temporarily. What is at stake is the production of a new modernity and of the impossibility of those conceptions of agency that have sustained us for centuries. This new modernity would seem to negate the very reality, and even the possibility, of the social or, more accurately, of social agency. What we are witnessing, what I have been trying to describe and imagine, is the production of a new context, a new modernity, out of the old. This production seems to require and seek the negation of many forms of individual and collective agency, including the very possibility of imagining alternative futures, of imagining the future as always holding open the possibility of alternatives.

That is, the attack on kids is about the relationship between individuality and time. It is a struggle to change our investment in and the possibility of imagining the future. And it is, as Bauman says, a struggle about escaping from the present.[38] Because as long as you believe in the future, there's always an escape route, there's always a way to get from here to there. And as long as there's an escape route, there is always a possibility of a community defined in opposition to the present. This struggle against modernity (in the name of a new modernity) must negate the possibility of imagination, of the imaginative power of the future. And in fact, the new modernity seems to demand that we deny the importance of the future. But if we are to take back control of our present, if we are to take back the possibility of imagining the future, we must somehow return to kids—all over the world—the possibility of embodying hope for themselves (without once again imposing on them the burden that they embody hope for us as well). We must also claim hope for ourselves as intellectuals. I recognize that my argument may stretch one's credulity, but I want to defend myself by agreeing with my good friend Meaghan Morris, who has suggested, "Things are too urgent now to be giving up our imagination."[39] I want to suggest that there is no other way except imaginatively to make sense of what is going on and that, in the end, it is precisely our ability to imagine that is at stake in the current political struggle.

Notes

Earlier versions of this argument have been published as "Why Does Neo-Liberalism Hate Kids? The War on Youth and the Culture of Politics," in *The Review of Education, Pedagogy, Cultural Studies* (2001); and "La guerra contro I giovani e il potere dell'immaginazione." In Lawrence Grossberg, *Saggi sui Cultural Studies: Media, Rock, Giovani* (Napoli: Liguori Editore, 2002). I am currently completing a book on this topic.

1. See my "Reflections of a Disappointed Popular Music Scholar" in this volume.
2. I want to thank Henry Giroux for, to paraphrase Kant, waking me from my dogmatic slumber and forcing me to engage with this issue. For the most important statement on this subject to date, see his book *Stealing Innocence: Youth, Corporate Power and the Politics of Culture* (New York: St. Martin's Press, 2000).
3. I have taken these statistics and those that appear at other points in this paper from a wide variety of sources. Wherever possible, I have tried to verify the figures and when necessary, I have chosen the most conservative figure. Of course, these figures change quite rapidly but I believe the trends remain the same.
4. Recent investigations suggest that many states are not claiming federal monies that are available to provide health care to families—and children—who have been forced off welfare rolls.
5. Mike Males, *The Scapegoat Generation* (Monroe, ME: Common Courage, 1996).
6. Henry Giroux, "Beating Up On Kids," *Z Magazine* (July/August 1996), 19: 7/8, 14–17.
7. Amazingly, the pediatricians' website has lots more to say about media consumption by youth than it has about the widespread use of adult psychotropic drugs (such as Ritalin) to treat vaguely diagnosed problems in children.
8. The following examples and quotations are taken from a report in the *Los Angeles Times*, reprinted in *The News and Observer* (October 17, 1999).
9. Deirdre Donahue, October 1, 1998, D1.
10. http://www.senate.gov/~judiciary/mediavio.htm.
11. Lawrence Grossberg, *We Gotta Get Out of This Place: Popular Conservatism and Postmodern Culture* (New York and London: Routledge, 1992).
12. Ann Hulbert, "So's Your Old Man." *Slate Magazine* (November 4, 1996). www.slate.com.
13. Andrew Clark, "How Teens Got the Power," *Macleans* (March 22, 1999), 42.
14. Henry Giroux, "Public Pedagogy and the Responsibility of Intellectuals: Youth, Littleton and the Loss of Innocence," *JAC* 20-1 (2000), 11.
15. Mike Males, "Bashing Youth: Media Myths about Teenagers," *Extra!* (March/April 1994).
16. Giroux, "Beating Up On Kids," 14.
17. David Blackenhorn of the "Nonpartisan" Institute for American Values, cited in *The News and Observer* (September 1, 1996).
18. J. Walker Smith of Yankelovich Partners, cited in *The News and Observer* (September 1, 1996).
19. Cited in Zygmunt Bauman, *In Search of Politics* (Stanford, CA: Stanford University Press, 1999), 157.
20. Shannon Brownlee, Roberta Hotinski, Bellamy Pailthorp, Erin Ragan, and Kathleen Wong, "Inside the Teen Brain," *U.S. News and World Report* (August 9, 1999).

21. Stuart Hall, "Popular-Democratic vs. Authoritarian Populism: Two Ways of 'Taking Democracy Seriously.'" In Stuart Hall, *The Hard Road to Renewal: Thatcherism and the Crisis of the Left* (London: Verso, 1988), 127.
22. Cited in Bauman, 20.
23. Paul Krugman, "The Spiral of Inequality," *Mother Jones* (November/December 1994), 44.
24. John Powers, "Beyond Prosperity, Outrage Simmers." *The News and Observer* (October 19, 1997), 25A.
25. "It Takes More than Anger to Fuel Mass Movement," *The News and Observer,* (October 19, 1997), 25A.
26. Bauman, 1.
27. Michael J. Sandel, "America's Search for a New Public Philosophy," *The Atlantic Monthly* (March 1996), 59.
28. Cited in Bauman, 92.
29. Cited in Bauman, 176.
30. It is worth noting that the current student movement against capitalism is based, as it were, on the experience and politicization of consumption. While many hold this new anticapitalist movement up against cultural studies, which is equated suddenly with identity politics, it is important to claim that in part, this current movement crucially depends on the move, advocated within cultural studies, to recognize the importance and political resonance of consumption.
31. Cited in Bauman, 20.
32. Doug Henwood, Lecture, Duke University, February 19, 1999.
33. Friedrich A. Hayek, *The Road to Serfdom* (Chicago: University of Chicago Press, 1944/1994).
34. This is visible in recent court and administrative decisions pertaining to the medical uses of marijuana, or the health threat of arsenic, or the reality of global warming, as well as in the very notion of a "faith based welfare system."
35. Lee Edelman, "The Future Is Kid Stuff: Queer Theory, Disidentification and the Death Drive," *Narrative* 6V1 (January 1998).
36. Richard T. Gill, *Posterity Lost: Progress, Ideology, and the Decline of the American Family.* (Lanham, MD: Rowman and Littlefield, 1997).
37. For example, a recent TV commercial has a young couple talking. The woman asks, "Are you worried about the future?" And the guy says, "Yes. I think we ought to be very careful about which car we buy. We want to make sure that our car can change with the future."
38. Bauman, 11.
39. Meaghan Morris, *The Pirate's Fiancee: Feminism Reading Postmodernism* (London: Verso, 1988), 186.

24

A Political Economy of Race, Urban Education, and Educational Policy

JEAN ANYON

A thorough political economy of race would entail an analysis of at least the wage, job, tax, and housing situation in urban neighborhoods, where the majority of low-income African Americans and Latinos reside (U.S. Census 2002, Tables 3-1, 3-14). Such an analysis would document the lack of living-wage and career-advancing jobs, and would explicate policies and practices that segregate poor and low-income people of color in underserved and underfinanced city neighborhoods and fiscally stressed, racially homogenous suburbs (see Anyon, 2005, for a full analysis).

In this chapter I focus on the wage and job situation for urban blacks and Latinos. I first describe the background, the overall wage and job picture in United States metro areas, and then provide a more finely honed analysis of the wages and jobs available to urban minority neighborhood residents.

Two consequences of a racial political economy for urban education will be drawn. First, the concentration of minority families without decent jobs in neighborhoods that are already underinvested, limits the level of financial investment in education by governments and business, and often limits the emotional investment of teachers and students in the schools. This situation of financial and emotional underinvestment leads to underresourced, underachieving classrooms and schools in those areas. I have described this situation in detail elsewhere (Anyon 1997).

A second consequence of a political economy of race for urban education, and one that will be discussed here, is that when the political economy prevents opportunity for decent jobs and wages in urban areas, and thereby maintains families in poverty, it diminishes the capacity of parents to provide rich, stable learning environments for their children. Recent empirical research demonstrates that this poverty and low income make it difficult for children to develop to their full potential, often derailing educational achievement early on (Lee and Burkham 2002; Brooks-Gunn et al. 1997). Fortunately, there is also evidence documenting that when income supports are provided to poor families, the educational achievement of the children typically improves significantly. This finding has important implications for the policies by which we expect to raise achievement for students of color in urban schools.

Wages and Jobs in U.S. Metro Areas

Almost three fourths (70%) of all American employees saw their wages fall between 1973 and 1995 (in constant dollars, i.e., adjusted for inflation); even with the boom of the late 1990s, a majority of workers made less in 2000 than they had in 1973. New college graduates earned $1.10 less per hour in 1995 (adjusted) than their counterparts did in 1973. The earnings of the average American family did improve slightly over this period, but only through a dramatic increase in the number of hours worked and the share of families in which both parents worked (Lafer 2002; Mishel, Bernstein, and Boushey 2003).

Some of the largest long-term wage declines have been among entry-level workers (those with up to five years of work experience) with a high school education. Average wages for male entry-level high school graduates were 28 percent lower in 1997 than two decades earlier. The decline for comparable women was 18 percent (Economic Policy Institute February 17, 2000).

Low wages are an important cause of poverty. Low-wage workers are those whose hourly wage is less than the earnings necessary to lift a family above the official poverty line: in 2003, $15,260 or less for a family of three, and $18,400 for a family of four.

In 2000, at the height of a booming economy, almost a fifth of all men (19.5%), and almost a third of all women (33.1%), earned poverty level wages working full time, year round. In 2000, over one in four black men (26.3%), one in three black women (36.5%) and Hispanic men (37.6%), and almost half of Hispanic women (49.3%) earned poverty wages working full time, year round (Mishel et al. 2003).

This author analyzed figures provided by the Economic Policy Institute to calculate the overall percent of people who work full time year round, yet make poverty zone wages. Poverty zone is defined here as wages up to 125% of the official poverty threshold needed to support a family of four at the poverty level (ibid). The analysis demonstrates that in 1999, during the economic boom, almost half of people at work in the United States (41.3%) earned poverty zone wages—in 1999, $10.24/hour ($21,299/year) or less, working full time year round (ibid, Table 2.10, 130). Two years later, in 2001, 38.4 percent earned poverty zone wages working full time year round (in 2001, 125% of the poverty line was a $10.88 hourly wage) (2003).

Who are the working poor? In 2000, more than half (59.5%) of the working poor were women; over 60 percent were white (60.4%); 35 percent were black or Latino (ibid, 353). Over 61.8 percent had a high school degree or less, while a quarter (24.2%) had some college, and 8 percent had a bachelor's degree (ibid, 03, 353). This last figure indicates that almost one in ten of the working poor is a college graduate.

Seventy percent of the working poor had jobs in services or retail trade and 10 percent worked in manufacturing (ibid, 03, 353). The vast majority (93.3%) were not in unions. More than half (57.7%) were under the age of thirty-five.

What job opportunities are available for Americans? For two decades, numerous politicians, educators, and corporate spokespeople have been arguing that the United States must improve education because people need advanced skills in order to get a job. This is a myth, however. Most job openings in the next ten years will not require either sophisticated skills or a college degree. Seventy-seven percent of new and projected jobs will be low paying. Most will require on-the-job training only, and will not require college; most will be in service and retail, where poverty zone wages are the norm. Only 12.6 percent of new jobs will require a bachelor's degree (U.S. Department of Labor 2002). Of the twenty occupations expected to grow the fastest, only six require college (these six are in computer systems and information technology (ibid), and there are relatively few of these jobs).

Only a quarter of new and projected jobs are expected to pay over $26,000 a year, which is not too far from the poverty line of $18,400 for a family of four in 2003. The typical job of the future is not in information technology. Most job openings will be in food preparation and service, and in fast food restaurants, as telephone customer service representatives, and as cashiers (U.S. Department of Labor 2002). In the next decade,

> about five million new jobs will be created for food workers, including kitchen help, waiters, and waitresses. Another four million will be for cashiers and retail salespeople. More than three million will be for clerks. Two million will be for helpers, packagers, and laborers. Openings for truck drivers will abound. Managerial and professional occupations will also need more workers, but their numbers pale compared with openings requiring less education. Employers will hire more than three times as many cashiers as engineers. They will need more than twice as many food-counter workers, waiters, and waitresses than all the systems analysts, computer engineers, and database administrators combined. (Rothstein 1999, 1)

A main determinant of whether one is poor or not is whether or not one has a decently paying job. The assertion that jobs are plentiful, if only workers were qualified to fill them, has been a central tenet of federal policy for twenty years (Lafer 2002). In 1982, the Reagan administration eliminated the Comprehensive Employment and Training Administration (CETA), which by 1978 had created almost 2 million full-time jobs, and substituted a major federal job training program (Job Partnership Training Act) (ibid). Since then, and continuing today, job training has been the centerpiece of federal and state efforts to solve both the unemployment problem and the poverty problem. For almost all of this time, however, the federal government has not collected data on job availability (vacancies). If they had, and if they had consulted studies that had been carried out, they would have found that all the evidence demonstrates that at any given time there are far more unemployed people than there are job openings (ibid; see also Pigeon and Wray 1999, among others). The federal government has spent $85 billion on job training since the Reagan years, claiming continually that there are jobs for those who want them (Lafer 2002).

Typically, new jobs are created every year, and other jobs are lost each year, as well. On average, the total (net) number of jobs increases by a million or more a year, in keeping with the country's overall population growth and economic expansion. But despite this growth, and despite government assumptions, there are not enough jobs for those who need them (Lafer 2002).

New data provided by the Bureau of Labor Statistics (the Job Openings and Labor Turnover Survey) allow us to compare job opening rates to unemployment rates. When employers' demand for workers decreases, the unemployment rate climbs. The job opening rate is typically considerably below the unemployment rate, and the differential has been growing. As of May 2002, for example, the number of jobs open was 3.46 million while the number of officially unemployed was 8.35 million persons. This is a surplus of nearly 5 million would-be workers (Economic Policy Institute, August 7, 2002).

However, when we add to the number of the officially unemployed the 3.7 million involuntary part-timers who wanted full-time work but could not get it, the 4.6 million nonjob seekers who want work but are not currently looking (the discouraged, those who lacked child care or transportation), we see that the actual number of people who need jobs is really 16.6 million. Yet there were only 3.46 million job openings in 2002 (National Jobs for All Coalition October 2002).

The Wage and Job Situation for Low-Income Minorities in Urban Areas

During the 1970s, African Americans made substantial economic progress: With mass migration to urban areas came increased years of education and rising wages; and civil rights laws and affirmative action conjoined to increase opportunities (Smith and Welch 1989). Indeed, by the late

1970s, wages of black and white college graduates were nearly equal, and the wages of black women surpassed those of white women (Freeman 1976). The numbers of black managers and professionals, especially in government agencies, increased significantly (Moss and Tilly 2001).

But there remained a large group living in concentrated poverty in America's inner cities. By 1990, there were more people living in concentrated poverty in America's cities than at any time since the 1960s. Prolonged unemployment, underemployment, and detachment from the labor market were prevalent (Wilson 1997; Eisenhower Foundation 1998; Anyon 1997).

During the 1980s, the wage gap between employed working- and middle-class blacks and whites began to increase. Black women were less likely to find work than in the 1970s and early 1980s (Bound and Dresser 1999). During this decade there was also a downward movement out of middle-wage employment for blacks into very low-wage employment for many, and relatively higher-wage employment for a few (Mishel, Bernstein, and Boushey 2003; see also Bound and Dresser 1999).

And by the early 1990s, in part because of the recessions of 1990 and 1991, young African American workers suffered wage and employment setbacks, even though blacks were obtaining higher levels of education than ever, and were closing the gap with whites in both educational attainment and test scores (Moss and Tilly 2001; see also Bound and Freeman 1992; and Jencks 1991). During the 1990s, wages diverged widely between young black and white male college graduates (Bound and Freeman 1992). Latinos also experienced economic regression in the 1990s (Moss and Tilly 2001; see also Corcoran, Heflin, and Reyes 1999).

In the 1990s, a larger divide existed between the wages of people of color and whites than in the 1980s; and by 2000, almost a third (31.8%) of black workers were in jobs paying less than poverty level wages and 40.4 percent of Hispanic workers were making below poverty level wages, while 20% of white workers made less than poverty level wages in 2000 (Mishel, Bernstein, and Boushey 2003).

What accounts for the deteriorated position of blacks and Latinos in the labor market during a decade in which they were obtaining higher levels of education? There are several constituents to a full answer to this question, including the lower quality of education in schools attended by many people of color. And in a landmark study of employer attitudes toward inner-city black and Latino workers, Philip Moss and Chris Tilly tested the assumption that relatively unskilled black and Latino inner-city high school graduates would have access to jobs that required only a high school education (2001).

The common explanation for why blacks and Latinos fare poorly in the labor market is that they do not have the skills required by the information/technology economy. The oft-noted increase in earnings inequality of the last two decades is laid to an upward shift in skill demands. Thus, it is said that because blacks and Latinos have less or lower quality education, they are not hired by employers. A corollary to this argument is that the "digital divide" is producing a growing racial divide (ibid, 43).

In order to assess the accuracy of this claim, Moss and Tilly undertook a project involving face-to-face interviews of 365 managers at 174 firms in four metropolitan areas (Atlanta, Boston, Detroit, and Los Angeles); they also utilized the results of a national telephone survey of 3,510 managers responsible for hiring in various industries, previously carried out by Harry Holzer (1996).

Moss and Tilly assessed employers' desires for workers' "hard skills" (literacy, numeracy, computer familiarity, cognitive abilities), which are said to be the basis of the digital divide, and "soft skills," which refer to interaction (ability to interact with customers, coworkers, and supervisors, including friendliness, teamwork, ability to fit in, and appropriate affect, language use, grooming, and attire), as well as motivation (which refers to enthusiasm, positive work attitudes, commitment, dependability, integrity, and willingness to learn) (2001).

The researchers discovered that, contrary to prevailing wisdom, but in agreement with Department of Labor data, hard skill demands have risen only moderately or not at all in most entry-level jobs—and although some entry-level workers were being required to take on a broader range of tasks such as interacting with customers, reading computer printouts, or using word processing skills in secretarial positions, other workers (e.g., cashiers) have been deskilled by recent technological trends (47–55).

As in other studies, the managers interviewed by Moss and Tilly fairly consistently reported increased need for skills. But, as in other research, the employers demand only modest increases in skill, and none reports dramatically increased demand for computer or other technological skills. "The weight of the evidence points to increased demands at the level of basic skills—reading and writing, soft skills such as motivation and communication, and to some degree, team and group problem-solving skills"—but not to drastically increased skill demands (2001, 47; see also Cappelli 1996; Holzer 1996; Moss and Tilly 1996; Murnane and Levy 1996; and Osterman 1995).

Since the mid-1990s, the mix of jobs has shifted to industries and occupations that require contact with customers. Retail and service industries totaled 36 percent of nonagricultural employment in 1979, but rose to 48 percent by 1999. Among occupations not including higher-skilled managers and professionals, sales and service employment climbed more modestly, from 32 to 37 percent since the mid-1980s (Moss and Tilly 2001). Indeed, Peter Cappelli (1995) concluded that the alleged "skill shortages" decried by employers in the first half of the 1990s referred mainly to issues of worker motivation (1996; see also Osterman 1995, who found, in a large, representative sample, that managers report behavioral traits as one of the two most important job criteria in about 82 percent of cases, and the top criterion in about half).

Indeed, managers interviewed by Moss and Tilly expressed increased demands for soft skills more frequently than for any hard skill, with the exception of computer literacy. Except for employers in manufacturing firms where workers needed to program computers or read printouts, "all other employers emphasized the soft skills of interaction with customers and motivation for work as just as important as basic reading and arithmetic skills" (or, to use these researchers' phrase, "attitude trumps technical facility" in large numbers of jobs) (61).

What Moss and Tilly also discovered is that managers' definition and evaluation of applicants' soft skills is highly subjective and is context bound. Moreover, employers typically conflated the two, aggregating appearance, ways of talking, and self-presentation, with possession of the hard skills. In interviews, managers mixed and entangled comments on inner city blacks' and Latinos' hard skills (education, intelligence) with evaluation of soft skills (use of language, dress, and attitudes) (44, 99).

Presentation of self, friendliness, or work ethic, of course, "cannot be measured with the same precision as, say, ability to use a word processing program or to calculate percentages" (44). Since most employers are white and middle class, their own cultural modes of expression differ from the high school educated applicants of color who present. Their attitudes toward potential groups of workers therefore influence most of their assessments of soft skills. "Cultural differences, prejudice and stereotype will cloud subjective assessment of a candidate's soft skills." Unfortunately, most employers do not screen applicants for entry-level jobs through formal measures; rather, they rely on the preemployment interview (ibid).

Moreover, soft skills are profoundly dependent on context. "How successfully a worker interacts with customers, coworkers, and supervisors depends decisively on how these other parties view and treat the worker. Pay level and his or her treatment by managers shape a worker's level of motivation" as do perceived chances for advancement (45).

Indeed, in most work settings successful performance of even narrowly defined technical tasks depends crucially on a set of relationships with other workers and managers (ibid). However, Moss and Tilly report that employers genuinely view interaction and motivation as skills that prospective workers either have or don't have (ibid; see also Capelli 1995).

The increased desire for soft skills makes it harder for nonwhite applicants because it may increase racial discrimination by employers.

> In some ways, race is becoming increasingly important [in the hiring process]. In particular, the growing stress on soft skills opens the door wider for biases and stereotypes to weigh in the hiring process, and on location decisions as well. This tells us that skill- or location-based policies that fail to address race are likely to fall short of the mark. Providing added training programs for black and Latino job seekers will not easily dissolve the suspicion that many employers harbor. And employers' unease may block access by workers of color to the critically important training that takes place on the job. Similarly, new transportation systems such as vanpools to crack inner city isolation will have limited effects if suburban business people remain chary of the urban minority workforce. *Policies to dissipate stereotypes, and to constrain employers' ability to act on them, are necessary complements* (254, italics added).

A smaller percentage of African American men are working now than in recent decades. Only 52 percent of young (aged 16 to 24) noninstitutionalized, out of school black males with high school degrees or less were employed in 2002, compared to 62 percent in the early 1980s. In contrast, the labor force activity of comparable white and Latino males has been steady over the last two decades, and employment among young black women has increased significantly. Remarkably, employment for young black men declined fairly continuously between 1989 and 1997, despite the strong economic recovery that occurred after 1992. Labor force participation for young black men suffered an even sharper 14 percentage point decline over the two-decade period. This contrasts sharply with the experience of young less educated Latino men, who essentially achieved employment parity with their white counterparts during this period (Offner and Holzer 2002; see also Mishel et al. 2003).

The percentage of young less educated black males employed in cities is much lower than in the suburbs, and the gap has widened since the mid-1990s. The employment rate for young, less educated black men living in central cities (46.99%) is now 16 percentage points lower than that for their suburban counterparts (63.09%) (Offner and Holzer 2002). The employment rate for young black male high school graduates dropped by over four times as much in cities (9 percentage points) as in suburbs (2 percentage points) over the course of the 1990s. The weakening attachment of young, less educated black males to the labor force occurred despite the higher educational attainment of the group: a much larger percentage of the group held high school degrees at the end of the period than at the beginning (ibid; see also Freeman 1991; Cherry and Rodgers 2000).

On the basis of Moss and Tilly's findings, one could argue that this decline in labor force participation of young black males is in large part a consequence of increased demands for soft skills and the stereotypical evaluation of these white middle-class managers, resulting in increased discrimination.

It is also the case, however, that a high current and former incarceration rate among members of this group may contribute to their declining employment. In 2000, 10 percent of black males aged twenty to twenty-four were incarcerated. Among high school dropouts, over *one third* were incarcerated (Mauer 2003a; Petit and Western 2004). Research by Holzer and Stoll found that many employers are reluctant to hire individuals with criminal records. Since substantial numbers of the 1,600 prisoners released every day in the United States return to low-income urban neighborhoods, their joblessness contributes to the low rates of employment in young black males (Holzer and Stoll 2001; Mauer 2003a, 2003b). Even young, less educated black males without criminal records may have trouble obtaining employment, if employers assume that they may be more likely to engage in criminal acts because they share age, race, and education characteristics with a high crime rate population (Holzer and Stoll 2001).

The reluctance of employers to hire young black males and workers of color in general, this widespread, illegal discrimination in hiring, has important implications for federal policies that will assist them. First, widespread discrimination suggests that increasing the level of education of young black males short of college completion may not be enough to improve their labor market opportunities. As economist Gordon Lafer suggests, federal policies that supported the right to organize labor unions might be more useful. Second, widespread employer discrimination implies that policies that might reduce overall unemployment in the hopes of employing significant numbers of black workers are not enough. During the nearly "full" employment economy of the late 1990s, the employment rate of young black women who did not finish high school rose by 14 points. However, the percentage of those young black women who were employed went from 23 to 37 percent, which is still very low. So policies that create jobs, with the federal government as employer of last resort, are what is indicated. Policies that would turn the minimum wage into a "living" wage will not necessarily assist less educated young black males, since so many are unemployed (Mishel et al. 2003; see also Nolan and Anyon 2004).

Educational Consequences of the Racial Political Economy

A growing body of research demonstrates ways in which poverty, especially in young children, and over the long term, limits children's chances for full development. In 2002, for example, Valerie Lee and David Burkham published the results of a large-sample assessment of the effects of poverty on cognitive development. They utilized data from the U.S. Department of Education's early childhood longitudinal kindergarten cohort, which is a comprehensive data set that provides a nationally representative portrait of kindergarten students. Lee and Burkham explored differences in young children's achievement scores in literacy and mathematics by race, ethnicity, and socioeconomic status as they began kindergarten. They also analyzed differences by social background in an array of children's homes and family activities (2002).

The study demonstrates that inequalities of children's cognitive ability by socioeconomic status (SES) are substantial even before children begin kindergarten, and that poverty has a detrimental impact on early intellectual achievement. Importantly, it demonstrates that the disadvantages of being poor outweigh by far the race or family structure of children as causes of the cognitive disadvantages (ibid).

Details of the national assessment include the following:

1. Before children enter kindergarten, the average cognitive scores of children in the highest SES group are 60 percent above the scores of the lowest SES group.
2. Cognitive skills are much *less* closely related to race/ethnicity after accounting for SES. After taking race differences into account, children from different SES groups achieve at different levels—before they begin kindergarten.
3. The impacts on cognitive skills of family structure (e.g., being in a single-parent family) are much smaller than either race or SES.
4. Socioeconomic status is very strongly related to cognitive skills; SES accounts for more of the variation in cognitive scores than any other factor by far.

Lee and Burkham also found that not only do disadvantaged children enter kindergarten with significantly lower cognitive skills than do their advantaged peers, but low-SES children begin school (kindergarten) in systematically lower-quality elementary schools than their more advantaged counterparts. "However school quality is defined— in terms of higher student achievement, more school resources, more qualified teachers, more positive teacher attitudes, better neighbor-hood or school conditions, private vs. public schools—the least advantaged U.S. children begin their formal schooling in consistently lower-quality schools. This reinforces the inequalities that develop even before children reach school age" (3; see also Entwistle and Alexander 1997; Phillips et al. 1998; Stipic and Ryan 1997; and White 1982).

What Can Be Done?

The argument in this chapter has been that a lack of jobs and decent incomes for African American and Latino families in cities is pervasive, and affects education and school achievement of the chil-dren, in part placing barriers to full cognitive development in their path. One policy that would provide a partial solution to the problem of low academic achievement in urban schools might lie, therefore, in providing financial support to low-income families.

Direct evidence that income supports improve educational achievement is available. In March 2001, for example, the Manpower Development Research Corporation (MDRC) published a syn-thesis of research on how welfare and work policies affect the children of single mothers (Morris et al. 2001). This synthesis reviewed data from evaluations of five programs that provided income supplements to poverty wage workers (Florida's Family Transition Program; the Minnesota Family Investment Program; the National Evaluation of Welfare-to-Work Strategies; the New Hope pro-gram; the Self-Sufficiency Project). These programs offered supports of various kinds to poverty wage workers: income supplements, earnings disregards (rules that allow working welfare recipi-ents to keep more of their income when they go to work), employment services, counseling, infor-mal get-togethers with project staff, and so on.

MDRC's review of the studies found that even relatively small income supplements to working parents (amounting to about $4,000 per year) improved children's elementary school achievement by about 10 to 15 percent of the average variation in the control groups. These improvements were seen on test scores and ratings by parents or teachers. The earning supplements had "consistently positive impacts on children's [school] achievement" (63). The positive effects were small, but were statistically significant (21–22).

Educational Policy

Indeed, providing income supports as a way to instigate raised educational achievement is common sense, since educational achievement in general, as well as for minorities, despite the gap with whites that remains (Ferguson 2000), has been found to increase with raised socioeconomic status: The more highly resourced the family, the better the educational environment typically available to children, and the stronger their educational achievement.

A policy of income supports for poor families could, in this sense, be understood as a crucial *educational* policy. If educators were to include in the panoply of policies they promote a set of strategies to provide income supports for poor and low-income families, and if such policies were passed and implemented in our cities, urban students could be provided with more highly resourced early learning environments. According to research findings, such an advantage could lead to increased school achievement for the students, and more highly performing urban schools.

References

Anyon, Jean. *Radical Possibilities: Public Policy, Urban Education, and a New Social Movement.* New York: Routledge, 2005.
Anyon, Jean. *Ghetto Schooling: A Political Economy of Urban Educational Reform.* New York: Teachers College Press, 1997.
Applebaum, Eileen. *What Explains Employment Developments in the U.S.?* Economic Policy Institute Briefing Paper. Wash-ington, DC: Economic Policy Institute, 2000.

Bound, John and Laura Dresser. "The Erosion of the Relative Earnings of Young African American Women during the 1980s." In *Latinas and African American Women at Work*, edited by Irene Browne. New York: Russell Sage, 1999. Cited in Moss and Tilly 2001, p. 6.

Bound, John and Richard Freeman. "What Went Wrong? The Erosion of Relative Earnings and Employment for Blacks." *Quarterly Journal of Economics* 107 (1992): 201–32.

Brooks-Gunn, Jeanne et al. "Lessons Learned and Future Directions for Research on the Neighborhoods in Which Children Live." In *Neighborhood Poverty*, vol. 1, *Contexts and Consequences for Children,* edited by Jeanne Brooks-Gunn, Greg Duncan, and Lawrence Aber, 379–98. New York: Russell Sage, 1997.

Cappelli, Peter. "Technology and Skill Requirements: Implications for Establishment of Wage Structures." In *Earnings Inequality,* edited by Philip Moss and Chris Tilly. Special issue, *New England Economic Review.* (May/June 1996). Cited in Moss and Tilly 2001, p. 47.

Cherry, Robert and William Rodgers. *Prosperity for All? The Economic Boom and African Americans.* New York: Russell Sage, 2000.

Corcoran, Mary, Colleen Heflin, and Belinda Reyes. "Latino Women in the U.S.: The Economic Progress of Mexican and Puerto Rican Women." In *Latinas and African American Women at Work,* edited by Irene Browne, 105–38. New York: Russell Sage, 1999.

Economic Policy Institute. *Entry Level Workers Face Lower Wages.* Washington, DC: Author, February 17, 2000.

Economic Policy Institute. *Decline in Job Openings Fuels Unemployment.* Washington, DC: Author, August 7, 2002.

Eisenhower Foundation. *Background Report.* Washington, DC: Author, 1998.

Entwistle, Doris. "The Role of Schools in Sustaining Early Childhood Program Benefits." *Future of Children* 5 (1985): 133–44.

Ferguson, Ronald. "Addressing Racial Disparities in High-Achieving Schools." *North Central Regional Educational Laboratory Policy Issues* 13 (December 13, 2002).

Freeman, Richard. "The Earnings and Employment of Disadvantaged Young Men over the Business Cycle." In *The Urban Underclass,* edited by Christopher Jencks and Paul E. Peterson. Washington, DC: The Brookings Institution, 1991.

Freeman, Richard. *Black Elite: The New Market for Highly Educated Black Americans.* Report prepared for the Carnegie Commission on Higher Education. New York: McGraw-Hill, 1976. In Moss and Tilly 2001, p. 35.

Holzer, Harry. *What Employers Want: Job Prospects for Less Educated Workers.* New York: Russell Sage, 1996.

Holzer, Harry and Michael Stoll. *Employers and Welfare Recipients: The Effects of Welfare Reform in the Workplace.* San Francisco: Public Policy Institute of California, 2001.

Holzer, Harry and Michael Stoll. *The Employment Rate of Adult African American Men.* Washington, DC: The Urban Institute, 2003.

Jencks, Christopher and Peterson, Paul E., eds. *The Urban Underclass.* Washington, DC: The Brookings Institution, 1991.

Lafer, Gordon. *The Job Training Charade.* Ithaca, NY: Cornell University Press, 2002.

Lee, Valerie E. and David T. Burkham. *Inequality at the Starting Gate: Social Background and Achievement at Kindergarten Entry.* Washington, DC: Educational Policy Institute, 2002.

Mauer, Marc. "Some Punishments Begin after Prison." *The Crisis* (May/June 2003a): 16–17.

Mauer, Marc. *Invisible Punishment: The Collateral Consequences of Mass Imprisonment.* New York: New Press, 2003b.

Mishel, Lawrence, Jared Bernstein, and Heather Boushey. *The State of Working America: 2000/2001.* Ithaca, NY: Cornell University Press, 2001.

Mishel, Lawrence, Jared Bernstein, and John Schmitt. *The State of Working America: 2002/2003.* Ithaca, NY: Cornell University Press, 2003.

Morris, Pamela et al. *How Welfare and Work Policies Affect Children: A Synthesis of Research.* Washington, DC: Manpower Development Research, 2001.

Moss, Philip and Chris Tilly. "'Soft' Skills and Race: An Investigation of Black Men's Employment Problems." *Work and Occupations* 23 (1996): 252–76.

Moss, Philip and Chris Tilly, eds. *Stories Employers Tell: Race, Skill, and Hiring in America.* New York: Russell Sage, 2001.

Murnane, Richard and Frank Levy. *Teaching the New Basic Skills: Principles for Educating Children to Thrive in a Changing Economy.* New York: Free Press, 1996.

National Jobs For All Coalition. *UnCommon Sense.* New York: Author, 2002.

Nolan, Kathleen and Jean Anyon. "Learning to Do Time: Willis's Model of Cultural Reproduction in an Era of Postindustrialism, Globalization, and Mass Incarceration." In *Learning to Labor in New Times,* edited by Nadine Dolby, Greg Dimitriadis, and Paul Willis. New York: RoutledgeFalmer, 2004.

Offner, Paul and Harry Holzer. *Left Behind in the Labor Market: Recent Employment Trends among Young Black Men.* Center on Urban and Metropolitan Policy. Washington, DC: Brookings Institution, 2002.

Osterman, Paul. "Skill, Training, and Work Organization in American Establishments." *Industrial Relations* 34 (1995): 2–13.

Petit, Becky and Bruce Western. "Mass Imprisonment and the Life Course: Race and Class Inequality in U.S. Incarceration." *American Sociological Review* 69 (2004): 151–69.

Phillips, Meredith, James Crouse, and John Ralph. "Does the Black/White Test Score Gap Widen after Children Enter School?" In *The Black/White Test Score Gap,* edited by Christopher Jencks and Meredith Phillips, 229–72. Washington, DC: Brookings Institute, 1998.

Pigeon, Marc-Andre and Randall Wray. *Down and Out in the U.S.: An Inside Look at the Out of the Labor Force Population.* Public Policy Brief No. 54. Annandale-on-Hudson, NY: The Jerome Levy Economics Institute of Bard College, 1999.

Rothstein, Richard. "Shortage of Skills? A High-Tech Myth." *The New York Times,* October 27, 1999.

Smith, James P. and Finis R. Welch. "Black Economic Progress after Myrdal." *Journal of Economic Literature* 27 (1989): 519–64..

Stipic, Deborah and Rosaleen Ryan. "Economically Disadvantaged Preschoolers: Ready to Learn but Further to Go." *Developmental Psychology* 33 (1997): 711–23.

U.S. Bureau of the Census. *American Housing Survey for the United States: 1999.* Washington, DC: Government Printing Office, 2002.

U.S. Department of Labor. *Occupation Projections to 2010.* Washington, DC: Author, 2002.

White, K. "The Relationship between Socioeconomic Status and Academic Achievement." *Psychological Bulletin* 91 (1982): 46–81.

Wilson, William Julius. *When Work Disappears: The World of the New Urban Poor.* New York: Vintage, 1997.

25

Magic Johnson's Urban Renewal

Empowerment Zones and the National Fantasy of HarlemUSA

MICHAEL D. GIARDINA AND CL COLE

"America" is an assumed relation, an explication of ongoing collective practices, and also an occasion for exploring what it means that national subjects already share not just a history, or a political allegiance, but a set of forms and the affect that makes these forms meaningful. (Lauren Berlant 1991, 5)

On the morning of October 17, 1994, over 400 New York City police officers—all dressed in riot gear—swept through 125th Street in Harlem, New York. Their goal? Stopping street vendors from plying their daily trade and forcibly relocating those who wished to stay in business to an empty lot some nine blocks away. The immediate result? For weeks following the sweep, Harlem was in disarray, as rallies were organized, marches held, local stores closed, and a magnified police presence became likened by residents to a "military occupation of a hostile foreign land" (Jackson 2002, 46). However, street vendors along 125th Street had been engaged in such "sidewalk" business practices since the 1960s, and had been at odds with local merchants who claimed the vendors were unwanted competition since the 1970s (Democracy Now 2001). Moreover, in 1979, the city itself brokered a compromise that led to the eventual opening of Mart 125, an indoor vendors market that catered to local Harlem residents, and which was located across the street from the famed Apollo Theater. Why, then, were street vendors all of a sudden rounded up, displaced, and, in some cases, arrested for doing what they had been doing for decades? Why, then, were the law-abiding vendors of Mart 125 served with eviction notices a few years later (in 1998)?

It has become the overriding conventional wisdom to suggest that such actions by the city of New York to remove street vendors from Harlem were only one in but a series of actions aimed at cityscape beautification and economic re/generation; among other developments, 1994 also saw a moratorium on the opening of sex-oriented video shops/bars/theaters, a full-scale push to "clean up" Times Square and make it "tourist friendly," and the start of an acrimonious public-private venture aimed at restoring Grand Central Station. However, and specific to the case of Harlem, credence is also ascribed to the fact that Upper Manhattan had just been selected as part of the Clinton administration's Empowerment Zone (EZ) initiative, and the race was on to attract name-brand global corporations to hock their wares. Surely the sight of street vendors composed primarily of

African Americans, West Africans, and West Indians scattered about one of the most historic—though, historically, economically impoverished—streets in the United States was not the public relations photo-op the Upper Manhattan Empowerment Zone's marketing planners and administrative liaisons had in mind when pitching Harlem as a future hotbed of investment opportunities, real estate development, and economic growth. And yet, even this set of talking points only scratches the surface in rationalizing the morphological changes occurring in Upper Manhattan, and there is more at stake here than the displacement of a few dozen street vendors (however unfortunate their situation undeniably is). Truth be told,

> the American urban center was—and is—a piece of a much larger puzzle of the proliferation of new social meanings that translate neoliberal forms of governmentality to the conduct of organizations (for example, as seen in American education debates regarding charter schools, corporate partnerships, and voucher programs) and the conduct of individuals; the "problems" of inner city life have become the new targets of self-management, regulation, the restraint of individual appetites and the moral voluntaristic investment of the inner-city dweller him- or herself (Giardina and McCarthy, forthcoming).

With the intersecting vectors of Clintonian neoliberalism, the stylization of urban culture, and the figure of the Black entrepreneur as our organizing tropes, we argue that emerging, interlaced narratives encompassing spatial identity, racialized consumption, and the celebration of transnational corporate expansion within the American urban environment serve to reproduce and reify a particular version of American national identity and collectivity whilst contributing to the further marginalization of local urban residents and the perpetuation of embodied deviance within such communities. We begin by focusing on specific (sociopolitical) moves made by the Clinton administration during the 1990s aimed at economic and community renewal. In this vein, we articulate the relationship of Clinton's "Third Way" political philosophy to the development of so-called Empowerment Zones. We then move to interrogate the Upper Manhattan Empowerment Zone initiative, specifically the so-named *HarlemUSA* project, a $65 million monument to transnational capitalism and the local, façadic refurbishment of urban space that stands at the heart of Harlem's (consumptive) renaissance. As part of this analysis on *HarlemUSA*, we turn to former National Basketball Association player Earvin "Magic" Johnson and his affiliation to this and other, similarly positioned urban renewal projects. In doing so, we unravel the much hyped entrepreneurial spirit currently projected onto and through the sphere of African-American popular culture. Ultimately, and informed by Lauren Berlant's (1991) understanding of national fantasy, it is our contention that *HarlemUSA* is representative of a new form of transracialized spatial commodification that hails the urban dweller (as well as the white, middle-class tourist-cum-consumer) "into an 'Imaginary' realm of identity and wholeness, where the subject becomes whole by being reconstituted as a *collective* subject, or citizen" of America's fictionalized National Symbolic (11, emphasis in original).

Empowerment Zones/Empowering Fictions

It has been widely acknowledged that since the early 1990s there has been a growing social trend within the United States that locates at its core a commitment to public–private investment, especially with respect to so-called "at risk" and "minority" populations. Whether in the form of Microsoft Corp. donating state-of-the-art computers to inner-city schools or Nike, Inc., implementing its P.L.A.Y. campaign to allegedly benefit America's youth (cf., Cole and Hribar 1995), such acts have generally been framed as either economic capital infusions or large-scale social activist endeavors. Truth be told, however, "The State, corporate interest and private individuals/groups now operate in tandem in a vigorous effort aimed at re-orienting the urban centers in the

United States from a Keynesian, welfarist ethos towards a post-Civil Rights, post-Keynesian, post-welfarist future" (Giardina and McCarthy, forthcoming). Such a position is located most specifically in the form of Bill Clinton's understanding of so-called Third Way politics, which, throughout the 1990s, forcefully entered into the vernacular of global politics, especially in connection with social democratic thinking, and was to define much of the public face of Clinton's agenda.

Loosely circulated during the 1992 presidential campaign, later forcefully unveiled by Clinton during his successful bid for reelection in 1996, and brought forth squarely to the American (and, in fact, global) audience during his 1998 State of the Union address, the Third Way designation was used by Clinton to identify a kind of "new progressivism" that could react and cope with changing global economic conditions and increasing transnational interconnectedness among individuals. Inherent in this so-called new progressive era is the belief that neither traditional liberal nor conservative political ideologies are adequately equipped to effectively govern in the late-capitalist moment. As Anthony Giddens (1998) has opined, "The overall aim of third way politics should be to help citizens pilot their way through the major revolutions of our time: globalization, transformations in personal life, and our relationship to nature" (64). Eventually playing off of British Prime Minister Tony Blair and instances of similar "radical center" debates taking place in Western Europe (most notably those involving German Chancellor Gerhard Schröder), Clinton likewise argued that the increasingly interconnected relations of the global age made it imperative for his administration to offer a "third way," something outside the main of standard Washington politics (cf., Klein 2001). The president spelled out the social dimension of his Third Way thinking—without ever mentioning it by name—in his 1996 monograph *Between Hope and History: Meeting America's Challenges for the 21st Century*:

> It was clear to me that if my vision of twenty-first century America was to become reality, we had to break out of yesterday's thinking and embark on a new and bold course for the future, with a strategy rooted in three fundamental American values: ensuring that all citizens have the *opportunity* to make the most of their own lives; expecting every citizen to shoulder the *responsibility* to seize that opportunity; and working together as a *community* to live up to all we can be as a nation. (7–8, emphasis in original).

This catchy tripartite slogan of opportunity, responsibility, and community established a rhetorical break with the previous Reagan/Bush administrations and signaled a distinct move away from Reagan's utilitarian individualism (Bellah et al. 1985) toward a modern-day form of *noblesse oblige*(d) inclusion, one that imagined all Americans "tak[ing] more responsibility, not only for ourselves and our families but for our communities and our country" (Clinton 1993, 2).

Pushed to the fore of American politics by the Democratic Leadership Council[1] (DLC)—a 501(c)(3) nonprofit organization dedicated to promoting centrist politics—Third Way political rationality within the United States seeks "a new balance of economic dynamism and social security, a new social compact based on individual rights and responsibilities, and a new model for governing that equips citizens and communities to *solve their own problems*" (DLC Press Release 1998, emphasis added). While scholars have debated for years what exactly Third Way philosophy is, and how it applies to contemporary social democratic societies and global political machinations, its early deployment within the United States under Clinton was not that of a fully realized political philosophy. Rather, as Giddens (2001) suggests, Clinton's Third Way was, first and foremost, developed as a "tactical response" to Democrat losses in the 1980, 1984, and 1988 presidential elections. This line of thinking is reinforced with Clinton's alignment with the DLC, an alignment he tactically used to gain nationwide name recognition for his initial candidacy in 1992. In a sense co-opting the banner of the Democratic Leadership Council—which has in the intervening years shifted to the hard-right periphery of the center-left movement, and is most notably embodied in the current positionality of Connecticut Senator Joseph Lieberman, North Carolina Senator John Edwards, and Indiana Senator Evan Bayh—one might not be too far off in calling Clinton's Third Way vision a remarkably successful marketing device (at least, in the beginning).

Despite the at-times-wandering philosophical mindset of the president, Clinton would in the end prove to hold true to the spirit of Third Way politics; much of the praise heaped on Clinton concerning economic growth and stability has been directly tied to his fiscal conservatism as informed by Third Way thinking. It is important to note here that his vision of the Third Way was not simply that of triangulation—or governing from the center (radical, or otherwise), as espoused most notably by former Clinton advisor (and now current Fox News Channel consultant Dick Morris)—but rather it was deployed as a kind of "modernized social democracy" that acceded to the economic imperatives of the right while maintaining its public commitment to progressive social policy.[2] In other words, as political observer and Clinton chronicler Joe Klein (2002) remarks, the very heart of Clinton's Third Way philosophy could best be described as "liberal ends through conservative means" (35).[3]

Put into tangible action—and specific to the case of urban centers and their attendant conjunctural vectors—the administration's above-mentioned talking points were couched within a (conservative) cultural context of family values, crime, and imagined community. Policies aimed at fiscal discipline, health care reform, investment in education and training, welfare-to-work legislation, urban renewal projects (e.g., Empowerment Zones), and taking a "hard line" (read conservative) on crime and punishment all became part of Clinton's (sociocultural) war of position (cf., Giddens, 1998, 2001). Within this type of neoliberalized Third Way framework, as Mary K. Coffey (2003) explains, community becomes "paradoxically asserted as a natural, pre-political zone yet also as a key terrain for the successful actualization of the goals and aspirations of government" (225). These "aspirations of government," at least in the Clintonian deployment of the Third Way, were grounded in a (corporate-minded centrist) belief, enumerated by Vice President Al Gore (1999), that "everyone has a positive contribution to make, and that all communities can create the climate that calls forth that contribution ... if we give them the tools they need" (2).

Perhaps most public of Clinton's Third Way policy-making initiatives can be seen in his move to positively impact urban and rural communities via socially aimed economic infusions. This is seen most especially through so-called Empowerment Zone initiatives that sprang to life in the early 1990s. An Empowerment Zone is a Clinton administration initiative designed to "revitalize distressed communities by using public funds and tax incentives as catalysts for private investment" (www.umez.org). Distressed communities, it should be noted, was taken as Clinton-speak for *inner city*, a term Clinton advisor George Stephanopoulos cautioned the President from using when publicly discussing Empowerment Zones (cf., Drew 1994, 126).[4] A nationwide initiative from the federal government authored by African-American U.S. Congressman Charles Rangel (D-NY), it is designed specifically to stimulate investments in low-income communities suffering from decentralization, exurbanization, and commercial flight (Bockmeyer 2000). The original program parameters consisted of six urban and three rural areas, as well as an additional sixty urban and thirty rural areas that were designated as "Enterprise Communities" (ECs) and thus subject to smaller packages (approximately $3 million each) of federal incentives (United States Department of Health and Human Services 2004, 107–65, 1). Under the inaugural initiative, each urban Empowerment Zone received $100 million in federal funds stretched over a ten-year period, and was made possible through the Title XX Social Service Block Grant (SSBG) program. Each rural Empowerment Zone received $40 million from this grant. An additional $1 billion was set aside by Housing and Urban Development (HUD) for loan guarantees, Community Development Block Grants (CDBG), and Economic Revitalization Grants (ERG). Further, the U.S. Department of

Treasury allocated $2.5 billion in tax benefits for those business ventures forming in EZs and ECs, presenting the corporate sector with a direct economic impetus for locating new franchises in such areas. The U.S. Department of Agriculture similarly set aside $400 million for rural Empowerment Zones, to be used for waste and water systems, business development, housing, and community facilities.

In the now post-Clinton moment, Empowerment Zones have not simply ceased to exist. In fact, under the Bush administration, the Department of Housing and Urban Development (HUD) added a third category (to go along with Empowerment and Enterprise), that of "Renewal Community." These Renewal Communities were eligible to take advantage of roughly $17 billion in tax incentives. However, unlike Clinton's acknowledged attempt to rebuild communities while at the same time offering a hand to the corporate community, the Bush administration makes clear its business-minded focus. HUD Secretary Mel Martinez stated the administration's goals: "[T]he aim is to help businesses grow in some of our country's most challenging communities. By creating the incentives that will promote job growth and economic development, we are joining with the private sector to restore economic vitality and restore whole communities in the process" (Martinez, quoted in City of Los Angeles 2002, 1).

Moreover, and related to being framed as an example of the Third Way in action, then-U.S. Secretary of Labor Robert Reich (1993) made clear that the Empowerment Zone initiative was not to be understood as "another 'top-down' mandate from Washington," but instead as a program locally designed—yet federally funded—to meet local needs by employing the most promising approaches developed at the grassroots level. He continued, "The Empowerment Zone program will be administered as a partnership among the private and non-profit sectors and the local, State, and Federal governments," the ultimate effectiveness and utility of such programs being to serve "as a model for reinventing government, breaking down bureaucratic barriers, minimizing red tape, and eroding old hostilities (1993, 51). Such thinking falls directly in line with Clinton's Third Way view of public–private engagement: he was always looking for a convergence of ideas between "those who said government was the enemy" and "those who said government was the solution" (Clinton 1998, 2).[5]

Although there are roughly two dozen Empowerment Zones to choose from—ranging from areas of Philadelphia and Los Angeles to Cleveland and Syracuse—we have chosen to focus on the New York Empowerment Zone. A special case, because it initially received $300 million (made possible because the city and state each gave an additional $100 million to the project), the New York zone—known officially as the Upper Manhattan Empowerment Zone (UMEZ)—spans the areas of Harlem (East, West, and Central), Inwood, and Washington Heights. Bordered on the east by the East River, on the west by the Hudson River, on the south by East 96th Street and West 110th Street, and on the north by 222nd Street, the Upper Manhattan Empowerment Zone is actually a subset of Upper Manhattan. Demographically speaking, approximately 521,000 people live in Upper Manhattan, with roughly 160,000 people living directly within the boundaries of the zone. The UMEZ's publicly stated focus is in the areas of entertainment and tourism, retail, health care, and business services. We make this choice to center our project on UMEZ/Harlem intentionally, because UMEZ is lauded not only as the prototypical (and, we may add, most controversial) iteration of current empowerment zones in existence, but also because of its strategic alliance with former National Basketball Association Hall of Famer turned business mogul, Earvin "Magic" Johnson and his corporate partners.

The National Fantasy of HarlemUSA

In the summer of 2000, a glassy, six-story, $65 million, 275,000 square foot retail and entertainment complex designated *HarlemUSA* opened to much fanfare and public acclaim (cf., DeSimone 1999;

see also Clark 2001, for a business-minded analysis). Located within the UMEZ boundary at Frederick Douglass Avenue (a.k.a. 8th Avenue) and 125th Street, the complex houses national retailers, including such widely known large-scale operations as Magic Johnson Movie Theaters, a Disney Store, T.G.I. Friday's Restaurant, HMV Records, Old Navy clothing store, and Chase Manhattan Bank (one of the main financial backers of the project). Since its opening, it has taken the shape of a "lavish, sterile, and conspicuous, ultramodern construct," that, like the multiplicity of new sporting stadia dominating the urban metropolis, embraces "a status-conscious, fastidious service culture" as it greets its privileged customers (Wilcox and Andrews 2003, 7). Made possible in part by an $11.2 million loan from the UMEZ project, it proclaimed the creation of 500 permanent jobs for the residents of the immediate community and marked an initial foray into the public–private reconstitution of the city. These days, business is booming in Harlem, which has become the most popular tourist destination in New York (surpassing both the Statue of Liberty and the Empire State Building) as busloads of European and Asian tourists clamor daily along 125th Street hoping to experience jazz and gospel music, soul food and historic sites like the legendary Apollo (now owned by AOL Time Warner!) Theater (Aidi 2000, n.p.). Drawing its cultural tradition from the legacies of Langston Hughes, Duke Ellington, Louis Armstrong, and Zola Neale Hurston, and from such institutions as the Cotton Club, Connie's Inn, and the Audubon Ballroom (where Malcolm X was assassinated), the century-old "Black capital of the world" is rapidly changing its face as the area itself evolves into a highly multicultural—though, increasingly, economically homogenous—community: Latina/os, Asians, and whites are relocating to Harlem in droves—to the ultimate displacement of poor and working-class African Americans and West African and West Indian immigrants who have been factored out by skyrocketing real estate prices and a lack of real economic possibility. Because of such developments, Harlem has gradually become more appealing to investors who, in the past, had shied away from the economically impoverished urban locality. However, all is not entirely copasetic.

The Changing Face of Harlem

There exists a vast literature as to the place of the (urban) city in the late-modern period of expansive globalizing processes and transnational interconnectedness (cf., Castells 1989; Clark 1996; Sassen 2001; Soja 1989). However, much of this literature tends to focus primarily on the *megacity*, to use Castell's term, and consider it in relation to and as part of larger international networks of entertainment, trade, and commerce. Thus, while we have Sassen's voluminous—and, moreover, enlightening—archive of research on New York City writ large, less has been written on cities that, while not towering Meccas of postindustrial capitalism, remain, in Silk's (2004) words, "engaged in aspirant and at times dramatic efforts of redevelopment" at the local and, even, national level of interaction with globalizing processes. These so-called second- or third-tier cities—or, in our case, enclaves located within larger metropolitan areas that find themselves residing on the margins—are cast in a liminal struggle to maintain their particularity of sub/urban locality while at the same time hoping to trade up, so to speak, to bigger and better redefinitions of imagined national or international importance. Thus, we see many instances of communities such as Memphis, Tennessee, San Diego, California, and Winnipeg, Manitoba, Canada, subsidizing (or attempting to subsidize) sports venues (cf., Andrews and Wilcox 2003; Scherer 2001; Silk 2004) or other retail and entertainment complexes (e.g., the Mall of America outside Minneapolis, Minnesota) in an effort to attract both investment capital and "brand" their city on the global playing field. And, further, we come face-to-face with the impact of these changing conditions on the ground level of such interactions.

Both in the imagined and geographic sense, Harlem exists in just such a liminal space: minutes away from some of the wealthiest census tracts in New York City, its residents are often caught on the inside looking out as the fruits of globalization reveal themselves time and again in Midtown and the

Upper West Side. For example, the neighborhood of East Harlem, home to approximately 110,000 people in 2.2 square miles of land, stands as one of Manhattan's poorest communities with a median income of $12,000 per year (Jackson, Jr. 2002, 8). It also happens to be located only a stone's throw from Wall Street, Madison Avenue, the site of the former World Trade Towers, and numerous other New York City landmarks. However, for as individually impoverished as Harlem's residents may seem (or, in some cases, may be racially stereotyped as being), its overall income density is estimated at $868 million per square mile, which astronomically outdistances cities such as Atlanta (only $56 million) and Cincinnati (only $72.2 million). This is so not because residents are earning at a pace ten times greater than elsewhere, but because, while there exist a highly concentrated number of residents living within such a condensed space, recent tourist and consumer upswings have dramatically altered the economic parameters of Harlem (DeSimone 1999, n.p.). Coupled with the nostalgic "mystique" of the area, the untapped buying power of Harlemites—old, new, and in the touristic sense—is especially appealing to corporations seeking to gain entry into and around the *HarlemUSA* site.

But, we hasten to add, just who is cleaning up on this economic resurgence? While a new influx of business has sprung up over the last several years, both local residents and established local businesses have decried that they are being displaced from their own community by skyrocketing rents made possible by the "renewal" of the urban landscape (Johnson 1998, 1). Brownstones now fetch upwards of $500,000 to $750,000, and some apartments in the neighborhood now regularly go for $3,000 per month (and this imposed on long-time residents used to paying far less than $1,000 per month in rent for comparable space and location) (Shipp 2000, 39).

More importantly, however, is that many longtime residents believe the erasure of small, minority-owned businesses is deliberate, not incidental (Johnson 1998). As *New York Times* columnist Kenneth Johnson (1998) reported in his focus piece on the UMEZ two years prior to the opening of *HarlemUSA*, the historic 125th Street area that has long stood as both an economic and cultural icon for African Americans "is being transformed … into a center of mainstream youth-culture merchandising: music, clothes and entertainment set in a kind of hipper Times Square in which Black culture will be only part of the *marketing* package" (1). Writing on similar developments in Memphis, Tennessee, Michael Silk (2004) theorizes that the "'symbolic commodification of place' is based around the manufacturing and promotion of a positive brand identity for a city … [giving an] enhanced role to those in the culture industries who produce the range of symbolic goods and experiences of 'culture' (holiday resorts, sports stadia, theme parks, department stores, shopping centers) within the contemporary city" (6). Charting this trend over the last five years, the cultural heritage and civic importance of Harlem has thus far been reduced to banal touristic caricatures that see "neighborhood radicalism and protest as entertainment, myth, human-interest story, or a peculiar spectacle to be gazed at by a curious middle class" (Mele 2000, 308). Rewriting Harlem's historical conventions as a simulacrum of imagined community leads us to agree with Sarah Vowell's (2003) appraisal that "there are few creepier moments in cultural tourism than when a site tries to rewrite its past" (2003, 36).

It is worth noting that such a rewriting of the urban communal landscape is, generally speaking, not limited solely to Harlem. As one of us has chronicled elsewhere (see Cole 2001), the Tompkins Square Park area of New York City's East Village has undergone similar changes organized around the systematic displacement of the so-called aesthetically disenchanting, albeit without the necessary large-scale invocation of transnational corporations or government initiatives found in post-1993 Harlem. Mele (2000) artfully reads the affect and effect thus:

The architectural features and interior designs of the East Village's new, high-end commercial and residential spaces produce a contrived sense of urban grittiness and feel of "downtown" without the risks and inconveniences of poverty. The effects are a symbolic gesture toward (but ultimately a rejection of) the surrounding landscape of tenement apartments occupied by poor and low-income families and individuals. (3)

Though speaking of the East Village, Mele's reading can be easily mapped onto Harlem's parallel re/development. The "branding dynamic," to borrow Mele's term, of the new Harlem is, like the new East Village, "embedded in highly marketable, sanitized styles and signs of subversion, antiauthoritarianism, and experimentation that designate it as an 'alternative space'" (Cole 2001, 117). But this alternative designation is a hollow vision: the counterculture experience of 1960s Harlem has been recast as the home to an "urban-themed" Starbucks coffee house affiliated with Magic Johnson and the reconstituted sites of past cultural traditions (e.g., Apollo Theater, Cotton Club, etc.). All things considered, the flashy, corporatist side of Harlem's façadic rebirth could be simulated in Disney/Epcot Center's "Parade of Nations Pavilions," because the difference is that there *is* no difference between the two.

Harlem Renaissance Redux

While on paper the UMEZ has incredible potential in both economic and socially progressive terms, there is a growing majority in Harlem (and elsewhere around the country specific to their own Empowerment Zone) that question just who benefits from such initiatives in Harlem. Says Lloyd William, President and CEO of the Greater Harlem Chamber of Commerce:

> Unfortunately, the major beneficiaries of the zone to date have been some of the large corporations. You have a Pathmark [grocery store] coming here and we need it. But it's the Pathmarks that are benefiting from the tax credits, employees' benefits and loans that are available, as opposed to the small mom-and-pop stores that really need to benefit from these zones. (quoted in Smith, 1997)

From one point of view, this "new kind of capitalism for a new Harlem"—an oft-repeated business slogan used to both justify and reinforce the public–private partnership made possible by Empowerment Zone initiatives—certainly *has* done wonders for established corporate giants such as Gap, Starbucks Coffee, and Barnes and Noble. Drew Greenwald, president of Grid Properties, which codeveloped the *HarlemUSA* complex, openly acknowledges that economic opportunities afforded transnational corporations such as Disney and Starbucks are at the core of Harlem's new (consumptive) renaissance: "Areas like Harlem have been looked over in the past, but now a lot of those companies realize there is a huge market that they're not reaching.... [I]t's easy to look at Harlem and realize that there are economic opportunities here" (quoted in Smith 1997). Against this position, noted author and community activist Mamadou Chinyelu—whose book *Harlem Ain't Nothing but a Third World Country* aggressively critiques the Upper Manhattan Empowerment Zone initiative—argues that projects such as *HarlemUSA* have done nothing but "merely make Harlem a cash cow for the masters of capitalism to milk" (1999). His main contention is that agglomerations such as *HarlemUSA* or "Harlem at the Piers" (an endeavor similar to Navy Pier in Chicago) will surely provide low-paying jobs for Harlem's working poor, but that they will not assist them in establishing businesses of their own or anything else resembling progressive political or economic empowerment (1999). Leon Griffith, owner of the Record Shack on 125th Street, agrees with Chinyelu: "It's corporate take-over. It's all about money.... [I] can't compete with HMV [industry giant in the music retail business]" (Griffith quoted in Aidi 2000). Thus, "due to the overdetermining forces of valorization, commodification, and professionalization" (Wilcox and Andrews 2003, 11) made visible in the public–private partnerships forged via Empowerment Zone legislation, community revitalization has nominally occurred only in a façadic sense, and at the cost of disenfranchising those very individuals whom the Zone was alleged to enfranchise (in both economic and political senses).

Another bone of contention has been directed to mismanagement on the part of UMEZ, as the "not another top-down Washington mandate," has, naturally, turned out to be mired by politics since its inception. In fact, UMEZ recently brought in Johnnie Cochran, Jr., Esq., (yes, *that* Johnnie Cochran!) to be the new chairman and add a public face of credibility to the project. In fact, at the halfway point of the ten-year period (1999), only $26 million of the original $300 million had even been distributed amongst those seeking economic relief (Moore 1999).[6] And that includes the $11.2 million allocated for *HarlemUSA*! Of course, this laxity in distributing funds was not for want of trying: to avoid the mistakes of previous urban renewal projects, as Keith Moore (1999) reports, federal rules stipulated unanimity among major decisions makers which, at the time of his article, amounted to New York City Mayor Rudolph Giuliani (now embattled Mayor Michael Bloomberg), New York Governor George Pataki, and local Democratic congressional representatives and business leaders. These individuals were never in agreement on anything remotely related to politics, let alone the administration of $300 million targeted toward urban regeneration.[7]

It is clear to us, however, that Empowerment Zones—and their attendant political rhetoric—are not simply about economic (re)generation, nor are they solely about the disproportionate dispersal of monetary funds vis-à-vis local entrepreneurs and transnational corporations under the guise of competition and up-market facilitation: the discursive formulation and active promotion of Empowerment Zones and the blithely propagated fiction that they serve the (local) community, and not simply the corporate sector, is fundamentally about the governing of desire and national subjectivity, the creation of national collectivity organized around "abstract universality and embodied particularity" (Berlant 1999). As an emblematic site of cultural production residing in the national symbolic, *HarlemUSA* and its attendant armatures both produce and are reproduced by national fantasy, by which we mean the nation's ever-evolving imagined origins, organization, and character. Leading the way in turning Harlem inside out and reducing it to a sort of Times Square lite in which neoliberal subjectivity is the order of the day? Earvin "Magic" Johnson.

Magic Johnson, CEO

Since his retirement from the NBA, Magic Johnson, much maligned during his playing days for not being active in giving back to the community, has gone on to amass a corporate empire of movie theaters, restaurants, and banks estimated at a value of over $500 million. As Larry Platt has written of Johnson:

> Though Michael Jordan is celebrated for his boardroom moves, he accumulated his wealth mostly by selling his name. [Magic] Johnson, by contrast, is an entrepreneur with Rockefeller-like ambitions who says he wants to do things no black man has ever done. He is becoming a post-Civil Rights Era role model for hip-hop jocks who reject the Jordan example and see Johnson as the walking embodiment of Malcolm X's dream—he is a black-run, inner-city business unto himself. (Platt 2002)

Morever, he has taken the bulk of his business ventures, such as Starbucks Coffee and T.G.I. Friday's, where they had never been before—the "inner city." Declaring himself as a product of the "inner city," Johnson proclaims that his knowledge of "what my people want" (i.e., what urban African Americans want) has been instrumental to the growth and success of his corporate empire. Yet, at the same time, we do not see the same growth and support of longtime local businesses in Harlem, many of which have been unable to garner UMEZ grants of any value. Unlike Tommie Smith, John Carlos, and Harry Edwards who, "rather than celebrating the suggestion that sports were at the forefront of racial advance ... increasingly came to assert that sports were tied to a racist, oppressive system" (Thomas 2004), Johnson trades on his sporting celebrity and remains firmly ensconced in a depoliticized narrative of so-called urban renewal: reinforced by his numerous product endorsements and slick corporate affiliations, Johnson's mediated persona reaches far into the Heartland of America and comes with it an always (al)ready attachment to a set of core national values and beliefs—he is the "safe" spokesman for the regeneration of the so-called urban jungle.

Yet, this narrative is inherently political, and goes straight to the conceptualization of (good) citizenship in the new millennia. While economic re/generation has become the *public* face of Empowerment Zone initiatives, it is interesting to note that in the official Empowerment Zone handbook authored by the President's Community Enterprise Board (1993) entitled *Building Communities Together: Guidebook for Community-Based Strategic Planning for Empowerment Zones and Enterprise Communities*, attention is overwhelmingly paid to issues of crime and criminality. For example, a letter from then United States Attorney General Janet Reno, included as part of this handbook, locates a "tough on crime" position as fundamentally *necessary* for a locality to receive any consideration for funding:

> If this program is to stabilize and reinvigorate neighborhoods, residents must be free from the fear of crime and violence. Job creation, improved housing, and enhanced service delivery are crucial in most potential empowerment zones and enterprise communities, but a commitment to the reduction of crime and violence through coordinated law enforcement is necessary to community stability, the delivery of health education, and other social services and economic development.... Unchecked violence, gun and drug trafficking, drug use, and other serious felonies will stifle investment, development and community building emphasis of the initiative. (1993, 45–46)

Upon closer inspection, however, such (de)moralizing jingoism is eerily reminiscent of something former President Ronald Reagan said in 1982:

> We must make America safe again, especially for women and elderly who face so many moments of fear.... Study after study shows that most serious crimes are the work of a relatively small group of hardened criminals. Let me give you an example—subway crime in New York City. Transit police there estimate that only 500 habitual criminal offenders are responsible for nearly half of the crimes in New York's subways last year.... It's time to get these hardened criminals off the street and into jail.... We can and must make improvements in the way our courts deal with crime.... These include revising the bail system so that dangerous offenders, and especially big-time drug pushers, can be kept off our streets. (*Public Papers of the Presidents of the United States 1982*, 1983, 2)

Though writing in response to Reagan's quote, David L. Andrews's (1993) words remain applicable to the Reno memo: "Without ever referring to race or ethnicity, it is manifest that the threat to American society [s]he vocalized was a black male inhabitant of America's anarchic urban jungles" (114–15). Framed in terms of community self-policing and "public safety innovations" (i.e., boot camps and diversionary programs for youth), the early Empowerment Zone blueprints were politically prepositioned so as to deflect any (neoconservative) calls that the administration (and the initiative itself) was in any way "soft on crime" (a deft sleight-of-hand by Clinton, to say the least). National security was thus mobilized around economic stability and corporate investment: incarcerating or evicting young black (and Latino) men became the naturalized, and accepted, outcome of "cleaning up" the inner city and paving the way for corporate expansion (a fate suffered by Harlem's street vendors and operators at Mart 125).[8]

Not surprisingly, and in keeping with the spirit of Janet Reno's memo, Johnson (and his corporate partners) perpetuates similar surveillance-under-the-guise-of-community-action-and-awareness practices. Such practices, in fact, reveal themselves as sine qua non for the opening and continued maintenance of many of his public retailer/foodworks endeavors. In all of the ventures—but specifically the movie theater operations—a code-of-conduct has been implemented that requires among other things: that patrons must be "appropriately" dressed in a manner reflecting that of an "upstanding citizen," and must not wear "gang colors," use beepers or cell phones, or be "disruptive" toward any other patrons. However, while Johnson does stipulate that anyone can come into his theater to take advantage of the concession stands, video game arcade, and meeting areas without purchasing a ticket to see a film, they must do so by following his "simple" rules appertaining to "proper" behavior for "good" citizens.

At the most basic of levels, Johnson and his corporate partners—titans in the business world—are re/producing highly stylized (and stereotypical) elements of the "inner city" for white middle-class consumers aching to experience a slice of the "urban" environment: his movie theater chain specializes in concession operations featuring chicken wings, buffalo shrimp, and Kool-Aid; his Starbucks outlets feature sweet potato pie; posters of Stevie Wonder, Ray Charles, and Louis Armstrong adorn the walls of his restaurant affiliations. At the same time, long-time Harlem residents are increasingly afforded fewer and fewer options: mom-and-pop businesses are closing, residents are being forced out to the fringes, and getting funding via the UMEZ is next to impossible unless you are from a brand-name conglomerate. Those who choose to stay are thus faced with the choice of acquiescing to the changing conditions of this new Harlem or, as has been the case of late, becoming evermore politically active in a attempt to take back their community.

Coda

In part, as Cameron McCarthy (2002) has alluded to with respect to our present conjuncture, technologies of truth and identification are increasingly deployed (for instance, in the "New Harlem") to "transform concrete individuals into mass cultural citizens whose lines of loyalty and affiliation now exceed the territory and social geography of the nation-state" as they become aligned with global corporations such as Disney, Starbucks, and AOL Time Warner (5–6). This national fantasy from the present works at representing a posthistorical future, one in which all subjects are free to imagine themselves outside their collective predicament, becoming a part of the national landscape. In fact, becoming visible as consumptive (and, now, may we add, patriotic) citizens is generatively organized around transnational lines of allegiance made national through an outlook of Harlem becoming a global site of touristic importance and a national site of consumerist desire and upward mobility. Spaces of consumption and its relation to citizenship (Miller 1998) in an age of multiplicity, hybridity, and difference have thus turned on cultural representations germane to a given (global) locality. The new Harlemitic consumer is thus imagined as the new *citizen* whose "aesthetics of existence are now ever more deeply imbricated in a universalization of the entrepreneurial spirit and the propagation of the redemptive neoliberal value of choice" (McCarthy 2002). From the start, however, such subjects are always already conceived of as having unfettered access to the (fictional) American Dream, and are correlatively imbricated in the formative mechanisms of such a discursive iteration.

But the center does not hold. Lauren Berlant (1997) articulates: the "promise" of this dream is continually "voiced in the language of *unconflicted* personhood" (4). Those without access (i.e., the "undesirable" now-ever-more-likely former residents of Harlem) have been factored out of the equation in both the literal and figural sense: Harlem, Black capital of the world and site of cultural memory for the Civil Rights movement, has become playground to the rich as they renarrate Harlem with a commodified history-book account filled with soundbite fictions of "Black" culture and correspondingly de/politicized commentary on the current state of American race relations. Magic Johnson, basketball legend and popularly conceived newfound hero to "the Black community," plays right along as he dishes his trademark no-look passes containing not basketballs but cheap rhetoric. And, so, the government-sanctioned pillaging of the American urban center continues unabated, this time under the guise of expanding Disney stores, Starbucks, and Gaps to a new consumer demographics (where, oh by the way, a few jobs may come out of it, if you're lucky). What, oh what, will it be next time?

Notes

1. Founded in part by Al From, the DLC is also associated with the Progressive Policy Institute (PPI), a centrist Washington think tank. In the 2003 run-up to the 2004 U.S. Presidential election, the DLC moved even further to the right of the center-left, and backed primary candidates such as Joseph Lieberman (D-CT) and John Edwards (D-NC) over perceived liberal candidates such as Howard Dean (D-VT) and John F. Kerry (D-MA). Following John Kerry's electoral loss to George W. Bush, the DLC suggested once again that moving the party to the Right—instead of energizing its base—was the key to victory (see From and Reed, December 8, 2004, p. 1).
2. For an economic-minded analysis of the Clintonian Third Way, see Meeropol (1998).
3. Correspondingly, the Blairist version of the Third Way would refer to such a strategy as "permanent revisionism … in the service of egalitarian values (and) of a fair distribution of the benefits of progress" (Rentoul 2001, 435).
4. It should also be noted that "Empowerment Zones" are not "Enterprise Zones," which was the previous Bush (George Herbert) administration's similar proposal. Clinton's version consisted of a community service requirement.
5. So much so, in fact, that it made it into his historic 1998 State of the Union Address: "My fellow Americans, we have found a Third Way. We have the smallest government in thirty-five years, but a more progressive one. We have a smaller government, but a stronger nation."
6. Another $35 million was spent as Moore's 1999 article was going to press.
7. Certainly, such revelations are not confined solely to the UMEZ project. Silk (2004), for example, reports that the Memphis, Tennessee, Empowerment Zone has revealed similar roadblocks and problems in which a shift of power from democratic local governing regimes to semiautonomous public/private authorities has "fragmented urban politics into a constellation of public/private institutions that operate largely independently from democracy and with little public accountability … can be seen as part of a 'revanchist' urban vernacular that suspends commitment to extend social justice to the whole of society, compelling the poor and disposed to be tightly disciplined through a range of legal and architectural methods" (Silk 2004, 10).
8. Yet, while some local residents took umbrage with the enforcement of Empowerment Zone strictures, Clinton's favorable ratings among African Americans soared. As Horne (1994) acknowledges, despite (or, perhaps, in spite of) Clinton's overwhelming support from the Black community, the president was always "willing to make certain gestures toward fulfilling the demands of minorities" while, at the same time, "willing to take swipes at African Americans and others to demonstrate his mainstream credentials" (184). Aside from his blundering foray into welfare reform, most notable among these instances was his much publicized tête-à-tête with New York City community activist and rapper Sister Souljah, in which the president lambasted her for her statement that "if black people kill black people every day, why not have a week and kill white people?" Clinton's remarks were part of a calculated strategy (his speech was written by top aide de camp Paul Begala) to appease white centrist Democrats who, during the 1992 presidential campaign, had suggested that he was swaying too far to the left of center in an effort to reach the so-called Jesse Jackson constituency. Through it all, Clinton maintained a high favorability rating when it came to dealing with race.

References

Aidi, H. "A 'Second Renaissance' in Harlem?" *Africana: Gateway to the Black World*. http://www.africana.com/DailyArticles/index_20001218.htm (December 18, 2000).

Andrews, D. L. Deconstructing Michael Jordan: Popular culture, politics, and postmodern America. PhD dissertation. University of Illinois, Urbana-Champaign, 1993.

Andrews, D. L. and M. Silk. "Beyond a Boundary: Sport, Transnational Advertising, and the Reimagining of National Culture." *Journal of Sport and Social Issues* 25 (2001): 180–201.

Bellah, R. N., R. Madsen, W. M. Sullivan, A. Swidler, and S. M. Tipton. *Habits of the Heart: Individualism and Commitment in American Life*. Berkeley: University of California Press, 1985.

Berlant, L. *The Anatomy of National Fantasy*. Chicago: University of Chicago Press, 1991.

Berlant, L. *The Queen of America Goes to Washington City*. Durham, NC: Duke University Press, 1997.

Bockmeyer, J. "A Culture of Distrust: The Impact of Local Political Culture on Participation in the Detroit EZ." *Urban Studies* 37 (2000): 2417–40.

Callinocos, A. *Against the Third Way: An Anti-Capitalist Critique*. Cambridge, UK: Polity Press, 2001.

Castells, M. *The Informational City: Information Technology, Economic Restructuring, and the Urban-Regional Process*. Oxford: Blackwell, 1989.

Chinyelu, M. *Harlem Ain't Nothin' but a Third World Country: The Global Economy, Empowerment Zones, and the Colonial Status of Africans in America*. New York: Mustard Seed Press, 1999.

City of Los Angeles. "Mayor Hahn, HUD Secretary Martinez Announce Renewal of Community Designation in Los Angeles. http://www.lacity.org/mayor/oldpress/ry3.pdf (January 23, 2002).

Clark, D. *Urban World/Global City*. London: Routledge, 1996.

Clark, S. "Mall of America." *Business and Management Practices* 3 (2001): 78.

Clinton, W. J. "Inaugural Address January 20, 1993." In *Public Papers of the Presidents*, book 1. Washington, DC: Government Printing Office, 1994, 3.

Clinton, W. J. *Between Hope and History: Meeting America's Challenges for the 21st Century*. New York: Random House, 1996.

Clinton, W. J. "Remarks by the President on Social Security." White House Press Office Online: http://www.whitehouse.gov (February 9, 1998).

Coffey, M. K. "From Nation to Community." In *Foucault, Cultural Studies, and Governmentality*, edited by J. Z. Bratich, J. Packer, and C. McCarthy, 207–42. Albany, NY: State University of New York Press, 2003.

Cole, CL "American Jordan: P.L.A.Y., Consensus, and Punishment." *Sociology of Sport Journal* 13 (1996): 366–97.

Cole, CL "Nike Goes to Broadway." *Journal of Sport and Social Issues* 25 (2001): 115–17.

Cole, CL and A. Hribar. "Celebrity Feminism—Nike-Style: Post-Fordism, Transcendence, and Consumer Power." *Sociology of Sport Journal* 12 (1995): 347–69.

Democracy Now. Radio program. http://www.democracynow.org/streampage.pl?issue=20010508 (May 8, 2001).

Democratic Leadership Council. "About the Third Way." http://www.ndol.org/ndol_ci.cfm?kaid=128&subid=187&contentid=895 (June 1, 2001).

DeSimone, E. "HarlemUSA Proves Neighborhood Is Seeing the Light." *Shopping Center World*, http://shoppingcenterworld.com/ar/retail_harlem_usa_proves/ (November 1, 1999).

Drew, E. *On the Edge: The Clinton Presidency*. New York: Simon and Schuster, 1994.

From, A. and B. Reed, B. "The Road Back: If Democrats Want to Be a Majority Party Again, They Need to Win Back the Middle Class. http://www.ndol.org/ndol_ci.cfm?kaid=127&subid=173&contentid=253054 (December 8, 2004).

Gore, A. "A Message from the Vice President of the United States." In *Building Communities, Together: Guidebook for Community-Based Strategic Planning for Empowerment Zones and Enterprise Communities*. Washington, DC: U.S. Government Printing Office, 1993.

Giardina, M. D. and C. McCarthy. The Popular Racial Order of 'Urban' America: Sport, Cinema, and the Politics of Culture." *Cultural Studies/Critical Methodologies*. Forthcoming.

Giddens, A. *The Third Way: The Renewal of Social Democracy*. London: Polity Press, 1998.

Giddens, A. *The Third Way and Its Critics*. London: Polity Press, 2000.

Giddens, A. *The Global Third Way Debate*. London: Polity Press, 2001.

Giddens, A. *What Now for New Labour?* London: Polity Press, 2002.

Horne, G. "Race: Ensuring a True Multiculturalism. In *State of the Union 1994: The Clinton Administration and the Nation in Profile*, edited by R. Caplan and J. Feffer. Bouldor, CO: Westview Press, 1994.

Jackson, Jr., J. L. *HarlemWorld: Doing Race and Class in Contemporary Black America*. Chicago: University of Chicago Press, 2001.

Johnson, K. "Uneasy Renaissance on Harlem's Street of Dreams." *The New York Times*, March 1, 1998.

Klein, J. *The Natural: The Misunderstood Presidency of Bill Clinton*. New York: Doubleday, 2001.

McCarthy, C. "Understanding the Work of Aesthetics in Modern Life: Thinking about the Cultural Studies of Education in a Time of Recession." Unpublished manuscript. Institute of Communications Research, University of Illinois, 2002.

McCarthy, C. "Afterword: Understanding the Work of Aesthetics in Modern Life." *Cultural Studies↔Critical Methodologies*, 3 (2003): 96–102

Meerpol, M. *Surrender: How the Clinton Administration Completed the Reagan Revolution*. Ann Arbor: University of Michigan Press, 1998.

Mele, C. *Selling the Lower East Side: Culture, Real Estate, and Resistance in New York City*. New York: New York University Press, 2000.

Miller, T. *Technologies of Truth: Cultural Citizenship and the Popular Media*. Minneapolis: University of Minnesota Press, 1998.

Moore, K. "From Red-Line to Renaissance: Things Are Looking Up in Harlem, but Some Poor Black Families Are Being Driven Out by the Neighborhood Renewal." *Salon.com*. http://www.archive.salon.com/news/feature/1999/0802/harlem (August 2, 1999).

Platt, L. *New Jack Jocks: Rebels, Race, and the American Athlete*. Philadelphia: Temple University Press, 2002.

President's Community Enterprise Board. *Building Communities, Together: Guidebook for Community-Based Strategic Planning for Empowerment Zones and Enterprise Communities*. Washington, DC: U.S. Government Printing Office, 1993.

Reagan, Ronald. *Public Papers of the Presidents of the United States: Ronald Reagan, 1982*, Washington, DC: U.S. Government Printing Office, 1983.

Reich, R. "A Message from Secretary of Labor Robert Reich." In *Building Communities, Together: Guidebook for Community-Based Strategic Planning for Empowerment Zones and Enterprise Communities*. Washington, DC: U.S. Government Printing Office, 1993.

Rentoul, J. *Tony Blair: Prime Minister*. London: Little, Brown and Company, 2001.

Sassen, S. *The Global City: New York, London, Tokyo*. 2nd ed. Princeton, NJ: Princeton University Press, 2001.

Scherer, J. "Globalization and the Construction of Local Particularities: A Case Study of the Winnipeg Jets." *Sociology of Sport Journal* 18 (2001): 205–30.

Shipp, E. R. "Sad Underside to Harlem Boom." *New York Daily News*, October 31, 2000.

Silk, M. "A Tale of Two Cities: Spaces of Consumption and the Façade of Cultural Development." Unpublished manuscript. Memphis, TN: The University of Memphis, 2004.

Smith, E. L. "Harlem Renaissance—Take Two." *Black Enterprise*, February 1997.

Soja, E. *Postmodern Geographies*. London: Routledge, 1989.

Thomas, D. "The Cold War Roots of the Mexico City Olympic Protest." Paper presented at the 5th International Biannual Crossroads in Cultural Studies Conference. Urbana: University of Illinois, Urbana-Champaign, 2004.

United States Department of Health and Human Services. "Empowerment Zones and Enterprise Communities Programs." http://www.2.acf.hhs.gov/programs/ocs/ez-ec/info.htm (2004).

United States Department of Housing and Urban Development. "Bush Administration Announces Renewal Community Initiative. www.hud.gov/news/release.cfm?content=pr02-013.cfm (2002).

Vowell, S. *The Partly Cloudy Patriot*. New York: Simon and Schuster, 2003.

Wilcox, R. C. and D. L. Andrews. "Sport in the City: Cultural, Economic, and Political Portraits." In *Sporting Dystopias: The Making and Meanings of Urban Sport Cultures*. Albany, NY: SUNY Press, 2003.

Woodward, B. *The Agenda*. New York: Simon and Schuster, 1994.

26

Crime Stories

A Critical Look through Race, Ethnicity, and Gender

MICHELLE FINE AND LOIS WEIS

Q: If Bill Clinton were to come to Jersey City/Buffalo to hold a town meeting, what problems
would you want him to pay attention to?

A: Crime and drugs, violence in the streets. The drug problem is out of hand.

In our recent interviews with 154 poor and working-class young adults, male and female, across racial
and ethnic groups (see Fine & Weis, 1998) in both Jersey City and Buffalo, we have wandered through
communities that have been ravaged by deindustrialization and a withering of the public sphere. Over
the past two decades, Buffalo, in particular, has lost a substantial portion of its blue-collar labor market, while Jersey City has watched its public safety net shrivel. Both cities, like cities all over the United
States, have suffered a withdrawal of private and public dollars, and each epitomizes one loss most
dramatically. Within this pattern of diminished economic and public resources sit young women and
men coming of age. Making families, shaping identities (both self and others), raising babies, searching for better, longing for a world of safety, prosperity, and comfort, they offer up analyses to explain
their own and others' economic and social defeat. And they are describing lives steeped in violence. It
is their explanations and narratives of this violence that our analysis draws upon.

With the support of the Spencer Foundation, we have collected life histories from Latino,
African-American, and White young adults, ages 23–35, as they narrate their educational, familial,
and economic biographies and they project and enact their parental involvements within their
communities, churches, and children's schools. Specifically, we have interviewed 154 individuals for
2–5 hours, across racial and ethnic groups (men and women) in Buffalo and Jersey City and have
conducted focus-group interviews with specified populations in each city in order to probe further
their perspectives and practices, unearthing, at once, their despair about and their envisioned
opportunities for individual, community, and social change. Group interviews have been held with
African-American mothers who struggle hard to raise the next generation in the midst of urban
poverty; Latina mothers who are probing the meaning of workfare programs in Jersey City;
African-American men who see the church as a way of envisioning both self and community differently from what they see as the dominant society's definition; White women who, although caught
in patriarchal working-class communities, both push and accept the limitations of their female

bodies and selves; and White men who patrol the borders of White masculinity, desirous of keeping others out of what they see as their rightful position.

We have assembled a rich array of interview material that enables us to narrate the experiences of the poor and working class during the 1980s and 1990s as well as press carefully into the policy realm given what we are finding. We have met with and are interviewing a broad range of policy makers in both cities in order to explore fully the situated nature of our findings as well as to impact broader social policy. We have testified and written "Op Ed" pieces on local and state policies as they affect constituents, e.g., on vouchers and school takeover in Jersey City and on welfare reform, and intend to do more (Weis & Fine, Spencer Grant Proposal, 1993 & 1996). However, as policies are written today for the poor and working class, we have yet to hear from them. Our goal, then, was to unearth the "voices" of people usually not heard and to excavate these voices across a range of life's activities.

We drew from a sample of young adults who have basically followed the social rules (attended school, sometimes beyond high school), focusing on people who were connected to "meaningful urban communities." We sampled from "communities," defined not by geographic location alone (given what Wilson, 1978, and Fine & Cook, 1991, have found about the lack of connection and trust in low-income urban communities), but by meaningful social connections. Our goal was to generate a broad analysis of the "coming of age in urban America" during the 1980s and 1990s. We focused, in both cities, on four sets of urban institutions:

1. schools and post-secondary institutions;
2. churches and spiritual sites;
3. social agencies and self-help groups;
4. community centers and activist organizations.

All individuals whom we interviewed were involved in at least one of these institutions. So, for example, White, African-American, and Latino men and women were drawn as equally as possible across the four sectors in each city. Schools refer to either their children's school or, in some cases, to their own. Churches that serve the poor and working class tend to be Catholic in urban northeastern White communities and Baptist and/or Holiness churches in the Black communities. Latinos/Latinas were drawn from both Catholic churches and Pentecostal churches. Social agencies refer to those agencies that actively seek (and receive funding) to train and place those who attend their programs in literacy, job training, public assistance, or domestic violence shelters. Community centers can at times double as social agencies, but also serve as spaces in which communities are drawn together, for example, a well-known community arts center located in the fruit belt in Buffalo, parental groups, a lesbian/gay center, and theater projects.

In spite of our desires, it was not possible to come up with exactly equivalent numbers in each category. White men, for example, are less well represented in social agencies (because they tend to attend in fewer numbers) than those in the other groups, and Latinos are disproportionately represented in community centers, owing to the prominence of particular community centers in the communities in which we worked. All in all, 154 Black, White, and Latino/Latina men and women were interviewed across the two cities.

In this piece we draw on those narrative data concerning crime and violence, and in so doing we bring together the literatures on critical race theory and the literatures on *crime* and *poverty*, which have spawned a number of important policy and theoretical conversations about causes and also consequences, particularly in communities of highly concentrated poverty. The brilliance of this literature noted, it is important to understand that from our data we can see that even experiences as seemingly clear cut as *crime* and *fear* are deeply classed, raced, ethnicized, and gendered. In the wake of the O. J. Simpson verdict, and the racially polarized responses to that verdict, it is no longer surprising to recognize that Americans' views on cops, crime, and violence differ dramatically by social position. If, indeed, this decision revealed a deep fissure in gendered and racialized points of view, then we as Americans need to recognize how profound are our differences. We can no longer assume consensus on social issues as charged as this one. With this essay, we hope to pry open a broad and inclusive conversation about violence in need of public shaping.

Crime, Violence and Poverty

The literature on crime and poverty, as reviewed by Fagan et al. (1993) and by Currie (1993), is relatively straightforward. Fagan and colleagues, in a rigorous review of available literature and a deep ethnographic look at eight urban communities across the United States, conclude that communities of concentrated poverty are today marked by what they call a "break in the intergenerational linkages that in the past helped each generation find their way to stable employment and immersion in conventional life roles" (p. 4). To paraphrase sociologist Elijah Anderson in his book *Streetwise* (1990), the "old heads" are gone or no longer respected. When jobs and factories vacated urban America, unions disappeared in the urban Northeast, and the predominantly White tradition of passing jobs and connections from generation to generation was threatened.

The consequences of this economic, community-based bankruptcy are multiple (Currie, 1993). Fagan et al. (1993) contend that this loss of social capital produces diminished economic expectations and social models for poor and working-class youth. In addition, the proliferation of the informal economy enables both gangs and immigrants to secure an (insecure) place in the economic structure, while squeezing out nongang members and native-born Americans from access to an adequate and legitimate income. With the withdrawal from urban America of primary or even secondary labor opportunities has come the well-established "institutionalization of drug markets" (Bourgois, 1995). Associated with the flight of capital and the rise of drugs is the loss of "social services, health care services, supermarkets and essential local services" (p. 7). This economic shift, in turn, breeds radical and devastating social transformations. Fagan et al. write:

> When drug trafficking moved from a low level indoor activity to an active street scene, violence moved outdoors with it and drove traffic from the street. In turn, legitimate informal economic activity was displaced by drug dealing. The mix of people on the street changed to sellers and their customers, and predictably violent street interactions followed. This issue (of services) is tied up with the larger ecology of street life, both social and economic, for it determines the nature of routine activities, routine interactions and the composition of street populations. (p. 7)

What Fagan et al. report, we too have documented in our own community-based interviews. As Bourgois (1995) notes, it is not, of course, that all inner-city residents are drug dealers, but that drug dealers now, in fact, control public space, thus exerting control over inner-city life far in excess of what their numbers would predict.

This literature on urban crime and violence is, by now, quite extensive. Ethnographic analyses, such as the studies of Jay MacLeod (1987) and Mercer Sullivan (1989), document powerfully the ways in which violence pierces the lives of urban young adults, with their participation ranging from perpetrators and witnesses to victims. Sullivan (1995), like Philip Bourgois, MacLeod, and other students of urban male crime, argues that violence may constitute a form of "socialization" for youth into systematic economic crime. Navigated in fights over territory and status, this socialization into violence has escalated today with the possession of knives and guns, particularly by younger and younger urban youth. In bold language Bourgois describes this scene simply as a "culture of terror, violence, intimidation, and performance on the streets" (p. 8).

Moving into the economics of crime, Sullivan invites readers to reconceptualize urban crime because:

> ...much of the economic life of the inner cities has been cut off from the labor market.... Unable to survive on the basis of the labor market, [inner city residents] rely on reciprocal sharing and redistribution for survival. Welfare and crime are both forms of redistribution that provide for the survival of inner city residents but also exacerbate their isolation from the mainstream of society and ultimately reproduce inequality. (p. 234)

While urban ethnographers of male youth culture document alarming rates of violence provoked, received, and/or witnessed in communities of poverty (see also Hsieh & Pugh, 1993), there is a parallel and growing scholarship on the severe consequences of urban violence on children and youths living amid the bullets, flying glass, the drive-bys, and the fears of same. Schwab-Stone et al. (1995) have documented high levels of violence exposure and feelings of being unsafe among 2248 urban youth in the Northeast: 40% of these youngsters witnessed a shooting or stabbing within the past year, and 74% reported feeling "unsafe" within a personal environmental setting. These researchers argue, then, that violence exposure bears serious consequence for psychological well-being, so much so that urban youth development theory should *assume* youth's sense of chronic threat and lack of safety in designing interventions for urban adolescent well-being.

The psychological consequences of violence documented by Schwab-Stone et al. have been confirmed neurologically in a disturbing study conducted by Margaret Wright Berton and Sally Stabb (Berton & Stab, 1996). With a particular interest in the symptomology characteristic of post-traumatic stress disorders (PTSD), Berton and Stabb found *high* rates of symptomology across this sample of urban youth. Indeed, the most precise predictor of PTSD was self-reported exposure to domestic or community violence. (This study is, by the way, one of the few to include domestic as well as community violence in the analysis.)

Not only does the exposure to violence in urban communities breed troubling attitudes and psychological difficulties, but a study by Attar, Guerra, and Tolan (1994) indicates that first through fourth graders exposed to high levels of "stressful life events," including violence, are also more likely to *display* high levels of aggression themselves and incrementally more within a year after the first measure. These authors conclude that "total number of stressful events and exposure to violence significantly interacted with neighborhood disadvantage, such that effects were only apparent under conditions of high neighborhood disadvantage" (p. 399). In this context, it is sobering to learn of a study of inner-city v. middle- and upper-class 12–24-year-olds' *exposure* to violence. Gladstein, Rusonis, and Heald (1992) report that inner-city youth were more often "victims, knew of victims, and witnessed more assaults, rapes, knifings, life threatening events and murders than their [middle-/upper middle-class comparison] group" (p. 277). Living in poverty, with exposure to violence, more often than not breeds violence (see also DuHart, Candenhead, Pendergrast, & Slavens, 1994).

Thus, we can see from both the ethnographic and the quantitative reviews that urban poverty bodes poorly for adolescents and children in terms of their exposure to, engagement with, and victimization by violence. In such communities, with neither economic opportunities nor social intervention, the likelihood is that exposure to violence will incite only more violence. While this story is by now at once riveting and predictable, it is also so markedly *gendered* that we find ourselves needing to turn, at this point, to the question of girls and women. We ask why the literature on urban crime and violence has been tucked away, so discretely but so precisely, severed from the research on domestic violence? Where do *me* look for crime and violence? Where are the women's and girl's stories? Whose lives matter in this realm of social research and social policy on violence?

Turning to Working-Class and Poor Girls and Women: Domestic Violence

For the women who have been physically abused in the home by the men with whom they live, the past two decades have seen both radical change and no change at all.... In many countries it is now well known that violence in the home is commonplace, that women are its usual victims and men its usual perpetrators.[1] It is also known that the family is filled with many different forms of violence and oppression, including physical, sexual and emotional, and that violence is perpetrated on young and old alike. It is the battered-women's movement, with the support of the media, who have put issues of the physical and sexual abuse of women and girls firmly on the social agenda. The now familiar stories of personal pain and degradation fill out the statistics with human dimension and make the social facts comprehensible. For some, familiarity with accounts of violence breeds indifference and inaction; for others they bring indignation and a call for action. (Dobash & Dobash, 1992, p. 266–267)

Quite separated from analyses of urban crime and violence, the literature on male violence against women spans a number of areas, ranging from discussion of the battered women's shelter movement (Shechter, 1982); to manuals on how to escape violent situations (Nicarthy, 1989; White, 1985); legal issues surrounding such violence (Fineman & Mykitiuk, 1994); and empirical and theoretical explorations involving what domestic violence is, what causes it, and to what it is related (Dobash, 1979; Hanmer & Maynard, 1987; Hoff, 1990; Jones, 1994; Roy, 1977; Steinmetz & Strauss, 1974; Walker, 1984). Within the latter category, discussions range from stressors that are linked to domestic violence, such as alcohol abuse and satisfaction with one's life situation and partner, to the extent to which such violence is linked to social class. While it is widely argued that violence in the home appears across social classes, it is now generally acknowledged that there is more such violence among poor and working-class families. In addition, while alcohol abuse is linked to violence, the removal of alcohol does not necessarily guarantee that violence will end (Downs, Miller, & Panek, 1993).

Rare in the literature are portraits of male violence against women drawn from *within* communities—within racial, ethnic, and social class communities. Specifically, we do not have much domestic violence research that locates White, Black, Latina, Native, Asian women at the intersectionality of their own class, race, and gender locations. Slowly, however, this silence is being broken, as for example, when Opal Palmer Adisa (1997) writes in *Undeclared War: African-American Women Writers Explicating Rape*:

For African-American women, rape continues as an ever present threat to their particular bodies. It is as June Jordan says, "the meaning of her identity." To be an African-American woman in this society means to be subject to rape. As such, rape is not a trope in the works of African-American women writers and poets; it is a lived experience that has left many scars, and is still the source of much suffering. (p. 208)

While we refuse essentialisms of race and gender, and must recognize enormous individual variation within group, we also need to emphasize that the intersectionalities of race, gender, and class lead to important questions and generalizations, on the ground and in policy, about life in communities. There is, furthermore, very little literature that explicitly explores the relationship between gendered violence, social class, and race (White, 1985; Marsh, 1993; Coley & Beckett, 1988). Indeed, our data, as you will see, have forced us into this discussion. We anticipated neither the prevalence nor the power of child sexual abuse and domestic violence in the women's lives. And we certainly did not anticipate the power the data would have over us.

One study that does attend closely to dynamics of class and race, within gender, was conducted by Kurz (1995), who randomly sampled divorced women from Philadelphia ($N = 129$) and found that *across classes and races* a full 70% of these 129 women had experienced violence at the hands of their husbands at least once. What started out as a study of divorce quickly and dramatically evolved into a study of domestic violence. Within her sample, Kurz also identified a set of characteristics that some families were involved with that included violence, alcohol abuse, drug abuse, and husbands' absence from homes. Kurz found these characteristics to be disproportionately reflective of life inside poor and working-class White homes. Concerned about the effects that, in particular, alcohol and drugs had on themselves and their children, many of these women left their partners.

As this growing literature indicates, even more profoundly, women living with violence have few options. Leaving a violent home is *no* guarantee that the violence will stop. In fact there is evidence of escalation after a woman leaves an abusive home. As Cecilia Castelano (1996) writes:

> A woman who leaves a violent partner is left with few, if any, necessary resources, and finds herself fearfully navigating a world in which the presence of the batterer and his violent and controlling behaviors are often shocking and deliberately far reaching, spatially across State borders and temporally several years after separation. The violence after separation escalates and sometimes becomes lethal. (p. 20)

In 1988, the National Crime Survey Data disaggregated their sample by marital status and found separated women to be the group most vulnerable to domestic violence, followed by divorced women and then married women. "Whereas only 15.6% of all assaults among married women are domestic, fully 55% of assaults among separated women are by a male intimate" (p. 308).

According to Castelano, separated or divorced women were found to be 14 times more likely than married women to report having been a victim of violence by a spouse or ex-spouse. Drawing from Castelano:

> In one study of spousal homicide, over one-half of the male defendants were separated from their victims.... In another study in Philadelphia and Chicago ... almost 25% of the women killed by the male partners were separated and divorced from the men who killed them; another 29% were attempting to end the relationship when they were killed. (p. 11)

In addition, a national comparison of the homicide rates between the years 1976–79 and 1980–84 indicates an increase in the killing of women partners after separation in 72% of the states (Jones, 1980). For poor and working-class men and women, life on the streets may be tough. But for the women, life may be tougher still at home.

Crime Stories

How should the nation think about crime? Right now this seems a particularly confusing question. Crime rates fall yet incarceration rises; law-and-order Republicans do battle with police chiefs over re-legalizing assault weapons; Reagan-appointed judges call for ending the war on drugs while Health and Human Services Secretary Donna Shalala greets those same proposals with derision.

For at least a generation, anxiety about crime has been central to the landscape of U.S. politics. This is emotional, contradictory and bewildering terrain. Most of us occupy it at least briefly when walking alone down the street at night as a footfall sounds a few yards to the rear; it is even more familiar to anyone who has contended with car theft or murder or anything in between. In this land, the story, not the logic and statistics, reigns supreme: the story of what we have suffered, what we have heard about, what we fear.

If the politics of crime seems especially muddled today, it is because not only the facts but the story itself is up for grabs. (Shapiro, 1996, p. 14)

The ways we see the world, the contradictions we perceive, the analyses we produce, the violence we experience, the stories we tell—and those we don't—derive from our position within social and economic hierarchies. While our position should not be seen as overdetermining point of view, our position does sharpen the lens through which the world is seen. Nancy Hartsock (1984) describes standpoint theory as follows:

> The concept of a standpoint carries several specific contentions. Most important, it posits a series of levels of reality in which the deeper level both includes and explains the surface or appearance. Related to the positing of levels are several claims: ... *Material life (class position in Marxist theory) not only structures but sets limits on the understanding of social relations.* (p. 231)

Standpoint theory enables theorizing through both structure and human agency; at one and the same time it recognizes the powerful influence of social position as well as the fluidity of personal dispositions. Here we position ourselves within standpoint theory because we wish to emphasize that material conditions as seemingly straightforward as "crime and poverty" nevertheless float through multiple lenses constituting community life.

To say this differently, in this article we script crime through the eyes and narrations of the 154 men *and* women who are Whites, African-Americans, and Latinos within poor and working class communities. We worry that research on crime and violence in poor urban America and policies stemming from this research have been written through a narrow, even singular, lens, and therefore this research speaks only from the perspective of *some* living within these communities. Our goal here is to decenter and complicate the representation of crime and violence.

In this essay, we analyze the narrative responses to the three following interview questions.

1. Think about Jersey City/Buffalo as it has changed over the past 12 years, particularly around crime. Do you see Jersey City/Buffalo as more violent today than it was in the 1980s? Do you see more, less, or the same amount of what could be called police brutality?
2. There are a lot of institutions in Jersey City/Buffalo that shape our lives—police, welfare, courts, schools, hospitals. Can you tell me about a time you had to struggle with one of these institutions for yourself or a relative? What happened?
3. There are a lot of young men in jails. How do you explain this? Why do you think this is the case?

Having reviewed all responses to these three questions and using grounded theory, a set of analytic codes were generated: (a) *focus* of the violence—that is, state, community, domestic; (b) *trust* in the police; (c) whether or not the respondent speaks in a *racialized discourse*; (d) whether or not the respondent indicated that the *police advised* him/her about how to "take justice into my own hands;" (e) whether the respondent sees *police brutality* on the rise, decline, or stabilized over the past decade. Using these codes as our lens, we hear quite distinct stories pouring out of each demographic category: White men, White women, Black men, Black women, Latinos and Latinas.[2]

Our data moved us toward two conclusions. First, the experience of urban terror associated with crime, violence, and drugs is articulated passionately and profoundly by poor and working-class men and women across racial and ethnic groups. Urban terror is democratically distributed among the poor. Second, while the terror may be universal, the *articulated site of violence* varies dramatically by race/ethnicity and gender. While all informants were similar in age (23–35), and class (poor to working class), their responses varied by race, ethnicity, and gender. When asked about violence in their communities, African-American men and Latinos (to a far lesser extent) focused their comments on *state-initiated* violence, detailing incidents of police harassment, the systemic flight of jobs and capital in poor communities of color, the over-arrest of men of color, and the revived construction of prisons. In response to the very same questions, however, White men in our sample report incidents of *street violence*, attributing these incidents almost universally to men of color. In sharp contrast with all three groups of men, White women, when asked about crime and violence, offer scenes of *domestic violence* among their parents, themselves and husbands, or sisters and husbands. African-American and Latina women likewise detail scenes of *home-based violence*, although African-American women, like men from the same community, equally often describe incidents of state-initiated violence, typically in the welfare office. And African-American women, like White men, passionately narrate incidents of street violence.

We hear, then, that depending on where you sit in the social hierarchy, the experience of urban terror will be traced to different sources. And yet with all the national talk about crime bills, prevention, and prosecution, the particular standpoint that has influenced social policy and scholarship most directly—that is, the standpoint that is best reflected in prevailing laws and academic writing—is the standpoint spoken in our data almost entirely by White men. The latter discuss neither state-initiated violence nor domestic violence; instead, they focus exclusively, almost fetishistically, on street violence initiated by men of color.

On White Men

The 1980s and 1990s have been decades in which White males have, indeed, lost a good bit of their privilege. Those most squeezed have been White working-class males, with the shrinkage of unionized and public sector jobs, the vibrant (if sometimes muzzled) energy of feminism, civil rights, and the unstoppable "coming out" of gay/lesbian rights. In our interviews with poor and working-class males in Jersey City and Buffalo, we hear a mantra of losses that they narrate, angrily, bitterly, with pointed fingers. From days gone by, they have lost wives whom they thought would stay home and cater to them, good jobs in the public sector and those protected by labor unions. Their schools and communities, according to these men, have been "invaded" by people of color. Their monopoly on power and privilege has been pierced. They are not happy.

Their stories of loss are voiced in a discourse of property rights. While it is the case that they have been economically dethroned, regendered, and reraced in the past two decades, they feel only mugged, but not by the global treachery of late capitalism, the flight of manufacturing jobs from the United States, or the erosion of strong labor unions, all of which are the real cause of their present circumstances. Instead, they feel erased by White women, men of color, gays and lesbians. Unable/unwilling to critique boldly and broadly, these men, for the most part, rehearse a noble loyalty to their American dreams.

Turning to the data on crime and violence, of all six groups, the White men emerged as the most distinct, that is, atypical narrators. A full half of these men spontaneously volunteered that they had a friend or relative who is a "cop." Quite distinct from the rest of the sample, 75% indicated a trust in the police, and only 25% alluded to police corruption in Jersey City, a city in which 75% of Latinos and African-American men reported instances of corruption and police brutality.

> *Alan:* Oh, the police. Well, I, last week when we had the break-in, the police came down. I thought it was kind of strange, you know, that the one cop said to me that it was too bad that you didn't catch him inside the house because then you would have killed him and we wouldn't have said anything. I, he said, it was too bad I didn't catch him; I could have beat the crap out of him. But they, um, I don't really think of anything that I've had a run-in, so to speak.

As you can hear, Alan feels he is protected by the police. Like Alan, three other men independently volunteered that the police, following their reporting of a crime, instructed them in how to "get the guy" next time. Twinned with their trust in the police, these men tell stories of street violence in which they typically identify the race of perpetrators. In fact, it is noteworthy that White men are the *only* group who insist on naming the race/ethnicity of their perpetrators—or at least naming those who are Black or Hispanic.

> *Joey*: Basically, because if you don't know someone in Jersey City, you can't get something in Jersey City. Like if you wanted a decent job, you have to be a political fuck boy, excuse my language, but to me that's what it boils down to, not having a fair shot. I recently went through several police officer tests, one for Port Authority, which may God strike me dead right now if I didn't score at least high 90s on its, and I didn't get anything. I heard it was the first time that they did not send back your exact score. They just sent a card stating that, congratulations, you passed with 70 percent or higher. Then, a friend of mine in administration told me that he was speaking to somebody, and the reason they did that was because they have to hire minorities and Blacks. So now, say, for instance, me and my friend Joe, who happens to be Black, took the same test. I got a 90 and he got a 60. They're going to take him and leave me, so they don't want to cause fights. They're not gonna disclose each score because they have to meet quotas. That's some of the reasons why. Other reasons are I'm getting to the age where I'd like to have a family, and Jersey City, I don't think, is the place to raise a family.

White men, further, when discussing fears, typically deny having their own fears but project fears onto "vulnerable" others—parents, children, sisters. In other words, White men narrate a racialized discourse of crime and punishment, attributing virtue and responsibility to the police who embody "us," criminality and degradation to "them"—men of color, all the while protecting elders, women, and children. In this triangle, these men don't see brutality by police. Or they don't, in the words of one, "see enough." A full 75% indicated that police brutality was on the wane, or fabricated, again unusual in a city in which most of our African-American and Latino respondents recited incidents of personal and/or witnessed acts of brutality. Sixty percent considered charges of police harassment to be "racially trumped up." Claims of police brutality were, for the most part, seen as a "crock."

> *Bob*: I don't know, I mean police brutality is such a crock sometimes. Most of the time people that are getting brutalized have done something one way or another to intimidate the police officer.

We do not dispute the accuracies, perspective, or authenticity of any of the crime stories we heard. We note, only, the dramatic discursive departures evident across groups. In this vein, many contemporary theorists argue that race theoretically *should not* make much of a difference, and this is how we began our work. Yet the life stories we collected were narrated as thoroughly raced. Personal stories of violence and family structure, narrative style, one's history with money, willingness to trash (and leave) men and marriages, access to material resources, relations with kin and the state, descriptions of interactions with police—all are profoundly narrated through "race" and, as you will see, through gender.

On White Women

Most White men whom we interviewed argued forcefully that they are feeling squeezed economically, in their neighborhoods and in the domestic sphere. Assuming deserved dominance, they sense that their "rightful place" is being unraveled by an economy that they argue privileges people of color over White men in the form of affirmative action and by pressure from Blacks and Latinos in their neighborhoods. In addition, they feel that their physical space is being compromised by women at home. Yes, even in their homes, their power wanes as women no longer listen, according to the men, and they—these men—are no longer in control. Lacking economic power, they attempt, we argue, to reassert power in the home/family sphere. As these White men enact border-patrolling strategies, all in the name of "protecting the family," the questions arise: Where does this leave the women? What does their existence look like? Where are crimes and violence in their lives?

Unfortunately, the story of the White working-class and poor women whom we interviewed is not a pretty one. The "secret" of childhood sexual abuse and domestic violence dripped through our interviews. It is so all encompassing that it is a story that we tell in graphic detail here. As we will argue, domestic violence is a distinct theme in Black and Latina women's lives as well, and it is no understatement to suggest that poor and working-class women's lives, across racial and ethnic groups, are saturated with domestic terror.

Amidst our two-city sample it was, initially, quite easy to distinguish between White women living in two *presumably* distinct domestic scenes. Borrowing Howell's categories (1972), "settled lives" women survive within what seem to be stable, intact family structures. In deceptively simple contrast, "hard living" women float between different types of households, move in and out of welfare, have less education and more (low paying) employment. Despite these apparent differences, however, our analysis leads us to conclude that almost all of the poor and working-class white women and their families are negotiating lives disrupted by an inhospitable economy, and almost all of these women are also surviving within scenes of domestic violence that span across generations. The distinction between the "settled lives" women and the "hard living" women may, sadly, only be determined by whether or not the woman has *exited* from her violent home. While current political debates romanticize the "settled lives" woman—the good woman who stays at home, cares for her children and husband, and "plays by the rules"—and demonizes the " hard living" woman—the bad woman who leaves her home, lives in poverty, flees her husband/boyfriend, and relies intermittently upon social services—our data suggest that both of these groups of women come from the same communities, have endured equivalent levels of violence, and differ only to the extent to which they expose their "private troubles" to public view (Mills, 1959).

White women in our sample, in contrast with White men, dropped the racialized discourse on street crime and 60% narrate stories of police and courts in terms of violence in their homes, in the homes of their mothers and their sisters. Unlike the White men, fewer than half of the White women " trust" the police. They, too, see little in the way of brutality, but 48% of those interviewed recognize corruption in the ranks.

Caroline: Well, like with my sister, my middle sister, she lived with a boyfriend who was a drug addict. Well, he was reformed and then he moved in with her and he was, the present one. And he became a problem. My parents were away, and he was, you know, threatening my sister and stuff. And he locked us in the house, and he was threatening to kill us and all this sick stuff. So, anyway, we had to call the police about eight times that day. And they had to arrest him and stuff. But it was, I mean, as far as the police go, it was a very … it was frustrating at first, and, then,

then, it was a good experience because they helped us. You know, they protected us and all that. At one point I didn't think they were going to, and I really was going a little bit crazy, you know. They kept sending him on his way, and he kept coming back, you know.... And I started screaming, you know. I'm like, you're giving him change and sending him on his way? He'll be back in an hour. Where is this guy going with a crack problem and a dollar? You know, so I'm, like, screaming at this cop and everything. And then the other two came, and, you know, I was pleading with this, the one who came back. I was, like, you swore you were going to put him in jail. My sister and me are scared to death. My father isn't here. We have nobody, you know.

Because the police potentially protect women from violent men, these women (unlike the women of color, as you will see) consider the police to be "responsive." Indeed, one woman, who had her husband locked up for domestic violence and brought to court on charges of nonpayment of child support, describes working with neighbors on a petition to get more police protection and succeeding. While most White women whisper incidents of domestic violence that have pervaded their lives, they tend not to call the cops, take out restraining orders, or bring their husbands to court. Most of the White women, in fact, have had few dealings with the police. Yet they are *more* likely than their White brothers to note police imperfections and *more* likely than women of color to trust them.

Cecilia: We had a situation where these people were coming from Duncan Projects, harassing our kids. Not mine, ours, meaning the neighborhood kids. And what we did was we called up the North District Police Department, and we asked to have them drive through occasionally because the kids were being harassed. They were being robbed and everything else, and at first it was, like, a problem, but then we got like this big list. I think it was like 4,000 people.

Sarah: Oh, a petition?

Cecilia: Yeah, and we brought it up to them and we got it [protection].

Sarah: The police are responsive to your needs?

Cecilia: Oh yeah, they are, yeah, they are. At first it was a little bit of a problem because they said they don't have enough cars. So we just blew it off, and they thought it was over with, but then we went and had the petition made and brought it to the Commissioner, and it was over with. We got it taken care of.

As the public sphere collapses, or more aptly is collapsed, by a Republican Congress eager to universalize cutbacks for the poor and support for the rich and by a President who recently signed a "welfare reform" act, women across racial and ethnic lines in the poor and working classes are being squeezed into tighter and tighter domestic corners and pushed out of the public worlds of work, welfare, and battered women's shelters. While escape from violence appears easy to those onlookers who ask, "Why doesn't she just leave?", we hear from these women that they can barely afford to exit, especially if they have children, and that male violence often follows them, whether they exit or not. They need "safe havens" to exit to, havens that are being taken away as moneys for battered women's shelters and welfare wither. Thus, the forecast is for family homelessness and intensified violence. As the public sphere shrinks, women will get beaten with more regularity, with fewer options and more muzzled critiques. They will be swept into the corners of a reinstitutionalized "private" sphere, secured in its violence by the hollowing of the economy and the retreat of public sector services for women and children.

On African-American Men

The discourse of violence spoken by Black men sits within a powerful, incisive, and painful social critique. When African-American men speak of violence, their analyses move directly to economic and state violence. This group of men speaks from a well of deep concern about the fate of their community. Surrounded by street-based violence and drugs as well as the violence perpetrated by police in their communities, African-American men throw a wide analytic net around the lack of jobs, racism, and police harassment. More than any other group, Black men offer a vivid and angry critique of American social and economic arrangements (Fine & Weis, 1998). This critique is sustained, however, in parallel with deeply held notions of the American dream—a strong sense that *their* failure in high school is *their* failure alone and that the future will be different if only *they* try harder.

When asked about violence in his community, Jon, an African-American gay man, poses a caustic analysis of political violence:

> *Jon*: The top people that control the society, they're the most angry, violent people in the world. They drop bombs. They spread diseases. They burn. They set up armies to do all kinds of things. I don't know all the violence that you talkin' about. Frankly, I don't see it. People stab each other. They always have. You know, so I see it, but it's just magnified on the television, but they don't show the real violence that they perpetrate, the economic violence.

In marked contrast with the White men, African-American men do not (with one exception, whose father is a police sergeant) describe police as friends or relatives. And they do not trust the police. In fact, 75% relay stories of corruption. Most think that brutality has gotten worse in the past decade, and almost all see the primary reason for the increase in proportion of men in jail as attributable to structural causes of state violence (Weis & Fine, 1996). Of the African-American men interviewed, almost all reported a story of being stopped, frisked, pulled over for no apparent reason. Some of the stories were told with fiery anger, others with a bitter sense of resignation. Carl tells about one incident:

> *Carl*: I remember one experience when, um, I had my car stolen and I had gotten the car back. And over a year my car was never taken off [the list] as stolen, alright.... So I had gotten pulled over because I made a wrong turn one time, and, um, I think you get a ticket for that, [laughs], I was pulled over. I gave him my license and registration. He was going to arrest me because he said my license was suspended. I said no.... Then they pushed me, one guy, one cop tried to put me into the cop car, and I'm telling them, I'm not, I said I'm not going in this cop car because I've done nothing wrong.... I had to drive to the police station because he had to help me take my car off my record as being stolen. And then he still couldn't help me. They're just not true to their position. They're supposed to serve the community [but]... that just made me look so bad to be surrounded by four cop cars. *I'm public enemy number one, you know* [emphasis added]. [laughs]

Demetrius, a calm, church-going civil servant, relays a story about his car breaking down:

> *Demetrius*: I'm walking back across the highway. I went to the grass and sidewalk, and the next thing I know a car came out of nowhere, all right? And he didn't have his headlights on. So all I hear is the engine, and it's pitch black out there, and I got another 50 yards to go before I get up under a streetlight. And I'm on a sidewalk, and the car's on the sidewalk. The car brushes by my leg, and we're on grass, and if he would have slightly lost control of that car, he would have took my leg out, okay? The car

just slid right past me. I was actually running across the street to get to the sidewalk, and that's when it happened. He jumps out of the car and he came to me ... and asked me if I wanted to fight. And my question was "Why?" And he started cursing and everything, uh, calling me all kinds of names, and so by then I'm getting mad. And so he approached me, and he pushed me, he pushed me in the chest. So I backed up, and he's like, "What you want to fight, black boy, you want a fight?"... And he was like, "I'm a police officer," like that, right, "I should run your big behind in," all this stuff. I'm like, "What are you talking about?" He was like, he's carrying on and carrying on, but he wasn't telling me what he was doing.... So he started patting me down. I'm saying, "If you're a cop, show me a damn badge!" And he's like, "I don't need to show you, this is enough." Like that, right?

Even Paul, whose father was a police sergeant, explains that the "police have a job to do," but notes, "If I go into a white neighborhood, I get stopped." These men repeat story after story of being suspect and narrate the toll that it takes. Vincent explains: "White women are scared of Black men. It makes you feel cheap." Robert is asked what he tells his children about police. He thinks, hesitates, and then:

Michelle: What would you tell a kid about the police? You know, they're supposed to be protecting you.

Robert: Well, my son, he loved policemen and cops and all this stuff. So, I'll let him see when he gets older, but now I'll tell him the cops are good, and when you are in trouble, call the police or an ambulance.

Michelle: So you do tell him?

Robert: I don't shatter his dreams cause he say he want to get to be a cop when he grows older, like, okay, you know.

Michelle: Do you think it would shatter him? If his dream was shattered?

Robert: If they're still going where they're going now, yeah, it will be shattered. Or if he have a struggle, I'll just focus on the other people, and don't be like the other cops, like the way they are now.

Black men are not only far more structural in their explanations of the root causes of crime and corruption, but they are far more devastated and hard pressed than other groups to imagine how to turn things around. Many note with regret the absence of community-based programs, the slashing of budgets for after-school programs. John remembers, fondly, that his community used to care for all the children, and now he's scared. "The neighbors used to be so nosey," but now "I don't know what to do to stop the violence." The Black men whom we interviewed were critical of the "system," longing for a past in which neighbors watched out for each other and beleaguered in their attempts to help the "young ones, still comin' up."

Stuart: Exactly, exactly, and, plus, the neighborhood isn't as close as it used to be. Everybody used to be nosey, as a way of saying it in street talk. You know, if something's happening, you would hear windows going up throughout the neighborhood, and now you don't hear it. Everybody is keeping to themselves, and if somebody's getting beat up or something outside or if there is a crime taking place, they're sheltered, they don't open windows as much as, you know, because they're scared they might get a bullet... Uh, I just recently got involved with something. I wasn't able to stop what happened. A guy in my neighborhood that's my sister's friend, he was literally beat down with baseball bats, and, you know, I just helped him out as far as getting him towels and ice and stuff like that, calling the police and ambulance ...

| *Judi*: | So you feel partly responsible for it? |
| *Stuart*: | Partly responsible, exactly. |

On African-American Women

The African-American women whom we interviewed sit at a vibrant and sometimes dangerous political intersection. They are African-American, female, and poor—in the evaporating years of the 20th century, the Clinton/Gingrich era, the era of dwindling public resources and economic opportunities. They are caretakers for their mothers and children, when few care for them; they are contributors to the social glue of impoverished communities when all else has failed, and they are demonized for "living off the state," when they barely manage to feed their families. Perched at a precarious intersection of race, class, and gender, they struggle to raise the next generation in the midst of a crack economy that claims many casualties and sustains few successes. Yet they do, feeling quite alone, in Jersey City and in Buffalo.

As to violence, the Black women we interviewed have much to report, although don't much trust police. While 25% think the cops are corrupt and while 25% report dealings with police in scenes of domestic violence, they are, overall, just tired of picking up the pieces for White society and, as many see it, for African-American men. These women narrate stories of exhaustion, few resources, fewer supports. They cast the widest net around their dealings with the law—noting landlord–tenant cases, child support, restraint orders, and run-ins with case workers:

| *Genette*: | So I said, all right, you can see the baby, you want to come see him, you can come see him, but just know, me and you, we have no business with each other except for this child. Don't touch me, don't act like you want me, I said, cause I don't want you.... He talkin' about, "Oh, I don't want you on welfare."... I said, "Well it's too late because he's on it," so he gets mad at me. I said, "Well, you're the man, you go get a job now before you go to jail" ... because the only reason why he didn't want me dealing with welfare because he knew the system would say who the father is and they would take him to court so he didn't want to go to the process of having to pay child support. |

Stories of male violence are not as frequent as they are for White and Latina women, but they are dramatic and devastating in consequence.

Tara:	Yeah, the time he was trying to hurt me, and I knew that he didn't want to hurt me, you know, to try to kill me. And when the judge asked me that, he didn't ask me that personally, he just said, Tara, do you have anything to say about the situation? And I didn't talk. I was scared. It was like [John] took over me. I didn't, I had just talked my piece. He wasn't a ruler over me. I just took it like I didn't have nothing to say.
Sarah:	Let's go back, okay. You pressed charges ...
Tara:	This was years ago.... He burnt my door and wouldn't let me out the door. And my brother and them came and moved the chair and I got out.
Sarah:	I understand that. Why did he do that?
Tara:	To scare me. Remember I told you he been trying to scare me. I think I did tell you.... But he didn't mean to do it. It wasn't like that. He was just trying to scare me, and he overdid it because he don't know how fire works.
Sarah:	Yeah, but still.

Tara:	And if you see *Backdraft*, you know how fire works. It goes wherever it wants to go. So he didn't know that then …
Sarah:	Did you call anybody? What did you do, cry?
Tara:	Cry? I panicked.
Sarah:	And what happened?
Tara:	I just got down on all fours … [laughs]
Sarah:	And prayed?
Tara:	Yeah. And woke up my kids. And …
Sarah:	Your kids were inside too?
Tara:	Yeah, all of us. And we all got down on all fours and sat in the house for fifteen minutes before the fire department came.

The African-American women with whom we spoke—even before "welfare reform"—were typically holding together their own families and caring for the children/parents of kin and doing so with almost no resources to speak of. Their anger at the police is matched by their anger at African-American men, case workers, African-American women who "make us look bad," and the younger generation who are committing crimes, rendering their neighborhoods terrifying for women and children. Women speak through a dual discourse of responsibility and blame. More than one quoted, "You do the crime, you do the time." More than one alluded to a domestic cycle of drugs, violence, *his* doing time … and then *his* not paying child support.

Women experience brutality in their own homes and witness it in neighbors' homes. Most stand firm—"I don't get involved." With little regret, they know that if they do "get involved," that is, call the cops on a neighbor's domestic violence, that they are vulnerable to retaliation. Living amidst and despite cycles of violence, knowing they and their children are ever vulnerable … they are ever so vigilant. From the eye of this hurricane, their anger is tempered by vulnerability. Violence keeps them in their homes, scared and angry.

On Latino Men

In poor northeastern communities like Buffalo and Jersey City, Puerto Rican men, in spite of great poverty, affirm a form of what Benmayor, Torruellas, and Juarbe (1992) call "cultural citizenship." As these authors describe:

Cultural citizenship expresses a process through which a subordinated group of people arrives at a common identity, establishes solidarity, and defines a common set of interests that binds the group together into action. Critical to this process is the affirmation and assertion of perceived collective rights which have been ignored or denied by the dominant society and its legal canon. Defined in this way, cultural citizenship is clearly oppositional, articulating the needs of people who do not hold state power. (p. 72)

Our interviews with Puerto Rican men alert us to the fact that these men do affirm, on a day-to-day basis, what Benmayor calls cultural citizenship. Far more aggressively than even the women whom we interviewed, Puerto Rican men put themselves forward as being Puerto Rican, as deserving of respect on the mainland, *for* preserving their heritage. The affirmation of cultural citizenship is, for men, however, threaded with inherited and constructed notions of masculinity, some of which are contested by Puerto Rican women today.

Turning to crime and violence, Latinos parted ways with the White men, and, sounding more like their African-American brothers, a full 100% of the Latinos in our sample described high levels of police corruption in the city of Jersey City.[3] Only one Latino describes a friend on the police force, while one other says he "trusts the cops." Most see police brutality everywhere, with the "police thinking they are above the law."

> *Pablo*:   Some of the police get me angry because in Food Town we have a police officer there, and they're there from five to eleven. I've finally, over the past five years or so, started to get to know them.... And they'll just have, you know, all types of conversations, you know, this scum was doing this and the way they term people that you already know they already have a bad outlook towards someone to begin with. And you'll have like two officers in front of me talking, and he goes, yeah, I went to a Rodriguez house, and he was talking about this, and I told him to shut up, and he didn't say nothing. I stand on the floor and kicked him and this and that, are you gonna shut up now, and you're looking at the, and you just say to yourself, you know, I feel like I'm gonna report this guy or whatever, but what can I get done because then I've seen so many officers that have something reported on them, and there's like a system you're not gonna, unless you get something like a Rodney King that's on video tape. The possibility of a police officer getting in trouble for doing something like that is rare.

Luis, below, resonated to the desire to be useful amidst violence in a war zone. He sounded like the African-American men when he said:

> *Luis*:   Oh, the police, they really think they're above the law. And they do what they want, and they get away with it. They really do.... There's more, like, this noncaring attitude; it's like, do what you want, do what you want. That's why I personally went and got a gun, but it's registered. And it sits right by my window. At night, if anything happens, the cars are parked right there. I won't hesitate to shoot. Because I'm sick of this place basically. The way it's going. I want to save it, but I don't know what to do.

Like Black men, these Latinos see state-initiated abuse as a problem, embodied by violence in blue. Both safety and trust have been eroded.

On Latinas

We heard poor and working-class Latinos working hard to reinstantiate cultural citizenship on the mainland. Performed and embodied in the face of anti-immigrant policies and practices and an elite control of an economy to which Latinos in the Unites States have little access, these men have embraced culture, history, and tradition that often presupposes gendered subordination. The data presented here suggest that Latinas in our sample are also reworking cultural citizenship. But these women are producing a version of "living Latina" in which gender as traditionally lived is being rewritten with neither economic nor domestic subordination of women assumed. As these women stretch the borders of gender *within Latino culture* and dare to raise their sons and daughters with revisionist definitions of culture, the rubs of gendered relations *within* Latino homes and communities grow more and more contested.

From White women, from African-American women, and from Latinas in our sample, we hear whispers and screams as they rethink and redesign the borders of gender and sexuality. The White women whisper their troubles and act rarely. The African-American women testify more boldly and act more often. The Latinas barely protest aloud, but they maneuver systematically and quickly to get themselves and their children out of the way of danger.

By far the most pronounced critique of the police among women came from the Latinas who, like African-American women, voice a profound disappointment in both the police and, for many, in their men. A full 75% of the Latinas believe the police are corrupt and violent, and an equal percentage have come into contact with police because of incidents of domestic violence. Asserting the will of God, these women often know how to get the police to do what they need to do, aware of the racial and ethnic politics that must be maneuvered in order to get the cops to respond:

Marta: Like, I see the cops go by, and they see the kids in the corner, and sometimes they'll say something and sometimes they won't. You know, like, they look the other way. You call 911 and say, "Okay, I'm calling from such and such a building. There's kids hanging outside. It's 3 o'clock in the morning. I can't sleep." The cops won't come. They won't come. They will never show up. Or, there's a domestic fight in apartment such and such. You'll sit there and die before they come. I mean the wife will be dead, and he'll beat her to death before the cops ever come.

Mun: Because they don't want to, because they don't care? Or because they don't want to walk in that neighborhood? Or because?

Marta: I think it's both of them. I think it's just, like, this society. I think the way they see it is, let them kill themselves. They'll take care of themselves. You know, Black people killing Black people. The Hispanics are killing each other. They're killing, they both take care of finishing, of terminating each other. I guess the cops just let them do it, you know. If they see two, if they see a White person and a Black person fighting, they'll stop it. But if they see a Hispanic and a Black person going at it, they'll, you know, they'll let it happen. If you call because there's a robbery, they'll let it happen. If you call because it's a domestic fight, they'll let it happen.... The cops, they are a joke, the cops. And most of the cops know the kids, and most of the cops, how can I tell you? The cops will tell them, look, I'm going to let you go this time, but next time I'm going to do something to you. And they really don't do anything. And some of the times, the cops are the ones who are dealing with them. You know, so it's inside jobs. And sometimes you see the cops talking to the kids outside. And the kids will tell you, no, man, he's with us. He's with us. So you have no type of police protection at all, at all.

Marta believes that the cops "don't care. When it comes to domestic violence in *our* community they think, 'Let them kill themselves.'"

Latinas, like White women, connect questions about violence to the domestic violence sphere:

Tamar: Because he was doing all the screaming and punching and she was the one doing all the crying, so you could tell. And I called the cops and said bring, you know, can you send me a car, there are kids involved. The man is hitting, and I said, please hurry up, and I was polite. She was telling me, she was a Black lady, and I'm like, but there are kids involved, you know, and I gave the information so she wanted to have my name and I told her, I'm not gonna give you my name and she's like, Well if you don't give me the name, I'm not gonna send the cops. So I told her if you don't send the cops, somehow there's gonna be a recording that I did call you, and you didn't do anything about it so, you know, and I hung up.

Mun: Did the police come?

Tamar: Yeah, they came. They came less than three minutes. If it wouldn't have been for me, forget it ...

Mun: How did that make you feel?

Tamar: It gave me flashbacks of me. And I wish that when they heard me screaming, somebody would have called the cops or knock on my door and tell me if I'm alright. They don't do that.

Margarita: Why do they beat their wives? I guess because that makes them in control. That's the only person they can control, maybe, you know, because that's why I say sometimes, like to the baby's father, don't be yelling at me, why don't you go and go do that to a man outside and see what happens. You'll get punched right in the face. You know, cause sometimes it's true. You haven't done nothing to that person, and they come and they, you know, treating you bad, and you say, "Wait a minute, what happened?" And I say, like, that, "Don't talk to me like that or treat me like that." You have an apartment, go to whoever gave you the problem, see, and do that face to face, you know, cause they'll slap the shit out of you or whatever, you know. But I think it's that, it's that they control, that they can control you or, yeah, control.

Mun: Do you think women are taking it? Do you think women are fighting back?

Margarita: Some of them are, but I think a lot of them, they still the same, they still, but you know what? It's because of the system.

Mun: What system?

Margarita: What do you mean, what, the system, the police system. You know how they say, like, in [a battered woman's] case, you know, um, uh, I think he went to jail for a couple of … He was only a week or two days, something like that.

Mun: They just locked him up a couple of days, then?

Margarita: That's why a lot of, I don't know, that's why, because I guess when a man sets his mind to do something, a little piece of paper is not gonna stop him, and I don't think even the police is gonna stop him. I think when they set their minds to, they're [men] gonna do this, they're gonna hurt you, or they're gonna do this, they're gonna do it.

Restraining orders have little effect, and many women think the police are prejudicial by virtue of race/ethnicity and gender. And, yet, with all the violence women report in their families of origin and families of procreation, their commitments to "familia" and fears of escape and retaliation run very deep:

Carmen: To finish college, everything. I want them [her children] to have, to be somebody. Like my son likes to, the airplanes, in the army, and I go, if you like that, you go for it and my, sometimes they say they want to be a judge, and the other one wants to be a cop because like, sees the cops, she'll take her father to jail and, like, my son is gonna be a judge, he'll put him in jail. That's what they say.

Michelle: But if you tell the police, the police would lock him up then. Your sister would be safe.

Carmen: I didn't know that. When he said I'm gonna hurt you, your sister and your mother, I'm gonna hurt you all, I believed he was gonna hurt us all. That's just the way it was.

Violence Across Poor and Working-Class Communities

America has long had a love affair with violence and guns. It's our history, we teach it to all of our young. The Revolution, the "taming of the West," the Civil War, the world wars, and on and on. Guns, justice, righteousness, freedom, liberty—all tied to violence. Even when we try to teach about non-violence, we have to use the Reverend Dr. Martin Luther King, Jr., killed by the violent. I'm sorry, America, but once you get past the rhetoric what we really learn is that might does make right. Poor people have just never had any might. But they want it. Oh how they want it.…

For the handgun generation there is no post-traumatic stress syndrome because there is no "post." We need a new term to describe what happens to people who never get out from under war conditions, maybe "continuing traumatic stress syndrome." I used to read that the thing that made the Vietnamese such fierce fighters was that they had been fighting for many decades. I don't know if this is true or not, but I've watched children grow up fighting with guns, and now they're young adults. The next generation might be called the Uzi generation because of their penchant for automatic weapons. These children, armed better than the police, are growing up as violent if not more so than the handgun generation. And the gun manufacturers in their greed continue to pump more and more guns into our already saturated ghettos.

Some may think that this violence is new, but it's not. Violence has always been around, usually concentrated amongst the poor. The difference is that we never had so many guns in our inner cities. The nature of the violent act has changed from the fist, stick, and knife to the gun. But violence, I remember. (Canada, 1995, x–xi)

From our data, we hear poor and working-class young adults in the grips of violence, as Geoffrey Canada would conclude. But we also hear the tilting influence of their relative position in analyzing this violence. So, for instance, we understand that all residents whom we interviewed carry around fears of violence and see police as very powerful players. For the White men, however, police are *protectors* of community. For people of color, and some of the White women, police are *perpetrators* of personal and community abuse. This, too, speaks clearly to questions of policy. If police are not trusted broadly, if they do not represent multiple voices, do not come from and represent the demographic and neighborhood groups and interests of all community members, if they appear to be and/or are unconcerned with violence within neighborhoods of color while far more responsive when the caller is White, we need ways to reimagine and redesign community policing so that the level of responsiveness and the time of arrival are not calculated through racism and institutional neglect.

We began our data analysis committed to an analytic strategy that would cut across these demographic groups. We intended to look for any apparent "differences" evident in demographic contrasts, but were determined *not* to organize our analyses around these "differences." And yet our data surprised us, as powerful data often do, forcing us to recognize the material and experiential consequences of particular race/ethnicity and gender positions in the United States. While the women and men we interviewed pledged the irrelevance of race/ethnicity and gender, "I don't think about it much," their stories are saturated with such evidence. Race, class and gender *are* socially constructed—*and* deeply engraved.

Across our sample, it is safe to say that every interviewee reported being aware of and frightened by violence and crime. But the commonality stops here. For African-American men, their most pronounced fears involve state violence. Indeed, Jersey City and Buffalo Criminal Index data show a dramatic "spike" in drug arrests from 1985 forward, particularly for African-Americans, which is perplexing given national surveys that indicate equal levels of drug *use* for Whites and African-Americans (U.S. Department of Justice, 1995). White men offer stories of violence that focus specifically on racially choreographed street violence. And, indeed, the Criminal Index does indicate a rise in robbery, rape, assault, burglary and larceny from 1975–90 in both Jersey City and Buffalo. Women across racial/ethnic groups voice terrors of domestic violence. And national data, confirmed by our numbers, suggest that women across racial/ethnic groups suffer roughly equivalent rates of violence, with low-income women far more susceptible to intimate violence than middle-class or upper-class women. We assert, then, in terms of policy recommendations, that a federal, state, or local "Crime Policy" must address simultaneously all three kinds of violence—state violence, community violence, and domestic violence. These three work as a set, a triplet, a collection of interrelated and embodied experiences of social life in poor and working-class communities. And as a set they affect children and youth—the next generation—with devastating predictability; whether these children witness, are victims, or, for some, are perpetrators of the violence.

A Note on Blame

As an epilogue we offer some commentary about the discourses that community members deploy when they talk about crime, violence, and responsibility. We do this in order to right a set of publicly advertised misconceptions. While the popular media continue to paint degenerated pictures of poor communities of color, our data paint a very different picture.

Indeed, the *only* group committed to an analysis of violence in which they, themselves, narrated no responsibility for the violence was White men. With important exceptions, White men as a group identified the source of the "problem" to be boys/men of color. The "solution," for White men, is the containment/confinement of these same boys/men. In contrast, the most pronounced discourse of responsibility could be heard from the African-American women, who are most likely to see criminal behavior as an outcome of bad personal choices and irresponsibility and *least* likely to offer up macro-structural explanations for why young boys/men are so heavily overrepresented in jails/prisons today. That is, African-American women tended not to assert that the absence of jobs or the presence of racism or hard economic times contribute to high rates of imprisonment. Because these women see entire communities as vulnerable to these conditions, most are unwilling to attribute criminal behavior simply to these structural conditions. Many assert, instead, with remarkable consistency that "if you commit the crime, you do the time." No fancy explanations or justifications. "If my children can struggle out here and stay away from jail—so can the others." A discourse of responsibility, perhaps even blame, is articulated most unambivalently from these women, who sound a bit like the conservatives who demonize them.

In analytic contrast with their African-American sisters, African-American men and Latinos assert broad-based structural explanations for why boys/men are overpopulating jails these days. Offering theories of "conspiracy," the "system," corruption, recession, no jobs, and racism, these men are *not*, however, shirking personal responsibility. Quite a few end their discussions of crime and violence with a sobering sense of personal powerlessness and responsibility. Filled out with a desire to create change, they voice frustration that few avenues are available. We remember the words of Luis who sits by his window with gun in hand, wanting to do something but not knowing what.

Concluding

The mid-90s mark yet another painful moment in racial history. As a people, we are reminded often and sharply of the enormous racial and class divides that continue to define community life in America. We watch Congress, and the President, pass legislation which portends negatively for working-class and poor families, people of color in particular, and will worsen conditions for both. We listen in relative silence, if not collusion, as these women and men are blamed for their own conditions.

Our data suggest a picture of social, racial, and class relations quite distinct from those drawn by Congress. We hear women and men of the poor and working class, White, Black, and Latino, disappointed by public and personal institutions ranging from welfare to the family to public schools, in pain about personal and collective tragedies but searching for ways to hold families together, protect communities, and take back their streets. We hear further that crime bills that would simply arrest, prosecute, and incarcerate; build more jails; cut school budgets; and deny job training will satisfy or assist no one. Not even poor and working-class White men.

The depth and consequence of social violence is enormous and multifaceted in poor and working-class urban communities. Street violence is a concern for White men, indeed, and it endangers even more profoundly the mobility and public life of poor and working-class women and men of color. But for women and men of color, state violence, police harassment, false arrests, exaggerated charges, and differential sentencing policies also figure prominently in their narrations of violence. And for most of the women—Whites, African-Americans, and Latinas—there is no respite from street violence. Going home is no safer, and perhaps more terrifying, than walking the streets at night. And leaving a violent home is no assurance of peace.

The news is not good. Our communities are fractured, and we come together only in our fears and finger-pointing. But, we would assert, the public policies that speak only from a privileged standpoint as if race, ethnicity, and gender neutral – incarcerating men and women from oppressed racial groups at unprecedented rates – contribute to the fracturing. There are policy answers for reinventing community and safety among our differences. Some of our respondents spoke of multi-racial/ethnic coalitions, community policing, diversion programs, reinvestment in education and job training, petition drives, and local organizing across race and ethnicity, within class, between genders. The question, today, is not just what do, but who is going to listen?

Notes

1. From *Women, Violence, and Social Change* (London: Routledge, 1992, pp. 1–14). Reprinted by permission.
2. Data presented here are drawn from Jersey City. We do, though, speak to the two-city sample since data drawn from both cities are remarkably similar by gender, race, and ethnicity.
3. These men in Jersey City author a critique of the police far more expansive than Latinos offered in Buffalo. We explain the discrepancy based on the physical proximity of Jersey City to New York, where discourses of police harassment and abuse are rampant; on the long, painful history of corruption in the Jersey City public sector; and on a distinct pattern of racial and ethnic discrimination in public sector hiring. With respect to City Hall, plus the schools, police, and fire departments, Jersey City has had a horrifying if celebrated history of patronage and favoritism—"cleaned up," in part, only recently. And yet on the ground, community-based suspicion of the schools, the mayor's office, the police, and the fire department remains widespread, particularly in communities of color.

References

Adisa, O. P. (1997). Undeclared war: African-American women writers explicating rape. In L. L. O'Toole & J. R. Schiffman (Eds.), *Gender violence: Interdisciplinary perspectives* (pp. 194–208). New York: New York University Press.

Anderson, E. (1990). *Streetwise: Race, class, and change in urban community*. Chicago: University of Chicago Press.

Attar, B. K., Guerra, N. G., & Tolan, P. H. (1994). Neighborhood disadvantages, stressful life events, and adjustment in urban elementary-school children. *Journal of Clinical Child Psychology, 23* (4), 391–400.

Bell, C. C., & Jenkins, E. J. (1993). Community violence and children on Chicago's southside. *Psychiatry Interpersonal and Biological Processes, 56* (1), 46–54.

Benmayor, R., Torruellas, R. M., & Juarbe, A. L. (1992). *Responses to poverty among Puerto Rican women: Identity, community, and cultural citizenship*. New York: Centro de Estudios Puertorriquenos, Hunter College.

Berton, M. W., & Stabb, S. D. (1996). Exposure to violence and post-traumatic stress disorder in urban adolescents. *Adolescence, 31* (122), 489–198.

Block, R., & Block, C. R. (1992). Homicide syndromes and vulnerability: Violence in Chicago community areas over 25 years. *Studies on Crime and Crime Prevention, 1* (1), 61–87.

Bourgois, A. (1995). *In search of respect: Selling crack in El Barrio.* New York: Cambridge University Press.

Browne, A. (1987). *When battered women kill.* New York: Free Press.

Canada, G. (1995). *Fist, stick, knife, gun: A personal history of violence in America.* Boston: Beacon Press.

Castelano, C. (1996). *Safe and healing spaces for women survivors of domestic violence: Immigrant Asian Indian women's perspectives.* Second year paper, Environmental psychology, City University of New York.

Coley, S. M., & Beckett, J. O. (1988). Black battered women: A review of the empirical literature. *Journal of Counseling and Development, 66* (6), 266–270.

Collins, P. H. (1990). *Black feminist thought: Knowledge, consciousness, and politics of empowerment.* Boston: Unwin Hyman.

Currie, E. (1993, November). *Missing pieces: Notes on crime, poverty, and social policy.* Paper prepared for the Social Science Research Council's Committee for Research on the Urban Underclass "Policy Conference on Persistent Urban Poverty," Washington, DC.

Dobash, R. E. (1979). *Violence against wives: A case study against the patriarchy.* New York: Free Press.

Dobash, R. E., & Dobash, R. P. (1992). *Women, violence and social change.* New York: Routledge.

Downs, W. R., Miller, B. A., & Panek, D. D. (1993). Different patterns of partner to woman violence: A comparison of samples of community, alcohol abusing, and battered women. *Journal of Family Violence, 8* (2), 113–135.

DuHart, R. H., Cadenhead, C., Pendergrast, R. A., & Slavens, G. (1994). Factors associated with the use of violence among urban Black adolescents. *American Journal of Public Health, 84* (4), 612–617.

Fagan, J., Conley, D., Debro, J., Curtis, R., Hamid, A., Moore, J., Padilla, F., Quicker, J., Taylor, C., & Vigil, J. D. (1993, November). *Crime, drugs and neighborhood change: The effects of deindustrialization on social control in inner cities.* Paper presented to the Social Science Research Council's Committee on Urban Underclass "Policy Conference on Persistent Urban Poverty," Washington, DC.

Fine, M., & Cook, D. (1991). *Evaluation report: "With and for parents."* Baltimore: National Committee of Citizens for Education.

Fine, M. & Weis, L. (1998) *The unknown city.* Boston: Beacon Press.

Fineman, M. A., & Mykitiuk, R. (Eds.) (1994). *The public nature of private violence: the discovery of domestic abuse.* New York: Routledge.

Gladstein, J., Rusonis, E. S., & Heald, F. P. (1992). A comparison of inner city and upper-middle class youths' exposure to violence. *Journal of Adolescent Health, 13* (4), 275–280.

Hanmer, J., & Maynard, M. (Eds.) (1987). *Women, violence, and social control.* Atlantic Heights, NJ: Humanities Press International.

Hartsock, N. (1984). *Money, sex, and power.* Boston: Northeastern University Press.

Hoff, L. A. (1990). *Battered women as survivors.* New York: Routledge.

Horowitz, K., Weine, S., & Jekel, J. (1995). PTSD symptoms in urban adolescent girls: Compounded community trauma. *Journal of the American Academy of Child and Adolescent Psychiatry, 34* (10), 1353–1366.

Howell, J. (1972). *Hard living on Clay Street: Portraits of bluecollar families.* New York: Anchor Books.

Jones, A. (1980). *Women who kill.* New York: Fawcett Crest.

Jones, A. (1994). *Next time she'll be dead.* Boston: Beacon Press.

Kurz, D. (1995). *For richer for poorer: Mothers confront divorce.* New York: Routledge.

Lieberg, M. (1995). Teenagers and public space. *Communication Research, 22* (6), 729–744.

MacLeod, J. (1987). *Ain't no makin' it: Leveled aspirations in a low-income neighborhood.* Boulder, CO: Westview Press.

Marsh, C. E. (1993). Sexual assault and domestic violence in the African-American community. *Western Journal of Black Studies, 17* (3), 149–155.

Mills, C. W. (1959). *The sociological imagination.* New York: Oxford University Press.

Nicarthy, G. (1989). From the sounds of silence to the roar of a global movement: Notes on the movement against violence against women. *Response to the Victimization of Women and Children 12* (2), 3–10.

Richters, J. E., & Martinez, P. (1993). The NIMH Community Violence Project, 1: Children as victims of a witness to violence. *Psychiatry Interpersonal and Biological Processes, 56* (1), 7–26.

Roy, M. (Ed.). (1977). *Battered women: A psychosociological study of domestic violence.* New York: Van Nostrand Reinhold.

Schechter, S. (1982). *Women and male violence.* Boston: South End Press.

Schwab-Stone, M. E., Ayers, T. S., Kasprow, W., & Voyce, C. (1995). No safe haven: A study of violence exposure in an urban community. *Journal of the American Academy of Child and Adolescent Psychiatry, 34* (10), 1343–1352.

Shapiro, B. (1996, April 22). How the war on crime imprisons America. *The Nation, 262,* 14–21.

Stark, E. (1993). The myth of Black violence. *Social Work, 38* (4), 485–490.

Stark, E., & Flitcraft, A. (1988). Violence against intimates: An epidemiological review. In Van Haselt, R. Morrison, A. Bellack, & M. Hersen (Eds.), *Handbook of family violence* (pp. 293–318). New York: Plenum Press.

Steinmetz, S., & Strauss, M. (Eds.) (1974). *Violence in the family.* New York: Dodd Mead.

Sullivan, M. L. (1989). *"Getting paid": Youth crime and work in the inner city.* Ithaca, N Y: Cornell University Press.

Walker, L. A. (1984). Battered women, psychology, and public policy. *American Psychologist, 39* (10), 1178–1182.

Weis, L. (1990). *Working class without work: High school students in a deindustrializing economy.* New York: Routledge.

Weis, L., & Fine, M. (1996). Writing the "wrongs" of field work: Confronting our own research/writing dilemmas in urban ethnographies. *Qualitative Inquiry, 2* (3), 251–274.

White, E. (1985). *Chain, chain change for Black women dealing with physical and emotional abuse.* Seattle: South End Press.

Wilson, W. J. (1978). *The declining significance of race: Blacks and changing American institutions.* Chicago: University of Chicago Press.

27

The Queer Character of Racial Politics and Violence in America

WILLIAM F. PINAR

[A]ll race relations tend to be, however subtle, sex relations.

—Calvin C. Hernton, 1988

Lynching has been called "America's National Crime" (Wells-Barnett 1977 [1901], 30). The centrality of castration to the lynching event underscores that racial politics and violence in this country have been—and still are—simultaneously sexual politics. (The widespread white rape of black female slaves confirmed the fact that racial domination was sexualized.) It is no accident that striking sanitation workers in Memphis in spring 1968—the same strike that took Martin Luther King, Jr., to Memphis—carried signs saying simply: I AM A MAN. Of course, that sentence means "I am a human being," and it means "I am a citizen." But striking sanitation workers did not choose *those* categories; instead, these black men chose a gendered term.

As nightmarish, as evil, as wantonly destructive as white men's sexual, political, and economic exploitation of black women has been, the oppression of black men contained—contains—one additional element. There is a specific psycho-sexual element to racial exploitation as white men have obsessed over the black man's sexuality, his body, his phallus, "his" alleged desire for the white "lady." While both black women and men were sexually violated by white men, the black man's subjugation was, by definition, *homo*sexual. That is to say, in addition to assaulting his dignity as a human being, his civic status as male citizen, his stature as father and husband, the white-male sexual subjugation of black men necessarily assaulted his sexual identity.[1]

To make things "perfectly queer" (Doty 1993), I have chosen lynching and prison rape to make explicit the male-male sexual assault that lace "race relations" and structures still, to a remarkable extent, to the gender of racial politics and violence in this country. Despite radical discontinuities among the various historical periods (from the antebellum and post-Reconstruction South to post-1960s urban prisons) in which these events occurred, there are, I submit, certain horrendous continuities. Making the research on these subjects available to teachers is one function of contemporary curriculum research.[2]

America's National Crime

Is not the lynching of the Negro a sexual revenge? (Frantz Fanon 1967, 159)

[C]astration is also an inverted sexual encounter between black men and white men. (Robyn Wiegman 1993, 458 n.)

Between 1882 and 1927, an estimated 4,900 persons—nearly all the victims were young black men—were lynched in the United States, although other estimates, including the Tuskegee Institute archival records, place the number slightly lower (Brown 1975; Harris 1984; see Hall 1979, 141; Zangrando, 1980, 4). James Elbert Cutler (1905) estimated that 3,837 human beings were lynched between 1882 and 1903. Sociologists Stewart Tolnay and E. M. Beck (1995) limit their estimates to the "lynching era," encompassing the five decades between the end of Reconstruction and the beginning of the Great Depression, 1882 through 1930. During these years, they estimate that there were 2,018 separate incidents of lynching in which at least 2,462 African American men, women, and children met their deaths at the hands of white men. Approximately fourteen percent of the 2,018 black lynching incidents involved more than one victim.

Of the 2,462 black victims Tolnay and Beck count, three percent (74) were female. Tolnay and Beck assert that there are no "hard data" for the five-year period between 1877 and 1881, or for the Reconstruction period from 1865 to 1877, even though there were certainly lynchings before 1882, especially during the first years of Reconstruction. In fact, George C. Wright (1990) argues that more lynchings occurred in the fifteen-year period from 1865 to 1880 than during any other fifteen-year period, even the years from 1885 to 1900, which most scholars and contemporary observers characterize as the zenith of lynching. Perhaps it is this knowledge upon which former slave and anti-lynching activist Ida B. Wells relies when she estimates that over 10,000 black lives were lost to "rope and faggot" (see White 1929).

Lynching statistics are not comprehensive, of course, as they report only *recorded* lynchings. Moreover, estimates of the number of *prevented* lynchings range from 648 during the years 1915–32 (Raper's 1969 [1933] estimate) to 762 for the 1915–42 period (Jessie Daniel Ames' [1942]; see Hall 1979). While the exact number is not known, these figures suggest that between one-half and two-thirds of threatened lynchings failed, usually due to the active intervention of the authorities (Griffin, Clark, and Sandberg 1997). When one takes into account how many lynchings were prevented, one can only guess how widespread the practice of lynching actually was (Zangrando 1980).

In the white popular imagination, lynching was a response to black male rape of white women. On occasion black men did assault white women, but, as Robert Zangrando (1980, 4) points out, "neither that nor the greater frequency of rape and sexual harassment inflicted on black women by white and black men accounted for mob violence." The gendered and specifically queer character of the practice is suggested in Hazel Carby's (1998, 76) lyrical and lingering question:

We must ask if the ritual of dismemberment and sadistic torture of black bodies is, in fact, a search to expose, and perhaps an attempt to claim, an essence of manhood that is both feared and desired, an essence of the possible which escapes its pursuers as the blood pours from their hands and soaks the earth.

Although they constituted a minority of all lynchings, some victims were lynched for even the most trivial "violations," including breaches of conduct such as "insulting a white woman," "grave robbing," or "running a bordello" (Tolnay and Beck 1995, 103). Young black men were lynched for any reason at all, including "for just acting troublesome" (Zangrando 1980, 4). The fact that most victims were tortured "suggests the presence of sadistic tendencies among the lynchers" (Raper

1969 [1933], 1). Indeed, over the history of the phenomenon, "lynching … seems to have become increasingly sadistic: emasculation, torture, and burning alive replaced the hangman's noose" (Hall 1979, 133). As the nationwide campaign to end the practice intensified, lynchings were slowly replaced by "legal lynchings," a phrase used to describe the mockery of the American judicial system that enabled whites to murder blacks "legally." Nearly all scholars acknowledge that only rarely—if indeed ever—did African Americans receive fair trials, especially in the South (Wright 1990).

Walter White (1929) notes that the rape myth apparently did not exist before 1830. Given that the first slaves were brought to North America in 1619, for more than two centuries charges of rape against African Americans were virtually unknown. White (1929, 88–9) emphasizes economic motives for lynching, commenting that "such accusations [of rape] were made only after a defective economic system had been upturned and made enormously profitable through inventions and in doing so had caused slave-labor to become enormously more valuable." Some forty years earlier, after the lynching of three businessmen, Ida B. Wells had perceived that economic motives were at work: "They [the three lynched men] had committed no crime against white women. This is what opened my eyes to what lynching really was. An excuse to get rid of Negroes who were acquiring wealth and property and thus keep the race terrorized and 'keep the nigger down'"(Wells 1970, 64). No doubt economic motives were at work, but there were other motives at work as well.

What was a "typical" lynching like? As historian Fitzhugh Brundage (1993) points out, there was no "typical" lynching. Tolnay and Beck (1995, 23) report, "Although most lynchings were straight-forward, albeit illegal, executions with little ceremony or celebration, many went far beyond a mere taking of a human life. At times lynchings acquired a macabre, carnival-like aspect, with the victim being tortured and mutilated for the amusement of onlookers." While not so in fact, there was a "typical" lynching in fiction, in the white male imagination, and not infrequently, this fiction became fact (see Baldwin 1998 [1965]; Harris 1984; Wiegman 1993, 1995).

After a precipitating event occurred (murder was the most common, but anything could be a pretext for violence, including nothing at all), white men assembled, determined to take revenge. Whether the "crime" was imaginary or real did not matter; a "guilty party"—usually a young black man—was "identified," and the "manhunt" was on. Once captured, public notices were circulated usually a day or two in advance of the lynching event itself. Sometimes the notices were distributed to distant communities. Sometimes trains made special trips, adding extra cars to meet the demands of crowds wishing to travel in order to watch the spectacle (Harris 1984). Anna Julia Cooper (quoted in Lemert and Bhan, 1998, 210) recalls, "Excursion trains with banners flying were run into place and eager children were heard to exclaim: 'We have seen a hanging, we are now going to see a burning!'"

The number of spectators on one occasion reached 15,000. The lynching itself was sometimes preceded by hours of physical torture and sexual mutilation, often climaxed by what whites euphemistically called "surgery below the belt." Those parts of the victim's body that had been dismembered were sometimes photographed for picture postcards, later to be sold as souvenirs. The remains were usually burned. The leaders of lynchings were often well known and seen by thousands. But nearly everyone, including law enforcement officers, participated in a conspiracy of silence; invariably the coroner would declare that the lynching was committed by unknown persons (Harris 1984; Brown 1975).

White women functioned in the nineteenth-century South as symbolic currency in a homosocial economy (Sedgwick 1985; Rubin 1975, Irigaray 1985). In the practice of lynching, they served as justifications for white men's sexual mutilation of black men. White men would have denied that lynching was sexual mutilation, of course. Nor were all victims of lynching black and male; black women and children (and a few whites) were also lynched. However, most victims were young black men. Not all black men who were lynched were also castrated, but many were. What did white men think as they assembled into mobs, tracked their prey, captured then tortured the young black man, now naked before them? White men insisted they were protecting white women, that they were doing nothing less than serving "popular justice," saving "civilization."

What caused lynching? Historians and sociologists point to a combination of economic and political factors. There is little doubt that lynching was a political and economic phenomenon, but it was as well, and perhaps most profoundly, a gendered, indeed "queer" phenomenon. In the final decade of the nineteenth century, at which lynching was at its zenith, there was, in addition to economic and political turmoil, a certain "crisis" in white masculinity, admittedly a problematic characterization given the wide and variable range of responses white men made to an imperiled sense of manhood. For example, some historians argue that nineteenth-century middle-class manhood was most characterized by a "chest-thumping virility, vigorous outdoor athleticism, and fears of feminization" (Bederman 1995, 7). Others stress white middle-class men's growing interest in hitherto strictly "feminine" occupations like parenthood and domesticity. White manhood was—is—no monolith; to appreciate the "polymorphous plurality of [this] subject position" (Zizek 1996, 15) enables us to understand these coextensive and apparently contradictory performances of late nineteenth-century manhood as multiple white sides of one racialized and gendered coin.

Nineteenth-century hegemonic masculinity became destabilized as a result of a series of dramatic historical developments. In the South, the Civil War forced white women to abandon their fixed, if imaginary, subject positions as "ladies" to do much of the supervisory and managerial labor absent husbands, fathers, and sons could not perform while off fighting the Yankees (Faust 1996). This shift in Southern white women's subject positions coupled with the crushingly complete military defeat of Southern white men, a profoundly gendered as well as political and military event, set the stage for a beleaguered, regressed, frighteningly destabilized series of white male subject positions in the South.

While Kaja Silverman (1992, 6) is surely right when she asserts that "identity and desire are so completely imbricated that neither can be explained without recourse to the other," in U.S. racial politics, even when its "queer" character gets expressed explicitly in prison, the emphasis in that sentence must be on "imbricated." Desire was not expressed in straightforward, easily decodable fashion, in no small measure due to the repression of same-sex desire, especially interracial same-sex desire. (Racial antagonism has never stopped white men from seeking sex with black women.) But the desire of white men was also embedded in political, regional, cultural, economic, and gendered events that masked its sexual nature.

Black women had no political power in the Jim Crow South, but that fact did not mean defeat or submission. A black woman who had been born a slave would make the first memorable intervention in this white-male compulsion to mutilate the black male body. That black woman was Ida B. Wells, a Memphis schoolteacher and journalist. Her moral courage, pedagogical brilliance, and political acumen mark her as one of the greatest Americans to have ever lived (Munro 1999; Schechter 1997; Franklin 1970; Carby 1987; Ware 1992).

Wells would be joined (be it thirty years later) by a white woman, a woman who sensed that lynching, presumably a practice conducted for white women's sake, had nothing to do with them. This white woman was Jesse Daniel Ames, a Texas suffragist who founded the Association of Southern Women for the Prevention of Lynching (Ames 1942; Hall 1979). It takes no mystic to divine that it would be men, specifically white men, who would resist these women's efforts and the efforts of black men, most notably, Walter White and James Weldon Johnson of the NAACP, to end the nightmare that was lynching. A mutilated and repressed sexual dynamic is not easily exorcised, especially when it appears masked as "constitutionality" and "states' rights" (see Pinar 2001, chapter 11). Federal antilynching legislation was never passed.

Lynching was a vicious, horrific performance of white men's obsession with the black male body, a body they had once owned, had had their way with, and would have their way with again. "Charles Johnson reminds us," Laurence Goldstein (1994, xi) writes, introducing Johnson's essay in *The Male Body*, "how the black body has been stereotyped as a phallus to suit the needs of a racist society." How does the "black body" as phallic "suit the needs" of racism? The white man has obsessed over the black man's phallus from the earliest slave days, examining genitalia to determine breeding potential, presumably (Jordan 1974). For most white men—straight and gay—black men remain firmly planted in their "place," inside the white man's head, a fragment of his (often eroticized) imagination (see Pinar 2001, chapters 13–15).

Because black men existed in a civic sense as the white man imagined him sexually, he was left (against his will) in a homoerotic, if not explicitly homosexual, position socially, politically, erotically. This position in an increasingly heterosexist, homophobic twentieth century (although there are contradictory movements and indications, overall I accept Foucault's general thesis that increased visibility of sexual minorities has been in the service of surveillance, that "repressive tolerance" requires a certain "outing") has necessarily meant for black masculinity an ongoing, at times explosive, crisis: sexual, political, and social. While, as Du Bois (1982 [1903]) knew, black men were an "oasis" in relation to the "desert" that was white masculinity—unself-knowing, predatory, desperate white masculinity—black men were imprisoned in the "social reality" white men imagined, and then enforced by law, institution, and culture.

The Racial Politics of Sex in Prison

Is it surprising that prisons resemble factories, schools, barracks, hospitals, which all resemble prisons? (Michel Foucault 1995 [1979], 228)

These scars and wounds [of lynching] are clearly etched on the canvass of black sexuality. (Cornell West 1993, 85)

If white racism is both expressed and experienced as sexualized, as an assault on "manhood," would we not predict that if there were an opportunity for political revenge, some black men might choose sex as its medium? In American prisons we find exactly that. My reasoning did not proceed as neatly as these sentences imply. I came to prison rape literature on a whim. If nineteenth-century Southern white men could be so mistaken about their rationale for lynching, namely that black men were raping white women (which was rarely the case), then perhaps (I reasoned) the white-male fantasy about interracial prison rape was just that, another fiction.

To my astonishment I discovered white men were not making this one up. Even in white majority prisons, heterosexually identified black men bypass willing and available homosexuals (both black and white) to rape and "turn out" young, white heterosexual men. Rope and faggot, to borrow the title of Walter White's 1929 study of lynching, still describe relations between white and black men, if racially reversed and punned. "In prison," Daniel Lockwood (1980, 2) found, "most aggressors are black; most targets are white."

Since Emancipation, criminalization has been profoundly racialized in the United States, as "legalized lynchings" came to replace the extra-legal kind (Wright 1990). In the late nineteenth century, black men were imprisoned for nearly any reason, and once imprisoned, exploited in a vicious convict-lease system that made slavery look almost attractive (Ayers 1984). A century later, black men are still imprisoned for almost any reason, often victims of a racialized "war on drugs," which is, in effect, a war on young black men (Miller 1996). Black men have been and remain the obsession of white men, white men who remain determined to keep black men incarcerated, if not in their minds, then certainly in their jails. There, however, black men have effected a racial and gendered reversal, often coming out "on top."

Sexual attacks are still feared in prisons today, but no longer do officials and students of the institution imagine that the fact of rape has to do with a disproportionate presence of homosexuals, as they did in the early decades of the twentieth century (see Pinar 2001, chapter 16). The head of one agency told researcher Anthony Scacco that "[h]omosexual rapes in prisons are not homosexual at all, but heterosexuals, usually black men raping white boys for power and revenge" (quoted in Scacco 1975, 4). Is this statement another "assassination" of the black male image, as Hutchinson (1997) might suggest? Studies of sexual assaults in jails and prisons conducted during the past several decades conclude that there *is* a disproportionate number of black aggressors and white victims. Perhaps this is because the majority of prisoners today are black? No, "[w]hether or not there is a black numerical supremacy within the walls of a penal institution, the victim is usually not a black but a white or Puerto Rican" (Scacco 1975, 47–8).

One white inmate explained the racial politics of prison sex in this way: "Blacks have more control in the jails than whites do. They call it revolution.... They turn the whites into punks. You don't see any black punks around here.... All blacks here try to be bad and stuff and show their masculinity.... The blacks want to bring slavery back to us now" (quoted in Bartollas, Miller, and Dinitz 1976, 60).

How do black prisoners understand the black rape of young heterosexual white men? Is it, as whites allege, "reverse racism"? Unlike the short memories of many white prisoners, black prisoners, time and again, speak about interracial rape in historical as well as political terms. One informant said, "Every can I been in that's the way it is.... It's gettin' even I guess.... You guys been cuttin' our balls off ever since we been in this country. Now we're just gettin' even" (quoted in Carroll 1974, 174; see also Bowker 1980, 92).

Why would rape—rather than fist-fighting or gambling, for instance—represent "gettin' even"? Could it be that the black men's political oppression has also been sexual, *homo*sexual? This is suggested by another prisoner who told his interviewer

> The black man's just waking up to what's been going on. Now that he's awake, he's gonna be mean. He's been raped - politically, economically, morally raped. He sees this now, but his mind's still small so he's getting back this way. But it's just a beginning. (quoted in Bowker 1980, 92–3).

A white rape victim named Alan reported how his black attackers repeatedly called him a "white punk," a "white bitch," and asked questions like, "How does it feel to have a black prick in you, white boy?" (quoted in Bowker 1980, 93). Such testimony suggests "a direct link between racism and sexual victimization" (Bowker 1980, 93–4). Alan is no isolated instance. After extensive interviewing, one prison researcher concluded, "The prison is merely an arena within which blacks may direct aggression developed through 300 years of oppression against individuals perceived to be representatives of the oppressors" (Carroll 1974, 184). Another student of prison rape was more cautious: "Putting all these observations together, it seems reasonable to conclude that racism is a major cause of some of the interracial victimization that occurs in prison, but it is not the only cause" (Bowker 1980, 94).

Several investigators seem unsurprised by the racial character of these violent events. In his study of prison rape, Goldfarb (1976, 96) concluded that "[a]t least in isolated cases, gang rapes of inmates are conducted as a special manifestation of deep racial antagonism that exist in society at large and which are exacerbated in jails." A study of the North Carolina prison system (Fuller, Orsagh, and Raber 1977) quantified racial differences in victimization. The black victimization rate was approximately forty-five percent lower than the white victimization rate. Approximately four out of every ten incidents were interracial; eighty-two percent involved a black aggressor and a white victim (Bowker, 1980)

The relationship between rape and race does not change in those prisons where the majority is white. In his study of an eastern penitentiary, Leo Carroll (1974) found that twenty-two percent of the men in that institution were black, yet the racialization of rape was quite similar to what Alan Davis (1968) found in the majority-black Philadelphia prison system. Fifty-six percent of rape incidents in Davis' study involved black aggressors and white victims; twenty-nine percent involved black aggressors and black victims; and fifteen percent involved white aggressors and white victims. One of Carroll's informants told him

> To the general way of thinking it's 'cause we're confined and we've got hard rocks. But that ain't it all. *It's a way for the black man to get back at the white man.* It's one way he can assert his manhood. Anything white, even a defenseless punk, is part of what the black man hates. It's part of what he's had to fight all his life just to survive, just to have a hole to sleep in and some garbage to eat…. It's a new ego thing. He can show he's a man by making a white guy into a girl. (Carroll 1977, 422; Bowker 1980, 9, emphasis added)

Carroll (1977) learned that nearly all of the black inmates in this prison had participated in sexual assault upon whites at some time during their incarceration.

A Racial Politics of Emasculation

> In patriarchy, men (not women) "castrate" each other. (Calvin C. Hernton 1987, 12)

The black "rapist" of the late nineteenth century—the victim of lynchings—has evolved through the twentieth century into "the stud." This is a promotion, perhaps, but both figures remain figments in the white male mind (again, no monolithic subject position: see Pfeil 1995). As Paul Gilroy (1990, 274) has observed, "[Today] the black body is celebrated as an instrument of pleasure rather than an instrument of labor." But who black men are white men seem to have no clue. Nor do they seem especially interested, as long as they are entertained by their physical prowess, as in sports (Edwards 1982).

Could it be that white men have no clue who black men are because they have no clue who they are? Opaque to themselves, how might they recognize others? To begin, it would seem that white men are neither (DiPiero 2002). "White" is a complicated imaginary constructed in relation to blackness, specifically because there was, whites imagined, something primitive and bestial that they identified as "black" (see, for instance, Wiegman 1995). White men constructed themselves oppositionally to what they imagined white women and black men and women to be. To be a man meant living in a "separate sphere" from women, a rugged sphere of the frontier (whether literal or metaphoric) in which men were "self-made" (see Kimmel 1996). Around the turn of the century "manliness" evolved into "masculinity," a more sexualized version of the gendered myth of character by which white men had measured themselves earlier (Bederman 1995). Trapped within their own imagination, white men mistook their fantasies—about themselves, about "others"—as real. To maintain the fantasy of white-male supremacy (that "whiteness" and "masculinity" even existed in any essential sense) required suppression of those whose agency, volition, and independence threatened the fragility of white men's minds.

By the final decade of the nineteenth century, a certain "crisis" of white masculinity was well under way. Shifts in the economy, the political and social gains of African Americans and of white women (including the campaign for suffrage), the disappearance of "romantic friendship," and in the South an ongoing racialization of a defeated white manhood all contributed to many white men feeling besieged, uncertain, indignant, and frightened. Not committed to working through such changes self-consciously and psychologically, the majority of men resorted to defensive and compensatory distractions, among them body building, sexual restraints (especially of adolescent boys), reactionary racial and gender politics (although both the suffrage and the civil rights movements continued), a "muscular" Christianity, and the construction of compulsory "heterosexuality." Like whiteness, this fantasy of hypermasculinity functioned as a standard to which all men must aspire; it was an ideal few men reached. To be a "man" now required exertion, self-policing, and continual demonstrations, even violent; one must *prove* that one was a "man" (see Pinar 2001, Chapters 4–6).

Add to this volatile mix the history of Africans in the "new world." From the Middle Passage to the auction block to the plantation, black bodies existed in subjugation to white bodies, specifically white male bodies, except for the Civil War years when, as Drew Faust (1996) points out, white women were forced to assume the male position. As Saidiya V. Hartman (1997) has explained, white men (even abolitionists) imagined, and in fact psychologically inhabited, black bodies, specifically black male bodies, as extensions of their own economic, political, and sexual desires. Not only black women were raped by white men. As Southern apologist Earl Thorpe (1967) boasts, there was in the antebellum American South a carnality unknown in the West since ancient Greece. Hardly the achievement Thorpe takes it to be, there was in fact a parallel: In both cases only white men were citizens and while (white) women were wives, young men were very much on old men's minds. The effects of this sexualized subjugation echo today:

> Every forty-six seconds of the school day, a black child drops out of school, every ninety-five seconds a black baby is born into poverty, and every four hours of every day in the year a black young adult, age twenty to twenty-four, is murdered, and one realizes that the much discussed crisis of the black male is no idle fiction. (Gates 1994, 12).

Black subjugation in America has been, of course, multidimensional; it remains simultaneously economic, political, psychological, and gendered. It has also been "queer."

The point bears emphasis. There was no white female analog to lynching. Even when white women knew white men were sleeping with black women, they devised no rituals of sexual torture and mutilation to "teach them a lesson." There is no evidence of white women collecting themselves in mobs, roving the countryside in search of black female (or male) "criminals" accused of sleeping with white men. Whatever white female sexual subjugation of black women occurred—apart from prison sex (and there such interracial sexual relationships are often consensual, with black women often playing the "butch" roles)—there seems to have been no sexual identity-threatening consequences to white female racism. Moreover, there seems no analog to black "hypermasculinity," no hyperfemininity that is driven by a compensatory effort to erase historical experience, a hypersexuality of denial and which guarantees a homoerotic undertow. While there is homosociality among women, it seems to lack any parallel to the misogyny, the group violence, of male groups. Women, black or white, do not gang rape men or women.

What is it about "men"—"men" who imagined themselves "white"—that required them to split white women into either madonnas or whores, black men into harmless uncles or rapists/superstuds, and black women into mammies or sluts? What is it about white men that they made black men the intense object of their obsession; why did those Europeans who first discovered Africans feel compelled to enslave them? The place black men have occupied in the imaginative life of European American writers is profound and constant, as Leslie Fiedler's remarkable commentary makes clear: "[W]hat they [these books] celebrate, all of them, [is] the mutual love of *a white man and a colored*" (Fiedler 1995 [1948], 531). That mutuality is in the white male mind only. At the center of American civilization (as a patriarchal, homosocial civilization) is the desire and longing the white man has felt and feels still for the black.

If only white men could feel what they have repressed, would the four hundred-year nightmare be over? Would racism disappear? The experience of black gay men with white suggests not. Still the surface of black male flesh shines with the desire white men feel; black male subjectivity remains effaced by the white objectification and commodification of the black male body. Of course, being a sex object is a promotion over being a slave, but as women know, not fundamentally, as objectification enslaves as well. The contemporary "studs"—actors, rappers, athletes, models—are at least paid for strutting their stuff, but the historical throughline is clear. Black men still strip, sweat, and move their muscles while white men watch. "The prize, the turf of struggle," Clyde Taylor (1994, 168) asserts, "may be focused less today on free black labor, only to shift to black experience as packaged and commodified in popular culture and entertainment." Elizabeth Alexander (1994, 92) sees the throughline as bodies in pain: "Black bodies in pain for public consumption have been an American spectacle for centuries. This history moves from public rapes, beatings, and lynchings to the gladiatorial arenas of basketball and boxing."

Prisons are not alien womanless worlds in which men resort to unimaginable acts. Prisons disclose the profoundly womanless worlds most men in fact inhabit, in which women are fundamentally fictive units of currency in a homosocial economy. What the fact of homosociality indicates is that the prison is not unique, that many, perhaps most, men "live" intrapsychically in all-male worlds from which women are aggressively banished. It is a mark of manhood (see Gilmore 1990, 2001). For most men, only fortunes and men's eyes are real. In prison, black men take revenge sexually for the civic subjugation, the political emasculation, they have suffered since the Middle Passage. Straight black men could have devised many forms of revenge: physical maiming for one, murder for another. But somehow black men knew exactly what form revenge must be once they were "on top," the same form that "race relations" have taken (and continue to take) in the United States. "Race" has been about castration, civic and literal, and being made into somebody's "punk," politically, economically, and, yes, sexually.

Notes

Thanks to Chris Myers, director of Peter Lang, New York, for allowing me to draw upon *The Gender of Racial Politics and Violence*.

1. While Foucault and others have argued persuasively that sexual identity is a twentieth-century phenomenon, the sexualization of racial politics influenced black male sexual identity not so much in terms of the gay/straight binary (after all, "blackness" became identified with hypermasculinity and hyperheterosexuality), but in even more complex and pervasive ways (see, for instance, Stokes 2001).

2. In drawing—promiscuously but critically—from various academic disciplines and popular culture, I propose that curriculum studies scholars work to create conceptual montages for public school teachers who understand that positionality as aspiring to create a public space (see Pinar in press).

References

Alexander, Elizabeth. "Can You Be BLACK and Look at This: Reading the Rodney King Video(s)." In *Black Male: Representations of Masculinity in Contemporary American Art*, edited by Thelma Golden, 91–110. New York: Whitney Museum of American Art (Harry N. Abrams, Inc.), 1994.

Ames, Jessie Daniel. *The Changing Character of Lynching*. Atlanta: Commission on Interracial Cooperation, 1942.

Ayers, Edward L. *Vengeance and Justice: Crime and Punishment in the Nineteenth Century American South*. New York: Oxford, 1984.

Baldwin, James. "Going to Meet the Man." In *Black on White: Black Writers on What It Means to Be White*, edited by David R. Roediger, 255–73. New York: Schocken Books, 1998. (Orig. pub. 1965.)

Bartollas, Clemens, Stuart J. Miller, and Simon Dinitz. *Juvenile Victimization: The Institutional Paradox*. New York: John Wiley, 1976.

Bederman, Gail. *Manliness and Civilization: A Cultural History of Gender and Race in the United States, 1880–1917*. Chicago: University of Chicago Press, 1995.

Bowker, Lee H. *Prison Victimization*. New York: Elsevier, 1980.

Brown, Richard Maxwell. *Strain of Violence: Historical Studies of American Violence and Vigilantism*. New York: Oxford University Press, 1975.

Brundage, W. Fitzhugh. *Lynching in the New South: Georgia and Virginia, 1880–1930*. Urbana: University of Illinois Press, 1993.

Carby, Hazel V. *Reconstructing Womanhood: The Emergence of the Afro-American Novelist*. New York: Oxford University Press, 1987.

Carby, Hazel V. *Race Men*. Cambridge, MA: Harvard University Press, 1998.

Carroll, Leo. "Race and Sexual Assault in a Prison." Paper presented at the annual meeting of the Society for the Study of Social Problems, 1974.

Carroll, Leo. "Humanitarian Reform and Biracial Sexual Assault in a Maximum Security Prison." *Urban Life* 5 (1977): 417–37.

Cutler, James Elbert. *Lynch Law: An Investigation into the History of Lynching in the United States*. New York: Longmans, Green & Co, 1905.

Davis, Alan J. "Sexual Assaults in the Philadelphia Prison System and Sheriff's Vans." *Trans-Action*, 6, 2 (1968): 8–16.

DiPiero, Thomas. *White Men Aren't*. Durham: Duke University Press, 2002.

Doty, A. *Making Things Perfectly Queer*. Minneapolis: University of Minnesota Press, 1993.

Du Bois, W. E. B. *The Souls of Black Folk*. New York: New American Library, 1982. (Orig. pub. 1903.)

Edwards, Harry. "Race in Contemporary American Sports." *National Forum* 62 (1982): 19–22.

Fanon, Frantz. *Black Skin, White Masks*. New York: Grove Weidenfeld, 1967. (Translated by Charles Lam Markmann.)

Faust, Drew Gilpin. *Mothers of Invention: Women of the Slaveholding South in the American Civil War*. Chapel Hill: University of North Carolina Press, 1996.

Fiedler, Leslie. "Come Back to the Raft Ag'in, Huck Honey!" In *Mark Twain, Adventures of Huckleberry Finn: A Case Study in Critical Controversy*, edited by Gerald Graff & James Phelan, 528–34. Boston & New York: Bedford Books of St. Martin's Press, 1995. (Originally appeared in *Partisan Review*, 1948.)

Foucault, M. *Discipline and Punish: The Birth of the Prison*. New York: Vintage, 1995. (Translated by Alan Sheridan.) (Orig. pub. 1979.)

Franklin, John Hope. "Foreword." In *Crusade for Justice*, by Ida B. Wells, ix–xi. Chicago: University of Chicago Press, 1970.

Fuller, Dan A., Thomas Orsagh, and David Raber. "Violence and Victimization within the North Carolina Prison System." Paper presented at the annual meeting of the Academic of Criminal Justice Sciences, 1977.

Gates, Jr., Henry Louis. "Preface." *Black Male: Representations of Masculinity in Contemporary American Art*, edited by Thelma Golden, 11–14. New York: Whitney Museum of American Art (Harry N. Abrams, Inc.), 1994.

Gilmore, David D. *Manhood in the Making*. New Haven: Yale University Press, 1990.

Gilmore, David D. *Misogyny: The Male Malady*. Philadelphia: University of Pennsylvania Press, 2001.

Gilroy, Paul. "One Nation under a Groove: The Cultural Politics of 'Race' and Racism in Britain." In *Anatomy of Racism*, edited by David Theo Goldberg, 263–82. Minneapolis: University of Minnesota Press, 1990.

Goldfarb, Ronald. *Jails: The Ultimate Ghetto of the Criminal Justice System*. Garden City, NY: Doubleday, 1976.

Goldstein, Laurence (Ed.). *The Male Body: Features, Destinies, Exposures*. Ann Arbor: University of Michigan Press, 1994.

Griffin, Larry J., Paula Clark, and Joanne C. Sandberg. "Narrative and Event: Lynching and Historical Sociology." In *Under Sentence of Death: Lynching in the South*, edited by W. Fitzhugh Brundage, 24–47. Chapel Hill: University of North Carolina Press, 1997.

Hall, Jacquelyn Dowd. *Revolt against Chivalry: Jessie Daniel Ames and the Women's Campaign against Lynching*. New York: Columbia University Press, 1979.

Harris, Trudier. *Exorcising Blackness: Historical and Literary Lynching and Burning Rituals*. Bloomington: Indiana University Press, 1984.

Hartman, Saidiya V. *Scenes of Subjection: Terror, Slavery, and Self-Making in Nineteenth Century America*. New York: Oxford University Press, 1997.

Haynes, Carolyn A. *Divine Destiny: Gender and Race in Nineteenth-Century Protestantism*. Jackson: University Press of Mississippi, 1998.

Hernton, Calvin C. *The Sexual Mountain and Black Women Writers*. New York: Anchor/Doubleday, 1987.

Hernton, Calvin C. *Sex and Racism in America*. New York: Doubleday, 1988. (Orig. pub. 1965.)

Hutchinson, Earl Ofari. *The Assassination of the Black Male Image*. New York: Simon & Schuster, 1997.

Irigaray, Luce. *This Sex Which Is Not One*. Ithaca: Cornell University Press, 1985. (Translated by Catherine Porter.)

Jordan, Winthrop D. *The White Man's Burden: Historical Origins of Racism in the United States*. New York: Oxford University Press, 1974.

Kimmel, Michael. *Manhood in America: A Cultural History*. New York: Free Press, 1996.

Lemert, Charles and Esme Bhan (Eds.) *The Voice of Anna Julia Cooper*. Lanham, MD: Rowan & Littlefield, 1998.

Lockwood, Daniel. *Prison Sexual Violence*. New York: Elsevier, 1980.

Miller, Jerome G. *Search and Destroy: African-American Males in the Criminal Justice System*. New York: Cambridge University Press, 1996.

Munro, Petra. "Political Activism as Teaching: Jane Addams and Ida B. Wells." In *Pedagogies of Resistance: Women Educator Activists, 1880–1960*, edited by Margaret Smith Crocco, Petra Munro, and Kathleen Weiler, 19–45. New York: Teachers College Press, 1999.

Pfeil, Fred. *White Guys*. London: Verso, 1995.

Pinar, William F. *The Gender of Racial Politics and Violence in America: Lynching, Prison Rape, and the Crisis of Masculinity.* New York: Peter Lang, 2001.

Pinar, William F. *What Is Curriculum Theory?* Mahwah, NJ: Lawrence Erlbaum, 2004.

Pinar, William F. "The Synoptic Text Today." *JCT*, in press.

Raper, Arthur F. *The Tragedy of Lynching.* Montclair, NJ: Patterson Smith, 1969. (Orig. pub. 1933.)

Rubin, Gayle. "The Traffic in Women: Notes on the 'Political Economy' of Sex." In *Toward an Anthropology of Women*, edited by Rayna Reiter, 157–210. New York: Monthly Review Press, 1975.

Scacco, Jr., Anthony M. *Rape in Prison.* Springfield, IL: Charles C. Thomas, 1975.

Schechter, Patricia A. "Unsettled Business: Ida B. Wells against Lynching, or How Antilynching Got Its Gender." In *Under Sentence of Death: Lynching in the South*, edited by W. Fitzhugh Brundage, 292–317. Chapel Hill: University of North Carolina Press, 1997.

Sedgwick, Eve Kosofsky. *Between Men: English Literature and Male Homosocial Desire.* New York: Columbia University Press, 1985.

Silverman, Kaja. *Male Subjectivity at the Margins.* New York and London: Routledge, 1992.

Stokes, Mason. *The Color of Sex: Whiteness, Heterosexuality, and the Fictions of White Supremacy.* Durham: Duke University Press, 2001.

Taylor, Clyde. "The Game." In *Black Male: Representations of Masculinity in Contemporary American Art*, edited by Thelma Golden, 167–74. New York: Whitney Museum of American Art (Harry N. Abrams, Inc.), 1994.

Thorpe, Earl E. *Eros and Freedom in Southern Life and Thought.* Durham: Seeman, 1967.

Tolnay, Stewart E. and E. M. Beck. *A Festival of Violence: An Analysis of Southern Lynchings, 1882–1930.* Urbana: University of Illinois Press, 1995.

Ware, Vron. *Beyond the Pale: White Women, Racism and History.* London: Verso, 1992.

Wells, Ida B. *Crusade for Justice: The Autobiography of Ida B. Wells.* Chicago: University of Chicago Press, 1970.

Wells-Barnett, Ida B. "Lynching and the excuse for it." In *Lynching and Rape: An Exchange of Views*, Jane Addams and Ida B. Wells (edited by Bettina Aptheker), (28–34). Chicago: University of Illinois, Occasional Paper No. 25, 1977. (Orig. pub. 1901.)

West, Cornel. *Race Matters.* Boston: Beacon Press, 1993.

White, Walter. *Rope and Faggot: A Biography of Judge Lynch.* New York: Alfred A. Knopf, 1929.

Wiegman, Robyn. "The Anatomy of Lynching." *Journal of the History of Sexuality* 3, 3 (1993): 445–67.

Wiegman, Robyn. *American Anatomies: Theorizing Race and Gender.* Durham: Duke University Press, 1995.

Wright, George C. *Racial Violence in Kentucky, 1865–1940: Lynchings, Mob Rule, and "Legal Lynchings."* Baton Rouge: Louisiana State University Press, 1990.

Zangrando, Robert L. *The N.A.A.C.P. Crusade against Lynching, 1909–1950.* Philadelphia: Temple University Press, 1980.

Zizek, Slavoj. "Re-visioning 'Lacanian' Social Criticism: The Law and Its Obscene Double." *Journal for the Psychoanalysis of Culture & Society* 1, 1 (1996): 15–25.

28

Diversity and Disciplinarity as Cultural Artifacts

ARJUN APPADURAI

Introduction

There is an implicit economy that informs us when we think of diversity and disciplinarity. Diversity suggests plenitude, an infinity of possibilities, and limitless variation. Disciplinarity suggests scarcity, rationing, and policing. They thus seem to be naturally opposed principles. I argue here that they need not be opposed and that it is important that they be brought into a certain sort of interaction in the American research university. The question is: what sort of interaction?

My observations have a background. First, I take as my context the research university in the United States, as well as those undergraduate colleges whose faculty were trained at research universities. In treating diversity as a cultural artifact, I have in mind the debate of the last decade or so over multiculturalism, political correctness, and affirmative action, which shows no signs of abating, even as it grows more sterile. I am also concerned with diversity as a slogan for the peculiarly American investment in cultural pluralism. I aim to return to the idea of diversity something of the technical sense it has in anthropology.

Images of Diversity

Even without recourse to the dictionary, it is possible to see that diversity is a tricky word. I began by suggesting that it suggests plenitude, an infinity of possibilities. There is something to this implication, even if the dictionary will not directly sustain it. Today, diversity is a word that contains all the force, all the contradictions, and all the anxieties of a specifically American utopianism. Let us call this a utopianism of the plural. To my knowledge the story of how the idea of "pluralism" enters American social, political, and academic thought has yet to be told. Briefly, I believe it is a twentieth-century idea, not really a part of the founding principles of the United States. It is a co-optative reaction to the great migrations from Europe of the late nineteenth and early twentieth century, and the fact that it has since become a central aspect of American society, civics, and political science is one of the interesting puzzles of the cultural history of this century. Be that as it may, today "diversity" as a slogan encompasses the strong fascination with the plural, and the even stranger idea that plurality and equality are deeply intertwined in a democratic society. The folk view that biological diversity is a good thing (which has become naturalized in American thought in the same way that the Oedipus complex and germ theory have become naturalized) creates a good part of the energy that animates debates about multiculturalism.

In spite of this Utopian subtext, which suggests that diversity means the infinite multiplication of difference, there is an uneasy sense among all participants in the debate about diversity, particularly in the academy, that it is not an infinitely elastic principle. This intuition is culturally and technically justified. If nothing else, it reflects the sense that even American wealth is not infinitely available to subsidize American dreams. The current discourse of the deficit, played out with remarkable uniformity in corporations, in the government, and in the university, certainly makes it difficult to sustain the idea of the plural as infinite.

When we speak of diversity, whatever our position in these debates, we all know that we are not speaking of just plurality, or variety, or difference. Diversity is a particular organization of difference. The question is: what kind of organization? The issue that does not seem to be engaged in much of the debate about diversity is not whether it is somehow organized (that is, rationed, policed, limited, and reproduced) but how it should be organized. In the wider society of the United States, this is the unspoken issue in debates about immigration, bilingualism, and citizenship. But my concerns here are with the academy, and in the academy the central problem is the reluctance to recognize that the economy of diversity is also a managed economy. If it is in the wider sense a managed economy, how then is it or could it be managed in the academy? What is at stake in its management?

There are many ways in which diversity could be managed in the academy, notably by the wholesale application or extension of larger principles, mechanisms, and ideas from outside the academy, such as quotas, censuses, and entitlements. These approaches tend to generate affirmative action babies, human and technical, whether we like them or not. Much of the official discourse of the university, notably in matters of recruitment, retention, and promotion, is premised on the assumption that diversity is a mechanical good, the aggregate outcome of good intentions applied case by case. By refusing to recognize that diversity requires more deliberation and more organization, universities allow the unfree play of the market—in students, in staff, and in faculty—to determine actual demographic outcomes. Furthermore, actual outcomes—specific statistical profiles about the presence of students of color, faculty of minority background, and a vaguely international milieu—are used as marketing tools by many colleges and universities to seek further diversity in their populations.

What is lacking is a sustained effort to examine the links between intellectual and cultural diversity. One way to approach diversity in the university is to see it as a particular organization of difference, in which intellectual and cultural diversity are interactive and mutually interlocutory. If we miss this link, the last vestiges of difference between the academy and other corporate organizational forms will disappear and the university will become just another workplace. This is not to deny that the university is *also* a workplace (involving issues of class, wages, safety, discrimination, mobility, and productivity) but to recall that it is a special sort of workplace concerned with thinking, with training, with ideas, and with knowledge.

One symptom of the current lack of critical thought about diversity in the academy is to be found in the canon debate. While much has been said in and about this debate, one feature of the debate is worthy of remark. There is a peculiar anxiety about quantity that characterizes much of it. This emerges in arguments over the form and shape of the canon—in particular of classic or "great" books in the undergraduate curriculum. In this debate of the last decade, there is a strange slippage between issues of quantity and quality. On the face of it, the debate is about the sort of standards that ought to govern the selection of classic books to be read by undergraduates—*prima facie* a question about quality. But this issue invariably tends to slip into a zero-sum discourse in which the addition of new sorts of classic works—by women and people from other societies and traditions, for example—is seen as unseating and eliminating a list, even if imaginary, of already time-tested classics. The debate often implies that for books to be truly great, they must belong to a closed and short list.

In one sense, this view reflects the deep and widespread idea that lists of the great, the rare, and the precious tend to be short and overlapping, with books as with other sorts of commodities. More salient is the fact that the issue of classic works involves a small fraction of the thirty or so courses that most American undergraduates take in their four or five years in college. In this sense, the list is finite, not by its nature but because the formal pedagogical opportunities to tell students what is really great about some books are relatively few. The true scarcity is not of great books—an odd idea—but of opportunities to impress upon students the right norms of quality-control.

Given this unconsciously apprehended scarcity of pedagogical opportunities to communicate ideas about great texts in the average college curriculum, it is no surprise that the sense of scarcity—and thus of urgency and of competition—tends to blur the line between the admission of books into various kinds of lists and the admission of students (and, to some extent, of faculty and of staff) into the social world of the university. There is a vague political intuition, shared by all sides in campus debates, that the demography of great books and the demography of students and faculty are somehow related. One aspect of this relationship, which has been widely noted, is that new kinds of students ("multicultural") tend to demand new kinds of books, but the sense of demographic anxiety runs deeper than this factor alone. It also reflects unease about the lack of principles with which to regulate intake in any of these lists. With human beings as with texts there is a sense that issues of quality (a.k.a. "standards") and issues of quantity are connected, but there are few explicit efforts to engage this connection.

Tied to the general absence of engagement with the links between intellectual and cultural diversity is another absence: the lack of any effort to distinguish between cultural diversity and the culture of diversity. By this I mean that the commitment to cultural diversity is dominated by numerical and categorical strategies that fundamentally involve addition and extension. A more serious effort to create a culture of diversity requires more than new categories and added numbers of people and books conceived to be different. What is required is a sustained effort to create a climate that is actually hospitable to diversity: one which puts diversity at the center of the curriculum and the demographics of the university, rather than at its statistical or conceptual margins. Affirmative action—in the narrow sense of entitlement by quota—is good neither for books nor for people. What is wrong with the narrow sense of affirmation is that addition of numbers—though good in itself—says little about the organization of the new or the transformation of what already exists by what is new. Put simply, the demographic and textual core of the university remains untouched if affirmative action is seen as a matter of a few more books, a few more courses, and a few more students and faculty of color.

More may be better, but it is not good enough. It is not good enough *for the university* unless the commitment to diversity transforms the way in which knowledge is sought and transmitted. That is, without a conscious commitment to the mutual value of intellectual and cultural diversity—which is really what I mean by a culture of diversity—the core mission of the university remains insulated from the commitment to diversity. Though the American academy has to some extent managed to put into practice a minimal commitment to cultural diversity, it has a long way to go before it can truly claim to have instantiated a culture of diversity. While the American university has managed to put into its official life (job advertisements, faculty and student recruitment, and courses of study) the principle that more difference is better, it has not succeeded in creating a habitus where diversity is at the heart of the apparatus itself. To deepen this appreciation requires a critical approach to the problem of disciplinarity, since it is in and through various kinds of discipline that the American university pursues its pedagogical and research projects.

The Idea of Disciplinarity

There has been much serious writing on the history of disciplines and disciplinarity, and an even larger literature about particular scholarly disciplines, their history and organization. There is also a substantial literature about the way in which the American research university adapted late nineteenth-century German models, which accounts for a good deal of the morphology of departments and disciplines for the ideology about teaching in relation to research, and for the value of research training. The "liberal arts" college is a more peculiarly American thing, which combines elements of the Oxbridge model of undergraduate life with the European model of disciplinary research. Notice that in neither European model (the British or the German) is there the slightest interest in diversity, especially in its social and cultural sense. That is an American preoccupation of this century, as I have already suggested. I am not going to engage this complicated set of literatures. Rather, I am going to propose a naive anthropology of the idea of disciplinarity as a cultural artifact.

One place to begin such an anthropology is the tension between historicity and authority. At least since the publication of Thomas Kuhn's *The Structure of Scientific Revolutions*, there has developed a broad consensus that the historicity of certain forms of inquiry is not the enemy of their productivity but perhaps its guarantee. This idea has leaked into various fields, institutions, and disciplinary cultures unevenly, but it seems clear that a simple model of accumulation and expansion no longer governs, even in such fields as philology, psychology, or musicology. Nevertheless, the virtues of historicity (or at least its undeniability) do not seem to blunt the rhetoric of permanence in many disciplinary contexts. This rhetoric usually underwrites the conservative discourse of standards, canons, taste, and anti-fashion that is most visible in public debates about the humanities, but in a quieter way appears in the social sciences and even in the natural sciences. The issue tends to show up in the invocation of quality and permanence—typically humanist tropes—in fields dominated by reading and interpretation. In the social and natural sciences the rhetoric of permanence relies on images of reliability and objectivism. It is thus also invoked in regard to ethnic identities, nationalist histories and the like, and often deployed against critiques couched in the idioms of invented traditions and constructed realities. The battle over trendiness, fashion, and the tradition of the new in the humanities seems to be fought largely at the annual meetings of the MLA and in cultural studies settings, but it is present throughout the academy.

One crucial question is why the humanities have become the site for the displacement and enactment of these large academic and social anxieties. I would suggest that this implosion into the humanities of issues of general cultural import reflects the peculiar status of the humanities and, at the college level, of the liberal arts, in an educational atmosphere increasingly driven by megascience, corporate sponsorship of research, the rollback of federal support for big research, and the continuing scramble for professional and pre-professional credentials among American students. Thus while many colleges and universities have increasingly become factories for specialized research, applied interests, and professional credentializing, the humanities have become the critical site for the idea that the university is also about thought and reflection, cultivation and conscience, disinterest and abstraction, literacy and cosmopolitanism. Since the humanities are simultaneously badly funded and seen to be infected by dangerous fashions—in art, literary theory, popular culture and the like—they are a serious site for cultural warfare. On their survival rests the image of the academy as being *independent* of wider social pressures, whether from science, state, or industry, and of the university as being the critical bastion, in modern American society, of the *cosmopolitan*.

In addition, there is the anxiety about quantity and quality that I alluded to in an earlier section of this essay and a widespread presumption that the four years of undergraduate life (when most students are roughly between eighteen and twenty-two years of age) constitute the crucial window for instilling cultural literacy. Before that age, students are seen as inadequately mature and after that, as given over to the full-time worship of Mammon. Whatever the reasons, we have a peculiar political economy behind the debates over the canon that assumes that ten or fifteen books, read in two or three courses, in a few thousand colleges and universities, in four years of the life-cycle of a modest number of Americans, are the decisive stage for the battle over literacy, standards, and cosmopolitanism. Is it expected that people will never read again? Or that they will never again read in a proper pedagogic setting? Whatever the reasons, the humanities have been elected for the role of hosting a series of dramas and debates about what constitutes cultural literacy for the educated elite. This implosion of large issues into a small and underfunded area of the American academy may well reflect the ambivalence about disinterested learning, passionate reading, and serendipitous discovery among those who hold power in American society as much as it reflects the left-wing discovery that the humanities are the place where existing ideas of the good, the true, and the beautiful are most easily exposed and challenged.

Debates about cultural studies—seen variously as an area, a field, a program, a discipline, or a conspiracy—reveal an overdetermined landscape of anxieties about the humanities. Two existing disciplinary fields that have much to lose (and also to gain) from the growth of cultural studies in the last decade are anthropology and English and American literature. In general, English departments have been the spaces within which cultural studies has grown and thrived. Recalling the origins of cultural studies in England in the work of Richard Hoggart and Raymond Williams (both students of literature), this is perhaps understandable. It was also doubtless inevitable that it would be in the space of English that Matthew Arnold's sense of culture (as civilizing process) would encounter the revenge of popular culture as a subject fit for literary study. As literary critics widened their lens to include all forms of representation, it was natural that the visual would enter their interests, with its accompanying cinematic, scopic, and feminist critiques. Exported to the colonies, English created many minor literatures, particularly of the "Commonwealth" variety, again rich materials for contesting the "white" canon. To all this must be added the seductions of theory (a.k.a. French post-structuralist thought), the special bête-noire of the literary neo-conservatives. A heady mix, mediated by a peculiar mixture of high formalisms (rightly traced back to the cold-bloodedness of New Criticism) and of low formalisms (feminism, music theory, rap, and consumer culture).

Of course, what looks like a vast and unruly expansion of the subject matter of literary studies in the United States (annually celebrated in the MLA fiesta and demonized by the National Association of Scholars and other conservative organizations) hardly passed without remark within English departments themselves, where scholars of Byron and Chaucer, of Joyce and of Whitman, did not greet this new imperialism of cultural studies without notable alarm and aggressive resistance.

But from the outside, in such fields as anthropology, cultural studies looked like a high-consensus conspiracy by literary scholars to steal CULTURE, or worse, to turn the study of cultural forms into a literary exercise. At this point, the protectionist wing of anthropology joined forces with the literary conservatives to decry—with the usual disregard for detail—all forms of the "postmodern," meaning all forms of cultural theory which emerged after they stopped reading. This war over culture (tied indirectly to the more publicly discussed "culture wars") takes on a special displaced force in anthropology, where the last few years have witnessed a growing anxiety about whether and why anthropology should remain the unified home of the "four fields"—socio-cultural anthropology, linguistic anthropology, biological anthropology, and archaeology.

In England and Europe, these fields are largely separate, but in the United States, because of the Boasian heritage, the special concern with cultural relativism, and the intense battle against racism in social science, anthropology retained the vision of a grand discourse on all forms of human variation, a vision sustained by explicit reference to evolutionary theory. For reasons that lie outside the scope of this essay, this foundation for normal interaction across the four fields has fallen on hard times lately and sustains uneven serious traffic. What is left is market niches, university politics, and shrinking budgets as the main motivations for holding the four fields together. In short, current arguments for holding the four fields together are grounded in calls to disciplinary patriotism rather than in high frequency, vibrant intra-disciplinary exchanges. The anxiety about holding the four fields together is tied up with a wish for a sort of general paradigm that is now plainly lacking. Since these matters are highly contingent, it is quite possible that such an integrating discourse—built around new understandings of material life: the body, work, space, death, warfare—may well emerge again, but calls to disciplinary arms have never been the best ways to hasten the progress of intellectual history.

At any rate, for anthropologists the threat from cultural studies comes just at the time when the center (at least in terms of the issue of the four fields) is seen as weak. Thus, although there is a healthy traffic on the borders of the two disciplines between groups who are happy to work in the gray economies typical of disciplinary borders, conservatives in both spaces have drawn the battle lines and are engaged in a vigorous tug-of-war about who really owns the study of culture. Of course, this is not helped by the fact that a whole slew of other fields, ranging from sociology and communication studies to romance languages and musicology, are happily grabbing pieces of the market.

One way in which the attack on cultural studies is formulated—by opponents from both anthropology and from literary studies—is to portray it as promiscuous in its choices of topic, loose and opportunistic in its methods, lax and consumerist in its pursuit of "trends." The charge of being victims of "trend" or "fashion" (hardly the first in the history of Western intellectual life) is levelled at cultural studies scholars as an omnibus characterization about its "theory" (too French), its topics (too popular), its style (too glitzy), its jargon (too hybrid), its politics (too postcolonial), its constituency (too multicultural). All this is usually accompanied by charges, both implicit and explicit, that the whole business of cultural studies is somehow not really scholarly, not truly disciplined, not about "real" research, and not about genuine knowledge. To see why cultural studies excites this anxiety about genuine scholarship, it is necessary to look more closely at some ambiguities that characterize ideas about discipline and disciplinarity, especially in the humanities.

Just as in regard to diversity there has been little thought about how to get from cultural diversity to a culture of diversity, likewise there is an aporia—or break—in thinking about disciplinarity in its two main senses: (a) care, cultivation, habit and (b) field, method, subject matter. The relationship between these two senses of discipline and of disciplinarity remains obscure in much debate, for example, about interdisciplinarity. The general contradiction in this sphere can be put something like this: much thinking about undergraduate curricula in the American academy presumes that care and cultivation—as expressed in habits of clear thinking, writing, and argumentation—must be divorced from the limitations of any single subject or field. This is what is liberal about the liberal arts. But graduate teaching (which is often and rightly described as training) presumes just the opposite, namely that discipline in the primary sense (care, cultivation, rigor, order) can only be formed in the context of special subjects, fields, and disciplinary departments. Caught in this contradiction is the idea of the undergraduate major (a messy creature) as well as the host of initiatives that multiply today under the rubric of the interdisciplinary (humanities institutes, interdisciplinary programs, interdepartmental colloquia and so forth.) All of these are efforts to restore the sense that discipline in the first—scholarly and critical—sense should be the conscience of disciplines in the second or departmental sense.

By and large, the political economy of the American university over the last fifty years or so (substantially driven by the needs for fiscal and bureaucratic accountability associated with large funds from the state and from industry) has resulted in the reverse situation: one in which departments (especially those defined by old and naturalized core disciplines, i.e. English, history, mathematics, physics) become the conscience and gatekeepers of discipline in the primary sense of care, cultivation, and habit. Yet scholarly discipline itself has a bifurcated history that is worth remarking.

There seem to be two senses of scholarly discipline, in the history of words and in the history of intellectual practices and institutions. On first glance, discipline in the sense of "care, cultivation, and habit" may appear to be best exemplified and institutionalized in the British ideal of the gentleman-scholar or amateur. This anti-professional sense of "discipline" (not unlike Hans-Georg Gadamer's sense of *bildung* in *Truth and Method*) may appear to be deeply antithetical to the sense of discipline (tied up with specialized techniques, standards, and interests) defining the vocation of the scholar. These two senses of scholarly discipline are the roots of what is now the very different, even opposed, milieus of graduate school and undergraduate learning, especially in the humanities. Graduate training, with its intense bias towards the vocational, the professional, and the specialized, appears directly contradictory to the idea of self-cultivation and liberality associated with the undergraduate ideology of the liberal arts.

The roots and implications of this tension between graduate school and college, between training and teaching, between teaching and scholarship, between the cultivation of a liberal self and the production of a professional scholar, has much to do with the archaeology of the idea of "research" in the Western academy. Briefly, I would like to suggest that sometime in the middle of the nineteenth century in Europe, the interest in discovery, reflection, observation, inquiry, and debate gave way to the idea of something radically new—the idea of research, the systematic pursuit of the not-yet-known. Research, in this sense, represents an inherently collective, replicable, and professionalized mode of inquiry into the world, first institutionalized in the natural sciences, then in history and the fledgling human sciences, all the way from philology to sociology. By the latter part of the nineteenth century, we get the idea of the research university, born in Germany and then taken up elsewhere in the world, including the United States.

This story is in many ways well studied and well documented. What I wish to highlight here is a matter I intend to take up in greater detail elsewhere—the newness and cultural strangeness of the idea of research itself. The main tension is not between teaching and research, or between teaching and training, or between professionals and amateurs, or even between two very different senses of the cultivated self which developed among academics in Europe in the course of the nineteenth century. Each of these tensions follows from a deeper institutional and epistemological change that occurs in Western Europe sometime during the nineteenth century, a change reflected in the emergence of the idea of research as the only legitimate way in which knowledge could be created in the framework of the modern university. Once this break occurs, the rest of the contradictions follow, one of which involves the tension between scholarly discipline and departmental disciplinarity. The latter reflects all the properties identified by Max Weber and others with the emergence of professional scholars, whereas the former harks back to an earlier, more broad ideal of knowledge associated with the formation of a cultivated self. This break is what, to pick one example among many, makes Goethe's treatise on color appear, in retrospect, as bad physics. If we can agree that the idea of research is both what is newest, strangest, and most interesting about the epistemology of the modern Western university, then the challenge is to establish whether there can be any coherent shared space between these two senses of scholarly discipline. Put another way, can liberal arts education and research co-exist to each other's benefit? This question might seem frivolous, in view of the fact that both in the United States and in Europe, as well as in many other parts of the world, they are encompassed either in the same institutions or in the same system of institutions. But does that mean they actually nurture each other?

In the folklore of the American academy the tension between teaching and research is frequently seen as a simple matter of faculty priorities and interests, with teaching represented as a chore and research as desirable and prestigious. There may be some truth to this perspective and to the increased pressure on faculty to do more justice to the classroom (and to the paying under-graduate consumer) and less to their research. But the issue is not just one of contradictions between faculty and student interests, or of different scales of prestige and reward associated with these activities for college and university teachers, or even of their apparently opposite budgetary properties: teaching pays the bills whereas research is often costly (especially in an era of shrinking federal support for research).

What is really at issue are the very different ideas of knowledge involved in the two kinds of discipline. The idea of discipline in the liberal arts aims to cultivate a certain sort of cosmopolitan liberal self among students. The idea of discipline that underpins the practice of research has very little to do—normatively—with any morally weighted sense of a liberal self, and has everything to do with the means and techniques for scrutinizing the world and producing knowledge that is both new and valid. The doing of research does, of course, involve certain ideals of ethics, voca-tion, and purpose but these ideals are means to the reliable pursuit of the not-yet-known. In the liberal arts ethos of discipline, by contrast, the formation of a certain sort of self is indeed the end, the telos of the activity.

What does this discussion of the idea of research have to do with disciplinarity and diversity? Departmental disciplinarity frequently advances its interests by invoking its special status in the fostering and protection of research. At the same time, when departments argue their interests (in matters of curriculum, certification, hiring, and budgets) against other departments or organized fields of study, they not only invoke the aura of research, but also imply that discipline in the prime sense of "care, cultivation, and habit" (the hallmark of the liberal arts and the building of cosmopolitan selves) is somehow an extension of the ideal of research. In fact, both conceptually and historically, just the reverse is true. Thus the first step towards articulating a more fruitful relationship between disciplinarity and diversity is to recognize the suture that the ideal of research permits between the discourse of departmental disciplinarity and the more general liberal ideal of scholarly discipline.

There is no easy solution to the co-existence of research and the formation of a cosmopolitan self as twin goals of the modern university. Yet one crucial step towards providing a moral basis for the pursuit of diversity (in both the intellectual and cultural senses) in the academy is by recourse to the more general, and historically prior, logic of the liberal arts, which was tied up with the production of a certain sort of liberal self.

How could this primary sense of "discipline" help to create what I earlier called a culture of diversity in the modern American university? Here I return to the idea of the liberal arts as quintes-sentially cosmopolitan: they were intended, that is, to widen the horizons, broaden the mental experiences, expand the imagination, and stretch the moral worlds of those exposed to them. To be sure, this sort of cosmopolitan ideal is also tied up with a particular bourgeois liberal conception of the self, with elite European conceptions of self and other, and with the many European imperial-isms of the last four hundred years, as a key component of the civilizing of European elites. Yet, it also contains the kernels of the idea that the key to self-formation is a disciplined encounter with the other. Gadamer, again, argues for the importance of the study of the classics of Greece and Rome because of their strangeness and their role in the dialectic of self-formation. Today, in the heat of the canon wars, it is hard to see Greek and Roman texts as truly "other," but the argument, in principle, is compelling.

The cosmopolitan self which is the object of humanistic pedagogy is tied up with a series of political, cultural, and social assumptions that might cause unease among some of us in an era in which liberalism has to be critically reconstructed and not just passively enjoyed. Yet there is no denying that in most of its Anglo-European variants, liberal education contains the germ of the sense of the cosmopolitan. This germ is often obscured by the other associations of liberal pedagogy, with democratic virtues, with class prerogatives, and with various forms of civilizing rhetoric. Yet it certainly contains the principle of self-expansion through engagements with the other. It is this principle that links the classic liberal sense of discipline with the values of diversity. Cosmopolitanism today, without a serious engagement with diversity, must degenerate either into tourism or into aestheticism, which are linked pursuits that can hardly advance the democratic potential of the modern university.

Diversity and Disciplinarity

In the context of the American research university as I have described it, and bearing in mind the artifactual and historical qualities of both diversity and disciplinarity, I suggest that diversity in all its senses poses a threat to departmentalized disciplines, both at their centers and at their boundaries. The canon wars, on which much ink has been spilt, are an excellent illustration of anxieties at the center: will Shakespeare be on the chopping block if Toni Morrison gets in? As regards the threat at the boundaries, there are numerous examples: anthropologists view English as a threat, just as political scientists worry that anthropologists are poaching on the nation-state; sociologists are moving to the Third World as media students begin to occupy domestic space in the United States; film scholars worry about members of the English department who have started teaching about film; and everyone is worried that cultural studies will take over the world.

Departmental disciplines operate increasingly like antagonistic nation-states, with much policing of boundaries, arcane loyalty tests, and rampant intellectual protectionism. Stimulated by ever-shrinking job markets and ever-growing budget cuts, there is much anxiety about disciplinary markets, and rhetorics of allegiance, mobilization, and interdisciplinary warfare are rife in the large universities.

This sort of border warfare (between disciplines-as-nation-states) usually indicates major internal problems, in the academy as in the wider social world. Debates within disciplinary departments typically ignore the fact that relations between fields and sub-fields cannot be legislated by economic externalities or by a misplaced sense of political solidarity in the budget wars. Such debates frequently betray the fraying relationship between departments and disciplines. This latter slippage, increasingly observable across the university, affects the entire tenor of debates about interdisciplinarity and indeed about diversity.

One potentially fruitful way to look at the relationship between diversity and disciplinarity is through the lens of "minors," "minorities," and "minor literatures." In a brilliant essay entitled "What is a Minor Literature?" Felix Guattari has shown that the key issue about minor literatures is that they expose the historicity of the majority of "major" literatures. This argument could be applied to literatures and knowledges across the entire terrain of the American academy, perhaps including the natural sciences, but certainly including the humanities and social sciences.

Today, calls for intellectual diversity in the curriculum (rather than just social diversity in the academy) are typically associated with calls for greater voice for "minor" texts. In more radicalized settings, advocates of "minor" literatures seek not just to add but to destabilize majority literatures (the textual foundation of all departmental disciplinarities). In even more radical cases, they seek to destabilize the very "majoritarianism" that underlies disciplinary authority. That Allen Bloom has now been followed by Harold Bloom in the debate about great books suggests that these efforts are successful as provocations in the academic world and the publishing world, even if they are hardly as powerful as they are sometimes made out to be. The regular flowering of Blooms suggests that the voice of the minor remains unsettling.

In the current dispensation of the culture of diversity and disciplinarity in the American academy, diversity is typically the voice of the "minor" whereas disciplines claim, generally successfully, the voice of the major (in all the senses of the senior, the larger, the more important). Here is where the tension between historicity and authority comes in. The idea of the minor can be used to explore the historicities that constitute the relationship between majority and minority in the history of disciplines. By extension, we can open up a serious way to interrogate the relationship between departmental disciplinarity and scholarly discipline in the life of the academy, since "minority" voices and texts can be the trojan horse both of the border in the center and a place to link intellectual to cultural diversity. It is with this last issue, tying "minor" to "minority" and intellectual to cultural diversity, that I would like to close.

One way to think about the links between diversity, the cosmopolitan, and the minor in the life of the academy is to consider the problems and potentials of area studies. By area studies I mean the particular organization of funds, centers, and pedagogical methods developed in the United States after 1945 to study those large areas of the world—Africa, Asia, Latin America, and the Middle East—considered both strategic for United States global interests and civilization. The debate over the future of area studies is now active and is deeply caught up with the effort of scholars, policy-makers, and funders to find a new way for American universities to internationalize themselves and participate in the making of a new world order. The question is: does the peace dividend have implications for how we study the rest of the world, as that world changes rapidly and in unexpected ways? This is not the place for an extended discussion of this topic, but a few observations might be helpful.

If the liberal arts (in the primary sense of the cultivation of a liberal self) have always involved a cosmopolitan agenda, then area studies—especially in the emerging cultural studies inflected forms that are gaining visibility—is surely one way to carry forward the cosmopolitan ideal without engaging in tourism or simple elite self-cultivation in the American college and university. Further, given that area studies remains both minor and endangered in most American universities and colleges (largely because of the steady decrease in government funds at the graduate level), it retains the value of the minor in unsettling the authority of disciplines. Often seen as dangerously anti-disciplinary (and thus as formless) area studies is simultaneously intensely demanding (especially as regards language training) and is inherently international, thus cosmopolitan, in its potential for American students and faculty. In current debates about the future of area studies, it has been shown that it contains the potential for a new, and critical, internationalism (Lee 1995). The critical revitalization of the cultural study of other parts of the world (area studies) is thus at least one way in which to restore the primacy of the liberal-cosmopolitan ideal of discipline over the later, research-driven ideal of disciplinarity.

Intellectual and Cultural Diversity

The major question originally proposed concerns how the interaction between disciplinarity and diversity could best be organized. A sub-question is: how can diversity be managed, assuming that there is an economy of diversity? A further question, which brings us to the matter of disciplinarity, is: how should intellectual and cultural diversity be linked in the academy?

An effective strategy for dealing with these questions runs something like this. Let us insist on the mutual interlocution of historicity and authority in the organization of disciplines and recognize that one entailment of this mutual interlocution is to resist the hegemony of departmental disciplinarity (tied to the dominance of the ideal of "research") over the more general disciplines of reading, writing, and argumentation. In so doing, let us invoke the minor and minority in the landscape of disciplines, not just as part of a program of distributive or affirmative reform, but as a way to destabilize the authority and establish the historicity of the "major" in whatever textual and interpretive world we inhabit.

This critical approach to the majoritarian thrust in departmental disciplinarity will ensure the constant historicizing of disciplinarity. It will also provide a principled, scholarly, textual, properly academic way to assure that the question of plurality—that is, cultural diversity—is driven by the academy rather than by electoral politics at large. In this strategy, intellectual diversity could drive cultural diversity within the academy, and could provide a critical basis for its organization. This should not be taken as a recipe for the isolation of the academy from politics, but as a proposal for the productive regulation of the ways in which politics-at-large enters the logic of cultural diversity in the academy.

Since questions of minority, historicity, and authority with respect to the disciplines inevitably invite an understanding of histories larger than those of the academy, the door might thus be opened for a genuinely dialectical relationship between the authority of disciplines and the diversity of texts and of readings. One result of this dialectical process could be to provide a way to assure that the plurality of readings and the plurality of readers (teachers and students) will drive each other while providing realistic constraints, in any given real university or college, on the actualization of the other. In this way, cultural diversity can create cultures of diversity not by fiat or by politics-as-usual but by a form of politics that is properly academic, that is, one that is disciplined without being merely disciplinary. This is a Utopia whose thinking does not depend on the prior admission of its impossibility.

Notes

This essay took shape before audiences at Bryn Mawr College, at Rutgers, and at the University of Illinois. The last of these was the most recent, and led to its publication in the present form. I am grateful for comments and suggestions made on all these occasions, particularly by Michael Bérubé, Dilip Gaonkar, George Levine, Cary Nelson, and Judith Shapiro. I am particularly grateful for suggestions about the penultimate draft from Dilip Gaonkar, who alerted me to the relevance of some of Gadamer's ideas to my arguments. This essay is part of a larger project that explores the anthropology of the modern American university. Many topics dealt with cursorily here await fuller treatment in that larger project. These include: the wider economy of debate about immigration, citizenship, and democracy that affect debates about diversity in the American university; the future of area studies as a distinctive knowledge form through which the American university grasps the world; and the genealogy of contemporary American practices and discourses surrounding "research." Because of the preliminary nature of this essay, the citation of other relevant work is minimal, though my reliance on a wider literature, especially on the canon wars, should be apparent to the reader.

References

Gadamer, H.G. (1990) *Truth and Method*. Trans. Joel Weinsheimer and Donald G. Marshall. New York: Crossroad Publishing Corporation.

Guattari, F. (1990) "What is a Minor Literature?" In R. Ferguson et al., eds. *Out There: Marginalization and Contemporary Cultures*, 59–69.

Lee, B. (1995) "Critical Internationalism," *Public Culture 7* (3), (Spring 1995): 559–92.

29
Asian American Studies after 9/11

KENT A. ONO

Many would argue that Asian American studies has changed significantly as a result of the advent of poststructuralism, postcolonialism, queer theory, feminism, diaspora and transnationalism, and globalization. Nevertheless, along with these changes—including impressive scholarship, strong undergraduate programs, and even graduate-level programs at some institutions—is an ever present risk of disassociation from the day-to-day struggles of communities. Forces leading to provincialism, elitism, and incorporation continue to affect Asian American studies as a growing, still relatively young, and not fully incorporated field (if it ever will be), within a still primarily segregated university system.

The risk of dissociation from community struggles is a particularly worrisome concern because, since 9/11, race has been fundamentally redefined. Tried and true racial categories have been reconfigured. Racial categories, such as Asian American, a category many treated as fixed, knowable, even dependable, have suddenly shifted. New racial identity categories have emerged. For instance, as Leti Volpp (2003) has recently written, "September 11 facilitated the consolidation of a new identity category that grouped together persons who appear to be 'Middle Eastern, Arab, or Muslim'" (147). Asian Americans, many of whom are Muslim, fall within this new category. Many Asian Americans are targets, because of physical appearance and not because of any professed self-identification as "Middle Eastern, Arab, or Muslim." Thus, the racial distance between being Arab and being Asian and being Asian American and being Arab American is shrinking. Asian Americans and Arab Americans, both of whom have been affected by historical orientalist constructions, are, post-9/11, both positioned (often without distinction) in orientalist ways.

The conflation of identity groups based on a racial imperative is an example of the changing racial scene; yet, it offers possibilities for cross-group concern, empathy, and political and sociocultural alliances, as well. 9/11 should move us to draw connections between what happened to Japanese Americans during World War II and what is happening to those in Guantanamo Bay, Cuba, as well as those who were in the Abu Ghraib prison.[1] It should lead us to think about the emerging uncertainty that exists around the meaning, protection, and even existence of civil rights. It should also move us to consider the ways in which Asian American studies needs to grow, self-redefine, and gain a rejuvenation of purpose. Asian American studies' relationship to Arab American studies is crucial to reconceptualizing Asian American studies. Given that Arab

American studies as a field is not yet established (and may not even have fledged), a significant amount of criticism of post-9/11 racism has taken place within the field of Asian American studies, which raises the question: If Arab American studies is not yet a field, where will Arab American studies occur? Where will Arab Americanists be housed, and what is the relationship of Arab American studies to Asian American studies?

This essay reflects on ways Asian American studies has been tested since 9/11 and discusses the ever-present need for renovation, renewal, collective struggle, and, most importantly, active engagement with the ever-changing social world. Powerful events, such as 9/11, are part of changing world politics and should be a constant reminder of how Asian American studies must continually respond to cultural, political, and institutional exigencies. In addition, this essay argues that continued attention to the ways in which race, ethnicity, nation, gender, class, sexuality, and ability continue to structure present conditions, even in a significantly changed environment, must also occur. While this essay argues that closer attention to globalization and changing world politics is needed, it also argues strongly for attention to deeply rooted material and structural relations. I will begin with a discussion of changes that have taken place within the field of Asian American studies. Then, I will discuss four essays that push the boundaries of Asian American studies post-9/11. Finally, I will develop ways Asian American studies might be reconceptualized in a post-9/11 era.

Association for Asian American Studies: 1994–2004

The development of Asian American studies is highly context-dependent, contingent upon social, political, economic, and historical realities. What Asian American studies has been, is, and becomes are very much determined by where Asian American studies is located. If Asian American studies, whether in the form of classes taught, faculty hired, or programs built, is a result of student and community protests, a particular *kind* of program will emerge. If, however, Asian American studies exists at a research university as an academic project dreamed up primarily by faculty, and in a university context that puts particular pressure on the unit to meet highly circumscribed scholarly standards and expectations, that too will affect the kind of program that emerges. Whether or not the college or university is located in a major metropolitan area or in a Club Med-like setting; whether or not the development of the program is driven by faculty or students; and whether or not the program is engaged by and involved in Asian American communities, or even created as a result of community pressure and involvement, all of these will affect the very kind of program that emerges.[2]

Given the context-dependence and context-specificity of the development of Asian American studies, one might ask three provocative questions in relation to 9/11: How might Asian American studies look were it to have emerged after 9/11? If conceived and developed after 9/11, which constituency groups would be central to the field?[3] And, more pertinent to the point of this chapter, how should Asian American studies be reconceived post-9/11? My goal in posing these questions is to talk about how the field of Asian American studies might begin to respond to changing social phenomena as they happen. These questions are particularly important when we consider that Asian American studies is a post-1960s phenomenon that came of age prior to the end of the Cold War. The field needs to be reformulated in a *post*–Cold War context, since U.S. international policy has shifted in many ways away from Asia and toward Arab nations. A fundamental reconceptualization of the field, which has focused heavily on histories of immigrants and immigrant communities migrating to the Americas prior to the 1924 and 1936 exclusion era, for example, is thus necessary.

One way to begin such a reconceptualization is by discussing the primary pan-college/university academic association devoted to Asian American studies. While quite different from the institutional structure of a university, an academic association, as a particular kind of institutional structure, has both advantages and disadvantages over intracampus institutional structures for Asian American studies activism and is thus an important site for analysis. Over the last decade, the primary academic organization associated with Asian American studies, the Association for Asian American Studies (AAAS), has undergone tremendous struggle, conflict, and division, and has faced many problems, primarily of a political nature.[4] Of course, it would be rhetorically unwise and perhaps even cynical to characterize the organization as being in perpetual turmoil, but it is important to say that, at least since the mid-1990s, issues of a political nature have dominated the Association's agenda. Despite the many challenges to the Association, its identity, and its mission, a thoroughgoing reconceptualization of the field in view of the many political circumstances that have arisen, both inside and outside of the Association, has *not* fully taken place. It is the purpose of this essay to suggest directions for a more widespread reconceptualization of the field in response to these many challenges and to other political transformations evolving out of fast-changing world affairs, such as 9/11.

One might begin narrating the current era of political conflict with the Association's handling of the move to boycott California as a conference site after Proposition 187 was passed by California voters. In November 1994, California voters passed the controversial statewide ballot Proposition 187, ostensibly in order to eliminate[5] health, education, and welfare benefits to undocumented migrants.[6] A debate ensued within AAAS over whether or not to hold its annual conference in Oakland, California, where it was scheduled to take place. Another option was for members to participate in an international boycott of California and thus join allied organizations and institutions opposed to the proposition. Although other organizations such as the National Association of Hispanic Journalists and the Rocky Mountain Asian American Student Coalition boycotted California, less than a month after voters approved Proposition 187 the Board of Directors of AAAS voted 7–4 not to boycott California and to continue planning for the conference to be held there. The conference in Oakland, CA, took place as originally planned in 1995; however, many members refused to go to the meeting, including myself.[7]

In 1998, at the annual AAAS conference held in Honolulu, Hawai'i, a controversy erupted over the selection of Lois Ann Yamanaka's novel, *Blu's Hanging* (1997), for the best fiction award given by the Association. The Filipino American Studies Caucus of AAAS and the Anti-Racism Coalition led and organized protests against the choice of book. Protesters mentioned that critiques had been made of the depiction of Filipino Americans in Yamanaka's earlier work and that the book's particular construction of deviant Filipino sexuality and depravity paralleled problematic historical depictions of Filipino Americans (Chuh 2003, 153, note 1). A resolution was put forth to rescind the award. After a vote of AAAS members present at the board meeting, the award was rescinded, and all of the Board of Directors of AAAS subsequently resigned simultaneously, noting possible legal repercussions that might result from the rescission of the award.

If Asian American studies as a field was experiencing growing pains prior to September 11, 2001, they certainly did not subside after 9/11. The most recent incident took place during the 2003 AAAS Conference and just prior to the 2004 conference. In 2003, the conference was held in San Francisco and a discussion/debate took place over whether or not to change the association's name to include Pacific Islanders. Prior to the conference, a detailed argument written by J. Kehaulani Kauanui (2004) about why AAAS should not change its name to include "Pacific"[8] was posted to the AAAS-community listserv[9] and circulated. Animated positions, pro and con, were heard during the organization's business meeting. A vote was then slated to be taken in January 2004. When the vote did not take place, e-mail messages were exchanged among the president, board members, and those both in favor and opposed to the resolution. Prior to the 2004 conference in Boston, challenges made to the AAAS president, Dana Takagi, and to other board members to call off an association-wide vote ultimately led to the rescission of the request for the name change—a request originally initiated by Asian/Pacific Islander Studies faculty at the University of Michigan.[10]

It is useful to consider these historical issues, to think about the degree to which the Association has or has not changed in response to them, and to imagine a reconfigured field in light of these challenges. Since the mid-1990s, then, AAAS has struggled over its political positioning with regard to key social and cultural issues, some on a national and some on a transnational scale. In the case of Proposition 187, the Association struggled over the issue of citizenship, and thus over the Association's identity in connection to U.S. national politics, its relationship with Chicana/os, Mexicana/os, Latina/os, in addition to its overarching commitment to the project of panracial, versus exclusively panethnic, politics. In the case of the *Blu's Hanging* controversy, the Association faced issues of internal racialization, structural inequality, and unequal access to political voice, especially as these issues affected Filipina/o Americans; in other words, there was a failure to address both the historical privilege of East-Asian Americans within the Association and the historical and continuing internal oppression of Filipina/o Americans. And, most recently in AAAS's decision about whether or not to add "Pacific" to Asian American studies, which would have meant changing the current acronym of "AA" to "APA" or to "AA and P,"[11] the Association came face to face with its own historical and continuing relationship to U.S. colonization, imperialism, exploitation, objectification, and the differential colonial processes that have affected Asian Americans and Pacific Islanders differentially.[12]

Questions and concerns about whether or not AAAS is a national and nationalist organization, to what degree it could serve as an arbiter of the quality of cultural work, and how the Association participates in partisan practices of governmentality that have real material effects, all became key issues. Moreover, the Association has had to contend with its own structural processes of incorporation and practices of appropriation. In short, AAAS has had to confront the contemporary positioning of (1) Asian American as a signifier of, and (2) Asian American studies as a forum for the expression of legitimate social resistance *and* of hegemonic control, as well as the roles that both the name and the field play within broader systems of racialization.

It would be convenient to explain all of these challenges as having resulted from contemporary transnational global transformations, the increasing fluidity of capitalism, the neoliberalization of economies, and consequently the pressures on national governments to sustain what is increasingly being understood to be the fiction of a constitutive nation. Most certainly, the fact that the primary issues confronting AAAS as an association over the past decade are very much responses to migration, colonization, racialization, and broader histories of imperialism does support and justify such a reading of these issues. However, desires to retain homelands and to create anew habitable and humane spaces, and the yearning and call for respect, appreciation, and honoring—hence informal, not only formal, citizenship—cannot only be seen as effects of transformations in capital and the movement of people across national borders. After all, all of the emerging issues affecting AAAS over the last decade have had to do with the dominant political centrism of the Association and the marginal, peripheral, or beside-the-point positionality of nonmainstream politics within, and in association with, the organization.[13] While globalizing forces are key to understanding the current context, the emergence of these particular issues *also* is about continuing historical relations, historical colonial and racial institutions and practices, hierarchical forms of power, and systems of power/knowledge that are deeply embedded in the spaces in which we live and labor.

The Changing Contours of Asian American Studies

However important the various contestations that have emerged within the Association have been, especially for those of us interested in creating more habitable spaces for people of color, women, queers, immigrants, and people with disabilities, a much broader set of challenges are now being posed to Asian America and Asian American studies. The internal disagreements, while at times volatile, exist in relationship to, but yet are of a different form and context from, changes to the Association born out of the aftermath of 9/11, which has deeply altered U.S./Middle East and U.S./ Asia politics. As a result, the racial politics exercised abroad have had serious consequences in the United States for Arab Americans, migrants from the Middle East, Muslims, Asian Americans, and migrants from Asia, in particular. The degree of suspicion cast on members of these many communities and the stigma resulting from the high visibility of their mediated bodies is acute. If their identities were not known to other people in the United States prior to 9/11, then the rash of visual and verbal discourses after 9/11 surely calls attention to and magnifies their significance and functions to represent them as inextricably linked to the violence associated with a U.S. national tragedy. Very much like Japanese Americans during World War II, scopic machineries are drawing unprecedented attention to "potential terrorists" today. Newspaper readers and TV audiences have been inundated with images of swarthy men, images that serve as mnemonic markers signifying potential terrorists.[14] Moreover, the principle correlation drawn between swarthy men and potential terrorism has been effected through rapid fire images linking dark men with the destruction of the World Trade Center and parts of the Pentagon. Contemporary media post-9/11 have worked to produce a kind of fixity of representation connecting swarthy men to terrorism and also to a U.S. tragedy, an articulation of imagery that, without an equivalent barrage of images challenging such associations, counterimages that might serve to disarticulate swarthy people from terrorism and U.S. tragedy, will be with us for a very long time.[15]

"Potential terrorists" serves as a useful concept to begin to address political and media discourses that produce a creative, if fictional, "network" or interconnection along racial, gender, national, sexual, political, and ideological lines. Hate crimes, surveillance by the repressive apparatus of the state, and surveillance and disciplining technologies have erected a powerful discursive barrier to full participation in society by those marked as "potential terrorist." Such forces produce an effect equivalent to an immediate threat to identity. Vast mechanisms to create a new public civility, a new nationalist ethos, and new conceptions of privileged citizenship have been put into place. Civilizing processes such as objectification, vilification, and ultimately acts of elimination of "potential terrorists" demonstrate the incredible degree to which new modes of public civility can shift in accordance with changes in social affairs. The massive violence unleashed upon "potential terrorist" communities and the legitimization of such practices through media demonization campaigns suggests the lengths to which historical identities, practices, institutions, networks, and hegemonies of whiteness will go to defend privileges and power scrupulously.

While racial profiling once focused primarily on African Americans, Latinas/os, Filipinas/os, surrounding 9/11, at least for a period of time, the targeting of a generic "potential terrorist" category (Volpp 2003) was aimed at those with features of visible difference associated (by way of media construction and U.S. racial logics) with South Asian Americans, South Asians, Muslims, Arabs, and Arab Americans, primarily.[16] Additionally, after 9/11 international students at universities (if they are ever able to return to the United States) and international student applicants to universities are now tracked to a much greater degree. University officials and staff, some of whom might have been confidantes of students prior to the enhancement of the mechanisms of the security state, are now agents of their surveillance and potential imprisonment. While the basis for this surveillance dates back to a 1996 piece of legislation,[17] it was the Patriot Act that was the trigger responsible for the enforcement of the 1996 provision. Among other things, the Act authorized $36.8 million to be spent *specifically* to help implement an infrastructure for tracking and monitoring international students.[18] The U.S.A. Patriot Act ensured universities would comply with the 1996 Act by prohibiting admissions of international students if monitoring and tracking systems were not put into place.[19]

At still another level—an abstract and perhaps larger one—is the global restructuration of the circulation of labor and capital, largely brought about through neoliberal economic forces, and the radically shifting racial and religious discourses that have predominated both prior to and after September 11, 2001. For the rest of this essay, then, I will discuss the need to reconceptualize Asian American studies in view of transformations of sexuality, racialization, and globalization. In particular, it would appear that fear and response to fear have saturated the public airwaves and ether lines post-9/11, as Ahmad (2002) suggests, and I would add the concatenation of local contexts, as well. And, attention has been focused on responding to these geopolitical events (e.g., protesting the U.S. war in Iraq, the illegal detention of prisoners in Guantanamo Bay, Cuba, the abuse of prisoners in Abu Ghraib prison, and George W. Bush and the administration's fabrication of justifications for war). But, in addition to rightful protests of oppression and imperialism, there also has to be time/space for reconceptualizing the relationship of those attempting to institutionalize and produce structures so often called on to respond to such circumstances. Seeking time for reflection, collaboration, and community (when the labors of life mitigate against such time) is a necessary part of the aftermath and may begin the very kinds of discussion necessary to create more proactive activism.

Here, I read four essays in terms of what they offer to a project that attempts to reconceptualize Asian American studies to be responsive to ever changing social relations. Then, I will discuss additional specific challenges Asian American studies faces resulting from changing legal-juridical transformations of domestic U.S. politics. Finally, I conclude with a call for greater openness to transformation and change, as well as a call for scholarship that challenges prior conceptualizations of Asian American studies in important ways.

In their essay, "Monster, Terrorist, Fag: The War on Terrorism and the Production of Docile Patriots," Jasbir K. Puar and Amit S. Rai delineate how the contemporary demonization of the terrorist draws on metaphors of monstrosity that have historically functioned to demonize nonheterosexual and racial others. Thus, they take the contemporary use of the concept of monster and trace the use of that framing as it has been applied to socially marginalized people historically. As they suggest, "Our contention is that today the knowledge and form of power that is mobilized to analyze, taxonomize, psychologize, and defeat terrorism has a genealogical connection to the West's abnormals, and specifically those premodern monsters that Western civilization had seemed to bury and lay to rest long ago" (124). In particular, they discuss racialized, sexualized, and classed monstrous figures from the eighteenth and nineteenth centuries, such as "the undesirable, the vagrant, the Gypsy, the savage, the Hottentot Venus" and "the Oriental" as historical counterparts to the "terrorist-monster" (124). They suggest that the use of rhetorics of monstrosity that have traditionally been used to mark queerness as a sexual deviancy are now being applied to terrorists and also function to discipline and normalize the broader society (126). They suggest that discourses contrast the "terrorist-monster," who is constructed as sexually deviant as well as a sexual threat, to the "docile patriot," who represents heteronormativity, as a means of producing polarities of positions that can be taken: either one can become an imprisoned and "quarantined" terrorist, or one can be a docile patriot by abiding by nationalist war-time imperatives.

Martin Manalansan's article, "Race, Violence and Neoliberal Spatial Politics in the Global City," traces the vacating of a site where queers of color used to socialize in New York, resulting from neoliberal economic forces, conservative "homonormative" politics, and the post-9/11 surveillance and disciplining practices of the repressive state apparatus. Germane to this essay is Manalansan's observation that post-9/11 antiterrorist surveillance has had specific effects on Middle-Eastern and South-Asian communities but also has produced a broader, more diffuse form of social scrutiny of Mexican and Latino men, many of whom are undocumented, and communities of queer men of color. While 9/11 is part of Manalansan's argument about the violent dissolution of urban spaces where queer of color communities formed, the broader social significance of neoliberal economic politics looms large in his telling of history. Central to his argument is that 9/11 became a ruse or an ideological excuse for the intensification of neoliberal economic, cultural, and political policies and practices.[20]

What is fascinating about Manalansan's essay for the purposes of my argument is the way he illustrates that what might appear to be surface changes of urban spaces are the result of changing social circumstances and forces. Moreover, the changes of urban spaces alter the demographics of the people who live there and their life activities, and do so along racial, sexual, and classed lines. Also key here is to suggest that the need for Asian American studies must not single-mindedly focus on race, on issues of class nationally, or even on a combination of race and class—in effect, on any single term of identification, subject positioning, or racialized and marginalized class. Critical social analysis requires a recognition of social variables beyond specific community or cultural ones.

In "The Language of Terror: Panic, Peril, Racism," Junaid Rana (2004) argues that in a period of moral panic Muslims can be constructed as, and reduced primarily to, enemies of the state. Rana details an event in which five people who entered the United States came to be conceived as a terrorist threat within the ensuing moral panic post-9/11. A heightened alert followed the destruction of the Twin Towers, but upon further investigation it was found that one of the men identified had not, in fact, even come to the United States; he had been misidentified as someone else. Another man was later understood to be a smuggler of Pakistani immigrants through Canada into the United States. So, even while his actions were understood to be threatening, he was not the threat he was originally deemed to be. Rana argues that in this case national identity is subsumed by race; hence, Muslims as a religious group come to be understood racially.

Rana traces the history of the use of moral panics, demonstrating the sedimented historical nature of the concept. In defining "moral panics," Rana writes, "Moral panics involve a process whereby social anxieties and fears become organized in a fashion that becomes known as rational and logical" (11). Such panics then lead to social control and the construction of images of "folk-devils." The result of such constructions is a broad attempt to justify popular consent to overweening state power. Migrants suffer from this, as they as a group come to be configured as dangerous and, hence, as part of the justification for state violence. As Rana suggests with regard to communities of color generally within the United States post-9/11, "The refusal to create legal mandates that control racial violence and hate crimes attests to the greater concern of the state in controlling communities of color rather than preventing and controlling racism" (17).

What is particularly useful about Rana's essay for my purposes is his discussion of Muslims and Asian Americans. He suggests that terrorism served to enhance suspicion and fear of immigrants in general post-9/11. Moreover, moral panics emerge in relation to historical conceptions of "the orient." As a result, Rana challenges ethnic studies and its various self-definitions, which he argues will have to be rethought with regard to Muslims, even as Muslims and Muslim American identity are not subsumed or subsumable under any existing area of race and ethnic studies, such as Asian American studies. Muslims clearly function under the sign of "oriental" post-9/11, and increasingly Indonesia, Pakistan, Egypt, Tunisia, and Palestine have come to be conflated within the larger construction of the "terrorist network." By tracing the historical construction of race for both Muslims and Asians in the United States, Rana is able to argue that, today, "moral panic surrounding the Islamic threat, the Muslim, the terrorist, brownness, illegality, and criminality, are all understood under one rubric" (28).

While Sunaina Maira's (2004) essay "A Moment of Empire: Doing Asian American Studies in the Metropole" is primarily an explication of an ethnography of South-Asian youth immigrant populations in Cambridge, Massachusetts, the beginning of her essay addresses issues specific to thinking about Asian American studies as a field post-9/11. Maira notes that 9/11 means hypersurveillance and documenting of Muslim migrant populations in particular. Such documentation is indeed a profoundly ethical and potentially problematic act. She says Arab American and South Asian American studies have come together at this nexus. She pushes for a much more explicit theorization of this intersection. Maira also notes the need for attention to anti-Zionism in Asian American studies, as well as the role of Arab American and Asian American studies. Responding to Robert Ku, who asks, "How has Asian American studies been able to center the discourse of Orientalism without acknowledging two of its primary signifiers, Palestine and Zionism?" Maira raises the issue of anti-Zionism. She challenges Asian American studies to consider the role of anti-Zionist politics in Asian American politics.

These four essays provide approaches to scholarship that help challenge Asian American studies to reconfigure its scope and field. All four try to draw a connection among targets of terrorist antipathy and the broader effects of such targeting on a much wider scale across history, race, ethnic groups, sexual groups, and the like. Puar and Rai suggest the need to work across the particulars of ethnic group representation and to configure, more broadly, difference and the other, both of which work in a broader sense to affix labels such as "monster," "terrorist," and "fag." Such constructions of the other are related; in order to understand the particular construction of otherness in a given period, attention to marginality across social divisions of sexuality, race, class, religion, nation, and gender is needed. Manalansan's essay asks us to think broadly about the convergence and time/history of neoliberal economic policies and political ideologies, as well as social and federal policy, and their relationship to the way people live their lives. He suggests we consider, in particular, the way in which queer men of color, and their dependency on the local and the geographical, and on the specifics of locale, influence and affect the possibilities for socialization and hence community. Rana's essay draws attention to the degree to which "Muslim" has come to be a catchword or "folk-devil" for broader racialized discourses, yet those discourses have their own particularities separate from but related to those of past historical racializations. Not only does he suggest that Asian American studies has to be rethought in relation to the way Muslims have come to be characterized, he suggests that "immigrant" itself is, in ways, the basis of the more specific and particularistic singling out and collapsing of the category Muslim.

It is worth stopping for a moment to articulate explicitly how representation both fails to fix groups in some instances, and then, if fixed in others, draws attention to particular features, and away from whole other groups. Thus, a focus on immigration might, because of the semiotic vectors of meaning contemporarily associated with it, draw attention away from some groups; whereas, a focus on Arabs might, at the same time, not immediately evoke groups traditionally understood to be immigrants. Maira makes the important observation that part of the challenge for Asian American studies is to come to terms with the politics of anti-Zionism. Without taking an explicit position on the subject, Asian American studies has been led to evacuate politics from its enterprise, and, arguably, to detach itself from continuing and changing world events. What is interesting here is that Asian American studies, perhaps because Arab Americans have not been conceptualized as part of the field, has not had to address in explicit terms politics relating to Palestine. Moreover, the larger U.S. politics that tends to bracket out Arab from Asian American/Latino/ Native American/African American means that traditional racializing processes that have affected Arab Americans, especially (but not only) since 9/11, have not had to be addressed by Asian American studies.

Toward a More Responsive Asian American Studies

In helping to build the field of Asian American studies, some may have assumed that at some point in the future the field would have been built, tools would have been put away, and the builders of the field would have then inhabited a completed and finalized structure. Once courses were on the books, faculty hired, programs started, and fields conceived,[21] there would then be a sense that protecting one's own space and fortifying what one has already built and accomplished was more important and more difficult than responding to world events as they happen. One might argue that, with those of us in the field so focused on programmatic and institutionalized discourses, we have been unable to respond adequately, sufficiently, and fully to the issues and events affecting a much broader range of people. Perhaps more importantly, because we have been put on the defensive so often, while continuing to struggle to do program building and maintenance, we have not been able to come up for air long enough to assess the current situation and to reconceptualize the field from its foundation forward according to what is really needed in the larger contemporary social context. But, perhaps we need to reconceive altogether our previous, tried and true, as well as well-worn institutionalizing practices.

If there is going to be work that addresses broad issues of significant social concern, if Asian American studies and race and ethnic studies more generally are going to be at the forefront of such work, and not made irrelevant, then most certainly they will need to be strongly included in any active project. This is because, unlike other kinds of academic fields, if they should even be compared, Asian American studies, like race and ethnic studies more generally, is always yoked inextricably to changing social conditions and relations. In the case of Joseph Ileto, the Filipino American postal worker who was shot and killed by Buford O. Furrow on August 10, 1999, those of us in Asian American studies had to respond. Not knowing that Ileto was going to be murdered did not prevent us from having to talk about it with newspaper reporters, protest it publicly, and discuss it with our students after it happened. Such is the case with regard to Proposition 187, the Los Angeles riots, Proposition 209, Proposition 227, John Huang, Wen Ho Lee, 9/11, and many other cases.

Prior to 9/11, geopolitical concerns over China's threat to U.S. world dominance had effects on Asian Americans and Asian immigrants in the United States, especially Chinese and Chinese Americans. Asian Americans such as John Huang and Wen Ho Lee were, in effect, feeling the heat resulting from increasingly tense U.S./China relations. The frenzied concern over China and the potential danger Chinese Americans posed to the nation-state, however, ended suddenly with 9/11. Where China had figured prominently on the nightly news, in headlines, and in federal intelligence research, 9/11 instantaneously shifted the government, military, and media's focus of concern. First came Afghanistan, then Iraq. Indonesia, North Korea, Iran, and Libya all were sited as possible adversaries[22] in relation to 9/11.

Thus, Asian American studies remains tightly connected to, if not interdependent on, material social circumstances. Priya Shah, for instance, in her (2004) paper theorizing the problematics of feminist (especially Western feminist) adjudication of (non-Western) forced marriage practices, which she presented at the Association for Asian American Studies in Boston, in 2004, demonstrated the ways in which women's lives can be generative of theoretical, cultural analyses. It is precisely the work that people like Shah are doing—to theorize transnational feminist politics in relation to ethnic, racial, religious, national, and gender relations and women's positionality within those relations—that should lead us to reconfigure Asian American studies. The trick is to put Asian American studies in continual conversation with the changing world and simultaneously to give serious attention to continuing historical material conditions. Both the changing global circumstances and long-standing features of historical material life are masked in contemporary popular discourses; hence, developing ways of responding to changing social events, globalizing forces, as well as embedded racial and ethnic relations, for instance, is part of the task. Asian American studies must not remain so rigid in terms of conceptualizing precisely the grounds of action/attack that we do not recognize the new features of the changed social terrain. Yet, Asian American studies should also not be so preoccupied with the changing social circumstances and globalizing forces that it ignores the deeply entrenched features of race, gender, class, nation, sexuality, and other social relations, all of which are inseparable from and generative of Asian American critique. As such, conceptualizing the field requires careful attention to how it responds to, adjusts to, makes way for, prepares for, and configures changing social circumstances.

I would strongly argue that the field should be proactive in orientation. It is obvious that Asian American studies is often caught unprepared by geopolitical events and their ramifications—that is, that response and reaction processes are, by the time a world event occurs, insufficiently prepared to respond to and overturn reactionary public sentiment—retooling Asian American studies in such a way as to transform the field proactively so that it might be able to address changing social events as they happen appears necessary. Cases such as John Huang's involvement in the campaign finance scandal and Wen Ho Lee's sudden emergence as a suspected traitor will likely "pop up" from time to time. While good research, good legal work, and smart and careful reading of newspapers could help one to prepare for such eventualities, no one has a crystal ball, and prediction in the social world is highly overrated. So, I am not suggesting that Asian American studies get into the business of trying to predict where the next high profile case of national concern relating to an Asian American will occur (although that would be a useful sideline). Rather, I am suggesting that taking the offensive, working not always, for instance, to have to react to media agenda setting but rather to participate in the construction of the media's agenda, is something that ought to be done, and done more systematically, and more often. Otherwise, those of us in the field are always placed in the position of having to respond to·the next Wen Ho Lee, the next 9/11, and so forth. If we are not proactive, then rather than being well-thought-out and planned, the field comes to be defined as a field on the defensive, always in the position of having to answer to others—a reaction formation.

While on the one hand going on the offensive and preparing for future international events that may directly impinge on Asian American studies is one kind of response, also important is to learn from tragedies that have already taken place. Hence, 9/11 does provide us with an opportunity to think through the parameters of the field in terms of Arabs, Arab Americans, Muslims, South Asians, and South Asian Americans, in particular, to see what can be done so that they are less likely to be targeted should something like 9/11 ever happen again. It is also an opportunity to reconceptualize the field, how Asian American is defined, and to understand the complexity of all that Asian American and Asian American studies represents. 9/11 provides Asian American studies with the opportunity to recall the abhorrent civil rights infringements that can occur when issues of national security emerge. 9/11 provides us with an opportunity to remember what happened to Japanese Americans during and after World War II, to learn from this comparison, and to discuss the legal casework that took place long after mass abridgement of civil freedoms took place. 9/11 should move us not to be so set in our ways, not to be secure in our definitions of such terms as *Asian American* and thus not to be so sure of who is to be included and who is to be excluded in what we conceive to be our "interest" group.

Reformulating our conception of Asian American studies requires, minimally, a willingness to change and adapt to shifting social circumstances and to remember the deep structures that undergird and inform contemporary social relations. Those of us involved in institutionalizing the field, reifying it on university campuses, and creating programs that we hope will be in place for a very long time, also have to be aware that what it is we are building, in fact, was never a fixed idea in the first place. What this means, in the recent post-9/11 context is, perhaps, that we have to reconfigure our curricula to be more conversant about the connection between Arab and Arab American studies, Muslim studies, and Asian and Asian American studies. Courses on South Asian Americans, on Muslim identity and culture, on the intersections between Arab American and Asian American studies would be appropriate. Searching to hire scholars doing Pakistani and Pakistani American studies as well as those doing research at the nexus between Iraqi and Asian American studies would be a start. Hiring scholars doing research at the intersection of national security, civil liberties, freedom of information, representations of women and queers, neoliberal economic forces, transnationalism, Muslim religious organizations, prison reform, political policy, and media activism might be another way to begin to meet the kinds of challenges facing us and to address a newly configured Asian American studies in the post-9/11 environment.

Pedagogy that encourages comparative understanding of groups, not only Asian American groups, but other groups marginalized by society, is needed. Thus, an internal comparative model and an external comparative model might be useful.[23] A theory of the role of geopolitical racial politics in relation to domestic racial politics (e.g., like Shah's), might be quite helpful and significant. Like Ahmad's work, an ability to understand racial and ethnic events in connection to sexual and gendered histories and experiences would be necessary. Courses that contain a social learning function, whereby students make connections between socially marginalized communities and other community members, continue to be needed.

One way to build flexibility, openness, and an ability to respond to changing social circumstances is simply to be more engaged in community life outside of the university auditorium. Asian American studies constantly risks intellectual provincialism, which is an ever-present danger of the academy more generally. Disengagement from social political life; emphasis on the intellectual above all else (hence, a reinscription of the mind/body and brain/brawn dualism replete throughout Western letters); and of course the diminishment of any positive place for rupture, antagonism, and fractiousness—in a word, activism—likely will encourage satisfaction with the status quo.

Flexibility, adaptability, a willingness to change, and a desire for shared social knowledge and improvement is key within our academic associations. In particular, more serious thought needs to be given to the way issues of marginalization, ethnic difference, and internal subjugation and colonization of groups are addressed within the Association. Theoretical work should turn to a discussion of imperialism within anti-imperial projects. Work should be done to address, treating with care, sincerity, vigilance, and long-term commitment, challenges to the Association. Hence, I would argue that Asian American studies, more generally, must turn to issues of marginalization within the Association and broader society. In that vein, such books as *Asian American Studies after Critical Mass* (2005) begin a conversation and provide an example in this direction.[24]

Coalition building across race and ethnic areas, in addition to building stronger networks that work actively to alter the prevailing military, security, surveillance, and control state, is needed. Nadine Naber (2004) calls for such work when she asks, "Will activists who organize themselves according to the category, 'people of color,' continue addressing domestic and international campaigns separately, or will they work from a place that recognizes the relationality of these efforts?" (235). She further suggests that "as a result, communities which define their primary battle as the national liberation of their homeland and the consequent opportunity to return home often are excluded from the analytical frameworks that shape racial/ethnic studies discourses and movements" (236). Naber argues that to build long-lasting coalitions requires hard work. She writes, "Coalition building since 9/11 has necessitated crafting frameworks for tackling racism that are flexible enough to expose sites of commonality and hierarchy between communities" (230). What I hope we learn from 9/11 is precisely what I hope we learn from other high profile events that affect Asian American studies, which is precisely what I hope we learn about changing cityscapes and the social worlds they enable: there is a fragile connection between Asian American studies and the changing sociopolitical environment, and Asian American studies should understand and engage with the material effects of such changes in order to reconceptualize continually its project and purpose within a changing social world.

Acknowledgments

I want to thank Cameron McCarthy for thinking my work worthy of further hearing; Shoshana Magnet and Rachel Dubrofsky for excellent research assistance; Laura Lindenfeld for having invited me to formulate some of these ideas in a presentation at the University of Maine; Martin Manalansan, Junaid Rana, Sunaina Maira, and Priya Shah for generously allowing me to read prepublication versions of their essays; and Nadine Naber, who continues to be a source of inspiration to me in struggles for social justice.

Notes

1. Several essays explicitly draw the connection between post-9/11 U.S. security measures and the incarceration of Japanese Americans during World War II in *Asian Americans on War and Peace*, edited by Russell C. Leong and Don T. Nakanishi.
2. Then there are other matters—such as the size of the budget, the number of faculty, the number of staff, kind and size of facilities, potential for curricular change, and most certainly quality of all of the above—that affect the kind of Asian American studies program that gets built in a given local context.
3. These first two questions are particularly important when one considers how the core of the field today was shaped by the particular historical conditions of the leaders of the field at the time. Thus, thinking about what the field would have been like had it emerged in a different cultural and historical context should give us pause about what the field is and where it should be going.
4. The creation and evolution of the East of California Caucus (EOC) of the Association for Asian American Studies being only one of those. EOC has become an association in and of itself, even as it is a caucus within AAAS, and has held its own conferences and has its own website, and at the 2004 AAAS EOC caucus meeting, the idea of EOC having its own secretariat came under consideration.
5. As has been suggested in many places, Proposition 187 was largely punitive, since most of the health, education, and welfare "benefits" the measure sought to eliminate were already unavailable to undocumented migrants. See Ono and Sloop, 4.
6. The initiative later encountered legal scrutiny within the courts and was basically annulled when then Governor Gray Davis chose not to appeal the District Court's decision negating most parts of the proposition (Ono and Sloop, 5).
7. It is interesting to think of the decision to boycott or not to boycott California as a conference site in light of the fact that California has been central to the historical experience of Asian Americans. The East of California Caucus of AAAS had formed in 1991, just three years prior to the Board voting not to boycott California. Perhaps for some, especially Californians, to boycott California, since California is in many ways seen as being definitive of Asian American experience, might be akin to boycotting Asian America. For more detailed discussion of the vote, see the e-mail message sent by Kenyon Chan regarding the Board's vote, dated November 29, 1994. For the record, I boycotted all the conferences in California that I normally would have attended, including AAAS in 1995, until Proposition 187 had been overturned in the courts. In hindsight of what happened in California during the 1990s, beginning with Proposition 187, moving to Proposition 209 eliminating affirmative action, and concluding with Proposition 227 eliminating bilingual education, had a more substantial political front been mobilized around Proposition 187, perhaps the subsequent political travesties might have been headed off.
8. In her e-mail message May 2003, Kauanui mentioned that she would not be at the conference and noted how ironic and problematic it was that Pacific Islanders who were not members of AAAS would not be able to vote as to whether or not Pacific was to be included in the Association's name.
9. aaascommunity@yahoogroups.com.
10. Another relevant issue arose over the release of Professor Antoinette Charfauros McDaniel, of Pacific Islander heritage, from her tenure track position at Oberlin College, October 30, 2001. As president of AAAS, Dana Takagi wrote a letter to the president of Oberlin College Nancy Dye about her and AAAS's concerns about the termination of Professor McDaniel's position.
11. For a detailed discussion of the relationship between Asian American studies and Pacific Islander studies, please see Kauanui (2004).
12. For a detailed discussion of the history of relations between Asian Americans and Pacific Islanders in general, please see Candace Fujikane.
13. It will be interesting to see, for instance, what the future holds for the Asian Latino Caucus within AAAS, given the history of the Association and Proposition 187.
14. Indeed, the images are heavily masculinized, hence rendering invisible, in many ways, women and children, notably women's activism and political participation.
15. In her introduction to a special issue of *Cinema Journal* on 9/11, "In Focus: Teaching 9/11," Louise Spence describes the impact of televisual images on her students' consciousness by suggesting that "the photographic images seemed to be so real that they fixed the events for posterity."

16. It is important to point out that racial profiling did not suddenly end for other groups. Articles after 9/11 suggested African Americans were experiencing relief from racial profiling as a result of the new "potential terrorist" racial profiling target. However, such stories ignored the likely outcome of 9/11, which was in fact greater suspicion of people of color more generally. See Junaid Rana.

17. The basic elements for implementing such a wide-ranging surveillance system had been laid out in section 641(a) of the Illegal Immigration Reform and Immigrant Responsibility Act of 1996 (8 U.S.C. 1372(a)). However, the financial capital to enforce the 1996 Act was key to the U.S.A. Patriot Act's successful, uniform, and thoroughgoing implementation of the 1996 Act's procedures.

18. This did not include money to pay for fees associated with international students being tracked. The Justice Department recommended to universities that the best way to pay for these fees would be to charge international students and applicants a $100 fee. Students across the United States have challenged this idea, suggesting that it is a form of taxation unfairly applied to international students as a specific class, because of who they are—international students—and that the fees associated with the implementation of surveillance and monitoring systems targeting international students should be borne by all.

19. At UC Berkeley, international admissions for the 2003 to 2004 school year dropped 18 percent over the previous year. See Cutler and Medrano (2004).

20. I thank Martin Manalansan for helping me describe this argument in this essay.

21. I think it is important to point out that there are tremendous anachronisms within the larger field of Asian American studies, with the early Asian American studies programs having emerged in the late 1960s and 1970s, with the Association for Asian American Studies having been founded in 1979, but programs east of California, for the most part, having been formed in the 1990s. The field's seeming inability to respond with seriousness to changing world events, demographics, and the interests such changes bring may be partly due to the anachronistic divisions that have emerged across the Association because of differential development of various parts of the field.

22. In his State of the Union address January 20, 2004, Bush named Iran and North Korea as serious threats to U.S. peace.

23. Clearly, this is one important reason why Asian studies and Asian American studies should interconnect, among many others Chuh and Shimakawa discuss in the introduction to *Orientations: Mapping Studies in the Asian Diaspora* and that I also discuss in my introduction to *Asian American Studies after Critical Mass*.

24. My introduction to *A Companion to Asian American Studies* also begins to address this point.

References

Ahmad, Muneer. "Homeland Insecurities: Racial Violence the Day after September 11." *Social Text* 20 (2002): 101–15.

Chan, Kenyon. "AAAS Response to 187." Foreword to aagpso@magnus.acs.ohio-state.edu. November 29, 1994.

Chuh, Kandice. *Imagine Otherwise: On Asian Americanist Critique*. Durham, NC: Duke University Press, 2003.

Chuh, Kandice and Karen Shimakawa, eds. *Orientations: Mapping Studies in the Asian Diaspora*. Durham, NC: Duke University Press, 2003.

Cutler, Kim-Mai and Medrano, Alberto, "Number of UC Applicants Drops: Fewer High School Graduates, Increased Fees Cited as Possible Reasons for First Dip in Decade." *Daily Californian*. January 28, 2004.

Fujikane, Candace. "Foregrounding Native Nationalisms: A Critique of Antinationalist Sentiment in Asian American Studies." In *Asian American Studies after Critical Mass*, edited by Kent A. Ono. Malden, MA: Blackwell, 2005.

Kauanui, J. Kehaulani. "Asian American Studies and the 'Pacific Question.'" In *Asian American Studies after Critical Mass*. edited by Kent A. Ono. Malden, MA: Blackwell, 2005.

Leong, Russell C. and Don T. Nakanishi, eds. *Asian Americans on War and Peace*. Los Angeles: UCLA Asian American Studies Center Press, 2002.

Maira, Sunaina. "A Moment of Empire: Doing Asian American Studies in the Metropole," 2004. Unpublished essay.

Manalansan, Martin F. IV. "Race, Violence, and Neoliberal Spatial Politics in the Global City." 2004. Unpublished essay.

Naber, Nadine C. "So Our History Doesn't Become Your Future: The Local and Global Politics of Coalition Building Post September 11th." *Journal of Asian American Studies* 5 (2002): 217–42.

Ono, Kent A., ed. *A Companion to Asian American Studies*. Malden, MA: Blackwell, 2004a.

Ono, Kent A., ed. *Asian American Studies after Critical Mass*. Malden, MA: Blackwell, 2004b.

Ono, Kent A. and John M. Sloop. *Shifting Borders: Rhetoric, Immigration, and California's "Proposition 187."* Philadelphia: Temple University Press, 2002.

Puar, Jasbir K. and Amit S. Rai. "Monster, Terrorist, Fag: The War on Terrorism and the Production of Docile Patriots." *Social Text* 20 (2002): 117–48.

Rana, Junaid. "The Language of Terror: Panic, Peril, Racism," 2004. Unpublished essay.

Shah, Priya J. "'A Choice by Right': Multiculturalism, Minority Group Rights, and Forced Marriage." Paper presented at the Association for Asian American Studies Conference, Boston, MA, March 27, 2004.

Spence, Louise. "Teaching 9/11 and Why I'm Not Doing It Anymore." *Cinema Journal* 43 (2004): 100–105.

Volpp, Leti. "The Citizen and the Terrorist." In *September 11 in History: A Watershed Moment?*, edited by Mary L. Dudziak, 147–62. Durham, NC: Duke University Press, 2003.

30
The Politics of Knowledge

EDWARD SAID

Last fall I was invited to participate in a seminar at a historical studies center of a historically renowned American university. The subject of the seminar for this and the next academic year is imperialism, and the seminar discussions are chaired by the center's director. Outside participants are asked to send a paper before their arrival; it is then distributed to the members of the seminar, who are graduate students, fellows, and faculty. They will have read the paper in advance, precluding any reading of a lecture to them by the visitor, who is instead asked to summarize its main points for about ten minutes. Then for an hour and a half, there is an open discussion of the paper—a fairly rigorous but stimulating exercise. Since I have been working for some years on a sequel to *Orientalism* (Said, 1978)—it will be a long book that deals with the relationship between modern culture and imperialism—I sent a substantial extract from the introduction, in which I lay out the main lines of the book's argument. I there begin to describe the emergence of a global consciousness in Western knowledge at the end of the nineteenth century, particularly in such apparently unrelated fields as geography and comparative literature. I then go on to argue that the appearance of such cultural disciplines coincides with a fully global imperial perspective, although such a coincidence can only be made to seem significant from the point of view of later history, when nearly everywhere in the colonized world there emerged resistance to certain oppressive aspects of imperial rule like theories of subject races and peripheral regions and the notions of backward, primitive, or undeveloped cultures. *Because* of that native resistance—for instance, the appearance of many nationalist and independence movements in India, the Caribbean, Africa, the Middle East—it is now evident that culture and imperialism in the West could be understood as offering support each to the other. Here I referred to the extraordinary work of a whole range of non-Western writers and activists, including Tagore, Fanon, C.L.R. James, Yeats, and many others, figures who have given integrity to anti-imperialist cultural resistance.

The first question after my brief resumé was from a professor of history, a black woman of some eminence who had recently come to the university but whose work was unfamiliar to me. She announced in advance that her question was to be hostile, "a very hostile one in fact." She then said something like the following: For the first thirteen pages of your paper you talked only about white European males. Thereafter, on page fourteen, you mention some names of non-Europeans. "How could you do such a thing?" she asked. I remonstrated somewhat and tried to explain my argument in greater detail—after all, I said, I was discussing European imperialism, which would not have been likely to include in its discourse the work of African American women. I pointed out that in the book I say quite a bit about the response to imperialism all over the world; that point was a place in my argument where it would be pertinent to focus on the work of such writers as—and here I again mentioned the name of a great Caribbean writer and intellectual whose work has a special importance for my own—C.L.R. James. To this my critic replied with a stupefying confidence that my answer was not satisfactory since C.L.R. James was dead! I must admit that I was nonplussed by the severity of this pronouncement. James indeed *was* dead, a fact that needn't, to a historian, have made further discussion impossible. I waited for her to resume, hoping that she might expatiate on what she meant by having suggested that even in discussions of what dead white European males said on a given topic it was inappropriate to confine oneself to what they said while leaving out the work of living African American, Arab, and Indian writers.

But she did not proceed, and I was left to suppose that she considered her point sufficiently and conclusively made: I was guilty of not mentioning living non-European nonmales, even when it was not obvious to me or, I later gathered, to many members of the seminar, what their pertinence might have been. I noted to myself that my antagonist did not think it necessary to enumerate what specifically in the work of living non-Europeans I should have used, or which books and ideas by them she found important and relevant. All I had been given to work with was the asserted necessity to mention some approved names—which names did not really matter—as if the very act of uttering them were enough. I was also left unmistakably with the impression that as a non-white—a category, incidentally, to which as an Arab I myself belong—she was saying that to affirm the existence of non-European "others" took the place of evidence, argument, discussion.

It would be pointless to deny that the exchange was unsettling. Among other things I was chagrined at the distortions of my position and for having responded to the distortions so clumsily. It did not seem to matter that a great deal of my own work has concerned itself with just the kind of omission with which I was being charged. What apparently mattered now was that having contributed to an early trend, in which Western and European intellectuals were arraigned for having their work constructed out of the suffering and deprivations of so many people of color, I was now allegedly doing what such complicit intellectuals had always done. For if in one place you criticize the exclusion of Orientals, as I did in *Orientalism*, the exclusion of "others" from your work in another place becomes, on one level, difficult to justify or explain. I was disheartened not because I was being attacked, but because the general validity of the point made in *Orientalism* still obtained and yet was now being directed at me. It was *still* true that various Others—the word has acquired a sheen of modishness that has become extremely objectionable—were being represented unfairly, their reality distorted, their truth either denied or twisted with malice. Yet instead of joining on their behalf, I felt I was being asked to get involved in an inconsequential academic contest. I had wanted to say, but didn't, "Is all that matters about the issue of exclusion and misrepresentation the fact that *names* were left out? Why are you detaining us with such trivialities?"

To make matters worse, a few minutes later in the discussion I was attacked by a retired professor of Middle Eastern studies, himself an Orientalist. Like me, he was an Arab, but he had consistently identified himself with intellectual tendencies of which I had always been critical. He now intervened to defend imperialism, saying in tones of almost comic reverence that it had accomplished things that natives couldn't have done for themselves. It had taught them, among other things, he said, how to appreciate the cuneiform and hieroglyphics of their own traditions. As he droned on about the imperial schools, railroads, hospitals, and telegraphs in the third world that stood for examples of British and French largesse, the irony of the whole thing seemed overpowering. It appeared to me that there had to be something to say that surrendered neither to the caricatural reductiveness of the two positions by then arrayed against me, and against each other, nor to that verbal quality in each that was determined to remain ideologically correct and little else.

I was being reminded, by such negative, flat-minded examples of thinking, that the one thing that intellectuals *cannot* do without is the full intellectual process itself. Into it goes historically informed research as well as the presentation of a coherent and carefully argued line that has taken account of alternatives. In addition there must be, it seems to me, a theoretical presumption that in matters having to do with human history and society any rigid theoretical ideal, any simple additive or mechanical notion of what is or is not factual, must yield to the central factor of human work, the actual participation of peoples in the making of human life. If that is so then it must also be true that, given the very nature of human work in the construction of human society and history, it is impossible to say of it that its products are so rarefied, so limited, so beyond comprehension as to exclude most other people, experiences, and histories. I mean further that this kind of human work, which is intellectual work, is worldly; that it is situated in the world and about that world. It is not about things that are so rigidly constricted and so forbiddingly arcane as to exclude all but an audience of like-minded, already convinced persons. While it would be stupid to deny the importance of constituencies and audiences in the construction of an intellectual argument, I think it has to be supposed that many arguments can be made to more than one audience and in different situations. Otherwise we would be dealing not with intellectual argument but either with dogma or with a technological jargon designed specifically to repel all but a small coterie or handful of initiates.

Lest I fall into the danger myself of being too theoretical and specialized, I shall be more specific now and return to the episode I was discussing just a moment ago. At the heart of the imperial cultural enterprise I analyzed in *Orientalism*, and also in my new book, was a politics of identity. That politics needed to assume, indeed needed firmly to believe, that what was true about Orientals or Africans was *not*, however, true about or for Europeans. When a French or German scholar tried to identify the main characteristics of, for instance, the Chinese mind, the work was only partly intended to do that; it was also intended to show how different the Chinese mind was from the Western mind.

Such constructed things—they have only an elusive reality—as the Chinese mind or the Greek spirit have always been with us; they are at the source of a great deal that goes into the making of individual cultures, nations, traditions, and peoples. But in the modern world considerably greater attention has generally been given to such identities than was ever given in earlier historical periods, when the world was larger, more amorphous, less globalized. Today a fantastic emphasis is placed upon a politics of national identity, and to a very great degree this emphasis is the result of imperialistic experience. For when the great modern Western imperial expansion took place all across the world, beginning in the late eighteenth century, it accentuated the interaction between the identity of the French or the English and that of the colonized native peoples. And this mostly antagonistic interaction gave rise to a separation between people, as members of homogenous races and exclusive nations, that was and still is one of the characteristics of what can be called the epistemology of imperialism. At its core is the supremely stubborn thesis that everyone is principally and irreducibly a member of some race or category and that that race or category cannot ever be assimilated to or accepted by others—except as itself. Thus came into being such invented essences as the Oriental or Englishness, as Frenchness, Africanness, or American exceptionalism, as if each of those had a Platonic idea behind it that guaranteed it as pure and unchanging from the beginning to the end of time.

One product of this doctrine is nationalism, a subject so immense that I can treat it only very partially here. What interests me in the politics of identity that informed imperialism in its global phase is that just as natives were considered to belong to a different category—racial or geographical—from that of the Western white man, it also became true that in the great anti-imperialist revolt represented by decolonization this same category was mobilized around, and formed the resisting identity of, the revolutionaries. This was the case everywhere in the third world. Its most celebrated instance is the concept of *négritude*, as developed intellectually and poetically by Aimé Césaire, Léopold Senghor, and, in English, W.E.B. Du Bois. If blacks had once been stigmatized and given inferior status to whites, then it has since become necessary not to deny blackness, and not to aspire to whiteness, but to accept and celebrate blackness, to give it the dignity of poetic as well as metaphysical status. Thus *négritude* acquired positive Being where before it had been a mark of degradation and inferiority. Much the same revaluation of the native particularity occurred in India, many parts of the Islamic world, China, Japan, Indonesia, and the Philippines, where the denied or repressed native essence emerged as the focus of, and even the basis for, nationalist recovery.

It is important to note that much of the early cultural resistance to imperialism on which nationalism and independence movements were built was salutary and necessary. I see it essentially as an attempt on the part of oppressed people, who had suffered the bondage of slavery, colonialism, and—most important—spiritual dispossession, to reclaim their identity. When that finally occurred in places such as Algeria, the grander nationalist efforts amounted to little short of a reconstructed communal political and cultural program of independence. Where the white man had once only seen lazy natives and exotic customs, the insurrection against imperialism produced (as in Ireland for example) a national revolt, along with political parties dedicated to independence, which (like the Congress party in India) were headed by nationalist figures, poets, and military heroes. There were remarkably impressive results from this vast effort at cultural reclamation, most of which are well known and celebrated.

But while the whole movement toward autonomy and independence produced in effect newly independent and separate states constituting the majority of new nations in the postcolonial world today, the nationalist politics of identity has nonetheless quickly proved itself to be insufficient for the ensuing period.

Inattentive or careless readers of Frantz Fanon, generally considered one of the two or three most eloquent apostles of anti-imperialist resistance, tend to forget his marked suspicions of unchecked nationalism. So while it is appropriate to draw attention to the early chapters on violence in *The Wretched of the Earth* (Fanon, 1963), it should be noticed that in subsequent chapters he is sharply critical of what he called the pitfalls of national consciousness. He clearly meant this to be a paradox: for the reason that while nationalism is a necessary spur to revolt against the colonizer, national consciousness must be immediately transformed into what he calls "social consciousness," just as soon as the withdrawal of the colonizer has been accomplished.

Fanon is scathing on the abuses of the postindependence nationalist party: on, for instance, the cult of the Grand Panjandrum (or maximum leader), or the centralization of the capital city, which Fanon said flatly needed to be deconsecrated, or most importantly, the hijacking of common sense and popular participation by bureaucrats, technical experts, and jargon-wielding obfuscators. Well before V.S. Naipaul, Fanon was arguing against the politics of mimicry and separatism that produced the Mobutus, Idi Amins, and Saddams, as well as the grotesqueries and pathologies of power that gave rise to tyrannical states and praetorian guards while obstructing democratic freedoms in so many countries of the third world. Fanon also prophesied the continuing dependency of numerous postcolonial governments and philosophies, all of which preached the sovereignty of the newly independent people of one or another new third world state and, having failed to make the transition from nationalism to true liberation, were in fact condemned to practice the politics, and the economics, of a new oppression as pernicious as the old one.

At bottom, what Fanon offers most compellingly is a critique of the separatism and mock autonomy achieved by a pure politics of identity that has lasted too long and been made to serve in situations where it has become simply inadequate. What invariably happens at the level of knowledge is that signs and symbols of freedom and status are taken for the reality: You want to be named and considered for the sake of being named and considered. In effect this really means that just to be an independent postcolonial Arab, or black, or Indonesian is not a program, nor a process, nor a vision. It is no more than a convenient starting point from which the real work, the hard work, might begin.

As for that work, it is nothing less than the reintegration of all those people and cultures, once confined and reduced to peripheral status, with the rest of the human race. After working through *négritude* in the early sections of *Cahier d'un retour* ([1947] 1969), Césaire states this vision of integration in his poem's climactic moment: "no race possesses the monopoly of beauty, of intelligence, of force, and there is a place for all at the rendez-vous of victory."

Without this concept of "place for all at the rendez-vous of victory," one is condemned to an impoverishing politics of knowledge based only upon the assertion and reassertion of identity, an ultimately uninteresting alternation of presence and absence. If you are weak, your affirmation of identity for its own sake amounts to little more than saying that you want a kind of attention easily and superficially granted, like the attention given an individual in a crowded room at a roll call. Once receiving such recognition, the subject has only to sit there silently as the proceedings unfold as if in his or her absence. And, on the other hand, though the powerful get acknowledged by the sheer force of presence, this commits them to a logic of displacement, as soon as someone else emerges who is as, or more, powerful.

This has proved a disastrous process, whether for postcolonials, forced to exist in a marginal and dependent place totally outside the circuits of world power, or for powerful societies, whose triumphalism and imperious willfulness have done so much to devastate and destabilize the world. What has been at issue between Iraq and the United States is precisely such a logic of exterminism and displacement, as unedifying as it is unproductive. It is risky, I know, to move from the realm of interpretation to the realm of world politics, but it seems to me true that the relationship between them is a real one, and the light that one realm can shed on the other is quite illuminating. In any case the politics of knowledge that is based principally on the affirmation of identity is very similar, is indeed directly related to, the unreconstructed nationalism that has guided so many postcolonial states today. It asserts a sort of separatism that wishes only to draw attention to itself; consequently it neglects the integration of that earned and achieved consciousness of self within "the rendez-vous of victory." On the national and intellectual level the problems are very similar.

Let me return therefore to one of the intellectual debates that has been central to the humanities in the past decade, and that underlies the episode with which I began. The ferment in minority, subaltern, feminist, and postcolonial consciousness has resulted in so many salutary achievements in the curricular and theoretical approach to the study of the humanities as quite literally to have produced a Copernican revolution in all traditional fields of inquiry. Eurocentrism has been challenged definitively; most scholars and students in the contemporary American academy are now aware, as they were never aware before, that society and culture have been the heterogeneous product of heterogeneous people in an enormous variety of cultures, traditions, and situations. No longer does T.S. Eliot's idea of the great Western masterpieces enduring together in a constantly redefining pattern of monuments have its old authority; nor do the sorts of patterns elucidated with such memorable brilliance in formative works like *Mimesis* (Auerbach, 1953) or *The Anatomy of Criticism* (Frye, 1957) have the same cogency for today's student or theorist as they did even quite recently.

And yet the great contest about the canon continues. The success of Allan Bloom's *The Closing of the American Mind* (1987), the subsequent publication of such works as Alvin Kernan's *The Death of Literature* (1990) and Roger Kimball's *Tenured Radicals* (1990), as well as the rather posthumous energies displayed in journals like *The American Scholar* (now a neoconservative magazine), *The*

New Criterion, and *Commentary*—all this suggests that the work done by those of us who have tried to widen the area of awareness in the study of culture is scarcely finished or secure. But our point, in my opinion, cannot be simply and obdurately to reaffirm the paramount importance of formerly suppressed or silenced forms of knowledge and leave it at that, nor can it be to surround ourselves with the sanctimonious piety of historical or cultural victimhood as a way of making our intellectual presence felt. Such strategies are woefully insufficient. The whole effort to deconsecrate Eurocentrism cannot be interpreted, least of all by those who participate in the enterprise, as an effort to supplant Eurocentrism with, for instance, Afrocentric or Islamocentric approaches. On its own, ethnic particularity does not provide for intellectual process—quite the contrary. At first, you will recall, it was a question, for some, of adding Jane Austen to the canon of male Western writers in humanities courses; then it became a matter of displacing the entire canon of American writers like Hawthorne and Emerson with best-selling writers of the same period like Harriet Beecher Stowe and Susan Warner. But after that the logic of displacement became even more attenuated, and the mere names of politically validated living writers became more important than anything about them or their works.

I submit that these clamorous dismissals and swooping assertions are in fact caricatural reductions of what the great revisionary gestures of feminism, subaltern or black studies, and antiimperialist resistance originally intended. For such gestures it was never a matter of replacing one set of authorities with another, nor of substituting one center for another. It was always a matter of opening and participating in a central strand of intellectual and cultural effort and of showing what had always been, though indiscernibly, a part of it, like the work of women, or of blacks and servants—but which had been either denied or derogated. The power and interest of—to give two examples particularly dear to me—Tayib Salih's *Season of Migration to the North* ([1969]1980) is not only how it memorably describes the quandary of a gifted young Sudanese who has lived in London but then returns home to his ancestral village alongside the Nile; the novel is also a rewriting of Conrad's *Heart of Darkness* ([1899]1967), seen now as the tale of someone who voyages into the heart of light, which is modern Europe, and discovers there what had been hidden deep within him. To read the Sudanese writer is of course to interpret an Arabic novel written during the late '60s at a time of nationalism and a rejection of the West. The novel is therefore affiliated with other Arabic novels of the postwar period including the works of Naguib Mahfouz and Yusuf Idris; but given the historical and political meaning of a narrative that quite deliberately recalls and reverses Conrad—something impossible for a black man at the time *Heart of Darkness* was written—Salih's masterpiece is necessarily to be viewed as, along with other African, Indian, and Caribbean works, enlarging, widening, refining the scope of a narrative form at the center of which had heretofore always been an exclusively European observer or center of consciousness.

There is an equally complex resonance to Ghassan Kanafani's *Men in the Sun* ([1956]1978), a compelling novella about the travails of three Palestinian refugees who are trying to get from Basra in Iraq to Kuwait. Their past in Palestine is evoked in order to contrast it with the poverty and dispossession of which they are victims immediately after 1948. When they find a man in Basra whose occupation is in part to smuggle refugees across the border in the belly of his empty watertruck, they strike a deal with him, and he takes them as far as the border post, where he is detained in conversation in the hot sun. They die of asphyxiation, unheard and forgotten. Kanafani's novella belongs to the genre of immigrant literature contributed to by an estimable number of postwar writers—Rushdie, Naipaul, Berger, Kundera, and others. But it is also a poignant meditation on the Palestinian fate, and of course eerily prescient about Palestinians in the current Gulf crisis. And yet it would do the subject of the work and its literary merit an extraordinary disservice were we to confine it to the category of national allegory, to see in it only a mirroring of the actual plight of Palestinians in exile. Kanafani's work is literature connected both to its specific historical and cultural situations and to a whole world of other literatures and formal articulations, which the attentive reader summons to mind as the interpretation proceeds.

The point I am trying to make can be summed up in the useful notion of worldliness. By linking works to each other we bring them out of the neglect and secondariness to which for all kinds of political and ideological reasons they had been previously condemned. What I am talking about therefore is the opposite of separatism, and also the reverse of exclusivism. It is only through the scrutiny of these works *as* literature, as style, as pleasure and illumination, that they can be brought in, so to speak, and kept in. Otherwise they will be regarded only as informative ethnographic specimens, suitable for the limited attention of experts and area specialists. *Worldliness* is therefore the restoration to such works and interpretations of their place in the global setting, a restoration that can only be accomplished by an appreciation not of some tiny, defensively constituted corner of the world but of the large, many-windowed house of human culture as a whole.

It seems to me absolutely essential that we engage with cultural works in this unprovincial, interested manner while maintaining a strong sense of the contest for forms and values that any decent cultural work embodies, realizes, and contains. A great deal of recent theoretical speculation has proposed that works of literature are completely determined as such by their situation, and that readers themselves are totally determined in their responses by their respective cultural situations, to a point where no value, no reading, no interpretation can be anything other than the merest reflection of some immediate interest. All readings and all writing are reduced to an assumed historical emanation. Here the indeterminacy of deconstructive reading, the airy insouciance of post-axiological criticism, the casual reductiveness of some (but by no means all) ideological schools are principally at fault. While it is true to say that because a text is the product of an unrecapturable past contemporary criticism can to some extent afford a neutral disengagement or opposed perspective impossible for the text in its own time, there is no reason to take the further step and exempt the interpreter from any moral, political, cultural, or psychological commitments. All of these remain at play. The attempt to read a text in its fullest and most integrative context commits the reader to positions that are educative, humane, and engaged, positions that depend on training and taste and not simply on a technologized professionalism, or on the tiresome playfulness of "postmodern" criticism, with its repeated disclaimers of anything but local games and pastiches. Despite Lyotard and his acolytes, we are still in the era of large narratives, of horrendous cultural clashes, and of appallingly destructive war—as witness the recent conflagration in the Gulf—and to say that we are against theory, or beyond literature, is to be blind and trivial.

I am not arguing that every interpretive act is equivalent to a gesture either for or against life. How could anyone defend or attack so crudely general a position? I am saying that once we grant intellectual work the right to exist in a relatively disengaged atmosphere and allow it a status that isn't disqualified by partisanship, we ought then to reconsider the ties between the text and the world in a serious and uncoercive way. Far from repudiating the great advances made when Eurocentrism and patriarchy began to be demystified, we should consolidate these advances, using them so as to reach a better understanding of the degree to which literature and artistic genius belong to and are some part of the world where all of us also do other kinds of work.

This wider application of the ideas I've been discussing cannot even be attempted if we simply repeat a few names or refer to a handful of approved texts ritualistically or sanctimoniously. Victimhood, alas, does not guarantee or necessarily enable an enhanced sense of humanity. To testify to a history of oppression is necessary, but it is not sufficient unless that history is redirected into intellectual process and universalized to include all sufferers. Yet too often testimony to oppression becomes only a justification for further cruelty and inhumanity, or for high-sounding cant and merely "correct" attitudes. I have in mind, for instance, not only the antagonists mentioned at the beginning of this essay, but also the extraordinary behavior of an Elie Wiesel who has refused to translate the lessons of his own past into consistent criticisms of Israel for doing what it has done and is doing right now to Palestinians.

So while it is not necessary to regard every reading or interpretation of a text as the moral equivalent of a war or a political crisis, it does seem to me to be important to underline the fact that whatever else they are, works of literature are not merely texts. They are in fact differently constituted and have different values, they aim to do different things, exist in different genres, and so on. One of the great pleasures for those who read and study literature is the discovery of longstanding norms in which all cultures known to me concur: such things as style and performance, the existence of good as well as lesser writers, and the exercise of preference. What has been most unacceptable during the many harangues on both sides of the so-called Western canon debate is that so many of the combatants have ears of tin and are unable to distinguish between good writing and politically correct attitudes, as if a fifth-rate pamphlet and a great novel have more or less the same significance. Who benefits from leveling attacks on the canon? Certainly not the disadvantaged person or class whose history, if you bother to read it at all, is full of evidence that popular resistance to injustice has always derived immense benefits from invidious distinctions made between ruling-class and subservient cultures. After all, the crucial lesson of C.L.R. James's *Black Jacobins* (1963) or of E.P. Thompson's *Making of the English Working Class* (1966; with its reminder of how important Shakespeare was to nineteenth-century radical culture) is that great antiauthoritarian uprisings made their greatest advances not by denying the humanitarian and universalist claims of the general dominant culture but by attacking the adherents of that culture for failing to uphold their own declared standards, for failing to extend them to all, as opposed to a small fraction, of humanity. Toussaint L'Ouverture is the perfect example of a downtrodden slave whose struggle to free himself and his people was informed by the ideas of Rousseau and Mirabeau.

Although I risk oversimplification, it is probably correct to say that it does not finally matter *who* wrote what, but rather *how* a work is written and *how* it is read. The idea that because Plato and Aristotle are male and products of a slave society they should be disqualified from receiving contemporary attention is as limited an idea as suggesting that *only* their work, because it was addressed to and about elites, should be read today. Marginality and homelessness are not, in my opinion, to be gloried in; they are to be brought to an end, so that more, and not fewer, people can enjoy the benefits of what has for centuries been denied the victims of race, class, or gender.

Published with the permission of the author. This essay first appeared in *Raritan*, 11 (1) (Summer 1991), pp. 17–31.

References

Auerbach, E. (1953). *Mimesis: The representation of reality in Western literature*. (W. R. Trask, Trans.). Princeton: Princeton UP.

Bloom, A. (1987). *The Closing of the American Mind*. New York: Simon.

Césaire, A. ([1947]1969). *Cahier d'un retour au pays natal*. [Return to my native land]. (A. Berger & J. Bostock, Trans.). Baltimore: Penguin.

Conrad, J. *Heart of Darkness*. ([1899])1967). In *Great short works of Joseph Conrad* (pp. 211–292). New York: Harper.

Fanon, F. (1963). *The Wretched of the Earth*. (H. Kirkpatrick, Trans.) New York: Grove.

Frye, N. (1957). *Anatomy of Criticism: Four essays*. Princeton: Princeton UP.

James, C. L. R. (1963). *The Black Jacobins: Toussaint l'Ouverture and the San Domingo revolution*. New York: Vintage.

Kanafani, G. ([1956]1978). *Men in the Sun*. Washington, DC: Three Continents.

Kernan, A. B. (1990). *The Death of Literature*. New Haven: Yale UP.

Kimball, R. (1990). *Tenured Radicals: How politics has corrupted our higher education*. New York: Harper.

Said, E. (1978). *Orientalism*. New York: Pantheon.

Salih, T. ([1969]1980). *Season of Migration to the North*. Washington, DC: Three Continents.

Thompson, E. P. (1966). *The Making of the English Working Class*. New York: Vintage.

Afterword

Foot Soldiers of Modernity

The Dialectics of Cultural Consumption and the 21st-Century School

PAUL WILLIS

Young people are unconscious foot soldiers in the long front of modernity, involuntary and disoriented conscripts in battles never explained. In particular, subordinate and working-class students are rendered by state-mandated education into the compulsory living materials of future imaginings and moldings. These institutional imaginings have immense social power but are usually undertaken by one generation for the next without the rudiments of a sociological or ethnographic imagination. The theories and qualitative methods of the social sciences are necessary to represent local experience at the grassroots and to understand its connections to the operations of larger institutional and macro forces. Power brokers and policy planners are transfixed by the internal logic of their "top-down" practices and initiatives; however, they fail to ponder the frequently ironic and unintended consequences of these practices and the creative cultural ways in which subordinate and working-class groups respond to them. These "bottom-up" responses are often informed by quite different social perceptions, practices, and assumptions.

What is crucial but missed is the recognition that the waves of attempted economic and technical modernization "from above" are often antagonistically related to waves of cultural modernization "from below," which are usually misunderstood. In part, technical modernization is fighting not chaos, a recalcitrant past, or the wrong type of future, but its own alter ego of late cultural modernism as articulated by working-class, dominated, and subordinated groups—what I will henceforth refer to as the popular classes. While often appearing to stand in the way of progress, the latter most often tend to believe in this goal and they profoundly condition, in unexpected ways, how it is played out socially and culturally.

Youth are always among the first to experience the problems and possibilities of the successive waves of technical and economic modernization that sweep through capitalist societies. Young people respond in disorganized and chaotic ways, but to the best of their abilities and with relevance to the actual possibilities of their lives as they see, live, and embody them. These responses are actually embedded in the flows of cultural modernization, but to adult eyes they may seem to be mysterious, troubling, and even shocking and antisocial. Schools are one of the principal sites for the dialectical playing out of these apparent disjunctions and contradictions, which, while misunderstood,

461

underlie some of the most urgent education debates—from traditionalism versus progressivism to the canon versus multiculturalism.

In this article, I argue that a social understanding of education needs to consider both top-down practices and bottom-up responses, and the ways in which they interact "on the ground" to produce the complex eddies, waves, and flows of modernization. The activities and processes I discuss in this article have currency throughout Western industrialized countries and exist in highly varied and often compressed versions in newly industrialized and industrializing countries. However, I draw on ethnographic arguments taken primarily from my own research in England. I deal with three waves of what I am calling cultural modernization "from below," which I discuss in the chronological order of my work. This order does not necessarily reflect their real occurrence in time, certainly not across all countries.

The first wave of modernization from below is based on the cultural responses of working-class and subordinate groups to "top-down" state programs and initiatives aimed at competitive modernization. The most important feature of these schemes has been the vastly expanded scale of compulsory education. This wave of modernization is disrupted by the effects of the second and third waves described below, and the subsequent responses of the popular classes to these waves. The social and cultural dislocations and crises resulting from the emergence of a postindustrial society drive the second wave of modernization. This wave brings a catastrophic decline in the demand for manual labor in industrialized Western countries and transforms the role of the state in the regulation of the youth labor market. We can understand this deindustrialization as one aspect of globalization whereby economic restructuring triggers the brutal arrival of the postindustrial society in the "first" world as industrial society finally takes root—unevenly—in the "third." The third wave of modernization from below arises from the common cultural responses of young people to the arrival of the global "commodity and electronic society." Young people creatively respond to a plethora of electronic signals and cultural commodities in ways that surprise their makers, finding meanings and identities never meant to be there and defying simple nostrums that bewail the manipulation or passivity of "consumers."

Although my main focus here will be on the third wave, all aspects and themes of the three waves continue as simultaneous and intertwined forces. In different ways, they continue to have broad relevance to the current conjunctures in various countries. The basic argument of this article is that the third wave cannot be understood except within the context of, and dialectical links with, the first two waves. Common cultural forms must be understood with respect to their interaction with other major forces sweeping through society and with the responses of the popular classes to these forces.

First Wave: Cultural Responses to Universal Schooling

Part of the political settlement between forces representing "capital" and "labor" in the United Kingdom (U.K.) after World War II was to give, at least theoretically, equal education rights to all children. In 1972, the U.K. raised the minimum school-leaving age from fifteen to sixteen. This marked the coming to full fruition of the early modernist drive to secure compulsory full-time education for all. Emile Durkheim (1956) comments on education as the instrument of modernization *par excellence* that is mobilized to raise the skill levels of workers in an internationally competitive industrial world. Always inherent in this drive is the tension between the socially integrative ideologies of aspiration and egalitarianism and the obvious practical logic of the continuing delivery of social agents into gendered hierarchies severely divided by skill, remuneration, and disposition. This tension helps us understand that even the extended support across the organized left in the U.K. for raising the school-leaving age failed to hide the disappointing response of a good section of the working class to the prospect of another year of enforced school attendance. Many working-class kids did not accept their new privilege with good grace. Instead, they simply wanted the earliest possible access to the wage. They did not want to be in school at all, never mind another year of it (Willis, 1977).

The Lads

Learning to Labour describes the informal school culture and interactions of a group of young White working-class boys in an English industrial midlands school in the mid-1970s (Willis, 1977). The "lads" resisted the mental and bodily inculcations of the school and rejected students who showed conformist attitudes to the school authorities. Their culture borrowed and recycled elements of traditional working-class culture and embodied an assertive masculine style, which was often aggressive and predicated on being able to "handle yourself" in a fight. The lads deployed a particularly concrete and sharp way of speaking and were devoted to a certain kind of omnipresent humor—"having a laff"—often directed cruelly against conformists and teachers. Their devotion to "the laff" was central to the culture, and its deployment was an ubiquitous form capable of turning almost any situation into material for jokes and ribbing: "It's the most important thing in life, even communists laff" (p. 29).

In *Learning to Labour*, I wanted to get at the inside story of this phenomenon, to try to see the world as the lads did, to get a feel for their social games and their fields of power from their point of view. They had little or no interest in studying and were not interested in gaining academic qualifications.[1] Vigorous opposition to the teachers' authority was the central vertical dynamic organizing the lads' lived culture: "Who are they, tellin' us what to do when they're no better than us?" The central horizontal dynamic that organized and arranged their cultural assumptions and practices was a rejection of conformist pupils labeled as "ear'oles":[2] "They'm prats, they never get any fun do they?" This rejection was felt as a kind of distinction and superiority: "We can make them laff, they can't make us laff." These positions and orientations were enacted and embodied through a strong "rough" masculine set of strategies, embellished in various ways through smoking, drinking, and stylish dressing.

From an educational point of view, the strangest thing about the lads' attitudes and behavior was their low interest in and/or hostility toward academic work and the gaining of qualifications. From a sociological point of view, the most interesting thing about their culture was the indifference it induced among the lads to the actual kind of work they thought of undertaking, ranging from readily available factory work to tire fitting and bricklaying. I argued in *Learning to Labour* that their own culture helped induct them voluntarily into the low-status jobs that most would shun. Their own culture was involved in processes of social reproduction, understood as the generational replacement of individuals in unequal class positions. There was a tragic irony at the heart of their culture; it was surprisingly more effective than any intended ideological mechanism aimed at promoting social reproduction.[3]

"Modern" Social Functions of Resistance

Although resistant cultures continue to be condemned in schools with teachers and administrators increasingly seeing them as pathological, they actually show some clear elements of rationality. In particular, these resistant cultures supply cultural forms and shields from stigma to blunt the cruel edge of individualism and meritocracy in capitalist societies. These ideologies and their associated mechanisms and practices can have only limited meaning for the majority of the working class who cannot all hope to attain the privilege of well-paid and high-prestige jobs at the end of the educational process. Individual logic says that it is worth working hard at school to gain qualifications to get a good job. However, this cannot be the case for all working-class individuals, even though all are asked to behave as if it were so.[4] Only a substantial minority from the working class can hope for mobility, and their cultures and dispositions are adapted accordingly. No one else discusses this, but the lads' culture, despite its disorders and chaos, tells them that no amount of extra qualification will improve the position of the whole class; that would constitute, in fact, the dismantling of the whole class society.

Meanwhile, the dominance of the individualistic and meritocratic ideology produces for the middle class a functional legitimacy for enjoying their privilege—they are there because they have passed exams. The capacities of the popular classes are subject to stultification in hopeless obedience to an impossible dream. Credentialism, or the proliferation of educational qualifications, works to prevent the working class from pursuing either alternative flowerings of their capacities or subversive courses of growth. It seeks to enslave their powers and trap them in the foothills of human development and can stand only as a fraudulent offer to the majority of what can really mean something only to the few. The student population is graded in a descending status order, from whose lowest ranks escape is usually impossible. The educational offer is to join an ever-multiplying classificatory system in which every increase further depresses its bottom layers (Gilborn & Mirza, 2000). The lads' culture exposes this dynamic, releasing them from collusion in their own exclusion and freeing up their potential for an alternative cultural expressivity.

Ironically, the lads' culture also had a stabilizing effect on the hierarchical social order. In their "tumble out of" and "escape" from what they felt was the oppressive atmosphere of the school, they went into manual work quite voluntarily, subsequently helping to reproduce the whole social order at its most difficult point. The lads also found a "culture of the shop floor" on arrival at work that was welcoming and familiar to them because it displayed many of the same qualities as their own counter-school culture. It gave them a collective and human means—even if sexist, anti-intellectual, and often racist—of surviving the harsh conditions and authority regimes of work. The lads' transition from school to work was, in part, a cultural vote with their feet for the working-class adult world of work. In this informal socialization process, there was also an enthusiastic taking up of rights to the only working-class inheritance bequeathed upon the lads—the wage. The power of the wage created possibilities for which their own culture had already precociously and only too well prepared them: smart dressing, pubbing and clubbing, and crosstown driving.

Hugely important to understand here is the antimental animus of the counter-school culture. While highly relevant in opposing and penetrating the demands of the school, it also becomes a kind of second nature that continues to orient bodily style, attitudes, and values during the transition from school to work and long after. This pattern impels them toward a certain kind of culturally mediated and experiential form of meaning-making throughout their lives. The danger is that this antimental attitude could lead to the whole world being divided into two—the mental and the manual. This makes hope for a "second chance" return to higher education much more difficult and unlikely. The lads' antimentalism reconciles them and those like them to manual work and often to job-hopping between dead-end jobs—now interspersed with long spells of unemployment, or even permanent unemployment—for the rest of their lives. It makes all jobs involving mental work, now and for the future, seem to be simply boring paperwork—"Who wants to spend their day pushing paper around?"

The Articulations of Gender with Antimentalism

Gender meanings and resources are also important elements within the articulations of cultural forces and practices resistant to the school. Symbolic structures of masculinity in the lads' culture help to embody and give an extra force to their school resistance. Masculinity gives them an axis of power over women, but it also gives them a realistic basis for feeling at least some ambiguous superiority over other less successful males, such as teachers and ear'oles. This response has a definite logic and is effective against the attempted domination of the school, and it gives alternative nonmental grounds for valuing the self and a whole solid, sometimes formidable, presence to resist belittling. As I argue in *Learning to Labour*, once formed, "hard" or "tough" masculine identities and the patterning of social relations that follow prove highly inflexible, intractable, and durable. This is perhaps especially so when they have been formed through the winning back of identity and dignity lost in inescapable institutional tensions in which they are trapped on the losing/receiving end. Masculinity and its reflexes henceforth help to organize the same repertoire of defensive/offensive responses no matter what the situation—as if all social sites and social relations contained somehow a mandatory threat. This produces an obvious danger for women in and out of the home, where a compensatory masculinity may seek proof and to exercise a felt superiority. Furthermore, shop floor and manual work relations are suffused with masculinity and masculinized social relations. These relations blunt the oppositional possibility of recognizing how specifically capitalist forms subordinate labor power.

There is a further twist here where the antimentalism and masculinity of the lads become intertwined with their sense of themselves and their own vital powers. For the lads, a manual way of acting in the world is a manly way, while a mental way is effeminate. These gendered associations reinforce and lock each other, producing a disposition and sensibility that may, quite literally, last a lifetime. In a final sealing of their subordinate future, mental work becomes not only pointless "paper pushing" but also "sissy" work for the lads. Teachers are seen as inferior because they are "sissies." Even higher paid mental work is considered sissy from the lads' point of view. Exhausting, exploited, and increasingly low paid, manual work can still somehow be seen in a masculine register, which prevents its true brutality from showing through.

Learning to Labour gives an account of the cultures of White, male, working-class resistance in school. It offers a perspective for understanding a particular stability in the first wave of cultural modernization in the U.K. and its contribution to the maintenance of a relatively peaceful class-divided society. Even after the advent of the Welfare State and formal educational equality for all, there was a settled—though unequal—relation between classes, where no over-ambition from the working class threatened either capitalist organization or the interests of the middle class. At the same time there was some real autonomy allowed to students and young workers, including, at least for an important section, their own transitions from childhood to adulthood. Arguably, this limited autonomy effectively sidelined, or at least profoundly modified, "modernizing" institutional attempts at controlling and regulating the passage into adulthood. Working-class and informal cultural forms and activities, while seen as antisocial by some, could take root and flower in inhospitable circumstances. This made those circumstances more livable and provided collective and mutual relations, communications, and meanings that sustained working-class identity and informal activity on a wider scale.

Although the social and political landscape has changed over the last twenty-six years, there continues to be very hard and persistent elements of resistant culture in schools. Despite their sometimes antisocial nature and the undoubted difficulties they produce for classroom teachers, these cultures continue to pose, in living form, crucial and collective questions from the point of view of the working class: What is "progress" for? What can I/we expect from the sacrifice of hard work and obedience in school? Why am I/are we compelled to be in school if there appears to be nothing in it for me/us?

Second Wave: Responses to the Postindustrial Society

In the early 1980s the U.K. became the first industrialized country to experience massive losses of the manual industrial work that had previously been available to the working classes. This trend is now firmly established across the old industrialized world. In the U.K., over half of the manufacturing jobs that existed in the 1970s have been destroyed with a slightly larger reduction in related trade union membership (Roberts, 2001). At the same time, there has been a virtually epochal restructuring of the kind of work available. From the point of view of the working class, work opportunities have shifted away from well to reasonably paid skilled or semi-skilled industrial work to much lower paid service and out-of-reach white-collar work.

Taken together, the new customer service call centers and the hotel and catering industries now employ more than double the number of workers as the old "smoke-stack" industries—cars, ship building, steel, engineering, coal mining (Roberts, 2001). The whole working class has been badly affected by the diminution in both the quality and quantity of jobs available, especially young people, older workers, and ethnic minorities. Recently, unemployment has dropped considerably to a general rate of 5.1 percent (Office of National Statistics, 2003). This figure, however, conceals a high turnover in part-time, casual, and insecure low-paid work. It also masks huge geographic variations, with large, predominantly middle-class areas enjoying virtually full employment while the older industrial areas and inner cities suffer from overall unemployment rates of 20 percent and more. One in two less-skilled men are without work and one in five households lack access to earned income (Gregg & Wadsworth, 1999; Willis, Bekenn, Ellis, & Whitt, 1988). Clearly, not everyone will find a role in the new weightless economy, and many continue to expect, against increasing odds, to be remunerated and respected for an ability and disposition to work in traditional manual ways.

The objective probabilities of a reliable and decent wage through manual work have been radically decreased for substantial parts of the working class, and the threat of its removal has become a permanent condition for all workers. This has to be understood as a threat, not only to the wage as an amount of money, but also to the wage as a particular kind of social inheritance and cultural, even moral, enfranchisement (Willis, 2000; Willis, Jones, Canaan, & Hurd, 1990). The wage provides access to cultural commodities and services and to the forms of informal meaning-making that these commodities and services frame and facilitate. It also provides the means to independent living, a place separate from the patriarchal dependencies of the parental home, and from the vicissitudes of the marketplace. The wage enables the formation of the couple and preparation for the nuclear family. Gaining access to the male family wage is still one of the important material bases for the courtship dance, romance, and "love-pairing."

In the U.K., we have been suffering from the breaking of these transitions for over two decades. The old processes and expectations often continue in some form but have been thrown into permanent crisis. There are still plenty of male working-class kids, like the lads, who are perhaps more willing than ever to take on exploited manual work in traditional masculine and anti-mentalist ways, but there is not enough work to go around, and many are left in suspended animation.[5] The lucky ones, at least to start with, feel grateful for any work. Even though the uncertainties associated with job insecurity—or the deceptive lure of job hopping—may seem like an antidote to the wearing down of repetitive or heavy labor, they threaten to throw workers back into a stagnant pool of labor at any moment. Nevertheless, simple gratitude and escape from vertiginous despair have become important reproductive mechanisms for those finding or holding on to work (Willis et al., 1988). The dramatic changes brought about by this second wave of modernization have destroyed or substantially weakened traditional forms of transition from school to work and have shaken the material foundations of traditional working-class cultural forms. While unemployment is seen from above as a price worth paying for competitive economic restructuring, economic adaptation produces continuing social and cultural crises at the bottom of social space.

The View from Below[6]

The young unemployed are much less physically mobile than the employed. They cannot afford cars and, therefore, have no access to the "crosstown car culture" of visits to pubs, clubs, and friends. In the Wolverhampton survey conducted for the *Youth Review* (Willis et al., 1988), half of the unemployed say that their activities are limited by the costs of travel, while three-quarters say that they are limited by lack of cash. A good proportion of them visit town centers and shopping malls during the day. They are attracted to the consumer meccas but have no economic role to play. Rather, they simply hang out or engage in activities that put them into conflict with shoppers, shop owners, and the police.

The dominant experience of the young unemployed is one of very limited sociability. They are isolated and homebound, traversing acres of boredom by themselves or in conflict with parents for whom their enforced dependence is often wholly unwelcome. The young unemployed have more free time than any other social group but, ironically, they are excluded from leisure activities, which overwhelmingly now require consumption and commercial power. For instance, whether we like it or not, drinking is by far the most popular activity among young people in the U.K., where three-quarters of them go to pubs nearly four times a week. However, only one-third of the long-term unemployed go drinking, and much less often. Furthermore, they do not spend the extra time engaging in sports or outdoor hobbies, nor do they participate in state-provided community and sports infrastructures any more than the employed. Another vivid aspect of this isolation, according to the *Youth Review* findings, is that, for the unemployed, courtship seems to lose the centrality that it holds for the employed. The young unemployed are much less likely to have a "steady" relationship, and thoughts of marriage or settling down seem very far away for most of them. They are prone to alienation, depression, and pessimism about their future prospects and are plagued by feelings of social shame and suspicions that other people blame them for their condition. Young people who experience long-term unemployment are uniquely open to drug abuse, often seen in distorted ways as forms of self-medication.

A whole succession of training programs and special labor market measures have been developed by the state to bridge the gaping wholes left by the collapse of the old transitions between school and work. In 1998, the British government introduced the New Deal program, which provides unemployed young people with two years of work experience, training, or work in the voluntary and charitable sector (Unemployment Unit, 1999). For the first time with such schemes, refusal to participate is not an option, and benefits are withdrawn if a young person fails to commit to one of these options. Essentially, the means of subsistence are made contingent upon flexibility and obedience, a qualitatively new coercive stage in the disciplining of labor power and attitude.

A significant minority of young people refuses this contractual submission to their own subordination. They are not accounted for in official figures and become invisible to the programs and to the state (Unemployment Unit, 1999; "One in Five Young People," 2003). Despite such refusal and widespread discontent, there is surprisingly little outright public or organized opposition. This may be explained in part by some bleak, internalized, and individualistic additions to the reproduction repertoire whereby many individuals blame themselves for their lack of work and for the lack of success attendance to state schemes brings. Individualizing and internalizing a structural problem, they shamefully reproach themselves for their inability to find work. Having been given so many training opportunities to develop their individual employability and having been told repeatedly that finding work is a question of permanent individual job search, it must be their individual fault when they cannot find work.

These are just some of the forces that corrode the main elements of the first wave modernist cultural settlement. The pride, depth, and independence of a collective industrial cultural tradition, forged from below and neither reliant on patronage nor punished for its cultural impertinence, is giving way to the regulated indignities of becoming a client to a reprimanding state. As the research for the *Youth Review* illustrates, young workers are forced into a reenvisioned reserve army of flexible and obedient labor. This army of workers is supposed to stand ready to occupy, at rock-bottom wages, the new menial functions of the postindustrial economy and to service the growing personal and domestic needs of a newly ascendant middle class. For those who refuse to join state schemes and the legitimate labor market, begging from parents and others, drug dealing, prostitution, hustling, and benefit fraud offer some income. They also lead to entanglements with youth justice systems and possible incarceration, which finally destroys any hope of a "proper" job. But for some, the highly ambiguous and self-defeating freedoms of the streets seem to offer a viable alternative to the mental incarceration of endless state schemes.

Schools in the Second Wave

The school is and will be a principal site for the early playing out of these contradictions and social tensions, thus placing students at the frontlines of these conflicts. A further condition is now added to devalue and question the role of schools at the level of cultural practice. Not only are young people able to challenge its underlying individualistic and meritocratic ideologies, but they can also expose the practical inability of schooling to connect many students to real prospects in the world of work. In these conditions, it is no longer possible to believe in a universal and positive role for the educational system in promoting benign and emancipatory effects for the popular classes. Are schools to prepare their students for unemployment? Are they to engage in remedial programs to equip individuals to fight each other for the very chance of low-paid service work? Are they to abandon altogether any hope of interrupting processes of social reproduction?

Meanwhile, many of the cultural experiences and disarticulations of the late adolescent or early adult unemployed find their way back into the school, importing with them their own hidden and not so hidden injuries and reinforcing attitudes of cynicism, detachment, and gender crisis. These cultural expressions are articulated within different formations of school culture, heightening the negative potential of an already existing atmosphere of disorder, violence, and social fear (Devine, 1997; Johnson, 1999; Paulle, 2003). Singular racial oppressions, exacerbated and magnified through even higher than expected unemployment rates, can add further impulses of anger and opposition (Sewell, 1997). School cultural practices have to be understood within this general context of disaffection with oppositional forms termed and understood as displaying "disassociated" or "disaffected" resistance, rather than the "simple" resistance of wave one. Resistance takes on a kind of futility, even potential pathology, when disassociated from traditional first wave cultural resources, from their sense of a future. After all, first wave resistance is solidified by a well-grounded social bet on capital's need for labor. It assumes and relies on a future of collective labor albeit actively and culturally formed to be relatively free from individualistic and meritocratic distortions and false promises. Even if not fitting official templates, there is a consequent materiality here to be worked on for economic, social, and cultural betterment, which still gives continuity to working-class forms. Second wave modernization deconstructs this working-class inheritance, and resistance spins freely without the context of any socially imagined future. It is hard to detect any link of disaffected or disassociated resistance with any kind of emancipatory political project.

Second Wave Gender Articulations

As in the first wave, gender registers and plays a part in these fundamental social and cultural shifts. In particular, forms of working-class masculinity are being thrown into crisis by the second wave of modernization, uprooted from their secure and central lodgings within proletarian relations of manualism, "pride in the job," and breadwinner power. This shift in the meaning of masculinity undermines the specific logic of masculinized resistance in school, as well as the continuities between male counter-school culture and what remains of shop floor culture. Further, the antimentalism of the counter-school culture cannot be securely cloaked in traditional proletarian masculinity. Antimentalism loses the counterpoint with a viable predictable future in manual work.

As the relationship between the wage and traditional meaning of masculinity shifts, the material base for the courtship dance disappears. For many young women, there is no longer the realistic prospect of gaining access to the family wage and to transition into a separate household through male earning power.[7] Questions of gender identity and sexuality may be rendered into matters of immediate attraction or non-attraction, rather than being informed by long-term expectations of commitment. Where a collective apprenticeship to a respectable future fails, for some young men a strategy for maintaining a sense of manhood may entail, and perhaps demand, immediate gender tributes extracted through heavy sexist language and humor and physical intimidation or its threat. This practice can be taken up into whole bodily dispositions, attitudes, and presence. Where masculinity cannot be about assuming the mantle and power of the wage, it can become a claim for power in its own right.[8]

Under conditions of chronic unemployment, social stability and reproduction may require that some of the young and potentially most disruptive of the unemployed of both sexes withdraw themselves into more or less self-pacified or marginalized positions. By excluding themselves permanently from the labor market, they withdraw from society the seeds of non-cooperation and rebellion. The development of an "underclass" (especially the degeneracies of its public imagery; see Adair, 2002), vastly expanding prison populations (the new "welfare" means for the poor), and the further economic victimization of single mothers may also provide socially reproductive object lessons in destitution *pour encourager les autres*, thereby enabling coercive control of working populations, present and future, without the use of explicit force. Substantial proportions of the student body may be influenced by oppositional cultures, but calculate that a state-regulated chance of a low-paid job beats incarceration or the tender mercies of the street. These are raw and open forms of social reproduction that are very different from the more settled, if mystified, forms associated with first wave modernization. But even through ambiguous and disassociated means, collective questions gain cultural articulation again: What's the point of school if there ain't no jobs to follow? If "progress" is so great, why is all I/we see at school, and in the schemes to follow, increased containment and discipline?

Third Wave: Commodity and Electronic Culture

Along with the upheavals in the material conditions of the subordinate classes described above come enormous changes at the cultural level that bring about disorganization to settled forms of working-class culture. New global electronic forms of communication are sidelining old sensuous communities—face-to-face interactions with known others—with now literally hundreds of TV channels available through digitalization. This is furthered by the huge growth of commercial leisure forms and the mass availability of cultural commodities. The postmodern cultural epoch is characterized by this qualitative expansion of commodity relations from the meeting of physical needs—food, warmth, and shelter—to the meeting and inflaming of mental, emotional, expressive, and spiritual needs and aspirations. You could say that the predatory productive forces of capitalism are now unleashed globally not only on nature but also on human nature.

At the level of culture, young people are becoming less defined by neighborhood and class than they are by these new relations of commodity and electronic culture. Even as their economic conditions of existence falter, most young working-class people in the U.K. would not thank you now for describing them as working class. They find more passion and acceptable self-identity through music on MTV, wearing baseball caps and designer shoes, and socializing in fast-food joints than they do through traditional class-based cultural forms.[9]

We should not underestimate the cultural offensive of capitalism against the young consumer. Young people may believe that they are free to choose, but the marketers have different ideas. Simon Silvester, executive planning director for Young & Rubicon Europe, writes recently in the "Creative Business" section of the *Financial Times*, "Marketers have concentrated on youth for 50 years for good reason—they [young people] are forming their brand preferences and trying out new things.... In 40 years, there'll be a generation of pierced grannies telling you they're brand-promiscuous and adventurous" (Silvester, 2002, p. 6). Ralph Nader (1996) writes in *Children First*:

> A struggle different than any before in world history is intensifying between corporations and parents over their children. It is a struggle over the minds, bodies, time and space of millions of children and the kind of world in which they are growing up.... The corporate marketing culture stresses materialism, money, sex, the power of violence, junk food and the status they bring; its power crowds out or erodes the values of the inherent worth and dignity of the human being. (pp. iii, vii)

Common Culture and the Expressive Subject

Such arguments are well known and, oddly enough, made with equal vigor from the Left and the Right.[10] There is much to be agreed with in Nader's pungently expressed views. However, my purpose is not so much to join a moral crusade as to establish the nature of an epochal shift in the symbolic order and its forms. It is crucial to better understand the consequences of these shifts on young people from a social scientific and ethnographic perspective.

The market, which provides an encompassing and saturating cultural Environment through its electronic forms, supplies the most attractive and use-able symbolic and expressive forms that are consumed by teenagers and early adults. Perhaps political parties, public cultures, or even properly functioning educational institutions should be the principal and principled source of symbolic forms and meanings. It is certainly necessary to continue to battle for the maintenance of the roles and influence of these institutions, but as Margaret Thatcher once said, "You cannot buck the market." Once penetrating the realm of culture and consciousness, a market economy of commodity relations must exert the same formative powers there as it does in the material realm. It drives out craft production and feudal relations of symbolic dependence and brings in an avalanche of commodity goods for consumers constituted as citizens (so long as they have money) who are free to choose and consume as they wish—now with their spirits as well as their bodies. It is not possible to throw out this influence without now throwing out market relations tout court.

My position is that the undoubted market power of capitalist cultural provision certainly determines the forms of production of cultural commodities, but that this cannot be seen as necessarily enforcing an isomorphic consumption reflecting only intended uses or meanings as coded within the production, advertising, and distribution of commodities. As the research reported in *Common Culture* (Willis et al., 1990) illustrates, the commodity form is certainly dominant. But while constricting and structuring the field, the commodity form does not determine it. Within bounds, the commodity form's built-in desperation to find use at any price incites and provokes certain kinds of appropriation. This appropriation is also not necessarily along standard lines: no two people look the same; no two living rooms look the same; no two people think the same; and yet they are all products of a social existence within a market economy.

What the production-oriented pessimists overlook is the other half of the equation—the processes and activities of the acculturation of consumer items. Acculturation refers to the processes and activities whereby human beings actively and creatively take up the objects and symbols around them for their own situated purposes of meaning-making. This process is well known to cultural anthropologists who have observed and commented on it in other contexts (see Clifford, 1997). But while anthropological dignity is accorded to the uses and contextual meanings of objects and artifacts in societies beyond far shores, the proximity and banality of commodity forms "at home" seem to have robbed them of such dignity. I would insist that no matter how disreputable their provenance, commodities and electronic messages are still subject to grounded processes, not only of passive consumption but also of active appropriation. Against the grain of dominant assumptions that aesthetics belong only to High Art and legitimate culture, I have argued that there is a "grounded aesthetics" in everyday practice whereby meanings are attributed to symbols and artifacts, now mostly commodities, in creative ways that produce new orders of symbolic meaning (Willis et al., 1990). These grounded aesthetics reset the possibilities for how every day is experienced and how the selection and appropriation of cultural materials will take place in the future.

Young and working-class people are caught up in the front line of engagement. They acculturate the materials of commodity culture almost as a matter of cultural life and death, not least because they find themselves with ever-diminishing inherited folk cultural resources and with little or no access to legitimate and bourgeois forms of cultural capital. In light of the multiple and complex possibilities of the grounded uses of new environmental resources—commodity and electronic—there is a strange emergence from subordinate cultural relations of a new kind of expressive subject. I would argue that it would have been better if this had occurred without exploitation and in planned developmental ways with more democratic control at the point of formal cultural production. But our hopes for an institutionally led and mutually cooperative cultural program for the popular classes have been rendered quaint and parochial by the new relations of desire brokered through the commodity.

The emergence of a subordinate expressive subject concerns members of the majority popular classes taking for themselves—on the alien and profane grounds of the commodity—something that only the elite have enjoyed as part of their sacred privilege. This privilege entails the formation of sensibilities to mark oneself culturally as a certain kind of person—rather than simply an unconscious carrier of traditional markers of class, race, and gender—or to "choose" to belong to these categories in distinctive, mannered, celebratory, or self-conscious ways. This is to take part in self-formation on relatively autonomous expressive grounds, rather than to be formed from outside on automatically ascribed grounds. The connection of the "given self" to variable external symbolic forms reflects the desire not just to take up social or material space in a way governed by others, but to matter culturally (Willis, 2000). Without some cultural marking, youth feel in danger of being culturally invisible, which increasingly means socially invisible. The choice to wear body jewelry may well last a lifetime, but it is a choice furnished in the conditions of a whole experienced life and life stage. It marks the self-consciousness of one's biography, a sense of self and specific social situation that simply cannot be reduced to the successful marketing of earrings.

It is crucial here to recognize the blurring of the lines between production and consumption in what I call *Common Culture* (Willis et al., 1990). Active consumption is a kind of production. Formal production—as in learning to play an instrument by listening to CDs—often arises first in relation to creative consumption. This is part of what separates the acculturation of popular cultural items from the usual notion of popular culture as materials that have their own inherent meanings and values. Selecting and appropriating popular cultural items for one's own meanings is a kind of cultural production. Though mediated through alien commodity materials, the attachment of an expressive identity to—or its workings through—a socially given mere existence is now a popular, and in its own way democratic, aspiration. While the continuing educational question for first wave modernization concerns whether state education is a means of liberation or ideological confinement for the unprivileged majority, the late modernist question for the same social group concerns whether the commodification and electrification of culture constitute a new form of domination or a means of opening up new fields of semiotic possibility. Are the young becoming culturally literate and expressive in new ways, or are they merely victims of every turn in cultural marketing and mass media manipulation?

However we judge the general tide of influence on this new front, it is incontestable that all school students are drawn in to the field of force of popular cultural provision. The basic point I want to make with respect to the overall theme of this Special Issue is that commodity-related expressive consumption—or common culture—does not take place in a vacuum or simply repeat the exploited meanings of commodity production. Furthermore, the acculturations that arise have to be understood as grounded in and informing other inherited social categories and positions as well as antagonisms between them. We must grant the freedoms of consumption that pedagogists begrudge, political economists deride, and antihumanists deny, but we must locate them at material and social interconnections and historical conjunctures that constrain and channel these freedoms in all kinds of ways. In the school, this points to the importance of understanding popular cultural consumption with respect to previously existing themes of school conformism, resistance, disaffection, variations, and points between them.

We must be alive to how cultural commodities are used to "body out"—give specific bodily expression to—the nature and practice of previously existent or socially articulated positions still organized ultimately by elementary class, race, and gender factors. Of particular importance is how the body-oriented and somatic emphasis of common cultural practices chime with, resonate with, and show an elective affinity with the antimentalism and manual emphases of working-class and subordinate bodily cultures. Bodybuilding, rave, and hip-hop dancing are some of the fields being opened up for the cultural exercise of the body, emphasizing its physical presence and showing its expressivity and superiority over desiccated mental ways of being. Commodity-related cultural practices are also producing new fields for the expression of gender in and out of the school. These practices include the trying on of new cloaks for the expression of masculinized resistance or independence from the school. This masculinity is no longer guaranteed by a proletarian industrial inheritance but is still targeted toward the school.

Common cultural practices can also wrap themselves up with second wave disaffected resistance producing a doubly articulated emphasis on the "now" of immediate consumer gratification to go along with the heavy extra weight placed on the present by the lack of a predictable social future. Where the moral and cultural benefits that flow from the proletarian inheritance of the wage are denied, a cultural expressivity through commodities may supply an instant social and cultural imaginary for resistance and alternatives to the felt oppressions of the school, providing, so to speak, something to resist "with." We must recognize that these practices include amplifications and resonances of misogyny and homophobia, as well as criminal and violent themes (hooks, cited in Marriott, 1993). The apparently boundless horizons of consumption have done little to remove the unconscious foot soldiers from their struggles, and have only added another front on which to contend.

These amplifications and resonances of opposition through common cultural means carry their own ironies for social reproduction and negation of subordinate interests. They remove students farther from what school might offer them and diminish the chances of a shot at a "proper" job (Sewell, 2002). Meanwhile, many students from less privileged backgrounds are inexorably drawn to exploited, dead-end, low-paid, intermittent, and part-time work in order to gain or maintain access to this world. The interest in any kind of paid work, no matter how exploited, can be motivated not by any intrinsic interest or delayed gratification, but by the necessity to earn the wages that allow access to the things that really energize and impassion them beyond the boring world of work. Unemployment, or the prospect of it, produces oppression by excluding young people from forms of identity-making and satisfaction provided by these new leisure and consumption fields. The old categories of judging a fair wage and a decent job are being capsized. The individualism inspired by cultural market relations can give a generalized sense of power and autonomy, often entirely misplaced with respect to the objective lack of real choice on youth labor markets, therefore concealing and mystifying it.[11]

Status Systems and Schools

Like the other authors in this Special Issue, I argue that popular culture should be understood in relation to the strong urge of young people to make and maintain a viable informal cultural identity acknowledged by others in shared social space. Commodity consumption and display (trainers, music, appearance, etc.) are major raw materials for the development of such expressive subjectivity and for the symbolic public marking of identity for self and others. But these forms of cultural expression are not simply about developing identity; they are also about putative, comparative, and hierarchical social placing of identity.[12] However, this comparative social dimension cannot be achieved within consumer relations themselves. Knowledgeable manipulations of symbolic markers of identity do not confer status on their own. While a necessary condition, these manipulations need to be part of an identity founded on other grounds. The school is a crucial site for these grounds where an over-mapping of distinctions takes place, with common culture positions and identities mapping onto distinctions within the school and these distinctions themselves mapping onto wider social distinctions.

There is not necessarily an automatic connection between basic social elements (class, race, and gender), school resistance or nonresistance (first wave), disaffection (second wave), and particular kinds of common cultural expression (third wave). Within the site of the school, each of these factors has a relatively independent life and can attach itself to other elements so that there is the possibility, among other things, for class and "ethnic cross-dressing" (McCarthy, 2002). However, there are likely to be some tendencies of strong association, which is the ethnographer's task to uncover. For instance, lower-working-class students are likely to be located at the bottom of the official school status system. From this position they are likely to be inclined to exploit popular culture and other resources to embody their resistance or disaffection with alternative status markers, mobilizing cultural "positional goods" that they can control.

Perhaps it is the singular nature of the modernist school, where people of the same age are forced into a common arena, that compels individuals and groups to find a place and identity within a single complex matrix. No matter how heterogeneous their backgrounds or how different their cultural destinies would have played out without the unnatural social atmospherics of the school, it is within the constraints of this institution that young people negotiate their identities. The previous section looked at some elements of the common cultural status system within the school and some of its points of contact with other systems. There are, in fact, several status systems in play at once in the school. The urgent and sometimes sulphurous social pressures built up in the pressure cooker of the school fuse and force into lived articulation a number of status-conferring symbolic relations derived from without and within the school. For example, the official academic status measures within the school create hierarchical levels among students, which reinforce the external cultural capital systems that confer likely status and advantage on middle-class students. Team sports provide a powerful system of status measurement and achievement,[13] and perceptions of sexual attractiveness provide a status system both inside and outside of schools. Furthermore, systems based on perceived bodily hardness and toughness provide working-class and Black students greater chances for privilege, while opposition to authority, derived from both the resistance of the first wave and the disassociation of the second, produce their own kinds of status systems. Lastly, but by no means least, new patterns of popular cultural consumption confer separate bases for evaluation and prestige.

Though forced into a common matrix, these symbolic relations are not aligned and do not point uniformly to common high-status positions. Conflict is ensured in the cauldron of the school, where students are competing for place and identity with reference to all of these positionalities. To change the metaphor, here is a complex cultural microecology, requiring considerable bravery and skill. On the one hand, failure in navigation skills may lead to victimhood, suffering, and even tragedy, while on the other, it may lead to involvement in serious crime and violence stretching beyond the school.

All schools are likely to manifest all or most of the themes discussed here, although there is likely to be wide variability in the cultural microecologies of particular schools and variation in the combination and alignment of systems. In different ways, common cultural systems are likely to become more central, inflecting how variations in the mix of social class, race, and ethnicities take root and grow in school ecologies. None of this can be read out automatically from social determinants, which again indicates a wide research agenda for ethnographic study.

There is a real autonomy and unpredictable chemistry in how status systems will mix in any given school. Successive and continuing waves of modernization and responses to them have added new layers of pressure and confusion. The contemporary school has been turned into a strange kind of hybrid, incorporating, under the same roof, the very different past and likely future trajectories of their very different students and the weighting of their stakes in different kinds of modernization, and whether these come from above or from below.

"Dominant Populars" in Schools

In predominantly working-class schools there is likely to be a polarization of the official culture and its hierarchies of status from the subterranean one. The latter develops and maintains its dominance by gathering for itself privileged positions within informal status systems that would include, most importantly, the status system of common culture. For instance, "popular" boys are likely to be tough, oppose the school, and be seen as stylish in their music and clothing tastes. To drop one of these attributes, would be to drop out of the "dominant popular"—the status system configuration that commands the most student prestige in a given school. To a greater or lesser extent, other social groups are likely to seek justifications for their own positions in relation to the dominant popular in the magnification of the mappings of distinction that are beneficial to them.

Of course, such dominant populars are socially subordinate in the wider frame. They invert not only the school's official hierarchies, but also some of the wider social hierarchies by appearing to confer on students deceivingly dominant roles even when they occupy subordinate economic and social positions outside the school. Unless they can convert informal skills and knowledge to market advantage in the informal or formal cultural industries, marked reproductive consequences are likely to continue for the members of such inverted fixings of the official cultural systems of the school. They may enjoy the ambiguous superiority of symbolic dominance only as a short prelude to and ironic preparation for extended economic disadvantage in the labor market. Middle-class students in predominantly working-class schools may take up positions within such subordinate dominant populars. If so, interesting competitions of influence will ensue between likely poor academic performance and effects flowing from inherited economic and cultural capital.

In schools with predominantly middle-class students, the weight of cultural capital is likely to give informal qualitative and quantitative ballast to the official system and its status prizes. Other systems are more likely to be aligned with this official system so that "popular" boys, for instance, are likely to achieve at least some academic success, get along with staff, and be seen as attractive and stylish. This produces a dominant popular more aligned with the school and with hierarchies outside of it, so to speak, a truly dominant dominant popular. Status systems that are out of line with the official system are likely to be attenuated in their power. A central point I wish to make is that the contents and meanings of the common cultural status system are likely to be very different when aligned with a dominant popular articulated in line with, rather than in opposition to, the school. In general, though, the conflicts and overlaps of various symbolic systems result in a cumulatively rising social atmosphere within the singular institution of the school. There are likely to be negative social and psychological effects associated with being excluded from the dominant popular in any given school.[14]

The School as Instrument and Site

The school is the direct instrument of the first wave; it suffers disorientation from the second wave; and it is an important site for the playing out of the third wave of modernization. You could say that all cultural forms and experiences now have an element of cultural diaspora. Even if you stop in the same place, change flows over you; when the young are still, symbolic borders pass them.

In this article, I have described three themes of cultural modernity "from below": continuing threads of institutionally based informal cultural resistance; responses of disaffection and depression to the continuing effects of postindustrial unemployment and tougher forms of state-regulated school-to-work transitions; and the new cultural and bodily relations and possibilities arising from grounded consumption and leisure. The combinations of these three themes are unstable and different in their implications for different social groups. Each wave affects the others and has to be understood in light of the others. In particular, issues of popular culture are too often treated for themselves and in their own vectors of effect on identity. These issues can be seen much more productively through the play and effect of preceding and continuing cultural and structural forces of modernization. These forces continue to play over particular groups still constituted in traditional categories of class, race, and gender. Thus there are multiple ways in which resistance (first wave) and disaffection (second wave) are given expression and development within common cultural practices (third wave).

It is true that in the last wave of modernization we can observe the cultural unconscious pushing back; that which was automatic seems willed. The tragedy is that what is sometimes called the aesthetization of experience does not actually change the material relation between freedom and necessity, between the chosen and the determined. These relations are actually tightening for the worse in the life space of the subordinate classes at the hands of second wave modernization, even as third wave modernization indicates symbolic space without borders. Cultural and material vectors seem to be out of kilter as never before. We must not overlook that the super-abundance of images and imaginary possibilities of apparently free-floating and classless forms of consumption intersect with materially worsening conditions for large sections of the working class. This is especially true, given the brute facts of youth unemployment and exploitative underemployment in low-wage service jobs for masses of young people. The blurring of consumption and production in third wave modernization might offer some young people hope of embarking on alternative "twilight" careers in the provision of cultural goods and services. But second wave conditions also produce heightened attractions to crime and to illegal activities in the informal economy. Meanwhile, schools continue to struggle, still formed by the ambitions and illusions of the first wave of modernization now breaking on very different shores.

In schools we can see a blunt, culturally mediated form of negotiation between young people and adults, both uncomprehending the meaning and effects of modernity. Antisocial behavior and associated common cultural forms can be vehicles for expression and for seizing space and autonomy where words fail. It must be understood that schooling is not only an instrument for producing modernity, but is also a site for the playing out of its contradictory forces and forms. Accepting popular culture does not mean a lazy throwing open of the school doors to the latest fad, but rather committing to a principled understanding of the complexity of contemporary cultural experience.

There is a wider set of issues here concerning the fullest understandings of cultural formations and the determinants of their direction for emancipation or alienation. The school is a social field as well as an instrument of social development. Therefore, educators, educational organizations, and their progressive allies should speak up unequivocally on behalf of young people in the middle and bottom of social space who are embroiled in the flux of this dialectical modernization. They can take up clues and themes from young peoples' emergent cultures, pains, and experience. If the consciousness, actions, and cultures of students need to change, so do the wider conditions and structural possibilities that help to structure those very responses. As this article addresses throughout, consciousness and structure are the two intertwined poles of continuous cultural processes. If consciousness has to change, so does structure. At the very least there are firm "voluntarist" limits on how far consciousness can be asked to change if questions of structure are firmly off the agenda. Rather than ever-more individualistic economic competition for the good life driven by the first wave, where are the means for the majority to find a collective place in the sun free from ideological straightjackets? Rather than shaming individualized insecurity and the state disciplining of working poverty described in the second wave, where are the guarantees for enhanced security and greater choice that globalized economic advance is supposed to bring? Rather than predatory market provisions of the third wave enflaming immediate desire, where are the means for the democratic production of new symbolic and informational goods?

The social impulses embodied in these arguments may have an ideological and Utopian tinge. Although in different ways, this is no more so than in the idealist figures of the top-down imaginary—dutiful students, an ever-retraining reserve army of the unemployed, passive grateful consumers—forced to progress through educational and economic institutions. These top-down efforts seek to bend consciousness to unremittingly inflexible and harsh structural conditions. It is the internal contradictions and social impossibility of these idealist figurations that unleash cultural modernization from below to forcibly demonstrate in return that everything cannot be as tidy and convenient for the powerful as the official ledger would have it. In this article, I have examined the counter effects, folding loops of irony, and unintended consequences unleashed from dominant imaginings and moldings of "progress," unavoidably set in motion by the institutional and economic power that backs them up. Maintaining a critique and indicating alternative views of "progress" are fundamental educational issues that are umbilically connected to debates over the canon and multiculturalism, or traditionalism and progressivism.

As for the specific questions of how to address issues of popular culture in the curriculum, I would argue that we should look beyond the products of popular culture to their uses in context—to the field of what I term common culture. Educators fret over the predatory view of popular culture, fearing the exploitations of the vulnerabilities and immoderate desires of the young. I am certainly not endorsing the ways market production scales away the remnants of organic community and institutional responsibility with imaginary relations and desires. Rather, I am trying to understand the processes of common culture to shed light on the grounded forms in which the young acculturate commodities into their everyday lives. In this way we may be able to separate the predatory from the creative and entertain a practical hope for practical action.

For all the predatory dangers of popular culture, within common cultural practices lies a new growth of awareness and identity within the individual or group. This growing awareness is a kind of variable and unpredictable mind-full-ness about individual choices and their limits and lodgings within complex social relations and structural determinants. These new, yet non-dominant, forms of identity and expression are precarious and open to further rounds of commodification. They also turn within new complexities and flows of social reproduction in situ. But there is nevertheless a dialectical site to be mined for clues to new kinds of public sphere. Within these public spheres, the subordinate mind-full-ness associated with consumer culture might become a purposeful self-conscious mindfullness of individual and collective action.

Educators and researchers within informal settings might explore a variety of ways that cultural consumption and production might be encouraged to operate in less exploitative ways. Their exploration might open new public realms that are seen not as compensating for or attacking commercial imperatives and their erosion of traditional values, but as going along with the flow of actually existing energies and passions. The conditions of existence within these new public realms would make young people more visible and give them more control over what is expressed and how.

Within formal settings, educators and researchers can use the resource of critical ethnographic texts to explore the meanings and rationalities of common cultural practices close to home. They may consider the products of popular culture not simply for their fetishized, immediate identities, but for their common cultural histories, and ask: How did these expressions become commodities and with what effects? How are they de-fetishized and turned into cultural possessions in situ? What do these appropriated expressions say about social position and location?

Pedagogic voices can be shockingly quiet about issues of social context, as if the four walls of the classroom, sanctuary-making as they can be, contain all that is necessary to understand and direct what goes on within them. Educators and researchers should utilize the cultural experiences and embedded bodily knowledge of their students as starting points, not for bemoaning the failures and inadequacies of their charges, but to render more conscious for them what is unconsciously rendered in their cultural practices. The experiences and knowledge of the students—foot soldiers of modernity—can help us, and them, to understand their own place and formation within flows of cultural modernization. This knowledge provides practical grounds for critical self-understandings of social reproduction and even perhaps for an appreciation of how far, under what conditions, and for whom Bourdieu's elusive enigma might hold true: "Resistance can be alienating and submission can be liberating" (quoted in Bourdieu & Wacquant, 1992, p. 24). While celebrating the "freedoms" of consumption, we must always locate them on the front lines where they are exercised.

I am extremely grateful for close and detailed critical comments on an earlier draft and suggestions generously offered by Philip Corrigan and Bowen Paulle. Thanks also for the detailed comments and suggestions from editors at HER, and especially for the close editorial attentions of Rubén Gaztambide-Fernández and Lionel C. Howard.

Notes

1. Not all working-class students failed. However, like today, middle-class students were about six times more likely to go into higher education than were working-class pupils.
2. "Ear'oles" is slang for the exterior bit of the human ear; the lads saw them as always listening and never doing.
3. Other forms of resistance and behavior leading to social reproduction have since been documented. Working-class girls perform more "silent" forms of resistance and disaffection, with similarly ironic processes of reproduction to be observed with respect to their destiny in unpaid domestic work and within low-paid "feminized" occupations (e.g., Anyon, 1983; Llewellyn, 1980; Payne, 1980). In the era of politically driven diaspora following and merging with continuing economic migration, other variants of informal and resistant cultures of school borrow from, recycle, and adapt to elements of various traditional race, ethnic, and national cultures (e.g., Fordham, 1996; Mac an Ghaill, 1988; fortes, 1995; Raissiguier, 1995).

4. Despite a marked spreading out and increase in the "nominal rate" of paper qualifications in the U.K. over the last twenty-five years, patterns of unequal attainment between the classes have remained remarkably constant (Arnot, 2002).
5. This job trend is compelling evidence of the inflexibility and long duration of locked cultural forms.
6. The following is based mainly on my work on *The Youth Review* (1988), Furlong and Cartmel's (1997) *Young People and Social Change*, and Starrin, Rantakeisu, and Hagquist's (1997) "In the Wake of Recession."
7. Single mothers may or may not find some mileage in the manipulation of an increasingly mean, disciplining, and coercive state to provide bare housing and subsistence, but various kinds of limitations on total lifetime welfare entitlements mean that they are running out of road on their way to a crossroads of enforced choice between workfare subservience and the dubious freedoms of subsistence in the informal economy (see Hofferth, Stanhope, & Harris, 2002).
8. On "hyper-masculinity" see Mac an Ghaill (1994).
9. For an overview of popular culture in the United States, see Traube (1996).
10. For a discussion of these arguments, see the articles by Dolby, Buckingham, and Trend in this issue.
11. See discussion of the "epistemological fallacy of late modernity" in Furlong and Cartmel (1997).
12. For an interesting parallel argument about the comparative importance of subcutural capital, see Thornton (1995).
13. This is especially true in the United States (see Holland & Andre, 1994; Spady, 1970).
14. For a biographic and life history ethnographic exploration of some of these issues, see Ortner (2002).

References

Adair, V. C. (2002). Branded with infamy: Inscriptions of poverty and class in the United States. *Signs: Journal of Women in Culture and Society, 27*, 451–471.

Anyon, J. (1983). Intersections of gender and class: Accommodation and resistance by working-class and affluent females to contradictory sex-role ideologies. In S. Walker & L. Barton (Eds.), *Gender, class and education* (pp. 19–37). Lewes, Eng.: Falmer Press.

Arnot, M. (2002). *Reproducing gender? Essays on educational theory and feminist politics.* London: Routledge Falmer.

Bourdieu, P., & Wacquant, L. (1992). *An invitation to reflexive sociology.* Chicago: University of Chicago Press.

Clifford, J. (1997). *Routes: Travel and translation in the late twentieth century.* Cambridge, MA: Harvard University Press.

Devine, J. (1997). *Maximum security: The culture of violence in inner-city schools.* Chicago: Chicago University Press.

Durkheim, E. (1956). *Education and sociology.* New York: Free Press.

Fordham, S. (1996). *Blacked out: Dilemmas of race, identity, and success in Capital High.* Chicago: University of Chicago Press.

Furlong, A., & Cartmel, F. (1997). *Young people and social change.* Philadelphia: Open University Press.

Gilborn, D., & Mirza, H. (2000). *Educational inequality: Mapping race, class and gender.* London: Office for Standards in Education.

Gregg, P., & Wadsworth, J. (Eds.). (1999). *The state of working Britain.* Manchester, Eng.: Manchester University Press.

Hofferth, S. L., Stanhope, S., & Harris, K. M. (2002). Exiting welfare in the 1990s: Did public policy influence recipients' behavior? *Population Research and Policy Review, 21,* 433–472.

Holland, A., & Andre, T. (1994). Athletic participation and the social status of adolescent males and females. *Youth and Society, 25,* 388–407.

Johnson, M. (1999). *Failing school, failing city: The reality of inner city education.* Charlbury, Eng.: Jon Carpenter.

Llewellyn, M. (1980). Studying girls at school: The implications of confusion. In R. Deem (Ed.), *Schooling for women's work* (pp. 42–51). Boston: Routledge & Kegan Paul.

Mac an Ghaill, M. (1988). *Young, gifted and Black.* Milton Keynes, Eng.: Open University Press.

Mac an Ghaill, M. (1994). *The making of men: Masculinities, sexualities and schooling.* Buckingham, Eng.: Open University Press.

Marriott, M. (1993, August 15). Hard core rap lyrics stir backlash. *New York Times,* p. 1.

McCarthy, C. (2002, April). *Understanding the work of aesthetics in modern life: Thinking about the cultural studies of education in a time of recession.* Paper presented at the annual meeting of the American Educational Research Association, New Orleans.

Nader, R. (1996). *Children first: A parent's guide to fighting corporate predators.* Washington, DC: Corporate Accountability Research Group.

Office of National Statistics. (2003). Work and joblessness. June assessment: Claimant count up. In *National Statistics Online.* Retrieved July 2, 2003 from http://www.statistics.gov.uk/cci/nugget.asp?id=12 [Last updates June 11, 2003].

One in five young people may drop out, says OFSTED. (2003, March 6). *London Times Higher Education Supplement,* p. 6.

Ortner, S. (2002). Burned like a tattoo: High school social categories and "American culture." *Ethnography, 3,* 115–148.

Paulle, B. (2003). Contest and collaboration: Embodied cultural responses of adolescents in an "inner city" school in the Bronx (New York) and a "zwarte" school in the Bijlmer (Amsterdam). In J. C. C. Rupp & W. Veugelers (Eds.), *Moreel-politieke heroriëntatie in het onderwijs* (pp. 17–51). Leuven, Belgium: Garant.

Payne, I. (1980). A working-class girl in a grammar school. In D. Spender & E. Sarah (Eds.), *Learning to lose: Sexism and education* (pp. 12–19). London: Women's Press.

Portes, A. (Ed.). (1995). *The economic sociology of immigration: Essays on networks, ethnicity and entrepreneurship.* New York: Russell Sage.

Raissiguier, C. (1995). The construction of marginal identities: Working-class girls of Algerian descent in a French school. In M. H. Marchand & J. L. Parpart (Eds.), *Feminism/postmodernism/development* (pp. 79–93). London: Routledge.

Roberts, K. (2001). *Class in modern Britain*. Basingstoke, Eng.: Palgrave.

Sewell, T. (1997). *Black masculinities and schooling: How Black boys survive modern schooling*. London: Trentham Books.

Sewell, T. (2002, December 15). I know why black boys fail at school – and racism isn't to blame. London: *Mail on Sunday*, p. 59.

Silvester, S. (2002, October 8). Grey hair, wrinkles, and money to burn. *Financial Times*, p. 6

Spady, W. G. (1970). Lament for the letterman: Effects of peer status and extracurricular activities on goals and achievement. *American Journal of Sociology, 75*, 680–702

Starrin, B., Rantakeisu, U., & Hagquist, C. (1997). In the wake of recession—economic hardship, shame and social disintegration. *Scandinavian Journal of Work and Environmental Health, 23*(4), 47–54.

Thornton, S. (1995). *Club cultures*. Cambridge, Eng.: Polity Press.

Traube, E. G. (1996) "The popular" in American culture. *Annual Review of Anthropology, 25*, 127–151.

Unemployment Unit. (1999). *Working brief 107 August/September*. London: Unemployment Unit and Youth-aid Research, Information, Campaigning.

Wills, P. (1977). *Learning to labour*. Aldershot, Eng.: Saxon House.

Wills, P. (2000). *The ethnographic imagination*. Cambridge, Eng.: Polity Press.

Wills, P., Bekenn, A., Ellis, T., & Whitt, D. (1988). *The youth review*. Aldershot, Eng.: Avebury.

Willis, P., Jones, S., Canaan, J., & Hurd, G. (1990). *Common culture*. Buckingham, Eng.: Open University Press.

Contributors

Jean Anyon is one of very few educational scholars whose work investigates the political economy of cities and schools. Her last book, *Ghetto Schooling: A Political Economy of Urban Education*, was reviewed in the *New York Times* and is widely used and cited. She has written many scholarly pieces on the confluence of social class, race, and education, several of which are classics and have been reprinted in over forty edited collections. Her forthcoming book is entitled *Radical Possibilities: Public Policy, Urban Education, and a New Social Movement*. On January 1, 2004, Jean and colleagues were awarded a $10 million grant from the National Science Foundation to set up a Center for Learning and Teaching Urban Mathematics. She teaches social and educational policy at the Graduate Center, Doctoral Program in Urban Education, City University of New York.

Arjun Appadurai is Provost and Senior Vice-President for Academic Affairs and John Dewey Professor in the Social Sciences at the New School for Social Research. He is the author of *Modernity at Large*.

Michael W. Apple is John Bascom Professor of Curriculum and Instruction at the University of Wisconsin, Madison. Among his recent books are *Educating the "Right" Way: Markets, Standards, God, and Inequality*; *The State and the Politics of Knowledge*, and the twenty-fifth anniversary third edition of *Ideology and Curriculum*.

Homi K. Bhabha is Anne F. Rothenberg Professor of English and American Literature and Language at Harvard University. He is the author of many important books and articles on postcolonial theory, globalization, and literature, including the widely influential *The Location of Culture*.

Deborah P. Britzman is Professor of Education at York University, Toronto, and author of the following books: *After-Education: Anna Freud, Melanie Klein and Psychoanalytic Histories of Learning*; *Lost Subjects, Contested Objects: Toward a Psychoanalytic Inquiry of Learning*; and *Practice Makes Practice: A Critical Study of Learning to Teach, Revised Edition*, all from State University of New York Press, Albany, New York.

Mary K. Coffey is Assistant Professor of Art History at Dartmouth College. Her manuscript "Sanctuaries of the Patria" traces the relationship between Mexican muralism and the development of federal museums after the Revolution. She has published widely on cultural policy, public art, and the politics of museums. Her essays appear in *Cultural Studies, Art Journal*, and edited volumes on Foucault and cultural studies and multicultural curricula.

CL Cole is Associate Professor of Gender and Women's Studies and Kinesiology and Affiliate Faculty in African American Studies and Sociology at University of Illinois, Urbana-Champaign. She is the editor of *Journal of Sport and Social Issues* and is currently on the editorial board of *Cultural Studies↔Critical Methodologies*. Cole has edited (with Michael Silk and David Andrews) *Sport and Corporate Nationalisms* and (with Susan Birrell) *Women, Sport, and Culture*.

Warren Crichlow is Associate Professor of Education at York University, Ontario. He is co-editor of the first edition of *Race, Identity, and Representation in Education*.

Antonia Darder is Professor of Educational Policy Studies and Latino/a Studies at the University of Illinois, Urbana-Champaign. She is the author of *Culture and Power in the Classroom* and *Reinventing Paulo Freire: A Pedagogy of Love*. She is the editor of several collections including *The Critical Pedagogy Reader*.

Greg Dimitriadis is Associate Professor in the Department of Educational Leadership and Policy at the University at Buffalo, The State University of New York. Dimitriadis is the author of *Performing Identity/Performing Culture: Hip Hop as Text, Pedagogy, and Lived Practice* and *Friendship, Cliques, and Gangs: Young Black Men Coming of Age in Urban America*. He is first co-author, with Cameron McCarthy, of *Reading and Teaching the Postcolonial: From Baldwin to Basquiat and Beyond*. He is first co-editor, with Dennis Carlson, of *Promises to Keep: Cultural Studies, Democratic Education, and Public Life* and second co-editor, with Nadine Dolby and Paul Willis, of *Learning to Labor in New Times*.

Nadine Dolby is Assistant Professor of Curriculum Studies at Purdue University. She is the author of *Constructing Race: Youth, Identity, and Popular Culture in South Africa*, and first co-editor, with Greg Dimitriadis and Paul Willis, of *Learning to Labor in New Times*. She has published in numerous journals including *Harvard Educational Review, Comparative Education Review, British Journal of Sociology of Education*, and *Teachers College Record*.

Rishma Dunlop is a poet, dramatist, fiction writer, and essayist and is currently Associate Professor of Education at York University, Toronto, Canada. Her most recent book of poetry is *Reading Like a Girl*, and she is a co-editor of *Red Silk: An Anthology of South Asian Canadian Women Poets*. Her Canadian Broadcast Corporation (CBC) radio play is titled *The Raj Kumari's Lullaby*.

Michelle Fine is Distinguished Professor of Social Psychology at the City University of New York Graduate Center. She is the author or editor of numerous books including *Off White: Readings on Power, Privilege, and Resistance, Second Edition*; *Working Method*; and *Framing Dropouts*.

Kelly A. Gates is Assistant Professor of Media Studies at CUNY, Queens College. Her work examines the social and cultural construction of new media technologies. She received her Ph.D. from the Institute of Communications Research at the University of Illinois.

Michael D. Giardina is Visiting Research Scholar in the Institute of Communications Research at the University of Illinois, Urbana-Champaign. He has written widely on race, sport, and the politics of culture and is the author of *Sporting Pedagogies: Performing Culture and Identity in the Global Arena*.

Lawrence Grossberg is the Morris Davis Distinguished Professor of Communication Studies and Cultural Studies at the University of North Carolina at Chapel Hill, where he is also the director of the University Program in Cultural Studies. He is the co-editor of the journal *Cultural Studies*. His book, *Caught in the Crossfire: Kids and the Dilemmas of American Politics*, will be released in 2005.

Susan J. Harewood is a doctoral candidate in the Institute of Communication Research at the University of Illinois, Urbana-Champaign. Her research interests center upon popular music, gender, and postcolonial studies. Her dissertation focuses on the construction and performance of identity in Caribbean popular culture.

Jonathan Xavier Inda is Assistant Professor of Chicano Studies at the University of California, Santa Barbara. He is co-editor of two books, including *The Anthropology of Globalization*.

Samantha King is Assistant Professor of Physical and Health Education at Queen's University, Ontario. Her work on the cultural politics of sport has appeared in *Social Text*, *Sociology of Sport Journal*, *Journal of Sport and Social Issues*, and *International Journal of Sport Marketing and Sponsorship*.

Vicky Lebeau teaches at the University of Sussex. She is the author of *Psychoanalysis and Cinema: The Play of Shadows*.

George Lipsitz is Professor and Chair of American Studies at the University of California, Santa Cruz. His publications include *American Studies in a Moment of Danger* and *The Possessive Investment in Whiteness*.

Alejandro Lugo is Associate Professor of Anthropology at the University of Illinois, Urbana-Champaign. He is the author of *Fragmented Lives, Assembled Parts: Culture, Capitalism, and Conquest at the U.S.-Mexico Border*.

Cameron McCarthy teaches mass communications theory and cultural studies at the University of Illinois, Urbana. He is Research Professor, Communications Scholar, and University Scholar in the Institute of Communication Research. McCarthy has authored or co-authored numerous research articles and books including *Race and Curriculum*, *The Uses of Culture: Education and the Limits of Ethnic Affiliation*, *Sound Identities: Youth Music and the Cultural Politics of Education*, *Multicultural Curriculum: New Directions for Social Theory, Practice and Policy*, and *Reading and Teaching the Postcolonial: From Baldwin to Basquiat and Beyond*. He has also published with his graduate students a book on Foucault and cultural studies, *Foucault, Cultural Studies and Governmentality*.

Luis Mirón is Professor of Educational Policy Studies at the University of Illinois, Urbana-Champaign. He is the author or editor of several books, including the recent *Reinterpreting Urban School Reform*.

Michael Omi is Chair of the Department of Ethnic Studies at the University of California, Berkeley. He is the author, along with Howard Winant, of *Racial Formation in the United States*.

Kent A. Ono is Director of and Professor in the Asian American Studies Program and Professor in the Institute of Communications Research at the University of Illinois, Urbana-Champaign. He conducts critical and theoretical analyses of print, film, and television media, specifically focusing on representations of race, gender, sexuality, class, and nation. He has contributed articles to numerous journals and anthologies. In addition to co-authoring *Shifting Borders: Rhetoric, Immigration, and California's Proposition 187*, he has co-edited *Enterprise Zones: Critical Positions on Star Trek*, *Asian American Studies after Critical Mass*, and *A Companion to Asian American Studies*. He is currently completing a book on films and videos about the incarceration of Japanese Americans during World War II, *Forgetting to Remember: Representations of Japanese American Incarceration on Film and Video*.

Nikos Papastergiadis is Associate Professor and Director of the Australian Centre, University of Melbourne. He has contributed to many academic and public panels on contemporary art and the impact of migration. His research and writing have focused on cultural theory and artistic practice in relation to place, migration, and globalization. Papastergiadis' recent work has focused on the transformation of urban environment in postindustrial cities. He has written three books, *Modernity as Exile*, *Dialogues in the Diaspora*, and *The Turbulence of Migration*, and has authored over 100 essays in various edited books, academic journals, and art magazines. In addition, he has edited or co-edited a number of books, including *Random Access*, *Ambient Fears*, *Art & Cultural Difference*, *Mixed Belongings*, *What John Berger Saw*, and *Complex Entanglements: Art, Globalization and Cultural Difference*. He has also served as special guest editor of *Arena*, *Chronico*, *Third Text*, *Art and Design*, *Annotations*, and *Photofile*.

Jin-Kyung Park is a doctoral candidate in the Institute of Communications Research at the University of Illinois, Urbana-Champaign. She is interested in postcolonial studies, feminist media studies, and cultural studies of science and technology. Her dissertation explores a cultural history of public health in colonial Korea. She is currently conducting her dissertation research in both Korea and Japan.

William F. Pinar teaches curriculum theory at Louisiana State University, where he serves as the St. Bernard Parish Alumni Endowed Professor. He has also served as the Frank Talbott Professor at the University of Virginia and the A. Lindsay O'Connor Professor of American Institutions at Colgate University. Pinar is the author of *What Is Curriculum Theory?*; *Autobiography, Politics, and Sexuality*; and *The Gender of Racial Politics and Violence in America*. He is the senior author of *Understanding Curriculum* and the editor of several collections, among them *Queer Theory in Education*, *The Passionate Mind of Maxine Greene*, *Contemporary Curriculum Discourses*, and the *International Handbook of Curriculum Research*.

Fazal Rizvi has been Professor of Educational Policy Studies at the University of Illinois, Urbana-Champaign since August 2001. Before that he held academic and administrative positions at a number of Australian universities. He has published extensively on a variety of subjects, including theories of globalization and the internationalization of education, racism, and the politics of multiculturalism in education, arts, and cultural policy, education and the politics of Asia-Australia relations, and problems of democratic reforms in educational governance. His books include a co-authored volume, *Education Policy and the Politics of Change*, and two co-edited volumes, *Disability and the Dilemmas of Education and Justice* and *Culture, Difference and the Arts*. Professor Rizvi was editor of the journal *Discourse: Studies in the Cultural Politics of Education* from 1993 to 2000 and the president of the Australian Association of Research in Education in 1996. He is currently researching issues of student mobility and the cultural politics of international education.

Leslie G. Roman is Associate Professor in the Department of Educational Studies at the University of British Columbia and publishes widely in cultural studies and education on the interrelations among various antioppression pedagogies, particularly antiracism, feminist materialism, and critiques of neocolonialism. Her work may be found in journals such as *Discourse, Educational Theory, Anglistica* (an Italian cultural studies journal), *The Journal of Educational Change, Environment and Planning: Society and Space, The International Journal of Qualitative Studies in Education*, and *Educacion y Sociedad* (translated into Spanish). Her published books are *Becoming Feminine: The Politics of Popular Culture* (co-edited with Linda Christian-Smith), *Views Beyond the Border Country: Raymond Williams and Cultural Politics* (co-edited with Dennis Dworkin), and *Dangerous Territories: Struggles for Difference and Equality in Education* (co-edited with Linda Eyre). She is currently working on a book tentatively entitled *Transgressive Knowledge: Relational Studies in Feminist Theory, Politics, and Pedagogies*.

Edward Said was Parr Professor of English and Comparative Literature at Columbia University. His books include *Orientalism* and *The World, the Text, and the Critic*.

Ella Shohat is Professor of Cultural Studies and Gender Studies at New York University. She has lectured and published extensively on the intersection of gender, post/colonialism, and multiculturalism, as well as on Zionist discourse, and the Arab-Jewish and Mizrahi question. Her award-winning publications include *Israeli Cinema: East/West and the Politics of Representation, Unthinking Eurocentrism: Multiculturalism and the Media* (with R. Stam), *Dangerous Liaisons: Gender, Nation and Postcolonial Perspectives* (co-edited), *Talking Visions: Multicultural Feminism in a Transnational Age, Forbidden Reminiscences*, and *Multiculturalism, Postcoloniality and Transnational Media* (co-edited). A recipient of a Rockefeller fellowship, she has served on the editorial board of such journals as *Social Text, Public Culture, Jouver, Critique*, and *Meridians*. Her writing has been translated into several languages, including French, Spanish, Portuguese, Arabic, Hebrew, German, Polish, and Turkish.

Christine E. Sleeter is Professor Emeritus of Education at California State University at Monterey Bay. She is the author or editor of several important books on multicultural education, including the recent *Culture, Difference, and Power*.

Gayatri Chakravorty Spivak is Avalon Foundation Professor in the Humanities at Columbia University. Her books including *Death of a Discipline, A Critique of Postcolonial Reason, In Other Worlds, The Post-Colonial Critic*, and *Outside in the Teaching Machine*.

Angharad N. Valdivia is Research Professor at the Institute of Communications Research at the University of Illinois. She is the author of *A Latina in the Land of Hollywood* and editor of *Feminism, Multiculturalism and the Media*, the Communications and Culture section of the *Routledge International Encyclopedia of Women*, and the *Blackwell Companion to Media*

Studies, Feminism, Multiculturalism, and the Media. She is also co-editor of the forthcoming *Geographies of Latinidad: Latina/o Studies into the Twenty-First Century.* Her research and teaching focus on transnational gender issues with a special emphasis on Latinas and Latin America in popular culture.

Lois Weis is Professor of Sociology of Education at the State University of New York at Buffalo. She is the author or editor of numerous books, including *Class Reunion; Off White: Readings on Power, Privilege, and Resistance, Second Edition;* and *Working Method.*

Cornel West is Professor of Religion and African American Studies at Princeton University. A preeminent cultural critic, his many important books include *Democracy Matters: Winning the Fight Against Imperialism, Race Matters, Keeping Faith: Philosophy and Race in America,* and *Beyond Eurocentrism and Multiculturalism.*

Paul Willis is trained in literary criticism at Cambridge and received his Ph.D. in 1972 from the Centre for Contemporary Cultural Studies, Birmingham University, where he remained as senior research fellow until 1980. During the 1980s, he served as youth policy adviser to Wolverhampton Borough Council in the English Midlands. There he produced *The Youth Review*, which formed the basis for youth policy in that city and for the formation of the democratically elected Youth Council, both still functioning. During the 1990s, he served first as head of the Division of Media, Communications and Cultural Studies and then as a member of the Professoriate at the University of Wolverhampton. He has held a variety of consulting posts, including membership of the Youth Policy Working Group of the Labour Party (1989–1990); at the English Arts Council (1992–1993); and at the Tate Gallery of the North (1995–1996). In 2000, he co-founded the Sage journal, *Ethnography*. Paul Willis's work has focused mainly but not exclusively on the ethnographic study of lived cultural forms in a wide variety of contexts, from highly structured to weakly structured, examining how practices of "informal cultural production" help to produce and construct cultural worlds "from below." Currently he is Professor of Social and Cultural Ethnography at Keele University, Staffordshire, England, and is working on conceptual and methodological ways of connecting or reconnecting a concern with identity/culture to economic structure, with particular reference to shop floor culture. His books include *Profane Culture, Learning to Labour, The Youth Review, Common Culture,* and *The Ethnographic Imagination.*

Howard Winant is Professor of Sociology at the University of California, Santa Barbara. His work focuses on the historical and contemporary importance of race in shaping economic, political, and cultural life, both in the United States and globally. He is the author of *The World Is a Ghetto: Race and Democracy Since World War II*, as well as *Racial Formation in the United States: From the 1960s to the 1990s*, co-authored with Michael Omi. His new book is *The New Politics of Race: Globalism, Difference, Justice.*

Index

Z